MIRRORS, PRISMS AND LENSES

A TEXT-BOOK OF GEOMETRICAL OPTICS

BY

JAMES P. C. SOUTHALL

Late Professor of Physics in Columbia University

THIRD EDITION

NEW YORK

DOVER PUBLICATIONS, INC.

This Dover edition, first published in 1964, is an unabridged and unaltered republication of the third edition, published by The Macmillan Company in 1933.

International Standard Book Number: 0-486-61234-1
Library of Congress Catalog Card Number: 64-25095

Manufactured in the United States of America
Dover Publications, Inc.
180 Varick Street
New York, N. Y. 10014

PREFACE TO THE FIRST EDITION

In spite of the existence of a number of excellent works on geometrical optics, the need of a text-book which will serve as an introduction to the theory of modern optical instruments appears to be generally recognized; and the present volume, which is the outgrowth of a course of lectures on optics given in Columbia University, has been written in the hope that it may answer this purpose. In a certain sense it may be considered as an abridgment of my treatise on *The Principles and Methods of Geometrical Optics*, but the reader will also find here a considerable mass of more or less new and original material which is not contained in the larger book. I have endeavored, however, to keep steadily in mind the limitations of the class of students for whom the work is primarily intended and to employ, therefore, only the simplest mathematical processes as far as possible. With this object in view I have purposely entered into much detail in the earlier and more elementary portions of the subject, following in fact the method which has been found to be most satisfactory with my own pupils; but I venture to hope that the book may be not without interest also to readers who already possess a certain knowledge of the subject.

Recent years have witnessed extraordinary progress in both ophthalmology and applied optics. Not many persons are aware of the rapid rate at which spectacle optics, in particular, is developing into a severe scientific pursuit; and there are certain portions of this volume which I think will be helpful to the modern oculist and optometrist. Thus, for example, I have been at some pains to explain the fundamental principles of ophthalmic lenses and prisms.

In general, however, I have necessarily had to omit much

v

that is essential to a thorough knowledge of the theory of
optical instruments. In fact, in the space at my disposal
it has been found quite impossible to describe a single one
of these instruments in detail. In the latter portion of the
book the theory of the chromatic and spherical aberrations
is treated as briefly as possible; and I have given Von Seidel's
formulæ for the five spherical aberrations in the case of a
system of infinitely thin lenses, chiefly because these formulæ
are exceedingly useful in the preliminary design of an optical
system. But a complete discussion of these subjects would
lie far beyond the plan of this volume.

The problems appended to each chapter were originally
collected for the use of my pupils and are generally of a very
elementary description. A few of them have been adapted
from other text-books, but in such cases I have now lost sight
of their sources.

If perchance this book should help to stimulate the study
of optics in our colleges and universities, the author will feel
abundantly repaid. Unfortunately, at present geometrical
optics would seem to be a kind of Cinderella in the curric-
ulum of physics, regarded perhaps with a certain friendly
toleration as a mathematical discipline not without value,
but hardly permitted to take rank on equal terms with her
sister branches of physics. On the contrary, it might be inferred that any system of knowledge which had already
placed at the disposal of scientific investigators such in-
comparable means of research as are provided by modern
optical instruments, and which has found so many useful
applications in the arts of both peace and war, would be deserving of the highest recognition and would be fostered and
encouraged in all possible ways. According to the maxim,
fas est et ab hoste doceri, the fact that from the time of Fraunhofer the Germans have not ceased to cultivate this field of
theoretical and applied science with notable achievements,
is certainly not without significance for us in this country
and in England. Indeed, both in England and in France,

apparently due to the exigencies of war, schools of applied optics have recently been organized.

Nearly all of the diagrams in this volume were drawn by my friends, Professor Joseph Hudnut, Dr. B. A. Wooten and Mr. J. G. Sparkes, to whom I am much indebted. I desire also to express my grateful acknowledgments to my colleague, Professor H. W. Farwell, for numerous valuable criticisms from time to time and especially for aid in making the photographic illustrations in Chapter II.

Any suggestions or corrections which may improve and extend the usefulness of the book will be appreciated.

JAMES P. C. SOUTHALL.

Columbia University,
  New York, N. Y.,
    April 4, 1918.

PREFACE TO THE SECOND EDITION

In the preparation of this volume a careful effort has been made to eradicate all the misprints and errors in both the text and diagrams of the first edition. The new problems which are to be found scattered here and there throughout the book constitute a large and important addition. Here it may be pointed out that the problems which are placed at the end of each chapter are not merely intended as good exercises for the student, valuable as they may be for that purpose. Many of them have a special value wholly apart from such uses and contain statements of general principles and methods which are not to be found explicitly in the text itself but which are corollaries perhaps of more practical utility than the theorems from which they are derived. Occasionally also a problem may have a certain historical interest or flavor: thus, for example, the formulæ given in No. 83, page 216, and No. 60, page 257, express the relations between conjugate foci which HUYGENS communicated to the

Royal Society in 1669 (*cf.* § 200) in the famous anagram:
"Tertia proportionalis in lente, quarta proportionalis in
superficie simplici dat punctum correspondens." So also
problem No. 20, page 557, gives incidentally the so-called
TSCHERNING equation for determining the form of a correction eye-glass which is free from astigmatism of oblique
bundles and adapted therefore for the mobile eye, as realized
in the modern "Punktal" spectacle lens.

Most important of all is an entire new chapter which has
been added at the end of the volume. Chapter XVI is called
an Appendix in the sense that it treats mainly of such subjects as have been already discussed in some measure in the
previous pages; but here, it may be, the serious student will
discover much new material not usually to be found in text-
books on optics which, however, is at the basis of some of
the best and most fruitful methods of modern optical engineering. Reflection prisms, new and approved schemes of
optical calculation, Cartesian optical surfaces—these are a
few of the topics that come under review in this chapter.
The brief outline of the historical development of geometrical
optics from EUCLID to NEWTON lends a human interest to
the subject and undoubtedly helps to clarify it.

The new diagrams, Figs. 59, 68 and 248–287, inclusive
(except two drawings which have been reproduced from HUY-
GENS' writings), have been executed with much skill and sym-
pathy by my pupil, Mr. F. J. RUCH. I am confident that the
readers of these portions of the book will be no less grateful
for his aid than I am myself. I am also much indebted to
my assistant, Mr. C. L. TRELEAVEN, for helping with the
proof-reading.

JAMES P. C. SOUTHALL.

Columbia University,
  New York, N. Y.,
    Feb. 1, 1923.

CONCERNING THE THIRD EDITION

Essentially this third edition of *Mirrors, Prisms and Lenses* consists in an enlargement of the volume by the addition of two entirely new chapters, namely Chapter XVII on the microscope considered as being more or less typical of optical instruments in general and Chapter XVIII which treats of various subjects (double refraction, ophthalmometer, visual acuity, color sensations, binocular perception of depth and the nature of light) pertaining more to physical and to physiological optics than to geometrical optics, yet all having a very direct bearing on the plan and purpose of the book as a whole. The inclusion of this new material comprising about 140 pages in all has made it necessary to revise the index completely.

Great care has been taken to eliminate as far as possible the typographical errors that were found in the second edition; otherwise no changes have been made in the main body of the book, Chapters I–XVI. Occasional misprints as well as other less excusable mistakes seem to be almost unavoidable in a work of this kind; I can only repeat that I shall be grateful for having my attention called to them and likewise for any helpful suggestions that will extend the usefulness of the book.

For the new diagrams in Chapters XVII and XVIII, I am much indebted to my colleague Professor C. L. TRELEAVEN and also to my former pupil Mr. H. J. HOFF.

JAMES P. C. SOUTHALL.

Columbia University,
New York, N. Y.,
Jan. 1, 1933.

CONTENTS

CHAPTER I

Lights and Shadows

SECTIONS	PAGES
1–11.	1–27
1. Luminous Bodies	1
2. Transparent and Opaque Bodies	1–3
3. Rectilinear Propagation of Light	3–5
4. Shadows, Eclipses, etc.	6–9
5. Wave Theory of Light	9, 10
6. HUYGENS's Construction of the Wave-Front	10–13
7. Rays of Light are Normal to the Wave-Surface	13–15
8. The Direction and Location of a Luminous Point	15–18
9. Field of View	18, 19
10. Apparent Size	20–22
11. The Effective Rays	23–25
Problems	25–27

CHAPTER II

Reflection of Light.   Plane Mirrors

SECTIONS	PAGES
12–25.	26–63
12. Regular and Diffuse Reflection	28–30
13. Law of Reflection	30–32
14. HUYGENS's Construction of the Wave-Front in case of Reflection at a Plane Mirror	33–37
15. Image in a Plane Mirror	37–40
16. The Field of View of a Plane Mirror	40–43
17. Successive Reflections from Two Plane Mirrors	43
18. Images in a System of Two Inclined Mirrors	43–48

xii   Contents

SECTIONS   PAGES
19. Construction of the Path of a Ray Reflected into
    the Eye from a Pair of Inclined Mirrors........   48–50
20. Rectangular Combinations of Plane Mirrors.......   50, 51
21. Applications of the Plane Mirror.................   52, 53
22. *Porte Lumière* and Heliostat....................   53–55
23. Measurement of the Angle of a Prism.............   55
24. Measure of Angular Deflections by Mirror and
    Scale..   56–58
25. HADLEY's Sextant.............................   58–60
    Problems......................................   60–63

CHAPTER III

Refraction of Light

SECTIONS   PAGES
26–39.   64–94

26. Passage of Light from One Medium to Another....   64, 65
27. Law of Refraction.............................   65–67
28. Experimental Proof of the Law of Refraction......   67–69
29. Reversibility of the Light Path..................   69
30. Limiting Values of the Index of Refraction........   70
31. HUYGENS's Construction of a Plane Wave Refracted
    at a Plane Surface...........................   70–72
32. Mechanical Illustration of the Refraction of a Plane
    Wave..   72, 73
33. Absolute Index of Refraction...................   74–76
34. Construction of the Refracted Ray..............   76–78
35. Deviation of the Refracted Ray.................   78
36. Total Reflection..............................   78–83
37. Experimental Illustrations of Total Reflection....   83–86
38. Generalization of the Laws of Reflection and Re-
    fraction.   Principle of Least Time (FERMAT's
    Law).......................................   86–89
39. The Optical Length of the Light-Path and the Law
    of MALUS....................................   89–91
    Problems......................................   92–94

CHAPTER IV

Refraction at a Plane Surface and also through a Plate with Plane Parallel Faces

SECTIONS   PAGES
40–47.   95–112

40. Trigonometric Calculation of Ray Refracted at a Plane Surface............................... 95, 96
41. Imagery in a Plane Refracting Surface by Rays which Meet the Surface Nearly Normally...... 96–98
42. Image of a Point Formed by Rays that are Obliquely Refracted at a Plane Surface............ 98, 99
43. The Image-Lines of a Narrow Bundle of Rays Refracted Obliquely at a Plane.................. 100
44. Path of a Ray Refracted Through a Slab with Plane Parallel Sides.............................. 101–103
45. Segments of a Straight Line.................... 104, 105
46. Apparent Position of an Object seen through a Transparent Slab whose Parallel Sides are Perpendicular to the Line of Sight................ 105–107
47. Multiple Images in the two Parallel Faces of a Plate Glass Mirror................................ 107–110
     Problems...................................... 110–112

CHAPTER V

Refraction through a Prism

SECTIONS   PAGES
48–62.   113–148

48. Definitions etc................................. 113
49. Construction of Path of a Ray Through a Prism.. 113–116
50. The Deviation of a Ray by a Prism 116, 117
51. Grazing Incidence and Grazing Emergence....... 117, 118
52. Minimum Deviation............................ 119–122
53. Deviation away from the Edge of the Prism....... 122, 123
54. Refraction of a Plane Wave Through a Prism..... 123, 124
55. Trigonometric Calculation of the Path of a Ray in a Principal Section of a Prism................. 124, 125

xiv Contents

SECTIONS   PAGES
56. Total Reflection at the Second Face of the Prism.. 125–128
57. Perpendicular Emergence at the Second Face of
    the Prism.......................................   129
58. Case when the Ray Traverses the Prism Symmet-
    rically..   129
59. Minimum Deviation............................   129–133
60. Deviation of Ray by Thin Prism............... 133, 134
61. Power of an Ophthalmic Prism. Centrad and
    Prism-Dioptry................................   134–138
62. Position and Power of a Resultant Prism Equiva-
    lent to Two Thin Prisms.....................   138–142
    Problems.....................................   142–148

CHAPTER VI

Reflection and Refraction of Paraxial Rays at a Spherical Surface

SECTIONS   PAGES
63–86.   149–216

63. Introduction. Definitions, Notation, etc.......... 149–153
64. Reflection of Paraxial Rays at a Spherical Mirror.... 153–156
65. Definition and Meaning of the Double Ratio...... 156–159
66. Perspective Ranges of Points................... 159–161
67. The Harmonic Range 161–164
68. Application to the Case of the Reflection of Par-
    axial Rays at a Spherical Mirror.............. 164–166
69. Focal Point and Focal Length of a Spherical Mirror 166–168
70. Graphical Method of Exhibiting the Imagery by
    Paraxial Rays............................... 168–171
71. Extra-Axial Conjugate Points................... 171–175
72. The Lateral Magnification...................... 176
73. Field of View of a Spherical Mirror.............. 176–179
74. Refraction of Paraxial Rays at a Spherical Surface...179–182
75. Reflection Considered as a Special Case of Refrac-
    tion....................................... 182, 183
76. Construction of the Point M' Conjugate to the
    Axial Point M.............................. 183–186

Contents

SECTIONS   PAGES

77. The Focal Points (F, F') of a Spherical Refracting Surface.................................... 186–190
78. Abscissa-Equation Referred to the Vertex of the Spherical Refracting Surface as Origin......... 190, 191
79. The Focal Lengths f, f' of a Spherical Refracting Surface.................................... 191–193
80. Extra-Axial Conjugate Points; Conjugate Planes of a Spherical Refracting Surface..............193, 194
81. Construction of the Point Q' which with respect to a Spherical Refracting Surface is Conjugate to the Extra-Axial Point Q...................... 194–196
82. Lateral Magnification for case of Spherical Refracting Surface............................ 196
83. The Focal Planes of a Spherical Refracting Surface...................................... 197–199
84. Construction of Paraxial Ray Refracted at a Spherical Surface................................ 199, 200
85. The Image-Equations in the case of Refraction of Paraxial Rays at a Spherical Surface........... 200, 201
86. The so-called SMITH-HELMHOLTZ Formula........ 201, 202
    Problems.................................... 203–216

CHAPTER VII

Refraction of Paraxial Rays through an Infinitely Thin Lens

SECTIONS   PAGES
87–98.   217–257

87. Forms of Lenses............................... 217–223
88. The Optical Center O of a Lens surrounded by the same Medium on both sides.................... 223–226
89. The Abscissa-Formula of a Thin Lens, referred to the Axial Point of the Lens as Origin........... 226–229
90. The Focal Points of an Infinitely Thin Lens....... 229–232
91. Construction of the Point M' Conjugate to the Axial Point M with respect to an Infinitely Thin Lens...................................... 232–234

Contents

SECTIONS   PAGES
92. Extra-Axial Conjugate Points Q, Q'; Conjugate
    Planes.................................... 234–236
93. Lateral Magnification in case of Infinitely Thin
    Lens...................................... 236, 237
94. Character of the Imagery in a Thin Lens......... 237–240
95. The Focal Lengths f, f' of an Infinitely Thin
    Lens...................................... 240–242
96. Central Collineation of Object-Space and Image-
    Space..................................... 242–244
97. Central Collineation (cont'd). Geometrical Con-
    structions................................. 244–247
98. Field of View of an Infinitely Thin Lens.......... 247–249
    Problems................................... 249–257

CHAPTER VIII

Change of Curvature of the Wave-front in Reflection and Refraction. Dioptry System

SECTIONS   PAGES
99–110.   258–299

99. Concerning Curvature and its Measure........... 258–265
100. Refraction of a Spherical Wave at a Plane Surface. 265–269
101. Refraction of a Spherical Wave at a Spherical Sur-
     face..................................... 269–274
102. Reflection of a Spherical Wave at a Spherical
     Mirror................................... 274–276
103. Refraction of a Spherical Wave through an In-
     finitely Thin Lens.......................... 276–279
104. Reduced Distance............................ 279–281
105. The Refracting Power........................ 281–284
106. Reduced Abscissa and Reduced "Vergence"....... 284–286
107. The Dioptry as Unit of Curvature............... 286–288
108. Lens-Gauge................................. 288, 289
109. Refraction of Paraxial Rays through a Thin Lens-
     System................................... 289–291
110. Prismatic Power of a Thin Lens................. 291–295
     Problems.................................. 295–299

Contents xvii

CHAPTER IX

Astigmatic Lenses

SECTIONS   PAGES
111–116.   300–328

111. Curvature and Refracting Power of a Normal Section of a Curved Refracting Surface 300–305
112. Surfaces of Revolution. Cylindrical and Toric Surfaces 305–310
113. Refraction of a Narrow Bundle of Rays incident Normally on a Cylindrical Refracting Surface ... 310–314
114. Thin Cylindrical and Toric Lenses 314–318
115. Transposing of Cylindrical Lenses 318–320
116. Obliquely Crossed Cylinders 320–326
    Problems 326–328

CHAPTER X

Geometrical Theory of the Symmetrical Optical Instrument

SECTIONS   PAGES
117–124.   329–255

117. Graphical Method of tracing the Path of a Paraxial Ray through a Centered System of Spherical Refracting Surfaces 329–331
118. Calculation of the Path of a Paraxial Ray through a Centered System of Spherical Refracting Surfaces 332–334
119. The so-called Cardinal Points of an Optical System 334–339
120. Construction of the Image-point Q' conjugate to an Extra-Axial Object-Point Q 339, 340
121. Construction of the Nodal Points, N, N' 340–342
122. The Focal Lengths f, f' 342–344
123. The Image-Equations in the case of a Symmetrical Optical System 344–349
124. The Magnification-Ratios and their Mutual Relations 349–351
    Problems 351–355

CHAPTER XI

Compound Systems. Thick Lenses and Combinations of Lenses and Mirrors

SECTIONS   PAGES

125–132.   356–396

125. Formulæ for Combination of Two Optical Systems 356–359
126. Formulæ for Combination of Two Optical Systems in terms of the Refracting Power 360–362
127. Thick Lenses Bounded by Spherical Surfaces 362–365
128. The so-called "Vertex Refraction" of a Thick Lens 365, 366
129. Combination of Two Lenses 366–370
130. Optical Constants of GULLSTRAND's Schematic Eye 370–374
131. Combination of Three Optical Systems 374–376
132. "Thick Mirror" 376–384
      Problems 384–396

CHAPTER XII

Aperture and Field of Optical System

SECTIONS   PAGES

133–143.   397–424

133. Limitation of Ray-Bundles by Diaphragms or Stops 397–399
134. The Aperture-Stop and the Pupils of the System . . . 399–401
135. Illustrations 401–404
136. Aperture-Angle. Case of Two or More Entrance-Pupils 404–406
137. Field of View 406–409
138. Field of View of System Consisting of a Thin Lens and the Eye 409–413
139. The Chief Rays 413, 414
140. The so-called "Blur-Circles" (or Circles of Diffusion) in the Screen-Plane 414–416
141. The Pupil-Centers as Centers of Perspective of Object-Space and Image-Space 416, 417
142. Proper Distance of Viewing a Photograph 417–419
143. Perspective Elongation of Image 419
144. Telecentric Systems 420–423
      Problems 423, 424

Contents

CHAPTER XIII

Optical System of the Eye. Magnifying Power of Optical Instruments

SECTIONS   PAGES
145–159.   425–464

145. The Human Eye.............................. 425–431
146. Optical Constants of the Eye................... 431–433
147. Accommodation of the Eye.................... 433, 434
148. Far Point and Near Point of the Eye............ 434, 435
149. Decrease of the Power of Accommodation with Increasing Age................................ 435, 436
150. Changes of Refracting Power in Accommodation.. 436, 437
151. Amplitude of Accommodation.................. 437–439
152. Various Expressions for the Refraction of the Eye.. 439
153. Emmetropia and Ametropia.................... 439–443
154. Correction Eye-Glasses........................ 443–446
155. Visual Angle................................. 446–448
156. Size of Retinal Image........................ 448, 449
157. Apparent Size of an Object seen Through an Optical Instrument................................. 449–452
158. Magnifying Power of an Optical Instrument Used in Conjunction with the Eye.................. 452–455
159. Magnifying Power of a Telescope................ 455–460
Problems.................................... 461–464

CHAPTER XIV

Dispersion and Achromatism

SECTIONS   PAGES
160–174.   465–507

160. Dispersion by a Prism........................ 465–471
161. Dark Lines of the Solar Spectrum............... 472
162. Relation between the Color of the Light and the Frequency of Vibration of the Light-Waves........ 473–476
163. Index of Refraction as a Function of the Wave-Length.................................... 476, 477

SECTIONS   PAGES
164. Irrationality of Dispersion...................... 477–479
165. Dispersive Power of a Medium................... 479–481
166. Optical Glass................................... 481–487
167. Chromatic Aberration and Achromatism.......... 487–489
168. "Optical Achromatism" and "Actinic Achroma-
     tism"....................................... 489–491
169. Achromatic Combination of Two Thin Prisms...... 491–493
170. Direct Vision Combination of Two Thin Prisms... 493–495
171. Calculation of AMICI Prism with Finite Angles.... 495–497
172. KESSLER Direct Vision Quadrilateral Prism....... 497–499
173. Achromatic Combination of Two Thin Lenses...... 499–502
174. Achromatic Combination of Two Thin Lenses in
     Contact.................................... 502–505
     Problems................................... 505–507

CHAPTER XV

Rays of Finite Slope. Spherical Aberration, Astigmatism of Oblique Bundles, etc.

SECTIONS   PAGES
175–193.   508–557

175. Introduction................................. 508, 509
176. Construction of a Ray Refracted at a Spherical Sur-
     face..................................... 509–512
177. The Aplanatic Points of a Spherical Refracting Sur-
     face..................................... 512, 513
178. Spherical Aberration Along the Axis............. 513–515
179. Spherical Zones.............................. 515, 516
180. Trigonometrical Calculation of a Ray Refracted at a
     Spherical Surface......................../..... 516–519
181. Path of Ray through a Centered System of Spheri-
     cal Refracting Surfaces. Numerical Calculation 519–522
182. The Sine-Condition or Condition of Aplanatism... 522–525
183. Caustic Surfaces.............................. 525, 526
184. Meridian and Sagittal Sections of a Narrow Bundle
     of Rays before and after Refraction at a Spherical
     Surface.................................... 526–529

Contents

SECTIONS   PAGES

185. Formula for Locating the Position of the Image-Point Q' of a Pencil of Sagittal Rays Refracted at a Spherical Surface.......................... 529, 530
186. Position of the Image-Point P' of a Pencil of Meridian Rays Refracted at a Spherical Surface.... 530–533
187. Measure of the Astigmatism of a Narrow Bundle of Rays...................................... 533, 534
188. Image-Lines (or Focal Lines) of a Narrow Astigmatic Bundle of Rays......................... 534–536
189. The Astigmatic Image-Surfaces.................. 536–538
190. Curvature of the Image....................... 538–540
191. Coma....................................... 540–543
192. Distortion; Condition of Orthoscopy.............. 543–545
193. SEIDEL's Theory of the Five Aberrations.......... 545–550
     Problems..................................... 551–558

CHAPTER XVI
Miscellaneous Notes

SECTIONS   PAGES

194–205.   559–634

194. Rectilinear Propagation of Light (Historical)....... 559–563
195. Reflection of Light; Mirrors.................... 563–569
196. Dioptrics (Historical)........................ 569–573
197. Reflection Prisms............................ 573–575
198. Single Reflection Prism....................... 575–585
199. Double Reflection Prism....................... 586–592
200. Optics in the Seventeenth Century.............. 592–598
201. Combination of Two Thin Lenses................ 599–602
202. Types of Optical Instruments.................. 602–606
203. Formula for Refracting Power ($F_{1, k}$) of Centered System of k Spherical Refracting Surfaces....... 606–611
204. Trigonometrical Calculation of Ray Refracted at a Spherical Surface........................... 611–617
205. Cartesian Optical Surfaces (or Surfaces which are free from Spherical Aberration along the axis)... 617–625
     Miscellaneous Problems....................... 626–634

Contents

CHAPTER XVII

The Microscope

Sections   Pages
206–220.   635–684

206. Introduction.................................. 635, 636

I. *The Magnifying Glass (or Simple Microscope)*

207. The Purpose of a Microscope..................... 636, 637
208. Simple Microscope; Magnifying Power............ 638–643
209. Useful Forms of Magnifying Glass................ 644–647
210. Practical Types of Simple Microscope............. 647–650

II. *The Compound Microscope*

211. General Characteristics of the Instrument.......... 650–655
212. The Ray-Procedure in the Compound Microscope... 655–661
213. Metric Relations in the Compound Microscope..... 661–663
214. The Numerical Aperture......................... 663–667
215. Brightness of the Image......................... 667–669
216. Resolving Power of a Microscope................. 669–673
217. Optical Requirements of the Objective of a Micro-
      scope....................................... 673–677
218. Types of Microscope Objectives.................. 677–680
219. The Ocular.................................... 680–683
220. Microphotography and Other Applications of the
      Microscope.................................. 683, 684

CHAPTER XVIII

Notes on Physical Optics and Physiological Optics

Sections   Pages
221–252.   685–771

221. Index of Refraction............................ 685–686

I. *Double Refraction*

222. Double Refraction in Iceland Spar................ 686–688
223. Huygens's Construction of the Wave-Surface in
      Iceland Spar................................ 688–693

Contents

SECTIONS   PAGES

224. The Variable Index of Refraction of the Extraordinary Ray in Iceland Spar 693, 694

225. WOLLASTON's Prism 694–696

II. *The Ophthalmometer*

226. The External Surface of the Cornea of the Human Eye 696–699

227. The Optical Theory of the Ophthalmometer 699–703

228. Clinical Ophthalmometer 703–706

III. *Visual Acuity in Daylight Vision*

229. Size of Retinal Image of Distant Object 707–709

230. Diffraction Disk Due to a Small Round Aperture ... 709–713

231. Resolving Power of the Eye in Central Daylight Vision 713–716

232. SNELLEN's Sight-Test Charts 716–719

IV. *The Color Sensations*

233. Color Vision 720–722

234. Elementary Facts of Color Mixing 722–725

235. Character and Distribution of the Spectral Colors.. 725–727

236. Complementary Spectral Colors 727, 728

237. The Gap in the Visible Spectrum 728–730

238. Hue, Saturation and Luminosity 730–732

239. The Color Triangle 732–735

240. Note concerning Homogeneous Projective Co-ordinates 735–738

241. The YOUNG-HELMHOLTZ Three-Components Color Theory 738–743

242. HERING's Opponent-Colors Theory 743–747

V. *Perception of Depth in Binocular (Stereoscopic) Vision*

243. Monocular Field of View (Eye at Rest) 747, 748

244. Field of Fixation of the Mobile Eye 748, 749

245. Field of Binocular Fixation 749–751

246. Binocular Perception of Depth 751, 752

247. Stereoscopic Vision 752–755

248. Simple Laws of Stereoscopic Projection 755–758

249. Telestereoscope and Binocular Telescopes 758–761

VI. *Concerning the Nature of Light*

SECTIONS	PAGES
250. FRESNEL's Wave Theory	761–764
251. MAXWELL's Electromagnetic Theory	764–767
252. Modern Theories	767–771
INDEX	773–806

MIRRORS, PRISMS AND LENSES

CHAPTER I

LIGHTS AND SHADOWS

1. Luminous Bodies.—The external world is revealed to the eye by means of light. With the rising sun night is changed into day, and animals, vegetables and minerals in all their manifold varieties of form and shade and color, which were quite invisible in the dark, are now revealed to view. Wherever the eye turns to gaze, there comes to it from far or near a messenger of light conveying information about the object which is under inspection. In an absolutely dark room everything is invisible, because the eye can perceive objects only when they radiate or reflect light into it. In the strict sense a source of light is a self-luminous body which shines by its own light, such as the sun or a fixed star or a candle-flame; but frequently the term is applied to a body which merely reflects or transmits light which has fallen upon it from some other body, as, for example, the moon and the planets which are illuminated by the light from the sun. In this latter sense the blue sky and the clouds, which, shining by light derived originally from the sun, contribute the greater portion of what is meant by daylight, are to be regarded as light-sources. A point-source of light or a luminous point is in reality a small element of luminous surface of relatively negligible dimensions or else a body like a star at such a vast distance that it appears like a point.

2. Transparent and Opaque Bodies.—In general, when light falls on a body, it is partly turned back or reflected at or very near the surface of the body, partly absorbed within

1

the body, and partly transmitted through it. An absolutely black body which absorbs all the light that falls on it does not exist; the best example we have is afforded by a body whose surface is coated with lamp-black. The color of a body as seen by reflected light is explained by the fact that part of the incident light is absorbed, whereas only light characteristic of the color in question is cast off or reflected from the body. Thus, when sunlight falls on a piece of red flannel, it is robbed of all its constituent colors except red, and thus it happens that the color by which we describe the body is in fact due to the light which it rejects. If the piece of red flannel were illuminated by pure blue light, it would appear black or invisible.

A substance such as air or water or glass, which is pervious to light, is said to be *transparent*. None of the light that traverses a perfectly transparent body will be absorbed; and, on the other hand, a perfectly *opaque* body is one which suffers no light at all to be transmitted through it. No substance is either absolutely transparent or absolutely opaque. These terms, therefore, as applied to actual bodies are merely relative, and so when we say that a body is opaque, we mean only that the light transmitted through it is so slight as to be practically inappreciable. Naturally, one thinks of clear water as transparent and of metallic substances generally as opaque; but a sufficiently large mass of water will be found to be impervious to light, whereas, on the other hand, gold leaf transmits green light. A perfectly transparent body would be quite invisible by transmitted light, although its presence could be detected by observing the distortion in the appearance of bodies viewed through it.

Again there are some substances which, while they are not transparent in the ordinary sense, are far from being opaque, such, for example, as ground glass, alabaster, porcelain, milk, blood, smoke, which contain imbedded or suspended in them fine particles of matter of a different optical quality from that of the surrounding mass. Light does penetrate through materials of this nature in a more or less irregular fashion, and accordingly they are described as *translucent*. In the interior of such granular structures or "cloudy media" light undergoes a so-called internal diffused reflection or scattering; so that while it may be possible to discern the presence of a body through an intervening mass of such material, the form of the object will be to some extent indistinct and unrecognizable.

An *optical medium* is any space, whether filled or not with ponderable matter, which is pervious to light. In geometrical optics it is generally assumed that the media are not only homogeneous and isotropic (meaning thereby that the substance possesses the same properties in all directions), as, for example, air, glass, water and vacuum, but perfectly transparent as well.

3. Rectilinear Propagation of Light.—When an opaque body is interposed between the observer's eye and a source of light, it is well known that all parts of the latter which lie on straight lines connecting the pupil of the eye with points of the opaque obstacle will be hid from view. We cannot see round a corner; we can look through a straight tube but not through a crooked one. A child takes note of such facts as these among the very earliest of his experiences and recognizes without difficulty the truth of the common saying that "light travels in straight lines," which in the language of science is called the law of the rectilinear propagation of light. The light that comes to us from a star traverses the vast stretches of interstellar space in straight lines until it reaches the earth's atmosphere, which is composed of layers of air of increasing density from the upper portions towards the surface of the earth; so that the medium through which the light passes in this short remainder of its downward journey is no longer isotropic, and, hence, also this part of the light path will, in general, be no longer straight but curved by a gradual and continuous bending from the less dense layers of air to the more dense layers below. This explains why it is necessary for an observer on the earth's surface looking through a long narrow tube at a star not directly overhead to point the tube not at the star itself but at its apparent place in the sky, which depends on the direction which the light has when it enters the eye; and, consequently, in accurate determinations of the position of a heavenly body, the astronomer is always careful to take account of the apparent displacement due to this so-called "atmospheric refraction," and a principal reason why astronomical observatories are nearly always located on high mountains is to obviate as much as possible the disturbing influence of the atmosphere. In aiming a rifle or in any of the ordinary processes we call "sighting," which are at the basis of some of the most delicate methods of measurement known to us, we rely with absolute confidence on this proved law of experience concerning the rectilinear propagation of light; and, in fact, the most conclusive demonstration that a line is straight consists in showing that it is the path which light pursues. The notion of a "ray of light" is derived from this law, and any line along which light travels is to be regarded as a ray of light. According to this idea, therefore, *the rays of light in an isotropic medium are straight lines.*

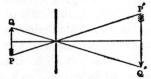

Fig. 1.—Rectilinear Propagation of Light.

A very striking proof of the rectilinear propagation of light is afforded by placing a luminous object (Fig. 1) in front of an opaque screen in which there is a very small round aperture. If now a second screen or a white wall is placed parallel to the first screen on the other side of it, there will be cast on it a so-called inverted image of the object, the size of which will be proportional to the distance between the two screens. From each point of the luminous object rays go out in all directions, and a narrow cone of these rays will traverse the perforated screen through the opening and illuminate a small area on the other screen, and thus every part of the object will be depicted in this way by little patches of light arranged in a figure which is similar in form to the object, but which is completely inverted, since not only top and bottom but right and left are reversed in consequence of the rectilinear paths of the rays of light. It may be remarked that this image is not an optical image in the strict sense of the term (see § 11), but the phenomenon can be explained only on the supposition that light proceeds in straight lines. If another small opening were made in the front screen very near the first hole, there would be two images formed which would partly overlap each other, so that the resultant image would be more or less blurred, and if we have a single large aperture, we could no longer see any distinct image at all.

The *pinhole camera*, invented by GIAMBATTISTA DELLA PORTA (*c*. 1543–1615), and sometimes called PORTA's camera, is constructed on the principle of the experiment which has just been described. It is very useful in making accurate photographic copies of the architectural details of buildings, because the image which is obtained is entirely free from distortion.

In the pinhole camera there is a certain relation between the size of the pinhole and the distance of the sensitive plate. According to ABNEY, in order to get the best results with an apparatus of this kind the diameter of the pinhole ought to be directly proportional to the square-root of the distance of the plate from the aperture, that is,

$$y = k\sqrt{x},$$

where x and y denote the distance of the plate and the diameter of the pinhole, respectively, and k denotes a constant, the value of which will depend on the unit of length. Thus, if x and y are measured in inches, $k = 0.008$; in centimeters, $k = 0.01275$.

4. Shadows, Eclipses, etc.—The forms of shadows are also easily explained on the hypothesis that light proceeds in straight lines, for the outline of the shadow cast by a body is precisely similar to that of the object as viewed from the place where the source of light is. Thus, for example, the

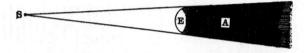

Fig. 2.—Shadow (umbra) of opaque globe E illuminated by point-source S.

shadow of a sphere held in front of a point-source of light has the form of a circle, and the shadow cast by a circular disk will have the outline of an ellipse of greater and greater eccentricity as the disk is turned more and more nearly edge-on towards the light. Passing a shop-window on Sunday when the shade is drawn down, if the sun is shining

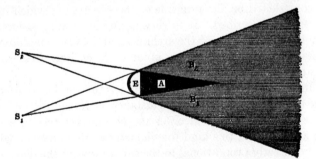

Fig. 3.—Shadow (umbra and penumbra) of opaque globe E illuminated by two point-sources S_1, S_2.

on the window, one can read the shadow of the sign painted on the glass quite as distinctly as the sign itself. The interposition of an opaque body between a source of light and a wall not only darkens a portion of the wall or casts its shadow there, but it converts an entire region of space between it and the wall into a dark tract either wholly or par-

tially screened from the light. Thus, for example, the space
A (Fig. 2) behind the body E which is comprised within the
cone of rays proceeding from the point-source S that are
intercepted by E gets no light from S, and this wholly un-
illuminated region is called the *umbra* or true shadow. When
there are two luminous points S_1 and S_2 (Figs. 3 and 4), the
region of shadow behind the opaque body E consists of the

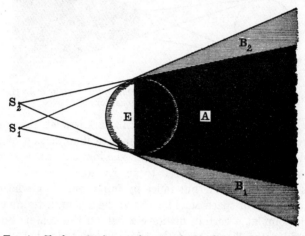

Fig. 4.—Shadow (umbra and penumbra) of opaque globe E
illuminated by two point-sources S_1, S_2.

umbra A which is wholly screened from both sources of light
and the so-called *penumbra* or partially illuminated space
composed of a space B_1 which gets light only from S_1 and
a similar space B_2 which gets light only from S_2. Points lying
beyond the *penumbra* will receive light from both sources.

If the light-source has an appreciable size, light will proceed from each of its shining points in all directions. Suppose, for example, that an opaque globe E (Fig. 5) is placed
in front of a luminous globe S: then the dark body will
intercept all rays that fall within the cone which is tangent
externally to the two spheres, and, consequently, the portion A of this cone which lies behind E will be completely

screened from all points of the source S, so that this portion constitutes the *umbra* where no light comes. In this case also there are two penumbral regions B_1 and B_2 which are partially illuminated, but the illumination is not uniform,

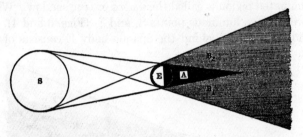

Fig. 5.—Shadow (umbra and penumbra) of opaque globe E illuminated by luminous globe S.

but increases gradually from total darkness at the outer borders of the *umbra* into the complete illumination of the region outside the shadow. The shadow cast on a screen by an opaque body exposed to an extended source of light has no sharp outline but fades by imperceptible gradations into the bright space outside. As to the *umbra*, it terminates in a point at a certain distance x behind the opaque body, provided the diameter of the latter is less than that of the luminous globe in front of it, that is, provided R is greater than r, where R, r denote the radii of luminous and opaque globes, respectively. If the distance d between the centers of the two globes is known, the length x of the *umbra* may be calculated from the proportion:

$$\frac{R}{r} = \frac{d+x}{x};$$

whence we find:

$$x = \frac{d}{\dfrac{R}{r} - 1}.$$

Thus, for example, the diameter of the sun is 109.5 times that of the earth, and the distance between the two bodies

is 93 millions of miles.   Accordingly, the *umbra* of the earth
is found to extend to a distance of more than 857 000 miles
behind it.   Sometimes the moon whose distance from the
earth is about 240 000 miles enters inside the shadow, and
becomes then totally eclipsed.   When the moon is only
partly inside the earth's *umbra*, there is a partial eclipse of
the moon.   On the other hand, if the earth or any part of it
comes inside the moon's shadow, there will be an eclipse
of the sun visible from points on the earth that are in the
shadow.

The angular diameter of the sun is 32′ 3.3″; whence it is
easy to calculate that the length of the *umbra* of an opaque
globe in sunlight is about 105 times the diameter of the globe.

On the other hand, if the light-source is smaller than the
interposed object, the *umbra*, instead of contracting to a
point, widens out indefinitely; and thus, whereas the shadow
cast on the opposite wall by a hand held in front of a broad
fire is smaller than the object, the shadow made by the same
hand in front of a small source of light like a candle-flame
may be prodigious in extent.

5. Wave Theory of Light.—The term "ray," as we have
employed it, is a purely geometrical conception, but in ordinary usage a ray of light implies generally an exceedingly
narrow beam of light such as is supposed to be obtained
when sunlight is admitted into a dark room through a pinhole opening in a shutter.   But when the experiment is
carefully made to try to isolate a so-called ray of light in
this fashion, new and unexpected difficulties arise, and,
contrary to our preconceived notions, we are disconcerted
by finding that the smaller the opening in the shutter, the
more difficult it becomes to realize the geometrical conception which is conveyed by the word "ray."   In fact, in consequence of this experiment and others of a similar kind,
we begin to perceive that the statement of the law of the
rectilinear propagation of light needs to be modified; for
among other phenomena we discover that when light pro-

ceeds through a very narrow aperture in a screen, it does not pass through it just as though the screen were not present, but it spreads out laterally from the point of perforation in all directions beyond the screen, proceeding, in fact, very much as it might do if the opening in the screen were the seat of a new and independent source of light.

The truth is, as has been ascertained now for a long time, light is propagated not by "rays" at all but by waves; and if, in general, it is found that light does proceed in straight lines and does not bend around corners as sound-waves do, the explanation is because the waves of light are excessively short, considerably less than one ten-thousandth of a centimeter. Wave-lengths of light are usually specified in terms of a unit called a "tenth-meter" or an "ÅNGSTROM unit," which is the hundred-millionth part of a centimeter (see § 162); that is, 1 ÅNGSTROM unit $= 10^{-10}$ meter $= 0.000\ 000\ 01$ cm. The wave-length of the deepest red light is found to be about 7667 of these units and the wave-length of light corresponding to the extreme violet end of the spectrum is a little more than half the above value or 3970 units.

According to the wave-theory the phenomena of light are dependent on an hypothetical medium called the *ether*, which may be compared to "an impalpable and all-pervading jelly" that not only fills empty space but penetrates freely through all material substances, solid, liquid and gaseous, and through which particles of ordinary matter move easily without apparent resistance, for it is imponderable and exceedingly elastic and subtle, insomuch that no one has ever succeeded in obtaining direct evidence of its existence. It is this ether which is the vehicle by which light-energy is transmitted and through which waves of light are incessantly throbbing with prodigious but measurable velocity, which *in vacuo* is about 300 million meters per second or about 186 000 miles per second.

6. Huygens's Construction of the Wave-Front.—The great Dutch philosopher HUYGENS (1629–1695), who was a contem-

porary of NEWTON's (1642–1727), and who is usually regarded
as the founder of the wave-theory of light, encountered his
greatest difficulty in trying to give a consistent and satisfactory explanation of the apparent rectilinear propagation of
light.   His mode of reasoning, as set forth in his " Treatise
on Light " published in 1690, while by no means free from
objection, leads to a simple *geometrical construction of the
wave-front* which corresponds with the known facts in regard
to the procedure of light.

Let O (Fig. 6) designate the position of a point-source of
light from which as center or origin ether waves proceed in
an isotropic medium with
equal speeds in all directions.   At the end of a
certain time the disturb-
ances will have arrived
at all the points which
lie on a spherical surface
σ_1 described around O as
center, and at the instant
in question this surface
will be the locus of all the
particles in the medium
that are in this initial
phase of excitation, and
so it represents the *wave-*

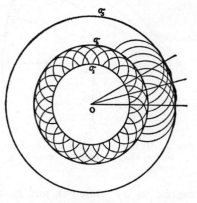

FIG. 6.—HUYGENS's construction of wave-
front.

front at this moment.   Now according to HUYGENS, every
point in the wave-front becomes immediately a new source
or center from which so-called secondary waves or wavelets spread out.   These innumerable ripples or wavelets
starting together from all the points affected by the
principal wave overlap and interfere with each other,
and HUYGENS inferred that their resultant sensible effects
are produced only at the points of the surface which at any
given instant touches or, as we say, envelops all the secondary
wave-fronts, and that accordingly the new principal wave-

front will be this enveloping surface; so that the effect is
the same as though the old wave-front had expanded into
the new, the disturbance marching forward along a straight
line in any given direction. Obviously, in an unobstructed
isotropic medium, such
as is here supposed,
the enveloping surface
or new wave-front will
be a sphere concentric
with the old wave-
front, and the straight
lines that radiate out
from the center will be
the paths of the dis-
turbance.

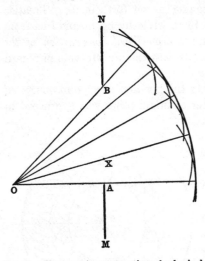

Now if a plane screen
MN (Fig. 7) is inter-
posed in front of the
advancing waves, and
if there is an opening
AB in the screen, each
point in the opening
between A, which is

FIG. 7.—Huygens's construction of spherical
waves passing through opening in a
screen.

nearest to the source O, and B, which is farthest from it,
will become in turn a new center of disturbance whence
secondary spherical waves will be propagated into the region on the other side of the screen. Since the disturbance
will have arrived at the point A before it has reached a point
X between A and B, the secondary wave emanating from
A will at the end of a given time t have been travelling for
a longer time than the secondary wave coming from X. If
the radius of the wavelet around X at the time t is denoted
by r, and if the distance OX is put equal to x, then $d = x + r$
will denote the distance from O which the disturbance will
have gone at the end of the time t; and since this distance
is constant, whereas the distances denoted by x and r are

variables depending on the position of the point X, it is evident that the farther X is from O, that is, the greater the value of x, the smaller will be the radius $r = d - x$ of the secondary wavelet around X. The enveloping surface in this case is seen to be that part of the spherical surface described around O as center with radius equal to d which is intercepted by the cone which has O for its vertex and the opening AB in the screen for a section. Within this cone, according to HUYGENS's view, the disturbance is propagated exactly as though the perforated screen had not been interposed, whereas points on the far side of the screen and outside this limiting cone are not affected at all.

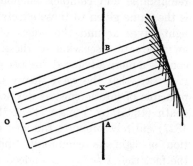

FIG. 8.—HUYGENS's construction of plane waves passing through opening in a screen.

It is plain that this mode of explanation is equivalent to the hypothesis of the rectilinear propagation of light.

If the luminous point O (Fig. 8) is so far away that the dimensions of the opening AB in the screen may be regarded as vanishingly small in comparison with the distance of the source, the straight lines drawn from O to the points A, X, B in the opening in the screen may be regarded as parallel, and the wave-front in this case will be plane instead of spherical, that is, the wave-front is a spherical surface with an exceedingly great radius as compared with the dimensions of the aperture in the screen.

7. Rays of Light are Normal to the Wave-Surface.—The most obvious objection to HUYGEN's construction is, What right has he to assume that the places of sensible effects are the points on the surface which is tangent to or envelops the secondary waves? And why is the light not propagated

backwards from these new centers as well as forwards?
Moreover, when the opening in the screen is very narrow,
it is found, as has been already stated (§ 5), that this construction does not correspond at all with the observed facts.

It is entirely beyond the scope of this book to attempt to
answer these questions here or to describe even briefly the
remarkable and complex phenomena of *diffraction* (which
is the name given to these effects due to the bending of the
light-waves around the edges of opaque obstacles). For
an adequate discussion of these matters the reader must
consult a more advanced treatise on physical optics. Suffice
it to say, that the wave-theory of light and especially the
principle of interference as developed long after HUYGENS's
death (1695) by YOUNG (1773–1829) and FRESNEL (1788–
1827) entirely supports the idea of the rectilinear propagation of light as commonly understood; notwithstanding
the fact that this law, as indeed is the case with nearly all
so-called natural laws, has to be accepted with certain reservations; but, fortunately, these latter do not concern us at
present.

Accordingly, a luminous point is said to emit light in all
directions, and the so-called light-rays in an isotropic medium
are straight lines radiating from the center of the spherical wave-surface. These rays may subsequently be bent
abruptly into new directions in traversing the boundary
between one isotropic medium and another, and under such
circumstances the wave-surfaces may cease to be spherical;
but no matter what may be the form of the wave-surface,
*the direction of the ray at any point is to be considered always as
normal to the wave-front that passes through that point* (see § 39).
In an isotropic medium the waves always march at right
angles to their own front, and the so-called rays of light in
geometrical optics are, in fact, the shortest optical routes
along which the disturbances in the ether are propagated
from place to place. With the aid of the principle of interference (alluded to above) and by the use of the higher

mathematics, it may indeed be shown that the effect produced at any point P in the path of a ray of light is due
almost exclusively to previous disturbances which have
occurred successively at all the points along the ray which
lie between the source and the point P in question, and that
disturbances at other points not lying on the ray which goes
through P are practically without influence at P, that is, their
effects there are mutually counteracted. And thus we arrive
also at the so-called *principle of the mutual independence of
rays of light*, which is also one of the fundamental laws of
geometrical optics. From this point of view a ray of light
is to be regarded as something more than a mere geometrical fiction and as having in some real sense a certain physical existence, although it is not possible to isolate the ray
from its companions.

8. The Direction and Location of a Luminous Point.—
When a ray of light comes into the eye, the natural inference as to its origin is that the source lies in the direction from
which the ray proceeded. There is no difficulty in pointing out
correctly the direction of an object which is viewed through
an isotropic medium; but if the medium were not isotropic,
the apparent direction of
the object might not be,
and probably would not
be, its real direction.
Thus, owing to the ef-
fects of atmospheric re-
fraction, to which allu-
sion has been made al-

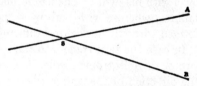

Fig. 9.—Direction and location of a luminous point.

ready (§ 3), the sun is seen above the horizon before it has
actually risen, and so also in the evening the sun is still
visible for a few moments after sunset. For the same reason
a star appears to be nearer the zenith than it really is.

In general, however, when a ray SA (Fig. 9) enters the
eye at A, it is correctly inferred that the source S lies somewhere on the straight line AS, but whether it is actually

situated at S or farther or nearer cannot be determined by means of a single ray. If the eye is transferred from A to another point B, the source will appear now to lie in the new direction BS. If the spectator views the source with both eyes simultaneously, one eye at A and the other at B, or if using only one eye he moves it quickly from A to B, the position of the source at S will be located at the point of intersection of the straight lines AS and BS; and this determination will be more accurate in proportion as the distance between the two points of observation A and B is greater or the more nearly the acute angle ASB approaches a right angle. That is the reason why in estimating the distance of a remote object one tries to observe it from two stations as widely separated as possible, and that explains also why a person shifts his head from side to side. If the object is comparatively near at hand, a single movement of the head may be sufficient in order to get a fairly good idea of its distance, or it may be that it is simply necessary to look at the object with both eyes at the same time. It is amusing to watch a person with one eye closed attempting to poke a pencil through a finger-ring suspended in the middle of a room on a level with his eye; by chance he may succeed after repeated failures, whereas with both eyes open, the operation is performed without the slightest difficulty.

In case the rays come into the eye after having traversed two or more isotropic media, it is easy to be deceived about the direction of the source where they emanated. In order for a bullet to hit a fish under water, the rifle must be pointed in a direction below that in which the fish appears to be. At the boundary-surface between two isotropic media the direction of a ray of light is usually changed abruptly by refraction (§ 26); so that, in general, the path of a ray will be found to consist of a series of line-segments. In Fig. 10 the broken line ABCD represents the course taken by a ray of light in proceeding through several media such as water, air and glass. The line-segments AB, BC and CD are portions of different straight lines of indefinite extent. For example, the actual route of the ray in air is along the straight line between B and C, and if the point P lies on this line between B and C, we say that the ray BC passes "really" through P, whereas we say that this same ray passes "virtually" through a point Q or R which lies in the prolongation of the line-segment BC in either direction.

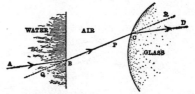

FIG. 10.—Points P, Q and R considered as lying on ray BC are to be regarded as lying in same medium as BC.

Moreover, thinking of the point Q or R as a point lying on the straight line BC which the light pursues in traversing the medium between the water and the glass, we must regard such a point as being optically in the same medium as the ray to which it belongs. Thus, the points Q and R in the figure considered as points on the ray BC are to be regarded as being optically in air, although in a physical sense Q is a point in the water and R is a point in the glass (see § 104).

Now let us suppose that two rays emanating originally

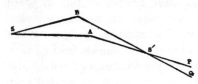

FIG. 11.—S′ is said to be a "real" image of point-source at S.

from a point-source S (Figs. 11 and 12) are bent at A and B into new directions AP and BQ, respectively, so as to enter the two eyes of an observer at P and Q. In such a case the observer will infer that the rays originated at the point S′ where the straight lines AP and BQ intersect. This point S′, which is called the *image* of S, may lie in the actual paths of the rays AP and BQ that enter the eyes, so that the light from S really does go through S′, and in this case (Fig. 11) the image S′ is said to be a *real image*. On the other hand, if the straight lines AP and BQ have to be produced backwards in order to find their point of intersection, the rays do not actually pass through S′, and in this case the image

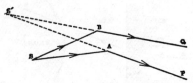

is said to be a *virtual image* of the point S (Fig. 12). However, it must be borne in mind in connection with these diagrams that in reality we do not see objects by means of single rays;

Fig. 12.—S′ is said to be a "virtual" image of point-source at S.

and, hence, we shall not be in a position to form an accurate idea of the term optical image until we come to consider bundles of rays in § 11.

9. Field of View.—The open or visible space commanded by the eye is called the field of view. Since the eye can turn in its socket, the field of view of the mobile eye is very much more extensive than that of the stationary eye, and, moreover, the field of view of both eyes is greater than that of one eye by itself. The spectator may also widen his field of vision by turning his head or indeed by turning his entire body. For the present, however, we shall employ the term field of view to mean that more limited portion of space which is accessible to the single eye turning in its socket around the so-called center of rotation of the eye. When a person gazes through a window, the outside field of view is limited partly by the size of the window and partly also by the position of the eye with reference to it; so that only such exterior objects will be visible as happen to lie within the conical region of space determined by drawing straight lines from the center of rotation of the eye to all the points in the edge of the window. Thus, for example, if the opening in the window is indicated by the gap GH in the straight line GH in Fig. 13, and if the point marked O is the position of the center of rotation of the eye, a luminous object at P

in front of the window and directly opposite the eye will
be plainly in view, because some of the rays from P may go
through the window and enter the eye. But if the object
is displaced far enough to one side to some position such as

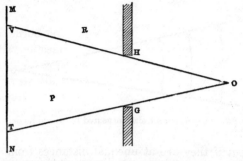

FIG. 13.—Field of view determined by contour of
window GH and position of the eye at O.

that marked R in the diagram, so that the straight line OR
does not pass through the window, the object will pass out
of the field of view. The straight line MN drawn parallel
to GH is supposed to represent a vertical wall opposite the
window. If this wall is covered with a mural painting, the
only part of the picture that can be seen through the window by the eye at O is the section included between the
points T and V where the straight lines OG and OH intersect
the straight line MN. The window acts here as a so-called
field-stop (§ 137) to limit the extent of the field of view. But
the limitation of the visible region depends essentially also
on the position of the eye, becoming more and more contracted the farther the eye is from the window. The size of
the window makes very little difference when the eye is
placed close to it, and a person sitting near an open window
can command almost as wide a view as if the entire wall of
the room were removed. If one is looking through a key-
hole in a door, he must put his eye close to the hole in order
to see objects that are not directly in front of it.

10. Apparent Size.—The *apparent size* of an object is measured by the *visual angle* which it subtends at the eye. Several objects in the field of view which subtend equal angles when viewed from the same standpoint are said to have the same apparent size; although their actual sizes will

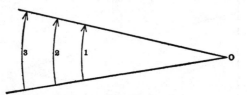

Fɪɢ. 14.—Apparent size measured by visual angle.

be different if they are at unequal distances from the eye. The objects marked 1, 2 and 3 in Fig. 14 appear to an eye at O to be all of the same size. Thus an elephant may appear no bigger than a man or a boy. Looking through a single pane of glass in a window, one may see a large building or an entire tree, because the apparent extent of the small area of glass is greater than that of the distant object. A fly crawling across the window may hide from view a large portion of the distant landscape outside. A mountain a few miles off may be viewed through a finger-ring.

The apparent size of an object, being measured by the visual angle which it subtends, is expressed in degrees or radians. The apparent diameter of the full moon in the sky, for example, is not quite half a degree, so that by holding a coin a little less than 9 mm. in diameter at a distance of one meter from the eye, the entire moon could be hid from view. In fact, instead of the angle itself it is customary to employ the tangent of the angle, especially in case the visual angle is not large. Thus, the apparent size of an object of height h at a distance d from the eye (in Fig. 15 AB = h, AO = d) is measured by the tangent of the angle BOA, that is,

Apparent size $= \dfrac{\text{linear dimension of the object}}{\text{distance from the eye}} = \dfrac{h}{d}.$

Accordingly, in order to determine the actual size (h) of the object, it is necessary to know its distance (d) as well as its apparent size, because the actual size is equal to the product of these two magnitudes. The apparent size of an

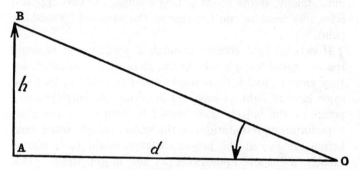

Fig. 15.—Apparent size varies inversely as distance d and directly as actual size h.

object at a distance of one foot is an hundred times greater than it is at a distance of an hundred feet, or, as we say, *the apparent size varies inversely as the distance.* As the object recedes farther and farther from the eye, its apparent size diminishes until at last it looks like a mere speck and the details in it have all disappeared. On the other hand, although the object is quite close to the eye, its actual dimensions may be so minute that it is not to be distinguished from a point. There is, indeed, a limit to the power of the human eye to see very small objects, which is reached when the object subtends in the field of view an angle that does not exceed one minute of arc. Two stars whose angular distance apart is less than this limiting value cannot be seen as separate and distinct by a normal eye without the aid of a telescope. Now $\tan 1' = \frac{1}{3438}$, and consequently the eye cannot distinguish details of form in an object which is viewed at a distance 3438 times as great as its greatest linear dimension. A silver quarter of a dollar is about 24 mm. in diameter and viewed from a distance of 82.5 meters (3438 times 24 mm. = 82 512 mm. = 82.5 m.) its apparent size will be 1' of arc and it will appear therefore like a mere point. The apparent width of a long straight street diminishes in proportion as the distance increases; until, finally, if the street is long enough, the two opposite sidewalks seem to run together at the so-called "vanishing point."

If rays of light coming through a window and entering the eye could leave marks in the glass at the points where they cross it, and if these marks could be made to emit the same kind of light as was sent out from the corresponding points of the object, there would be formed on the glass a pictorial representation of the object which when held before the eye at the proper distance would have almost exactly the same appearance as the object itself. This principle of *perspective* is made use of in the art of painting, and the artist, with his lights and shades and colors, tries to portray on a plane canvas a scene which will produce as nearly as possible the same visual impression on a spectator as would be produced by the natural objects themselves. So far as apparent size is concerned, such a representation may be perfect. In a good drawing the various figures are delineated in such dimensions that when viewed from the proper standpoint they have the same apparent sizes as the realities would have if seen under the aspect represented in the picture. No one looking at a photograph of a Greek temple will notice (unless his attention is specially directed to it) that the more distant pillars are much shorter in the picture than the nearer ones. Indeed, generally we pay little heed to the apparent sizes of things, but always try to conceive their real dimensions. When two persons meet and shake hands, neither is apt to observe that the other appears much taller than he did when they were fifty yards apart.

11. The Effective Rays.—All the rays that enter the eye and fall on the retina must pass through the circular window in the iris or colored diaphragm of the eye which is called the *pupil of the eye* and which is sometimes spoken of as the "black of the eye," because it appears black against the dark background of the posterior chamber of the eye. The pupil of the eye is about half a centimeter in diameter, although within certain limits its size can be altered to regulate the quantity of light which is admitted to the eye. So far as the spectator's vision is concerned, it is only these rays that go through the pupil of his eye that are of any use, and these are the *effective rays.* When the pupil dilates, more rays can enter, and consequently the source appears brighter. The brightness of the source will depend also on its distance, because for a given diameter of the pupil, the aperture of the cone of rays from a nearer source will be wider than that of the cone of rays from a more distant source. In general, therefore, the pupil of the eye regulates the angular apertures of the cones of rays that enter the eye from each point of a luminous object and acts as the so-called *aperture-stop* (§ 134). Thus, while the extent of the field of view is controlled by the field-stop (§ 9), the brightness of the source depends essentially on the size of the aperture-stop.

A series of transparent isotropic media each separated from the next by a smooth, polished surface constitutes an *optical system.* An *optical instrument* may consist of a single mirror, prisms or lens, but generally it is composed of a combination of such elements, which may be in contact with each other or separated by air or some other medium. In the great majority of actual constructions the instrument is symmetrical with respect to a straight line called the *optical axis.* Not all the rays emitted by a luminous object will be utilized by the instrument; generally, in fact, only a comparatively small portion of such rays will be transmitted through it, in the first place because its lateral dimensions are limited, and in the second place because, in addition to the lens-fastenings and other opaque obstacles (sides of the tube, etc.), nearly all optical instruments are provided with perforated screens or diaphragms called "stops," specially placed and designed to intercept such rays as for one reason or another it is not desirable to let pass (§133). The planes of these stops are placed at right angles to the optical axis with the centers of the openings on the axis. Accordingly, each separate point of the object is to be regarded as the vertex of a limited cone or *bundle of rays*, which, with respect to the instrument, are the so-called *effective rays*, because they are the only rays coming from the point in question that traverse the instrument from one end to the other without being intercepted on the way.

Moreover, in every bundle of rays there is always a certain central or representative ray, coinciding perhaps with the axis of the cone or distinguished in some special way, called the *chief ray* of the bundle (§ 139). In a symmetrical optical instrument the chief ray of a bundle of effective rays is generally defined to be that ray which in traversing a certain one of the series of media crosses the optical axis at a prescribed point, which is usually at the center of that one of the stops which is the most effective in intercepting the rays and which, therefore, is called the aperture-stop, as will be explained more fully hereafter (see Chapter XII). According to this definition, the chief rays coming from all the various points of the object constitute a bundle of rays which in the medium where the aperture-stop is placed (sometimes called the "stop medium") all pass through the center of the stop.

We shall employ the term *pencil of rays* to mean a section of a ray-bundle made by a plane containing the chief ray.

The effective rays in the first medium before entering the instrument are called the *incident rays* or *object rays;* and these same rays in the last medium on issuing from the instrument are called the *emergent rays* or *image rays.* If we

select at random any point X lying on one of the rays of
the bundle of emergent rays which had its origin at the luminous object-point P, in general, no other ray of this bundle
will pass through X, since in a given optical system there
will usually be one single route by which light starting from
the point P and traversing the instrument can arrive finally,
either really or virtually (§ 8), at a selected point X in the
last medium. However, there may be found a number of
singular points where two or more rays of the bundle of
emergent rays intersect; and under certain favorable and
exceptional circumstances it may indeed happen that there
is one special point P′ where *all* the emergent rays emanating
originally from the object-point P meet again; and then we
shall obtain at P′ a perfect or *ideal image* of P, which is
described by saying that P′ *is the image-point conjugate to
the object-point at* P. This image will be real or virtual
according as the actual paths of the image-rays go
through P′ or merely the backward prolongations of these
paths (§ 8).

In order to obtain an image in this ideal sense, the optical
system must be such as to transform a train of incident
spherical waves spreading out from the object-point P into
a train of emergent spherical waves converging to or diverging from a common center P′ in the image-space. When
all the rays of a bundle meet in one point, the bundle of rays
is said to be *homocentric* or *monocentric*. In general, however, a monocentric bundle of rays in the object-space will
be transformed in the image-space into an *astigmatic bundle*
of emergent rays, which no longer meet all in one point;
and in fact this is a usual characteristic of a bundle of optical rays.

PROBLEMS

1. Why are the shadows much sharper in the case of an
arc lamp without a surrounding globe than with one?

2. Draw a diagram to show how a total eclipse of the

moon occurs; and another diagram to illustrate a total eclipse of the sun. Give clear descriptions of the drawings.

3. An opaque globe, 1 foot in diameter, with its center at a point C, is interposed between an arc lamp S and a white wall which is perpendicular to the straight line SC. If the wall is 12 feet from the lamp, and if the distance SC = 3 feet, what is the area of the shadow on the wall?   Ans. 12.57 sq. ft.

4. What is the apparent angular elevation of the sun when a telegraph pole 15 feet high casts a shadow 20 feet long on a horizontal pavement?   Ans. 36° 52′ 10″.

5. What is the height of a tower which casts a shadow 160 feet long when a vertical rod 3 feet high casts a shadow 4 feet long?   Ans. 120 feet.

6. An object 6 inches high is placed in front of a pinhole camera at a distance of 6 feet from the aperture. What is the size of the inverted image on the ground glass screen if the length of the camera-box is 1 foot?   Ans. 1 inch.

7. A small hole is made in the shutter of a dark room, and a screen is placed at a distance of 8 feet from the shutter. The image on the screen of a tree outside 120 feet away is measured and found to be 3 feet long. How high is the tree?
     Ans. 45 feet.

8. If the sensitive plate of a pinhole camera is 20 cm. from the pinhole, what should be the diameter of the pinhole, according to ABNEY's formula?   Ans. 0.57 mm.

9. What is the apparent size of a man 6 feet tall at a distance of 100 yards? How far away must he be not to be distinguishable from a point?   Ans. 1° 8′ 45″; 3.9 miles.

10. If the moon is 240 000 miles from the earth and its apparent diameter is 31′ 3″, what is its actual diameter?
     Ans. 2168 miles.

11. A person holding a tube 6 inches long and 1 inch in diameter in front of his eye and looking through it at a tree moves backwards away from the tree until the entire

tree is just visible. What is the apparent height of the tree?   Ans. $9°\ 27'\ 44''$.

12. Assuming that the resolving power of the eye is one minute of arc, at what distance can a black circle 6 inches in diameter be seen on a white background?   Ans. 1719 feet.

13. The shadow of an opaque circular disk which is interposed between a screen and a similar luminous disk of larger size is composed of the central dark umbra and the surrounding penumbra. The straight line joining the centers of the disks is perpendicular to their faces and to the plane of the screen. The diameter of the luminous disk is $2r$, the distance between the disks is d, and the distance of the screen from the opaque disk is x. Show that the width of the penumbra ring projected on the screen is equal to $2rx/d$, and that it is therefore independent of the diameter of the opaque object.

CHAPTER II

12. Regular and Diffuse Reflection.—When a beam of sunlight, admitted through an opening in a shutter in a dark room, falls on a piece of smoothly polished glass, although the glass itself may be almost or wholly invisible, a brilliant patch of light will be reflected from the glass on the walls of the room or the ceiling or on some other adjacent object. If a person in the room happens to be looking towards the piece of glass along one special direction, he will be almost blinded by the light that is reflected into his eyes. The glass acts like a mirror and reflects the sunlight falling on it in a definite direction which depends only on the direction of the incident rays and on the orientation of the reflecting surface, and in such a case the light is said to be *regularly reflected*. Thus, for example, signals may be communicated to distant and inaccessible stations by reflecting thither the rays of the sun by a plane mirror adjusted in a suitable position.

If the surface is not smooth, the light will be reflected in many directions at the same time. The long sparkling trail of sunlight seen on the surface of a lake or a river on a bright day is caused by the reflections of the sun's rays into the eyes of the spectator from countless little ripples on the surface of the water.

The bright spot of light on the wall of a dark room at the place where a beam of sunlight falls, which shines almost as though this portion of the wall were itself a self-luminous body, is visible from any part of the room by means of the light which is reflected from it; and although the incident rays have a perfectly definite direction, the reflected light

28

is scattered in all directions. Some of this reflected light
will fall on other bodies in the room, which will be more or
less feebly illuminated thereby and rendered dimly visible
by the light which they reflect in their turn; until at last
the light after undergoing in this way repeated reflections
from one body to another becomes too faint to be perceptible. Light which is reflected or scattered in this way is
said to be *diffusely reflected* or *irregularly reflected,* although,
strictly speaking, there is nothing irregular about it. Ordinarily it is in this way that bodies illuminated by daylight or by artificial light are rendered visible to a whole
group of spectators at the same time.

The paper on the walls of an apartment which gets very
little light through the windows should be a dull white in
order to scatter and diffuse as much as possible the light
that comes into the room. The walls of a dark chamber
used for developing photographic plates should be painted
a dull black in order to absorb the light that falls on them.
An absolutely black body (§ 2) exposed to the direct rays
of the sun will be completely invisible, except by contrast
with its surroundings. If the walls of a dark room and all
the objects within it were coated with lampblack, and if
the air inside were entirely free from dust and moisture,
a beam of sunlight traversing the room could not be seen
and the only way to detect its presence would be by placing
the eye squarely in its path. But if a little finely divided
powder were scattered in the air or if a cloud of smoke were
blown across the beam of light, the course of the rays would
immediately become manifest to a spectator in any part of
the room, because some of the light reflected from the floating particles of matter in practically every direction would
enter the eye. But the light itself is quite invisible.

Any surface that is not too rough, that is, whose scratches
or ridges are not wider than about a quarter of a wave-
length of light, will reflect light in a greater or less degree
depending on the smoothness of the surface. Waves of

light falling on a sheet of white paper are broken up or
scattered in all directions, and we can get some idea of the
quantity of light that is diffusely reflected from such a surface by letting the light of a lamp shine on the paper when
it is held near an object that is in shadow. It is almost
startling to see how under the influence of this indirect
illumination the details of the obscure body suddenly appear as if summoned forth by magic. A highly polished
metallic surface makes the best mirror, reflecting sometimes as much as three-fourths of the incident light. Our
ordinary looking-glasses are really metallic mirrors, because
they are coated at the back with silver, and the glass merely
serves as a protection for the reflecting surface.

13. Law of Reflection.—A ray of light represented in
Fig. 16 by the straight line AB is incident at B on a smooth
reflecting surface whose trace in the plane of the diagram
is the line ZZ. The straight line BN normal to the surface

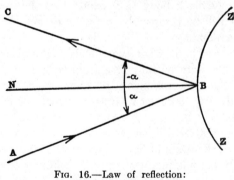

Fig. 16.—Law of reflection:
∠ NBA = -∠ NBC = ∠ CBN.

at B is called the *incidence-normal,* and the plane ABN which
contains the *incident ray* AB and the normal BN is called
the *plane of incidence,* which corresponds here with the
plane of the diagram. The *angle of incidence* is the angle
between the incident ray and the incidence-normal; or, to

define this angle more exactly, *the angle of incidence is the acute angle (a) through which the incidence-normal has to be turned about the point of incidence in order to make it coincide with the incident ray;* thus, $a = \angle$NBA. Counter-clockwise rotation is to be reckoned as positive and clockwise rotation as negative. This rule will be consistently observed in the case of all angular measurements.

The *reflected ray* corresponding to the incident ray AB is represented by the straight line BC; and if in the above definition of the angle of incidence we substitute "reflected ray" for "incident ray," we shall obtain the definition of the *angle of reflection* (β); that is, $\beta = \angle$NBC. The sense of the rotation is indicated by the order in which the letters specifying the angle are named; thus, $\angle$ABC is the angle described by rotating the straight line AB around the point B until it coincides with the straight line BC; whereas $\angle$CBA $= -\angle$ABC denotes the equal but opposite rotation from CB to BA. The student should take note of this usage, which will be uniformly employed throughout this book.

The law of the reflection of light, which has been known for more than 2200 years, is contained in the following statement:

The reflected ray lies in the plane of incidence, and the incident and reflected rays make equal angles with the normal on opposite sides of it; that is, $\beta = -a$.

A very accurate experimental proof of this law may be obtained by employing a meridian circle to observe the light reflected from an artificial mercury-horizon, that is, from the horizontal surface of mercury contained in a basin. In fact, this is the actual method used by astronomers in measuring the altitude of a star. The telescope is pointed at the star and then at the image of the star in the mercury mirror, and it will be found that the axis of the telescope in these two observations will be equally inclined to the vertical on opposite sides of it.

A simple lecture-table apparatus for verifying the law of reflection of light consists of a circular disk (Fig. 17) made of ground glass, about one foot or more in diameter, and graduated around the circumference in degrees. This disk is mounted so as to be capable of rotation in a vertical plane

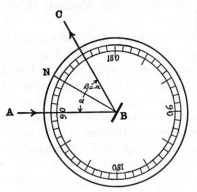

about a horizontal axis perpendicular to this plane and passing through the center of the disk. A small piece of a plane mirror B with its plane perpendicular to that of the disk is fastened to the disk at its center, and the mirror is adjusted so that it is perpendicular to the radius BN drawn

Fig. 17.—Optical disk used to verify law of reflection.

on the disk. A beam of sunlight falling on the

mirror in the direction NB will be reflected back from the mirror in the opposite direction BN, so that in this adjustment of the disk the paths of the incident and reflected rays coincide $(\beta = -\alpha = 0)$. Now if the disk is turned so that the incident ray AB makes with the normal BN an angle NBA, the reflected ray will proceed in a direction BC such that $\angle NBC = \angle ABN = -\alpha$.

If, without changing the direction of the incident ray, the disk is turned through an angle θ, the plane of the mirror together with the incidence-normal will likewise be turned through this same angle, and the angles of incidence and reflection will each be changed in opposite senses by the amount θ, so that the angle between the incident and reflected rays will be changed by 2 θ. Accordingly, *when a plane mirror is turned through a certain angle, the reflected ray will be turned through an angle twice as great.*

14. Huygens's Construction of the Wave-Front in Case of Reflection at a Plane Mirror.

1. *The case of a plane wave reflected from a plane mirror.*
The rebound of waves from a polished surface affords a very simple and instructive illustration of HUYGENS's Principle (§ 5). In Fig. 18 the straight line AD represents the trace in the plane of the diagram of a plane mirror, and the straight line AB represents the trace of a portion of the front of an incident plane wave (§ 6) advancing in the direction of the wave-normal BD. At the first instant under consideration the wave-front is supposed to be in the position AB when the disturbance h a s just reached the point A of the reflecting surface, and from this time forward, according to HUYGENS's theory, the point A is to be regarded as itself a center of disturbance f r o m which secondary hemispherical

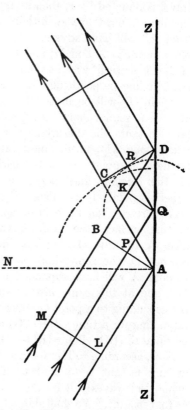

FIG. 18.—HUYGENS's construction of plane wave reflected at plane mirror.

waves are reflected back into the medium in front of the mirror. Exactly the same state of things will prevail at this instant ($t = 0$) at all points of the plane reflecting surface lying on a portion of the straight line perpendicular

to the plane of the paper at the point A, and the envelop
of the hemispherical wavelets originating from these points
will be a semicylindrical surface whose axis is the straight
line just mentioned. If the speed with which the waves
travel is denoted by v, then at the end of the time $t = PQ/v$
the disturbance that was initially at the point P in the wave-
front AB will have advanced to a point Q on the reflecting
plane between A and D; and from this moment a new set
of hemispherical wavelets having their centers all on a
straight line perpendicular to the plane of the diagram at
the point Q will begin to develop, and their envelop will
also be a semicylinder. And so at successively later and
later instants the disturbance will arrive in turn at each
point along AD; until, finally, after the time $t = BD/v$ the
farthermost point D will be reached. Meanwhile, around
all the straight lines perpendicular to the plane of the
paper at points lying along AD semicylindrical elementary
wave-surfaces will have been spreading out from the reflecting surface, the radii of these cylinders diminishing
from A towards D. At the time when the disturbance
reaches D, the semicylindrical wavelet whose axis passes
through A will have expanded until its radius is equal to
BD, and at this same instant the semicylindrical wavelet
corresponding to a point Q between A and D will have been
expanding for a time $(BD - PQ)/v$, and hence its radius will
be equal to $(BD - PQ) = (BD - BK) = KD$.

Now, according to Huygens's Principle, the surface which
at any instant is tangent to all these elementary semicylindrical waves will be the required reflected wave-front
at that instant. We shall show that the reflected wave-front
is a plane surface which at the moment when the disturbance reaches the point D contains this point; or, what
amounts to the same thing, we shall show that if a straight
line DC in the plane of the diagram is tangent at C to the
semicircle in which this plane cuts the semicylinder whose
axis passes through A, it will be a common tangent to all

such semicircles; for example, it will also be tangent to
the semicircle in which the plane of the diagram cuts the
semicylinder belonging to the point Q. From D draw DC
tangent at C to the semicircle described around A as center
with radius AC = BD and DR tangent at R to the semicircle described around Q as center with radius QR = KD.
The right triangles ABD and ACD are congruent, and hence
∠DAB = ∠CDA; and, similarly, in the congruent right triangles QKD and QRD ∠DQK = ∠RDQ. But ∠DQK =
∠DAB, and therefore ∠RDQ = ∠CDA, and hence the two
tangents DR and DC coincide. Accordingly, the trace of
the reflected wave-front in the plane of the diagram is the
straight line CD. This reflected plane wave will be propagated onwards, parallel with itself, in the direction shown
by the reflected rays AC, QR, etc. It is evident from the
construction that the ray incident at A, the normal AN to
the reflecting surface at the incidence-point A, and the reflected ray AC lie all in the same plane; and the equality of
the angles of incidence and reflection is an immediate consequence of the congruence of the triangles ABD and ACD.

2. *The case of a spherical wave reflected at a plane mirror*.
In Fig. 19 the light is represented as originating from a
point-source L and spreading out from it in the form of
spherical waves which presently impinge on the plane reflecting surface represented in the diagram by the straight
line AD. The nearest point of the reflecting plane to the
source at L is the foot A of the perpendicular let fall from
L on the straight line AD, and this, therefore, is the first
point of the mirror to be affected. Obviously, on account
of symmetry with respect to LA, it will be quite sufficient
to investigate the procedure of the waves in the plane of
the figure. The wave-front at the time the disturbance
reaches A will be represented by the arc of a circle described
around L as center with radius equal to LA; let P designate the position of a point on this arc, and draw the straight
line LP meeting AD at Q. After a time $t = PQ/v$ the dis-

turbance will have advanced from P to Q, and from this
moment the point Q will begin to send back wavelets from
the reflecting surface.   And so in succession one point of
the mirror after another will be affected until presently the
disturbance reaches the farthest point D.   Meanwhile, all

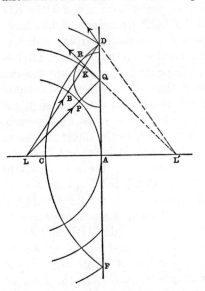

the points along AD on
one side of AL and
along AF on the other
s i d e (AF = DA) will
have been sending out
wavelets whose radii will
be greater and greater
the nearer these new
centers are to the point
A midway between D
and F. D r a w t h e
straight line LD meet-
ing the arc AP in the
point B: then at the
moment $t = BD/v$ when
the disturbance from L
has just arrived at D,
the reflected wavelet

FIG. 19.—HUYGENS's construction of spheri- proceeding from A as
cal wave reflected at plane mirror.   center will have ex-

panded until its radius is equal to BD, and at this same
instant there will also be a wavelet around Q as center
of radius (BD—PQ) = (BD—BK) = KD.   According to
HUYGENS, the problem consists, therefore, in finding the
surface which is tangent at a given instant to all these
secondary waves.   Produce the straight line LA on the
other side of the reflecting surface to a point L' such
that AL' = LA, and draw the straight line L'Q, and mark
the point R where this straight line produced meets
the semicircle described around Q as center with radius
KD = QR.   Since LQ + QR = LK + KD = LD, obviously,

L′R = L′D; and therefore a circle described around L′ as center with radius equal to L′D will touch at R the semicircle described around Q as center with radius equal to QR. Moreover, it will also touch at a point C on the straight line LA the semicircle described around A as center with radius AC = BD. Consequently, this circle will be the envelop of all these semicircles. The reflected wave-front, therefore, is obtained by revolving the arc DCF around LL′ as axis. The straight line QR is the path of the reflected ray corresponding to the incident ray PQ; the angle of incidence at Q is equal to the angle ALQ and the angle of reflection is equal to AL′Q, and these angles are evidently equal, in agreement, therefore, with the law of reflection.

15. Image in a Plane Mirror.—In Fig. 19 the plane mirror bisects at right angles the straight line LL′, and since the

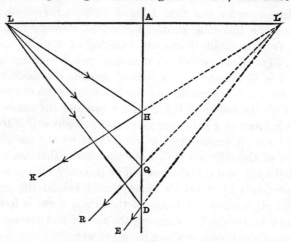

Fig. 20.—L′ is image of object-point L in plane mirror AD;
AL = L′A.

position of the point L′ is independent of the position of the incidence-point Q (Fig. 20), all the rays coming from the luminous point L and falling on the plane mirror will be reflected along paths which, when prolonged backwards, all meet in the point L'. Thus, *to a homocentric bundle of incident rays reflected at a plane mirror there corresponds also a homocentric bundle of reflected rays.* This remarkable property of converting a homocentric bundle of rays into another homocentric bundle is characteristic of a plane mirror, because no other optical device is capable of it except under conditions that are more or less unrealizable in practice. Thus, the image L' of an object at L is found by drawing a straight line from L perpendicular to the plane mirror, and producing this line on the other side of the mirror to a point L' such that the line-segment LL' is bisected by the plane of the mirror; so that an object in front of a plane mirror is seen in the mirror at the same distance behind it. The image in this case is *virtual* (§ 8). The late Professor SILVANUS THOMPSON in his popular lectures published under the title *Light Visible and Invisible* describes the following simple method of showing how the rays from a candle flame are reflected at a plane mirror (Fig. 21). If a vertical pin mounted on a horizontal baseboard is illuminated by a lighted candle, the position of the shadow is determined by the line joining the top of the pin with the source of light. If the pin and the candle are both in front of a plane mirror placed at right angles to the base-board, a second shadow will be cast by the pin on account of the reflected rays from the candle that are intercepted by it, and this shadow will be precisely such as would be produced by a candle flame placed behind the mirror at the place where the image of the actual flame is formed, as may be proved by removing the mirror and transferring the candle to the place where its image was.

If the bundle of incident rays instead of diverging from a point L in front of the plane mirror converged towards a point L behind it (as could easily be effected with the aid of a convergent lens), a *real image* (§ 8) will be produced at a point L' at the same distance in front of the mirror as the *virtual object-point* L was beyond it.

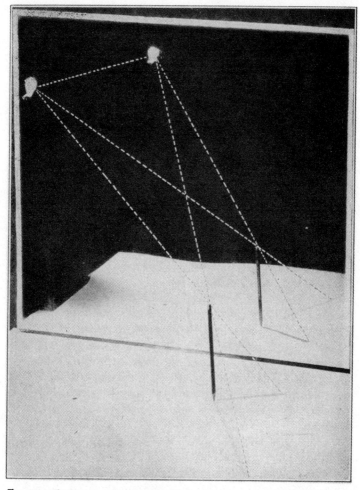

FIG. 21.—Shadows cast by an object in front of a plane mirror when object is illuminated by point-source (from actual photograph), showing that the source and its image are at equal distances from the mirror.

Fig. 23.—Image of object in plane mirror (from actual photograph).

The image of an extended object is the figure formed by
the images of all of its points separately. The diagram
(Fig. 22) shows, for example, how an eye at E would see
the image L'M' of an object LM reflected in a plane mirror.
The series of parallel lines joining corresponding points of

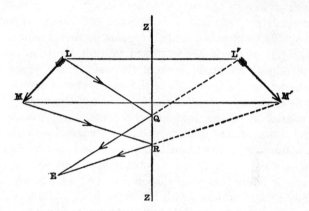

Fig. 22.—Image L'M' of object LM in plane mirror ZZ.

object and image will be bisected at right angles by the
plane of the mirror.

The dimensions of the image in a plane mirror are exactly the same as those of the object. Moreover, the top
and bottom of the image correspond with the top and bottom of the object, that is, the image is *erect*. Also, the
right side of the image corresponds with the right side of
the object, and the left side of the image with the left side
of the object (Fig. 23), although it is frequently stated in
books on optics that when a man stands in front of a mirror
the right side of the image shows the left side of the person,
and that if the man extends his right hand, the image will
extend its left hand. The true explanation of the so-called
"perversion" of the image in a plane mirror, which is strikingly seen when a printed page is held in front of the mirror,
is that it is *the rear side of the image that is opposite the front*

side of the object. The image of a printed page in a mirror has exactly the same appearance as it would have if the page were held in front of a bright light and it was viewed from behind through the paper. When a person looks in a mirror at his own image, his image appears to be looking back at him in the opposite direction, if he faces east, his image faces west, and if we call the east side of object or image its front side and the west side its rear side, then the rear side of the image is turned towards the front side of the object; although, because this side of the image corresponds to the front side of the object, it is a natural mistake to regard it as also the front side of the image. The explanation of the common impression that, whereas up and down remain unchanged in the image of an object in a plane mirror, right and left are reversed, is probably because a person regarding his own image under such circumstances is unconsciously disposed to transfer himself mentally into coincidence with his image by a rotation of 180°, not around a horizontal, but around a vertical axis, thus producing a confusion of mind as to right and left but not as to top and bottom. The reason why this mental revolution is performed around the vertical axis seems to be due partly to the circumstance that this movement can be readily executed in reality, and partly also perhaps to the fact that the human body happens to be very nearly symmetrical with respect to a vertical plane.

16. The Field of View of a Plane Mirror.—In the adjoining diagram (Fig. 24) the straight line GH represents the trace in the plane of the paper of the surface of a plane mirror, and the point marked O′ shows the position of the center of the pupil of the eye of a person who is supposed to be looking towards the mirror. Evidently, the straight lines HO′, GO′ drawn to O′ from the points G, H in the edge of the mirror will represent the paths of the outermost reflected rays that can enter the eye at O′, and therefore the field of view (§ 9) is limited by the contour of the mirror just as if the observer were looking into the image-space through a hole in the wall that exactly coincided with the place occupied by the mirror. Corresponding to the pair of reflected rays HO′ and GO′ intersecting at O′ there would be a pair of incident rays directed along the straight lines HO

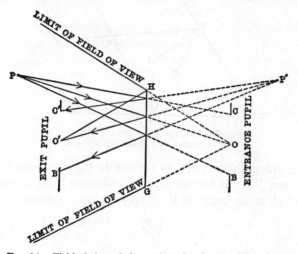

Fig. 24.—Field of view of plane mirror for given position of eye.

and GO towards a point O on the other side of the mirror, and it is evident that O′ will be the real image of a virtual object-point at O (§ 15). Any luminous point lying in front of the plane mirror within the conical surface formed by drawing straight lines such as OG, OH from O to all the points in the edge of the mirror will be visible by reflected light to an eye placed at O′, and hence this cone limits the field of view of the object-space.

Through O′ draw a straight line parallel to GH, and take on it two points C′, B′ at equal distances from O′ on opposite sides of it, and let us suppose that B′C′ represents the diameter in the plane of the diagram of the pupil of the eye. Construct the image BOC of the eye-pupil B′O′C′. Then if P designates the position of a luminous point lying anywhere within the field of view of the object-space, it is clear that the incident rays PO, PC and PB will be reflected at

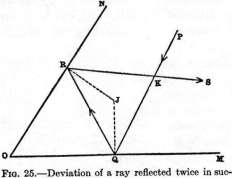

Fig. 25.—Deviation of a ray reflected twice in succession from a pair of inclined mirrors.

the mirror into the pupil of the eye in the directions P′O′, P′C′ and P′B′, as though they had all come from the point P′ which is the image of P. This imaginary opening or vir-

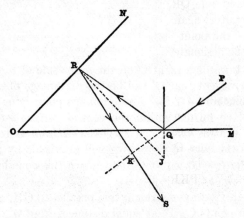

Fig. 26.—Deviation of a ray reflected twice in succession from a pair of inclined mirrors.

tual stop BOC towards which the incident rays must all be directed in order to be reflected into the eye-pupil B′O′C′ is called the *entrance-pupil* of the optical system consisting of the plane mirror and the eye of the observer; and the pupil of the eye itself is called here the *exit-pupil* (see Chapter XII). Since the entrance-pupil limits the apertures of the bundles of rays that ultimately enter the eye, it acts as the *aperture-stop* of the system (§ 11).

17. Successive Reflections from two Plane Mirrors.— Any section made by a plane perpendicular to the line of intersection of the planes of a pair of inclined mirrors is called a *principal section* of the system. *If a ray lying in a principal section is reflected successively at two plane mirrors, it will be deviated from its original direction by an angle equal to twice the dihedral angle between the mirrors.*

Let the plane of the principal section intersect the planes of the mirrors in the straight lines OM, ON (Figs. 25 and 26); and let $\gamma = \angle\,MON$ denote the angle between the mirrors. The ray PQ lying in the plane MON is incident on the mirror OM at the point Q, whence it is reflected along the straight line QR, meeting the mirror ON at the point R, where it is again reflected, proceeding in the direction RS. Let the point of intersection of the straight lines PQ and RS be designated by K. Then $\angle\,PKR$ is the angle between the original direction of the ray and its direction after undergoing two reflections, and we must show that this angle is equal to $2\,\gamma$.

Draw the incidence-normals at Q and R, and prolong them until they meet at J. Then by the law of reflection the straight lines QJ and RJ bisect the angles PQR and QRS, respectively.

In Fig. 25, $\quad \angle\,PKR = \angle\,PQR + \angle\,QRS = 2(\angle\,JQR + \angle\,QRJ)$
$$= 2(180° - \angle\,RJQ) = 2\gamma;$$

and in Fig. 26, $\angle\,PKR = \angle\,PQR - \angle\,SRQ$
$$= 2(180° - \angle\,RQJ - \angle\,JRQ)$$
$$= 2\angle\,QJR = 2\gamma.$$

18. Images in a System of Two Inclined Mirrors.—When a luminous point lies in the dihedral angle between two plane mirrors, some of its rays will fall on one mirror and some on the other, and consequently there will be two sets of images. In Fig. 27 the plane of the diagram is the principal section which contains the point-source S, and the straight lines OM, ON represent the traces of the mirrors

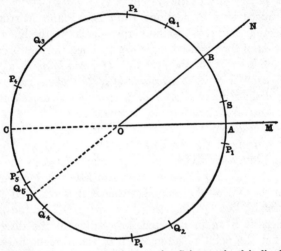

FIG. 27.—Images of a luminous point S in a pair of inclined mirrors OM and ON.

in this plane. The rays which fall first on the mirror OM will be reflected as though they came from the image P_1 of the luminous point S in this mirror. Some of these rays falling on the mirror ON will be again reflected and proceed thence as though they came from the point P_2 which is the image of P_1 in the mirror ON. Thus, by successive reflections, first at one of the mirrors and then at the other, a series of images P_1, P_2, etc., will be formed by those rays which fall first on the mirror OM; let us call this the P-series of images. Similarly, the rays that fall first on the mirror ON will produce another series of images Q_1, Q_2, etc., which will be called the Q-series. Each of these series will terminate with an image which lies behind both mirrors in the dihedral angle COD opposite the angle MON between the mirrors themselves; because rays which, after reflection at one of the mirrors, appear to come from a point thus situated cannot fall on the other mirror, and so there will be no more images after this one.

Since the straight line OM is the perpendicular bisector of the line-segment SP_1, the points S and P_1 are equidistant from every point in the straight line OM; and, similarly, since P_2 is the image of P_1 in the plane mirror ON, these two points are likewise equidistant from every point in the straight line ON. Accordingly, the three points S, P_1, P_2 are all equidistant from the point O where the straight lines OM and ON intersect. Applying the same reasoning to all the other images, we perceive that *the images of both series are ranged on the circumference of a circle whose center is at O and whose radius is* OS.

In the following discussion of the angular distances of the images from the luminous point S, the angles will be reckoned always in the same sense, either all clockwise or all counter-clockwise. Let $\gamma = \angle AOB$ denote the angle between the two mirrors, the letters A and B referring to the points where the circle crosses the planes of the mirrors OM and ON, respectively. Also, let $\alpha = \angle AOS$, $\beta = \angle SOB$ denote the angular distances of S from A, B, respectively, so that $\alpha + \beta = \gamma$. Then

$$\angle P_1OS = 2\alpha;$$
$$\angle SOP_2 = \angle SOB + \angle BOP_2 = \beta + \angle P_1OB = 2(\alpha + \beta) = 2\gamma;$$
$$\angle P_3OS = \angle P_3OA + \alpha = \angle AOP_2 + \alpha = \angle SOP_2 + 2\alpha$$
$$= 2\gamma + 2\alpha;$$
$$\angle SOP_4 = \angle SOB + \angle BOP_4 = \beta + \angle P_3OB$$
$$= 2\beta + \angle P_3OS = 2(\alpha + \beta + \gamma) = 4\gamma;$$
$$\angle P_5OS = \angle P_5OA + \alpha = \angle AOP_4 + \alpha = \angle SOP_4 + 2\alpha$$
$$= 4\gamma + 2\alpha.$$

In general, therefore,

$$\angle SOP_{2k} = 2k\gamma, \qquad \angle P_{2k+1}OS = 2k\gamma + 2\alpha,$$

where P_{2k}, P_{2k+1} designate the positions of the $2k$th and

$(2k+1)$th images of the P-series, k denoting any integer, and where the angles SOP_{2k}, $P_{2k+1}OS$ are the angles subtended by the arcs SBP_{2k}, $P_{2k+1}AS$, respectively. Similarly, for the Q-series of images we find:

$$\angle Q_{2k}OS = 2k\gamma, \qquad \angle SOQ_{2k+1} = 2k\gamma + 2\beta,$$

where these angles are the angles subtended by the arcs $Q_{2k}AS$, SBQ_{2k+1}, respectively.

Evidently, the image P_{2k+1} will fall on the arc CD behind both mirrors, if arc $P_{2k+1}AS >$ arc DAS, that is, if

$$2k\gamma + 2a > 180° - \beta;$$

and, by adding $(\beta - a)$ to both sides of this inequation, and dividing through by γ, this condition may be expressed as follows:

$$2k+1 > \frac{180° - a}{\gamma}.$$

In the same way we find that the image P_{2k} will fall between C and D if

$$2k > \frac{180° - a}{\gamma}.$$

Thus, *the total number of images of the P-series, whether it be odd or even, will be given by the integer next higher than* $(180° - a)/\gamma$; and, similarly, *the total number of images of the Q-series will be given by the integer next higher than* $(180° - \beta)/\gamma$.

The only exception to this rule is when the angle γ is contained in $(180° - a)$ or $(180° - \beta)$ an exact whole number of times; in the former case the last image of the P-series falls at C, and in the latter case the last image of the Q-series falls at D; and instead of taking the integers next above the quotient $(180° - a)/\gamma$ or $(180° - \beta)/\gamma$, we must take the actual integer obtained by the division. An example will make the matter clear. Thus, suppose $\gamma = 27°$, $a = 8°$, then $\beta = 19°$, and the integers next higher than $(180° - a)/\gamma$ and $(180° - \beta)/\gamma$ will be 7 and 6, respectively; hence in this case there will be 7 images of the P-series and 6 images of the Q-series or 13 images in all. But if $a = 10°$ and $\beta = 17°$, each series will be found to have 7 images, 14 images in all. The exceptional case occurs when $\alpha = 9°$ and $\beta = 18°$, for then $(180° - \beta)/\gamma = 6$, and hence there will be 7 P-images and 6 Q-images.

If the angle γ between the mirrors is an exact multiple of 180°, that is, if $180°/\gamma = p$, where p denotes an integer, the integers next higher than $(180° - \alpha)/\gamma$ and $(180° - \beta)/\gamma$ will both be equal to p, no matter what may be the special position of the object between the two mirrors; so that in such a case the number of images in each series will be equal, but the last image of one set will co-incide with the last of the other. In fact, the points S, P_2, P_4, . . . Q_4, Q_2 and the points P_1, P_3, . . . Q_3, Q_1 are the vertices of two equal

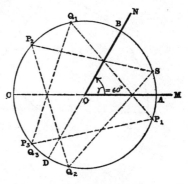

Fig. 28.—Images of a luminous point in a pair of plane mirrors inclined to each other at an angle of 60°.

regular polygons, of p sides each; and if p is odd, the polygon P_1P_3 . . . Q_3Q_1 will have one of its corners between C and D, whereas if p is even, one of the corners of the polygon SP_2P_4 . . . Q_4Q_2 will fall between C and D; in either case this vertex is the position of the last image of both series. Thus, for example, if $\gamma = 60°$ (Fig. 28), then $p = 3$, and the two polygons are the equilateral triangles SP_2Q_2 and $P_1P_3Q_1$ (or $P_1Q_3Q_1$).

The toy called a *kaleidoscope*, devised by Sir David Brewster (1781–1868), consists essentially of two long narrow strips of mirror-glass inclined to each other at an angle of 60° and inclosed in a cylindrical tube. One end of the tube is closed by a circular piece of ground glass whereon are loosely disposed a lot of fragments of colored glass or

beads, and at the other end of the tube there is a peep-hole.
When the instrument is held towards the light, an observer
looking in it will see an exquisitely beautiful and symmetrical
pattern formed by the colored objects and their images, the
form of which may be almost endlessly varied by revolving
the tube around its axis so that the bits of glass assume new

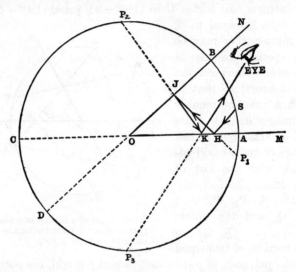

Fig. 29.—Path of ray reflected into eye from a pair of inclined
mirrors.

positions. In fact, this device has been turned to practical
use in making designs for carpets and wall-papers.

**19. Construction of the Path of a Ray Reflected into the
Eye from a Pair of Inclined Mirrors.**—In order to trace the
paths of the rays by which a spectator standing in front of a
pair of inclined mirrors sees the image of a luminous point,
it is convenient to assume, for the sake of simplicity, that
the eye at E in Fig. 29 lies in the plane of the paper. The
first step in the construction of the path of the ray is to draw
the straight line from the given image-point to the eye,
because if the eye sees this point the light that enters the

eye must arrive along this line. If this line does not cross the mirror in which the image is produced, this particular image will not be visible from the point E. Now join the point where this line meets the mirror with the preceding image in the same series; the part of this line that lies between the two mirrors will evidently show the route of the

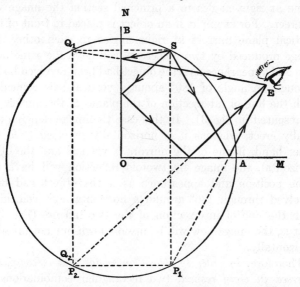

FIG. 30.—Showing how an eye at E sees the images of a luminous point S in a rectangular pair of plane mirrors.

light before its last reflection. Proceeding in this fashion from one mirror to the other, we shall trace backwards the zigzag path of the ray until we arrive finally at the luminous source at S. Consider, for example, the image P_3 formed in the mirror OA in Fig. 29. This image is visible to the eye at E because the straight line P_3E cuts at K the mirror OA. If J and H designate the points where the straight lines KP_2 and JP_1 meet the mirrors OB and OA, respectively, the broken line SHJKE will represent the path of the ray from the source at S into the eye at E. Fig. 30 shows how an eye at E in front of two perpendicular plane mirrors can see the images P_1, P_2, Q_1 and Q_2.

20. Rectangular Combinations of Plane Mirrors.—In a rectangular combination of two plane mirrors ($\gamma = 90°$) the image formed by two successive reflections will be inverted in the principal section of the system, but in any plane at right angles to a principal section the image will be erect. For example, if an object is placed in front of two vertical plane mirrors at right angles to each other, the image produced by two reflections will have the same position and appearance as if the object had been revolved bodily through an angle of 180° about a vertical axis coinciding with the line of intersection of the planes of the mirrors, as represented in Fig. 31. In this case the image remains vertically erect, whereas it is horizontally inverted. On the other hand, if one of the mirrors is vertical and the other horizontal, the image by twofold reflection will have the same position and appearance as if the object had been revolved through 180° around a horizontal axis coinciding with the line of intersection of the two mirrors (Fig. 32); that is, the image now will be upside down but not inverted horizontally.

Therefore, *in order to obtain an image that is completely reversed in every respect*, two rectangular combinations of plane mirrors may be employed with their principal sections mutually at right angles, so disposed that the rays coming from the object will be reflected in succession from each of the four plane surfaces. An auxiliary system of this description is sometimes used in connection with an optical instrument for the purpose of *rectifying the image* which otherwise would be seen inverted. A rectifying device depending on this principle is the so-called PORRO prism-system (1852), utilized by ABBE (1840–1905) in the design of the famous prism binocular telescope or field-glasses (*c.* 1883). A sketch of the arrangement is shown in Fig. 33. Two rectangular prisms are placed in the tube of the instrument, between the objective and the

Fig. 31.—Image of an object in a rectangular pair of plane mirrors (from actual photograph); showing how the last image is obtained by rotating the object through 180° around the line of intersection of the mirrors. Both mirrors in vertical planes.

Fig. 32.—Image of an object in a rectangular pair of plane mirrors (from actual photograph); showing how the last image is obtained by rotating the object through 180° around the line of intersection of the mirrors. One mirror vertical, the other horizontal.

ocular, with their principal sections at right angles to each other. The axial ray, after traversing the objective, crosses normally the hypothenuse-face of the first prism and is totally reflected (see § 36), in the plane of a principal section, at each of its two per-pendicular faces so as to emerge from the hypoth-enuse-face in a direction precisely opposite to that which it had when it first crossed this surface. This ray now undergoes a simi-lar cycle of experiences in a principal section of the second prism, and finally emerges from this prism in the same direction as it had when it met the

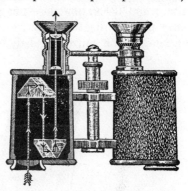

FIG. 33.—PORRO prism-system in prism binocular field glasses.

first prism. A ray parallel to the axial ray and lying above a horizontal plane containing the axis will be converted by virtue of the two reflections in the first prism into a ray whose path lies below this plane; and, similarly, a ray par-allel to the axis and lying on one side of a vertical plane containing the axis will, in consequence of the two reflec-tions within the second prism, be converted into a ray whose path lies on the opposite side of this vertical plane. Thus, the combined effect of the two reflecting prisms together will be to reverse completely the position of the ray with respect to the horizontal and vertical meridian planes, so that the ray will issue from the system on opposite sides of both these planes. If the system of prisms were removed, the image in the instrument would appear inverted, but by interposing the prisms in this fashion the image will be rectified and oriented exactly in the same way as the object; which in the case of many optical instruments is an essential consideration.

21. Applications of the Plane Mirror.—It is hardly
necessary to say that the plane mirror for various purposes has been in use among civilized peoples of all ages;
although the use of mirrors as articles of household fur-
niture and decoration does not go back farther than the
early part of the 16th century. By a combination of two
or more plane mirrors a lady can arrange the back of

Fig. 34.—Porte lumière.

her dress and in fact see herself as others see her. With
the aid of a mirror or combination of mirrors many ingenious "magical effects" are produced in theaters. The
plane mirror also constitutes an essential part of numerous
useful scientific instruments in some of which its only duty
is to alter the course of a beam of light, whereas in various
forms of goniometrical instruments and contrivances for determining an angular magnitude that is not easily measured

directly the angle in question is ascertained indirectly by
observing the angle turned through by a ray of light which
is reflected from a plane mirror.

22. Porte Lumière and Heliostat.—As good an illustration as can be given of the use of a plane mirror for changing the direction of a beam of sunlight is afforded by the

Fig. 35.—Heliostat.

porte lumière (Fig. 34), which consists essentially of a plane
mirror ingeniously mounted so as to be capable of rotation
about two rectangular axes, whereby it may be readily adjusted in any desired azimuth and reflect a beam of sunlight through a suitable opening in the wall of the building
to any part of the interior of the room.

However, owing to the diurnal movement of the sun,

a continual adjustment of the mirror is necessary in order
to keep the spot of light for any length of time at the place
in the room where it is needed, and sometimes this manipulation is very inconvenient and annoying, especially in the
case of a laboratory experiment extending perhaps over
a considerable part of a day. Thus, for example, in studying the solar spectrum it is often desirable to illuminate the
slit in the collimator tube of the spectrometer for hours at
a time. For such purposes it is better to use a *heliostat*
(Fig. 35), which is contrived so that the plane mirror is continuously revolved by clockwork around an axis parallel
to the earth's axis so as to preserve always the same relative
position with respect to the sun in its apparent diurnal
motion in the sky. The mirror can also be turned about

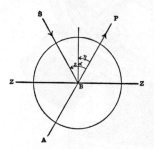

a horizontal axis, and it has first
to be adjusted about this axis so
that the rays of the sun are reflected towards the north pole
of the celestial sphere, that is,
parallel to the axis of the earth.
The mirror being adjusted at
this angle, which will depend on
the declination of the sun above
or below the celestial equator,
and turning at the rate of 15°

FIG. 36.—Principle of heliostat.

per hour around an axis parallel to the axis of rotation of
the earth, it is evident that the rays of the sun will continue
to be reflected constantly in the same direction. Suppose,
for example, that the mirror is adjusted in the position
ZZ (Fig. 36) so that the ray SB coming from the sun at S is
reflected at B in the direction BP parallel to the axis of the
earth and therefore parallel to the axis of rotation AB of the
mirror. If the polar distance of the sun is denoted by
$2a = \angle PBS$, and if the angle between the normal to the
mirror and the axis of rotation is denoted by η, then, evidently, $\eta = a$. If the sun's declination on a certain day

is $+10°$, then $2\alpha = 90° - 10° = 80°$, and $\eta = 40°$. If, on the other hand, the sun is $10°$ below the equator, $2\alpha = 100°$ and $\eta = 50°$.

The heliostat is provided also with a fixed mirror which reflects the rays from the rotating mirror in a definite direction, as desired, usually in a horizontal direction into the room where the sunlight is to be used. Generally, the instrument is mounted on a permanent ledge outside the window; sometimes it is placed on the roof of the building and the fixed mirror adjusted so as to send the sun's rays down a vertical tube at the bottom of which there is another mirror placed at an angle of 45° with the vertical where the rays are once more reflected so that the beam of sunlight which enters the room will be horizontal.

23. Measurement of the Angle of a Prism.— Another laboratory application of the principle of a plane mirror is seen in the method of using a goniometer to ascertain

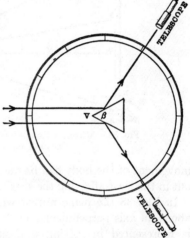

Fig. 37.—Measurement of angle of prism.

the dihedral angle between two plane faces of a glass prism (§ 48). The angle that is actually measured by the goniometer is the angular distance between the images of a distant object as seen in the two faces of the prism. Parallel rays coming from a far-off source at S (Fig. 37) and incident on the two faces of the prism that meet in the edge V are reflected as shown in the diagram, and the angle between the two directions of the reflected rays is obviously equal to twice the dihedral angle β.

24. Measure of Angular Deflections by Mirror and Scale.

—The angular rotation of a body, for example, the deflection of the magnetic needle of a galvanometer, is frequently measured by attaching a mirror to the rotating body from which a beam of light is reflected. This reflected light acts as a long weightless pointer whereby the actual

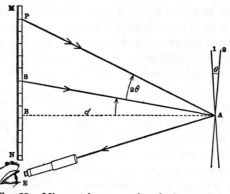

FIG. 38.—Mirror, telescope and scale for measurement of angles.

movement of the body can be magnified to any extent without in the least affecting the sensitiveness of the apparatus.

In Fig. 38 the plane mirror which is capable of rotation about an axis perpendicular at A to the plane of the paper is represented in its initial position by the line-segment marked 1. The straight line MN in front of the mirror and at a known distance (d=AB) from it represents a scale graduated in equal divisions. An eye at E looking through a telescope pointed towards A will see the image in the mirror of the scale-division at S, the so-called "zero-reading," because the light from S incident at A on the mirror in the position 1 ("equilibrium-position") is reflected along AE into the eye at E. If now the mirror is turned through an angle θ into the position marked 2, another scale-division will come into the field of view of the telescope and coincide with the cross-hair in the eye-piece. If this scale-division corresponds to the point marked P, it is the light that comes along PA that is now reflected along AE into the eye at E; and evidently, according to § 13, $\angle\,\text{PAS} = 2\,\theta$. In making a measurement by this method, the three points designated by S, B and E are generally adjusted so as to be very near together, if not actually coincident. If they were coincident, the planes of the mirror and scale would be parallel, and the axis of the telescope would coincide with the straight line BA perpendicular to the scale at B. But in any case the $\angle\,\text{BAS} = \epsilon$ will be a constant, depending partly on the initial position of the mirror and partly on the direction of the axis of the telescope; thus,

$$\tan \epsilon = a/d,$$

where $a = \text{BS}$. If, therefore, we put $x = \text{SP}$, we have:

$$\frac{x}{d} = \tan\,(\epsilon + 2\,\theta) - \tan \epsilon\,;$$

whence, since the value of x can be read off on the scale, it will be easy to calculate the value of the required angle θ through which the mirror has been turned. In many cases where this method is employed the angles denoted by θ and ϵ are both so small that there will be little error in substituting the angles themselves in place of their tangents. Under these circumstances the above formula will be greatly simplified, for the angle ϵ will disappear entirely, and we shall obtain:

$$\theta = \frac{x}{2d},$$

where, however, it must be noted that this expression gives the value of the angle θ in radians. The value of θ in degrees is found by multiplying the right-hand side of this formula by $180/\pi$, so that we obtain:

$$\theta = \frac{90.x}{\pi.d} \text{ degrees.}$$

A lamp and scale is sometimes used instead of a telescope and scale, the light of the lamp being reflected from the mirror on to the scale which is usually made of translucent glass, so that it is easy to read the position of the spot of light.

25. Hadley's Sextant.—Another instrument which utilizes the principle of § 17 is the sextant, which is employed for

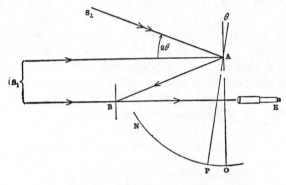

FIG. 39.—Principle of sextant.

measuring the angular distance between two bodies, for example, the altitude of the sun above the sea-horizon. The plan and essential features of this apparatus are shown in Fig. 39. At the center A of a graduated circular arc ON a small mirror is set up in a plane at right angles to that of the arc. This mirror can be turned about an axis perpendicular to the plane of the paper and passing through A. Rigidly connected to this mirror and turning with it is a long solid arm AP whose other end P, provided with a vernier scale, moves over the arc ON, whereby the angle through which the mirror turns can be accurately measured. A little beyond the extremity N of the graduated part of the arc, a second mirror B is erected facing the first mirror. The plane of this mirror is likewise perpendicular to that of the circle, but from the upper half of it the silver has been removed, so that this portion of the mirror B is transparent. Moreover, this mirror is fixed with respect to the instrument. An observer looking through a peep-hole or tele-

scope attached to the instrument towards the mirror B may
see a distant object through the upper transparent part of
this mirror, and at the same time he may also see just below
it the image of a second object reflected in the lower half
of the glass.   When the planes of the two mirrors A and B
are parallel, the zero-mark of the vernier on the movable
arm coincides with the zero-mark O of the graduated arc.
Suppose, for example, that when the two mirrors are parallel to each other, the instrument is pointed at a distant

FIG. 40.—Model of mirror sextant.

object, say, a star at S_1, which will be seen directly through
the upper half of the fixed mirror B.   At the same time the
observer will see an image of the object S_1 by rays which
have been reflected from the mirror A to the mirror B and
thence into the eye at E; for if the two mirrors are parallel,
the direction of a ray after two reflections will be the same
as its initial direction.   If now the mirror A is turned until
the image of another object at S_2 comes into the field of
vision, the two objects S_1 and S_2 will be seen simultaneously,
for with the mirror at A in this new position the incident ray
S_2A will be the ray that is reflected from A to B and thence,
as before, into the eye at E.   Moreover, since the angle between
the original direction S_2A of this ray and its final direction

S_1A is equal to double the angle between the planes of the two mirrors, that is, is equal to $2\,\theta$, where $\theta = \angle \mathrm{OAP}$, the angular distance between the objects at S_1 and S_2 must be equal to $2\,\theta$, that is, $\angle S_1AS_2 = 2\,\theta$. In order to save trouble in making the readings, half-degrees on the graduated arc are reckoned as degrees, so that the value of the angle $2\,\theta$ is read directly on the scale. As the angular distance between the objects will seldom exceed 120°, and since, in fact, the method is not very accurate for angles greater than this, the actual length of the graduated arc need not be greater than about 60° or one-sixth of the circumference; whence the name sextant is derived.

A simple model of a mirror sextant is shown in Fig. 40. For accurate measurements the instrument is made of metal with a scale etched on a silver strip. Moreover, a telescope is used instead of a peep-hole; so that with a fine sextant it is comparatively easy to measure the angular distance between two points to within one-half minute of arc. One great advantage of this instrument is its portability, and since it does not have to be mounted on a stand, it is very serviceable on shipboard for measurements of altitude and determinations of latitude, etc.

PROBLEMS

1. The top of a vertical plane mirror 2 feet high is 4 feet from the floor. The eye of a person standing in front of the mirror is 6 feet from the floor and 3 feet from the mirror. What are the distances from the wall on which the mirror hangs of the farthest and nearest points on the floor that are visible in the mirror?   Ans. 6 ft.; 18 in.

2. A ray of light is reflected at a plane mirror. Show that if the mirror is turned through an angle θ, the reflected ray will be turned through an angle $2\,\theta$.

3. Show that the deviation of a ray reflected once at each of two plane mirrors is equal to twice the angle between the mirrors.

4. If a plane mirror is turned through an angle of 5°, what is the deflection indicated by the reading on a straight scale 100 cm. from the mirror?   Ans. About 17.6 cm.

5. Find the angle turned through by the mirror when the deflection on the scale in the preceding example is 10 cm.?
                                                    Ans. 2° 52′.

6. What must be the length of a vertical plane mirror in order that a man standing in front of it may see a full length image of himself? Ans. The length of the mirror must be equal to half the height of the man.

7. Show that a plane mirror bisects at right angles the line joining an object-point with its image.

8. A ray of light proceeding from a point A is reflected from a plane mirror to a point B. Show that the path pursued by the light is shorter than any other path from A to the mirror and thence to B.

9. Give HUYGENS's construction, (1) for the reflection of a plane wave at a plane mirror, and (2) for the reflection of a spherical wave at a plane mirror.

10. Explain clearly how to determine the limits of the field of view in a plane mirror for a given position of the eye of the spectator.

11. A candle is placed between two parallel plane mirrors. Show how an observer can see the image of the candle produced by rays which have been twice reflected at one mirror and three times at the other. Draw accurate diagram showing the paths of the rays, the positions of the images, etc.; and give clear explanation of the figure.

12. OA and OB are two plane mirrors inclined at an angle of 15°, and P is a point in OA. At what angle must a ray of light from P be incident on OB in order that after three reflections it may be parallel to OA?   Ans. 45°.

13. Show that the images of a luminous object placed between two plane mirrors all lie on a circle.

14. Show how by means of two plane mirrors a man standing in front of one of them can see the image of the back

of his head. Trace the course of the rays from the back of his head into his eye and explain clearly.

15. Show by a diagram, with clear explanations, how one sees the image of an arrow in a plane mirror.

16. Construct the image of an arrow formed by two reflections in a pair of inclined mirrors, (1) when the mirrors are at right angles, and (2) when the angle between the mirrors is 60°.

17. Show how a horizontal shadow of a vertical rod can be thrown on a vertical screen by a point-source of light with the aid of a plane mirror. Draw a diagram.

18. An object is placed between two plane mirrors inclined at an angle of 45°. Show by a figure how a spectator may see the image after four successive reflections. Give clear explanation.

19. Two plane mirrors are inclined at an angle of 50°. Show that there will be 7 or 8 images of a luminous point placed between them, according as its angular distance from the nearer mirror is or is not less than 20°.

20. Find the number of images formed when a bright point is placed between two plane mirrors inclined to each other at an angle of 25°. Ans. 15 or 14 images according as the angular distance of the luminous point from the nearer mirror is or is not less than 5°.

21. A luminous object moves about between two plane mirrors, which are inclined at an angle of 27°. Prove that at any moment the number of images is 13 or 14 according as the angular distance of the luminous point from the nearer mirror is or is not less than 9°.

22. The angle between a pair of inclined mirrors is 80°. Find the position of an object which is reproduced by 5 images. Ans. The object must be less than 20° from the nearer mirror.

23. Describe a sextant with the aid of a diagram, and explain its use.

24. Describe and explain the heliostat.

25. Construct the image of the capital letter F as seen in a plane mirror.

26. When a candle-flame is placed in front of a screen with a pin-hole opening, an image of the flame is formed on a second screen placed parallel to the first. But if the second screen is replaced by a plane mirror, the image will be formed on the back of the first screen. Explain how this happens.

27. Explain clearly (with diagram, formula, etc.) the method of using a mirror and scale for measurement of angles.

28. Describe how the dihedral angle of a g'ass prism is measured on a goniometer-circle.

29. AB is an object in the form of an arrow placed in front of a plane mirror, and A'B' is its image in the mirror. P and P' are two points at equal distances from the mirror on opposite sides of it. Show how an eye at P can see the image A'B'; and also how an eye at P' would see the object AB if the mirror were removed. Explain how the image in the mirror is "perverted."

CHAPTER III

26. Passage of Light from One Medium to Another.— Hardly any one can have failed to observe that the course of light in passing obliquely from water to air is abruptly changed at the surface of the water. For example, if a coin is placed at A in the bottom of a china bowl (Fig. 41), and if the eye

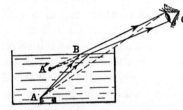

is adjusted at a point C so that the coin is hid from view by the side of the vessel, then, without altering the position of the eye, the coin can be made visible merely by pouring water in the bowl up to a certain level.

Fig. 41.—Coin at bottom of bowl rendered visible by filling bowl with water.

The broken line ABC illustrates how a ray proceeding from A may be bent at the surface of the water so as to pass over the edge of the bowl and enter the eye at C. It is true the coin will will not appear to be at A but at a point A′ nearer the surface of the water and displaced a little sideways towards the eye, because the rays that come to the eye intersect at this point A′ (§ 42). A clear pool of water seems to be shallower than it really is, and this illusion is greater in proportion as the line of sight is more oblique, so that bright objects at the bottom of the pool appear to be crowded together towards the surface. When a stick is partly immersed in water, the part under water appears to be bent up towards the surface (§ 42).

This bending of the rays which takes place when light crosses the boundary between two media is called *refraction*.

The path of a beam of sunlight through water can easily be shown by mixing a little milk in the water or by stirring in it a minute quantity of chalk-dust, while a puff of smoke will at once reveal the track of the beam in the air, so that the phenomena of refraction can readily be exhibited to the eye. In every case it will be found that the ray is bent farther from the incidence-normal in the rarer or less dense medium (see § 30); and here also, as in the case of reflection, there is a perfectly definite connection between the direction of the incident ray and that of the corresponding refracted ray.

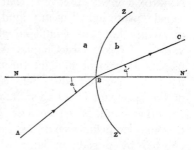

FIG. 42.—Law of Refraction.

27. Law of Refraction.—In Fig. 42 the straight line AB represents the path of a ray incident at the point B on a smooth refracting surface separating two media which for the present will be designated by the letters a and b. The straight line NN′ drawn perpendicular to the plane which is tangent to the refracting surface at B represents the incidence-normal; and the plane of the paper which contains the incident ray and the incidence-normal is the plane of incidence, as already defined (§ 13). The line ZZ represents the trace of the refracting surface in this plane. And, finally, the path of the refracted ray is shown by the straight line BC. The angles of incidence and refraction are defined to be the acute angles through which the incidence-normal has to be turned in order to bring it into coincidence with the incident and refracted rays, respectively. Thus, if these angles are denoted by a, a', then

$$a = \angle\,\mathrm{NBA}, \qquad a' = \angle\,\mathrm{N'BC}.$$

In the figure as drawn the angle a is represented as greater than the angle a', so that, according to the statement at the end of § 26, the medium a is less dense or "rarer" than the medium b.

Before stating the relation which is found to exist between the angles α and α', it is necessary to allude to NEWTON'S great discovery that sunlight and indeed so-called "white light" of any kind, as, for example, the light of an arc lamp, is composed of light of an innumerable variety of colors (see Chapter XIV), as may be shown by passing a beam of sunlight through a glass prism, whereby it will be seen that white light is a mixture of all the colors of the spectrum in all their infinite varieties of hues. On the other hand, *monochromatic light*, as it is called, is light of some one definite color, as, for example, the yellow light emitted by a sodium flame which may be obtained by burning common salt in the flame of a BUNSEN burner. In geometrical optics, unless we are specially concerned with the investigation of color-phenomena (as in Chapter XIV), it is nearly always tacitly assumed that the source of the light is monochromatic.

The *law of refraction*, as found by experiment, may now be stated as follows:

The refracted ray lies in the plane of incidence on the opposite side of the normal in the second medium from the incident ray in the first medium; and the sines of the angles of incidence and refraction are to each other in a constant ratio, the value of which depends only on the nature of the two media and on the color (or wave-length) of the light.

This constant ratio, denoted by the symbol n_{ab}, is called *the relative index of refraction from the first medium* (a) *to the second medium* (b) *for light of the given color;* thus,

$$\frac{\sin \alpha}{\sin \alpha'} = n_{ab};$$

the value of this constant, as a rule, being greatest for violet and least for red light, so that the violet rays are the most "refrangible" of all. When light is refracted from air (*a*) to water (*w*) the relative index of refraction is, approximately,

$n_{aw} = 4/3$, and hence under these circumstances $\sin a' = \frac{3}{4} \sin a$. Although there are many different varieties of optical glass, for rough calculations the value of the relative index of refraction from air (a) to glass (g) may be taken as $n_{ag} = 3/2$; which means that the sine of the angle which the ray makes with the normal in glass is about two-thirds of the sine of the angle which the corresponding ray makes with the normal in air.

Although the law of refraction is quite simple, it somehow eluded discovery until early in the seventeenth century when the true relation between the angle of refraction and the angle of incidence was first ascertained by WILLEBRORD SNELL (1591–1626) or SNELLIUS, of Leyden, and the law is, therefore, often referred to as SNELL's Law of Refraction. The law was first published by the French philosopher DESCARTES (1596–1650), who had probably seen SNELL's papers, although he does not allude to him by name.

28. Experimental Proof of the Law of Refraction.—The relation between the angles of incidence and refraction can be very strikingly exhibited with the aid of the optical disk that was mentioned in § 13 in connection with a lecture-table experiment for verifying the law of reflection of light. The vertical ground glass disk is adjusted in the track of a narrow beam of sunlight (or parallel rays from a lantern) in such a position that the path of the light is shown by a band of light crossing the face of the disk along one of its diameters. The glass body through which the light is refracted has the form of a semicylinder, the two plane parallel sides being ground rough so as to be more or less opaque, whereas the curved surface and the diametral plane face are both highly polished. This half-disk has a radius of about 2 inches and is about one-half inch thick or more. It can be fastened against the vertical face of the optical disk with its axis horizontal and coinciding with the axis of rotation of the disk, as represented in the diagram Fig. 43. If this adjustment is made, and the disk turned so that the incident ray AB meets the polished plane face of the glass body at its center B, the refracted ray BC will proceed through the glass along a radius of the semicylinder, and therefore meeting the curved surface normally, it will emerge again

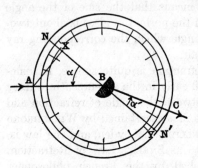

into the air without being further deviated. The diameter NN′ which is marked on the face of the optical disk is normal to the plane surface of the glass body, and if from the points A and C where the incident and refracted rays cross the circumference of the disk perpendiculars are let fall on the normal NN′, the lengths of these

Fig. 43.—Optical Disk used to verify law of refraction.

perpendiculars AX and CY will be proportional to the sines of the angles of incidence and refraction NBA and N′BC, respectively. Now it will be found that, no matter how we turn the disk, the perpendicular AX will always be about one-and-a-half times as long as the perpendicular CY. If we substitute for the half-disk of solid glass a hollow vessel of the same form and size with thin glass walls, and if we fill this vessel with water, we shall find now that the length of the perpendicular AX will always be about one-and-one-third times that of the perpendicular CY, because the relative index of refraction from air to water is 4/3, as above stated.

But the best proof of the law of the refraction of light is to be found in the fact that this law is at the basis of the theory and construction of nearly all optical instruments, and it has been subjected, therefore, to the most searching tests. The law of refraction may also be regarded as completely verified by the methods that are employed in the determination of the indices of refraction of transparent bodies, solid, liquid and gaseous; which are described in treatises on experimental optics usually under the title of "refractometry."

29. Reversibility of the Light Path.—When a ray of light AB is reflected at B in the direction BD, a plane mirror placed at D at right angles to BD will turn the reflected ray back on itself; arriving again at B, the light will obviously be reflected there so as to return finally to the point A where it started. This is a simple instance of a general law of optics known as the *principle of the reversibility of the light path*. Experiment shows that the same rule holds likewise in the case of the refraction of light, and that if ABC is the route pursued by light in going from a point A in one medium to a point C in an adjoining medium by way of the incidence-point B, and if then the light is reversed by some means so as to be started back along the path CB, it will be refracted at B into the first medium along the path BA. And, in general, if the final direction of the ray is reversed, for example, by falling normally on a plane mirror, the light will retrace its entire path, no matter how many reflections or refractions it may have suffered. Thus, in any optical diagram, in which the directions of the rays of light are indicated by arrow-heads, these pointers may all be reversed, if we wish to ascertain how the rays would go through the system if they were to enter it from the other end.

It follows, therefore, since

$$\frac{\sin \alpha}{\sin \alpha'} = n_{ab}, \qquad \frac{\sin \alpha'}{\sin \alpha} = n_{ba},$$

that we have the relation:

$$n_{ab} \cdot n_{ba} = 1;$$

that is, *the relative indices of refraction from* (a) *to* (b) *and from* (b) *to* (a) *are reciprocals of each other.* Thus, for example, since $n_{aw} = 4/3$ is the index from air to water, the index from water to air is $n_{wa} = 3/4$. Similarly, if $n_{ag} = 3/2$, the index from glass to air is $n_{ga} = 2/3$.

30. Limiting Values of the Index of Refraction.—Accordingly, we see that the value of the relative index of refraction may be greater or less than unity. If $n_{ab} > 1$, the second medium (b) is said to be *more highly refracting* or (*optically*) *denser* than the first medium (a); and since in this case $\sin a > \sin a'$, it follows that $a > a'$, which means that *the refracted ray is bent towards the normal*, as happens when light is refracted from air to water ($n_{ab} = 1.33$). On the other hand, if $n_{ab} < 1$, the second medium (b) is said to be *less highly refracting* or (*optically*) *rarer* than the first medium (a), and now the angle of refraction (a') will be greater than the angle of incidence (a), so that in this case the refracted ray will be *bent away from the normal*, as, for example, when light is refracted from water into air ($n_{wa} = 0.75$). Glass is more highly refracting than water, and diamond has the greatest light-bending power of all optical media, the index of refraction from air to diamond being about 2.5. The values of the constant n_{ab} for pairs of media a, b that are available for optical purposes are comprised within comparatively narrow limits, say, between 1/2 and 2. In the exceptional case when $n_{ab} = 1$, the angles of incidence and refraction will be equal, and the rays pass from a to b without change of direction. This is the reason why a glass rod is invisible in oil of cedar. Sometimes accidental differences of refrangibility between two adjacent layers of the same medium enable us to distinguish one part of a transparent medium from another. Similarly, also, the presence of air-bubbles in water or glass is made manifest by the refractions that take place at the boundaries. A fish swimming in water does not see the water around him, but the phenomena of refraction may make him aware of the existence of a different medium above the surface of the water.

31. Huygens's Construction of a Plane Wave Refracted at a Plane Surface.—The straight lines AB and AD (Fig. 44) show the traces in the plane of the diagram of the plane wave-front advancing in the first medium (a) in the direc-

tion BD and the plane refracting surface, respectively. The
disturbance is supposed to have just arrived at the point A
of the refracting plane, which from this moment $(t=0)$
becomes a new origin
from which secondary
hemispherical wavelets
are propagated into the
second medium (b). Now
light is propagated with
different velocities in different media; thus, for
example, the velocity of
light in water is only
about three-fourths of
what it is in air and the
velocity in glass is about
two-thirds of the velocity
in air.   Consequently,
when waves of light pass
from air into water or

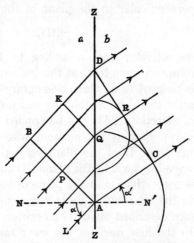

FIG. 44.—HUYGENS's construction of plane
wave refracted at plane surface.

glass, the part of the wave-front that is in the denser medium
advances more slowly than the part that is still in the air,
so that the direction of the wave-front is changed in passing
from one medium to another.   Let the velocities of light
in the media a and b be denoted by v_a and v_b, respectively.
Then after a time $t=\mathrm{BD}/v_a$, when the disturbance which
was at B has just arrived at D on the boundary between
the two media, the secondary wavelets which have been
spreading out from A as center will have been propagated
in the second medium (b) to a distance $\mathrm{AC}=v_b.t=\dfrac{v_b}{v_a}.\mathrm{BD}$;
and, similarly, at the same instant from any intermediate
point Q lying on AD between A and D the disturbance will
have proceeded into the second medium (b) to a distance

$$\mathrm{QR}=\frac{v_b}{v_a}(\mathrm{BD}-\mathrm{PQ})=\frac{v_b}{v_a}\mathrm{KD},$$

where K (not shown in the figure) designates the foot of the perpendicular let fall from Q on BD. Thus, the radii of the elementary cylindrical refracted waves whose axes are perpendicular to the plane of the diagram at A and Q are

$$\frac{v_b}{v_a}BD, \qquad \frac{v_b}{v_a}KD,$$

respectively; and, according to HUYGENS's principle, the refracted wave-front at this instant will be the surface which is tangent to all these elementary cylindrical surfaces. Exactly the same method as was used in the similar problem of reflection (§ 14) can be applied here; and thus it may be shown that at the moment when the disturbance reaches the point D of the plane refracting surface, the refracted wave-front will be the plane CD containing this point, which is perpendicular to the plane of the figure and tangent at C to the elementary wave represented by the spherical surface described about C as center with radius equal to AC. In the first medium the wave marches forward in the direction LA and in the second medium in the direction AC.

SNELL's law of refraction (§ 27) may be deduced from the figure by observing that $BD=AD.\sin a$, where $a = \angle NAL = \angle DAB$ denotes the angle of incidence, and $AC = AD.\sin a'$, where $a' = \angle N'AC = \angle ADC$ denotes the angle of refraction. Consequently,

$$\frac{\sin a}{\sin a'} = \frac{BD}{AC} = \frac{v_a}{v_b} = a \text{ constant,}$$

which constant must, therefore, be identical with the relative index of refraction n_{ab}.

The diagram is drawn for the case when the light travels faster in the first medium than it does in the second ($v_a > v_b$), that is, when the second medium is more retarding or "optically denser" (§ 30) than the first.

32. Mechanical Illustration of the Refraction of a Plane Wave.—A simple mechanical illustration of the refraction of a plane wave at a plane surface may be devised as follows:

Two boxwood wheels each about two inches in diameter
are connected by an iron axle about 4 inches long passing
through the centers of the wheels at right angles to their
planes of rotation (Fig. 45). If this body is placed on a
smooth rectangular board, about a yard long and about
18 inches wide, which is
slightly tilted, and allowed
to roll diagonally down the
board, its path will be
along a straight line. But
if a piece of felt cloth or
velveteen cut in the form
of a rectangle is glued in
the middle of the board,
with its long side parallel
to the edge of the board,
then when the body de-
scends the inclined plane
obliquely, one of the wheels
will arrive at the edge of
the cloth before the other,

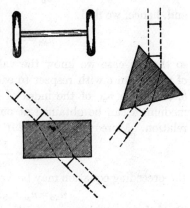

FIG. 45.—Mechanical illustration of
refraction.

so that it will be suddenly slowed up while the other wheel
continues to move on the bare board under the same conditions as before. Consequently, the axle will be made to swing
round until both wheels get on to the cloth piece, the direction of motion having been abruptly changed in this process.
At the opposite edge of the cloth rectangle, a similar change
of the direction of motion takes place in an opposite sense,
so that when the roller leaves the retarding surface and
emerges again on to the bare board, it will be found to be
going approximately in the same direction as at first. These
bendings in the course of the roller descending the inclined
plane at the places where it crosses the parallel sides of the
cloth rectangle are analogous to the deviations in the line
of march of a plane wave of light in traversing a glass slab
surrounded by air.

33. Absolute Index of Refraction.—If v_a, v_b and v_c denote the velocities of light in the media a, b and c, respectively, then, as we have just seen (§ 31), according to the wave-theory of light, the relative indices of refraction will be:

$$n_{ab} = \frac{v_a}{v_b}, \; n_{ac} = \frac{v_a}{v_c}, \; n_{bc} = \frac{v_b}{v_c};$$

and, hence, we find:

$$n_{ab} = \frac{n_{ac}}{n_{bc}};$$

so that in case we know the values n_{ac}, n_{bc} of the indices of a medium c with respect to each of the two media a and b, the value n_{ab} of the index of medium b with respect to medium a can be obtained at once by means of the above relation. Moreover, since (§ 29)

$$n_{cb} = \frac{1}{n_{bc}},$$

the preceding equation may be written as follows:

$$n_{ab} = n_{ac}.n_{cb}.$$

Thus, for example, suppose the three media a, b and c are water, glass and air, respectively; since $n_{ac} = 3/4$ and $n_{cb} = 3/2$, the index of refraction from water to glass is found by the above formula to be $n_{ab} = 9/8$.

In fact, if there are a number of media a, b, c, . . . , i, j, k it is obvious that we shall have the following relation between the relative indices of refractions:

$$n_{ab}.n_{bc} \; \cdots \; n_{ij}.n_{jk} = n_{ak},$$

which is easily remembered by observing the order in which the letters occur in the subscripts. In particular, if the last medium k is identical with the first medium a, as is the case in an optical instrument surrounded by air, then $n_{ak} = n_{aa} = 1$, and accordingly we obtain:

$$n_{ab}.n_{bc} \; \cdots \; n_{ij}.n_{ja} = 1.$$

A special case of this general relation, viz.,

$$n_{ab}.n_{ba} = 1,$$

has already been remarked (§ 29).

Since $n_{ac}.n_{ca}=n_{bc}.n_{cb}=1$ and $n_{ab}.n_{bc}=n_{ac}$, we may write also:

$$n_{ab}=\frac{n_{cb}}{n_{ca}},$$

and this formula suggests immediately the idea of employing some suitable medium c as a *standard optical medium* with respect to which the indices of refraction of all other media may be expressed. The natural medium to choose for this purpose is the ether itself which light traverses in coming to the earth from the sun and stars; and so the index of refraction of a medium with respect to empty space or vacuum is called its *absolute index of refraction* or simply its refractive index. Thus, the absolute index of refraction of vacuum (c) is equal to unity, that is, $n_c=1$. Similarly, the symbols n_a, n_b will be employed to denote the absolute indices of the media a, b, respectively; so that here they are really equivalent to the magnitudes denoted by n_{ca}, n_{cb} in the preceding formula, which, therefore, may be written:

$$n_{ab}=\frac{n_b}{n_a};$$

that is, *the relative index of refraction of medium* b *with respect to medium* a *is equal to the ratio of the absolute index of medium* b *to that of medium* a.

The absolute indices of refraction of all known transparent substances are greater than unity. The velocity of light in ordinary atmospheric air is so nearly equal to its velocity *in vacuo* that for all practical purposes we may generally take the absolute index of refraction of air as also equal to unity. The actual value for air at 0°C. and under a pressure of 76 cm. of mercury, for sodium light, is 1.000293.

With every isotropic medium there is associated, therefore, a certain numerical constant n called its (absolute) index of refraction; and, hence, when a ray of light is refracted from a medium of index n into another of index n', *the trigonometric formula for the law of refraction* may be written thus:

$$\frac{\sin a}{\sin a'} = \frac{n'}{n},$$

which may also be put in the following symmetric form:

$$n'.\sin a' = n.\sin a.$$

This latter mode of writing this relation suggests also another way of stating the fundamental fact in regard to the

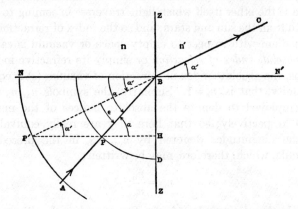

FIG. 46.—Construction of refracted ray ($n' > n$)

refraction of light, as follows: *Whenever a ray of light is refracted from one medium to another, the product of the index of refraction and the sine of the angle between the ray and the normal to the refracting surface has the same value after refraction ($n'.\sin a'$) as before refraction ($n.\sin a$).* This product $K = n.\sin a = n'.\sin a'$ which does not vary when the light crosses a surface separating a pair of isotropic media is called the *optical invariant of refraction.*

34. Construction of the Refracted Ray.—Let the absolute indices of refraction of two media separated from each other by a smooth refracting surface be denoted by n, n', and let the straight line AB (Figs. 46 and 47) represent the path in the first medium (n) of a ray incident on the boundary-

surface at the point B. The straight line NN′ represents
the normal to the refracting surface at this point, and hence
the plane of the diagram is the plane of incidence. The
straight line ZZ shows the trace in this plane of the plane
tangent to the refracting surface at the incidence-point B;
in the special case when the refracting surface is itself plane,
this straight line will be the trace of the surface of separation between the two media. With the point B as center

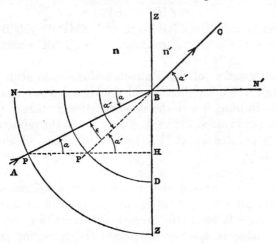

FIG. 47.—Construction of refracted ray $(n' < n)$

and with any radius r describe in the plane of incidence the
arc of a circle cutting the incident ray AB in a point P lying
in the first medium; and in the same plane, with radius
n'/n times as great, that is, with radius $n'r/n$, describe also
the arc of a concentric circle intersecting at P′ the straight
line HP drawn through P perpendicular to ZZ at H. If
the second medium is more highly refracting than the first,
that is, if $n' > n$, the radius of the second circle will be greater
than that of the first, as represented in Fig. 46; whereas
when $n' < n$, the second circle is inside the first, as in Fig. 47.
The path of the refracted ray correspodinng to the given

incident ray AB will be represented by the prolongation
BC in the second medium of the straight line P'B.

The proof of this construction consists simply in showing
that the $\angle$N'BC between the normal and the straight line
BC is equal to the angle of refraction a' as given by the
formula $n'.\sin a' = n.\sin a$, where $a = \angle$NBA denotes the
given angle of incidence. Evidently, from the figure, we have:

$$\frac{\sin\angle\text{HPB}}{\sin\angle\text{HP'B}} = \frac{\text{BP'}}{\text{BP}} = \frac{n'}{n},$$

and since $\angle$HPB $= \angle$NBA $= a$, and $\angle$HP'B $= \angle$N'BC, we
obtain immediately the relation: $n'. \sin\angle$N'BC$= n.\sin a$ and
therefore $\angle$N'BC$= a'$.

35. Deviation of the Refracted Ray.—The acute angle
through which the direction of the refracted ray has to be
turned to bring it into the same direction as that of the incident ray is called the *angle of deviation* of the refracted ray
and is denoted by ϵ; thus, $\epsilon = \angle$P'BP (Figs. 46 and 47).
Obviously,

$$\epsilon = a - a'.$$

The only ray incident at B whose direction will remain unchanged after the ray enters the second medium is the one
that proceeds along the normal NB ($a = a' = \epsilon = 0$). The
more obliquely the ray AB meets the refracting surface,
that is, *the greater the angle of incidence, the greater also will
be the deviation-angle.* The truth of this statement will be
apparent from an inspection of the relation between the
angles a and ϵ as exhibited in Fig. 46 or Fig. 47. The intercept PP' included between the circumferences of the two
construction-circles, which remains constantly parallel to the
incidence-normal, increases in length as the angle of incidence increases, whereas the other two sides BP, BP' of
the triangle BPP', being always equal to the radii of the
circles, remain constant in length; and hence the angle ϵ
must increase in absolute value as the angle a increases.

36. Total Reflection.—In ordinary refraction, as we have
seen, there can only be one refracted ray corresponding to

a given incident ray, but the question may be asked: Is it
possible that, under certain circumstances, there will be
no refracted ray, so that the incident light will be *totally
reflected* at the surface without being refracted at all? Evidently such will be the case whenever in the foregoing construction (§ 34) the point P′ (Figs. 46 and 47) cannot be
located, because the path of the refracted ray is determined
by the straight line P′B.

Let us examine, first, the case when the second medium
is more highly refracting than the first, $n' > n$ (Fig. 46).

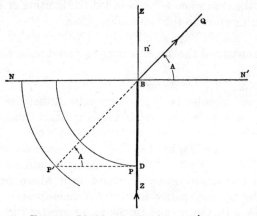

Fig. 48.—Limiting refracted ray $(n' > n)$

Suppose that the straight line AB which represents the
path of the incident ray is initially in the position NB, and
that it is rotated from this position around the point B as
a pivot until it has turned through a right angle in the plane
of the figure. While the point P on AB describes a quadrant
of the circumference of the circle of radius BP, the point
P′ will trace out an arc of the concentric circle of radius
BP′, which, however, will never be equal to a quadrant of
this circumference; for when the point P has completed its
quadrant and arrived at the point D (Fig. 48) on the tangent plane drawn to the refracting surface at B, the point

P′ will likewise have reached the extremity of its arc where the tangent to the inner circle at D meets the circumference of the outer circle. The incident ray ZB just *grazes* the refracting surface at B or skims along it, and most of the light is reflected and does not enter the second medium at all, but the portion that is refracted pursues the path BQ corresponding to this extreme position of the point P′, and this will be the outermost of all the refracted rays that enter the second medium at the point B. The $\angle N′BQ = A$ which is the greatest value that the angle of refraction can have in the case when $n′ > n$ is called the limiting or *critical angle* with respect to the two media. Since

$$\sin\angle N′BQ = \sin\angle PP′B = BD/BP′ = n/n′,$$

the magnitude of the angle A may be found from the relation:

$$\sin A = n/n′, \qquad (n < n′);$$

which may likewise be derived by substituting the values $a = 90°$, $a′ = A$ in the refraction-formula. Thus, if the first medium is air $(n = 1)$ and the second medium is glass $(n′ = 3/2)$, $\sin A = 2/3$, so that the critical angle for air-glass is found to be $A = 41° 49′$. For air-water $\sin A = 3/4$, $A = 48° 35′$; and, consequently, a ray of light whose path lies partly in air and partly in water cannot possibly make an angle with the normal in the water greater than about $48° 30′$. For example, when a star is just rising or setting, the rays coming from it will fall very nearly horizontally on the surface of tranquil water and will be refracted into the water, therefore, at an angle of approximately $48° 30′$ with the vertical, so that if these rays entered an eye under the water, the star would appear to be nearly halfway to the zenith. In fact, all the rays coming into an eye placed under water from the entire overhanging arch of the sky would be comprised in the water within a cone whose axis points to the zenith and whose angular aperture is about $97°$. In this connection it is interesting and instructive to examine a photograph of an air-scene made with a so-called

"fish-eye" camera immersed below the level of a clear pool
of water, which affords some idea of how the world outside
the pond must look to a fish. Professor WOOD, of the Johns
Hopkins University, has obtained a number of pictures of
this kind, some of which are reproduced in illustrations in
his very original book on *Physical Optics*, where also a brief
description of the essential features of the ingenious pin-

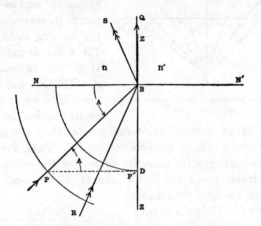

FIG. 49.—Limiting incident ray $(n' < n)$

hole camera which was used in making these pictures is
also given.

Accordingly, when light is refracted from a rarer to a
denser medium, there will always be a refracted ray corresponding to a given incident ray, because it is always
possible under these circumstances to locate the position
of the point P' opposite P, or, to express it in another way,
because when $n < n'$ there will always be a certain acute
angle a' that will satisfy the equation $\sin a' = n.\sin a/n'$ for
values of a comprised between 0° and 90°. But in the opposite case when the first medium is denser than the second
$(n > n')$, for example, when the light is refracted from water
to air, the statement just made is no longer true. The es-

sential difference in the two cases may be seen at once by reversing the arrow-heads in the diagram Fig. 48, at the same time making corresponding changes in the letters and symbols. Fig. 49 is a special diagram to illustrate this case. The refracted ray BQ which grazes the surface at the point B corresponds to the limiting incident ray PB which is incident at B at the critical angle A = ∠NBP; and, consequently, any ray, such as RB, which meets the surface at an angle of incidence greater than the angle A will be *totally reflected* in the direction BS. Thus, for values of a which are greater than the value A of the critical angle of incidence, there will be no value of a' that will satisfy the equation $\sin a' = n.\sin a/n'$ when $n > n'$. Only those rays incident at B which lie within the cone generated by the revolution of the limiting incident ray around the incidence-normal as axis will be refracted into t h e second medium; and all rays falling on the refracting surface at B and lying outside this cone will be totally reflected.

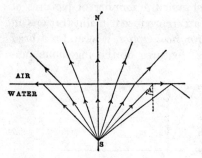

Fig. 50.—Refraction from water to air; total reflection.

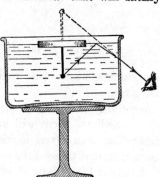

Fig. 51.—Experiment illustrating total reflection.

Fig. 50 shows how rays proceed from a radiant point below the horizontal free surface of still water.

If a pin is stuck in the under side of a flat circular cork floating on water, as represented in Fig. 51, and if the

diameter of the cork is (say) 6 inches and the head of
the pin is not more than 2.5 inches below the water-level
and vertically beneath the center of the cork, an eye placed
anywhere above the level of the water will be unable to see
the pin, because all the rays coming from it that meet the
surface of the water beyond the edge of the cork will be
totally reflected back into the water.

In Fig. 49 since $\sin \angle \mathrm{NBP} = \sin \angle \mathrm{P'PB} = \mathrm{BP'}/\mathrm{BP}$, we find
in this case when $n' < n$ that $\sin A = n'/n$, which will also be
obtained by putting $a = A$, $a' = 90°$ in the refraction-
formula $n.\sin a = n'.\sin a'$. Comparing this result with
the formula $\sin A = n/n'$ obtained for the case when $n' > n$,
and recalling the fact that the sine of an angle is never
greater than unity, we may formulate the following rule:

*The sine of the so-called
critical angle (A) with respect to two media is the
ratio of the index of refraction of the rarer to that of
the denser medium. Or,
the sine of the critical angle
(A) of a substance is the
reciprocal of the absolute
index of refraction of the
substance:* thus,

$$\sin A = \frac{1}{n}.$$

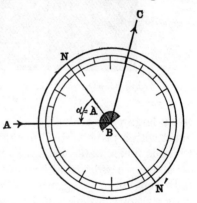

Fig. 52.—Optical Disk used to show total
reflection.

**37. Experimental Il-
lustrations of Total Re-
flection.**—The phenomenon of total reflection may be exhibited with the aid of the optical disk and the semicylinder
of glass described in § 28. If the disk is turned so that the
beam of incident parallel rays falls first on the curved surface
of the semicylinder, as shown in Fig. 52, the rays meet this
surface normally and proceed through the glass to the plane
face without being deviated. At the plane surface a por-

tion of the beam is reflected and, in general, a portion is refracted from glass to air. If the disk is turned until the
angle of incidence at the plane surface is just equal to the
critical angle (A), the rays emerging into the air will proceed along the plane face, and if the disk is turned a little
farther in the same sense, so that the angle of incidence
exceeds the critical angle, the light will be totally reflected.

An ingenious contrivance for exhibiting the procedure of
light in passing from water to air consists of a compara-

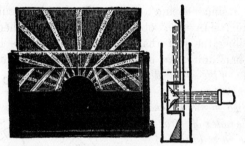

Fig. 53.—Demonstration of refraction from water to
air and total reflection.

tively large glass tank (Fig. 53) filled with water and provided with a plane vertical metallic screen the lower half of
which is under water while the upper half extends into the
air above. A cylindrical beam of light is directed horizontally and normally against the lower part of the vertical
glass wall of the tank, which is behind the screen and parallel to it. The rays entering the water are received first
on the surface of a solid reflecting cone of aperture-angle
90° placed in the water under the screen and mostly in front
of it, the axis of the cone being horizontal and its apex
turned towards the on-coming light. From the surface of
this cone the rays are reflected through the water in all directions in a vertical plane coinciding as nearly as possible
with the front side of the screen turned towards the spectators. Surrounding the conical reflector and co-axial with

it, there is a cylindrical cavity of diameter very little larger than that of the base of the cone. The surface of this cylinder is made of thin sheet-metal blackened on the inside, wherein a number of equal horizontal slits are cut at equal angular distances apart, and through these slits narrow beams of light reflected from the surface of the cone are permitted to pass upwards towards the surface of the water, their courses being shown by the bright traces on the screen. Some of these beams will be refracted out into the air, whereas others, meeting the water-surface more obliquely, will be totally reflected.

If rays are incident normally on one of the two perpendicular faces of a glass prism (§ 48) whose principal section is an isosceles right-triangle (Fig. 54), they will enter the prism without deviation, and falling on the hypothenuse-face at an angle of 45°, which is greater than the critical angle of glass, they will be totally reflected there and turned through a right angle, so that they will emerge in a direction normal to the other of the two perpendicular faces of the prism.

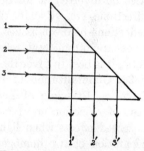

Fig. 54.—Total reflection prism

A prism of this kind is frequently employed in optical systems. It is used, for example, in connection with a photographic lens to rectify the image focused on the sensitive plate of the camera, so that the right and left sides of the negative will correspond to the right and left sides of the object. None of the light is lost by the total reflection in the prism, and if the prism is made of good optical glass of high transparency there will be comparatively little loss of light by absorption in the prism or by reflection on entering and leaving it. The same optical effect can be produced by a simple plane mirror, but as a rule a polished metallic surface absorbs the incident light to a considerable extent.

However, the loss of light in the case of a mirror silvered on glass is very slight; but on the other hand, the fine layer of silver may easily be injured mechanically or tarnished by exposure to the air. If the glass mirror is silvered on the back side, the light will be reflected from both surfaces of the glass and there will be confusion. Moreover, a glass mirror may easily get broken or become dislocated in an optical instrument; whereas a prism made of a solid piece of glass is much more substantial and durable.

Optical prisms consisting of solid pieces of highly transparent homogeneous glass with three or more polished plane faces are very extensively used in the construction of modern optical instruments for rectifying images which would otherwise be inverted or for bending the rays of light into new directions, etc. Usually the light undergoes several interior reflections before it issues from the prism, and these reflections are often total reflections. If the reflection is not total, it is best to silver the surface.

38. Generalization of the Laws of Reflection and Refraction. Principle of Least Time (Fermat's Law).—The laws of reflection and refraction, which merely describe the observed effects when light falls on the common surface of separation of two homogeneous media, and which are capable of simple explanation on the basis of the wave-theory, as has been illustrated in certain special cases (§§ 14 and 31), may be combined into a general law which was first announced about 1665 by the French philosopher FERMAT, and which may be stated as follows: *The actual path pursued by light in going from one point to another is the route that, under the given conditions, requires the least time.*

In case the reflections and refractions take place only at plane surfaces, the truth of the above statement is easily proved. Consider, first, the case *when the light is reflected from a plane mirror*. The straight line ZZ (Fig. 55) represents the trace of the plane mirror in the plane of the diagram, and A and C designate the positions of a pair of points lying in this plane in front of the mirror. Now if a point X in the plane of the mirror is connected with A and C by the straight lines XA, XC, the route AXC will be shortest when the normal to the mirror at X lies in the plane AXC and bisects the angle AXC. The point X must lie, therefore, in the plane of the diagram at the point B, so that when AB is the direction of an incident ray, BC will be the direction of the reflected ray. Obviously, if A′ is the image of A in the mirror, then AB+BC=A′B+BC =A′C, and since the straight line A′C is shorter, for example, than (A′D+DC)=(AD+DC), where D is

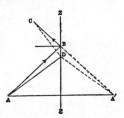

Fig. 55.—Fermat's principle of least time in case of reflection at a plane mirror.

another point on the mirror different from the point B, it is evident that the route from A to C by way of B is shorter than the route *via* any other point on the mirror. Moreover, if the ray is reflected at a number of plane mirrors in succession, its entire path will be the shortest possible route from the starting point to the terminal point, subject to the condition that it must touch at each mirror in turn. The principle of least time in the case of reflection of light at a plane mirror dates back to the time of Hero of Alexandria (150 B. C.).

When light is refracted at a plane surface, the route pursued between a point A in one medium to a point C in the other is indeed the quickest way but generally not the shortest. The following illustration will help to make the problem clear in this case. Suppose a level field is divided into two parts by a straight line ZZ (Fig. 56), on one side of which the ground is bare and smooth while on the other side it is plowed and rough; and let us also suppose that a man can walk only half as fast over the rough part of the field as over the smooth part, and that he desires to march as quickly as possible from a point A in the smooth ground to a certain other point C in the plowed ground. The question is, Where should he cross the dividing line ZZ? Of course, his shortest route would be along the straight

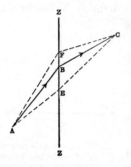

line from A to C which intersects ZZ at the point marked E in the figure, but unless the straight line AC happens to be perpendicular to ZZ this will not be his quickest way. Instead of crossing at E, suppose he selects a point F on ZZ which is a little nearer to his objective at C; then although the length FC in the plowed ground is shorter than before, on the other hand the distance AF over the smooth ground is longer, but on the whole we may assume that

FIG. 56.—Quickest route from A to C *via* path ABC.

the route AFC will take less time than the shortest route AEC. But if the point of crossing ZZ is taken too far from E, the advantage of the shorter dis-

tance in the rough ground will presently be more than offset by the increasing length of the distance that has to be traversed in the smooth ground. Accordingly, there is a certain point B on ZZ such that the time taken along the route ABC will be the quickest of all routes. Now we shall see that this is also the very path that light would take if it were refracted from A to C across ZZ, supposing that the ratio of the velocities of light on the two sides

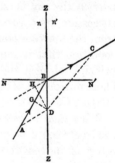

FIG. 57.—FERMAT's principle of least time in case of refraction at plane surface.

of ZZ were the same as the ratio of the velocities of walking in the two parts of the field.

In the accompanying diagram (Fig. 57) the broken line ABC represents the actual path of a ray of light from a point A in the first medium (n) to a point C on the other side of the plane refracting surface ZZ in the second medium (n'); so that if NBN′ is the normal to the surface at B, then by the law of refraction:

$$\frac{\sin\angle \mathrm{NBA}}{\sin\angle \mathrm{N'BC}} = \frac{n'}{n} = \frac{v}{v'},$$

where v, v' denote the speeds with which light travels in the media n, n', respectively. The time taken to go over the route ABC is

$$t = \frac{\mathrm{AB}}{v} + \frac{\mathrm{BC}}{v'},$$

and we wish to show that this time t is less than the time

$$\frac{\mathrm{AD}}{v} + \frac{\mathrm{DC}}{v'}$$

along any other route ADC, where D designates the position of any point on ZZ different from the point B. Draw DG, DH perpendicular to AB, BC, respectively; then, since

$$\angle \mathrm{BDG} = \angle \mathrm{NBA}, \qquad \angle \mathrm{BDH} = \angle \mathrm{N'BC},$$

evidently we have:

$$\frac{\sin\angle \mathrm{BDG}}{\sin\angle \mathrm{BDH}} = \frac{\mathrm{GB}}{\mathrm{HB}} = \frac{v}{v'}, \text{ or } \frac{\mathrm{GB}}{v} = \frac{\mathrm{HB}}{v'}.$$

Now

$$\frac{\mathrm{AB}}{v} + \frac{\mathrm{BC}}{v'} = \frac{\mathrm{AG} + \mathrm{GB}}{v} + \frac{\mathrm{BC}}{v'} = \frac{\mathrm{AG}}{v} + \frac{\mathrm{HC}}{v'};$$

and since $\mathrm{AG} < \mathrm{AD}$ and $\mathrm{HC} < \mathrm{DC}$, therefore

$$\left(\frac{\mathrm{AB}}{v} + \frac{\mathrm{BC}}{v'}\right) < \left(\frac{\mathrm{AD}}{v} + \frac{\mathrm{DC}}{v'}\right),$$

and hence the time *viâ* ABC is less than it would be *viâ* any other route from A to C.

It should be remarked, however, that when the boundary-surface between two media is *curved*, the time taken by light to go from a point A across the surface to another point C is not always a minimum. It may, indeed, be a maximum, but it is always one or the other.

39. The Optical Length of the Light-path, and the Law of Malus.—In the time t that light takes to go along the path

ABC from a point A in one medium (n) to a point C in an adjacent medium (n') it would traverse *in vacuo* the distance

$$V.t = V\left(\frac{AB}{v} + \frac{BC}{v'}\right),$$

where V denotes the velocity of light *in vacuo*. But by the definition of the absolute index of refraction (§ 33), $n = V/v$, $n' = V/v'$; and hence the equivalent d i s t a n c e *in vacuo* is:

$$n.AB + n'.BC.$$

The *optical length* of the path of a ray in a medium

Fig. 58.—Optical length of ray-path $= \Sigma nl.$

is defined to be the product of the actual length (l) of the ray-path by the index of the medium (n) that is, $n.l.$ Suppose, for example, that light traverses a series of media n_1, n_2, etc., as represented in Fig. 58; the total optical length along a ray will be:

$$n_1.l_1 + n_2.l_2 + \ldots\ldots + n_m.l_m = \sum_{k=1}^{k=m} n_k.l_k;$$

where l_k denotes the actual length of the ray-path in the kth medium.

Now the wave-front at any instant due to a disturbance emanating from a point-source is the surface which contains all the farthest points to which the disturbance has been propagated at that instant. Thus, *the wave-surface* may be defined as *the totality of all those points which are reached in a given time by a disturbance originating at a point.* In a single isotropic medium the wave-surfaces, as we have seen, will be concentric spheres described around the point-source as center; but if the wave-front arrives at a reflecting or refracting surface μ, at which the directions of the so-called rays of light are changed, the form of the wave-surface thereafter will, in general, no longer be spherical; and even in those exceptional cases when the reflected or refracted wave-front is spherical, the waves will spread out from

a new center which is seldom identical with the original
center. The function Σnl has the same value for all actual ray-paths between one position of the wave-surface and
another position of it; so that when the form and position
of the wave-front and the paths of the rays at any instant
are known, the wave-front at any subsequent instant may
be constructed by laying off equal optical lengths along the
path of each ray.

A consequence of this definition of the wave-surface is
that the ray is always normal to the wave-surface (§7), as will
be evident from the following
reasoning.   Suppose   t h a t   the
straight line AB (Fig. 59) represents the path of a ray incident
on the refracting surface ZZ at
the point B, and that the straight
line BC represents the path of
the corresponding refracted ray.
Moreover, let the wave-surface
which passes through the point

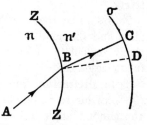

FIG. 59.—Law of MALUS: Ray
normal to wave-front.

C be designated by σ. From the incidence-point B draw
any other straight line, as BD, meeting the wave-surface σ
in the point D.   Then by the principle of least time, the
route ABC is quicker, that is, optically shorter, than the
route ABD, because the natural or actual route between the
points A and D would not be by way of the incidence-point
B.   Hence, the straight line BC must be shorter than BD,
and therefore BC is the shortest line that can be drawn from
the incidence-point B to the wave-surface σ.

The same reasoning is applicable to all cases of reflection
and refraction, and hence we may make the following general statement:

Rays of light meet the wave-surface normally; and, conversely, *The system of surfaces which intersect at right angles
rays emanating originally from a point-source is a system of
wave-surfaces.*

This law was published by MALUS in 1808.

PROBLEMS

1. (*a*) A ray is refracted from vacuum into a medium whose index of refraction is $\sqrt{2}$, the angle of incidence being 45°: find the angle of refraction.

(*b*) Find the angle of incidence of a ray which is refracted at an angle of 30° from vacuum into a medium of index equal to $\sqrt{3}$.

(*c*) Find the relative index of refraction when the angles of incidence and refraction are 30° and 60°, respectively.   Ans. (*a*) 30°; (*b*) 60°; (*c*) $\sqrt{3}$: 3.

2. Assuming that the indices of refraction of air, water, glass and diamond have the values 1, $\frac{4}{3}$, $\frac{3}{2}$ and $\frac{5}{2}$, respectively, calculate the angle of refraction in each of the following cases:

(*a*) Refraction from air to glass, angle of incidence 40°; (*b*) from air to water, angle of incidence 60°; (*c*) from air to diamond, angle of incidence 75°; (*d*) from glass to water, angle of incidence 30°; (*e*) from diamond to glass, angle of incidence 36° 52′ 11.6″.   Ans. (*a*) 25° 22′ 26″; (*b*) 40° 30′ 19″;
(*c*) 22° 43′ 44″; (*d*) 34° 13′ 44″; (*e*) 90°.

3. The height of a cylindrical cup is 4 inches and its diameter is 3 inches. A person looking over the rim can just see a point on the opposite side 2.25 inches below the rim. But when the cup is filled with water, looking in the same direction as before, he can just see the point of the base farthest from him. Find the index of refraction of water.

Ans. 4:3.

4. The index of a refracting sphere is $\sqrt{3}$; it is surrounded by air. A ray of light, entering the sphere at an angle of incidence of 60° and passing over to the other side, is there partly reflected and partly refracted. Show that the reflected ray and the emergent ray are at right angles to each other.

5. In the preceding problem, show that the reflected ray will cross the sphere again and be refracted back into the

air in a direction exactly opposite to that which the ray had before it entered the sphere.

6. A straight line drawn through the center C of a spherical refracting surface meets the surface in a point designated by A. If J, J' designate the points where an incident ray and the corresponding refracted ray intersect the straight line AC, and if $CJ = \frac{n'}{n} . AC$, show that $CJ' = \frac{n}{n'} . AC$, where n, n' denote the indices of refraction of the first and second media, respectively.

7. Construct the path of a ray refracted at a plane surface. Draw diagrams for the cases when n' is greater and less than n. Construct the critical angle in each figure.

8. The velocity of light in air is approximately 186000 miles per second. How fast does it travel in alcohol of index 1.363?   Ans. Approximately, 136 460 miles per sec.

9. A fish is 8 feet below the surface of a pool of clear water. A man shooting at the place where the fish appears to be points his gun at an angle of 45°. Where will the bullet cross the vertical line that passes through the fish? (Take index of water as 1.33, and neglect any deflection of the bullet caused by impact with the water.)

Ans. 3 feet above the fish.

10. Assuming that the velocity of light in air is 30 000 000 000 cm. per sec., calculate its velocity in water and in glass.

11. Prove that $n_{ab} = n_{cb} : n_{ca}$.

12. Show that the sine of the critical angle of an optical medium is equal to the reciprocal of the absolute index of refraction.

13. Assuming same values of the indices of refraction as in problem No. 2, calculate the values of the critical angle for each of the following pairs of media: (a) air and glass, (b) air and water, (c) air and diamond.

Ans. (a) 41° 48′ 40″; (b) 48° 35′ 25″; (c) 23° 34′ 41″.

14. A 45° prism is used to turn a beam of light by total internal reflection through a right angle. What must be

the least possible value of the index of refraction of the glass?   Ans. $\sqrt{2}$.

15. Show that when a ray of light passes from air into a medium whose index of refraction is equal to $\sqrt{2}$, the deviation cannot be greater than 45°.

16. The absolute index of refraction of a certain transparent substance is $\frac{5}{3}$. Show that a luminous point at the center of a cube of this material cannot be seen by an eye in the air outside, if at the center of each face of the cube a circular piece of opaque paper is pasted whose radius is equal to three-eighths of the edge of the cube.

17. What will be the greatest apparent zenith distance of a star to an eye under water?

18. Explain why it is that it is not possible for a person by merely opening his eyes under water to see distinctly objects in the water around him or in the air above the water; whereas, if he is provided with a diver's helmet with a plate glass window in it, he will experience no difficulty in distinguishing such objects clearly.

19. Rays of light are emitted upwards in all directions from a luminous point at the bottom of a trough containing a layer of a transparent liquid 3 inches in depth and of refractive index 1.25. Show that all rays which meet the surface outside a certain circle whose center is vertically above the point will be totally reflected; and find the radius of this circle.   Ans. 4 inches.

20. A pin with a white head is stuck perpendicularly in the center of one side of a flat circular cork, and the cork is floated on water with the pin downwards. Assuming that the head of the pin is 2 inches below the surface of the water, find the smallest diameter the cork can have so that a person looking down through the water (index $\frac{4}{3}$) from the air above (index unity) could not see the head of the pin.
                                        Ans. 4.535 inches.

21. Plot a curve showing the deviation ϵ as a function of the angle of incidence a for the case when the refraction is from water ($n=4/3$) to air ($n'=1$).

CHAPTER IV

REFRACTION AT A PLANE SURFACE, AND ALSO THROUGH A PLATE WITH PLANE PARALLEL FACES

40. Trigonometric Calculation of Ray Refracted at a Plane Surface.—A geometrical construction of the path of the refracted r a y was given in § 34. The path of a ray refracted at a plane surface may also be easily determined by trigonometric calculation. The straight line yy in Figs. 60 and 61 represents the plane refracting surface separating the two media of indices n, n',

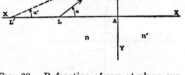

FIG. 60.—Refraction of ray at plane surface: $v = AL$, $v' = AL'$ $(n' > n)$.

and the straight line LB shows the path of a ray which is incident on yy at the point marked B. The straight line LA perpendicular to yy at A

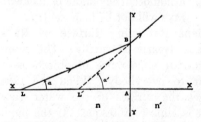

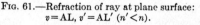

FIG. 61.—Refraction of ray at plane surface: $v = AL$, $v' = AL'$ $(n' < n)$.

is the *axis* of the refracting plane with respect to the position of the point L. The magnitudes $v = AL$ $a = \angle ALB$ which determine completely the position of the incident ray are sometimes called t h e ray-coördinates. Let L′ designate the point where the refracted ray L′B intersects the axis xx, and let $v' = AL'$, $a' = \angle AL'B$ denote the coördinates of the refracted ray. The

95

problem is: Given the incident ray $(v,\ \alpha)$, determine the refracted ray $(v',\ \alpha')$.

From either diagram we obtain immediately the relation:

$$\frac{v'}{v}=\frac{\tan \alpha}{\tan \alpha'};$$

and since $n.\sin \alpha = n'.\sin \alpha'$, we obtain finally the following formulæ for calculating the refracted ray:

$$v'=\frac{v}{n}\ \frac{\sqrt{n'^2 - n^2.\sin^2 \alpha}}{\cos \alpha},\ \sin \alpha'=\frac{n}{n'}.\sin \alpha.$$

Now if the point L is a luminous point, rays will emanate from it in all directions, and, whereas the magnitude v will

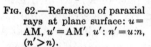

FIG. 62.—Refraction of paraxial rays at plane surface: $u=$ AM, $u'=$AM', $u': n'=u:n$, $(n'>n)$.

remain the same for all these rays, the angle α will vary from ray to ray. But for different values of α, in general we shall obtain different values of the magnitude v', and, consequently, the position of the point L' on the axis will be different for different incident rays coming from L. Accordingly, the bundle of refracted rays corresponding to a homocentric bundle of incident rays will not be homocentric.

41. Imagery in a Plane Refracting Surface by Rays which Meet the Surface Nearly Normally.—The more or less blurred and distorted appearance of objects seen under water is familiar to everybody. When the rays that enter the eye meet the surface of the water very obliquely, the distortion is almost grotesque. If the pupil of the eye were not comparatively small, it would indeed be practically almost impossible to recognize an object under water, even if the eye were placed in the most favorable position vertically over the object. It is only because the apertures of the bundles of effective rays that enter the eye are quite narrow, that there is any true image-effect at all in the case of refraction at a plane surface.

When the eye looks directly along the normal to the plane refracting surface at an object-point M on the other side of the surface (Figs. 62 and 63), the effective rays coming from M will meet the surface very nearly perpendicularly, and the incidence-points will all be so close to the point A that there will be practically no difference between the lengths of the straight lines MA and MB, and accordingly under these circumstances we may write sin a in place of tan a. Similarly, also, with respect to

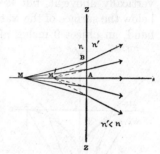

FIG. 63.—Refraction of paraxial rays at plane surface: $u = AM$, $u' = AM'$, $u':n' = u:n$, $(n' < n)$.

the refracted ray, sin a' can be substituted here for tan a'. And if in this case we put $AM = u$, $AM' = u'$, where M, M' designate the points where a ray which is very nearly normal to the refracting plane crosses the normal before and after refraction, we have therefore,

$$\frac{u'}{u} = \frac{\tan a}{\tan a'} = \frac{\sin a}{\sin a'},$$

and, hence, by the law of refraction:

$$\frac{n'}{u'} = \frac{n}{u}, \quad \text{or} \quad u' = \frac{n'}{n} . u.$$

The angle a has disappeared entirely from this formula, and the value of u' may be found as soon as the value of u is given. This means that corresponding to a given position of the object-point M there is a perfectly definite image-point M', and the points M, M' are said to be a pair of *conjugate points*. Accordingly, *when a narrow bundle of homocentric rays is incident nearly normally on a refracting plane, the corresponding bundle of refracted rays will be homocentric also.* And if the aperture of the bundle is infinitely narrow, the imagery will be ideal.

For example, a pebble at the bottom of a pool of water 12 inches deep will be seen distinctly from a point in the air vertically above it, but it will appear to be only 9 inches below the surface of the water, since $n'/n = 3/4$. On the other hand, an object 9 inches above the surface will seem to be 12 inches above it to an eye in the water vertically beneath the object, because in this case $n'/n = 4/3$.

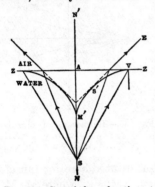

FIG. 64.—Caustic by refraction at plane surface from water to air.

42. Image of a Point Formed by Rays that are Obliquely Refracted at a Plane Surface.— But if the bundle of rays coming from the luminous point S (Fig. 64) is a wide-angle bundle of considerable aperture, no distinct image will be formed by these rays after refraction at a plane, but the points of intersection of the refracted rays will be spread over a so-called *caustic surface*, which in this case is a surface of revolution around the normal SA drawn from S to the refracting plane. The figure shows a meridian section of this surface for the case when the rays are refracted from a denser to a rarer medium ($n' < n$), the curve in this case being the evolute of an ellipse. Each refracted ray produced backwards touches the caustic surface. The cusp of the meridian curve is on the normal SA at the point M′ where the image of S is formed by rays that meet the refracting plane nearly perpendicularly, as explained in the preceding section. Wherever the eye is placed in the second medium, only a narrow bundle of rays coming from S can enter it through the pupil of the eye. The nearest approach to an image of the source at S as seen by rays that are refracted more or less obliquely will be the little element of the caustic surface which is the assemblage of the points where the effective rays that enter the eye touch this surface. Thus, rays entering the eye at E appear to come from the point S′ where the tangent from E touches the caustic. It is evident now why an object S under

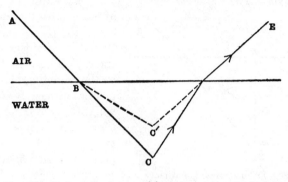

FIG. 65.—Rod partly immersed in water appears to be bent upwards.

water appears to be raised towards the surface and at the same time also to be shifted towards the spectator more and more as the eye at E is brought nearer to the surface of the water, until finally when the eye is on a level with the surface of the water, the image of S appears now to be at V on the refracting plane. Rays from S that meet the surface beyond this limiting point V where the caustic curve is tangent to the straight line ZZ will be totally reflected. The image of S seen by the eye at E is blurred and distorted, because the image-point S′ is the point of intersection of a very limited portion of the bundle of refracted rays that enter the eye.

The above explanation makes it clear why a straight line ABC (Fig. 65) which is partly in air and partly in water will appear to an eye at E to be bent at B into the broken line ABC′. The image BC′ of the part BC under water can be plotted point by point for any position of the eye.

43. The Image-lines of a Narrow Bundle of Rays Refracted Obliquely at a Plane.—The diagram (Fig. 66) shows the paths of two rays SBD and SCE which originating at S and falling on the refracting plane ZZ at the points B and C are refracted in the directions CE and BD into the eye of an observer. The refracted rays produced backwards intersect

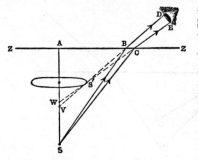

at S' and cross the normal SA at the points marked W and V. Evidently, all the rays from S that fall on the refracting plane at points between B and C will, after refraction, intersect SA at points between V and W. Suppose that the figure is revolved around SA as axis, then each ray will generate a conical surface, and the vertices of these cones will

FIG. 66.—Oblique refraction at plane surface $(n' < n)$.

be at the points S, V, and W for the rays that are actually drawn in the diagram. The bundle of rays that enter the eye at DE will be a small portion of the refracted rays that are contained between the conical surfaces whose vertices are at V and W. These conical surfaces intersect each other in the circle which is described by the point S' when the figure is rotated around the axis SA, and it is a little element of arc of this circle perpendicular to the plane of the diagram at S' that contains the points of intersection of the rays that enter the eye. This is called the *primary image-line* (§188) of the narrow bundle of refracted rays. There is another image line at V called the *secondary image-line*, which lies in the plane of the paper, and which is generally taken as perpendicular to the axis of the bundle of refracted rays, though sometimes it is considered as the segment VW of the axis of revolution. But these are intricate matters that can be only alluded to in this place. (See Chapter XV.)

44. Path of a Ray Refracted Through a Slab with Plane Parallel Sides.—When a ray of light traverses several media in succession, then

$$n_1 . \sin a_1 = n_2 . \sin a_1', \quad n_2 . \sin a_2 = n_3 . \sin a_2', \text{ etc.,}$$

where n_1, n_2, n_3, etc., denote the indices of refraction of the media, and a_1, a_1'; a_2, a_2'; etc., denote the angles of incidence and refraction at the various surfaces of separation. In the

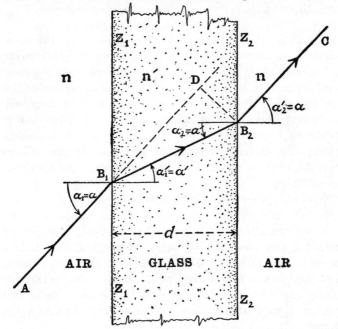

Fig. 67.—Path of ray refracted through plate with plane parallel sides.

special case when these refracting surfaces are a *series of parallel planes*, the angle of incidence at one plane will be equal to the angle of refraction at the preceding plane ($a_{k+1} = a_k'$, where the integer k denotes the number of the plane).

The simplest case of this kind occurs when there are only *two parallel refracting planes*, and when the last medium is the same as the first, as, for example, in the case of a slab of glass bounded by plane parallel sides and surrounded by air, as represented in Fig. 67. Then

$$n_3 = n_1 = n, \ n_2 = n',$$

and $$a_1' = a_2 = a'.$$

Accordingly, we have the following pair of equations:

$$n . \sin a_1 = n' . \sin a', \ n' . \sin a' = n . \sin a_2';$$

and, therefore:

$$a_2' = a_1 = a;$$

which means that the ray emerges from the slab in the same direction as it entered it. Thus, *when a ray of light traverses a slab with plane parallel sides which is bounded by the same medium on both sides, the emergent ray will be parallel to the incident ray.* Obviously, this statement may be amplified as follows: *When a ray of light traverses a series of media each separated from the next by one of a series of parallel refracting planes, the final and original directions of the ray will be parallel, provided the first and last media have the same index of refraction.*

The only effect of the interposition of the glass plate (Fig. 67) in the path of the ray is to shift the path to one side without altering the direction of the ray. It might be inferred, therefore, that the apparent position of an object as seen through such a plate of glass would not be altered, but this is not true in general, as we shall proceed to explain. Every ray that traverses the plate will be found to be displaced at right angles to its original position through a distance

$$B_2D = \frac{\sin(a - a')}{\cos a'} d,$$

where d denotes the thickness of the plate. Since

$$\cos a' = \frac{\sqrt{n'^2 - n^2 . \sin^2 a}}{n'},$$

the formula above may be put also in the following form:

$$B_2D = \frac{\sin a \ (\sqrt{n'^2 - n^2 \sin^2 a} - n . \cos a)}{\sqrt{n'^2 - n^2 . \sin^2 a}} . d.$$

Accordingly, the shift B_2D varies with the slope of the incident ray. If the object is very far away, the rays that enter the eye will be parallel, so that the apparent position of a distant object will not be altered in the slightest by viewing it through a plate of glass with plane parallel sides, no matter what may be the angle of incidence of the rays, and consequently the plate may be turned to the rays at dif-

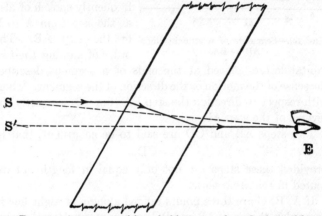

Fɪɢ. 68.—Apparent position of object seen through plate with plane parallel sides

ferent angles without producing any change in the appearance of the object as seen through it. But if the object-point S (Fig. 68) is near at hand, an eye at E will see it in the direction ES, but when the glass is interposed, it will appear to lie in the direction ES' which is sensibly different from ES, and this difference can be increased or diminished by rotating the plate around an axis perpendicular to the plane of the figure. This principle is utilized very ingeniously in the original form of ophthalmometer designed by HELM-HOLTZ (1821–1894) for measuring the curvatures of the refracting surfaces of the eye. It is employed also in an instrument for measuring the diameter of a microscopic object, which Professor POYNTING has called the "parallel plate micrometer" (see *Proc. Opt. Convention*, London, 1905, p. 79).

45. Segments of a Straight Line.—The finite portion of a straight line included between two points is called a *segment* of the line, while each of the other two parts of the line is to be regarded as a prolongation of the segment. Considered as generated by the motion of a point along a straight line from a starting-point or origin A to an end-point or terminus

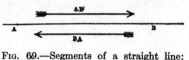

B, the segment AB is frequently spoken of also as the *step* from A to B or the step AB. The order of naming the two capital letters placed at the ends of a segment describes the sense of the motion or the direction of the segment. Thus, with respect to direction the step BA (Fig. 69) is exactly the reverse of the step AB.

Fig. 69.—Segments of a straight line: AB = –BA.

Two steps AB and CD are said to be congruent, that is,
$$AB = CD,$$
provided these steps are not only equal in length but executed in the same sense.

If A, B, C are three points ranged along a straight line in any order, that is, if AB and BC are two steps along the same straight line such that the end of one step is the starting point of the other, then the step AC is said to be equal to the sum of the steps AB and BC; thus,
$$AB + BC = AC;$$
and hence also:
$$AB = AC - BC, \quad BC = AC - AB.$$
Moreover, if we suppose that the point C is identical with the point A, it follows that
$$AB + BA = 0 \text{ or } AB = -BA.$$
Thus, if one of the two directions along a straight line is regarded as the *positive direction*, the opposite direction is to be reckoned as *negative*. For example, if the distance between A and B is equal to 12 linear units, and if we put AB = +12, then BA = −12.

Similarly, also, we may write:

$$AB+BC+CA=0;$$

or if X designates the position of any fourth point on the straight line, then

$$AB+BC+CX=AX.$$

These ideas will be found to be of great service in treating a certain class of problems in geometrical optics; and an application of this method of adding line-segments occurs in the following section.

46. Apparent Position of an object seen through a transparent Slab whose Parallel Sides are perpendicular to the Line of Sight.—In Fig. 70 the line of sight joining the object-point M_1 with the spectator's eye at E is perpendicular at A_1 and A_2 to the parallel faces of the transparent slab, and all the rays that enter the eye will pass through the slab close to this axial line.

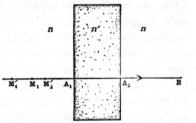

FIG. 70.—Displacement of object viewed perpendicularly through plate with plane parallel sides.

Inside the slab they will proceed as if they had originated at a point M_1' on the line of sight, but being again refracted, they will emerge into the surrounding medium as if they had come from a point M_2', which is the apparent position of the object-point as seen by rays that are very nearly perpendicular to the faces of the slab. If n, n' denote the indices of refraction of the two media, then, according to §§ 41 and 45, we may write the following equations:

$$\frac{A_1M_1}{n}=\frac{A_1M_1'}{n'}, \quad A_2M_1'=A_2A_1+A_1M_1', \quad \frac{A_2M_1'}{n'}=\frac{A_2M_2'}{n}.$$

Hence, the apparent displacement of the object is:

$$M_1M_2' = M_1A_1 + A_1A_2 + A_2M_2'$$

$$= M_1A_1 + A_1A_2 + \frac{n}{n'}A_2M_1'$$

$$= M_1A_1 + A_1A_2 + \frac{n}{n'}(A_2A_1 + A_1M_1')$$

$$= M_1A_1 + A_1A_2(1 - \frac{n}{n'}) + A_1M_1 = \frac{n'-n}{n'}A_1A_2;$$

accordingly, if the thickness of the plate is denoted by $d = A_1A_2$,

$$M_1M_2' = \frac{n'-n}{n'}d.$$

Thus, we see that the apparent displacement in the line of sight depends only on the thickness of the plate and on the relative index of refraction $(n':n)$, and is entirely independent of the distance of the object-point from the slab. Hence, also, the size of the image of a small object viewed directly through a glass plate is the same as that of the object, but its apparent size will be different, because since the image and object are at different distances from the eye, the angles which they subtend will be different.

An object viewed perpendicularly through a glass plate surrounded by air $(n':n=3:2)$ will appear to be one-third the thickness of the plate nearer the eye than it really is.

If the displacement of the object is denoted by x, that is, if we put $M_1M'_2 = x$, then

$$\frac{n'}{n} = \frac{d}{d-x}.$$

This relation has been utilized in a method of determining the relative index of refraction $(n':n)$. A microscope S pointed vertically downwards is focused on a fine scratch or object-point O. A plate of the material whose index is to be determined is then inserted horizontally between the object and the objective of the microscope. The interposition of the plate necessitates a re-focusing of the microscope in order to see the object distinctly, which will now appear to be at a point O' nearer the microscope by the distance $x = OO'$. This distance x is easily ascertained in terms of the distance through which the objective of the microscope has to be raised in order to obtain a distinct image of the object. The thickness of the plate is easily measured,

and, consequently, we have all the data for determining the value of n'/n. This method is especially convenient for obtaining the index of refraction of a liquid (Fig. 71).

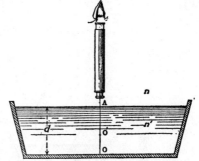

Fig. 71.—Measurement of index of refraction of a liquid.

47. Multiple Images in the two Parallel Faces of a plate glass Mirror.—An object is reproduced in a metallic mirror by a single image, but in a glass mirror which is silvered on the back side there will be a series of images of an object in front of the glass, which may be readily seen by looking a little obliquely at the reflection of a candle-flame in an ordinary looking glass. The first image will be comparatively faint, the second one the brightest and most distinct of all, and behind these two principal images other images more or less shadowy may also be discerned whose intensities diminish rapidly until they fade from view entirely. These multiple images by reflection may also be seen in a transparent block of glass with plane parallel sides.

The light falling on the first surface is partly reflected and partly refracted. It is this reflected portion that gives rise to the first image of the series. The rays that are refracted across the plate will be partly reflected at the second face, and, returning to the first face, a portion of this light will be refracted back into the air and give rise to the second image of the series; while the other portion of the light will be reflected back into the glass to be again reflected at the back face, and so on. In the diagram (Fig. 72) the source of the light is supposed to be at the point marked S, and the straight

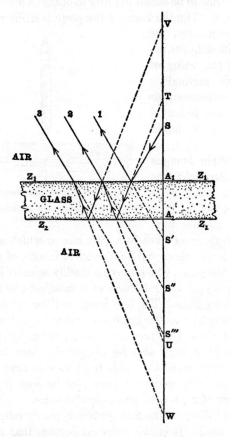

Fig. 72.—Multiple images by reflection from the two parallel faces of a plate of glass.

line drawn from S perpendicular to the parallel faces of the glass slab meets these faces in the points marked A_1 and A_2. The path of one of the rays coming from S is indicated in the figure, and it can be seen how it zigzags back and forth between the two sides of the slab, becoming feebler and feebler in intensity at each reflection. We consider here only such rays from S as meet the surface very nearly normally. The series of images of S will be formed at S′, S″, S‴, etc., all lying on the prolongation of the normal SA_1A_2, and it is because these images are all ranged in a row one behind the other, that ordinarily when we look in a mirror we do not see the images separated.

The reflected ray 1 proceeds as if it had come from S′, the position of this point being determined by the relation $A_1S′ = SA_1$. But the refracted ray crosses the slab as if it had come from the point T, the position of which is determined by the relation $TA_1 = n.SA_1$, where n denotes the index of refraction of the glass (the other medium being assumed to be air of index unity). Arriving at the second face, this ray will be reflected as if it had come from a point U such that $A_2U = TA_2$. Returning to the first surface, it will be partly refracted out into the air as the ray marked 2 proceeding as if it came from the second image-point S″, the position of which is determined by the relation $A_1S″ = A_1U/n$; and also partly reflected as if it had come from a point V such that $VA_1 = A_1U$. The ray is reflected a second time at the second face, as if it came from the point W, where $A_2W = VA_2$; and being once more refracted at the first face, emerges into the air as the ray marked 3, appearing now to come from the image-point marked S‴ determined by the relation $A_1S‴ = A_1W/n$.

What is the interval between one image and the next? For example, let us try to obtain an expression for the interval S″S‴. This may be done as follows:

$$S″S‴ = S″A_1 + A_1S‴;$$
$$\begin{aligned}A_1S‴ &= A_1W/n = (A_1A_2 + A_2W)/n = (A_1A_2 + VA_2)/n\\ &= (A_1A_2 + VA_1 + A_1A_2)/n = (A_1U + 2A_1A_2)/n\\ &= A_1S″ + 2d/n;\end{aligned}$$

where $d = A_1A_2$ denotes the thickness of the glass plate. Hence, we find:

$$S''S''' = \frac{2d}{n}.$$

It appears, therefore, that the distance between one image and the next is constant and equal to $\frac{2}{n}$ times the thickness of the plate. Thus, for a glass plate for which $n = 3/2$ the distance from one image to the next is equal to 4/3 the thickness of the plate.

PROBLEMS

1. A ray of light traverses in succession a series of isotropic media bounded by parallel planes, and emerges finally into a medium with the same index of refraction as that of the first medium. Show that the final path of the ray is parallel to its original direction.

2. Construct accurately the paths of six rays proceeding from a point below the horizontal surface of water and refracted into air; and show where the object-point will appear to be as seen by an eye above the surface of the water, for three different positions of the eye.

3. Why does the part of a stick obliquely immersed in water appear to be bent up towards the surface of the water? Explain clearly.

4. Derive the formula $\frac{n'}{u'} = \frac{n}{u}$ for the refraction of paraxial rays (§63) at a plane surface.

5. A ray of light incident on a plane refracting surface at an angle α crosses a straight line drawn perpendicular to the surface at a distance v from this surface. How far from the surface does the refracted ray cross this line?

6. If a bird is 36 feet above the surface of a pond, how high does it look to a diver who is under the water? What is the apparent depth of a pool of water 8 feet deep?

Ans. 48 feet above the surface; 6 feet.

7. What will be the effect on the apparent distance of an object if a slab of transparent material with plane parallel sides is interposed at right angles to the line of vision?

Ans. It will appear to be nearer the eye by the amount $(n-1)d/n$, where d denotes the thickness of the slab and n denotes the index of refraction of the material.

8. A cube of glass of index of refraction 1.6 is placed on a flat, horizontal picture; where does the picture appear to be to an eye looking perpendicularly down on it?

Ans. It will appear to be raised three-eighths of the thickness of the cube.

9. A microscope is placed vertically above a small vessel and focused on a mark on the base of the vessel. A layer of transparent liquid of depth d is poured in the vessel, and then it is found that the image of the mark has been displaced through a distance x which is determined by re-focusing the microscope. Show that the index of refraction of the liquid is equal to $d/(d-x)$.

10. In an actual experiment made by the above method to determine the index of refraction of alcohol, the depth of the liquid was 4 cm., and the displacement of the image was found to be 1.06 cm. What value was found for the index of alcohol?   Ans. 1.36.

11. A candle is observed through a tank of water with vertical plane glass walls. The line of sight is perpendicular to the sides of the tank, the candle being 15 cm. from one side and 39 cm. from the opposite side. What is the apparent position of the candle? (Neglect the effect of the thin glass walls.)   Ans. It appears to be 9 cm. from the near side.

12. If an object viewed normally through a plate of glass with plane parallel faces seems to be five-sixths of an inch nearer than it really is, how thick is the glass?

Ans. 2.5 inches.

13. A layer of ether 2 cm. deep floats on a layer of water 3 cm. deep. What is the apparent distance of the bottom of

the vessel below the free surface of the ether?   (Take index of refraction of water = 1.33 and of ether = 1.36.)

Ans. 3.73 cm.

14. A person looks perpendicularly into a mirror made of plate glass of thickness one-half inch silvered on the back. If his eye is at a distance of 15 inches from the front face, where will his image appear to be?

Ans. $15^2/_3$ inches from the front face.

15. When a stick is partly immersed in a transparent liquid of index n at an angle θ with the free horizontal surface, what is the angle θ' which the part of the stick below the surface appears to make with the horizon as seen by an eye looking vertically down on it from the air above the liquid?

Ans. $\tan \theta' = \dfrac{\tan \theta}{n}$.

16. Calculate the values of the angles of refraction for all angles of incidence from $0°$ to $90°$, at intervals of $5°$, for each of the following values of the relative index of refraction, namely: 2.40, 2.00, 1.75, 1.50, 1.25 and 1.00; and plot the results on a sheet of coördinate paper, obtaining a set of curves representing the angle of refraction as a function of the angle of incidence.

17. The critical angle of an optical medium of index n is given by the formula $\sin A = 1/n$. Give n in succession the values $n = 1.0$, $n = 1.2$, $n = 1.4$, etc., up to $n = 3.0$; and calculate the corresponding values of the angle A. On a sheet of coördinate paper plot a curve which represents the critical angle as a function of the index of refraction. (It will be convenient to take the vertical axis of coördinates as corresponding to the value $n = 1$.)

CHAPTER V

48. Definitions, etc.—An optical prism is a limited portion of a highly transparent substance with polished plane faces where the light is reflected or refracted. Prisms in a great variety of geometrical forms and combinations are employed in many types of modern optical instruments (*cf.* §§ 20, 37); but in this chapter the term *prism* will be restricted to mean a portion of a transparent, isotropic substance included between two polished plane faces that are not parallel. The straight line in which the planes of the two faces meet is called the *edge* of the prism, and the dihedral angle between these planes is called the *refracting angle.* This angle, which will be denoted by the symbol β, may be more precisely defined as *the convex angle through which the first face of the prism has to be turned around the edge of the prism as axis in order to bring this face into coincidence with the second face.* The first face of the prism is that side where the rays enter and the second face is the side from which the rays emerge. Every section made by a plane perpendicular to the edge of the prism is a *principal section,* and we shall consider only such rays as traverse the prism in a principal section, not only because the problem of oblique refraction through a prism presents some difficulties which are beyond the scope of this volume, but especially because in actual practice the principal rays are usually confined to a principal section of the prism. It will also be assumed, for simplicity, that the prism is surrounded by the same medium on both sides.

I. *Geometrical Investigation*

49. Construction of Path of a Ray Through a Prism.—The plane of the diagram (Fig. 73) represents the principal

section of a prism whose edge meets this plane perpendicularly at the point marked V. The traces of the two plane
faces are shown by the straight lines Z_1V, Z_2V intersecting at
V. The straight line AB_1 represents the path of the given
incident ray lying in the plane of the principal section and

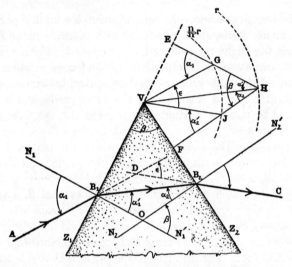

FIG. 73.—Construction of path of ray through principal section
of prism $(n' > n)$.

falling on the first face of the prism at the incidence-point B_1.
The problem of constructing the path of the ray both within
the prism and after emergence from it is solved by a method
essentially the same as that employed in § 34.

Let n denote the index of refraction of the medium surrounding the prism and n' the index of refraction of the prism-
medium itself. With the point V as center, and with radii
equal to r and $\frac{n}{n'}.r$, where the radius r may have any convenient length, describe the arcs of two concentric circles both
lying within the angle Z_2VE, where E designates a point on
the prolongation of the straight line Z_1V beyond V. Through

V draw a straight line VG parallel to AB_1 meeting the arc of radius nr/n' in the point designated by G; and through the point G draw a straight line GE perpendicular at E to the first face of the prism (produced if necessary), and let H designate the point where the straight line GE (likewise produced if necessary) meets the circumference of the other of the two circular arcs. Then the straight line B_1B_2 drawn parallel to the straight line VH will represent the path of the ray within the prism. For if the straight line N_1N_1' is the incidence-normal to the first face of the prism at the point B_1, and if the angles of incidence and refraction at this face are denoted by $a_1 = \angle N_1B_1A$, $a_1' = \angle N_1'B_1B_2$, then by the law of refraction:

$$n \cdot \sin a_1 = n' \cdot \sin a_1'.$$

But by the construction:

$$\frac{\sin \angle EGV}{\sin \angle EHV} = \frac{VH}{VG} = \frac{n'}{n},$$

and since $\angle EGV = \angle N_1B_1A = a_1$, it follows that $\angle EHV = a_1'$; and hence the path of the ray within the prism must be parallel to VH.

Again, from the point H let fall a perpendicular HF on the second face of the prism, where F designates the foot of this perpendicular; and let J designate the point where HF intersects the arc of radius nr/n'. Then the straight line B_2C drawn from the incidence-point B_2 parallel to the straight line VJ will represent the path of the emergent ray. For if we draw N_2N_2' perpendicular to the second face of the prism at B_2, and if the angles of incidence and refraction at this face are denoted by $a_2 = \angle N_2B_2B_1$, $a_2' = \angle N_2'B_2C$, respectively, then $n' \cdot \sin a_2 = n \cdot \sin a_2'$. But

$$\frac{\sin \angle FJV}{\sin \angle FHV} = \frac{VH}{VJ} = \frac{n'}{n},$$

and since by construction $\angle FHV = a_2$, it follows that $\angle FJV = a_2'$, and hence the path of the emergent ray will be parallel to VJ.

The diagram (Fig. 73) is drawn for the case when $n'>n$, as in the ordinary case of a glass prism surrounded by air. The student should draw also a diagram for the other case when $n'<n$, showing the procedure of a ray through a prism of less highly refracting substance than that of the surrounding medium, for example, an air prism surrounded by glass, such as is formed by the air-space between two separated glass prisms.

50. The Deviation of a Ray by a Prism.—The *total deviation* of a ray refracted through a prism, which is equal to the algebraic sum of the deviations produced by the two refractions (§ 35), may be defined as the angle $\epsilon = \epsilon_1 + \epsilon_2$ through which the direction of the emergent ray must be turned in order to bring it into the direction of the incident ray; thus, in Fig. 73, $\epsilon = \angle JVG$; and if the angle ϵ is measured in radians, the arc $JG = \epsilon.JV$. In order to specify completely an angular displacement, it is necessary to give not only the magnitude of the angle and the sense of rotation of the radius vector, but also the plane in which the displacement occurs. This plane may be specified by giving the direction of a line perpendicular to it, which in the case of the angle here under consideration may be the edge of the prism or any line parallel to it; because any such line will be perpendicular to the principal section of the prism in which the ray lies. In fact, the angle ϵ may be completely represented in a diagram by a straight line drawn parallel to the edge of the prism, which by its length indicates the magnitude of the angle and by its direction shows the sense of rotation. Thus, for example, the line may be drawn along the edge of the prism itself from a point V in the plane of the principal section and always in such a direction that on looking along the line towards that plane $\angle JVG = \epsilon$ will be seen to be a counter-clockwise rotation. A deviation of 20° in a principal section coinciding, say, with the plane of the paper would be represented, therefore, by a straight line perpendicular to this plane of length 20 cm., if each degree were to be represented by one centimeter. If $\epsilon = +20°$, this line would point out from the paper towards the reader, and if $\epsilon = -20°$, it would point away from him. Thus, if the prism, originally "base down," is turned "base up" (as the opticians say), everything else remaining the same, the sign of the angle ϵ will be reversed, and so also will be the direction of the vector which represents this angle.

51. Grazing Incidence and Grazing Emergence.—The angle GHJ between the normals to the two faces of the prism is equal to the refracting angle β; and hence for a given prism this angle will remain always constant. No matter how the direction of the incident ray AB_1 (or VG) may be varied, the vertex H of this angle will lie always on a certain portion of the circumference of the construction-circle of radius r, and the sides HG, HJ will remain always in the same fixed directions perpendicular to the faces of the prism. Obviously, there will be two extreme or limiting positions of the point H marking the ends of the arc on which it is confined, namely, the positions which H has when one of the sides of the angle GHJ is tangent to the circle of radius nr/n'; which can occur only for the case when $n' > n$, because otherwise the point H will lie inside the circumference of this circle and therefore it will be impossible for either HG or HJ to be tangent to it.

If the side HG is tangent to the inner circle at G, as shown in Fig. 74, the point G will lie in the plane of the first face of the prism, and accordingly the corresponding ray incident on the first face of the prism at the point B_1, which must have the direction VG, will be the ray Z_1B_1 which, entering the prism at "*grazing*" incidence ($\alpha_1 = 90°$), traverses the prism as shown in the figure.

On the other hand, when the side HJ of the angle GHJ is tangent at J to the construction-circle of radius nr/n' (Fig. 75), the point J will lie in the second face of the prism, and the straight line VJ will coincide with the straight line VZ_2. Under these circumstances the ray emerges from the prism at B_2 along the second face in the direction $B_2Z_2(\alpha_2' = -90°)$.

The straight line KB_1 shows the path of the ray incident on the first face of the prism at B_1 which "grazes" the second face on emerging from the prism. Any ray incident at B_1 and lying in the principal section of the prism within the angle KB_1Z_1 will succeed in getting through the prism and emerging

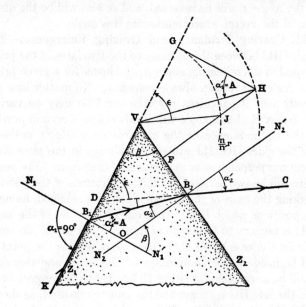

Fig. 74.—Case when ray "grazes" first face of prism.

into the surrounding medium again; whereas if the ray incident at B_1 lies anywhere within the angle VB_1K, it will be *totally reflected* at the second face of the prism. The ray KB_1 is called the *limiting incident ray* and $\angle N_1B_1K = \iota$ is the *limiting angle of incidence*. These relations will be discussed more fully in the analytical investigation of the path of a ray through a prism (§§ 55, foll.); but it may be remarked that $\angle GHV = \alpha_1'$ in Fig. 74 and $\angle JHV = \alpha_2$ in Fig. 75 are both equal to the critical angle A (§ 36) with respect to the two media n, n' $(\sin A = n/n')$.

52. Minimum Deviation.—Between the two extreme or terminal positions of the vertex H of ∠GHJ shown in Figs. 74 and 75, there is also an intermediate place which is of special interest and importance and to which, therefore, attention must be called. In general, the sides HG, HJ inter-

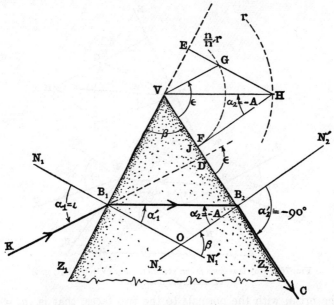

Fig. 75.—Case when ray "grazes" second face of prism.

cepted between the two construction-circles (Fig. 73) will be unequal in length, but if HG = HJ, as in Fig. 76, the angles GVJ, GHJ and EVF will evidently all be bisected by the diagonal VH of the quadrangle VGHJ. When this happens, the path B_1B_2 of the ray inside the prism, which is parallel to VH, *crosses the prism symmetrically*, that is, the triangle VB_1B_2 is isosceles. In fact, the points designated in the diagram by the letters V, D and O will be the summits of isosceles triangles having the common base B_1B_2, and they will all lie therefore on the bisector of the refracting angle $\beta =$

$\angle Z_1VZ_2$, which is perpendicular to VH. The angle of incidence at the first face and the angle of emergence at the second face are equal in magnitude, although they are described in opposite senses, so that $a_2' = -a_1$. The same is true also in regard to the angles which the ray makes inside

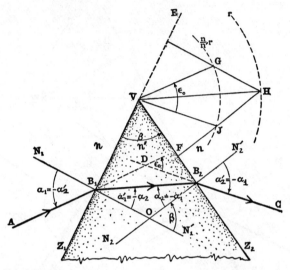

FIG. 76.—Ray traverses prism symmetrically (VB$_1$ = VB$_2$); case of minimum deviation.

the prism with the normals to the two faces, that is, $a_2 = -a_1'$.

Now when the ray traverses the prism symmetrically, as represented in Fig. 76, the deviation ϵ has its least value ϵ_0. In order to show that this is true, it will be convenient to reproduce the symmetrical quadrangle VGHJ in Fig. 76 in a separate diagram, as in Fig. 77. Suppose that H′ designates the position of a point infinitely near to H lying likewise on the arc of the circle of radius r, and draw H′G′, H′J′ parallel to HG, HJ and meeting the arc of the other circle in the points G′, J′, respectively. In the figure the point H′ is taken *below* the point H, and in this case it is plain that the two parallels HJ, H'J' will meet the circumference of the inner circle more obliquely than the other pair of parallel lines HG, H'G', and, consequently, the infinitely small arc

J'J intercepted between the first pair will be greater than the arc G'G intercepted between the second pair. Hence, the small angle J'VJ will be greater than ∠G'VG, and therefore

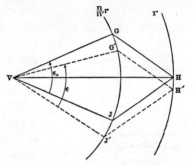

FIG. 77.—Case of minimum deviation.

$$\angle J'VG' > \angle JVG.$$

The angle JVG here is the angle of deviation (ϵ_o) of the ray that goes symmetrically through the prism; whereas $\angle J'VG' = \epsilon$ is the angle of deviation of a ray which traverses the prism along a very slightly different path. And according to the above reasoning (for we shall arrive at the same result if we take the point H' also above H), we find:

$$\epsilon > \epsilon_o.$$

Accordingly, we see that *the ray which traverses the prism symmetrically in the plane of a principal section is also the ray which is least deviated.*

It is easy to verify this statement experimentally. Thus, for example, if a bundle of parallel rays is allowed to fall on an isosceles triangular prism, so that while some of the rays are incident on one of the equal faces and are transmitted through the prism, the other rays of the bundle are reflected from the base of the prism, as represented in (1) in Fig. 78; and if then the prism is gradually turned around an axis parallel to its edge, first, into position (2), which is the position of minimum deviation, and then past this position into a third position (3), it will be observed that when the prism is in the position of minimum deviation the rays reflected from the base will be parallel to the rays which emerge at the second face of the prism; which can only be the case when the rays cross the prism symmetrically.

In spectroscopic work and in many other scientific uses of the prism, the position of minimum deviation, which is easily found, is frequently the most convenient and advantageous adjustment of the prism for purposes of observation.

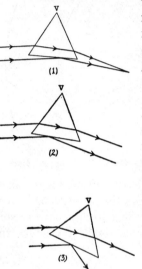

53. Deviation away from the Edge of the Prism.—*When a ray of light passes through a prism of more highly refracting material than that of the surrounding medium $(n'>n)$, the deviation is always away from the edge towards the thicker part of the prism.*

If the angles of the triangle VB_1B_2 (Fig. 79) at B_1 and B_2 are both acute, the incident and emergent rays lie on the sides of the normals at B_1 and B_2 away from the prism-edge, so that at both refractions the ray will be bent away from the edge. If

FIG. 78.—Experimental proof that ray which traverses prism symmetrically is ray of minimum deviation.

one of the angles, say, the angle at B_2, is a right angle, the ray will not be deviated at all by the refraction at this point, but at the other incidence-point it will be bent away from the edge. And, finally, if one of the angles at B_1 or B_2 is obtuse, for example, the angle at B_1 (Fig. 80), the deviation on entering the prism will, it is true, be towards the edge of the prism, but this deviation will not be so great as the subsequent deviation away from the edge which is produced at the second refraction when the ray issues from the prism, as may be easily seen from the diagram. Thus, in every case when $n' > n$, the total deviation will be away from the prism-edge.

If $n' < n$, all these effects will be reversed.

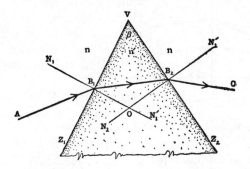

FIG. 79.—Deviation away from edge of prism.

54. Refraction of a Plane Wave Through a Prism.— The diagram (Fig. 81) shows a principal section of the prism, and the straight line B_1D represents the trace of a plane wave (supposed to be perpendicular to the plane of the paper and parallel therefore to the edge of the prism) advancing towards the first face of the prism in the direction DV at right angles to B_1D. If around the point B_1, which lies in the first face of the prism, the arc of a circle is described with radius $BE = \dfrac{n}{n'}$DV, then, according to

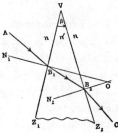

FIG. 80.—Deviation away from edge of prism.

HUYGENS's principle (§ 5), the straight line VE tangent to this circle at E will represent the trace of the wave-front inside the prism. Let the straight line B_1E meet the second face of the prism at B_2. Around V as center with radius $VF = \dfrac{n'}{n} EB_2$ describe the arc of a circle; then the straight line B_2F tangent to this circle at F will represent the trace of the emergent wave-front.

The disturbance at any point C will have emanated from

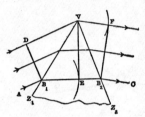

some point on AB_1, and the time taken by the light to go from B_1 to B_2 inside the prism will be the same as that required to go from D to F in the surrounding medium (§ 39); that is, the optical lengths along these two routes are equal. For, as appears from the construction,

FIG. 81.—Refraction of plane wave through prism.

$$n(DV+VF) = n'.B_1B_2.$$

An excellent and most instructive mechanical illustration of the refraction of a plane wave through a prism can be obtained by using the roller and tilted board described in § 32 with a triangular piece of plush cloth glued in the middle of the board to represent the prism (see Fig. 45).

II. *Analytical Investigation*

55. Trigonometric Calculation of the Path of a Ray in a Principal Section of a Prism.—The angles of incidence and refraction at the first and second faces of the prism, denoted by a_1, a_1' and a_2, a_2', are, by definition (§ 27), the acute angles through which the normals to the refracting surfaces at the incidence-points have to be turned in order to bring them into coincidence with the incident and refracted rays at the two faces of the prism; thus, in Fig. 73, $\angle N_1B_1A = a_1$, $\angle N_1'B_1B_2 = a_1'$, $\angle N_2B_2B_1 = a_2$, $\angle N_2'B_2C = a_2'$.

Assuming that the prism is surrounded by the same medium on both sides, and being careful to note the sense of rotation of each of the angles, we obtain by the law of refraction, taken in conjunction with the obvious geometrical relations as shown in the figure, the following system of equations for calculating the path of a ray through a principal section of a prism:

$$n' . \sin a_1' = n . \sin a_1, \quad a_2 = a_1' - \beta, \quad n . \sin a_2' = n' . \sin a_2.$$

Combining these formulæ so as to eliminate a_1' and a_2, we may derive the following convenient expression for determining the angle of emergence (a_2') at the second face of the prism:

$$\sin a_2' = \sin a_1 . \cos \beta - \sin \beta \frac{\sqrt{n'^2 - n^2 . \sin^2 a_1}}{n} .$$

Thus, if we know the value of the relative index of refraction (n'/n) and the refracting angle of the prism ($\beta = \angle Z_1 V Z_2$), we can calculate the angle of emergence (a_2') corresponding to any given direction (a_1) of the ray incident on the first face of the prism.

The total deviation (ϵ) of a ray refracted through a prism is measured, as defined above (§ 50), by $\angle JVG$, and since this angle is equal to the external angle at D in the triangle DB_1B_2, we have:

$$\epsilon = \angle B_2B_1D + \angle DB_2B_1$$
$$= \angle N_1'B_1D - \angle N_1'B_1B_2 + \angle DB_2N_2 - \angle B_1B_2N_2$$
$$= a_1 - a_1' - a_2' + a_2;$$

and since $a_1' - a_2 = \beta$, we obtain finally the following expression for the angle of deviation:

$$\epsilon = a_1 - a_2' - \beta.$$

These formulæ contain the whole theory of the refraction of a ray through a prism in a principal section. It will be interesting to discuss analytically some of the special cases which we have already studied in the preceding sections of this chapter.

56. Total Reflection at the Second Face of the Prism.— If the angle of emergence at the second face of the prism is a right angle, that is, if $a_2' = -90°$, the emergent ray B_2C will issue from the prism along the second face in the direction B_2Z_1 (Fig. 75). Hence, $\sin a_2 = \frac{n}{n'} . \sin a_2' = -\frac{n}{n'}$, and therefore $a_2 = -A$, where A denotes the critical angle (§ 36) of the media n, n', defined by the relation $\sin A = \dfrac{n}{n'}$. If the absolute value of the angle a_2 is greater than A, the ray will be *totally reflected* at the second face of the prism, and there will be no emergent ray. This case may be discussed in some detail.

For a prism of given refracting angle (β), there is a certain limiting value (ι) of the angle of incidence (a_1) at the first face of the prism (§ 51) for which we shall have at the second

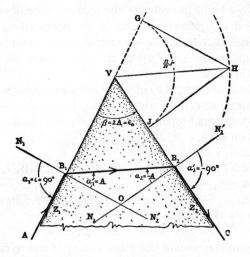

FIG. 82.—Prism with refracting angle $\beta = 2A$.

face the values $a_2 = -A$, $a_2' = -90°$; so that *a ray which is incident on the first face of the prism at an angle less than the limiting angle ι will not pass through the prism but will be totally reflected at the second face.* Putting $a_2 = -A$, we find $a_1' = \beta - A$, and therefore, since $a_1 = \iota$,

$$\sin \iota = \frac{n'}{n} \sin (\beta - A),$$

which is the trigonometric formula for computing the value of the limiting angle of incidence for a given prism. It will be worth while to examine this formula for certain particular values of the refracting angle β.

(1) If $\beta > 2A$, then, since $\sin A = \dfrac{n}{n'}$, the formula shows that sin ι will be greater than unity, so that for a prism of this form there is no angle corresponding to the limiting angle ι. *No ray can be transmitted through a prism whose refracting angle is more than twice as great as the critical angle of the two media in question.* A prism of this size is called a *totally*

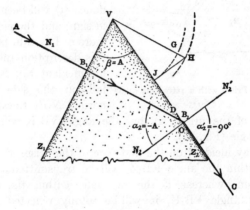

Fig. 83.—Prism with refracting angle $\beta = A$.

reflecting prism; if it is made of glass of index 1.5 and surrounded by air, the refracting angle should be about 84° at least.

(2) If $\beta = 2A$, we find that $\iota = 90°$; which is the case represented in Fig. 82. The only ray that can get through this prism is the ray that traverses it symmetrically, entering the prism along one face and leaving it along the other.

(3) If $\beta > A$ but $< 2A$ (that is, if $2A > \beta > A$), the value of the angle ι as determined by the formula above will be comprised between 90° and 0°. This is the case which was shown in Fig. 73. The direction of the limiting incident ray is be-

tween Z_1B_1 and N_1B_1; that is, $\angle V_1BK$ will be an obtuse angle.

(4) If $\beta = A$, we find $\iota = 0°$, and then the limiting incident

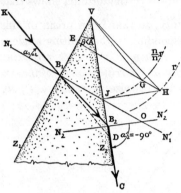

ray will proceed along the normal N_1B_1, as shown in Fig. 83, and $\angle VB_1K$ (or $\angle VB_1A$) will be a right angle.

(5) Finally, if $\beta < A$, the limiting angle of incidence (ι) will be negative in sign; and therefore in a more or less thin prism of this description the limiting incident ray KB_1 will

Fig. 84.—Prism with a refracting angle $\beta < A$.

fall on the side of the normal N_1B_1 towards the apex V of the prism, so that the angle VB_1K will be an acute angle (Fig. 84).

Any ray incident on the first face of the prism at B_1 and lying within the angle KB_1Z_1 will be transmitted through the prism; whereas if the ray falls within the supplementary angle VB_1K, it will be totally reflected at the second face.

In KOHLRAUSCH's method of measuring the relative index of refraction $(\frac{n'}{n})$, the prism is adjusted so that the incident ray "grazes" the first face, and then if the refracting angle of the prism (β) is known, and if the angle of emergence (α_2') is measured, the value of $n' : n$ may be calculated by means of the formula:

$$\sqrt{\left(\frac{n'}{n}\right)^2 - 1} = \frac{\cos\beta - \sin\alpha_2'}{\sin\beta}, \ (\alpha_1 = 90°).$$

The principle of total reflection is also employed in the prism refractometers of ABBE and PULFRICH for measurement of the index of refraction.

57. Perpendicular Emergence at the Second Face of the Prism.—For this case we have $a_2 = a_2' = 0°$, and therefore $a_1' = \beta$, $a_1 = \beta + \epsilon$, and hence:

$$\frac{n'}{n} = \frac{\sin(\beta + \epsilon)}{\sin \beta};$$

which is also a convenient formula for the experimental determination of the value of the relative index of refraction. A description of the apparatus and the method of procedure may be found in the standard treatises on physics.

58. Case when the Ray Traverses the Prism Symmetrically.—As has been pointed out already (§ 52), a special case of great interest occurs when the ray traverses the prism symmetrically. Under these circumstances, the general prism-equations given in § 55 take the following forms:

$$a_1 = -a_2' = \frac{\beta + \epsilon_0}{2}, \quad a_1' = -a_2 = \frac{\beta}{2},$$

$$\frac{n'}{n} = \frac{\sin \dfrac{\beta + \epsilon_0}{2}}{\sin \dfrac{\beta}{2}};$$

where ϵ_0 denotes the angle of deviation of this symmetric ray. The last of these formulæ is the basis of the FRAUNHOFER method of determining the relative index of refraction, the angles β and ϵ_0 being both capable of easy measurement.

This last formula may also be transformed into the following form:

$$\tan\frac{\beta}{2} = \frac{n \cdot \sin\dfrac{\epsilon_0}{2}}{n' - n \cdot \cos\dfrac{\epsilon_0}{2}};$$

whereby the refracting angle β can be calculated in terms of n, n' and ϵ_0.

59. Minimum Deviation.—The prism itself is defined by its refracting angle (β) and the relative index of refraction (n'/n). The total deviation (ϵ) of a ray refracted through a given prism depends only on the angle of incidence (α_1), according to the formula:

$$\epsilon = \alpha_1 - \alpha_2' - \beta;$$

for the angle α_2' may be expressed in terms of α_1, β and n'/n, as we have seen (§ 55). Hence, for a given value of these three magnitudes the angle ϵ will be uniquely determined. On the other hand, for a given value of the angle ϵ there will always be *two* corresponding values of the angle of incidence α_1; for it is obvious from the principle of the reversibility of the light-path (§ 29) that a second ray incident on the first face of the prism at an angle equal to the angle of emergence of the first ray will emerge at the second face at an angle equal to the angle of incidence of the first ray at the first face, and these two rays will be equally deviated in passing through the prism. For example, suppose that the values of the angles of incidence and emergence in the case of the first ray are $\alpha_1 = \gamma$, $\alpha_2' = \gamma'$: a second ray incident on the first face of the prism at the angle $\alpha_1 = -\gamma'$ will emerge at the second face at an angle $\alpha_2' = -\gamma$, and each of these rays will suffer precisely the same deviation, viz., $\epsilon = \gamma - \gamma' - \beta$. Thus, corresponding to any given value of the angle ϵ, within certain limits, there will always be a pair of rays which are deviated by this same amount. One pair of such rays consists of the *two identical rays* determined by the relation

$$\alpha_1 = \gamma = -\alpha_2'.$$

In fact, this is the ray which traverses the prism symmetrically, and a little reflection will show that the deviation of this ray must be either a maximum or a minimum.

But while the best way of demonstrating that *the ray which goes symmetrically through the prism is the ray of minimum deviation* (§ 52) involves the employment of the methods of the differential calculus, the following analytical proof demands of the student a knowledge of only elementary mathematics.

The deviation at the first face of the prism is $\epsilon_1 = \alpha_1 - \alpha_1'$, and that at the second face is $\epsilon_2 = a_2 - a_2'$ (§ 35), and hence the total deviation is

$$\epsilon = \epsilon_1 + \epsilon_2 = (a_1 - a_1') + (a_2 - a_2'),$$

or, since $a_1' - a_2 = \beta$, $\epsilon = a_1 - a_2' - \beta$, as has been already remarked, for example, in § 55. *Assume now that $n' > n$*, and, consequently, that *the angle ϵ is positive*, as is always the case when the ray is bent away from the edge of the prism (§ 53); then it is evident that the angle ϵ will have its least value (ϵ_0) in the case of that ray for which the function ($a_1 - a_2'$) is least. Now since

$$n . \sin a_1 = n' . \sin a_1', \quad n . \sin a_2' = n' . \sin a_2,$$

we obtain by subtraction:

$$n(\sin a_1 - \sin a_2') = n'(\sin a_1' - \sin a_2),$$

and hence by an obvious trigonometric transformation:

$$n . \sin \frac{a_1 - a_2'}{2} . \cos \frac{a_1 + a_2'}{2} = n' . \sin \frac{a_1' - a_2}{2} . \cos \frac{a_1' + a_2}{2},$$

which may be written as follows:

$$\sin \frac{a_1 - a_2'}{2} = \frac{n'}{n} . \sin \frac{\beta}{2} . \frac{\cos \dfrac{a_1' + a_2}{2}}{\cos \dfrac{a_1 + a_2'}{2}}.$$

According as $a_1 \gtreqless - a_2'$, the deviation ϵ_1 at the first face of the prism will (see § 35) be greater than, equal to, or less than, the deviation ϵ_2 at the second face; that is, according as $a_1 \gtreqless - a_2'$, we shall have $(a_1 - a_1') \gtreqless (a_2 - a_2')$, and hence also

$$\frac{a_1 + a_2'}{2} \gtreqless \frac{a_2 + a_1'}{2}.$$

If we suppose, first, that $a_1 > - a_2'$, then $a_1' > - a_2$ and $(a_2 + a_1') > 0$; and since the cosine of a positive angle decreases as the angle increases, it follows that here we must have:

$$\cos \frac{a_1' + a_2}{2} > \cos \frac{a_1 + a_2'}{2}.$$

On the other hand, if we suppose, second, that $a_1 < - a_2'$, then

$a_1' < - a_2$ and $(a_2 + a_1') < 0$; but in this case $(a_2 + a_1') >$ $(a_1 + a_2')$, so that although $(a_2 + a_1')$ and $(a_1 + a_2')$ are both negative, the absolute value of the former is greater than that of the latter, and hence here also we find exactly the same result as before.

Thus, whether a_1 is greater or less than $- a_2'$, the ratio

$$\frac{\cos \dfrac{a_1' + a_2}{2}}{\cos \dfrac{a_1 + a_2'}{2}} > 1;$$

and only in the case when $a_1 = - a_2'$ will this ratio equal to unity. Hence, $\sin \dfrac{a_1' - a_2'}{2}$ has its least value when $a_1 = - a_2'$, and then also the deviation (ϵ) is a minimum and equal to

$$\epsilon_0 = 2 a_1 - \beta.$$

The same process of reasoning applied to the case when $n' < n$ leads to the conclusion that the angle ϵ will be a maximum for the ray which traverses such a prism symmetrically, for example, an air-prism surrounded by glass; but in this case the angle ϵ will be negative in sign, and since a maximum value of a negative magnitude corresponds to a minimum absolute value, the actual deviation of the ray is least in this case also.

60. Deviation of Ray by Thin Prism.—If the refracting angle of the prism (β) is small, as represented, for example, in Fig. 85, the deviation (ϵ) will likewise be a small angle of the same order of smallness; for if $\beta = a_1' - a_2$ is small, then $(a_1 - a_2')$ will be small also, and the angle ϵ is the difference between these two small magnitudes. In fact, the deviation ϵ produced by a thin prism will not only always be small, but it will never be very different from its minimum value ϵ_0. Accordingly, in the case of a thin prism, we may put $\epsilon = \epsilon_0$ without much error; and therefore very approximately (see § 58):

$$\frac{n'}{n} = \frac{\sin \dfrac{\epsilon + \beta}{2}}{\sin \dfrac{\beta}{2}}.$$

Consequently, the deviation ϵ, as calculated by this formula, will depend only on the prism-constants (β, $n' : n$) and not on the angle of incidence (α_1). The smaller the angle β, the more nearly correct this formula will be; and if the angle β is so small that we may substitute $\dfrac{\beta}{2}$ and $\dfrac{\epsilon + \beta}{2}$ in place of $\sin \dfrac{\beta}{2}$ and $\sin \dfrac{\epsilon + \beta}{2}$, respectively, we obtain the exceedingly

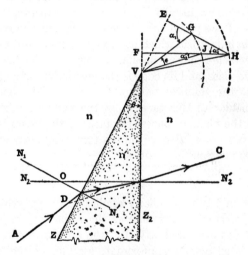

Fig. 85.—Prism with comparatively small refracting
angle.

useful and convenient practical relation for the angle of deviation of a ray refracted through a thin prism, viz.:

$$\epsilon = (\frac{n'}{n} - 1)\,\beta,$$

which, however, is more frequently written:

$$\epsilon = (n - 1)\,\beta,$$

where n is employed now to denote the relative index of refraction. Accordingly, *in a thin prism the deviation is di-*

rectly proportional to the refracting angle. For example, the deviation in the case of a thin glass prism surrounded by air for which $n = 1.5$ is one-half the refracting angle.

61. Power of an Ophthalmic Prism. Centrad and Prism-Dioptry.—An ophthalmic prism is a thin glass prism, whose index of refraction is usually about 1.52, which is used to correct faulty tendencies and weaknesses of the ocular muscles which turn the eye in its socket about the center of rotation of the eye-ball. In an ordinary laboratory prism the two faces are usually cut in the form of rectangles having the edge of the prism as a common side; but the contour of an ophthalmic prism which has to be worn in front of the eye in a spectacle-frame is circular or elliptical like that of any other eye-glass, and its edge is the line drawn tangent to this curve at the thinnest part of the glass. The line drawn perpendicular to this tangent at the point of contact and lying in the plane of one of the faces of the prism is the so-called *"base-apex" line*, which is a term frequently employed by writers on spectacle-optics.

The formula

$$\epsilon = (n-1)\beta$$

obtained in § 69 is peculiarly applicable to the weak prisms used in spectacles. As long as the refracting angle of the prism does not exceed, say, 10°, the error in the value of ϵ as calculated by this approximate formula will be less than 5 per cent.

Formerly it was customary to give the strength or power of an ophthalmic prism in terms of its refracting angle β expressed in degrees; but the proper measure of this power is the deviation produced by the prism. However, instead of measuring this angle in degrees, DENNETT has suggested that the deviation of an ophthalmic prism shall be measured in terms of a unit angle called a *centrad*, which is the one-hundredth part of a radian and equal therefore to the angle subtended at the center of a circle of radius one meter by an arc of length one centimeter. Since π radians = 180°, the relation between the centrad and the degree is given as follows:

$$1° = \frac{100\,\pi}{180} \text{ centrads},$$

or

$$1° = 1.745 \text{ ctrd.}, \quad 1 \text{ ctrd.} = 0.573°.$$

Prior to this suggestion, Mr. C. F. PRENTICE, of New York, had proposed in 1888 to measure the deviation of an ophthalmic prism in terms of the linear or tangential displacement in centimeters on a screen placed at a distance of one meter from the prism.

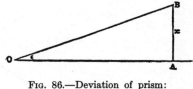

FIG. 86.—Deviation of prism: tan ϵ = AB : OA.

If the straight lines OA, OB (Fig. 86) represent the directions of the incident and emergent rays, respectively, then $\angle$AOB will be the angle of deviation of the prism; and if a plane screen placed at right angles to OA at A is intersected by OB at B, then $\tan\angle\text{AOB} = \dfrac{\text{AB}}{\text{OA}}$.

Now if the distance OA = 100 cm. and if AB = x cm., then, according to PRENTICE's method, the $\angle$AOB would be an angle of x units and the power of the prism would be denoted by x. Dr. S. M. BURNETT suggested that the name *prism-diopter* or *prism-dioptry* be given to this unit. (The term "prismoptrie" was proposed by Professor S. P. THOMPSON.) The prism-dioptry is the angle corresponding to a deviation of one centimeter on a tangent line at a distance of one meter; and, accordingly, when the angle of deviation is equal to the angle whose trigonometric tangent is $x/100$, the power of the prism is said to be x prism-dioptries or $x\triangle$, where the symbol $\triangle$ stands for prism-dioptry. The chief objection to be urged against this unit of angular measurement is that the angle subtended at a given point O (Fig. 87) by equal line-segments on a line Ay perpendicular to Ox at A diminishes as the segment on Ay is taken farther and farther from A. In other words, since $\tan^{-1} x/100$ is less than $x.\tan^{-1} 1/100$, x prism-dioptries is less than x times one prism-dioptry. Ordinarily, the variability in the magnitude of a unit would constitute an insuperable objection to it; but so long as the

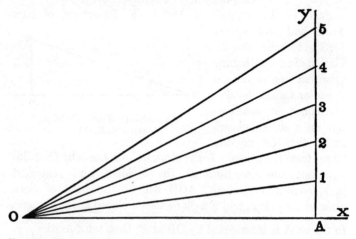

Fig. 87.—Unequal angles subtended at O by equal intervals on straight line Ay drawn perpendicular to OA.

angles to be measured are always small, as is the case with ophthalmic prisms, the prism-dioptry may be regarded as invariably equal to the $\tan^{-1} 1/100$ or about $34' 22.6''$ without sensible error; and hence we may say, for example, that $2\triangle + 3\triangle = 5\triangle$, although this statement is not quite accurate. At any rate, whatever may be the theoretical objections, this unit of measurement of the strength of a thin prism is so convenient and satisfactory that it has been generally adopted in ophthalmic practice.

In point of fact, with the small angular magnitudes which are here pre-supposed (the power of an ophthalmic prism seldom exceeds 6 ctrd.), there is practically no distinction to be made between the angle itself and the tangent of the angle, so that *we may regard the centrad and the prism-dioptry as identical in most cases;* that is,

$$1\triangle = 1 \text{ ctrd.} = 0.573°.$$

Accordingly, we obtain the following relation between the power (p) of an ophthalmic prism expressed in prism-dioptries or centrads and the refracting angle (β) given in degrees:

$$p = \frac{100\ \pi}{180}\ (n-1)\beta = 1.745(n-1)\beta,$$

where n denotes the relative index of refraction. If $n = 1.5$, then the power of a prism of refracting angle β degrees is $0.873\ \beta$ prism-dioptries.

However, in order to exhibit the actual relations still more clearly, the following table gives the values in degrees, minutes and seconds of all integral numbers of prism-dioptries and centrads from 1 to 20; and incidentally it will be seen that whereas an angle of k centrads contains k times as many degrees, minutes and seconds as an angle of 1 centrad, where k denotes any integer from 1 to 20, the same statement is not strictly true of the prism-dioptry.

Prism-Dioptries	Equivalent in degrees, minutes and seconds	Centrads	Equivalent in degrees, minutes and seconds
1	0° 34′ 22.6″	1	0° 34′ 22.7″
2	1° 8′ 44.8″	2	1° 8′ 45.3″
3	1° 43′ 6.1″	3	1° 43′ 8.0″
4	2° 17′ 26.2″	4	2° 17′ 30.6″
5	2° 51′ 44.7″	5	2° 51′ 53.3″
6	3° 26′ 1.1″	6	3° 26′ 15.9″
7	4° 0′ 15.0″	7	4° 0′ 38.6″
8	4° 34′ 26.1″	8	4° 35′ 1.2″
9	5° 8′ 33.9″	9	5° 9′ 23.9″
10	5° 42′ 38.1″	10	5° 43′ 46.5″
11	6° 16′ 38.3″	11	6° 18′ 9.2″
12	6° 50′ 34.0″	12	6° 52′ 31.8″
13	7° 24′ 24.9″	13	7° 26′ 54.5″
14	7° 58′ 10.6″	14	8° 1′ 17.1″
15	8° 31′ 50.8″	15	8° 35′ 39.8″
16	9° 5′ 25.0″	16	9° 10′ 2.4″
17	9° 38′ 53.0″	17	9° 44′ 25.1″
18	10° 12′ 14.3″	18	10° 18′ 47.7″
19	10° 45′ 28.7″	19	10° 53′ 10.4″
20	11° 18′ 35.8″	20	11° 27′ 33.0″

62. Position and Power of a Resultant Prism Equivalent to Two Thin Prisms.—In ascertaining the prismatic correction of the eye of a patient, the oculist or optometrist sometimes finds it convenient and advantageous to employ a combination of two thin prisms placed one in front of the other with their edges inclined to each other at an angle γ which can be measured; and having obtained the necessary correction in this way, he has to prescribe a single prism which will produce precisely the same resultant effect as t h e t w o superposed prisms of the trial-case. In general, it would be exceedingly laborious and difficult to calculate the power of this resultant prism, but, fortunately, the problem in this case is enormously simplified

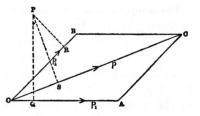

FIG. 88, *a*.—Parallelogram law for finding single prism equivalent to a combination of two thin prisms.

by the fact that the refracting angles are so small that it is quite simple to obtain an approximate solution which is sufficiently accurate and reliable for ordinary practical purposes.

Let the deviation-angles or powers of the two prisms, denoted by p_1 and p_2, be represented, according to the method

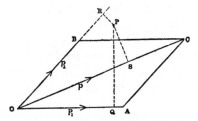

FIG. 88, *b*.—Parallelogram law for finding single prism equivalent to a combination of two thin prisms.

explained in § 50, by the vectors OA, OB, respectively (Fig. 88), which are drawn parallel to the edges of the prism, so that $\angle\,AOB = \gamma$. Complete the parallelogram OACB and draw the diagonal OC. The vector OC will represent on the same scale the deviation-angle or power p of the resultant prism, as we shall proceed to show.

If a point P is taken anywhere in the plane of the parallelogram OACB, it may easily be proved that the area of the triangle POC is equal to the sum or difference of the areas of the triangles POA and POB according as the point P lies

outside the $\angle$ AOB, as in Fig. 88 (a), or inside this angle, as in
Fig. 88 (b), respectively.   And, therefore, if PQ, PR and PS are
drawn perpendicular to OA, OB and OC, respectively, then
$$SP . OC = QP . OA \pm RP . OB.$$

For simplicity, let us assume that the deviations p_1, p_2
produced by the two component prisms are indefinitely
small. Now suppose that the point P is turned, first, about
OA as axis through a very small angle p_1 and then about OB
as axis through the small angle p_2. In consequence of the
first rotation it will move perpendicularly out from the plane
of the paper towards the reader through a tiny distance
corresponding to the arc of a circle described around Q as
center with radius QP, the length of this arc being equal
to the product of the radius by the angle, that is, equal to
QP . OA, since the length of OA is made equal to the magnitude of the angle p_1. If now in this slightly altered position
the point P is again rotated, this time, however, around OB
as axis, through another small angular displacement $p_2 =$ OB,
either it will move a little farther out from the plane AOB,
as in the case shown in Fig. 88 (a), or it will move back
away from the reader, as in the case shown in Fig. 88 (b),
by an additional amount equal to RP . OB. And as this
latter displacement will also be very nearly at right angles to
the plane of the paper, the resultant angular displacement
of the point P may be regarded as equal to the algebraic
sum of its two successive displacements and numerically
equal, therefore, to
$$QP . OA \pm RP . OB,$$
where the upper sign is to be taken in case the point P lies
outside the angle AOB and the lower sign in case it lies inside
this angle. In either case, therefore, the resultant displacement of P will be equal to SP . OC. But this product is equal
to the linear displacement which the point P would have if
it experienced an angular displacement represented by the
vector OC.

Hence, if the straight lines OA, OB drawn parallel to the

edges of the two thin prisms represent the components of the total deviation of a ray which traverses both prisms, the diagonal OC of the parallelogram OABC will represent the resultant or total deviation, and this effect will be produced by a single prism of power $p = OC$ placed with its edge inclined to the edge of the prism of power p_1 ($= OA$) at an angle $\theta = \angle AOC$. If the powers p_1, p_2 of the two component prisms are given in prism-dioptries (or in terms of any other suitable unit, for example, degree, centrad, etc.), and if also the angle γ between the edges of the prisms is given in degrees, the power p of the resultant prism may, therefore, be computed by the formula:

$$p = \sqrt{p_1^2 + p_2^2 + 2p_1 . p_2 . \cos\gamma} \ ,$$

and the angle θ which shows how the resultant prism is to be placed may be calculated by the formula:

$$\tan\theta = \frac{p_2 . \sin\gamma}{p_1 + p_2 . \cos\gamma}.$$

In particular, if $\gamma = 90°$, then $p = \sqrt{p_1^2 + p_2^2}$, $\tan\theta = \dfrac{p_2}{p_1}$.

As an illustration of the use of these formulæ, suppose that the deviations produced by the two prisms separately are 3° and 5°, and that the edges of the prisms are inclined to each other at an angle of 60°. Then $p_1 = 3°$, $p_2 = 5°$, $\gamma = 60°$, and hence the deviation produced by the two prisms together will be $p = \sqrt{9 + 25 + 15} = 7°$; and since $\tan\theta = \dfrac{5\sqrt{3}}{11}$, the resultant prism in this case is found to be a prism of power 7° placed with its edge at an angle of nearly 38° 13′ with that of the weaker of the two component prisms.

A "rotary prism" used for finding the necessary prismatic correction of a patient's eye is an instrument, circular in form, which consists of two ophthalmic prisms of equal power ($p_1 = p_2$) conveniently mounted so that the prisms can be rotated about an axis perpendicular to the plane of the instrument, one in front of the other, the angle between the prism-edges being shown by the positions of two marks which move as the prisms are turned over a circular arc graduated in degrees. In the initial position when the two marks are at opposite ends of a diameter of the circular scale the base of one prism corresponds with the edge of the other, so that in this position the two prisms are equivalent to a glass plate with plane parallel faces ($\gamma = 180°$, $p = p_1 - p_2 = 0$). The maximum effect is obtained when the edges of the prism correspond ($\gamma = 0°$, $p = p_1 + p_2 = 2p_1$). With a device of this kind, we can obtain, therefore, any prismatic power from $p = 0$ to $p = 2p_1$.

On the other hand, we can resolve the effect of a given prism of power p into a component $p \cdot \cos \theta$ in one direction and a component $p \cdot \sin \theta$ in a direction perpendicular to the first. Thus, a prism of power 5 centrads with its edge at an angle of 30° to the horizontal is equivalent to a combination of two prisms of powers $\dfrac{5\sqrt{3}}{2}$ and $\dfrac{5}{2}$ centrads, with their edges horizontal and vertical, respectively.

PROBLEMS

1. Show how to construct the path of a ray refracted through a prism in a principal section; and prove the construction. Discuss the following special cases, and draw separate diagrams for each of them: (a) Incident ray normal to first face of prism, (b) Emergent ray " grazes " second face; (c) Ray traverses prism symmetrically; (d) Ray is incident on first face on side of normal towards the edge of the prism.

2. Show that the total deviation of a ray in a principal section of a prism of more highly refracting material than the surrounding medium is always away from the prism-edge. Discuss each of the three possible cases, viz., When the point where the two incidence-normals intersect falls (a) inside the prism, (b) outside the prism, and (c) on one of the two faces of the prism. Draw diagram for each case.

3. Obtain a formula for calculating the magnitude of the

angle of incidence at the first face of the prism of the ray
which emerges from the prism along the second face; and discuss this formula for the cases when the refracting angle of
the prism is (a) greater than 2A, (b) equal to 2A, (c) less
than 2A but greater than A, (d) equal to A, and (e) less than
A; where A denotes the so-called critical angle of the two
media concerned. Draw diagram for each case.

4. Show that the deviation of a ray which goes symmetrically through a prism in a principal section is less than
that of any other ray.

5. Show that the point of intersection of the incidence-
normals to the two faces of a prism is equidistant from the
incident ray and its corresponding emergent ray.

6. Construct the path of a ray refracted through a prism
of small refracting angle; and show that the angle of deviation
will also be a small angle of the same order of smallness, no
matter how the ray falls on the prism.

7. What is the smallest angle that a glass prism $(n=1.5)$
can have so that no ray can be transmitted through it?
What is the magnitude of this angle for a water prism
$(n=1.33)$? (Assume in each case that the prism is surrounded by air of index unity.)

Ans. 83° 37′ 14″; 97° 30′ 25″.

8. What must be the refracting angle of a prism whose
index of refraction is equal to $\sqrt{2}$ in order that rays that
are incident on one of its faces at angles less than 45° will
be totally reflected at the other face?   Ans. 75°.

9. The refracting angle of a prism is 60° and the index of
refraction is equal to $\sqrt{2}$. Show that the angle of minimum
deviation is 30°, and draw accurate diagram showing the
construction of the path of this ray through the prism.

10. The refracting angle of a glass prism $(n=1.5)$ is 60°,
and the angle of incidence is 45°. Find the angle of deviation.
What is the angle of minimum deviation for this prism?

Ans. 37° 22′ 52.5″; 37° 10′ 50″.

11. If the angle of minimum deviation of a ray traversing

a principal section of a prism is 90°, show that the index of refraction cannot be less than $\sqrt{2}$.

12. Find the angle of minimum deviation in the case of a glass prism ($n = 1.54$) of refracting angle 60°.

Ans. 40° 42′ 28″.

13. The minimum deviation for a prism of refracting angle 40° is found to be 32° 40′. Find the value of the index of refraction.   Ans. 1.7323.

14. A glass prism of refracting angle 60° is adjusted so that the ray "grazes" the first face, and in this position the angle of emergence is found to be 29° 25′ 49″. Determine the index of refraction.   Ans. 1.52.

15. A prism is made of glass of index 1.6, and the angle of minimum deviation is found to be 28° 31′ 20″. Calculate the refracting angle.   Ans. 42° 39′ 44″.

16. The refracting angle of a water prism ($n = \frac{4}{3}$) is 30°. How must a ray be sent into this prism so that it will emerge along the second face?

Ans. Ray must lie on the side of the normal towards the edge of the prism, and make with the normal an angle of 25° 9′ 15″.

17. The angle of incidence for minimum deviation in the case of a prism of refracting angle 60° is 60°. Find the index of refraction.   Ans. $\sqrt{3}$.

18. Find the index of refraction of a glass prism for sodium light for the following measurements: Refracting angle of prism = 45° 4′; angle of minimum deviation = 26° 40′.

Ans. 1.53.

19 The refracting angle of a prism is 30° and its index of refraction is 1.6. Find the angles of emergence and deviation for each of the following rays: (a) Ray meets first face normally; (b) Angle of incidence at first face is equal to 24° 28′; (c) Angle of incidence at first face is equal to 53° 8′; and (d) Ray "grazes" first face.

Ans. (a) 53° 8′; 23° 8′; (b) 24° 28′; 18° 56′; (c) 0°; 23° 8′; (d) 13° 59′; 46° 1′.

20. Find the refracting angle of a glass prism $(n = 1.52)$ for which the minimum deviation is $15°$. Ans. $27° 44' 36''$.

21. The refracting angle of a flint glass prism is measured and found to be $59° 56' 22.4''$; and the angles of minimum deviation for rays of light corresponding to the FRAUNHOFER lines D, F and H are also measured and found to have the following values: $46° 31' 4.15''$; $47° 35' 59.2''$; and $49° 30' 5.7''$, respectively. Calculate the values of the indices of refraction n_D, n_F, and n_H.

Ans. $n_D = 1.603528$; $n_F = 1.614771$; $n_H = 1.634183$.

22. The refracting angle of a crown glass prism is measured and found to be $60° 2' 10.8''$; and the angles of minimum deviation for rays of light corresponding to the FRAUNHOFER lines D, F and H are also measured and found to have the following values: $38° 38' 14.3''$; $39° 10' 51.8''$; and $40° 3' 49.4''$, respectively. Calculate the values of the indices of refraction n_D, n_F, and n_H.

Ans. $n_D = 1.516274$; $n_F = 1.522437$; $n_H = 1.532370$.

23. A prism is to be made of crown glass of index 1.526, and it is required to produce a minimum deviation of $17° 20'$. To what angle must it be ground? Ans. $31° 20'$.

24. A ray of light falls on one face of a prism in a direction perpendicular to the opposite face. Assuming that the refracting angle of the prism (β) is an acute angle, show that the ray will emerge along the opposite face if
$$\cot \beta = \cot A - 1,$$
where A denotes the critical angle of the prism-medium.

25. A ray "grazes" the first face of a prism and emerges at the second face in a direction perpendicular to the first face: show that the refracting angle (β) is such that
$$\cot \beta = \sqrt{n^2 - 1} - 1,$$
where n denotes the index of refraction of the prism-medium.

26. The refracting angle of a prism is $60°$ and the index of refraction is $\sqrt{7/3}$. What is the limiting angle of incidence of a ray that will be transmitted through the prism?
Ans. $30°$.

27. Show that if ϵ_0 denotes the angle of minimum deviation of a prism of refracting angle β, the angle β cannot be greater than $(\pi - \epsilon_0)$ and the index of refraction cannot be less than $\sec\dfrac{\epsilon_0}{2}$.

28. Show that the minimum deviation of a prism of given index of refraction increases with increase of the refracting angle of the prism.

29. Derive the formula for the angle of deviation of a thin prism, and show that the deviation is approximately constant for all angles of incidence.

30. Show that when a thin glass prism of index $\frac{3}{2}$ is immersed in water of index $\frac{4}{3}$ the deviation of a ray will be only one-fourth of what it would be if the prism were surrounded by air.

31. The refracting angle of a prism of rock salt is $1°\ 30'$. How much will a ray be deviated in passing through it? And what should be the refracting angle of a rock salt prism which is to produce a deviation of $48'$? (Index of refraction of rock salt $= 1.54$.)   Ans. $48'\ 36''$; $1°\ 29'$.

32. What must be the refracting angle of a water prism of index $\frac{4}{3}$ to produce the same deviation as is obtained with a glass prism of index $\frac{3}{2}$ whose refracting angle is equal to $2°$?   Ans. $3°$.

33. A glass prism of index 1.5 has a refracting angle of $2°$. What is the power of the prism in prism-dioptries?
     Ans. 1.745 prism-dioptries.

34. The power of a prism is 2 prism-dioptries and $n = 1.5$. Find the refracting angle.   Ans. $2.29°$.

35. A prism of refracting angle $1°\ 25'$ bends a beam of light through an angle of $1°\ 15'$. Calculate the index of refraction and the power of the prism in prism-dioptries.
     Ans. $n = 1.882$; 2.18 prism-dioptries.

36. Two thin prisms are crossed with their edges at an angle of $30°$. The first prism produces a deviation of $6°$ and the second a deviation of $8°$. Find the deviation produced

by the single prism which is equivalent to this combination
and the angle which the edge of the resultant prism must
make with the edge of the first prism.

Ans. Deviation of resultant prism $= 13.53°$; angle between its edge and that of the $6°$-prism $= 17°$ $11'$.

37. Two prisms, each of power 5 prism-dioptries, are
combined base down with their base-apex lines inclined to
the horizontal at angles of $45°$ and $135°$. Find the equivalent
single prism.

Ans. A prism of power a little more than 7 prism-dioptries,
base down, vertical meridian (edge horizontal).

38. What will be the horizontal effect of a prism of power
10 placed with its base-apex line at an angle of $20°$ with the
horizontal?

Ans. It will be the same as the effect of a prism of power
nearly 9.4 in horizontal meridian (edge vertical).

39. The base-apex line of a prism of power 4 centrads makes
an angle of $120°$ with the vertical. Show that it is equivalent to a combination of two prisms, one of power 2 centrads in
the vertical meridian (edge horizontal) and the other of power
3.46 centrads in the horizontal meridian (edge vertical).

40. Find the single prism equivalent to a combination of
two prisms superposed with their base-apex lines at right
angles to each other, the power of one being 3 and that of
the other 4.

Ans. A prism of power 5 with its base-apex line inclined to
that of the weaker prism at an angle of nearly $53°$ $8'$.

41. Two equal prisms, each of power 3, are superposed
in meridians inclined to each other at an angle of $120°$.
Find the equivalent single prism.

Ans. A prism of power 3 in a meridian halfway between
the meridians of the two components.

42. The angle between the base-apex lines of a combination of two unit prisms is $82°$ $50'$, and the bisector of this
angle is horizontal. What is the horizontal effect of the
combination?   Ans. 1.5 units.

43. ABCDE is the principal section of a pentagonal prism. AB=BC, AE=CD, $\angle$ABC=90°, $\angle$EAB=$\angle$BCD=112.5°. A ray of light RS lying in the principal section is incident on the face BC at the point S. The ray enters the prism at this face, and is reflected, first, from the face AE, and then from the face DC, and emerges finally at a point P in the face AB in the direction PQ. Show that PQ makes a right angle with RS.

44. ABC is a principal section of a triangular prism, $\angle$B=2$\angle$A. A ray of light lying in the plane ABC is refracted into the prism at the side BC, and after undergoing two internal reflections, first, from the side AB and then from the side CA, emerges into the surrounding medium at the side AB. Show that the total deviation of the ray will be equal to the angle at B.

45. If β denotes the refracting angle of a prism and if ϵ denotes the deviation (defined as in §§ 50, foll.), show that the angle of incidence of the ray at the first face of the prism must be such that

$$\tan a_1 = \frac{A \pm B}{C},$$

where A, B and C are abbreviations for the following expressions:

$A = \sin(\beta + \epsilon) \left\{ \cos\beta - \cos(\beta + \epsilon) \right\}$;

$B = \sin\beta \sqrt{n^2 \left\{ 2 - n^2\sin^2\beta - 2\cos\beta\cos(\beta + \epsilon) \right\} - \sin^2(\beta + \epsilon)}$;

$C = (n^2 - 1) \sin^2\beta - \left\{ \cos\beta - \cos(\beta + \epsilon) \right\}^2$.

In these expressions n denotes the relative index of refraction of the two media.

46. Show that the two values of a, for a prism of glass (n = 1.5) and of refracting angle 60° which give a deviation of 40° are 63° 27′ 28″ and 36° 32′ 32″.

CHAPTER VI

63. Introduction. Definitions, Notation, etc.—The center
of the spherical refracting or reflecting surface ZZ (Fig. 89)
will be designated by C. The *axis* of the surface with respect
to a given point M is the
straight line joining M
with C, and the point A
where the straight line
MC (produced if neces-
sary) meets ZZ is called the
pole or *vertex* of the surface
with respect to the point
M. Evidently, the spheri-
cal surface will be sym-
metrical around MC as
axis, and the plane of the
diagram which contains the axis is a meridian section of the
surface.

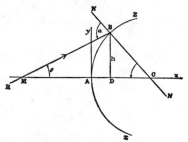

Fig. 89, *a.*—Ray incident on convex
spherical surface crosses axis at
point M in front of surface.

It will be convenient to take the vertex A as the *origin*
of a system of plane rectangular coördinates; the axis of
the surface being chosen as the x-axis and the tangent to the
surface at its vertex, in the meridian plane of the diagram,
being taken as the y-axis. *The positive direction of the x-axis
is the direction of the incident ray which coincides with this
line,* and since *the diagrams are all drawn on the supposition
that the incident light goes from left to right,* a point lying on
the x-axis to the right of A will be on the positive half of
the axis. The positive direction of the y-axis is the direction
found by rotating the positive half of the x-axis through a

149

right angle in a sense opposite to that of the motion of the
hands of a clock in the meridian plane of the diagram. Accordingly, if the positive direction of the x-axis is along a

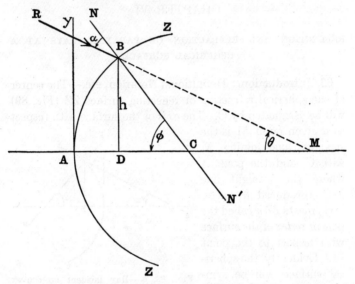

Fɪɢ. 89, b.—Ray incident on convex spherical surface crosses axis at point
M on the other side of the surface.

horizontal line from left to right, the positive direction of
the y-axis will be vertically upwards.

According as the center C lies on the same side of the
spherical surface as that from which the incident light comes
or on the opposite side, it is said to be *concave* (Fig. 89, *c*
and *d*) or *convex* (Fig. 89, *a* and *b*), respectively. The radius
r of the spherical surface is the abscissa of the center C, that
is, $r = $ AC. It is the step from A to C, and this is always a
positive step for a convex surface (Fig. 89, *a* and *b*) and a
negative step for a concave surface (Fig. 89, *c* and *d*). The
radius of a convex surface whose center is 60 cm. from its
vertex is $r = +60$ cm., and the radius of a concave surface of
the same size is $r = -60$ cm.

It will be assumed in this chapter that any ray with which we are concerned lies in a meridian plane of the spherical surface; so that any straight line such as RB which represents the path of an incident ray will intersect the axis either "really" (Fig. 89, *a* and *c*) or "virtually" (Fig. 89, *b* and *d*) at some point designated here by M (see § 8). The point designated by R is any point on the incident ray RB at which the light arrives before it gets to either M or the incidence-point B. The straight line BC which joins the point of incidence with the center of the surface will be the incidence-normal, and if N designates a point on this normal lying in front of the spherical surface, then $\angle NBR = \alpha$ will be the

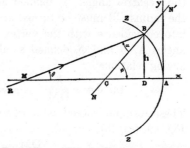

Fig. 89, *c.*—Ray incident on concave spherical surface crosses axis at point M in front of the surface.

angle of incidence (§§ 13 & 27). The plane of this angle is the plane of incidence, which is the meridian plane of the diagram.

From the incidence-point B draw BD perpendicular to the *x*-axis at D; the ordinate $h = DB$ is called the incidence-height of the ray. The *slope of the ray* is the acute angle through which

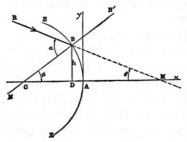

Fig. 89, *d.*—Ray incident on concave spherical surface crosses axis at point M on the other side of the surface.

the *x*-axis has to be turned around the point M in order that it may coincide in position (but not necessarily in direction) with the rectilinear path of the ray. If this angle is denoted by θ, then $\angle AMB = \theta$. Here, as always in the case of angular magnitudes (§ 13), counter-clockwise rotation is to be reckoned as positive. And, finally, the acute angle at the center C of the spherical surface subtended by the arc BA will be denoted by ϕ. This angle, sometimes called the "central angle," is defined as the angle through which the radius CB must be turned around C in order to bring B into coincidence with the vertex A; thus, $\phi = \angle$ BCA. The angles A, θ and ϕ, defined as above, are given by the following relations:

$$\tan \theta = -\frac{h}{DM}, \quad \sin\phi = \frac{h}{r}, \quad a = \theta + \phi.$$

These formulæ should be verified for each of the diagrams Fig. 89, (a), (b), (c), (d).

Moreover, since $BM = \dfrac{DM}{\cos \theta}$, and since (see § 45)

$$DM = DC + CA + AM = r.\cos\phi - r + AM,$$

we find:

$$BM = \frac{r(\cos\phi - 1) + AM}{\cos \theta}.$$

Now in the special case *when the incidence-point* B *is very close to the vertex* A *of the spherical surface*, the angle of incidence a will be exceedingly small as will be also the angles denoted by θ and ϕ; and if these angles expressed in radians are all such small fractions that we may neglect their second and higher powers, so that in place of the sines (or tangents) we can write the angles themselves and put $\cos \theta = \cos \phi = \cos a = 1$. Obviously, in such a case we shall have BM = AM. Under these circumstances the ray RB is called a *paraxial ray*, sometimes also a "central" or "zero" ray, $a = \theta = \phi = 0$, approximately.

A paraxial ray is one whose path lies very near the axis of the spherical surface and which therefore meets this surface at a point close to the vertex and at nearly normal incidence: the angles denoted by a, θ *and* ϕ *being all so small that their second powers may be neglected.*

In this chapter and for several subsequent chapters we shall be concerned entirely with the procedure of paraxial rays; that is, we shall consider only such rays as are comprised within a very narrow cylindrical region immediately surrounding the axis of the spherical surface which is likewise the axis of the cylinder. Accordingly, the only portion of the spherical surface that will be utilized for reflection or refraction will be a small zone whose summit is at A; so that,

so far as paraxial rays are concerned, the rest of the spherical surface may be regarded as if it had no optical existence or at any rate as if it were opaque and non-reflecting. Thus, for example, the surface might be painted over with lampblack leaving bare and exposed only the small effective zone

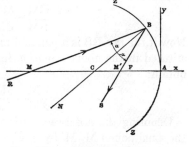

FIG. 90, *a.*—Reflection of ray at concave mirror.

in the immediate vicinity of the vertex; or a screen might be set up at right angles to the axis close to the vertex with a small circular opening in it. Even then a source of light

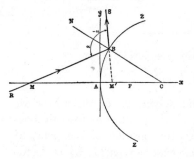

FIG. 90, *b.*—Reflection of ray at convex mirror.

lying at a considerable distance off the axis would send rays which notwithstanding that they were incident near the vertex would not be paraxial rays.

64. Reflection of Paraxial Rays at a Spherical Mirror.—In the accompanying diagrams (Fig. 90, *a* and *b*) the straight line RB represents the path of an incident ray crossing the axis of a spherical mirror ZZ at the point M and incident on the mirror at the point B, and the straight line BS shows the path of the corresponding reflected ray crossing the axis, "really" (Fig. 90, a) or "virtually" (Fig. 90, b), at the point marked M'. By the law of reflection $\angle NBR = \angle SBN$ where BN is the incidence-normal and N designates a point on it which lies in front of the mirror. Since the normal bisects the interior or exterior angle at B of the triangle MBM', the following proportion may be written:

$$\frac{CM}{BM} = \frac{M'C}{BM'}.$$

Now if the ray RB is a paraxial ray, the letter A may be substituted in the above equation in place of B, and thus * we obtain:

$$\frac{CM}{AM} = \frac{M'C}{AM'}.$$

Denoting the abscissae, with respect to the vertex A, of the axial points M, M' by u, u', respectively, that is, putting $AM = u$, $AM' = u'$, and also, as stated in § 63, putting $AC = r$, we may write:

$$CM = CA + AM = -r + u = u - r,$$
$$M'C = M'A + AC = -u' + r = -(u' - r);$$

so that, introducing these symbols in the equation above, we obtain:

$$\frac{u - r}{u} = -\frac{u' - r}{u'}$$

which may be put in the form (see § 67):

$$\frac{1}{u} + \frac{1}{u'} = \frac{2}{r}.$$

If, therefore, the form and dimensions of the mirror are known (that is, if the value of r is assigned as to both magnitude and sign), and if also the position of the point M

---

* In writing this proportion, care must be taken to see that the two members of it shall have the same sign. For example, in each of the diagrams in Fig. 90, as they are drawn, the segments CM and AM have the same direction along the axis, so that for each of these figures the ratio CM : AM is positive. Now if the ratio M'C : AM' is to be put equal to this ratio, it must be positive also, that is, the segments M'C and AM' in each diagram must have the same direction.

where the incident paraxial ray crosses the axis of the spherical mirror is given, the abscissa u' of the point M' where the corresponding reflected ray crosses the axis may be calculated by means of the expression:

$$u' = \frac{r.u}{2u - r}.$$

But the most noteworthy conclusion to be drawn from this formula is the fact that, provided the rays are paraxial, their actual slopes do not matter, for none of the angular magnitudes α, θ, or ϕ appears in the formula; which means that all paraxial rays which cross the axis at the point M before reflection will cross the axis after reflection in the spherical mirror at one and the same point M'. Thus, *a homocentric bundle of paraxial rays incident on a spherical mirror remains homocentric after reflection.* If, therefore, M designates the position of a luminous point in front of the mirror, and if the mirror is screened so that only such rays as proceed close to the axis are incident on it, the bundle of reflected rays will form at a point M' on the straight line MC an ideal image of the luminous point M. According as the image-point M' lies in front of the mirror (Fig. 90, *a*) or beyond it (Fig. 90, *b*), the image will be real or virtual, respectively. Thus, for a real image in a spherical mirror, the value of u' as found by the formula above will be negative, whereas for a virtual image it will be positive.

It may be noted also that the formula is symmetrical with respect to u and u', so that the equation will not be altered by interchanging the symbols u and u'; and hence it follows that *if M' is the image of M, then likewise M may be regarded as the image of M'.* This is indeed merely an illustration of the general law known in optics as the "principle of the reversibility of the light-path" (§ 29). But the symmetry of the equation implies more than is involved in this principle; for it indicates that in the case of reflection object-space and image-space coincide completely, the actual paths of the incident and reflected rays both lying in the space in front of the mirror. Accordingly, an incident ray and its corresponding reflected ray are always so related that when either is regarded as object-ray the other will be an image-ray.

THE DOUBLE RATIO OF FOUR POINTS ON A STRAIGHT LINE

65. Definition and Meaning of the Double Ratio.—It will be convenient and profitable at this place to turn aside from the special problem which is here under investigation in order to devote a few paragraphs to a brief explanation of the simpler metrical processes of modern projective geometry, which are of great utility in geometrical optics, especially when we are concerned with imagery by means of the so-called paraxial rays.

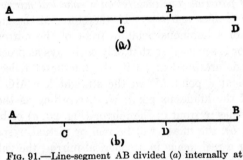

FIG. 91.—Line-segment AB divided (a) internally at C and externally at D, and (b) internally at C and D.

If L designates the position of a point on a straight line determined by the two points A, B, the line-segment AB is said to be divided at L in the ratio AL : BL. If the point L lies between A and B, the steps (see § 45) AL and BL are in opposite senses along the line, and the ratio AL : BL will be negative, and in this case we say that the segment AB is "divided internally" at L. On the other hand, if the point L does not lie between A and B, the ratio AL : BL will be positive, and we say that the segment AB is "divided externally" at L.

Accordingly, if A, B, C, D (Fig. 91, a and b) designate a

series of four points all ranged along a straight line in any
order of sequence, the segment AB will be divided at C and
D in the ratios AC : BC and AD : BD, respectively; and
the quotient of these two ratios is called the *double ratio* (or
"cross ratio") of the four points A, B, C, D. This double
ratio is denoted symbolically by inclosing the four letters
ABCD in parentheses; thus, according to the above definition,

$$(ABCD) = \frac{AC}{BC} : \frac{AD}{BD},$$

where the first two letters in the parentheses mark the end-
points of the segment and the last two letters designate the
points of division. The line-segment CD is divided in the
same way by the points A and B; for

$$(CDAB) = \frac{CA}{DA} : \frac{CB}{DB} = \frac{AC}{BC} : \frac{AD}{BD} = (ABCD).$$

According as the two ratios AC : BC and AD : BD have
the same sign or opposite signs, the value of the double ratio
(ABCD) will be positive or negative, respectively. Suppose,
for example, that the segment AB is divided internally at C,
as represented in both *a* and *b* of Fig. 91. Then the ratio
AC : BC will be negative. Now if AB is divided also internally at D, as in Fig. 91, *b* the ratio AD : DB will likewise
be negative. Accordingly, if C and D are both points of internal division (or both points of external division), the
double ratio (ABCD) will be positive. But if one of these
points divides AB internally while the other divides it externally (Fig. 91, *a*), the double ratio (ABCD) will be negative.

In order to form a clear idea of the values which (ABCD)
may assume, let us suppose that the points designated by
A, B and C in Fig. 92 represent three stationary points on a
straight line *x*, and that O designates another fixed point not
on this line. The straight line *x* and the point O together
determine a plane which is the plane of the diagram. Now
let *y* designate a second straight line lying in this plane and

passing through O, and let the point of intersection of the straight lines x and y be designated by Y. And if the straight line y is supposed to turn around O as a pivot in a

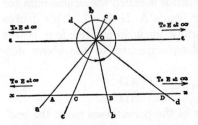

sense, say, opposite to that of the motion of the hands of a clock, the point Y will be a variable point moving along the straight line x constantly in the same sense, namely, in Fig. 92 from left to right. Assume, for example, that the three stationary points A, C, B

FIG. 92.—Central projection from O of the point-range ABCDE lying on the straight line x.

are ranged along the straight line x from left to right in the order named, as shown in the figure; and suppose that the variable point Y starts originally at B, so that the revolving line OY or y coincides initially with the "ray" marked b in the figure and $BY = BB = 0$, and, consequently, the ratio $AY : BY = \infty$, Hence, under these circumstances the initial value of the double ratio of the four points A, B, C, Y will be:

$$(ABCY) = \frac{AC}{BC} : \frac{AY}{BY} = 0.$$

When the revolving ray has turned through $\angle BOD$, where D designates a point lying on the straight line x to the right beyond B, the point Y will be at D outside the segment AB and the double ratio (ABCY) will be negative, as explained above. As y continues to revolve around O, the point Y will move farther and farther to the right along the straight line x, until when y is parallel to x, and in the position of the ray marked e in the figure, the point Y will then coincide with *the infinitely distant point* E *of the straight line* x. Now $AE = BE = \infty$, and hence $AE : BE = 1$; and therefore when Y is at E,

$$(ABCY) = \frac{AC}{BC} : \frac{AE}{BE} = \frac{AC}{BC}.$$

When the revolving ray y has turned beyond the position represented by the straight line e, the point Y which had just vanished at one end E of the straight line x now reappears from the other end E, proceeding along it still in the same sense from left to right. Thus, before the ray y has executed a complete revolution, the point Y will pass through A, and at this moment, $AY = AA = 0$, and

$$(ABCY) = \frac{AC}{BC} : \frac{AY}{BY} = \frac{AC}{BC} : \frac{AA}{BA} = - \infty \; ;$$

and thus we see that as the point Y has traversed the straight line x from B *via* the infinitely distant point E to A, the double ratio $(ABCY)$ has assumed all negative values from 0 to $- \infty$. Finally, as the ray y completes its revolution by turning from the position a to its initial position b, the point Y moves from A *via* C to B. When Y is at C, $AY = AC$, $BY = BC$, and

$$(ABCY) = \frac{AC}{BC} : \frac{AY}{BY} = +1 \; ;$$

so that in passing along x from A to C, $(ABCY)$ assumes all positive values comprised between $+ \infty$ and $+1$. Between C and B, it has all positive values less than unity. Thus, as the point Y traverses the straight line x continually in the same sense until it has returned to its starting point, the double ratio $(ABCY)$ will assume all possible values both positive and negative.

In general, since

$$(ABCD) = \frac{AC}{BC} : \frac{AD}{BD} = \frac{BD}{AD} : \frac{BC}{AC} = \frac{CA}{DA} : \frac{CB}{DB} = \frac{DB}{CB} : \frac{DA}{CA} \, ,$$

we may write:

$$(ABCD) = (BADC) = (CDAB) = (DCBA).$$

66. Perspective Ranges of Points.—If A, B, C, etc., designate the positions of the points of a point-range x (Fig. 92) these points are said to be "projected" from a point O outside of x by the straight lines or "rays" OA, OB, OC, etc.; and if these rays intersect another straight line x' (Fig. 93) in the points A', B', C', etc., the two point-ranges x, x' are said to be in *perspective* with respect to the point O as *center* *of perspective.* The points A, A′; B, B′; C, C′; etc., are called pairs of corresponding points of the two perspective point-ranges *x, x′.*

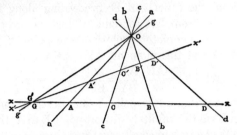

Fig. 93.—The point-ranges ABCD and A′B′C′D′ are in perspective relation with respect to the point O as centre of perspective.

If A, B, C, D designate the positions of any four points of *x,* and if A′, B′, C′, D′ designate the corresponding points on *x′,* then

$$(A'B'C'D') = (ABCD),$$

as we shall proceed to show.

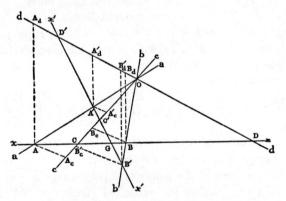

Fig. 94.—Straight lines *x, x′* are bases of two point-ranges in perspective, so that (ABCD) = (A′B′C′D′).

Through the points A, B, A′ and B′ (Fig. 94) draw four parallel lines AA$_c$, BB$_c$, A′A$_c$′ and B′B$_c$′ meeting the ray OC or c in the points A_c, B_c, A_c' and B_c', respectively; and through these same points draw four other parallel lines AA_d, BB_d, $A'A_d'$ and $B'B_d'$ meeting the ray OD or d in the points A_d, B_d, A_d' and B_d', respectively. Then, evidently,

$$\frac{AC}{BC} = \frac{AA_c}{BB_c}, \quad \frac{AD}{BD} = \frac{AA_d}{BB_d},$$

$$\frac{A'C'}{B'C'} = \frac{A'A_c'}{B'B_c'}, \quad \frac{A'D'}{B'D'} = \frac{A'A_d'}{B'B_d'};$$

hence,

$$(ABCD) = \frac{AC}{BC} : \frac{AD}{BD} = \frac{AA_c}{BB_c} : \frac{AA_d}{BB_d},$$

$$(A'B'C'D') = \frac{A'C'}{B'C'} : \frac{A'D'}{B'D'} = \frac{A'A_c'}{B'B_c'} : \frac{A'A_d'}{B'B_d'}.$$

Now

$$\frac{A\,A_c}{A'A_c'} = \frac{A\,A_d}{A'A_d'}, \quad \frac{B\,B_c}{B'B_c'} = \frac{B\,B_d}{B'B_d'},$$

and, consequently,

$$(A'B'C'D') = (ABCD),$$

as was to be proved.

67. The Harmonic Range.—The special case when the points C and D divide the line-segment AB internally and externally in the same numerical ratio, so that

$$\frac{AC}{BC} = -\frac{AD}{BD},$$

demands attention, particularly because it is a case that we shall meet again in the theory of the reflection of paraxial rays at a curved mirror. Under these circumstances, the value of the double ratio is

$$(ABCD) = -1;$$

and then we say that *the segment AB is divided harmonically at C and D*, or also the segment CD is divided harmonically at A and B. For example, the perpendicular bisectors of the exterior and interior angles of a triangle divide the opposite side of the triangle harmonically in the ratio of the other two sides.

Four harmonic points may be defined not merely by the metrical relation that their double ratio is equal to -1, but also by a geometrical relation, as we shall now show.

Let P, Q, R, S (Figs. 95 and 96) designate the positions of

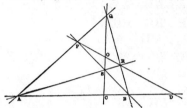

four points lying all in one plane, no three of which are in the same straight line. These four points will determine six straight lines, viz., PQ, PR, PS, QR,

FIG. 95.—Complete quadrilateral PQRS; (ABCD) = -1.

QS, and RS, which are called the *sides* of the

complete quadrilateral whose four vertices are at the points P, Q, R, and S. Any two of these lines which together contain all the vertices form a pair of opposite sides of the quadrilateral. Accordingly, there are three pairs of opposite

sides, viz., PQ and RS which meet in a point designated by A, PS and QR which meet in a point designated by B, and QS and PR which meet in a point designated by O. The three points A, B and O are sometimes called the

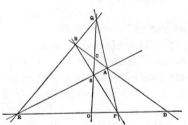

FIG. 96.—Complete quadrilateral PQRS; (ABCD) = -1

secondary vertices of the quadrilateral. We shall explain now what connection this figure has with a harmonic range of points.

The secondary vertices A and B are determined by the two pairs of opposite sides PQ, RS and PS, QR; and the points C and D where the third pair of opposite sides QS and PR meet the straight line AB divide the segment AB harmonically. For, since A, B, C, D and P, R, O, D are in perspective relation with respect to the point Q as center of perspective (§ 66), therefore

$$(\text{ABCD}) = (\text{PROD}).$$

But P, R, O, D and B, A, C, D are also in perspective to each other with respect to the point S as center of perspective; consequently,

$$(\text{PROD}) = (\text{BACD}).$$

It follows therefore that

$$(\text{ABCD}) = (\text{BACD}).$$

But by the definition of the double ratio

$$(\text{BACD}) = \frac{1}{(\text{ABCD})} \, .$$

Accordingly, here we must have:

$$(\text{ABCD}) = \frac{1}{(\text{ABCD})},$$

or

$$(\text{ABCD})^2 = 1.$$

According to this equation, therefore, the double ratio (ABCD) must be equal to $+1$ or -1. But we saw above (§ 65) that the double ratio of four points A, B, C, D in a straight line can be equal to $+1$ only in case one of the points A, B is coincident with one of the pair C, D; which cannot happen in case of the four points A, B, C, D of the quadrilateral PQRS. Therefore, we must have here:

$$(\text{ABCD}) = -1;$$

and hence, by definition, the points A, B are harmonically separated by the points C, D. Similarly, also, the points P, R are harmonically separated by the points O, D.

If A, B, C, D is a harmonic range of points, then

$$\frac{\text{BC}}{\text{AC}} = \frac{\text{DB}}{\text{AD}}, \text{ or } \frac{\text{BA} + \text{AC}}{\text{AC}} = \frac{\text{DA} + \text{AB}}{\text{AD}} \, ,$$

that is,

$$\frac{\text{AC} - \text{AB}}{\text{AC}} = \frac{\text{AB} - \text{AD}}{\text{AD}} \, ;$$

which may finally be written in the form:

$$\frac{1}{A\ C}+\frac{1}{A\ D}=\frac{2}{A\ B};$$

an equation that is characteristic of a harmonic range of four points A, B, C, D (*cf.* § 64).

68. Application to the Case of the Reflection of Paraxial Rays at a Spherical Mirror.—When paraxial rays are reflected at a spherical mirror whose center is at C, we saw (§ 64) that CM : AM = M′C : AM′, where M, M′ designate the positions of a pair of conjugate points lying on a central ray which crosses the mirror at the point marked A (Fig. 90, *a* and *b*); and therefore

$$\frac{CM}{CM'}:\frac{AM}{AM'}= -1 \text{ or } (CAMM')= -1.$$

Consequently, the four points C, A, M, M′ are a harmonic range of points lying on the central ray AC, and we may say that the pair of conjugate points M, M′ is harmonically separated by the center of the mirror C and the point A where the central ray meets the mirror. Thus, if we know the positions of three of these points, we can construct the position of the fourth point by the aid of the properties of the complete quadrilateral (§ 67). For example, the image-point M′ conjugate to a given point M with respect to a spherical mirror may be constructed as follows:

Draw a straight line *x* (Fig. 97, *a* and *b*) to represent the axis of the mirror, and mark on it the positions of the three given points, A, C and M, which may be ranged along this line in any sequence whatever depending on the form of the mirror and on whether the object-point M is real or virtual. Through M draw another straight line in any convenient direction, and mark on it two points which we shall call Q and S, and draw the straight lines AQ and CS meeting in a point R and the straight lines AS and CQ meeting in a point P. Then the straight line PR will intersect the straight line *x* in the point M′ which is conjugate to M with respect to a spherical mirror whose vertex is at A and whose center is at C. It will be remarked that in performing this construction the only drawing instrument that is needed is a straight-edge.

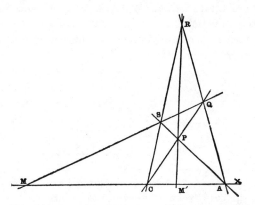

Fig. 97, *a.*—Concave Mirror: Construction of point
M′ conjugate to axial point M in front of the mirror.

If the mirror is concave, the possible sequences of these four points on the axis are M, C, M′, A; M′, C, M, A; and C, M, A, M′, when the object-point M is real, and C, M′,

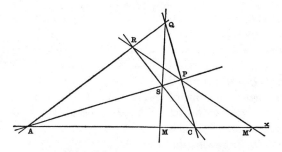

Fig. 97, *b.*—Convex Mirror: Construction of point M′
conjugate to virtual object-point M on axis of mirror.

A, M, when the object-point M is virtual. In the case of a convex mirror the points may occur in any one of the following arrangements: M, A, M′, C, when the object-point M is real, and M′, A, M, C; A, M, C, M′ and A, M′, C, M, when the object-point M is virtual. The student should satisfy himself as to the accuracy of these statements by drawing a diagram for each of these eight sequences according to the directions for the construction as given above. Fig. 97, *a* shows the case of a concave mirror with the points in the order M, C, M′, A; whereas Fig. 97, *b* represents

a convex mirror with a virtual object-point at M, the order in this case being A, M, C, M′.

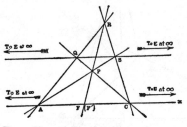

Fig. 98, *a*.—Focal point of convex mirror (AF = FC)

69. Focal Point and Focal Length of a Spherical Mirror.

—In the special case when the object-point M coincides with the infinitely distant point E of the *x*-axis, the conjugate point M′ will lie at a point F′ (Fig. 98, *a* and *b*) determined by the relation:

$$(CAEF') = -1,$$

and since here CE = AE = ∞, we must have:

$$AF' = F'C.$$

This means that a cylindrical bundle of incident paraxial rays parallel to the axis of a spherical mirror will be transformed into a conical bundle of reflected rays with its vertex at a point F′ which is midway between the vertex A and the center C.

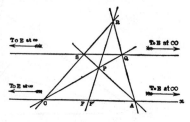

Fig. 98, *b*.—Focal point of concave mirror (AF = FC)

If, on the other hand, the image-point M′ coincides with the infinitely distant point E, the conjugate object-point M will lie on the axis at a point F determined by the relation:

$$(CAFE') = -1,$$

and therefore we obtain here in the same way as above:
$$AF = FC.$$
Accordingly, a conical bundle of incident rays with its vertex at a point F midway between the vertex of the mirror and its center will be transformed into a cylindrical bundle of reflected rays parallel to the axis of the mirror. The letters F and F′ will be used to designate the positions of the so-called *focal points* of an optical system which is symmetric around an axis. They are not a pair of conjugate points, as might naturally be inferred from the fact that they are designated by the same letter. In the case of a spherical mirror these two points, as we have seen, are coincident with each other, which is a consequence of the identity of object-space and image-space to which reference was made at the conclusion of § 64. The focal point of a concave mirror lies in front of the mirror, as shown in Fig. 98, *b*, so that paraxial rays parallel to the axis will be reflected at a concave mirror to a real focus at F; whereas in the case of a convex mirror the focal point F lies behind the mirror (virtual focus), as shown in Fig. 98, *a*.

The *focal length f* of a spherical mirror may be defined as the abscissa of the vertex A with respect to the focal point F as origin; that is, $f = FA$. Hence, *according as the mirror is concave or convex, the focal length will be positive or negative, respectively*. It may be remarked that the signs of f and r are always opposite, the relation between these magnitudes being given by the following formula:
$$f = -\frac{r}{2} \text{ or } r = -2f.$$
Hence, also, the abscissa-relation obtained in § 64 may be written in terms of f instead of r as follows:
$$\frac{1}{u} + \frac{1}{u'} + \frac{1}{f} = 0;$$
where, however, it must be borne in mind that, whereas the abscissæ u, u' are measured from the vertex A as origin, the focal length f is measured from the focal point F.

If the abscissæ, with respect to the focal point F, of the pair of conjugate axial points M, M' are denoted by x, x', that is, if $FM=x$, $FM'=x'$, then, since

$$AM = AF+FM, \qquad AM' = AF+FM',$$

the connection between the u's and the x's is given by the following equations:

$$u = x-f, \qquad u' = x'-f;$$

and substituting these values in the formula above and clearing of fractions, we derive the so-called *Newtonian formula*, viz.:

$$x.x' = f^2;$$

which is an exceedingly simple and convenient form of the abscissa-relation between a pair of conjugate axial points. The right-hand side of this equation is essentially positive, and hence the abscissæ x, x' must always have like signs. Consequently, *in a spherical mirror the conjugate axial points M, M' lie always both on the same side of the focal point F.*

70. Graphical Method of exhibiting the Imagery by Paraxial Rays.—The points M, M' in Fig. 99, a and b desig-

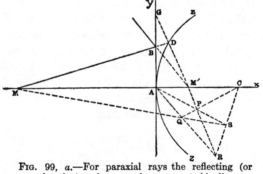

Fig. 99, a.—For paraxial rays the reflecting (or refracting) surface must be represented in diagram by the straight line Ay, not by the curved line AZ.

nate the positions on the axis of a spherical mirror of a pair of conjugate points constructed according to the method explained in § 68. On the reflecting sphere ZZ take a point D, and draw the straight lines MD, M'D meeting the tangent A*y* in the plane of these lines in the points B, G, respectively. Also, draw the straight line M′B. Now if the point D were very close to the vertex A of the mirror, then the straight line MD would represent the path of an incident

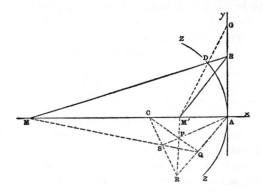

Fɪɢ. 99, *b*.—For paraxial rays the reflecting (or refracting) surface must be represented in diagram by the straight line A*y*, not by the curved line A*Z*.

paraxial ray crossing the axis at M, and the path of the corresponding reflected ray would be along the straight line DM′. But under these circumstances, the three points designated here by the letters D, B, G would all be so near together that even when we cannot regard D as absolutely coincident with A, we may consider D, B and G as all coincident with one another. Therefore, when the ray is paraxial, we may, and, in fact, in the diagram we *must*, regard the straight line BM′ as showing the path of the reflected ray. It is quite essential that this point which is seldom clearly explained should be rightly apprehended by the student. In diagrams showing the imagery by means of paraxial rays the duty of the straight lines that are drawn is not primarily to represent the actual paths of the rays themselves but to locate by their intersections the correct positions of the pairs of corresponding points in the object-space and image-space.

In the construction of such diagrams, a practical difficulty is encountered due to the fact that, whereas in reality paraxial rays are comprised within the very narrow cylindrical region immediately surrounding the axis of the spherical surface (§ 63), it is obviously quite impossible to show them this way in the figure, because it would be necessary to take the dimensions of the drawing at right angles to the axis so small that magnitudes of the second order of smallness would no longer be perceptible at all; thus, for example, the points B, D, G in Fig. 99 would have to be shown as one point. On the other hand, if the lines in the diagram are not all drawn close to the axis, the relations which have been found above will cease to be applicable, so that, for instance, the rays shown in such a drawing would not intersect in the places demanded by the formulæ.

Accordingly, in order to overcome this difficulty, a method of constructing these figures has been very generally adopted, which, although it is confessedly in the nature of a compromise, has been found to be on the whole quite satisfactory, and wherein at any rate the geometrical relations are in agreement with the algebraic conditions, which is the essential requirement. In this plan, while the dimensions parallel to the axis remain absolutely unaltered, the dimensions at right angles to the axis are all prodigiously magnified in the same proportion. Thus, for example, if the incidence-height $h = DB$ (Fig. 89) is a small magnitude of the order, say, of one-thousandth of the unit of length, it will be shown in the figure magnified a thousand times; whereas another ordinate whose height was only one one-millionth of the unit of length and which, therefore, would be of the second order of smallness as compared with h, would appear even in the magnified diagram as a magnitude of the first order of smallness. And if the ordinate denoted by h, although in reality infinitely small, is represented in the drawing by a line of finite length, an ordinate of the second order of smallness as compared with h will be entirely unapparent in the magnified diagram.

Of course, as already intimated, one effect of this lateral enlargement will be to misrepresent to some extent the relations of the lines and angles in the figure. For instance, the circle in which the spherical mirror (or refracting surface) is cut by the plane of a meridian section will thereby be transformed into an infinitely elongated ellipse with its major axis perpendicular to the axis of the spherical surface, and this ellipse will appear in the diagram as a straight line Ay tangent to the circle at A. The minor axis of the ellipse remains unchanged and equal to the diameter $2r$ of the circle, and moreover the center of the ellipse remains at the center C of the circle. But the most apparent change will be in the angular magnitudes which will be completely altered and distorted. For example, every straight line drawn through the center C really meets the circle ZZ (Fig. 89) normally, but in the distorted figure the axis of symmetry will be the only one of such lines which will be perpendicular to the straight line Ay which takes the place of the circular arc ZZ. Angles which in reality are equal will appear unequal, and *vice versa*. However—and after all this is the really essential matter—*the absolute dimensions of the abscissæ and the relative dimensions of the ordinates will not be changed at all;* and therefore lines which are really straight will appear as straight lines in the figure, and straight lines which are parallel will be shown as such. The abscissa of the point of intersection of a pair of straight lines in the drawing will be the true abscissa of this point.

In such a diagram, therefore, any ray, no matter what slope it may have nor how far it may be from the axis, is to be considered as a paraxial ray. The meridian section of the spherical reflecting or refracting surface *must* be represented in the figure by the straight line Ay (y-axis), and the position of the center C with respect to the vertex A will show whether the surface is convex or concave.

71. Extra-Axial Conjugate Points.—If we suppose that the axis of the spherical mirror is rotated about the center C through a small angle ACU, so that the vertex A moves along the mirror to a neighboring point U, the conjugate axial points M, M' will describe also small arcs MQ, M'Q' of concentric circles; and, evidently, the points Q, Q' will be

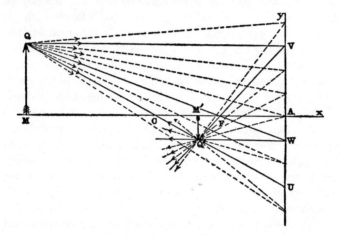

Fig. 100.—Concave mirror: Object is a small line MQ perpendicular to axis; its image M'Q' is real and inverted.

harmonically separated (§§ 67, 68) by the points C, U, so that $(CUQQ') = (CAMM') = -1$. Thus, we see how the point Q' is the image-point conjugate to the extra-axial object-point Q. In the diagram (Fig. 100) the circular arcs AU, MQ and M'Q' will appear as straight lines perpendicular to the axis, as explained in § 70. We derive, therefore, without difficulty the following conclusions:

(1) *The image, in a spherical mirror, of a plane object perpendicular to the axis is likewise a plane perpendicular to the axis; (2) A straight line passing through the center of the spherical mirror intersects a pair of such conjugate planes in a pair of conjugate points; and (3) To a homocentric bundle of incident paraxial rays proceeding from a point Q in a plane perpendicular to the axis of a spherical mirror there corre-*

sponds a homocentric bundle of reflected rays with its vertex Q′
lying in the conjugate image-plane.

In order to *construct the image-point* Q′ *of the extra-axial
object-point* Q, we have merely to find the point of intersection after reflection at the spherical mirror of any two

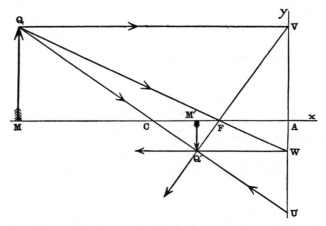

Fig. 101, *a.*—Lateral magnification and construction of image in
concave mirror.

rays emanating originally from Q. The diagrams (Fig. 101,
a and *b*), which are drawn according to the method explained
in § 70, exhibit this construction for the cases when the mirror
is concave and convex. Of the incident rays proceeding
from Q, it is convenient to select for this purpose two of the
following three, namely: the ray QC which proceeding towards the center C meets the spherical mirror normally at
U, whence it is reflected back along the same path; the ray
QV which proceeding parallel to the axis and meeting the
mirror in the point designated by V is reflected at V along
the straight line joining V with the focal point F; and the
ray QW which being directed towards the focal point F is
reflected at W in a direction parallel to the axis. The point
where these reflected rays intersect will be the image-

point Q'. Moreover, having located the position of Q', we can draw QM, Q'M' perpendicular to the axis at M, M', respectively; and then M'Q' will be the image of the small object-line MQ. In Fig. 101, a the image M'Q' is real and inverted, whereas in Fig. 101, b it is virtual and erect.

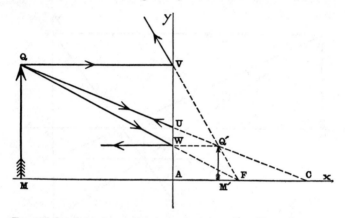

FIG. 101, b.—Lateral magnification and construction of image in convex mirror.

Whether the image is real or virtual and erect or inverted will depend both on the position of the object and on the form of the mirror.

If the object-point Q is supposed to move, say, from left to right along the straight line QV drawn parallel to the axis of the mirror, the corresponding image-point Q' will traverse the straight line VF continuously in the same direction. Thus, in the diagrams (Fig. 102, a & b) the numerals 1, 2, 3, etc., ranged in order from left to right along a straight line parallel to the axis of the mirror, show a number of successive positions of the object-point, while the primed numbers 1', 2', 3', etc., lying along the straight line VF, show the corresponding positions of the image-point. The straight lines 11', 22', 33', etc., all meet at the center C of the mirror.

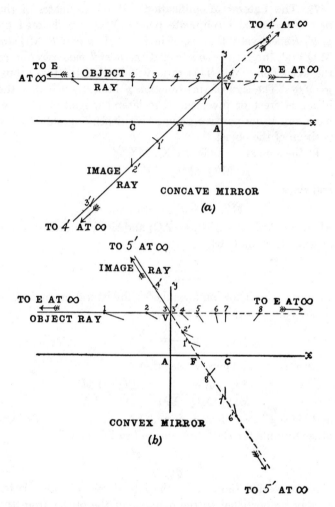

FIG. 102, *a* and *b*.—Imagery in (*a*) concave mirror, (*b*) convex mirror.

72. The Lateral Magnification.—If the ordinates of the pair of extra-axial conjugate points Q, Q' are denoted by y, y', respectively, that is, if in Fig. 101, a and b, MQ=y, M'Q'=y', the ratio y'/y is called the *lateral magnification* at the axial point M. This ratio will be denoted by y; thus, $y = y'/y$. The sign of this function y indicates whether the image is erect or inverted. The lateral magnification may have any value positive or negative depending only on the position of the object.

In the similar triangles MCQ, M'CQ'

$$M'Q' : MQ = M'C : MC;$$

and since

$$M'C = r - u', \qquad MC = r - u,$$

where $u = AM$, $u' = AM'$, $r = AC$; and since according to the abscissa-formula (§ 64)

$$\frac{r - u'}{r - u} = -\frac{u'}{u},$$

we derive the following formula for the lateral magnification in the case of a spherical mirror:

$$y = \frac{y'}{y} = -\frac{u'}{u}.$$

Also, from the figure we see that

$$\frac{M'Q'}{MQ} = \frac{AW}{MQ} = \frac{FA}{FM} = \frac{M'Q'}{AV} = \frac{FM'}{FA};$$

and since FM=x, FM'=x', and FA=f, we derive also another formula for the lateral magnification, as follows:

$$y = \frac{y'}{y} = \frac{f}{x} = \frac{x'}{f}.$$

This expression shows that the lateral magnification is inversely proportional to the distance of the object from the focal plane.

73. Field of View of a Spherical Mirror.—When the image of a luminous object is viewed in a spherical mirror, the axis of the mirror is determined by the straight line O'C

(Fig. 103, *a* and *b*) joining the center O′ of the pupil of the observer's eye with the center C of the mirror; and, on the assumption that the image is formed by the reflection of paraxial rays, the actual portion of the mirror that is utilized

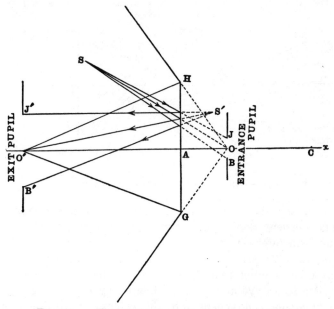

FIG. 103, *a*.—Field of view for eye in front of convex mirror.

consists of a small circular zone immediately surrounding the vertex A where the axis meets the reflecting surface. According to the method of drawing these diagrams which was described in § 70, the line-segment GH which is perpendicular to the axis at A and which is bisected at A will represent a meridian section of this zone in the plane of the figure, so that the points designated by G, H are opposite extremities of a diameter of the effective portion of the mirror.

All the reflected rays that enter the eye at O′ must necessarily lie within the conical region determined by revolving the isosceles triangle O′GH around the axis of the mirror.

The outermost rays that can possibly be reflected into the eye at O′ will be the rays that are reflected along the straight lines HO′ and GO′.   In order to see a real image in a concave mirror (Fig. 103, *b*), the eye must be placed in front of the

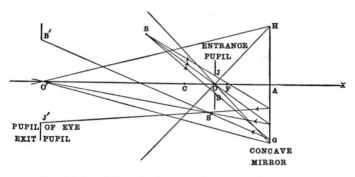

Fig. 103, *b*.—Field of view for eye in front of concave mirror.

mirror at a distance greater than the length of the radius. The incident rays corresponding to the extreme reflected rays will intersect in a point O which is conjugate to O′; and hence the *field of view* (§ 9) within which all object-points must lie in order that their images in the mirror may be visible to an eye at O′ will be limited by the surface of a right circular cone generated by the revolution of the isosceles triangle OHG around the axis of the mirror.   Thus, exactly as in the case of the corresponding problem in connection with the field of view of a plane mirror (§ 16), the contour of the effective portion of the spherical mirror acts also as a *field-stop* for the imagery produced by paraxial rays.

Through O′ draw B′J′ at right angles to the axis of the mirror, and mark the points B′, J′ at equal distances from O′ on opposite sides of the axis.   Then B′J′ may be supposed to represent the diameter in the plane of the diagram of the iris opening of the pupil of the observer's eye.   Construct by the method described in § 71, the object-line BJ whose image in the mirror is B′J′.   Evidently, any ray which after reflection enters the pupil of the eye between B' and J' must before reflection have passed, really or virtually, through the conjugate point on the straight line between B and J. In fact, the circle described around O as center in the transversal plane perpendicular to the axis at O with radius OB will act like a material stop to limit the apertures of the bundles of incident rays.   It is the so-called *entrance-pupil* of the system, while the pupil of the eye plays the part of the *exit-pupil* (see § 16).   Thus, for example, if S designates the position of a luminous point lying anywhere within the field of view, the eye at O' will see the image of S at S' by means of a bundle of rays which are drawn from S to all points of the entrance-pupil and which after reflection at the mirror are comprised within the cone which has its vertex at S' and the exit-pupil as base.   The entrance-pupil BJ is the aperture-stop of the system (§ 11).

74. Refraction of Paraxial Rays at a Spherical Surface.— In the accompanying diagrams Fig. 104, *a* and *b*, the straight line RB represents an incident ray meeting the spherical refracting surface ZZ at B, while the straight line BS shows

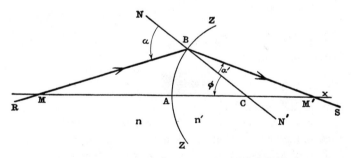

Fig. 104, *a*.—Convex spherical refracting surface ($n' > n$).

the path of the corresponding refracted ray.   If the position of the point M where the incident ray crosses the axis is given, the problem is to determine the position of the point M' where the refracted ray meets the axis.   The angles of incidence and refraction are $\angle NBR = \alpha$, $\angle N'BS = \alpha'$, and by the law of refraction:

$$n' . \sin\alpha' = n . \sin\alpha,$$

where n, n' denote the indices of refraction of the first and second media, respectively. In the triangles MBC, M'BC, we have:

$$CM : BM = \sin\alpha : \sin\phi, \qquad CM' : BM' = \sin\alpha' : \sin\phi,$$

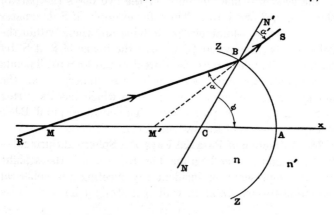

FIG. 104, b.—Concave spherical refracting surface $(n' > n)$.

where $\phi = \angle BCA$. Dividing one of these equations by the other, we obtain:

$$\frac{CM}{CM'} . \frac{BM}{BM'} = \frac{n'}{n} .$$

Now if the ray RB is a paraxial ray, the incidence-point B will be so near the vertex A of the spherical refracting surface that A may be written in place of B, according to the definition of a paraxial ray as given in § 63. Therefore, in the case of the refraction of paraxial rays at a spherical surface the four points C, A, M, M' on the axis are connected by the following relation:

$$\frac{CM}{CM'} . \frac{AM}{AM'} = \frac{n'}{n}$$

which may be written (§ 65):

$$(\text{CAMM}') = \frac{n'}{n};$$

that is, *the double ratio of the four axial points* C, A, M, M′ *is constant and equal to the relative index of refraction from the first medium to the second.*

Thus, for a given spherical surface (that is, for known positions of the points A and C), separating a pair of media of known relative index of refraction (n'/n), the point M′ on the axis corresponding to a given position of the axial point M has a perfectly definite position, entirely independent of the actual slope of the incident paraxial ray RB; whence it may be inferred that M′ is the image of M, so that *to a homocentric bundle of incident paraxial rays with its vertex lying on the axis of the spherical refracting surface there corresponds also a homocentric bundle of refracted rays with its vertex on the axis.*

In Fig. 104, *a* the image at M′ is real, whereas in Fig. 104, *b* it is virtual. Since the relative index of refraction is never less than zero, the value of the double ratio (CAMM′) in the case of refraction at a spherical surface is necessarily positive; consequently, the pair of conjugate points M, M′ is not "separated" (§ 65) by the pair of points A, C, as was found to be the case in reflection at a spherical mirror (§ 68). Thus, if M, M′ designate the positions of a pair of conjugate axial points with respect to a spherical refracting surface, it is always possible to pass from M to M′ along the axis one way or the other without going through either of the points A or C, although in order to do this it may sometimes be necessary to pass through the infinitely distant point of the axis (see § 65). Accordingly, depending only on the form of the surface and on whether n is greater or less than n', there will be found to be sixteen possible orders of arrangement of these four points, viz.:

A, C, M, M′; A, C, M′, M; A, M, M′, C; A, M′, M, C; M, A, C, M′; M′, A, C, M; M, M′, A, C; M′, M, A, C;

together with the eight other arrangements obtained by reversing the order of the letters in each of these combinations;
in other words, exactly the series of combinations that are
not possible in the case of a spherical mirror where the pair
of conjugate axial points M, M' is harmonically separated
by the pair of points A, C, so that $(CAMM') = -1$ (§ 68).
The student should draw a diagram similar to Fig. 104 for
each of the possible arrangements of the four points above
mentioned. Fig. 104, a shows the case M, A, C, M' and
Fig. 104, b shows the case M, M', C, A.

Moreover, if $(CAMM') = n'/n$, then also $(CAM'M) = n/n'$, as follows from the definition of the double ratio (§ 65).
Consequently, if a paraxial ray is refracted at a point B of
a spherical surface from medium n to medium n' along the
broken line RBS, a ray directed from S to B will be refracted
from medium n' to medium n in the direction BR; which is
in accordance with the general principle of the reversibility
of the light-path (§ 29). If therefore M' is the image of M
when the light is refracted across the spherical surface in a
given sense, then also M will be the image of M' when the
refraction takes place in the reverse sense.

**75. Reflection Considered as a Special Case of Refrac-
tion.**—It was implied above that if it were possible for the
ratio n'/n to have not only positive values but also the unique
negative value -1, the single formula $(CAMM') = n'/n$
would express the relation between a pair of conjugate axial
points M, M' both for a spherical refracting surface and
for a spherical mirror. The question naturally arises, therefore, Is there a general rule of this kind applicable also to
other problems in optics that are not necessarily concerned
with paraxial rays or particular conditions? Returning to
fundamental principles and recalling the laws of reflection
and refraction, we observe that while the angles of incidence
and refraction always have like signs, the angles of incidence
and reflection, on the contrary, have opposite signs. In
order, therefore, that the refraction-formula $n' . \sin\alpha' = n . \sin\alpha$

may include also the law of reflection as well, the values of n and n' in the latter case must be such that $a' = -a$ is a solution of the equation in question; and obviously this solution can be obtained only by putting

$$n' = -n, \text{ or } \frac{n'}{n} = -1.$$

Accordingly, the rule discovered above to be true in a special case is found to be entirely general, so that, at least from a purely mathematical point of view, the reflection of light may be regarded as a particular case of refraction back again into the medium of the incident light, provided we assign to this medium two equal and opposite values of the absolute index of refraction. The convenience of this artifice is apparent, since it makes it quite unnecessary to investigate separately and independently each special problem of reflection and refraction; for when in any given case the relation between an incident ray and the corresponding refracted ray has been ascertained, it will be necessary merely to impose the condition $n' = -n$ in order to derive immediately the analogous relation between the incident ray and the corresponding reflected ray. Thus, for example, any formula hereafter to be derived concerning the refraction of paraxial rays at a spherical surface may be converted into the corresponding formula for the case of a spherical mirror by putting $n' = -n$.

76. Construction of the Point M′ Conjugate to the Axial Point M.—In order to construct the point M′ conjugate to the axial point M with respect to a spherical refracting surface, we may proceed as follows:

Through the vertex A (Fig. 105, a, b, c and d) and the center C draw a pair of parallel straight lines (preferably but not necessarily) at right angles to the axis; and on the line going through C take two points O and O′ such that

$$\text{CO} : \text{CO}' = n' : n.$$

Join the given axial point M by a straight line with the point O, and let B designate the point where this straight line,

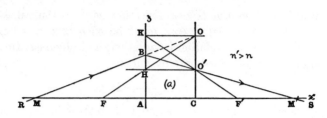

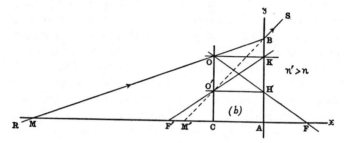

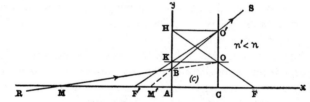

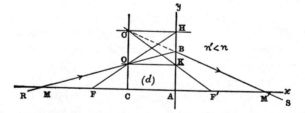

Fig. 105.—Spherical refracting surface: Construction of image-point M'
conjugate to axial object-point M; construction of focal points F, F'.
(a) Convex surface, $n' > n$; order MACM'.
(b) Concave surface, $n' > n$; order MM'CA.
(c) Convex surface, $n' < n$; order MM'AC.
(d) Concave surface, $n' < n$; order MCAM'.

produced if necessary, meets the line drawn through A parallel to CO; then the required point M′ will be at the place where the straight line BO′, produced if necessary, intersects the axis.

The straight line Ay drawn perpendicular to the axis at A will be tangent to the spherical surface at its vertex; and this line will represent the spherical surface in the diagram, since we are concerned here only with paraxial rays (§ 70). Thus, to the incident ray RB crossing the axis at M and incident on the surface at B, there will correspond the refracted ray BS crossing the axis at M′.

The proof of the construction consists in showing that the double ratio (CAMM′) is equal to $\dfrac{n'}{n}$, in accordance with the relation which, as we saw above (§ 74), connects the two conjugate points M, M′.

In the pair of similar triangles CMO, AMB,

$$CM : AM = CO : AB;$$

and in the pair of similar triangles CM′O′, AM′B,

$$AM' : CM' = AB : CO'.$$

Multiplying these two proportions, we obtain:

$$\frac{CM}{CM'} \cdot \frac{AM'}{AM} = \frac{CO}{CO'},$$

or

$$\frac{CM}{CM'} : \frac{AM}{AM'} = \frac{n'}{n},$$

and hence

$$(CAMM') = \frac{n'}{n}.$$

The diagrams illustrate four cases, viz., the cases when the points A, C, M, M′ are ranged along the axis from left to right in the orders MACM′, MM′CA, MM′AC and MCAM′. In the diagrams Fig. 105, a and b, the second medium is represented as more highly refracting than the first $(n'>n)$, whereas in the two other diagrams Fig. 105, c and d, the opposite case is shown $(n'<n)$; in a and c the surface is convex, and in b and d it is concave.

77. The Focal Points (F, F') of a Spherical Refracting Surface.—The object-point F which is conjugate to the infinitely distant image-point E and the image-point F' which is conjugate to the infinitely distant object-point E of the axis are the so-called *focal points* of the spherical refracting surface. A conical bundle of incident paraxial rays with its vertex at the *primary focal point* F will be converted into a cylindrical bundle of refracted rays all parallel to the axis and meeting therefore in the infinitely distant point E of the axis; and, similarly, a cylindrical bundle of paraxial rays proceeding from the infinitely distant point E of the axis will be transformed into a conical bundle of refracted rays with its vertex at the *secondary focal point* F'.

According to the method explained in § 76, the focal point F may be constructed by drawing the straight line O'H (Fig. 105, a, b, c and d) through O' parallel to the axis meeting the straight line AB in the point designated by H; and then the straight line OH will intersect the axis in the primary focal point F. Similarly, if the straight line OK is drawn through O parallel to the axis meeting AB in a point K, the point of intersection of the straight line KO' with the axis will determine the position of the secondary focal point F'. In brief, the diagonals of the parallelogram OO'HK meet the axis in the focal points F, F'. The spherical refracting surface is said to be *convergent* or *divergent* according as the focal point F' is real or virtual, respectively. Thus, in the diagrams Fig. 105, a and d, incident rays parallel to the axis are brought to a real focus at F', so that the surface is convergent for each of these cases; whereas in the diagrams Fig. 105, b and c, incident rays parallel to the axis are refracted as if they proceeded from a virtual focus at F'.

Moreover, certain characteristic metric relations may be derived immediately from the diagrams Fig. 105, a, b, c, and d.

For example, in the two pairs of similar triangles FAH, HO'O and F'CO', O'HK, we obtain the proportions:

$$\text{FA} : \text{HO}' = \text{AH} : \text{O}'\text{O}, \qquad \text{CF}' : \text{HO}' = \text{CO}' : \text{HK},$$

and since CO' = AH, HK = O'O, we find:

$$\text{FA} = \text{CF}';$$

and hence also:

$$\text{F}'\text{A} = \text{CF}.$$

Accordingly, concerning the positions of the focal points of a spherical refracting surface we have the following rule:

The focal points of a spherical refracting surface lie on the axis at such places that the step from one of them to the center is identical with the step from the vertex to the other focal point.

This statement should be verified for each of the diagrams. Not only will the center C be seen to be at the same distance from the primary focal point as the secondary focal point is from the vertex A, but the direction from F to C will always be the same as that from A to F'.

This relation may also be expressed in a different way; for, since

$$\text{FA} = \text{CF}' = \text{CA} + \text{AF}',$$

we have the following equation:

$$\text{FA} + \text{F}'\text{A} = \text{CA}; \text{ or } \text{AC} = \text{AF} + \text{AF}';$$

which may be put in words by saying that *the step from the vertex to the center of a spherical refracting surface is equal to the sum of the steps from the vertex to the two focal points.*

And, finally, since in the pair of similar triangles FAH, FCO, we have:

$$\text{FC} : \text{FA} = \text{CO} : \text{AH} = \text{CO} : \text{CO}' = n' : n,$$

and since FC = −CF = −F'A, we obtain also another useful and important relation, viz.:

$$\frac{\text{F}'\text{A}}{\text{F A}} = -\frac{n'}{n},$$

and, consequently: *The two focal points F, F' of a spherical refracting surface lie on opposite sides of the vertex A, and at distances from it which are in the ratio of n to n'.* If, therefore, we are given the positions of one of the two focal points,

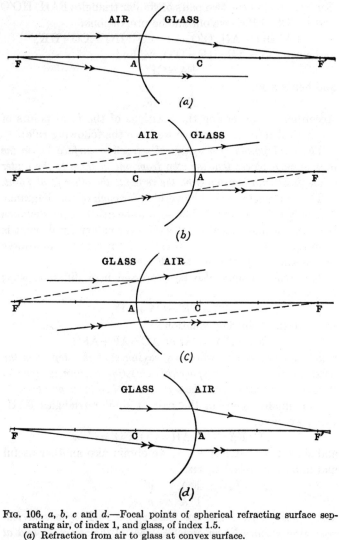

Fig. 106, a, b, c and d.—Focal points of spherical refracting surface separating air, of index 1, and glass, of index 1.5.
(a) Refraction from air to glass at convex surface.
(b)   "   "   "   " "   "   " concave   "
(c)   "   " glass to air " convex   "
(d)   "   "   "   " "   "   " concave   "

F or F', as well as the positions of the points A, C which determine the size and form of the spherical surface, we have
all the data necessary to enable us to locate the point M'
conjugate to a given axial object-point M.   For we can
locate the position of the other focal point and thus determine
the value of the ratio $n':n$.

Whether the secondary focal point will lie on one side or
the other of the spherical refracting surface, that is, whether
the surface will be convergent or divergent, will depend on
each of two things, viz.: (1) Whether the surface is convex
or concave, and (2) Whether n' is greater or less than n.   For
example, if the rays are refracted from air to glass ($n'/n =$
$3/2$), according to the above relations we find that $AF = 2\,CA$,
$AF' = 3\,AC$; so that starting at the vertex A and taking the
step CA twice we can locate the primary focal point F; and
returning to the vertex A and taking the step AC three
times, we arrive at the secondary focal point F'.   The diagrams Fig. 106, a and b, show the positions of the focal points
for refraction from air to glass for a convex surface and for
a concave surface.   In this case the convex surface is convergent and the concave surface is divergent.   On the other
hand, when the light is refracted from glass to air ($n'/n =$
$2/3$), we find $AF = 3\,AC$, $AF' = 2\,CA$ (Fig. 106, c and d), and
in this case the concave surface is convergent and the convex
surface is divergent.

In conclusion, it may be added that the constructions and
rules which have been given above for the case of a spherical
refracting surface are entirely applicable also to a *spherical
mirror*.   In fact, here we have an excellent illustration of
the method of treating reflection as a special case of refraction, which was explained in § 75.   For if we take $n' = -n$,
the two points O, O' (Fig. 107, a and b) will lie on a straight
line passing through the center C of the mirror at equal distances from C in opposite directions.   The point M' conjugate to the axial object-point M and the focal points F,
F' will be found precisely according to the directions for

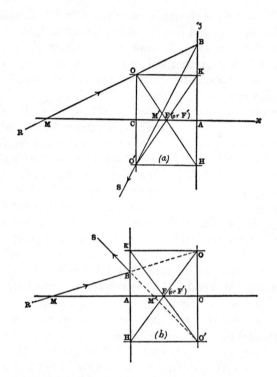

FIG. 107, *a* and *b*.—Reflection at spherical mirror: Construction of image-point M′ conjugate to axial object-
point M; construction of focal point.
(*a*) concave mirror, (*b*) convex mirror.

drawing the diagrams of Fig. 105. Obviously, the focal
points of a spherical mirror will coincide with each other
at a point midway between the vertex and center (§ 69).

**78. Abscissa-Equation referred to the Vertex of the
Spherical Refracting Surface as Origin.**—If the vertex A of
the spherical refracting surface is taken as the origin (§ 63)
from which distances or steps along the axis are reckoned,
and if the symbols *r*, *u* and *u′* are employed as in the case
of a spherical mirror (§ 64) to denote the abscissæ of the

center C and the pair of conjugate axial points M, M', that is, if $AC = r$, $AM = u$, $AM' = u'$, then

$$CM = CA + AM = u - r, \qquad CM' = CA + AM' = u' - r;$$

and since the formula $(CAMM') = \dfrac{n'}{n}$ may evidently be written as follows:

$$n' \cdot \frac{CM'}{AM'} = n \cdot \frac{CM}{AM},$$

we obtain:

$$n' \cdot \frac{u' - r}{u'} = n \cdot \frac{u - r}{u}.$$

Dividing both sides by r, we derive the so-called *invariant relation* in the case of refraction of paraxial rays at a spherical surface, in the following form:

$$n'\left(\frac{1}{r} - \frac{1}{u'}\right) = n\left(\frac{1}{r} - \frac{1}{u}\right).$$

Usually, however, this equation is written as follows:

$$\frac{n'}{u'} = \frac{n}{u} + \frac{n' - n}{r},$$

which is to be regarded as one of the fundamental formulæ of geometrical optics. If the two constants r and n'/n are known, the abscissa u' corresponding to any given value of u may easily be determined. Putting $n' = -n$ (§ 75), we obtain the abscissa-formula for reflection of paraxial rays at a spherical mirror (§ 64); and if we put $r = \infty$, we derive the formula $\dfrac{n'}{u'} = \dfrac{n}{u}$ for the refraction of paraxial rays at a plane surface (§ 41). It is because this linear equation connecting the abscissæ of a pair of conjugate axial points includes these other cases also that some writers have proposed that the formula above should be called the *characteristic equation of paraxial imagery*.

79. The Focal Lengths f, f' of a Spherical Refracting Surface.—*The steps from the focal points* F *and* F' *to the vertex*

A *are called the focal lengths of the spherical refracting surface;
the primary focal length, denoted by f, is the abscissa of* A *with
respect to* F (f=FA), *and the secondary focal length, denoted
by f', is the abscissa of* A *with respect to* F'(f'=F'A).

Since FA+F'A=CA (§ 77), and since CA=$-r$, the focal
lengths and the radius of the surface are connected by the
following relation:

$$f+f'+r=0,$$

and hence if two of these magnitudes are known, the value
of the third may always be determined from the fact that their
algebraic sum is equal to zero. For example, starting at any
point on the axis and taking in succession in any order the
three steps denoted by f, f' and r, one will find himself at
the end of the last step back again at the starting point.

Moreover, the focal lengths are connected with the indices
of refraction by the following relation (§ 77):

$$\frac{f'}{f}=-\frac{n'}{n} \text{ or } n.f'+n'.f=0;$$

and, hence, *the focal lengths of a spherical refracting surface
are opposite in sign and in the same numerical ratio as that of
the indices of refraction.* This formula, as we shall see (§ 122),
represents a general law of fundamental importance in geometrical optics.

Expressions for the focal lengths in terms of the radius
r and the relative index of refraction $(n' : n)$ may be derived
immediately from the pair of simultaneous equations above
by solving them for f and f'. The same expressions may
likewise be easily obtained by substituting in succession in
the abscissa-formula (§ 78) the two pairs of corresponding
values, viz., $u=-f$, $u'=\infty$ and $u=\infty$, $u'=-f'$. And,
finally, they may also be obtained geometrically from one of
the diagrams of Fig. 107 by observing that, since by construction CO : CO'=n': n, it follows that

$$CO': O'O=n: (n'-n), \qquad CO: O'O=n': (n'-n).$$

Now from the two pairs of similar triangles FAH, HO′O and F′AK, O′HK we obtain the two proportions:

$$FA:HO'=AH:O'O, \qquad F'A:O'H=AK:HK;$$

and since

$$FA=f, \ HO'=AC=r, \ AH=CO', \ F'A=f', \ AK=CO, \text{ and}$$
$$HK=O'O,$$

we have, finally:

$$f=\frac{n}{n'-n}\cdot r, \quad f'=-\frac{n'}{n'-n}\cdot r;$$

which are exceedingly useful forms of the expressions for the focal lengths.

Since

$$\frac{n}{f}=\frac{n'-n}{r}=-\frac{n'}{f'},$$

the abscissa-relation connecting u and u' may be expressed in terms of one of the focal lengths instead of in terms of the radius r, for example, in terms of the focal length f, as follows:

$$\frac{n'}{u'}=\frac{n}{u}+\frac{n}{f}.$$

80. Extra-Axial Conjugate Points; Conjugate Planes of a Spherical Refracting Surface.—If the axis AC of a spherical refracting surface is revolved in a meridian plane through a very small angle about an axis perpendicular to this plane at the center C, so that the vertex of the surface is displaced a little to one side of its former position A to a point U on the surface, the pair of conjugate points M, M′ will likewise undergo slight displacements into the new positions Q, Q′; and, evidently, the same relation will connect the four points C, U, Q, Q′ on the central line UC as exists between the four points C, A, M, M′ on the axis AC, and accordingly (§ 76) we may write:

$$(CUQQ')=\frac{n'}{n};$$

and hence it is obvious that the points Q, Q′ are a pair of extra-axial conjugate points with respect to the spherical refracting surface. Thus, if the points belonging to an object are all congregated in the immediate vicinity of the axis on an element of a spherical surface which is concentric with the refracting sphere, the corresponding image-points will all be assembled on an element of another concentric spherical surface, and any straight line going through C will determine by its intersections with this pair of concentric surfaces two conjugate points Q, Q′. In order that the rays concerned may all be incident near the vertex A, it is necessary to assume that ∠ UCA is very small, which means that the little elements of the surfaces described around C may in fact be regarded as plane surfaces perpendicular to the axis AC. Accordingly, the imagery produced by the refraction of paraxial rays at a spherical surface may be described by the following statements:

(1) *The image of a plane object perpendicular to the axis of a spherical refracting surface is similar to the object, and will lie likewise in a plane perpendicular to the axis;* (2) *A straight line drawn through the center C will intersect a pair of conjugate planes in a pair of conjugate points Q, Q′;* and (3) *Incident rays which interesct in Q will be transformed into refracted rays which intersect in Q′.*

Diagrams showing the refraction of paraxial rays at a spherical surface should be drawn therefore according to the plan explained in § 70, as has been already stated. The spherical refracting surface *must* be represented in the figure by the plane tangent to the surface at its vertex A, whose trace in the meridian plane of the drawing is the straight line Ay which is taken as the y-axis of the system of rectangular coördinates whose origin is at A (§ 63).

81. Construction of the Point Q′ which with Respect to a Spherical Refracting Surface is Conjugate to the Extra-axial Point Q.—The point Q′ conjugate to the extra-axial point Q is easily constructed. Having first located the focal points F, F′ (§ 77), we draw through Q (Figs. 108 and 109) a straight line parallel to the x-axis meeting the y-axis in the point designated by V; then the point of intersection of the

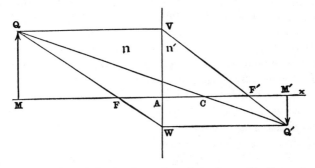

Fig. 108.—Spherical refracting surface: Lateral magnification and construction of image. Convex surface, $n' > n$.

straight lines VF′ and QC will be the required point Q′. A third line may also be drawn through Q, viz., the straight line QF meeting the y-axis in the point marked W; and if a

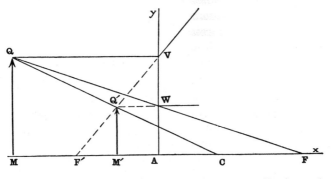

Fig. 109.—Spherical refracting surface: Lateral magnification and construction of image. Convex surface, $n' < n$.

straight line is drawn through W parallel to the x-axis, it will likewise pass through Q′.

If M, M′ designate the feet of the perpendiculars let fall

from Q, Q' respectively, on the x-axis, then M'Q' will be the image of the small object-line MQ. In both Fig. 108 and Fig. 109 the refracting surface is convex to the incident light. In Fig. 108 ($n' > n$) the image is real and inverted, whereas in Fig. 109 ($n' < n$) the image is virtual and erect.

If the object-point Q coincides with the point marked V, the image-point Q' will also be at V, and image and object will be congruent. The pair of conjugate planes of an optical system for which this is the case are called the *principal planes* (see § 119); and hence *the principal planes of a spherical refracting surface coincide with each other and are identical with the tangent-plane at the vertex.*

82. Lateral Magnification for case of Spherical Refracting Surface.—The ratio M'Q' : MQ (Figs. 108 and 109) is the so-called *lateral magnification* of the spherical refracting surface with respect to the pair of conjugate axial points M, M'. Since

$$M'Q' : MQ = CM' : CM,$$

and since (§ 74)

$$\frac{CM'}{CM} = \frac{n}{n'} \cdot \frac{AM'}{AM},$$

we find:

$$\frac{M'Q'}{MQ} = \frac{n}{n'} \cdot \frac{AM'}{AM}.$$

If y, y' denote the heights of object and image, that is, if $y = MQ$, $y' = M'Q'$, and if we put the lateral magnification equal to $\boldsymbol{y}$, as in § 72, then, evidently:

$$\boldsymbol{y} = \frac{y'}{y} = \frac{n}{n'} \cdot \frac{u'}{u},$$

where $u = AM$, $u' = AM'$. The lateral magnification depends, therefore, on the position of the object, and the image is erect or inverted according as this ratio is positive or negative.

83. The Focal Planes of a Spherical Refracting Surface.
—The focal planes are the pair of planes which are perpendicular to the axis at the focal points F, F'. "The infinitely
distant plane of space," which, according to the notions of
the modern geometry, is to be regarded as the locus of the
infinitely distant points (§ 65) of space, is the image-plane
conjugate to the *primary focal plane*, which is the plane
perpendicular to the axis at F. On the other hand, regarded as belonging to the object-space, the infinitely distant plane is imaged by the *secondary focal plane* perpendicular to the axis at F'.

The rays proceeding from an infinitely distant object-point
I (Fig. 110) constitute a cylindrical bundle of parallel in-

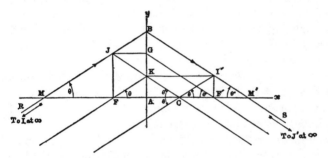

Fig. 110.—Focal planes and focal lengths of spherical refracting surface.

cident rays. Since I lies in the infinitely distant plane of
space, its image I' will be formed in the secondary focal
plane, and the position of I' in this plane may be located by
drawing through the center C of the spherical refracting
surface a straight line parallel to the system of parallel
rays which meet in the infinitely distant point I. Thus, for
example, the image of a star which may be regarded as a
point infinitely far away will be formed in the secondary
focal plane; and if the apparent place of the star in the firma-
ment is in the direction CI, the star's image will be at the

point I′ where the straight line CI meets the secondary focal plane.

Similarly, if J designates the position of an object-point lying in the primary focal plane, its image J′ will be the infinitely distant point of the straight line JC. Thus, *to a homocentric bundle of incident paraxial rays with its vertex in the primary focal plane, there corresponds a cylindrical bundle of refracted rays; and to a cylindrical bundle of incident paraxial rays there corresponds a homocentric bundle of refracted rays with its vertex in the secondary focal plane.*

The directions of the infinitely distant points I and J′ are given by assigning the values of the slope-angles

$$\theta = \angle \text{FCI} = \angle \text{F'CI'}, \qquad \theta' = \angle \text{FCJ} = \angle \text{F'CJ'};$$

and the points I′ and J conjugate to them will lie in the secondary and primary focal planes on straight lines passing through the center C and inclined to the axis at the angles θ and θ', respectively. The angle θ, which is the measure of the angular distance from the axis of the infinitely distant object-point I, determines the *apparent size* of an object in the infinitely distant plane of the object-space; and, similarly, the angle θ' is the measure of the apparent size of the infinitely distant image of the object FJ.

Draw the straight lines JG and I′K paralled to the optical axis and meeting the y-axis in the points designated by G and K, respectively; then the straight lines FK and CI′ will be parallel to each other, and the same will be true with respect to the straight lines GF′ and JC. Hence, $\angle \text{AFK} = \theta$, $\angle \text{AF'G} = \theta'$; and since $\text{AK} = \text{F'I'}$ and $\text{AG} = \text{FJ}$, we find:

$$\frac{\text{F'I'}}{\text{FA}} = \tan \theta, \quad \frac{\text{FJ}}{\text{F'A}} = \tan \theta'.$$

Putting $\text{FA} = f$ and $\text{F'A} = f'$ (§ 79), we obtain the following expressions for the focal lengths:

$$f = \frac{\text{F'I'}}{\tan \theta}, \quad f' = \frac{\text{FJ}}{\tan \theta'};$$

and since the tangents of the small angles θ, θ' are indistinguishable from the angles themselves (see § 63), we obtain new definitions of the focal lengths, as follows:

The primary focal length is the ratio of the height of the image, in the secondary focal plane, of an infinitely distant object to the apparent size of the object; and the secondary focal length is the ratio of the height of an object in the primary focal plane to the apparent size of the infinitely distant image.

The ratio of the apparent size of the infinitely distant image to the height of an object in the primary focal plane is a measure of the *magnifying power* of the optical system (see § 158), and in this sense we may say that *the magnifying power of a spherical refracting surface is equal to the reciprocal of the secondary focal length.*

84. Construction of Paraxial Ray Refracted at a Spherical Surface.—The refracted ray corresponding to a paraxial ray IB (Fig. 110) incident on a spherical refracting surface at the point B may easily be constructed, for example, in one of the following ways:

(*a*) Through the primary focal point draw the straight line FK parallel to IB meeting the *y*-axis in the point K; and through K draw a straight line parallel to the *x*-axis meeting the secondary focal plane in the point I'; the path of the refracted ray will lie along the straight line BI'.

(*b*) Through the center C draw a straight line CI' parallel to the given incident ray meeting the secondary focal plane in the point I'; the path of the corresponding refracted ray will be along the straight line BI'.

(*c*) Let J designate the point where the given incident ray crosses the primary focal plane, and draw the straight line JG parallel to the *x*-axis meeting the *y*-axis in the point designated by G; then the path of the required refracted ray will lie along the straight line BI' drawn through the incidence-point B parallel to the straight line GF', where F' designates the position of the secondary focal point.

(d) Finally, the required refracted ray will be along the straight line BI′ drawn parallel to the straight line JC.

85. The Image-Equations in the case of Refraction of Paraxial Rays at a Spherical Surface.—The rectangular coördinates of the image-point Q′ may easily be expressed in terms of the coördinates of the object-point Q. But the forms of these expressions will depend partly on the particular pair of constants $(n'/n, r$ and $f, f')$ which define the surface and partly on the system of axes to which the coördinates are referred. The axis of the spherical surface will always represent the axis of abscissæ (x-axis), and the y-axis will be at right angles to it; but the origin may be taken at any place along the x-axis. If the vertex A is taken as the origin (§ 63), the coördinates of Q, Q′ will be (u, y) and (u', y'); that is, $u=$AM, $u'=$AM′, $y=$MQ, $y'=$M′Q′; and since (§§ 78 and 82)

$$\frac{n'}{u'}=\frac{n}{u}+\frac{n'-n}{r}, \qquad \frac{y'}{y}=\frac{n\,u'}{n'u},$$

we obtain by solving for u' and y';

$$u'=\frac{n'ru}{(n'-n)\,u+nr}, \qquad y'=\frac{nry}{(n'-n)\,u+nr}.$$

In terms of the same coördinates, but with a different pair of constants, viz., f, f', instead of $n': n, r$, the image-equations may be put also in other forms, as follows:

It will be recalled that in § 79 the abscissa-formula was written:

$$\frac{n'}{u'}=\frac{n}{u}+\frac{n}{f},$$

and since (§ 79) $n'/n=-f'/f$, n and n' may be eliminated and the image-equations will become:

$$\frac{f}{u}+\frac{f'}{u'}+1=0, \quad \frac{y'}{y}=\frac{f}{f+u}=\frac{f'+u'}{f'}=-\frac{fu'}{f'u};$$

which are also frequently employed. These formulæ may also be easily derived from the geometrical relations in Figs. 108 and 109, since we have the proportions:

FM : AM = VA : VW = AF′ : AM′.

Instead of a single system of rectangular coördinates, we may have two systems, one for the object-space and the other for the image-space. For example, if the focal points F, F' are selected as the origins of two such systems, and if the abscissæ of the pair of conjugate axial points M, M' are denoted by x, x', that is, if $x = FM$, $x' = F'M'$, then, since

$$u = AM = AF + FM = x - f, \qquad u' = AM' = AF' + F'M' = x' - f',$$

the abscissæ, u, u' may be eliminated from the equations above, and the image-equations will be obtained finally in their simplest forms, as follows:

$$\frac{y'}{y} = \frac{f}{x} = \frac{x'}{f'}.$$

These relations may be derived directly from the two pairs of similar triangles FMQ, FAW and F'M'Q', F'AV in Figs. 108 and 109. The abscissa-relation

$$x \cdot x' = f \cdot f'$$

is the so-called *Newtonian formula* (see § 69). If the x's are plotted as abscissæ and the x''s as ordinates, this equation will represent a rectangular hyperbola.

86. The so-called Smith-Helmholtz Formula.—In Fig. 111 if $M'Q' = y'$ represents the image in a spherical refracting

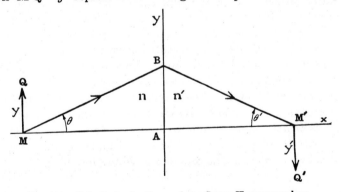

Fig. 111.—Spherical refracting surface: **Smith-Helmholtz** law.

surface Ay of a small object-line $MQ = y$ perpendicular to the axis at M, and if B designates the incidence-point of a paraxial ray which crosses the axis before and after refraction at M and M', respectively, then in the triangle MBM'

$$\sin \theta : \sin \theta' = BM' : BM,$$

where $\theta = \angle AMB$, $\theta' = \angle AM'B$ denote the slopes of the incident ray MB and the corresponding refracted ray BM'. Since the ray is paraxial, we may put $\theta = \sin \theta$, $\theta' = \sin \theta'$ and also $BM = AM = u$, $BM' = AM' = u'$ (§ 63). Hence,

$$\frac{\theta}{\theta'} = \frac{u'}{u}, \quad \text{or} \quad u' \cdot \theta' = u \cdot \theta.$$

But (§ 82)

$$\frac{n' \cdot y'}{u'} = \frac{n \cdot y}{u};$$

and, therefore, by multiplying these two equations so as to eliminate u and u', we obtain the important invariant-relation in the case of refraction of paraxial rays at a spherical surface, viz.:

$$n' \cdot y' \cdot \theta' = n \cdot y \cdot \theta.$$

This formula states that the function obtained by the continued product of the three factors n, y, θ has the same value after refraction at a spherical surface as it had before refraction. It is a special case of a general law which is found to apply to a centered system of spherical refracting surfaces (§ 118) and which is usually known as LAGRANGE's law; but undoubtedly ROBERT SMITH who announced the law for the case of a system of thin lenses as early as 1738 is entitled to the credit of it. The importance of the relation was recognized by HELMHOLTZ(1821–1894), and the form in which it is written above is due to him. On the whole it seems proper to adopt the suggestion of P. CULMANN and to refer to this equation as the SMITH-HELMHOLTZ formula.

PROBLEMS

1. If A designates the vertex and C the center of a spherical mirror, and if M, M′ designate the points where a paraxial ray crosses the straight line AC before and after reflection, respectively, show that

$$\frac{1}{u}+\frac{1}{u'}=\frac{2}{r},$$

where $r=$ AC, $u=$ AM, $u'=$ AM′.

2. The radius of a concave mirror is 30 cm. Paraxial rays proceed from a point 60 cm. in front of it; find where they are focused after reflection.

Ans. At a point 20 cm. in front of the mirror.

3. The radius of a concave mirror is 60 cm. A luminous point is placed in front of the mirror at a distance of (a) 120 cm., (b) 60 cm., (c) 30 cm., and (d) 20 cm. Find the position of the image-point for each of these positions of the object.

Ans. (a) 40 cm. in front of mirror; (b) 60 cm. in front of mirror; (c) at infinity; and (d) 60 cm. behind mirror.

4. A candle is placed in front of a concave spherical mirror, whose radius is 1 foot, at a distance of 5 inches from the mirror. Where will the image be formed?

Ans. 30 inches behind the mirror.

5. An object is 24 inches in front of a concave mirror of radius 1 foot; where will its image be formed? If the object is displaced through a small distance z, through what distance will the image move?

Ans. Image is 8 inches in front of mirror; distance through which image moves will be $2z/(z-18)$.

6. An object is placed 1 foot from a concave mirror of radius 4 feet. If the object is moved 1 inch nearer the mirror, what will be the corresponding displacement of the image?

Ans. The image moves 3.7 inches nearer the mirror.

7. An object-point is 10 cm. in front of a convex mirror of radius 60 cm. Find the position of the image-point.

Ans. 7.5 cm. behind the mirror.

8. Given the positions on the axis of a spherical mirror of the vertex A, the center C and an object-point M; show how to construct the position of the image-point M'. There are eight possible arrangements of these four points; draw a diagram for each one of them.

9. If x, x' denote the abscissæ, with respect to the focal point F as origin, of a pair of conjugate points on the axis of a spherical mirror, show that

$$x . x' = f^2,$$

where f denotes the focal length of the mirror. How are object and image situated with respect to the focal plane?

10. An object is placed at a distance of 60 cm. in front of a spherical mirror, and the image is found to be on the same side of the mirror at a distance of 20 cm. What is the focal length of the mirror, and is it concave or convex?

Ans. Concave mirror of focal length 15 cm.

11. How far from a concave mirror of focal length 18 inches must an object be placed in order that the image shall be magnified three times?

Ans. 1 ft. or 2 ft. from the mirror, according as image is erect or inverted.

12. A candle-flame one inch high is 18 inches in front of a concave mirror of focal length 15 inches. Find the position and size of the image.

Ans. The image will be real and inverted, 90 inches from the mirror, and 5 inches long.

13. A small object is placed at right angles to the axis of a spherical mirror; show how to construct the image, and derive the magnification-formula:

$$\frac{y'}{y} = -\frac{u'}{u}.$$

14. A luminous point moves from left to right along a straight line parallel to the axis of a spherical mirror. Show by diagrams for both concave and convex mirrors how the conjugate image-point moves.

15. The center of a spherical mirror is at C, and the

straight line QQ′ joining a pair of conjugate points meets the mirror in a point U. If P designates the position of a point which is not on the straight line QQ′, and if a straight line is drawn cutting the straight lines PU, PQ, PC and PQ′ in the points V, R, Z and R′, respectively; show that R, R′ are a pair of conjugate points with respect to another spherical mirror whose center is at Z and whose radius is equal to VZ.

16. Show by geometrical construction that the focal point of a spherical mirror lies midway between the center and the vertex.

17. An object is placed 5 inches from a spherical mirror of focal length 6 inches. Assuming that the object is real, where will the image be formed, and what will be the magnification? Draw diagrams for both convex and concave mirrors.

Ans. For concave mirror, image is 30 in. behind the mirror, magnification $= +6$; for convex mirror, image is $2\frac{8}{11}$ inches behind the mirror, magnification $= +\frac{6}{11}$.

18. How far from a concave mirror must a real object be placed in order that the image shall be (a) real and four times the size of the object, (b) virtual and four times the size of the object, and (c) real and one-fourth the size of the object? Draw diagrams showing the construction for each of these three cases.

Ans. Distance of mirror from the object is equal to (a) $5f/4$, (b) $3f/4$, and (c) $5f$, where f denotes the focal length.

19. What kind of image is produced in a concave mirror by a virtual object? Illustrate and explain by means of a diagram.

Ans. Image is real and erect and smaller than object.

20. Determine the position and magnification of the image of a virtual object lying midway between the vertex and focal point of a convex mirror. Draw diagram showing construction.

Ans. The vertex of the mirror will be midway between the

axial point of the image and the focal point of the mirror, and
the image will be real and erect and twice as large as object.

21. Show that when an object is placed midway between
the focal point and the vertex of a concave mirror the image
will be virtual and erect and twice as large as the object.

22. An object 3 inches high is placed 10 inches in front of
a convex mirror of 30 inches focal length. Find the position
and size of the image.

Ans. Virtual image 7.5 inches from the mirror and $2\frac{1}{4}$
inches high.

23. An object is placed in front of a concave mirror at a
distance of one foot. If the image is real and three times as
large as the object, what is the focal length of the mirror?

Ans. 9 inches.

24. The radius of a concave mirror is 23 cm. An object,
2 cm. high, is placed in front of the mirror at a distance of
one. meter. Find the position and size of the image.

Ans. A real image, 0.26 cm. high, 13 cm. from the mirror.

25. Find the position and size of the image of a disk 3
inches in diameter placed at right angles to the axis of a
spherical mirror of radius 6 feet, when the distance from the
object to the mirror is (a) 1 ft., (b) 3 ft., and (c) 9 ft.

Ans. For a concave mirror: (a) Virtual image, 4.5 inches
in diameter, 18 inches from mirror; (b) Image at infinity;
(c) Real inverted image, 1.5 inches in diameter, 4.5 feet from
the mirror.

26. Assuming that the apparent diameter of the sun is
30′, calculate the approximate diameter of the sun's image
in a concave mirror of focal length 1 foot.

Ans. A little more than one-tenth of an inch.

27. A gas-flame is 8 ft. from a wall, and it is required to
throw on the wall a real image of the flame which shall be magnified three times. Determine the position and focal length
of a concave mirror which would give the required image.

Ans. The mirror must have a focal length of 3 ft. and must
be placed at a distance of 4 ft. from the object.

28. It is desired to throw on a wall an image of an object magnified 12 times, the distance of the object from the wall being 11 feet. Find the focal length of a concave mirror which will do this, and state where it must be placed.

Ans. The focal length of the mirror must be $\frac{12}{13}$ ft., and it must be placed 1 ft. from the object.

29. Assuming that the eye is placed on the axis of a spherical mirror, and that the rays are paraxial, explain how the field of view is determined. Draw accurate diagrams for concave and convex mirrors.

30. A man holds, halfway between his eye and a convex mirror 3 feet from his eye, two fine parallel wires, so that they are seen directly and also by reflection in the mirror. Show that if the apparent distance between the wires as seen directly is 5 times that as seen by reflection, the radius of the mirror is 3 feet.

31. A scale etched on a thin sheet of transparent glass is placed between the eye of an observer and a convex mirror of focal length one foot. When the distance between the eye and the scale is three feet, one of the scale divisions appears to cover three divisions of the image in the mirror. Find the position of the mirror.

Ans. The mirror is one foot from the scale.

32. A scale etched on a thin sheet of transparent glass is interposed between the eye of an observer and a convex mirror of focal length f. When the distance of the scale from the eye is b feet, one division of the scale appears to cover m divisions of its image in the mirror. If now the scale is displaced through a distance c in the direction of the axis of the mirror, it is found that one division of the scale appears to cover k divisions in the mirror. Find an expression for f in terms of m, k, b and c.

Ans.

$$f = -\frac{(k-m)\ (b-c)\ bc}{\{b(k-m)-(k-1)c\}\ \{b(k-m)-(k+1)c\}}$$

33. A concave and a convex mirror, each of radius 20 cm., are placed opposite to each other and 40 cm. apart on the same axis. An object 3 cm. high is placed midway between them. Find the position and size of the image formed by reflection, first, at the convex, and then at the concave mirror. Draw accurate diagram, and trace the path of a ray from a point in the object to the corresponding point in the image.

Ans. The image is $12\frac{8}{11}$ cm. from the concave mirror, real and inverted, and $1\frac{3}{11}$ cm. high.

34. Same problem as No. 33, except that in this case the image is formed by rays which have been reflected first from the concave mirror and then from the convex mirror.

Ans. The image is $6\frac{2}{3}$ cm. behind the convex mirror, virtual and inverted, and 1 cm. high.

35. Two concave mirrors, of focal lengths 20 and 40 cm., are turned towards each other, the distance between their vertices being one meter. An object 1 cm. high is placed between the mirrors at a distance of 10 cm. from the mirror whose focal length is 20 cm. Find the position and size of the image produced by rays which are reflected first from the nearer mirror and then from the farther mirror.

Ans. A real inverted image, 1 cm. long, at a distance of 60 cm. from the mirror that is farther from the object.

36. The distance between the vertices A_1 and A_2 of two spherical mirrors which face each other is denoted by d, that is, $d = A_2A_1$. The focal points of the mirrors are at F_1 and F_2, and the focal lengths are $f_1 = F_1A_1$ and $f_2 = F_2A_2$. An object is placed between the mirrors at a distance u_1 from A_1. Rays proceeding from the object are reflected, first, from the mirror A_1 and then from the mirror A_2; show that the distance of the final image from the mirror A_2 is

$$\frac{\{f_1.u_1 - (f_1+u_1)\ d\}\ f_2}{(f_1+u_1)\ (f_2+d) - f_1.u_1},$$

and that the magnification is

$$\frac{f_1.f_2}{(f_1+u_1)\ (f_2+d) - f_1.u_1}.$$

37. If the rays fall first on the mirror A_2 and then on A_1, these letters having exactly the same meanings as in No. 36, then the distance of the image from mirror A_1 will be

$$\frac{f_1\{(f_2+d)\ (u_1+d)+f_2d\}}{(f_1-d)\ f_2+(u_1+d)\ (f_1-f_2-d)};$$

and the magnification will be

$$\frac{f_1 \cdot f_2}{(f_1-d)\ f_2+(u_1+d)\ (f_1-f_2-d)}.$$

38. If the mirror A_1 in Nos. 36 and 37 is a plane mirror, show that when the light is reflected from the plane mirror first the distance of the image from the curved mirror is

$$\frac{(u_1-d)\ f_2}{f_2+d-u_1},$$

and that the magnification is

$$\frac{f_2}{f_2+d-u_1};$$

and that when the light is reflected from the curved mirror first, the distance of the image from the plane mirror is

$$\frac{(f_2+d)\ (u_1+d)+f_2d}{f_2+u_1+d},$$

and that the magnification is

$$\frac{f_2}{f_2+u_1+d}.$$

If both the mirrors are plane, the magnification will be unity, and the image after two reflections, first at A_1 and then at A_2, will be formed at a distance of (u_1-d) from A_2; whereas if the light falls first on mirror A_2, the distance of the image from the other mirror will be (u_1+2d).

39. If M, M' are a pair of conjugate points on the axis of a spherical refracting surface which divides two media of indices n and n', show that

$$(\text{CAMM}') = \frac{n'}{n},$$

where A and C designate the vertex and the center of the spherical surface.

40. Show how to construct the position of the point M'

conjugate to a given point M on the axis of a spherical refracting surface; and draw diagrams for all the possible arrangements of the four points A, C, M, M'. Prove the construction, and derive the formula $n'/u' = n/u + (n'-n)/r$, where n, n' denote the indices of refraction, and $u = $ AM, $u' = $ AM', $r = $ AC.

41. Show how the formula in No. 40 includes as special cases the case of refraction of paraxial rays at a plane surface and the case of reflection at a spherical mirror.

42. From the formula in No. 40 derive expressions for the focal lengths f, f' of a spherical refracting surface, and show that

$$f + f' + r = 0, \qquad nf' + n'f = 0.$$

43. Does the construction found in No. 40 apply to the case of a spherical mirror? Explain with diagrams.

44. Apply the construction employed in No. 40 to determine the positions of the focal points F, F' of a spherical refracting surface, and show that

$$\text{FA} = \text{CF}', \qquad \text{F}'\text{A} = \text{CF}, \qquad \text{F}'\text{A} : \text{FA} = -n' : n.$$

45. Where are the focal points of a plane refracting surface? Explain clearly.

46. Explain how the results of No. 44 are applicable to a spherical mirror.

47. Air and glass are separated by a spherical refracting surface of radius $r = $ AC. Find the positions of the focal points F, F' for the cases when the refraction is from air to glass and from glass to air and when the surface is convex and concave; illustrating your answers by four accurately drawn diagrams. (Take indices of refraction of air and glass equal to 1 and 1.5, respectively.)

48. From the figures used in No. 44 for constructing the positions of the focal points F, F', derive the formulæ for the focal lengths which were obtained in No. 42.

49. Light falling on a concave surface separating water $(n = 1.33)$ from glass $(n' = 1.55)$ is convergent towards a point 10 cm. beyond the vertex. The radius of the surface

is 20 cm. Find the point where the refracted rays cross the axis.

Ans. 12.7 cm. beyond the vertex of the sphere in the glass medium.

50. Light is refracted from air to glass $(n': n=3: 2)$ at a spherical surface. If the vertex of the bundle of incident rays is in the glass and 20 cm. from the vertex of the refracting surface, and if the refracted rays are converged to a point in the glass and 5 cm. from the vertex, determine the form and size of the surface.

Ans. Convex surface of radius 2 cm.

51. A small air-bubble in a glass sphere, 4 inches in diameter, viewed so that the speck and the center of the sphere are in line with the eye, appears to be one inch from the point of the surface nearest the eye. What is its actual distance, assuming that the index of refraction of glass is 1.5?

Ans. 1.2 inches.

52. The radius of a concave refracting surface is 20 cm. A virtual image of a real object is formed at a distance of 40 cm. from the vertex, and the distance from the object to the image is 60 cm. The first medium is air $(n=1)$. Find the index of refraction of the second medium.

Ans. $n'=1.6$.

53. Light diverging from a point M in air is converged by a spherical refracting surface to a point M′ in glass of index 1.5. The distance $MM'=18$ cm., and the point M is twice as far from the surface as the point M′. Find the radius of the surface.   Ans. 1.5 cm.

54. Find the positions of the focal points F, F′ of a concave spherical refracting surface separating air from a medium of index 1.6, having found that the image of a luminous point 30 cm. in front of the surface is midway between the luminous point and the surface.

Ans. AF = + 13.64 cm.;   AF′ = −21.82 cm.

55. A convergent bundle of rays is incident on a spherical refracting surface of radius 10 cm. The relative index of

refraction from the first medium to the second medium is equal to 2 (n': $n=2$:1). If the incident rays cross the axis at M and the refracted rays at M', and if M'M$=+60$ cm., determine the positions of the points M, M'.

Ans. If the surface is convex, AM$=+77.72$ cm., AM' $=+17.72$ cm. If the surface is concave, then either AM$=$ $+30$ cm., AM'$=-30$ cm. or AM$=+20$ cm., AM'$=-40$ cm.

56. A beam of parallel rays passing through water ($n=$ 1.3) is refracted at a concave surface into glass ($n'=1.5$). If the radius of the surface is 20 cm., where will the light be focused?   Ans. Virtual focus, 150 cm. from the surface.

57. A small air-bubble is imbedded in a glass sphere at a distance of 5.98 cm. from the nearest point of the surface. What will be the apparent depth of the bubble, viewed from this side of the sphere, if the radius of the sphere is 7.03 cm., and the index of refraction from air to glass is 1.42?

Ans. 5.63 cm.

58. Assuming that the cornea of the eye is a spherical refracting surface of radius 8 mm. separating the outside air from the aqueous humor (of index $\frac{4}{3}$), find the distance of the pupil of the eye from the vertex of the cornea, if its apparent distance is found to be 3.04 mm. Also, if the apparent diameter of the pupil is 4.5 mm., what is its real diameter?   Ans. 3.6 mm.; 4 mm.

59. Construct the image M'Q' of a small object MQ perpendicular at M to the axis of a spherical refracting surface, and derive the magnification-formula in terms of the distances of M and M' from the vertex of the surface. Draw two diagrams, one for convex, and one for concave surface.

60. Derive the image-equations of a spherical refracting surface referred to the focal points as origins.

61. Derive the image equations of a spherical refracting surface in the forms
$$f/u+f'/u'+1=0, \qquad y'/y=f/(f+u)=(f'+u')/f'.$$

62. Show that there are two positions on the axis of a spherical refracting surface where image and object coincide.

63. Locate the two pairs of conjugate planes of a spherical refracting surface for which image and object have the same size.

64. A real object, 1 cm. high, is placed 12 cm. from a convex spherical refracting surface, of radius 30 cm., which separates air $(n=1)$ from glass $(n'=1.5)$. Find the position and size of the image.

Ans. Image is virtual and erect, 1.25 cm. high, 22.5 cm. from vertex.

65. In the preceding example, suppose that the object is a virtual object at the same distance from the spherical refracting surface. Find the position and size of the image in this case.

Ans. Image is real and erect, $\frac{5}{6}$ cm. high, and 15 cm. from vertex.

66. Solve Nos. 64 and 65 for the case when the surface is concave; and draw diagrams showing construction of the image in all four cases.

67. Solve No. 64 on the supposition that the first medium is glass and the second medium air.

Ans. Image will be virtual and erect, $\frac{15}{17}$ cm. high, and $\frac{120}{17}$ cm. from vertex.

68. (a) The human eye from which the crystalline lens has been removed (so-called "aphakic eye") may be regarded as consisting of a single spherical refracting surface, namely, the anterior surface of the cornea. If the radius of this surface is taken as 8 mm., and if the index of refraction of the eye-medium (both the aqueous and vitreous humors) is put equal to $\frac{4}{3}$, what will be the focal lengths of the aphakic eye? (b) Assuming that the length of the eye-ball of an aphakic eye is 22 mm., where will an object have to be placed to be imaged distinctly on the retina at the back of the eye?

Ans. (a) $f=+24$ mm., $f'=-32$ mm.; (b) $u=+52.8$ mm., which means that the object must be virtual and lie behind the eye.

69. LISTING's "reduced eye" is composed of a single convex spherical refracting surface of radius 5.2 mm. separating air ($n=1$) from the vitreous humor ($n'=1.332$). Calculate the focal lengths.

Ans. $f = +15.66$ mm., $f' = -20.86$ mm.

70. In DONDERS' "reduced eye" the focal lengths are assumed to be $+15$ and -20 mm. Calculate the radius of the equivalent spherical refracting surface and the index of refraction of the vitreous humor for these values of the focal lengths.   Ans. $r=+5$ mm.; $n'=\frac{4}{3}$.

71. The angular distance of a star from the axis of a spherical refracting surface which separates air ($n=1$) from glass ($n'=1.5$) is $10°$. The surface is convex and of radius 10 cm. Find the position of the star's image.

Ans. A real image will be formed in the secondary focal plane about 3.5 cm. from the axis.

72. What is the size of the image on the retina of LISTING's "reduced eye" (No. 69) if the apparent size of the distant object is $5°$?   Ans. 1.36 mm.

73. A hemispherical lens, the curved surface of which has a radius of 3 inches, is made of glass of index 1.5. Show that rays of light proceeding from a point on its axis 4 inches in front of its plane surface will emerge parallel to the axis.

74. A paraxial ray parallel to the axis of a solid refracting sphere of index n' is refracted into the sphere at first towards a point X on the axis, and after the second refraction crosses the axis at a point F'. If the first and last media are the same and of index n, show that the point F' lies midway between the second vertex of the sphere and the point X.

75. A small object of height y is placed at the center of a spherical refracting surface in a plane at right angles to the axis. Determine the position and size of the image. Show how the SMITH-HELMHOLTZ formula (§ 86) is applicable to a part of this problem.

Ans. Image is in same plane as object, erect, and of size $y' = n.y/n'$.

76. A plane object is placed parallel to a plane refracting surface. Show that its image formed by paraxial rays is erect and of same size as object. Is the SMITH-HELMHOLTZ formula (§ 86) applicable to a plane refracting surface? Is it applicable to a spherical mirror? Explain clearly.

77. In a convex spherical refracting surface of radius 0.75, which separates air $(n=1)$ from water $(n'=\frac{4}{3})$, the image is real, inverted and one-third the size of the object. Find the positions of object and image. If a ray proceeding from the axial point of the object is inclined to the axis at an angle of 3°, what will be the slope of the corresponding refracted ray?

Ans. Object is in air and image is in water, their distances from the surface being 9 and 4, respectively; slope of refracted ray is −6.75°.

78. In a spherical refracting surface

$$a = \theta + \varphi, \qquad a' = \theta' + \varphi,$$

where a, a' denote the angles of incidence and refraction, θ, θ' denote the inclinations of the ray to the axis before and after refraction, and φ denotes the so-called central angle ($\angle BCA$). For a paraxial ray the law of refraction may be written

$$n'.a' = n.a.$$

From these formulæ deduce the abscissa-relation in the form

$$\frac{n'}{u'} = \frac{n}{u} + \frac{n'-n}{r}.$$

79. The curved surface of a glass hemisphere is silvered. Rays coming from a luminous point at a distance u from the plane surface are refracted into the glass, reflected from the concave spherical surface, and refracted at the plane surface back into the air. If r denotes the radius of the spherical surface and n the index of refraction of the glass, show that

$$\frac{1}{u} + \frac{1}{u'} + \frac{2n}{r} = 0,$$

where u' denotes the distance of the image from the plane surface.

80. A plane object of height one inch is placed at right angles to the axis of a spherical mirror. The slope of the reflected ray corresponding to an incident paraxial ray which emanates from the axial point of the object at a slope of $+5°$ is $+10°$. Is the image erect or inverted, and what is its size?

　　　　　　　　　　Ans. Inverted image, one-half inch high.

81. A paraxial ray crosses the axis of a spherical refracting surface before and after refraction at points whose distances from the center of the surface are denoted by z and z', respectively. If n, n' denote the indices of refraction of the two media and if f denotes the focal length, show that

$$\frac{n}{z'} = \frac{n'}{z} + \frac{n}{f}.$$

82. In a spherical refracting surface separating two media of indices n, n', show that

$$AF : CF = CF' : AF' = n : n',$$

where A, C, F and F' designate the positions of the vertex, center and focal points, respectively.

83. M, M' designate the positions of a pair of conjugate points on the axis of a spherical refracting surface whose center, vertex and first focal point are designated by C, A and F, respectively: show that

$$MF : MA = MC : MM'.$$

CHAPTER VII

87. Forms of Lenses.—In optics the word *lens* is used
to denote a portion of a transparent substance, usually
isotropic, comprised between two smooth polished surfaces,
one of which may be plane. These surfaces are called the
faces of the lens. The curved faces are generally spherical,
and this may always be considered as implied unless the
contrary is expressly stated. Lenses with spherical faces
are sometimes called "spherical lenses" to distinguish them
from cylindrical, sphero-cylindrical and other forms of
lenses which are also quite common, especially in modern
spectacle glasses. A plane face may be regarded as a spherical or cylindrical surface of infinite radius.

The *axis* of a lens is the straight line which is normal to
both faces, and, consequently, a ray whose path lies along
the axis (the so-called axial ray) will pass through the lens
without being deflected from this line. The axis of a spherical lens is the straight line joining the centers C_1, C_2 of
the two spherical faces, and since a lens of this kind is symmetric around the axis, it may be represented in a plane
figure by a meridian section showing the arcs of the two
great circles in which this plane intersects the spherical
faces. Depending on the lengths of the radii in comparison
with the length of the line-segment C_1C_2, these arcs intersect in two points equidistant from the axis or else they do
not intersect each other at all.

(*a*) If they intersect, then C_1C_2 is less than the arithmetical sum but greater than the arithmetical difference
of the radii, and the lens may be a *double convex lens*

217

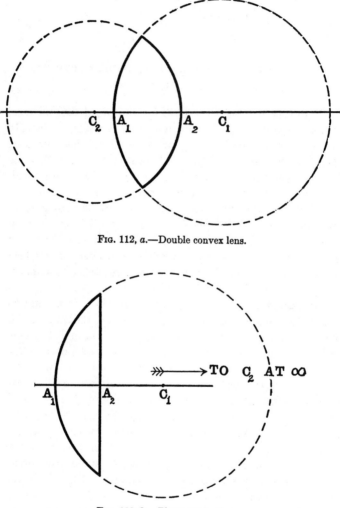

Fig. 112, *a.*—Double convex lens.

Fig. 112, *b.*—Plano-convex lens.

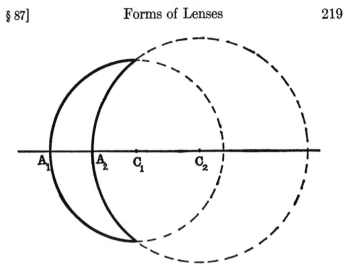

Fig. 112, c.—Convex meniscus.

(Fig. 112, *a*) or a *convex meniscus* (Fig. 112, *c*). A particular case of a double convex lens is a *plano-convex lens* (Fig. 112, *b*).

(*b*) If they do not intersect, then either one circle lies wholly outside the other, the distance between the centers being, therefore, greater than the arithmetical sum of the radii, so that the lens is a *double concave lens* (Fig. 113, *a*), or, in case one of the surfaces is plane, a *plano-concave lens* (Fig. 113, *b*); or else one circle lies wholly inside the other, so that the distance between the centers is less than the arithmetical difference of the radii, and then the lens has the form of a *concave meniscus* (Fig. 113, *c*).

The *first face* of a lens is the side turned towards the incident light. The points where the axis meets the two faces are called the *vertices*, and the distance from the vertex A_1 of the first face to the vertex A_2 of the second face, which is denoted by d, is called the thickness of the lens; thus, $d = A_1A_2$. Since the direction which the light takes in going across the lens from A_1 to A_2 is *the positive direction along the axis* (see § 63), the thickness d is essentially a positive magnitude.

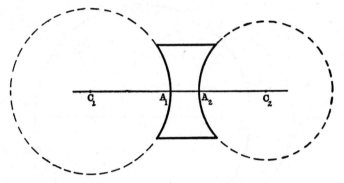

FIG. 113, *a.*—Double concave lens.

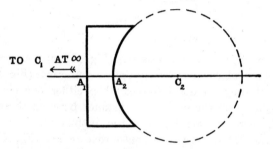

FIG. 113, *b.*—Plano-concave lens.

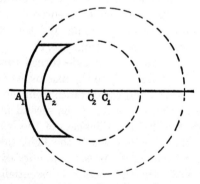

FIG. 113, *c.*—Concave meniscus.

The radii of the surfaces, denoted by r_1, r_2, are the abscissæ of the centers C_1, C_2 with respect to the vertices A_1, A_2, respectively; thus, $r_1 = A_1C_1$, $r_2 = A_2C_2$.

Certain *special forms of spherical lenses* may be mentioned here, viz.:

(a) *Symmetric Lenses*, which are double convex or double concave lenses whose surfaces have equal but opposite curvatures ($r_1 + r_2 = 0$). A particular case of double convex symmetric lens is one whose two faces are portions of the same spherical surface; a lens of this kind being sometimes called a *solid sphere* ($d = r_1 - r_2 = 2r_1$).

(b) *Concentric Lenses*, whose two faces have the same center of curvature ($C_1C_2 = 0$). A concentric lens may be

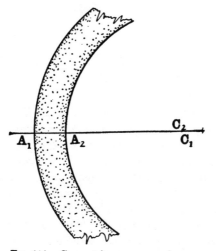

Fig. 114.—Concentric concave meniscus.

a double convex lens characterized by the relation $d = r_1 - r_2$, of which a "solid sphere" is a special case; or it may have the form of a concave meniscus for which either $r_1 > r_2 > 0$ and $d = r_1 - r_2$ (Fig. 114) or $r_1 < r_2 < 0$ and $d = r_2 - r_1$.

(c) *Lenses of Zero Curvature*, in which the axial thickness

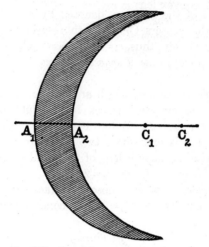

FIG. 115.—Lens of zero curvature ($r_1 = r_2$).

of the lens is equal to the distance between the centers ($d = A_1A_2 = C_1C_2$). This lens is a convex meniscus characterized by the condition that $r_1 - r_2 = 0$ (Fig. 115).

Lenses may also be conveniently classified in two main groups, viz., *convex lenses* and *concave lenses*, depending on the relative thickness of the lens along the axis as compared with its thickness at the edges. The thickness of a convex lens is greater along the axis than it is out towards the edge, whereas a concave lens is thinnest in the middle. Each of these two main divisions includes three special forms which have already been mentioned. Thus, the three types of convex lenses are the double convex, the plano-convex and the convex or "crescent-shaped" meniscus, as shown in Fig. 112; and, similarly, the types of concave lenses are the double concave, plano-concave and the concave or "canoe-shaped" meniscus (Fig. 113).

A convex glass lens of moderate thickness held in air with its axis towards the sun has the property of a burning glass and converges the rays to a real focus on the other side of the lens. A convex lens is called therefore also a *convergent lens* or a *positive lens*. On the other hand, under the same circumstances, a concave lens will render a beam of sunlight divergent, and, accordingly, a concave lens is called also a *divergent lens* or a *negative lens*. The explanation of the terms "positive" and "negative" as applied to lenses will be apparent when we come to speak of the positions of the focal points of a lens (§ 90).

Finally, if the curvatures of the two faces of the lens are opposite in sign, the lens is double convex or double concave; if the curvatures have the same sign, the lens is a meniscus; and if the curvature of one face is zero, the lens is plano-convex or plano-concave.

88. The Optical Center O of a Lens surrounded by the same medium on both sides.—When a ray of light emerges at the second face of a lens into the surrounding medium in the same direction as it had when it met the first face, the path of the ray inside the lens lies along a straight line which crosses the axis at a remarkable point O called the *optical center* of the lens, which is indeed the (internal or external) "center of similitude" of the two circles whose arcs are the traces of the spherical faces of the lens in the meridian plane which contains the ray.

In order to prove this, draw a pair of parallel radii C_1B_1 and C_2B_2 (Fig. 116), and suppose that a ray enters the lens at B_1 and leaves it at B_2, so that the straight line B_1B_2 represents the path of the ray through the lens. If the straight line RB_1 represents the path of the incident ray, a straight line B_2S drawn through B_2 parallel to RB_1 will represent the path of the emergent ray; because, since the tangents to the circular arcs at B_1, B_2 are parallel to each other, the lens behaves towards this ray which enters it at B_1 exactly like a slab of the same material with plane parallel sides (§ 44). Consequently, the position of the point O where the straight line B_1B_2, produced if necessary, crosses the axis of the lens is seen to be entirely dependent on the

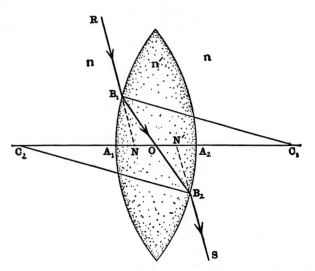

Fig. 116.—Optical center of lens.

geometrical form of the lens. In particular, the position of this point will not depend on the direction of the incident ray, as will be shown by the following investigation. From the similar triangles OC_1B_1 and OC_2B_2, we derive the proportion:

$$OC_1 : OC_2 = B_1C_1 : B_2C_2 = A_1C_1 : A_2C_2.$$

Accordingly, we may write:

$$\frac{OA_1 + A_1C_1}{OA_2 + A_2C_2} = \frac{A_1C_1}{A_2C_2},$$

and, consequently:

$$\frac{A_1O}{A_2O} = \frac{r_1}{r_2}.$$

Now $A_2O = A_2A_1 + A_1O = A_1O - d$; so that we obtain finally:

$$A_1O = \frac{r_1}{r_1 - r_2}d.$$

The function on the right-hand side of this equation depends only on the form of the lens, so that the position of the point O with respect to the vertex of the first face of the lens may be found immediately as soon as we know the magnitudes denoted by r_1, r_2 and d.

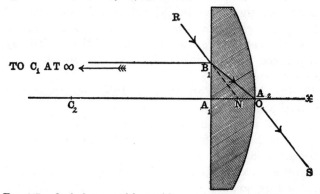

FIG. 117.—Optical center of lens with one plane face is at the vertex of curved face.

If the lens is double convex or double concave, the optical center O will lie inside the lens between the vertices A_1 and

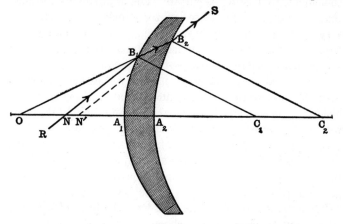

FIG. 118.—Optical center of meniscus lies outside lens.

A_2; if one face of the lens is plane (Fig. 117), the optical center will coincide with the vertex of the curved face: and, finally, if the lens is a meniscus (Fig. 118), the optical center will lie outside the lens entirely.

In general, the positions of the points designated in the diagrams by the letters N, N' will vary for different ray-paths $B_1 B_2$ within the lens; but if the rays are paraxial, the positions of N, N' are fixed. In fact, if the ray $RB_1 B_2 S$ is a paraxial ray, the points N, N' are the so-called nodal points of the lens (see § 119).

89. The Abscissa-Formula of a Thin Lens, referred to the axial point of the lens as origin.—Ordinarily, the axial thickness of a lens is much smaller than either of the radii of curvature, so that in many lens-problems this dimension is negligible in comparison with the other linear dimensions that are involved. Moreover, the lens-formulæ are greatly simplified by ignoring the thickness of the lens. However, in using these formulæ one must be duly cautious about taking too literally results that are strictly applicable only to an *infinitely thin lens*, whose vertices are regarded as coincident, that is, $A_1 A_2 = d = 0$. The approximate formulæ that are obtained for lenses of zero-thickness are often of very great practical utility, especially in the preliminary design of an optical instrument composed, it may be, of several lenses whose thicknesses are by no means negligible.

The optical center O of an infinitely thin lens coincides with the two vertices A_1, A_2, and hereafter these three co-incident points in which the axis meets an infinitely thin lens will be designated by the simple letter A. An infinitely thin lens is represented in a diagram by the segment of a straight line which is bisected at right angles by the axis of the lens; the actual form of the lens being indicated by assigning the positions of the centers C_1, C_2 of the two faces. In order to tell at a glance the character of a lens, the form of it at the edges may be indicated, as shown in Fig. 119. Fig. 119,*a* is a conventional representation of an infinitely thin con-vex lens, and Fig. 119, *b* is a similar diagram for an infinitely thin concave lens.

Let us assume that the lens is surrounded by the same medium on both sides; and let n denote the index of refrac-

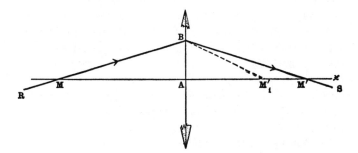

Fig. 119, a.—Infinitely thin convex lens; M, M′ conjugate points on axis.

tion of this medium, while n' denotes the index of refraction of the lens-substance itself.

The broken line RBS (Fig. 119) represents the path of a paraxial ray which enters and leaves the infinitely thin

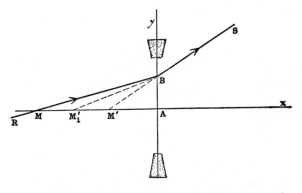

Fig. 119, b.—Infinitely thin concave lens; M, M′ conjugate points on axis.

lens at the point marked B. The points where the ray crosses the axis before and after passing through the lens will be designated by M, M′, respectively. The straight line BM_1' which intersects the axis at the point marked M_1' shows the path the ray takes after being refracted at the first face of the lens. Obviously, the points M, M_1' are a pair of conjugate axial points with respect to the first surface of the lens, and, similarly, the points M_1', M' are a pair of conjugate axial points with respect to the second surface of the lens, and, therefore, M, M' are a pair of conjugate axial points with respect to the lens as a whole, so that M' will be the image in the lens of an axial object-point M. The abscissæ of these points with respect to the axial point A as origin will be denoted by u, u'; thus, $u = AM$, $u' = AM'$. Also, put $u_1' = AM_1'$. The radii of curvature of the two faces are $r_1 = AC_1$, $r_2 = AC_2$.

Accordingly, in order to obtain the formulæ connecting u and u', we have merely to apply the fundamental equation (§ 78) for the refraction of paraxial rays at a spherical surface to each face of the lens in succession, bearing in mind that the first refraction is from medium n to medium n', while the second refraction is from medium n' to medium n. Thus, we obtain:

$$\frac{n'}{u_1'} - \frac{n}{u} = \frac{n'-n}{r_1}, \quad \frac{n}{u'} - \frac{n'}{u_1'} = -\frac{n'-n}{r_2}.$$

Eliminating u_1' by adding these equations, and dividing through by n, we derive the *abscissa-formula for the refraction of paraxial rays through an infinitely thin lens*, in the following form:

$$\frac{1}{u'} - \frac{1}{u} = \frac{n'-n}{n}\left(\frac{1}{r_1} - \frac{1}{r_2}\right).$$

The expression on the right-hand side of this equation, involving only the lens-constants r_1, r_2 and n'/n, has for a given lens a perfectly definite value, which may be computed once for all. And so if we put

$$\frac{1}{f} = \frac{n'-n}{n}\left(\frac{1}{r_1} - \frac{1}{r_2}\right),$$

where the magnitude denoted by f is a constant of the lens (which we shall afterwards see is the *focal length* of the lens), the formula above may be written:

$$\frac{1}{u'} - \frac{1}{u} = \frac{1}{f};$$

which is the form of the lens-formula that is perhaps most common. For a given value of u we find $u' = f.u/(f+u)$.

Incidentally, it may be observed that the equation above is symmetrical with respect to u and $-u'$; that is, the equation will remain unaltered if $-u$ is written in place of u' and $-u'$ in place of u. Accordingly, if the positions of a pair of conjugate points on the axis are designated by M, M'

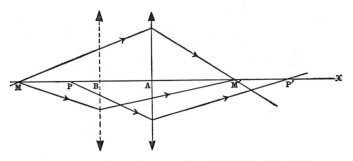

Fig. 120.—Infinitely thin lens: AP = M'A = BM, AP' = MA.

(Fig. 120), the pair of axial points designated by P, P' will likewise be conjugate, provided AP = M'A and AP' = MA; so that the thin lens at A bisects the two segments PM' and P'M. Another and more striking way of exhibiting this characteristic property of an infinitely thin lens consists in saying, that if M' is the image of an axial object-point at M, and if then the lens is shifted from its first position at A to a point B such that MB = AM', the object-point M will again be imaged at M'.

90. The Focal Points of an Infinitely Thin Lens.—If the object-point M is at the infinitely distant point on the axis of the lens, its image will be formed at a point F' whose position on the axis may be found by putting $u = \infty$, $u' = AF'$

in the formula $1/u'-1/u=1/f$; thus, we find $AF'=f$. Similarly, the object-point F conjugate to the infinitely distant point of the axis is found by substituting in the same equation the pair of values $u=AF$, $u'=\infty$, whence we obtain $AF=-f$. These points F, F' are *the primary and secondary focal points*, respectively, and, accordingly, it is evident that *the focal points of an infinitely thin lens are equidistant from the lens and on opposite sides of it.*

The character of the imagery in the case of an infinitely thin lens is completely determined as soon as we know the positions of the two focal points F, F'; and since the point A where the axis meets the lens lies midway between F and F', it is obvious that the natural division of lenses is into two classes depending on the order in which the three points above mentioned are ranged along the axis.

(1) *If the primary focal point is in front of the lens* (Fig. 121, *a*), that is, if the order of the points named in the se-

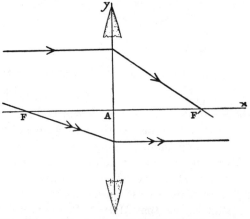

Fig. 121, *a*.—Focal points (F, F'),of infinitely thin lens (FA=AF'=*f*). In a positive (or convex or convergent) lens the first focal point (F) lies on same side of lens as incident light (real focus).

quence in which they are reached by light traversing the axis of the lens is F, A, F', then incident rays parallel to

the axis will be converged to a real focus at F′ on the other
side of the lens, and the lens is a *convergent lens* (§ 87). It
is also called a *positive lens*, because the lens-constant (or
primary focal length) $f = FA = AF′$ is measured along the
axis in the positive sense. If it is assumed that $n′ > n$ (as,
for example, in the case of a glass lens in air), the sign of
this constant f, according to the formula above which defines $1/f$, will be the same as that of the term $(1/r_1 - 1/r_2)$,
which is the algebraic expression of the difference of curvatures (§ 99) between the two faces of the lens. If the lens
is double convex, plano-convex or a crescent-shaped meniscus—that is, in all forms of lenses that are thicker in
the middle than out towards the edges—the difference of
curvatures $(1/r_1 - 1/r_2)$ will be found to be positive. And
hence, as already stated (§ 87), thin lenses of this description are convergent if $n′ > n$.

(2) *If the secondary focal point is in front of the lens* (Fig.
121, *b*), that is, if the points F′, A, F are ranged along the

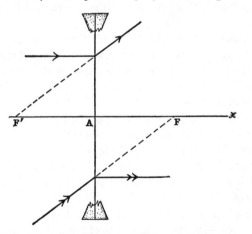

Fig. 121, *b*.—Focal points (F,F′) of infinitely thin
lens (FA = AF′ = *f*). In a negative (or concave or
divergent) lens the first focal point (F) lies on
the other side of the lens from the incident light
(virtual focus).

axis in the order named, incident parallel rays will be made to diverge from a virtual focus at F', and in this case the lens is said to be a *divergent* or *negative lens*, since now the lens-constant $f = \text{FA} = \text{AF}'$ is measured along the axis in the negative sense. For lenses which are thinner in the middle than at the edges, that is, for double concave, plano-concave and canoe-shaped meniscus lenses the difference of curvatures $(1/r_1 - 1/r_2)$ will be found to be negative; and hence for such lenses the constant f will be negative if $n' > n$.

A case of rather more theoretical than practical interest is afforded by an *infinitely thin concentric lens* (§ 87) for which $r_2 = r_1$, and which is therefore uniformly thick in a direction parallel to the axis, so that according to the above classification it should be neither convergent nor divergent. In fact, the value of the lens-constant f for this lens is infinity, and hence $u' = u$, so that object-point M and image-point M' are coincident always. A bundle of parallel rays traversing an infinitely thin concentric lens will emerge from the lens just as though the lens had not been interposed in the path of the rays.

91. Construction of the Point M' Conjugate to the Axial Point M with respect to an Infinitely Thin Lens.—The planes which are perpendicular to the axis of the lens at the focal points F, F' are called the *primary* and *secondary focal planes*, respectively.

The point M' conjugate to a point M on the axis of an infinitely thin lens surrounded by the same medium on both sides may be constructed as follows:

Through the given point M (Fig. 122, *a* and *b*) draw a straight line MB meeting the lens at B, and through the axial point (A) of the lens draw a straight line AI' parallel to MB and meeting the secondary focal plane in the point I'; then the point where the straight line BI', produced if necessary, crosses the axis will be the required point M' conjugate to M.

The point M' may also be constructed in another way,

as follows: Let J designate the point where the straight line MB crosses the primary focal plane, and through B draw a straight line parallel to the straight line JA, which

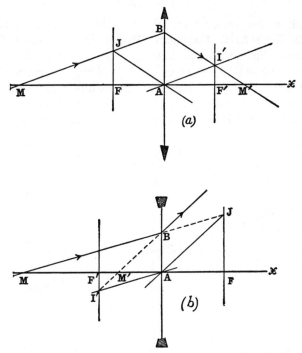

Fig. 122, *a* and *b*.—Infinitely thin lens: Construction of point M′ conjugate to axial object-point M. (*a*) Convex, (*b*) Concave lens.

will intersect the axis of the lens in the required point M′. Fig. 122, *a* shows the construction in the case of a convex lens and Fig. 122, *b* shows it for a concave lens.

The proof is obvious. From the two pairs of similar triangles MAB, AF′I′ and MM′B, AM′I′, we obtain the proportions:

$$\frac{MA}{AF'} = \frac{MB}{AI'} = \frac{MM'}{AM'};$$

and if we introduce the symbols $u=\mathrm{AM}$, $u'=\mathrm{AM}'$, $f=\mathrm{AF}'$, we get:

$$\frac{-u}{f}=\frac{u'-u}{u'};$$

which is the same as the abscissa-relation found in § 89.

92. Extra-Axial Conjugate Points Q, Q′; Conjugate Planes.—Since the axial point A of an infinitely thin lens is also the optical center of the lens (§ 89), a straight line drawn through A will represent the path of a ray both before and after passing through the lens at this point. If the axis of the lens is rotated in a meridian plane through

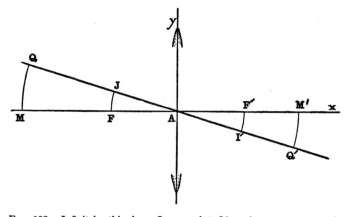

Fig. 123.—Infinitely thin lens: Image-point Q′ conjugate to extra-axial object-point Q.

a very small angle FAJ (Fig. 123) around the point A as vertex, the focal points F, F′ will describe the small arcs FJ, F′I′ and the straight line JI′ will represent the path of a paraxial ray traversing the lens at A. The points Q, Q′ at the ends of the arcs MQ, M′Q′ traced out in this angular movement of the axis by a pair of conjugate axial points M, M′ will evidently occupy the same relation to each other on the straight line JI′ as M, M′ have to each other

on the straight line FF', and therefore Q, Q' are a pair of
extra-axial conjugate points.

Accordingly, if the points of an object lie in the vicinity
of the axis on an element of a spherical surface described

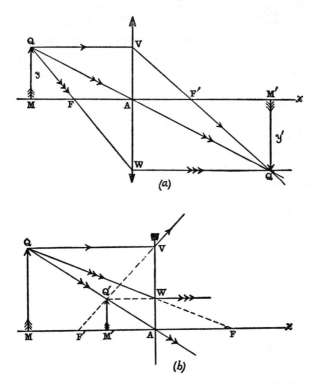

Fig. 124, *a* and *b.*—Infinitely thin lens: Lateral magnification
and construction of image M'Q' conjugate to short object-
line MQ perpendicular to axis. (a) Convex, (b) Concave lens.

around the vertex A of the infinitely thin lens as center,
the corresponding points of the image will be assembled
on a concentric spherical surface; and since, within the
region of paraxial rays, these spherical elements may be
regarded as plane, it follows that a small plane object at

right angles to the axis will be reproduced by a similar plane image also at right angles to the axis.

Conjugate planes are pairs of parallel planes perpendicular to the axis of the lens; and any straight line drawn through the center of an infinitely thin lens will pierce a pair of conjugate planes in a pair of conjugate points.

In particular, the planes conjugate to the focal planes are the infinitely distant planes of the image-space and object-space, according as the infinitely distant plane is regarded as belonging to one or the other of these regions.

The construction of the point Q′ conjugate to an extra-axial object-point Q (Fig. 124, *a* and *b*), with respect to an infinitely thin lens, is made by a method precisely similar to that employed in the corresponding problem in the cases both of a spherical mirror (§ 71) and of a spherical refracting surface (§ 81); the only difference in this case being that the center of the lens takes the place of the center of the spherical surface and that the focal points of the lens are at equal distances on opposite sides of it.

93. Lateral Magnification in case of Infinitely Thin Lens. —The lateral magnification in the case of an infinitely thin lens, defined, as in §§ 72 and 82, as the ratio of the height of the image ($y′ = $ M′Q′) to the height of the object ($y = $ MQ), may be obtained from the diagram (Fig. 124) and is evidently given by the following formula:

$$\boldsymbol{y} = \frac{y′}{y} = \frac{u′}{u};$$

so that *the linear dimensions of object and image are in the same ratio as their distances from the thin lens.* Moreover, it appears that *the image is erect or inverted according as object and image lie on the same side or on opposite sides of the lens.*

Another expression for the lateral magnification may be derived by considering the two pairs of similar right triangles FMQ, FAW and F'M'Q', F'AV, from which we obtain the proportions:

$$\frac{AW}{MQ} = \frac{FA}{FM}, \qquad \frac{M'Q'}{AV} = \frac{F'M'}{F'A};$$

and since

$$AW = M'Q' = y', \qquad AV = MQ = y, \qquad FA = AF' = f,$$

we find:

$$y = \frac{y'}{y} = \frac{f}{x} = -\frac{x'}{f},$$

where $x = FM$, $x' = F'M'$ denote the abscissæ of M, M' with respect to the focal points F, F', respectively, as origins. Accordingly, *the lateral magnification varies inversely as the distance of the object from the primary focal plane, and directly as the distance of the image from the secondary focal plane.*

94. Character of the Imagery in a Thin Lens.—The Newtonian form of the abscissa-relation (*cf.* § 85) for an infinitely thin lens surrounded by air is:

$$x.x' = -f^2,$$

which shows that object and image lie on opposite sides of the focal planes; so that if M is a point on the axis to the right of the primary focal point F, the conjugate point M' will be found on the axis at the left of the secondary focal point F', and *vice versa.*

The character of the imagery produced by the refraction of paraxial rays through an infinitely thin lens is exhibited in the diagrams Fig. 125, *a* and *b*. The numerals 1, 2, 3, etc., mark the successive positions of an object-point which is supposed to traverse a straight line parallel to the axis (so-called "object-ray") from an infinite distance in front of the lens to an infinite distance on the other side of it. Until it reaches the lens at the point marked V the object is real, thereafter it is virtual. The corresponding numerals with primes, viz., 1', 2', 3', etc., ranged along the straight line VF' (called the "image-ray") mark the successive positions of the image-point, which, starting, from the secondary focal point F′, moves along this line always in the same direction out to infinity and back again to its starting point. The straight lines 11′, 22′, 33′, etc., con-

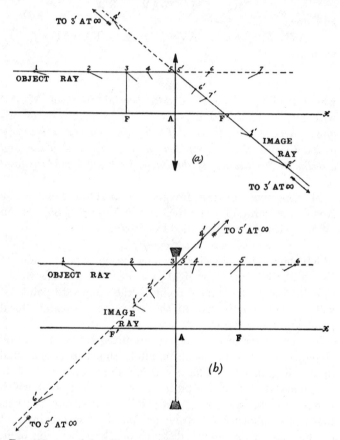

Fig. 125, *a* and *b*.—Character of imagery in infinitely thin lens. (*a*) Convex, (*b*) Concave lens.

necting corresponding positions of object-point and image-point form a pencil of rays all passing through the optical center A of the lens, which is the center of perspective of object-space and image-space. At the point V object and image coincide with each other in the lens itself, and here object and image are congruent. The so-called *principal planes* (§ 119) *of an infinitely thin lens coincide with each other in the plane perpendicular to the axis of the lens at its optical center* A. The fact that object-point and image-point coincide with each other at V is expressed geometrically by saying *the y-axis is the base of a range of self conjugate points.*

In a convex lens (Fig. 125, *a*) the image of a real object is seen to be real and inverted as long as the object lies in front of the lens beyond the primary focal plane; whereas the image is virtual and erect if the object is placed between the primary focal plane and the lens. The image of a virtual object in a convex lens is formed between the lens and the secondary focal plane and is real and erect.

In a concave lens (Fig. 125, *b*) the image of a real object lies between the lens and the secondary focal plane, and it is virtual and erect. If the object is virtual, its image in a concave lens will be real and erect if the object lies between the lens and the primary focal plane, but it will be virtual and inverted if the object lies beyond the primary focal plane.

If $z=MM'$ denotes the distance between a pair of conjugate axial points M, M', then $u'=u+z$, where $u=AM$, $u'=AM'$. Substituting this value of u in the formula $1/u'-1/u=1/f$, we obtain a quadratic in u, which implies, therefore, that for a given value of the interval z between object and image, there are always *two* positions of the object-point M with respect to the lens (§ 89). But under some circumstances the assigned value of the interval z may be such that the roots of the quadratic prove to be imaginary, and then it will be quite impossible with the given lens to produce an image at the given distance z from the object. For example, if the object lies in front of a *convex lens* ($f>0$) at a distance greater than the focal length, then $u<0$ and $z>0$. Put $a=\mathrm{MA}=-u$, so that the magnitudes denoted by f, z and a are all positive. Eliminating u' from the abscissa-formula, we obtain a quadratic in a whose roots are given by the following expression:

$$a=\frac{z\pm\sqrt{z(z-4f)}}{2};$$

which will be imaginary if $(z-4f)<0$. Hence, *the distance (z) between a real object and its real image in a convex lens cannot be less than four times the focal length f.*

95. The Focal Lengths f, f′ of an Infinitely Thin Lens.—The focal lengths of a thin lens are defined exactly in the same way as the focal lengths of a spherical refracting sur-

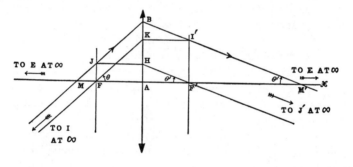

Fig. 126.—Focal planes and focal lengths of infinitely thin lens
$(f=\mathrm{FA}=-f'=\mathrm{AF'})$.

face (§ 83). Thus, *the primary focal length of a lens is the ratio of the height of the image, in the secondary focal plane, to the apparent size of the infinitely distant object.* In Fig. 126 F′I′ is the height of the image of the infinitely distant object EI which is seen under the angle $\theta=\angle\mathrm{EFI}=\angle\mathrm{AFK}$, and the primary focal length is, therefore, F′I′/tan $\theta=$ AK/tan $\theta=\mathrm{FA}=f$; and hence, as already observed, the primary focal length is identical with the lens-constant denoted by f, which, as we have seen (§ 90), is the abscissa of the axial point A of a thin lens with respect to its primary focal point F. Similarly, *the secondary focal length (f′) is*

*the ratio of the height of an object in the primary focal plane of
the lens to the apparent size of its infinitely distant image.*
For example, in the diagram the image of the object FJ
lying in the primary focal plane is E'J', which lying in the
infinitely distant plane of the image-space, subtends the
angle $\theta' = \angle EF'J' = \angle AF'H$; and hence $f' = FJ/\tan \theta' =$
$AH/\tan \theta' = F'A$; so that the secondary focal length may
also be defined as the abscissa of the axial point A of an infinitely thin lens with respect to the secondary focal point F'.
And since $F'A = -AF' = -FA$, evidently:

$$f' = -f.$$

Accordingly, *the focal lengths (f, f') of a lens surrounded by
the same medium on both sides are equal in magnitude and
opposite in sign.*

If the lens is reversed by turning it through 180° about
an axis perpendicular to the axis of the lens, that is, if the
light is made to traverse the lens in a sense exactly opposite
to that which it had at first, the focal lengths f, f' will not
be altered. This is evident from the fact that the expression for the focal length f, viz.,

$$f = -f' = \frac{n.r_1.r_2}{(n'-n)\ (r_2-r_1)},$$

remains the same when $-r_1$, $-r_2$ are substituted in place of
r_1, r_2, respectively. Thus, the character of the lens (§ 90)
and its action are not changed by presenting the opposite
face to the incident rays.

The focal length of an infinitely thin symmetric lens
(§ 87), for which $r_1 = -r_2 = r$ (say) is $f = \dfrac{n.r}{2(n'-n)}$; and if
$n = 1$, $n' = 1.5$, we find $f = r$. Accordingly, *the focal length
of an infinitely thin symmetric glass lens surrounded by air
$(n = 1,\ n' = 1.5)$ is equal to the radius of the first face.* Spectacle glasses were at first symmetric lenses, and in the old
inch system of designation a No. 10 spectacle glass, for example, was a lens whose radius of curvature on each surface
was 10 inches and whose focal length was 10 inches.

If one face of the lens is plane, for example, if $r_1 = \infty$, $r_2 = r$, we find $f = -\dfrac{n.r}{n'-n}$; or if $r_1 = r$, $r_2 = \infty$, then $f = \dfrac{n.r}{n'-n}$, where in each case r denotes the radius of the curved surface. Comparing this with the value of f obtained in the preceding case, we see that *if one of the faces of a symmetric lens be ground off plane, the focal length of the lens will thereby be doubled.*

96. Central Collineation of Object-Space and Image-Space.—Comparing the methods and results of this chapter with those obtained in the preceding chapter, the serious student cannot have failed to remark a striking parallelism that exists between the imagery by paraxial rays in a spherical refracting surface and the imagery under the same conditions in an infinitely thin lens. In some instances the formulæ are actually identical, and a closer examination will show that this similarity extends even to comparative details. For example, the focal points lie on opposite sides of a lens just as they were found to do in the case of a spherical refracting surface, and the resemblance goes still farther. For in a spherical refracting surface the connection between the focal lengths (f, f') and the indices of refraction (n, n') is expressed by the formula $n'.f + n.f' = 0$ (§ 79); and if in this formula we put $n' = n$, we obtain the relation $f + f' = 0$, which is the algebraic statement of the fact that the focal lengths of a lens surrounded by the same medium on both sides are equal and opposite (§ 95).

It has already been pointed out that the imagery in a spherical mirror may be regarded as a special case of refraction at a spherical surface (§§ 75, 77 and 78); and now it is proposed to advance a step farther in this generalization process and to show that all these types of imagery which have been investigated separately and independently are in reality embraced in a concept of geometry known as *collinear correspondence* between one space and another (called in the theory of optical imagery "object-space" and "image-space"). Moreover, these types of imagery belong to a particularly simple kind of collinear correspondence to which the name *central collineation* has been given.

A lens or an optical instrument is said to divide the surrounding space into two parts, viz., the object-space and the image-space; but these are not to be thought of as separate and distinct regions but as interpenetrating and including each other; so that a point or ray may be regarded at one time as belonging to the object-space and at another time as belonging to the image-space, depending merely on the point of view. Thus, for example, the infinitely distant plane of space may be viewed as the image of the primary focal plane of a lens, and then it is a part of the image-space; but if the secondary focal plane is regarded as the image of the infinitely distant plane, the latter is a part of the object-space.

Now the distinguishing characteristics of the optical imagery which is produced by the refraction of paraxial rays at a single spherical surface or through an infinitely thin lens may be summarized in the two following statements:

(a) *All straight lines joining pairs of conjugate points intersect in one point,* viz., the center (C) of the spherical refracting surface or the optical center (A) of the thin lens. This point which is the center of perspective of object-space and image-space is called the *center of collineation,* and will be referred to here as the point C.

(b) *Any pair of corresponding incident and refracted rays lying in a meridian plane meet in a straight line* Ay *called the axis of collineation* (or the y-axis) *which is perpendicular at A to the optical axis* (or the x-axis).

Any straight line going through the center of collineation is called a *central ray. Every central ray is a self-corresponding ray;* that is, image-ray and corresponding object-ray lie along one and the same straight line. Moreover, any point lying on the axis of collineation is a *self-conjugate point;* that is, *along this line object-point and image-point are coincident with each other.* The center of collineation is also a self-conjugate point, and hence, *in general, there are two self-conjugate points on a central ray,* viz., the center of collineation and the point where the ray meets the axis of collineation. Only in case the center of collineation lies on the axis of collineation will there be only one self-conjugate or so-called double point on a central ray.

97. Central Collineation (cont'd). **Geometrical Constructions.**—Starting from these simple propositions, we can easily develop a complete theory of optical imagery for the simple cases mentioned above. Thus, for example,

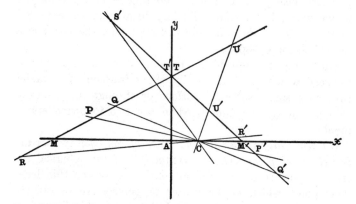

Fig. 127.—Central collineation: Construction of pairs of conjugate points M, M'; P, P'; Q, Q'; R, R'; S, S'; T, T'; and U, U'. Axis of collineation Ay; center of collineation C.

being given the axis of collineation (Ay) and the center of collineation (C), together with the positions of a pair of conjugate points P, P', we can construct the position of a point Q' conjugate to a given point Q, as follows:

(a) In general, the straight line PQ (Fig. 127) will not pass through the center of collineation. Let the self-conjugate point in which the straight line PQ meets the axis of collineation be designated by T; the image-ray corresponding to the object-ray PT will lie along the straight line TP', and since this ray must pass likewise through the point Q' conjugate to Q, the required point will be at the intersection of the straight lines TP', QC.

(b) But in the special case when the straight line PQ is a central ray (Fig. 128) the construction which has just been given fails, and we must resort to a different procedure,

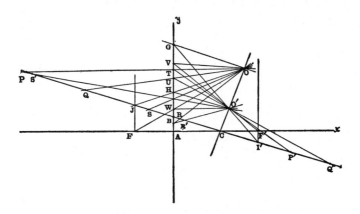

FIG. 128.—Central collineation: Straight line PQ passes through center of collineation (C). Diagram shows case when C does not lie on axis of collineation Ay; as in spherical refracting surface (c > 1).

as follows: Through the points P and C draw a pair of straight lines PO, CO meeting in a point O, and let the point where the straight line PO meets the axis of collineation be designated by T. Also, let O' designate the point of intersection of the straight lines TP' and CO. Then if the point where the straight line QO meets the axis of collineation is designated by U, the required point Q' will be the point of intersection of the straight lines UO' and QC.

The image-point I' conjugate to the infinitely distant object-point I of the pencil of parallel rays whose central ray is PP' may be constructed exactly as described above in (b), provided we have the same data. The straight line

OG is drawn parallel to PP′ meeting the axis of collineation in G, and the required point I′ is the point of intersection of the straight lines GO′ and PP′.

Similarly, the position of the object-point J conjugate to the infinitely distant image-point J′ of the central ray PP′ is found by drawing the straight line O′H parallel to PP′ meeting the axis of collineation in H; then the point of intersection of the straight lines OH, PP′ will be the required point J.

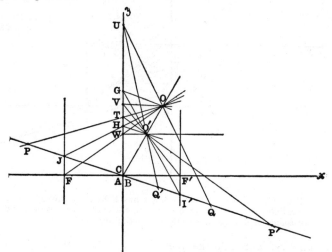

FIG. 129.—Central collineation: Straight line PQ passes through center of collineation (C). Diagram shows case when C lies on axis of collineation Ay, as in infinitely thin lens ($c = 1$).

The focal points F, F′ on the optical axis are constructed in precisely the same way as the two points J, I′ on the central ray PP′.

The special case when *the center of collineation* (C) *lies on the axis of collineation*, that is, when the two points A and C are coincident, is shown in Fig. 129, which evidently corresponds to the case of an infinitely thin lens surrounded by the same medium on both sides.

It would be easy to show by the methods of projective geometry that the straight lines FJ, F'I' are parallel to the axis of collineation and that we have the following relations between the points J, I' and the two self-conjugate points B, C on the central ray JI':

$$JB = CI', \quad I'B = CJ, \quad \frac{I'B}{BJ} = c,$$

where c denotes a constant called *the invariant of central collineation*, which has the value $n':n$ for a spherical refracting surface and the value $+1$ for a thin lens surrounded by the same medium on both sides. For a spherical mirror, $c = -1$. For the axial ray the above relations may be written:

$$FA = CF', \quad F'A = CF, \quad \frac{F'A}{AF} = c.$$

The reader who wishes to pursue this subject will find a complete discussion at the end of Chapter V of the author's *Principles and Methods of Geometrical Optics* published by The Macmillan Company of New York.

98. Field of View of an Infinitely Thin Lens.—If it is assumed that there are no artificial stops present except in the plane of the lens, and that the imagery is produced by means of paraxial rays only, the field of view in the case of an observer looking through the lens along its axis is easily determined by drawing the straight lines O'G, O'H (Fig. 130, *a* and *b*) in a meridian plane of the lens from the center O' of the eye-pupil to the ends G, H of the diameter of the lens-opening. For the lens-opening acts here just like a round window or port-hole in an opaque wall to limit the field of view in the image-space of the lens. If O designates the position of the axial object-point which is reproduced by the image-point O', then the straight lines OG, OH determine the limits in the meridian plane of the diagram of the field of view of the object-space. Let the straight line B'C' bisected at right angles at O' by the axis of the lens represent the diameter of the pupil in the meridian plane of the lens; and construct the line BOC whose image in the lens is the diameter B'O'C' of the pupil of the eye. Then the image S' of the luminous point S lying within the object-side field of view may be constructed by drawing through S the straight lines SB, SC to meet the lens in two points which

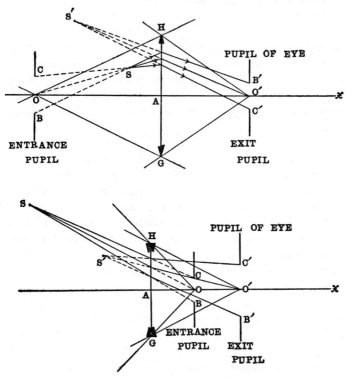

Fig. 130, *a* and *b*.—Field of view of infinitely thin lens for given position of eye on axis of lens. (*a*) Convex, (*b*) Concave lens.

must be joined with B', C', respectively; and the point of intersection of these latter lines will be the required point S' conjugate to S. In brief, the circular opening whose diameter is BC is the common base of all the cones of effective rays in the object-space of the lens, just as the pupil of the eye itself is the common base of the cones of effective rays in the image-space. Assuming that the lens-opening is large enough to permit the entire pupil of the eye to be filled with rays emanating from an axial object-point, the lens-opening GH acts as field-stop and the pupil of the eye as aperture-stop (Chapter XII).

PROBLEMS

1. Show how to construct the optical center of a lens. Draw diagrams for the various forms of convex and concave lenses; and prove that the distance of the optical center from the vertex of the first face is equal to $r_1 d/(r_1 - r_2)$, where r_1, r_2 denote the radii of the two surfaces and d denotes the axial thickness of the lens.

2. In each of the following lenses the axial thickness is 2 cm. Find the position of the optical center, and draw a diagram for each lens showing the position of this point.

(a) Double convex lens of radii 10 and 16 cm.; (b) Double concave lens of radii 10 and 16 cm.; (c) Plano-convex lens; (d) Positive meniscus of radii 10 and 16 cm.; (e) Negative meniscus of radii 20 and 16 cm.; (f) Lens of zero curvature.

3. Rays of light diverging from a point one foot in front of a thin lens are brought to a focus 4 inches beyond it. Find the focal length.   Ans. $f = +3$ inches.

4. An object is placed one foot in front of a thin convex lens of focal length 9 inches. Where is the image formed?
                    Ans. 3 feet from the lens on the other side.

5. Rays coming from a point 6 inches in front of a thin lens are converged to a point 18 inches on the other side of the lens. Find the focal length.   Ans. $f = +4.5$ inches.

6. An object is placed in front of a thin lens at a distance of 30 cm. from it. The image is virtual and 10 cm. from the lens. Find the focal length.   Ans. $f = -15$ cm.

7. The radius of the first face of a thin double convex lens made of glass of index 1.5 is 20 cm. If the focal length of the lens is 30 cm., what must be the radius of the second face?   Ans. 60 cm.

8. A thin convex lens made of glass of index 1.5 has a focal length of 12.5 cm. If the radius of the second face is +17.5 cm., what is the radius of the first face? And if the lens is concave, and the radius of the first face is +17.5 cm., what is the radius of the second face?

Ans. In both cases the radius is +4.6 cm.

9. The focal length of a double convex lens was found to be 30.6 cm., and its radii 30.4 and 34.5 cm. Find the index of refraction of the glass. Ans. 1.528.

10. The focal length of a glass lens in air is 5 inches. What will be the focal length of the lens in water, assuming that the indices of refraction of air, glass and water are 1, $\frac{3}{2}$ and $\frac{4}{3}$, respectively? Ans. 20 inches.

11. Show that any thin lens which is thicker in the middle than out towards the edges is convergent, provided the lens-medium is more highly refracting than the surrounding medium.

12. Show that the focal length of a thin plano-convex lens is twice that of a double convex lens, if the curvatures of the curved surfaces are all equal in magnitude.

13. Find the focal length of a thin double convex diamond lens, of index 2.4875, the radius of each surface being 4 cm. Ans. 13.4 mm.

14. The curved surface of a thin plano-convex lens of glass of index 1.5 has a radius of 12 inches. Find its focal length. What must be the radii of a symmetric double convex lens of same material which has same focal length?

Ans. $f = 24$ inches; $r = 24$ inches.

15. The radii of a thin double convex lens are 9 cm. and 12 cm. The lens is made of glass of index 1.5. If light diverges from a point 18 cm. in front of the lens, where will it be focused? Ans. Real image, 24 cm. from lens.

16. A thin lens is made of glass of index n. If the focal length of the lens in air is a, and if its focal length in a liquid is b, show that the index of refraction of the liquid is

$$\frac{bn}{b+a(n-1)}.$$

17. Draw figures, approximately to scale, showing the paths of the rays of light, and the positions of the images formed when a luminous object is placed at a distance of (a) 1 inch, (b) 6 inches from a convex lens of focal length 2 inches.

18. An object is placed 8 inches from a thin convex lens, and its image is formed 24 inches on the other side of the lens. If the object were moved nearer the lens until its distance was 4 inches, where would the image be?

Ans. Virtual image, 1 foot from lens.

19. A virtual image of an object 30 cm. from a thin lens is formed on the same side of the lens at a distance of 10 cm. from it. Find the focal length of the lens.

Ans. $f = -15$ cm.

20. Light converging towards a point M on the axis of a lens is intercepted and focused at a point M′ on the same side of the lens as M. The distances of M and M′ from the lens are 5 cm. and 10 cm., respectively. Find the focal length of the lens.   Ans. $f = -10$ cm.

21. A far-sighted person can see distinctly only at a distance of 40 cm. or more. How much will his range of distinct vision be increased by using spectacles of focal length +32 cm.?

Ans. The spectacles will enable him to see distinctly objects as near to his eye as 17.78 cm., so that his range of distinct vision will be increased by 22.22 cm.

22. The projection lens of a lantern has a focal length of one foot. If the screen is 1024 feet away, how far back of the lens must the glass slide be placed?   Ans. 1024/1023 ft.

23. An engraver uses a magnifying glass of focal length +4 inches, holding it close to the eye. At what distance must the lens be from the work so that the magnification may be fourfold?   Ans. 3 inches.

24. Assuming that the optical system of the eye is equivalent to a thin convex lens of focal length 15 mm., what will

be the size of the retinal image of a child 1 meter high at a distance of 15 meters from the eye?   Ans. 1 mm.

25. A millimeter scale is placed at a distance of 84 cm. in front of a convex lens, and it was found that 10 mm. of the scale corresponded to 29 mm. of its real inverted image. Find the focal length of the lens.   Ans. $f = +62.5$ cm.

26. If X, X' and Y, Y' are two pairs of conjugate points on the axis of an infinitely thin lens, and if the lens is midway between X and Y', show that it is also midway between X' and Y.

27. M and M' are a pair of conjugate axial points with respect to an infinitely thin lens whose optical center is at a point designated by A. Show that when the lens is shifted from A to a point B such that $MB = AM'$, the points M and M' will be conjugate to each other with respect to the lens in this new position.

28. Given the positions of the focal points F, F' of an infinitely thin lens, show how to construct the image-point M' conjugate to an axial object-point M. Draw diagrams for convex and concave lenses.

29. At the optical center (A) of a thin lens erect a perpendicular to the axis of the lens, and take a point L on this perpendicular such that $AL = f$, where f denotes the primary focal length. Through A draw a line AP in such a direction that $\angle F'AP = 45°$, where F' designates the secondary focal point of the lens. Take a point M on the axis of the lens, and draw the straight line ML meeting the straight line AP in a point S. If M' designates the foot of the perpendicular let fall from S to the axis of the lens, show that M, M' are a pair of conjugate axial points. Draw two diagrams, one for a convex and the other for a concave lens.

30. Derive the image-equations in the case of an infinitely thin lens in the form: $1/u' = 1/u + 1/f$, $y'/y = u'/u$.

31. Show that the focal points of an infinitely thin lens are at equal distances on opposite sides of the lens.

32. A candle is placed at a distance of 2 meters from a wall, and when a lens is placed between the candle and the wall at a distance of 50 cm. from the candle, a distinct image of the latter is cast upon the wall. Find the focal length of the lens and the magnification of the image.

Ans. $f = 37.5$ cm.; image is 3 times as large as object.

33. The distance between a real object and its real image in an infinitely thin lens is 32 inches. If the image is 3 times as large as the object, find the position and focal length of the lens.

Ans. The lens is a convex lens of focal length 6 inches placed between object and image at a distance of 8 inches from the object.

34. When an object is held at a distance of 6 cm. from one face of a thin lens, the image of the object formed by reflection in this face is found to lie in the same plane as the object. If the object is placed at a distance of 20 cm. from the lens, the image produced by the lens is inverted and of the same size as the object. The lens is made of glass of index 1.5. Find the radii of the two surfaces.

Ans. The lens is a convex meniscus of radii 6 and $\frac{30}{11}$ cm.

35. In a magic lantern the image of the slide is thrown upon a screen by means of a thin convex lens. Show that the adjustment for focusing is always possible provided that the distance from the slide to the screen is not less than 4 times the focal length of the lens, and provided that the lens can move in its tube to a distance from the slide equal to twice the focal length.

36. A person holds a lens in front of his eye and observes that by reflection at the nearer surface an object which is 6 feet from the lens appears upright and diminished to one-twentieth of its height. Looking through the lens at an object on the other side 6 feet from the lens, its image is inverted and diminished in height to one-tenth. The lens is a glass lens of index 1.5. Find the radii of its surfaces.   Ans. A double convex lens of radii $\frac{12}{19}$ and $\frac{12}{25}$ ft.

37. How far from a lens must an object be placed so that its image will be erect and half as high as the object?

Ans. The object must be in the second focal plane of the lens. (Draw diagram showing construction of image for convex lens and also a diagram for concave lens.)

38. How far from a thin lens must an object be placed so that its image will be inverted and half as high as the object? Draw two diagrams, showing construction of image for convex lens and for concave lens.

Ans. If the optical center of the lens and the primary focal point are designated by A and F, respectively, and if the axial point of the object is designated by M, then AM = 3AF.

39. An object is to be placed in front of a convex lens of focal length 18 inches in such a position that its image is magnified 3 times. Find the two possible positions, and draw diagram for each position showing the construction of the image.

Ans. If image is inverted, object must be 2 ft. from lens; if it is erect, object must be 1 ft. from lens.

40. In the preceding example if the lens were concave, where would the object have to be?

Ans. The object would be virtual, at a distance of 1 ft. from the lens for an erect image, and at a distance of 2 ft. for an inverted image.

41. A person can see distinctly at a distance of 1 foot, and he finds that when he holds a certain lens close to his eye small objects are seen distinctly and magnified 6 times. Find the focal length of the lens.   Ans. $f = +2.4$ inches.

42. Derive the Newtonian formula $x.x' = -f^2$ for a lens.

43. A convex lens is used to produce an image of a fixed object on a fixed screen. Show that, in general, there will be two possible positions of the lens, and prove that the height of the object is the geometrical mean between the heights of the two images.

44. A copper cent is 19 mm. in diameter and a silver

half dollar is 30.4 mm. in diameter. How far from a convex lens of focal length 10 cm. must the smaller coin be placed so that its image in the lens will be just the size of the larger one?

Ans. It must be placed in front of the lens at a distance of either 16.25 cm. or 3.75 cm.

45. What must be the radius of the curved surface of a thin plano-convex lens made of glass of index 1.5 which will give a real image of an object placed 2 cm. in front of the lens and magnified 3 times?   Ans. 7.5 mm.

46. Find the magnification of a convex lens of focal length 0.2 inch for an eye whose distance of most distinct vision is 14 inches.   Ans. 71 times.

47. An object is placed in front of a convex lens at a distance from it equal to 1.5 times the focal length. Find the linear magnification. If the object is removed to twice this distance, what will be the magnification?   Ans. -2; $-\frac{1}{2}$.

48. An object 5 cm. high is placed 12 cm. in front of a thin lens of focal length 8 cm. Find the position, size and nature of the image (a) for a convex lens, and (b) for a concave lens; and draw accurate diagram for each case.

Ans. (a) Real, inverted image, 10 cm. high, 24 cm. from lens; (b) Virtual, erect image, 2 cm. high, 4.8 cm. from lens.

49. When an object is placed at a point R on the axis of a thin lens of focal length f, the image is erect, and when the object is moved to a point S the image is the same size as before but inverted; show that

$$\mathrm{SR} = \frac{2f}{m},$$

where m is a positive number denoting the value of the ratio of the size of the image to that of the object.

50. A screen, placed at right angles to the axis of a thin lens of focal length f, receives the image of a small object. If the image is 20 times as large as the object, show that the distance of the screen from the lens is equal to $21f$.

51. Given a convex lens, a concave lens, a concave mirror and a convex mirror, each of focal length 20 cm. An object is placed in front of each in turn at distances of 40, 20 and 10 cm. Draw diagrams showing the construction of the image for each lens and each mirror and for each of the three given positions of the object; and find the position and character of the image in each case.

52. A plane mirror is placed anywhere behind a convex lens with its plane at right angles to the axis of the lens. A needle is set up perpendicular to the axis in the primary focal plane of the lens. Show that the image of the needle produced by rays that have passed twice through the lens will lie also in the primary focal plane and will be of the same size as the object but inverted.

53. An object is placed in front of a thin convex lens at a distance a from it not greater than twice its focal length f; and a plane mirror is adjusted in the secondary focal plane of the lens. Show that a real image formed by rays which have passed twice through the lens will be formed at a distance b in front of the lens; and that $f = (a+b)/2$. Show also that the image is of the same size as the object but inverted. Draw a diagram showing the construction of the image.

54. A convex lens of focal length 10 cm. is placed at a distance of 2 cm. in front of a plane mirror which is perpendicular to the axis of the lens. Where must an eye be placed in front of the lens so that it may see its own image by means of rays which, after having traversed the lens twice, return into the eye as bundles of parallel rays?

Ans. 3.75 cm. from the lens.

55. A thin convex lens of focal length 10 inches is placed in front of a concave mirror of focal length 5 inches. The distance between the lens and the mirror is 10 inches. An object is placed in front of the lens at any distance from it. Show that its image formed by rays which have passed twice through the lens will lie at an equal distance from the

lens on the other side of it, and that it will be of the same size as the object but inverted.

56. A thin convex lens of focal length 12 inches is placed 12 inches in front of a concave mirror of focal length 8 inches. An object is placed 3 inches in front of the lens. Show that its image formed by rays which have passed twice through the lens is in the same plane as the object and of the same size, but inverted.

57. The focal length of a thin symmetric double concave lens made of glass of index 1.5 is five inches. A luminous point lies on the axis so far away that it may be considered as being at infinity. Prove that its image formed by rays which are reflected at the first surface is 2.5 inches in front of the lens; the image formed by rays which are refracted twice at the first surface and reflected once at the second surface is on the other side of the lens at a distance of 1.25 inches from it; and, finally, the image formed by rays which after being reflected twice at the second surface have emerged again into the surrounding air is 0.5 inch from the lens on the side away from the source.

58. A concave mirror, of radius r, has its center at the optical center of a thin lens, of focal length f, and the axes of lens and mirror are in the same straight line. Rays coming from an axial object point at a distance u from the lens traverse the lens and after being reflected at the mirror pass through the lens again and emerge from it as a bundle of rays parallel to the axis. Prove that

$$\frac{1}{u}+\frac{2}{r}+\frac{2}{f}=0.$$

59. Being given the axis and the optical center of an infinitely thin lens and also the positions of a pair of conjugate points on the axis, construct the positions of the focal points.

60. The positions of the focal points of an infinitely thin lens are designated by F, F′ and the position of the optical center by A: show that

FM : AM = AM : M′M and F′M′ : AM′ = AM′ : MM′,

where M, M′ designate the positions of a pair of conjugate points on the axis.

CHAPTER VIII

99. Concerning Curvature and its Measure.—Since the
rays or lines of advance of the light-waves are always at
right angles to the wave-surface (§ 7), one way of investigating the procedure of light is to study the form of the
wave-surface; for, in general, the effect of reflection and refraction will be to produce an abrupt change of curvature
of the wave-front.   In this method attention is concentrated primarily on the wave-surface rather than on the
rays themselves; but in reality the only difference between
it and the ray-method consists in a new point of view, which
may, however, be serviceable.   Thus, when a plane wave
is incident on a lens, the wave-front on emergence will no
longer be plane but curved in such fashion that the light-
waves either converge to or diverge from a point in the second
focal plane of the lens.   The effect of the lens or optical
system is to imprint a new curvature on the wave-front,
and if the change of curvature which is thus produced can
be ascertained, the final form of the wave can be determined
by mere algebraic addition of the initial and impressed
curvatures.   It will be necessary, however, to explain precisely what is meant by this term curvature and how it is
measured.

In passing along an arc of a plane curve from a point A
(Fig. 131) to a point B, the *total curvature* of the arc AB is
the change of direction of the curve between A and B, which
is evidently measured by the angle between the tangents
to the curve at these two places.   This angle is equal to
the angle at O between the normals AO and BO which are

258

perpendicular to the tangents at A and B. The *mean curvature* between A and B is the change of this angle per unit length of the arc AB. If, therefore, the length of the arc AB is denoted by a and the magnitude of the angle BOA

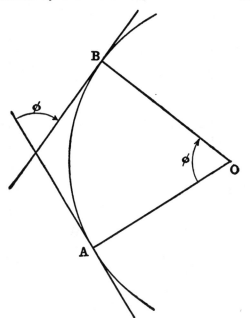

Fig. 131.—Mean curvature of arc AB measured by ϕ/a, where a-denotes length of arc and ϕ denotes angle between the normals AO and BO.

by φ, the mean curvature between A and B is equal to φ/a. And the limiting value of this quotient when the point B is infinitely near to A is the measure of the actual curvature at the point A or, as we say, *the curvature at* A. If the curvature at A is denoted by the capital letter R, then R is equal to the limiting value of φ/a when the arc a is indefinitely small.

In Fig. 132 the point B is supposed to be infinitely near to A; and the point of intersection C of the normals drawn to the two contiguous points A, B on the curve passing through these two points is called the *center of curvature* of the curve at the point A; the circle described in the plane of the curve around this point C as center with radius

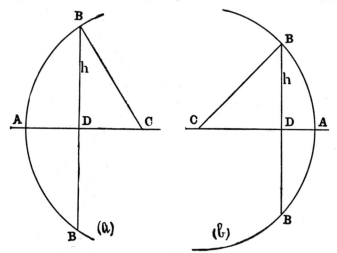

Fig. 132, *a* and *b*.—Curvature of arc BAB at point A midway between B and B is measured by the sagitta AD. (*a*) Convex, (*b*) Concave arc.

$r = $AC, which will coincide with the given curve throughout the infinitely small arc AB, is called the *circle of curvature* and its radius r is called the *radius of curvature* at the point A. Now since by definition the angle φ is equal to the arc BA divided by the radius r, that is, since $\varphi = a/r$, the curvature at A is equal to $1/r$; that is, *the curvature at any point on a curve is equal to the reciprocal of the radius of curvature at that point*, or

$$R = \frac{1}{r}.$$

The sign of the curvature is the same as that of the radius of curvature. Accordingly, *if the surface is convex with respect to the incident light, the curvature is to be counted as positive*, in accordance with our previous usage in this respect.

Thus, for example, when spherical waves spread out from a point-source, the wave-front at any instant is concave and its curvature is reckoned, therefore, as negative. If a convex lens is interposed at a distance from the point-source greater than its focal length, the light-waves will thereby be converged to a focus on the other side of the lens whence they will ultimately diverge again. While the wave-front is advancing from the lens to the focus, its curvature is positive; at the focus itself the wave-front collapses into a point, the curvature of the wave at this place being infinite; and beyond the focus the curvature becomes negative. As long as the wave does not undergo any reflection or refraction, its curvature varies continuously; whereas a sudden change of curvature is imprinted on the wave when there is a transition from one medium to another.

Another method of measuring the curvature of a small arc BB (Fig. 132) is in terms of its bulge AD, where the points designated by A and D are the middle points of the arc and its chord. If the points A and B are so close together that they may be regarded as lying on the circle of curvature corresponding to the point A, the ordinate $DB = h$ will be a mean proportional between the two segments into which the diameter of the circle is divided by the point D, so that we have the proportion:

$$AD : h = h : (2r - AD).$$

Since the segment AD is always very small in comparison with the diameter of the circle of curvature, only a vanishingly small error will be introduced by writing $2r$ in place of $(2r - AD)$ in the above proportion. Thus, we obtain:

$$AD = \frac{h^2}{2r},$$

or since $R = 1/r$,

$$AD = \frac{h^2}{2} R.$$

If the arc BB is not infinitely small, this equation contains a certain error which is more and more negligible in proportion as the arc is taken smaller and smaller. For a small arc, therefore, we may say that the segment AD is proportional to the curvature (R) at the point A, and hence it may be said to measure the curvature at this place. This segment AD was called by KEPLER the *sagitta* of the arc BB because of its resemblance to an "arrow" on a bow.

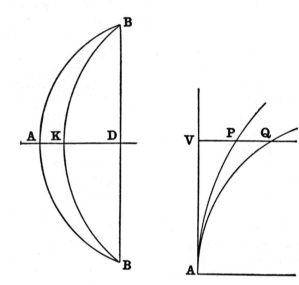

FIG. 133.—Curvatures of arcs BAB and BKB are in same ratio as their sagittæ AD and KD.

FIG. 134.—Curvatures of arcs AP and AQ in same ratio as their sagittæ VP and VQ.

Obviously, it does measure the bulge or "sag" of the curve at A. In Fig. 133, where the straight line BDB is the common chord of the small arcs BAB and BKB, the curvatures at A and K are evidently in the ratio of AD to KD. Or, again, consider Fig. 134, where the two arcs AP and AQ have a common tangent at A. If on this tangent a point V is taken very close to A, and if through V a straight line is drawn perpendicular to AV intersecting the two arcs in the points designated by P and Q, the curvatures at A will be in the ratio of VP to VQ.

In many optical problems (as has been explained in the last two chapters) we are concerned only with a very small portion of the reflecting and refracting surface (case of paraxial rays), and under such circumstances it is especially convenient and simple to measure the curvatures of the wave-fronts before and after refraction or reflection and the curvatures of the mirrors or lenses by means of their sagittæ. In fact, the ordinary method of determining the curvature of an optical surface with an instrument called a *spherometer* (Fig. 135) consists essentially in employing a micrometer screw to measure the *sagitta* of the arc whose chord is equal to the diameter of the circle circumscribed about the equilateral triangle formed by the conical points of the tripod which supports the instrument on the curved surface to be measured. The simple *lens-gauge* (Fig. 136) used by opticians to measure the power of a spectacle lens is based on the same principle. In size and external appearance it resembles a watch, except that on its lower side it has three metallic pins projecting from it in parallel lines which all lie in a plane parallel to the face of the gauge. The two outer pins are stationary and symmetrically placed so that when the instrument is held in a vertical plane with the pins pointing downwards, the straight line BB (Fig. 132) joining the conical points of the outer pins is horizontal; whereas

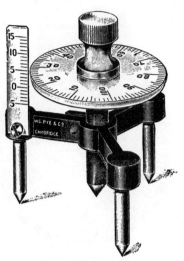

FIG. 135.—Spherometer.

the other pin which is midway between the two outer ones is capable of being pushed upwards by a slight pressure so that its tip A which left to itself falls a little below the straight line BB can be made to ascend a little above this line. The vertical displacement of the tip A of the middle pin above or below the level of the chord BB, which is equal to the *sagitta* of the arc BAB whose curvature is to be measured, is registered on the dial (see § 108) by the angular movement of a light hand or pointer with which the movable pin is connected. If the circle is drawn which passes through the end-points of the three pins B, A and B, the

Fig. 136.—Lens-gauge.

diameter drawn through A will bisect the chord BB at a point D; and since the products of the segments of two intersecting chords of a circle are equal, we obtain immediately:

$$AD\,(2r - AD) = h^2,$$

where r denotes the radius of the circle and $2h$ = chord BB. Hence, exactly as above, we obtain here also:

$$AD = \frac{h^2}{2r}\ , \text{ approximately;}$$

thus proving again that the *sagitta* AD is proportional to the curvature $1/r = R$. In using the lens-gauge care must be taken to see that the plane of the instrument is not tilted out of the vertical, and this is one reason why a spherometer is more accurate. On the other hand, the lens-gauge, besides being more handy and convenient, possesses a decided advantage over a spherometer supported on a tripod by reason of the fact that it can be used to measure the curvatures in different meridians of a non-spherical surface of revolution, for example, the curvatures of the normal sections (§ 111) of a cylindrical or of a toric surface (§ 112). How the lens-gauge is graduated will be explained presently (§ 108).

100. Refraction of a Spherical Wave at a Plane Surface. —The whole duty of an optical system, therefore, whether

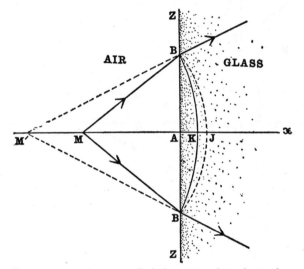

Fig. 137, *a.*—Divergent spherical waves refracted at plane surface from air to glass.

it be a single lens or mirror or a combination of such parts is to imprint a certain curvature on the surface of the incident wave; and if we consider only such portions of the wave-fronts as lie very close to the axis of symmetry of the instrument, it is evident that this method of investigating the change of curvature that is produced in the wave-front at the point where the axis meets it should lead to precisely the same results as have been found already in the corresponding problems concerning the reflection and refraction of paraxial rays. In fact, according to this method, these results should be found to apply not merely to the case when the reflecting and refracting surfaces are plane or spherical, but equally also to the more general case when these surfaces have any form whatever, provided they are symmetrical around the optical axis.

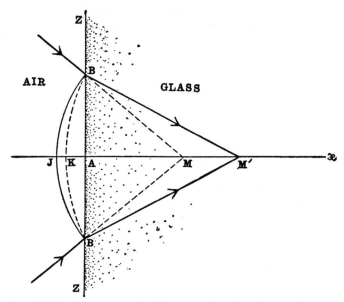

Fig. 137, b.—Convergent spherical waves refracted at plane surface from air to glass.

We shall begin by investigating the simple case of the refraction of a spherical wave at a plane surface.

In the diagrams (Fig. 137, a, b, c, and d) the straight line ZZ represents the trace in the plane of the paper of a plane refracting surface separating two media of indices n, n'. Around the point M as center spherical waves are supposed to be advancing in the first medium (n) towards the refracting surface, and at a certain instant when the disturbance has begun to affect a point B on this surface the incident wave will be represented in the plane of the figure by the circular arc BJB described around M as center with radius equal to BM; the point designated by J lying on the arc midway between its two ends B, B, so that the straight line MJ is the perpendicular bisector at A of the chord BB. The two points M, J will be found to lie always on opposite

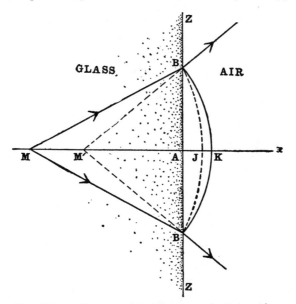

Fig. 137, *c.*—Divergent spherical waves refracted at plane surface from glass to air.

sides of the refracting plane. In Fig. 137, *a* and *c*, where the point M is shown as lying in front of the surface ZZ, the arc BJB is indicated by a dotted line, because it marks the position which the incident wave-front would have had if the refracting surface had not been interposed. But the waves travel faster in the rarer medium (air) than in the denser medium (glass); and, consequently, the vertex of the refracted wave-front instead of being at the point J on the axis will be at a point K on this line, and therefore the position of the refracted wave-front at the moment when the disturbance arrives at B will be represented by the arc BKB of a circle whose center is at a point M′ on the axis. If, for example, the waves are refracted from air to glass, that is, if $n'>n$, the velocity v in the first me-

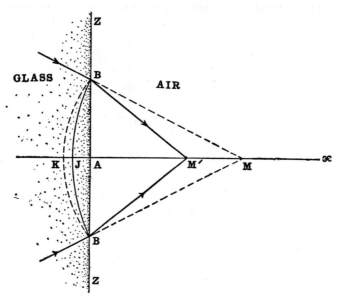

FIG. 137, d.—Convergent spherical waves refracted at plane surface from glass to air.

dium will be greater than the velocity v' in the second medium, so that for this case AK will be shorter than AJ, and the effect of the retardation will be to flatten the wave-front, as shown in Fig. 137, a and b. On the other hand, if $n'<n$, then $v'>v$, so that now AK will be longer than AJ, and the effect of the refraction will be to increase the curvature or bulge of the wave-front, as shown in Fig. 137, c and d. Since (see § 31)

$$AJ : AK = v : v' = n' : n,$$

it follows that
$$n'.KA = n.JA.$$
Now JA and KA are the *sagittæ* (§ 99) of the small arcs
BJB and BKB, respectively, and hence they are proportional to the curvatures of these arcs, that is, to 1/JM and
1/KM′. If the point B is infinitely near to A, we may put
JM = AM = u, KM′ = AM′ = u'; and thus we obtain:
$$\frac{n'}{u'} = \frac{n}{u} ;$$
which will be recognized as the relation which we found
for the refraction of paraxial rays at a plane surface (§ 41).

**101. Refraction of a Spherical Wave at a Spherical Sur-
face.**—Here the same method is employed as in the preced-

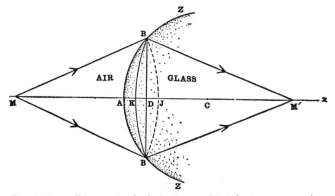

Fig. 138, *a*.—Divergent spherical waves refracted at convex surface
from air to glass.

ing section. In each of the diagrams (Fig. 138, *a*, *b*, *c*, *d*,
e, *f*, *g*, and *h*) the circular arc ZZ represents the trace in the
plane of the paper of a meridian section of the spherical
refracting surface with its vertex at A and center at C. The
surface is convex in Fig. 138, *a*, *b*, *c*, and *d* and concave in
Fig. 138, *e*, *f*, *g*, and *h*. The point M on the axis is the center
of a system of spherical waves which are advancing in the
first medium, of index *n*, towards the refracting surface.
In Fig. 138, *a*, *c*, *e*, and *g* the point M lies in front of the re-

fracting surface, whereas in Fig. 138, *b*, *d*, *f*, and *h* this point is situated on the other side of the surface. The points

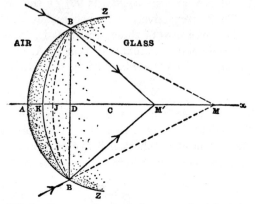

FIG. 138, *b*.—Convergent spherical waves refracted at convex surface from air to glass.

marked B, B are two points on the arc ZZ very close together but at equal distances on opposite sides of the op-

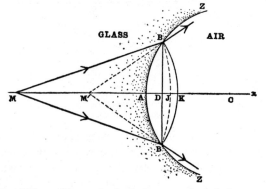

FIG. 138, *c*.—Divergent spherical waves refracted at convex surface from glass to air.

tical axis, so that the arc BJB described around M as center with radius equal to BM shows the position of the wavefront of the incident waves at the instant when the disturbance begins to affect the points B, B; the point where this arc crosses the optical axis being designated by J.

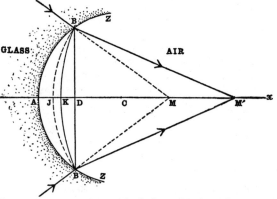

FIG. 138, *d.*—Convergent spherical waves refracted at convex surface from glass to air.

When the waves enter the second medium, of index n', they will proceed with augmented or diminished speed ac-

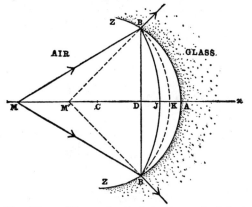

FIG. 138, *e.*—Divergent spherical waves refracted at concave surface from air to glass.

cording as n is greater or less than n'. In the diagrams Fig. 138, *a, b, e, f,* the case is represented where $n' > n$; and in the diagrams Fig. 138, *c, d, g, h* the second medium is

supposed to be less highly refracting than the first $(n' < n)$.
The center of curvature of the refracted waves will lie at

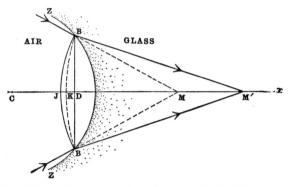

FIG. 138, *f*.—Convergent spherical waves refracted at concave
surface from air to glass.

a point M′ on the axis, so that the wave-front in the second
medium which passes through B, B will be represented by

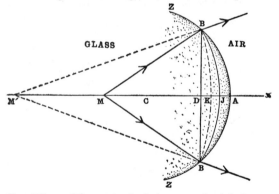

FIG. 138, *g*.—Divergent spherical waves refracted at concave surface from glass to air.

the arc BKB of a circle described around M′ as center with
radius equal to BM′; the point where this arc crosses the
axis being designated by K.

In each of the diagrams of Fig. 138 one of the two arcs

BJB and BKB is shown by a dotted line, because, on account of the interposition of the refracting surface ZZ, the part of one or the other of these wave-fronts which is comprised between B, B does not actually materialize; but this circumstance does not in the least affect the geometrical relations.

Thus, during the time the light takes to go in the first medium from J to A (or from A to J), it will travel in the

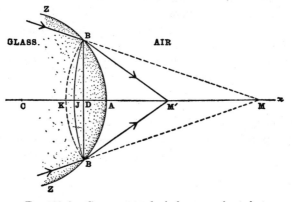

FIG. 138, h.—Convergent spherical waves refracted at concave surface from glass to air.

second medium from K to A (or from A to K). In other words, the optical lengths (§ 39) of the axial line-segments AJ and AK are equal, and therefore:

$$n.\mathrm{AJ} = n'.\mathrm{AK}.$$

This shows how the position of the point M' may be found, for we have only to lay off on the axis a piece

$$\mathrm{AK} = \frac{n}{n'}\,\mathrm{AJ},$$

and to locate the point M' at the place where the perpendicular bisector of the chord BK intersects the optical axis.

Draw the chord BDB crossing the optical axis at right

angles at the point D; then, evidently, since

AJ = AD + DJ = AD − JD, AK = AD + DK = AD − KD,

we have: $n(AD − JD) = n'(AD − KD)$.

Now recalling the fact that the points B, B were assumed to be very close to the vertex A of the spherical refracting surface, we remark that the arcs whose summits are at A, J and K are all very small; and hence the segments AD, JD and KD may be regarded as the *sagittæ* of these arcs and proportional to their curvatures (§ 99), viz., $1/r$, $1/u$ and $1/u'$, respectively, where $r = AC$, $u = AM = JM$, $u' = AM' = KM'$, approximately. Introducing these values in the equation above, we obtain the characteristic invariant relation for the case of the refraction of paraxial rays at a spherical surface, viz.,

$$n\left(\frac{1}{r} - \frac{1}{u}\right) = n'\left(\frac{1}{r} - \frac{1}{u'}\right),$$

in the same form as was found in § 78.

102. Reflection of a Spherical Wave at a Spherical Mirror.—The problem of reflection at a spherical mirror may

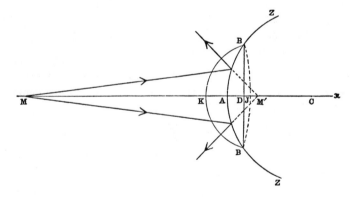

Fɪɢ. 139, *a*.—Divergent spherical waves reflected at convex mirror.

be investigated in the same way. In Fig. 139, *a* and *b*, the arcs BAB, BJB and BKB represent the traces of the mirror and of the wave-fronts of the incident and reflected waves, respectively. In the case of reflection the condition evidently is:

$$KA = AJ,$$

because while the incident wave advances along the optical axis through the distance AJ or JA, the reflected wave will travel in the opposite direction through an equal distance

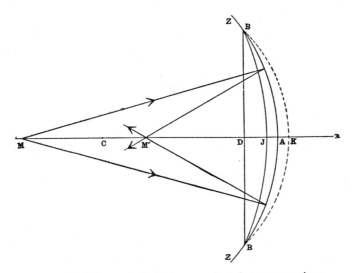

Fig. 139, *b.*—Divergent spherical waves reflected at concave mirror.

KA or AK. Therefore the center M′ of the reflected wave may be found by laying off AK = JA and locating the point where the perpendicular bisector of the chord KB intersects the axis.

Here also the segments AD, JD and KD are to be regarded as the measures of the curvatures of the small arcs BAB, BJB and BKB, respectively, and proportional, therefore, to the reciprocals of the radii of curvature, viz., $1/r$, $1/u$ and $1/u'$, where $r = AC$, $u = AM = JM$, $u' = AM' = KM'$ in the limit when the arcs are infinitely small. Now

$$KD = KA + AD = AJ + AD = AD + DJ + AD,$$

that is,

$$JD + KD = 2AD;$$

hence, substituting the symbols u, u' and r, we derive the abscissa-formula for the reflection of paraxial rays at a spherical mirror (§ 64), viz.,

$$\frac{1}{u} + \frac{1}{u'} = \frac{2}{r} \; ;$$

which may be expressed in words by saying that *the curvature of the mirror is the arithmetical mean of the curvatures of the incident and reflected waves at the vertex of the mirror;* that is,

$$R = \frac{U + U'}{2} \; ,$$

where $U = 1/u$, $U' = 1/u'$ denote the curvatures of the incident and reflected waves, and $R = 1/r$ denotes the curvature of the mirror. Thus, for example, if an incident plane wave ($U = 0$) is advancing parallel to the axis of the mirror, the curvature of the reflected wave will be twice that of the mirror, and consequently, the center F of the reflected wave-front will lie midway between the vertex A and the center C of the mirror (§ 69).

Of course, the condition $KA = AJ$ might have been derived at once from the condition $n.AJ = n'.AK$, which was found in § 101, by putting in this equation $n' = -n$, in accordance with the general rule given in § 75.

103. Refraction of a Spherical Wave through an Infinitely Thin Lens.—Since, as has been shown (§ 89), a homocentric bundle of incident paraxial rays with its vertex at a point M on the axis of a thin lens is transformed into a homocentric bundle of emergent rays with its vertex at the conjugate point M', we know that if the waves are spherical before traversing the lens, they will issue from it as spherical waves, at least in the neighborhood of the axis.

Each of the diagrams (Fig. 140, *a* and *b*) represents a meridian section of the lens which is convex in one figure and concave in the other. As a matter of fact the lens is assumed to be infinitely thin, and perhaps it is well to call particular attention to this fundamental consideration, because in the diagrams, in order to exhibit the relations by means of the *sagittæ*, the lens-thickness is shown very much exaggerated.

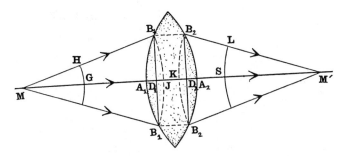

Fɪɢ. 140, *a*.—Divergent spherical waves refracted through thin convex lens.

Take a point B_1 on the first surface of the lens not very far from the vertex A_1 of this surface, and around the axial object-point M as center with radius equal to B_1M describe the circular arc B_1JB_1 which is bisected by the axis of the lens in the point designated by J; evidently, this arc will represent the trace in the plane of the diagram of the wave-front of the incident waves at the moment when the disturbance reaches B_1. Now the disturbance which is propagated onwards from B_1 will proceed across the lens to a point B_2 on the second face of the lens, and since the lens is supposed to be infinitely thin, the distances of B_1, B_2 from the axis are to be regarded as equal, that is, $D_1B_1 = D_2B_2$, where D_1, D_2, designate the feet of the perpendiculars let fall from B_1, B_2, respectively, to the axis of the lens. If, therefore, around the point M' conjugate to M an arc B_2KB_2 is described with radius equal to B_2M', which is bisected by the axis at the point designated by K, this arc will represent the trace in the plane of the diagram of the wave-front of the emergent waves at the same instant that the arc B_1JB_1 shows the wave-front of the incident waves.

With M, M' as centers and with any convenient radii describe also the arcs GH, SL intersecting the axis of the

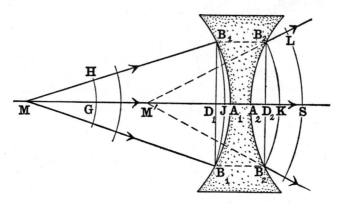

Fig. 140, *b*.—Divergent spherical waves refracted through thin concave lens.

lens at G, S and meeting the straight lines B_1M, B_2M', in H, L, respectively; so that these arcs represent, therefore, successive positions of the wave-front before and after transmission through the lens. Now the optical length of the light-path from H to L is equal to that along the axis of the lens from G to S (§ 39); and, hence, if n, n' denote the indices of refraction of the two media concerned, we may write:

$$n.HB_1 + n'.B_1B_2 + n.B_2L = n.GA_1 + n'.A_1A_2 + n.A_2S;$$

and since

$$n(MH + LM') = n(MG + SM'),$$

we obtain by addition of these two equations:

$$n(MB_1 + B_2M') + n'.B_1B_2 = n(MA_1 + A_2M') + n'.A_1A_2.$$

Now $MB_1 = MJ,$ $B_2M' = KM',$ $B_1B_2 = D_1D_2;$ and therefore:

$$n(MJ - MA_1 + KM' - A_2M') = n'(A_1A_2 - D_1D_2).$$

Substituting in this equation the following expressions, viz.:
$$MJ - MA_1 = A_1M + MJ = A_1J = A_1D_1 + D_1J = A_1D_1 - JD_1,$$
$$KM' - A_2M' = KM' + M'A_2 = KA_2 = KD_2 + D_2A_2$$
$$= KD_2 - A_2D_2,$$
$$A_1A_2 = A_1D_1 + D_1D_2 + D_2A_2 = A_1D_1 + D_1D_2 - A_2D_2,$$
we obtain:
$$n(A_1D_1 - JD_1 + KD_2 - A_2D_2) = n'(A_1D_1 - A_2D_2);$$
which may be put finally in the following form:
$$n(KD_2 - JD_1) = (n' - n)(A_1D_1 - A_2D_2).$$
It has been assumed here that the lens is surrounded by the same medium (n) on both sides, but the same method would lead to a more general formula for which the initial and final media were different.

Evidently, since the points B_1, B_2 are very near the vertices A_1, A_2, the segments A_1D_1, JD_1, A_2D_2, KD_2 may be regarded as the *sagittæ* of the small arcs $B_1A_1B_1$, B_1JB_1, $B_2A_2B_2$, B_2KB_2, respectively; and since these arcs all have equal chords, the reciprocals of the radii of curvature may be substituted in the equation above in place of the *sagittæ*. Accordingly, if the radii of the lens-surfaces are denoted by r_1, r_2, and if we put $AM = JM = u$, $A_2M' = KM' = u'$, as is permissible in this case, we derive immediately the familiar lens-formula for the refraction of paraxial rays (§ 89), viz.:
$$n\left(\frac{1}{u'} - \frac{1}{u}\right) = (n' - n)\left(\frac{1}{r_1} - \frac{1}{r_2}\right) = \frac{n}{f},$$
where f denotes the primary focal length of the lens.

104. Reduced Distance.—If P, Q designate the positions of two points lying both in the same medium of refractive index n, a distinction has already been pointed out (see § 39) between the actual or absolute distance of these points from each other and the so-called "optical length" of the segment PQ of the straight line joining these points, which is obtained by multiplying the absolute length by the index of refraction of the medium, and which is equal therefore to $n \cdot PQ$. A further distinction, due originally to GAUSS, is to be made now by employing the term *reduced distance* between P and Q to mean, not the product, but *the quotient of the distance* PQ *by the index of refraction of the medium in which the two points* P *and* Q *lie;* that is, the reduced distance from P to Q is equal to $\dfrac{PQ}{n}$. Thus, for example, if the medium is glass of index 1.5, and if the distance PQ = 12 inches, the optical distance or equivalent light-path in air will be 18 inches, whereas the reduced distance will be 8 inches. The reduced thickness of a lens is $c = \dfrac{d}{n}$, where $d = A_1A_2$ denotes the distance of the second vertex A_2 of the lens from the first vertex A_1 and n denotes the index of refraction of the lens-substance. The optical distance is never less, and the reduced distance is never greater, than the actual distance. If the medium is air $(n = 1)$, the optical distance and the reduced distance are both equal to the absolute distance. Apparently, the first use of the term "reduced distance" in this sense in English occurs in PENDLEBURY'S *Lenses and systems of lenses, treated after the manner of* GAUSS (Cambridge, 1884). A distinct advantage in the direction of simplification is usually gained in mathematical formulation by denoting a more or less complex function by a single symbol; and modern optical writers, notably GULLSTRAND and his disciples in Germany, have recognized the convenience of this idea of "reduced distance" and utilized it to express the relations between object and image in their simplest forms; as we shall show presently by several examples.

In this connection the attention of the student needs to be called to a point which has been alluded to before (see § 8), but which is not always clearly understood. Although two points P, Q may be situated physically in different media, they may be regarded as optically in the same medium. Thus, any point which is on the prolongation, in either direction, of the line-segment which represents the actual path of a ray of light through a certain medium, *may*, and in fact generally *must*, be regarded as a point belonging to the medium in question, no matter what may be its actual physical environment. No better illustration of this notion can be given than is afforded by considering the focal points on the axis of a spherical refracting surface. The points F and F' lie always on opposite sides of the vertex A, but no matter whether the first focal point F is on one side of A or on the other, it is to be considered always as a point in the first medium; and, similarly, the second focal point F' is to be considered always as a point in the second medium, so that the reduced distance between F and F' is $FA/n + AF'/n'$ both for a convergent and for a divergent system. The *reduced focal lengths* of a spherical refracting surface are $\dfrac{f}{n}$ and $\dfrac{f'}{n'}$; so that the reduced distance of F' from F is equal to $\dfrac{f}{n} - \dfrac{f'}{n'}$.

The boundary between two optical media is a "twilight zone," so to speak, which cannot be said properly to belong to either medium; and hence linear magnitudes which refer specifically to the interface or surface of separation cannot be definitely assigned to one medium or the other. This applies, for example, to the radius of curvature of a mirror or of a refracting surface. Whether a surface which separates air from glass is convex or concave, we have no right to say that the radius of curvature lies in the air or in the glass; and thus we never speak of the "reduced radius" of a reflecting or refracting surface.

105. The Refracting Power.—In the *u*-form of the abscissa-equation which gives the relation between a pair of conjugate points on the axis, we are concerned not so much with the linear magnitudes themselves, that is, with the abscissæ, as with the reciprocals of these magnitudes, which, as we have seen, represent the curvatures of the surfaces of which these abscissæ are the radii. It is partly for this reason that many teachers of geometrical optics regard the so-called "curvature method" of studying these problems as both more natural and more direct than the "ray method." There is certainly much to be said in its favor, but the truth is, both methods have their advantages, and neither is to be preferred to the other. The student who desires to have more than a mere elementary knowledge of optics will find it necessary to be acquainted with both points of view; and when he has attained this position, he will realize that the two methods are perfectly equivalent and that the distinction between them is more or less artificial.

But whether we have the so-called "curvature method" in mind or not, it will evidently be a step in the direction of simplifying the abscissæ-formula if we introduce symbols for the reciprocals of the abscissæ, and thereby get rid of the fractional forms. Thus, instead of employing the reduced focal length, it will be better to introduce a term for the reciprocal of this magnitude. Accordingly, the *refracting power* of an optical system is defined to be *the reciprocal of the reduced primary focal length*. These reciprocal magnitudes will be denoted by capital italic letters. For example, the refracting power of an optical system will be denoted by F; that is, according to the above definition:

$$F = \frac{n}{f}.$$

The refracting power of a *spherical refracting surface* (see § 79) is:

$$F = \frac{n}{f} = -\frac{n'}{f'} = (n'-n)R,$$

where $R = \frac{1}{r}$ denotes the curvature of the surface. If the first medium is air ($n = 1$), then $F = \frac{1}{f}$. The refracting power of a spherical refracting surface is directly proportional to the curvature of the surface.

The *reflecting power* of a *spherical mirror* $(n' = -n,\ f' = f)$ is defined in the same way, viz.,

$$F = \frac{n}{f} = -2n.R,$$

where n denotes the index of refraction of the medium in front of the mirror. Thus, although the position of the focal point (F) and the magnitude of the focal length (f) of a curved mirror will not be altered by changing the medium in front of the mirror, its reflecting power will be affected; and this will be the case whether the mirror is concave or convex. If the focal length of a mirror is 8, its reflecting power will be one-eighth when the mirror is in contact with air $(n = 1)$, but it will be raised to one-sixth if the medium in front of the mirror is water $(n = \frac{4}{3})$.

The refracting power of a *lens* surrounded by the same medium (n) on both sides is

$$F = \frac{n}{f} = -\frac{n}{f'}\ .$$

If the curvatures of the two faces of an *infinitely thin lens* are denoted by R_1 and R_2, that is, if

$$R_1 = \frac{1}{r_1},\ \ R_2 = \frac{1}{r_2},$$

then

$$F = (n' - n)\ (R_1 - R_2),$$

where n' denotes the index of refraction of the lens-substance and n denotes the index of refraction of the surrounding medium. If either one of these media is changed, other things remaining the same, the refracting power of the lens will be altered.

If F_1, F_2 denote the refracting powers of the two surfaces of a lens, then

$$F_1 = (n' - n)R_1, \qquad F_2 = (n - n')R_2,$$

and in place of the preceding equation we may write:

$$F = F_1 + F_2;$$

and thus it appears that *the refracting power of an infinitely thin lens is equal to the algebraic sum of the refracting powers of the lens-surfaces.*

The refracting power of a lens depends, therefore, on the curvatures of both faces, but evidently a lens of given material and of prescribed refracting power may have very different forms. One of the minor problems of optical construction is to *"bend" a lens*, as the technical phrase is, that is, being given the curvature of one face of the lens, to find the curvature of the other face so that the refracting power of the lens may have a given value. If, for example the magnitudes denoted by n, n', R_2 and F are assigned, the curvature of the first face must be:

$$R_1 = R_2 + \frac{F}{n'-n}.$$

If *the media are different on the two sides of the lens*, and if the indices of refraction of the three media in the order in which they are traversed by the light are denoted by n_1, n_2 and n_3, we find easily the following formula for the refracting power of an infinitely thin lens:

$$F = \frac{n_1}{f} = -\frac{n_3}{f'} = (n_2-n_1)R_1 + (n_3-n_2)R_2 = F_1 + F_2,$$

where the symbols have precisely the same meanings as before.

It will be seen from these examples that one effect of introducing the term refracting power is a simplification in consequence of the fact that the two magnitudes denoted by f and f' are now expressed in terms of a single magnitude F.

106. Reduced Abscissa and Reduced " Vergence ".—The reduced abscissæ of a pair of conjugate axial points M, M' are defined in exactly the same way as the reduced focal lengths. The point designated by M is to be regarded always as lying in the first medium of the system, and, similarly, the point designated by M' is to be regarded as lying in the last medium, entirely irrespective of the question as to whether either of these points is "real" or "virtual," as explained in § 104.

By way of illustration, suppose that the optical system consists of a single spherical refracting surface separating two media of indices n and n'. If the origin of abscissæ is taken at the vertex A, so that $u = $ AM, $u' = $ AM', then the reduced abscissæ will be $\dfrac{u}{n}$, $\dfrac{u'}{n'}$. The reciprocals of these magnitudes, denoted by U, U' are called the *reduced "vergences,"* with respect to the point A; thus,

$$U = \frac{n}{u}, \qquad U' = \frac{n'}{u'}.$$

These functions U, U' are the measures of the convergence or divergence of the bundles of object-rays and image-rays; and in this illustration these magnitudes are evidently proportional to the curvatures of the incident and refracted wave-fronts at the instant when the disturbance arrives at the surface of separation of the two media.

Since (§ 79) the abscissa-formula for a *spherical refracting surface* may be written in the form:

$$\frac{n'}{u'} = \frac{n}{u} + \frac{n}{f},$$

this relation may now be expressed in the elegant and convenient form:

$$U' = U + F.$$

This same formula holds in the case of a *spherical mirror*, in which case $U' = -n/u'$, where n denotes the index of refraction of the medium in front of the mirror.

Moreover, the same formula $U' = U + F$ is found to be applicable to the case of an *infinitely thin lens*. If the lens is surrounded by the same medium (n) on both sides, then we must put $U = n/u$, $U' = n/u'$ and $F = n/f$, where n' denotes the index of refraction of the lens-substance. Or in case the last medium (n_3) is different from the first medium (n_1), then $U = n_1/u$, $U' = n_3/u'$, and $F = n_1/f$. In both cases the formula will be found to be identical in form with that given above. In fact, as we shall see in Chapter X, the formula $U' = U + F$ is perfectly general and applicable to any optical instrument which is symmetrical about an axis. The advantage of a single formula which has such wide applicability is obvious. It is easy to remember that *the reduced vergence* (U') *on the image-side of the instrument is equal to the algebraic sum of the reduced vergence* (U) *on the object-side and the refracting power* (F).

If the abscissæ are measured from the focal points F, F', that is, if we put $x = $ FM, $x' = $ F'M', the magnitudes

$$X = \frac{n}{x}, \qquad X' = \frac{n'}{x'}$$

are called the *reduced focal point vergences;* and the relation between X, X' is expressed by the equation:

$$X \cdot X' = -F^2.$$

107. The Dioptry as Unit of Curvature.—Obviously, the magnitudes which have been denoted above by capital italic letters, since they are all equal or proportional to the reciprocals of certain linear magnitudes, are essentially measures of curvature, and hence they must be described or expressed in terms of some *unit of curvature*, which will itself be dependent on the unit of length. Opticians guided by purely practical considerations were the first to recognize the need of a suitable optical unit for this purpose. The unit of curvature which is now almost universally used in spectacle optics and which is coming to be employed more and more in all other branches of optics is the curvature of an arc whose radius of curvature is one meter. To this unit the name *dioptry** has been given. Originally, the

---

* The name "dioptrie" was first suggested by MONOYER of France in 1872 (see *Annales d'oculistique*, LXVIII, 111), being derived from the Greek τὰ διοπτρικά, whence came also the term "dioptrics" which was formerly much used by scientific writers as applying to the phenomena of refraction, especially through lenses. The word is generally written *dioptre* in French and *Dioptrie* in German. Etymologically, the correct English form would appear to be *dioptry*, and this spelling has been adopted by the American translators of both

dioptry was defined as the refracting power of a lens in air
of focal length one meter. Consequently, a lens whose focal
length was 50 cm. or half a meter would have a refracting
power of 2 dptr., whereas another lens of focal length 2 meters
would have a refracting power of $\frac{1}{2}$ dptr. In general, if
the focal length of a lens surrounded by air is f centimeters,
its refracting power will be $100/f$ dptr. But according to
the definition which we have given, the dioptry is a unit
not of refracting power only but of any similar magnitude
of the nature of a curvature. Thus, for example, if the
radius of a mirror or of a spherical refracting surface is half
a meter, its curvature is 2 dptr. If the distances denoted
by f, r, u, x, etc., are expressed in meters, the magnitudes
denoted by the corresponding capital letters F, R, U, X,
etc., will be in dioptries. Dr. DRYSDALE has suggested
that we introduce also the convenient terms *millidioptry*
($=0.001$ dptr.), *Hectodioptry* ($=100$ dptr.) and *Kilodioptry*
($=1000$ dptr.) corresponding, respectively, to the Kilo-
meter, centimeter and millimeter as units of length. Thus,
the refracting power of a lens of focal length 10 cm. might
be variously described as equal to 100 millidioptries, to
10 dioptries, to 0.1 Hectodioptry or to 0.01 Kilodioptry.
But these terms have not come into general use.

If the focal length of a lens in water ($n=1.3$) is 13 cm.,
its refracting power will be the same as that of a lens in
air ($n=1$) of focal length 10 cm., viz., 10 dptr. If the primary focal point of a spherical refracting surface is situated

LANDOLT's and TSCHERNING's books on physiological optics; notwithstanding the fact that the word is usually spelled and pronounced
dioptre in England and *diopter* in America. Dr. CREW in his well known
text-book of physics writes *dioptric*. The author has concluded that
on the whole it is best to adopt the spelling used in the text.

The usual abbreviation of dioptry is a capital D.; but as this letter
is liable to be confused with the symbols of magnitude employed in the
formulæ, it seems preferable to follow the usage of VON ROHR and
other modern writers on optics who have adopted the abbreviation
dptr., although doubtless many will object to this long form.

(optically) in air $(n=1)$ at a distance of 1 meter from the vertex, the refracting power of the surface will be 1 dptr. and the radius of the surface will be equal to $(n'-1)$ meters, where n' denotes the index of refraction of the second medium. If the radius of curvature of a mirror is 50 cm., its reflecting power will be 4 dptr. if the reflecting surface is in contact with air $(n=1)$, but it will be $5\frac{1}{3}$ dptr. if the surface is in contact with water $(n=\frac{4}{3})$. These examples are given merely to illustrate how the term dioptry is used.

108. Lens-Gauge—The dial of the opticians' lens-gauge described in § 99 is usually graduated so as to give in dioptries the refracting power of the surface which is measured. The refracting power of a spherical refracting surface is proportional to its curvature, as we have seen (§ 105), but it is dependent also on the indices of refraction of the two media. If the first medium is air and if the index of refraction of the second medium is denoted by n, then $F = (n-1)R$. The gauge actually measures the curvature R, and the readings on the dial correspond to the values of R multiplied by the factor $(n-1)$. Direct readings of the refracting power (F) imply, therefore, that the maker has assumed a certain value of the index of refraction n; and if the actual value of n is different from this assumed value, the readings will be erroneous. The value of n assumed by the maker is a constant of the instrument, which should be marked on it, although it may easily be determined empirically by comparing the readings with the determination of the curvature as obtained with an ordinary spherometer.

Suppose that this constant is denoted by c, and that we wish to use the gauge to measure the refracting power (F) of a lens of negligible thickness made of glass of index n. If the refracting powers of the two surfaces of the lens are denoted by F_1 and F_2 and the curvatures by R_1 and R_2, then $F = F_1 + F_2$ where $F_1 = (n-1)R_1$, $F_2 = -(n-1)R_2$, the minus sign in front of the last expression being necessary because the refraction in this case takes place from glass to air. But if the constant c has a value different from n, the readings of the instrument for the two faces of the lens will not give the correct values F_1, F_2 of the refracting powers. Suppose the readings are denoted by F_1', F_2', so that $F_1' = (c-1)R_1$, $F_2' = -(c-1)R_2$. Then evidently

$$F_1 = \frac{n-1}{c-1} F_1', \qquad F_2 = \frac{n-1}{c-1} F_2',$$

and hence

$$F = \frac{n-1}{c-1} (F_1' + F_2').$$

The gauge-readings must be multiplied therefore by the factor

$$\frac{n-1}{c-1}$$

in order to obtain the correct values of the refracting powers. Suppose, for example, that the graduations on the dial correspond to a value $c = 1.54$ and that the index of the lens to be measured is $n = 1.52$. Then the value of the factor is 0.963; so that if the lens-gauge gives for the refracting power F the value 6.25 dptr., the correct value is obtained by multiplying this value by 0.963, that is, the correct value will be 6.02 dptr.

109. Refraction of Paraxial Rays through a Thin Lens-System.—Let M_1' designate the position of a point conjugate to an axial object-point with respect to an infinitely thin lens of refracting power F_1, and let the point where the axis crosses the lens be designated by A_1. If the lens is surrounded by air, and if we put $u_1 = A_1M_1$, $u_1' = A_1M_1'$, $U_1 = 1/u_1$, $U_1' = 1/u_1'$, then

$$U_1' = U_1 + F_1.$$

If now at a point A_2 on the axis of the lens beyond A_1 (such that the distance $d = A_1A_2$ is measured in the direction in which the light is going) another infinitely thin lens is set up with its axis in the same straight line with that of the first lens, then M_1' may be regarded as an axial object-point

M_2 with respect to the second lens; and if M_2' designates the position of the point conjugate to M_2 (or M_1') with respect to this lens, then also (supposing that the second lens is surrounded by air and that its refracting power is denoted by F_2),

$$U_2' = U_2 + F_2,$$

where $U_2 = 1/u_2$, $U_2' = 1/u_2'$, $u_2 = A_2M_2 = A_2M_1'$, $u'_2 = A_2M_2'$. Obviously, the point M_2' is the image-point conjugate to the axial object-point M_1 with respect to the two lenses; so that regarding the system as a whole, we may write M, M' in place of M_1, M_2' and U, U' in place of U_1, U_2', respectively.

Now let us impose the condition that *the two thin lenses are in contact with each other* or that they are as close together as possible; in other words, that the axial distance d between the lenses is negligible. If this is the case, the points A_1, A_2 are to be regarded as a pair of coincident points, and hence

$$U_1' = U_2;$$

and, therefore, we may write now:

$$U_1' = U + F_1, \qquad U' = U_1' + F_2.$$

Eliminating U_1', we obtain:

$$U' = U + (F_1 + F_2);$$

and if we put

$$F = F_1 + F_2,$$

we have finally:

$$U' = U + F.$$

Since this formula is seen to be identical in both form and meaning with the formula for a single thin lens, it appears therefore that *a combination of two thin coaxial lenses in contact is equivalent to a single lens of refracting power F equal to the algebraic sum of the refracting powers F_1 and F_2 of the component lenses.*

Theoretically, this rule can be applied to a centered system of *any number of thin lenses in contact.* Thus, the total refracting power of a *thin lens-system* will be

$$F = F_1 + F_2 + \ldots + F_m,$$

where the total number of lenses is denoted by m. This formula may be written:

$$F = \sum_{i=1}^{i=m} F_i ,$$

where F_i denotes the refracting power of the ith lens.

In the case of actual lenses placed together in this fashion it will always be a question, How far are we justified in neglecting the total thickness of the system? Two adjacent lenses may be placed in actual contact, but a third lens cannot be in contact with the first. Moreover, even when there are only two lenses, their outward forms may be such that it will not be possible to place them in tangential contact at their vertices, although they can always be made to touch at two points symmetrically situated with respect to their common axis. Attention is directed to this question chiefly in connection with the method of *neutralization* of lenses which is practiced extensively in the fitting of spectacle glasses. Two infinitely thin lenses of equal and opposite refracting powers are said to "neutralize" each other, because when they are placed in contact their total refracting power $(F_1 + F_2)$ is equal to zero. Strictly speaking, the neutralization of a negative glass by a positive glass implies not only that the focal lengths are equal in magnitude but also that the primary focal point of one lens shall coincide with the secondary focal point of the other. Both of these conditions are realized in a combination of a plano-concave with a plano-convex lens fitted together so as to form a slab with plane parallel sides. But even with the relatively thin lenses employed in spectacles sensible errors may be introduced by assuming, as is usually done, that the condition $F_1 + F_2 = 0$ is the sole or even the main consideration for neutralization.

110. Prismatic Power of a Thin Lens.—Only such rays as go through the optical center (§ 88) emerge from a lens without being deviated from their original directions. The prismatic power of a thin lens, which, like the power of a

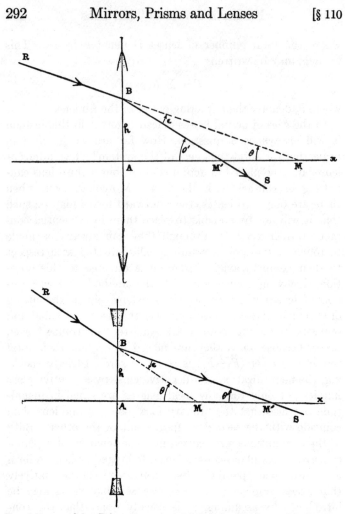

Fig. 141, *a* and *b*.—Prismatic power of infinitely thin lens.   (*a*) Convex, (*b*) Concave lens.

thin prism (§ 70), is measured by the deviation of a ray in passing through it, depends not only on the refracting power of the lens but also on the place where the ray enters the lens. In the accompanying diagram (Fig. 141, *a* and *b*)

the point A designates the axial point of a thin lens of refracting power F. A ray RB incident on the lens at B passes
out in the direction BS. If M, M' designate the points
where the incident and emergent rays cross the axis, then
$\angle$ M'BM = ϵ is the angle of deviation; and if $\theta = \angle$ AMB denotes the slope of the incident ray and $\theta' = \angle$ AM'B denotes
the slope of the emergent ray, evidently we have the relation:

$$\epsilon = \theta - \theta'.$$

The distance $h =$ AB of the incidence-point B from the axis
of the lens or the incidence-height of the ray is called by
the spectacle-makers the *decentration* of the lens. Since
the decentration of an ophthalmic lens is always comparatively small, the ray RB may be regarded as a paraxial
ray, and hence we can put θ and θ' in place of $\tan\theta$ and
$\tan\theta'$ and write:

$$\theta = -\frac{h}{u} = -h.U, \qquad \theta' = -\frac{h}{u'} = -h.U',$$

where $u =$ AM, $u' =$ AM', $U = 1/u$, $U' = 1/u'$, since the lens
is supposed to be surrounded by air ($n = 1$). Accordingly,

$$\epsilon = h(U' - U),$$

the deviation-angle ϵ being expressed in radians if h, u and
u' are all expressed in terms of the same linear unit. But

$$U' - U = F;$$

and hence

$$\epsilon = h.F \text{ radians.}$$

In this formula the decentration h must be expressed in
meters if the refracting power F is given in dioptries. The
above relation may be derived immediately also from
Fig. 142, where the incident ray RB is drawn parallel to
the axis of the lens, so that in this case $\theta' + \epsilon = 0$; and
since $\tan \theta' = \theta' = \dfrac{AB}{F'A} = \dfrac{h}{f'} = -\dfrac{h}{f} = -h.F$, we obtain, as above,
$\epsilon = h.F$. If a screen is placed perpendicular to the incident
light coming in the direction RB, a spot of light will be produced on the screen at the point N where the straight line

RB meets the screen; and if now a lens is interposed at a certain known distance from the screen, the deviation ϵ can easily be determined by measuring the distance NL through which the spot of light is deflected.

However, both the radian and the meter are inconveniently large units for expressing the values of the small mag-

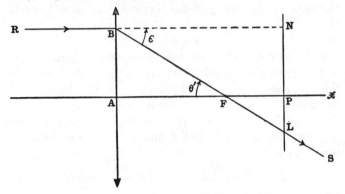

Fig. 142.—Prismatic power of infinitely thin lens; incident ray parallel to axis.

nitudes denoted by ϵ and h. Opticians measure the deviation in terms of the *centrad* or in terms of the *prism-dioptry*, which in the case of small angles, as we have seen (§ 70), is practically the same unit as the centrad. If the angle of deviation expressed in centrads or prism-dioptries is denoted by p, while ϵ denotes the value of this angle in radians, then

$$p = 100 \ \epsilon.$$

Moreover, if the decentration h is given in centimeters instead of in meters, we obtain the following formula:

$$p = h.F;$$

that is, *the deviation (p) in prism-dioptries (or centrads) produced by a thin lens in any zone is equal to the product of the refracting power (F) of the lens in dioptries by the radius (h) of the zone in centimeters;* or as the opticians usually express it, *the prismatic power of a thin lens in prism-dioptries is equal to the product of the refracting power of the lens in dioptries by the decentration in centimeters.* For example, a spectacle glass of refracting power 5 dptr. must be decentered about 0.4 cm. or 4 mm. in order to have a prismatic power of 2 prism-dptr.

If in Fig. 142 the distance AP of the screen from the lens is 1 meter, the deflection LN in centimeters of the spot of light will be equal to the prismatic power of a lens of focal length $f = AF'$ decentered by the amount $h = AB$.

PROBLEMS

1. How is the curvature of a wave affected by reflection at a plane mirror? How is the curvature of a plane wave affected by reflection at a spherical mirror?

2. The distance between a luminous point and the eye of an observer is 50 cm. A plate of glass ($n = 1.5$), 10 cm. thick, is interposed midway between the point and the eye with its two parallel faces perpendicular to the line of vision. Spherical waves spreading out from the luminous point are refracted through the plate and into the eye. Find the curvature of the wave-front: (*a*) just before it enters the glass, (*b*) immediately after entering the glass, (*c*) immediately after leaving the glass, and (*d*) when it reaches the eye.

Ans. (*a*)-5 dptr.; (*b*)$-3\frac{1}{3}$ dptr.; (*c*)$-3\frac{3}{4}$ dptr.; (*d*) $-2\frac{1}{7}$ dptr.

3. What is the refracting power of a spherical refracting surface of radius 20 cm. separating air ($n = 1$) from glass ($n' = 1.5$)?

Ans. $+2.5$ dptr. or -2.5 dptr., according as the surface is convex or concave, respectively.

4. If the cornea of the eye is regarded as a single spherical refracting surface of radius 7.7 mm. separating air ($n = 1$) from the aqueous humor ($n' = 1.336$), what is its refracting power?   Ans. 43.6 dptr.

5. Using the data of the preceding problem, find the refracting power of the cornea when the eye is under water $(n=1.33)$.   Ans. Nearly 0.78 dptr.

6. What is the reflecting power of a concave mirror of radius 20 cm. when the reflecting surface is in contact with (a) air $(n=1)$ and (b) water $(n=\frac{4}{3})$?

Ans. (a) 10 dptr.; (b) 13.33 dptr.

7. A convex spherical surface of radius 25 cm. separates air $(n=1)$ from glass $(n'=1.5)$. Find the refracting power and the reflecting power of the surface.

Ans. Refracting power is $+2$ dptr.; reflecting power is -8 dptr.

8. The reflecting power of a spherical mirror in contact with air is $+2$ dptr. Determine the form of the mirror.

Ans. A concave mirror of radius 1 meter.

9. A spherical mirror is in contact with a liquid of refractive index n. If the reflecting power of the mirror is $+2$ dptr., show that the mirror is a concave mirror of radius n meters.

10. The index of refraction of carbon bisulphide is 1.629. What is the reflecting power of a concave mirror of radius 25 cm. in contact with this liquid?   Ans. $+13.032$ dptr.

11. What is the refracting power of a thin symmetric convex lens made of glass of index 1.5, if the radius of curvature of each surface is 5 cm.?   Ans. $+20$ dptr.

12. The refracting power of a thin plano-convex lens made of glass of index 1.5 is 20 dptr. Find the radius of the curved surface.   Ans. 2.5 cm. or nearly 1 inch.

13. A thin convex meniscus lens is made of glass of index 1.5. The radius of the first surface is 10 and that of the second surface is 25 cm. Assuming that the lens is surrounded by air $(n=1)$, find its refracting power.

Ans. $+3$ dptr.

14. If the lens in the preceding example were made of water of index $\frac{4}{3}$, what will be its refracting power?

Ans. $+2$ dptr.

15. If the first surface of the lens in No. 13 were in contact with water $(n_1 = \frac{4}{3})$ and the second surface in contact with air $(n_3 = 1)$, what will be the refracting power?

Ans. $-\frac{1}{3}$ dptr.

16. If the first surface of the lens in No. 13 were in contact with air $(n_1 = 1)$ and the second surface in contact with water $(n_3 = \frac{4}{3})$, what will be the refracting power?

Ans. $+4\frac{1}{3}$ dptr.

17. In examples 13, 14, 15 and 16 suppose the lens were reversed so that the opposite face was turned to the incident light. What would be the answers to these problems then?

Ans. The same answers would be obtained for Nos. 13 and 14; but the answers for Nos. 15 and 16 would be interchanged.

18. Show that the lateral magnification in a spherical mirror, a spherical refracting surface or an infinitely thin lens is equal to the ratio of the reduced " vergences " U and U'.

19. Describe the spherometer and the lens-gauge and explain their principles.

20. Show how a plane wave is refracted through a thin lens, and derive from a diagram for this case the formula for the refracting power.

21. Show how a plane wave is refracted through a thin prism, and derive the formula for the deviation in terms of the refracting angle of the prism and the relative index of refraction.

22. The refracting power of a thin lens is $+6$ dptr. It is made of glass of index 1.5 and surrounded by air $(n = 1)$. If the radius of the first surface is $+10$ cm., what is the radius of the second surface?   Ans. $r_2 = -50$ cm.

23. A convex lens produces on a screen 14.4 cm. from the lens an image which is three times as large as the object. Find the refracting power of the lens.   Ans. 27.78 dptr.

24. A lens-gauge graduated in dioptries for glass of index 1.5 is used to measure a thin double convex lens made

of glass of index 1.6.   The readings on the dial give $+4$ for both surfaces.   Find the refracting power of the lens, assuming that its thickness is negligible.   Ans. $+9.6$ dptr.

25. Modern spectacle glasses are meniscus lenses with the concave surface worn next the eye.   If the glass is to give the proper correction, it is very important for it to be adjusted at a certain measured distance from the eye.   In determining this distance it is necessary to ascertain the "vertex depth" of the concave surface, that is, the perpendicular distance (t) of the vertex from the plane of the edge or contour of the surface.   If the diameter of this contour expressed in millimeters is denoted by $2h$, and if the refracting power of the surface next the eye, expressed in dioptries, is denoted by F_2, and, finally, if the index of refraction of the glass is denoted by n, show that the vertex depth of the surface is approximately:

$$t = -0.0005 \frac{h^2 F_2}{n-1} \text{ millimeters.}$$

26. What is the refracting power of a lens which is equivalent to two thin convex lenses of focal lengths 15 and 30 cm., placed in contact?   Ans. 10 dptr.

27. A concave lens of focal length 12 cm. is placed in contact with a convex lens of focal length 7.5 cm.   Find the refracting power of the combination.   Ans. 5 dptr.

28. The refracting power of a thin concave lens is 5 times that of a thin convex lens in contact with it.   If the focal length of the combination is 8 cm., find the refracting power of each of the components.   Ans. $-15\frac{5}{8}$ and $+3\frac{1}{8}$ dptr.

29. Two thin lenses, made of glass of indices 1.5 and 1.6, are fitted together with the second surface of the first lens coincident with the first surface of the second lens ($r_3 = r_2$).   The radii of the surfaces are all positive and equal to 4, 11 and 6 cm. taken in the order named.   Find the refracting power of the combination.   Ans. 3.41 dptr.

30. What is the prismatic effect of a lens of power $+4$ dptr. decentered 0.75 cm.?   Ans. 3 prism-dioptries.

31. Two thin convex lenses have each a focal length of 1 inch. Find the position of the second focal point of the combination of these two lenses when they are placed with their axes in the same straight line: (*a*) when they are in contact, (*b*) when they are separated by 1.5 inches, and (*c*) when they are separated by 3 inches. Draw a diagram for each case showing the path of a beam of light coming from a distant axial object-point.

Ans. (*a*) Half an inch beyond the combination; (*b*) between the lenses and 1 inch from second lens; (*c*) 2 inches beyond second lens.

32. A convex lens of focal length 20 cm. and a concave lens of focal length 5 cm. are placed 16 cm. apart. Find the positions of the focal points of the combination.

Ans. One of the focal points is 420 cm. from the convex lens and 436 cm. from the concave lens; and the other focal point is 36 cm. from the convex lens and 20 cm. from the concave lens.

33. How much must a lens of 5 dptr. be decentered in order to produce a deviation of 3° 30′?   Ans. 1.22 cm.

34. The radius of a spherical surface is measured by a spherometer and found to be 14.857 cm. Measured by a lens-gauge the reading is 3.5 dptr. What is the index of refraction of the glass for which the readings on the dial of the gauge have been calculated?   Ans. 1.52.

35. The radius of each surface of a thin symmetric double convex glass lens is 6 inches. The lens is supported with its lower face in contact with the horizontal surface of still water. Assuming that the sun is in the zenith vertically above the lens, and that its apparent diameter is 30′, find the position and size of the sun's image. (Take the indices of refraction of air, glass and water equal to 1, $\frac{3}{2}$ and $\frac{4}{3}$, respectively.)

Ans. A real image 9 inches below the surface of the water, 0.0785 inch in diameter.

CHAPTER IX

111. Curvature and Refracting Power of a Normal Section of a Curved Refracting Surface.—The refracting power (F) of a spherical surface is proportional to the curvature (R) of the surface, that is, $F = (n' - n)R$, where n and n' denote the indices of refraction of the media on opposite sides of the surface (§ 105). A spherical surface has the same curvature in every meridian, and hence also its refracting power is uniform, so that the refracted rays in one meridian plane are brought to the same focus as those in another meridian plane. But the surfaces of a lens are not always spherical (§ 87), and therefore, in order to ascertain what happens when a narrow bundle of rays is incident perpendicularly on a curved reflecting or refracting surface of any form, we must investigate the reflecting or refracting power in different sections of the surface; and this means that we must investigate the curvature of these sections. In general, this is a problem of some difficulty and involves a more or less extensive knowledge of the theory of curved surfaces and the methods of infinitesimal geometry. No attempt can be made to explain this theory here, but for the student who is not already familiar with it, certain general definitions and propositions of geometry which have a direct bearing on the optical problems to be treated in this chapter will be stated as succinctly as possible.

The normal to a curved surface at any point is a straight line drawn perpendicular to the tangent plane at that point. The curved line which is traced on the surface by a plane containing the normal at a point A of the surface is called a *normal section* through this point. The normal sections of a sphere, like the meridians of longitude of the earth (assumed to be a perfect sphere), are all great circles of the sphere, and their curvatures are equal. But, generally,

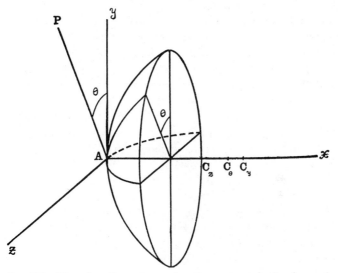

FIG. 143.—Normal sections of curved surface: xAy and xAz planes of principal sections; xAP plane of oblique normal section.

the curvatures of the normal sections through a point on a curved surface will vary from one section to the next; so that if we imagine a plane containing the normal to be turned around this line as axis, we shall find that for one special azimuth of this revolving plane the curved line which it carves out on the surface will have the greatest curvature, and that then as the plane continues to revolve the curvature of the section decreases and reaches its least value for an azimuth which is exactly 90° from that for which the curvature was greatest. Thus, for example, in a cylindrical surface the curvature at any point is least and equal to zero in a normal section whose plane is parallel to the axis of the cylinder, and it is greatest in a normal section made by a plane perpendicular to the axis. *At each point* A *of a curved surface the normal sections of greatest and least curvatures lie always in two perpendicular planes,* which are called the planes of the *principal sections* of the surface at A. The lines of intersection of these planes with each other and with the tangent plane at A may be chosen as the axes of reference of a system of rectangular coördinates x, y, z whose x-axis is the normal Ax (Fig. 143). The centers of curvature of the principal sections made by the xy-plane and the xz-plane will be designated by C_y and C_z, respectively; and the curvatures of the principal sections will be denoted by R_y and R_z, so that if $r_y = AC_y$ and $r_z = AC_z$ denote the principal radii of curvature of the surface at the point A, we must have here (§ 99) $R_y = 1/r_y$ and $R_z = 1/r_z$.

Now there is a remarkable geometrical relation between the curvature of any normal section at A and the curvatures of the principal sections of the surface at this point which will be stated also without giving the proof. Let a plane containing the normal Ax intersect the tangent plane (or yz-plane) in the straight line AP (Fig. 143) and put $\angle y$AP $= \theta$. The center of curvature of the normal section made by this plane lies also on the normal Ax at a point which may be designated as C_θ, so that the radius of curvature is $AC_\theta = r_\theta$, and the curvature itself is $R_\theta = 1/r_\theta$. The connection between R_θ and the principal curvatures R_y and R_z is expressed by the following formula:

$$R_\theta = R_y . \cos^2 \theta + R_z . \sin^2 \theta,$$

where θ denotes the angle which the normal section makes with the xy-plane.

In a normal section at right angles to the first we should have, therefore,

$$R_{\theta + 90°} = R_y . \cos^2 (\theta + 90°) + R_z . \sin^2 (\theta + 90°),$$

or, since $\qquad \cos (\theta + 90°) = - \sin \theta, \quad \sin (\theta + 90°) = \cos \theta,$

$$R_{\theta + 90°} = R_y . \sin^2 \theta + R_z \cos^2 \theta.$$

Adding the curvatures $R\theta$ and $R\theta+90°$, we obtain the relation:

$$R\theta + R\theta+90° = R_y + R_z;$$

that is, *the algebraic sum of the curvatures of any two normal sections intersecting each other at right angles at a point on a curved surface has a constant value, which is equal to the algebraic sum of the principal curvatures at this point.*

These theorems concerning the curvatures of the normal sections at a point of a curved surface are due to the great mathematician EULER (1707–1783), who made notable contributions also to the theory of optics.

Since, therefore, the curvature of a surface at the point A varies from one azimuth to another as has just been explained, the power of a refracting surface will vary in exactly the same way. Accordingly, the principal sections for which the curvature of a refracting surface has its greatest and least values (R_y, R_z) are also the sections at this place of greatest and least refracting powers (F_y, F_z), because

$$F_y = (n' - n)R_y, \qquad F_z = (n' - n)R_z.$$

The refracting power at this place in an oblique normal section which is inclined to the xy-plane at an angle θ will be:

$$F\theta = (n' - n)R\theta;$$

and the relation between $F\theta$ and F_y, F_z is given by the formula:

$$F\theta = F_y.\cos^2 \theta + F_z.\sin^2 \theta;$$

and moreover:

$$F\theta + F\theta+90° = F_y + F_z;$$

that is, *the algebraic sum of the refracting powers in any two perpendicular normal sections through a point on a curved refracting surface is constant and equal to the algebraic sum of the principal refracting powers.*

For example, in Fig. 144, let A designate a point of a curved refracting surface, and let the normal at this point be represented by the straight line Ax, which in accordance with the preceding discussion is to be taken as the x-axis of a system of rectangular coördinates with its origin at A.

The y-axis is represented by a straight line drawn in the plane of the paper perpendicular to Ax.   The plane of the paper represents the plane of one of the principal sections, whereas the xz-plane at right angles to this plane represents

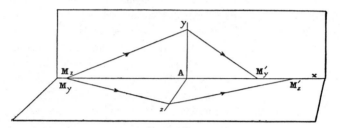

Fig. 144.—Chief ray of narrow bundle of rays normal to curved refracting surface: Principal sections xAy, xAz; tangent plane yAz.

the plane of the other principal section.   The tangent-plane at A is represented by the yz-plane perpendicular to the normal.   Consider now a narrow bundle of rays which proceeding from a point M on the normal are incident on the curved refracting surface at points which are all very close to A.   This point M may be designated also by M_y or by M_z according as it is regarded as lying in the one or the other of the two principal sections; or it may be designated also by M_θ if it is to be considered as lying in an oblique normal section which is inclined to the xy-plane at an angle θ.   The chief ray of the bundle is the ray which coincides with the normal to the surface at A and which proceeds therefore into the second medium without being deviated.   A plane containing this chief ray will cut out from the bundle a pencil of rays which will be refracted at points of the surface which lie in a normal section.   The pencil of rays proceeding from M_y in the xy-plane will be refracted to a point M_y', while the pencil of rays proceeding from M_z will be refracted to a point M_z'; and, in general, these points M_y' and M_z' will be two different points on the normal Ax.   Now if U_y, U_y' denote the reduced "vergences" (§ 106) of the pair of conjugate points M_y, M_y' in one principal section; and, similarly, if U_z, U_z' denote the reduced "vergences" of the pair of conjugate points M_z, M_z' in the other principal section, evidently we shall have the following relations:

$$U_y' = U_y + F_y, \qquad U_z' = U_z + F_z.$$

Similarly, also, a pencil of rays proceeding from M_θ and meeting the refracting surface at points in an oblique normal section will be refracted to a point M_θ' which will lie on Ax between M_y' and M_z', so that

$$U_\theta' = U_\theta + F_\theta.$$

If the bundle of incident rays is homocentric, that is, if the points designated by M_y, M_z and M_θ are all coincident, then $U_y = U_z = U_\theta = U$. The peculiarity of the imagery consists in the fact that instead of obtaining a single image-point M′ corresponding to an object-point M, as in the case of a spherical refracting surface, we find here a whole series of such points lying on the segment $M_y'M_z'$ of the normal Ax. This will be explained more fully in § 113.

112. Surfaces of Revolution. Cylindrical and Toric Surfaces.—The curved reflecting and refracting surfaces of optical mirrors and lenses are almost without exception *surfaces of revolution*, that is, surfaces generated by the revolution of the arc of a plane curve around an axis in its plane. Accordingly, it is desirable to call attention to some of the special properties of these surfaces. The curve traced on a surface of revolution by a plane containing the axis of revolution is called a *meridian section*. The normals to the generating curve are also normals to the surface; and since the normal at any point of the surface lies in the meridian section which passes through that point, it follows that the normals to a surface of revolution all intersect the axis of revolution.

The two principal sections at any point of a surface of revolution are the meridian section which passes through that point and the normal section which is perpendicular to the meridian section. The center of curvature of the latter principal section lies on the axis of revolution at the point where the normal crosses it.

Not only are the surfaces of mirrors and lenses generally surfaces of revolution, but usually they are very simple types of such surfaces. A spherical surface may be considered as generated by the revolution of a c i r c l e around one of its diameters. The o t h e r chief forms of reflecting and refracting surfaces are *cylindrical* and *toric surfaces*, which are also comparatively easy to grind.

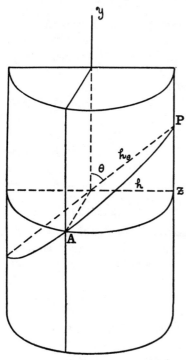

A *cylindrical surface* of revolution is generated by the revolution of a straight line about a parallel straight line as axis, called the *axis of the cylinder*. A meridian section of a cylinder at a point A on the surface (Fig. 145) will be a straight line of z e r o curvature, whereas the other principal section at right angles to

FIG. 145.—Refracting power of cylindrical surface: Principal sections made by planes Ay and Az; oblique section AP.

the axis of the cylinder will be the arc of a circle whose curvature is $R = 1/r$, where r denotes the radius of the cylinder. If the y-axis is drawn parallel to the cylinder-axis, then $R_y = 0$, $R_z = R$; and hence according to EULER's formula given in § 111, the curvature in an oblique normal section AP inclined to the axis of the cylinder at an angle θ will be

$$R_\theta = R.\sin^2\theta.$$

This result may be obtained also independently by observing that although the arcs Az and AP in Fig. 145 have the same *sagitta* (§ 99), their chords denoted by 2h and 2h_θ are unequal in length, because $h = h_\theta.\sin\theta$.   Now the curvatures of two arcs having the same *sagitta* are inversely proportional to the squares of their chords; consequently,

$$\frac{R_\theta}{R} = \frac{h^2}{h_\theta{}^2},$$

and hence

$$R_\theta = R.\sin^2\theta,$$

exactly as above.   Moreover, in a normal section perpen-

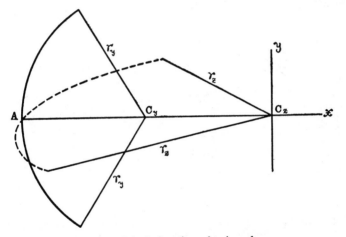

Fig. 146.—Principal sections of toric surface.

dicular to the section AP, we find, by writing $(\theta + 90°)$ in place of θ,

$$R_{\theta+90°} = R.\cos^2\theta;$$

and therefore

$$R_\theta + R_{\theta+90°} = R.$$

Accordingly, in the case of a cylindrical refracting surface, if the maximum refracting power is denoted by F, the refracting power in an oblique section inclined to the

axis at an angle θ will be $F.\sin^2\theta$, and in a section at right
angles to this $F.\cos^2\theta$. The refracting power F of a cylindrical refracting surface may, therefore, be considered as
in a certain sense capable of resolution into a refracting
power $F.\sin^2\theta$ in one oblique section and a refracting power

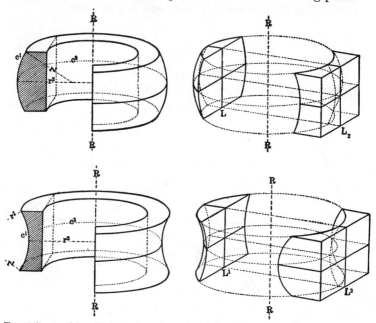

FIG. 147, a and b.—Toric surfaces (reproduced from PRENTICE's *Ophthalmic Lenses and Prisms* by permission of the author).

$F.\cos^2\theta$ in a section at right angles to the first; and since
$$F_\theta + F_{\theta+90°} = F,$$
we can say that *the algebraic sum of the refracting powers in
any two mutually perpendicular sections of a cylindrical refracting surface is constant and equal to the maximum refracting power.*

A *toric* or *toroidal surface* (so-called from the architectural term *torus* applied to the molding at the base of an
Ionic column) is a surface shaped like an anchor-ring which

is generated by the revolution of a conic section around an axis which lies in the plane of the generating curve but does not pass through its center. The surface of an automobile tyre is a toric surface, being generated by the revolution of the circular cross-section of the tyre around an axis per-

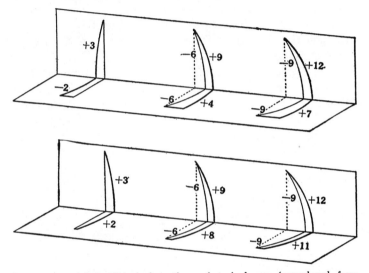

Fig. 148, *a* and *b*.—Principal sections of toric lenses (reproduced from PRENTICE's *Ophthalmic Lenses and Prisms* by permission of the author).

pendicular to the plane of the wheel at its center. Toric refracting surfaces are generated always by the revolution of the arc of a circle (Fig. 146). The arcs of the two principal sections of a toric surface of a lens bisect each other at the vertex A of the surface, so that the normal Ax is an axis of symmetry. If the axis of revolution is parallel to the y-axis of the system of rectangular coördinates, the center of the meridian section through A is at the center C_y of the generating circle, whereas the center of the other principal section at A is at the point of intersection C_z of the normal Ax with the axis of revolution.

The diagrams, Fig. 147, *a* and *b* (which are copied from

the beautiful drawings of Mr. PRENTICE in his valuable
and original essay on "Ophthalmic Lenses and Prisms" in
the *American Encyclopædia of Opthhalmology*) show the two
principal forms of toric surfaces. The principal sections of
some types of toric lenses are indicated in Fig. 148, *a* and *b*.

A cylindrical surface of revolution may be considered as
a special form of toric surface by regarding the segment of
the generating straight line as the arc of a circle with an
infinite radius.

**113. Refraction of a Narrow Bundle of Rays incident
Normally on a Cylindrical Refracting Surface. Sturm's
Conoid.**—In order to obtain a clear idea of the character
of a bundle of rays refracted at a cylindrical surface or
through a thin cylindrical lens, suppose, by way of illustra-

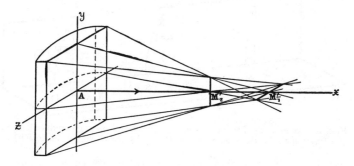

FIG. 149.—Chief ray of narrow bundle meets cylindrical refracting surface
normally; astigmatic bundle of refracted rays. Principal sections *xAy*
and *xAz*.

tion, that we consider a special case of the problem which we
had in § 111 in connection with Fig. 144, namely, the case in
which a narrow homocentric bundle of incident rays, originally converging towards a point M, is intercepted before it
reaches this point by being received on a cylindrical refracting surface which is placed so that the chief ray of the bundle
meets the surface normally at a point A and proceeds, therefore, along the normal A*x* (Fig. 149) without being deflected.

For convenience of delineation, the cylindrical surface is represented in the figure as the first surface of an infinitely thin plano-cylindrical lens, but the explanation is not essentially affected by the fact that it applies to a bundle of rays which have undergone also a second refraction at the plane face of the lens. The bundle of incident rays is not represented in the figure. The point where the chief ray meets the lens is designated by A. In the drawing this point A is marked on the second or plane face of the lens, but since the lens is supposed to be infinitely thin, this point may be regarded also as lying on the first face. The plane of the paper represents the meridian section of the cylindrical surface through the vertex A, and hence the axis of the cylinder is in this plane and parallel to the straight line Ay perpendicular to Ax in the meridian or xy-plane. This meridian plane is one of the principal sections at the vertex A of the cylindrical surface; whereas the other principal section is the xz-plane at right angles to the plane of the paper. The bundle of rays is cut by these principal sections in a *pencil of meridian rays* lying in the meridian xy-plane and a *pencil of sagittal rays* (named by analogy with the so-called "sagittal suture" in anatomy) lying in the xz-plane; the chief ray of the bundle being common to both of these pencils, since it is the line of intersection of the two principal sections of the bundle. Now the meridian rays traversing the infinitely thin cylindrical lens in a section containing the axis of the cylinder will be entirely unaffected in transit and will proceed therefore to the point M just as though the thin piece of glass had not been interposed in the way; so that this point regarded now as the point of rendezvous, so to speak, of the meridian rays after they have passed through the lens may also be designated by M_y', as in fact it is marked in the diagram. On the other hand, the rays of the sagittal pencil meet the surface in points lying on the arc of the section made by the xz-plane, and the rays in this plane are refracted just as they would be through a plano-spherical lens of the same curvature as that of the cylinder; and accordingly after passing through the lens they will be brought to a focus at a point M_z' on the chief ray Ax, which in the case here supposed will be between the lens and the point M_y', as represented in the figure.

The bundle of rays after refraction is no longer homocentric, so that an object-point is not reproduced in a cylindrical lens by a single image-point or even by a pair of image-points, since only the meridian and sagittal image-rays intersect in the so-called image-points M_y' and M_z', respectively. Under such circumstances, the bundle of image-rays is said to be *astigmatic* (or without focus), which, in fact, is the general character of a bundle of optical rays, as will be further explained in Chapter XV.

Rays which are incident on the cylindrical surface in an oblique section made by a plane containing the normal Ax will be brought to a focus at a point lying between M_y' and M_z', as explained in § 111. But the two points M_y' and M_z' have a superior right to be regarded as the image-points of the astigmatic bundle of rays, not only because they are the image-points of the two principal pencils of the bundle, but also because the so-called *image-lines* of the astigmatic bundle of rays are located at these places, as we shall proceed to show.

Imagine a straight line drawn on the surface of the cylinder parallel to the y-axis and at a short distance from the xy-plane, and consider the pencil of rays which meet the surface in points lying along this line; these rays after passing through the lens will meet in a point in the xz-plane a little to one side of the image-point M_y'; and the assemblage of these image-points will form a very short image-line perpendicular to the meridian section of the bundle of rays at the point M_y'; just as though the pencil of meridian rays had been rotated through a very small angle around an axis parallel to the y-axis and passing through M_z'. And, similarly, if the pencil of sagittal rays is rotated slightly on both sides of the xz-plane around an axis parallel to the z-axis and passing through the image-point M_y', the image-point M_z' will trace out a little image-line perpendicular to the sagittal section of the astigmatic bundle of rays. Thus, instead of a point-like image of a point-like object or point-to-point correspondence between object and image, that is, instead of the so-called *punctual imagery* which we have when paraxial rays are reflected or refracted at a spherical surface, we obtain here something essentially different; for in this case each point of the object is reproduced by *two*

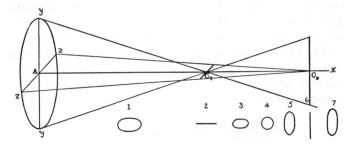

FIG. 150.—STURM'S conoid.

tiny image-lines, each perpendicular to the chief ray of the bundle, one in one principal section and the other in the other principal section; so that if one of the image-lines is vertical, the other will be horizontal. The image-line which passes through the image-point of the meridian rays lies in the plane of the sagittal section, and *vice-versa*.

The case in which an object-point is reproduced by two short image-lines is the simplest form of astigmatism, and it is only under exceptionally favorable circumstances that it can be actually realized as described above. The astigmatic bundle of rays represented in Fig. 150, which is completely symmetrical in the two principal sections is known as STURM'S *conoid* after the celebrated mathematician who appears to have been the first to make a systematic investigation (1838) of the characteristics of a narrow bundle of optical rays. If the lens-opening is determined by a small circular stop in a plane at right angles to the optical axis (or x-axis) and with its center on this axis, the transverse sections of the astigmatic bundle of refracted rays made by planes perpendicular to the chief ray (that is, parallel to the yz-plane) will be ellipses with their major axes parallel to the y-axis in one part of the bundle and parallel to the z-axis in the other part. These elliptical sections become narrower and narrower as they approach either of the image-lines, at both of which places the elliptical section collapses into the major-axis of the ellipse. At some intermediate point between the two image-lines the section of the bundle will be a circle (the so-called "circle of least confusion").

114. Thin Cylindrical and Toric Lenses.—Optical lenses may now be classified in two principal groups, namely, *anastigmatic* (or simply *stigmatic*) *lenses* and *astigmatic lenses*, according as the imagery produced by the refraction of par-

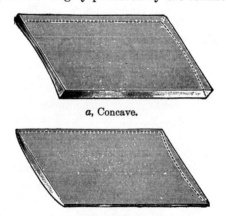

a, Concave.

b, Convex.
Fig. 151, *a* and *b*.—Plano-cylindrical lenses.

axial rays through the lens is punctual imagery or not (§ 113). Anastigmatic lenses are single focus lenses, whereas astigmatic lenses may be said to be double focus lenses. The essential requirement is that the optical axis of the lens, which is generally an axis of symmetry, shall meet both faces normally (§ 87); and another condition that must always be fulfilled in an actual lens is that the planes of the principal sections at the vertex of the first surface shall also be the planes of the principal sections at the vertex of the second surface. Astigmatic lenses are generally cylindrical or toric.

Cylindrical lenses are made in three forms, namely, *plano-cylindrical* (one surface cylindrical and the other plane,

FIG. 152.—Sphero-cylindrical lens.

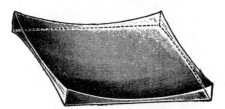

FIG. 153.—Sphero-cylindrical lens.

Fig. 151, *a* and *b*), *cross-cylindrical* (both surfaces cylindrical, the axes of the cylinders being at right angles), and *sphero-cylindrical* (one surface cylindrical and the other spherical, Figs. 152 and 153). All of these forms are quite common in modern spectacle glasses, but prior to 1860 cylindrical lenses were hardly employed at all. The first scientific use of a cylindrical lens seems to have been made by FRESNEL (1788–1827) in 1819 for the purpose of obtaining a luminous line. In 1825 Sir GEORGE AIRY (1801–1892), afterwards the distinguished astronomer-royal at Greenwich, employed a con-

cave sphero-cylindrical glass to correct the myopic astigmatism of one of his eyes.   But it was not until DONDERS
(1818–1889) published his treatise on astigmatism and cylindrical glasses in 1862 that their importance began to be
recognized by ophthalmologists all over the world.

   In a toric lens usually only one of the surfaces is toric
(§ 112), while the other is plane or spherical.   The diagrams,
Fig. 147, a and b, and Fig. 148 show the principal types of
toric lenses.

   Let $F_{y,1}$, $F_{y,2}$ and $F_{z,1}$, $F_{z,2}$, denote the refracting powers
of the two surfaces of an astigmatic lens in the xy-plane and
xz-plane, respectively, which are the planes of the principal
sections of the thin lens with respect to its optical center A.
Now the total refracting power (F) of a thin lens was found
(§ 105) to be equal to the algebraic sum (F_1+F_2) of the
powers of the two surfaces of the lens; so that applying this
formula to an astigmatic lens, we obtain for the refracting
power in the two principal sections:
$$F_y = F_{y,1} + F_{y,2}, \qquad F_z = F_{z,1} + F_{z,2}.$$
   In each of the following special cases the lens is supposed
to be surrounded by the same medium (n) on both sides,
while the index of refraction of the lens itself is denoted by n'.

   (1) Consider, first, the case of a *plano-cylindrical lens*,
which in a principal section containing the axis of the cylinder acts, as was remarked (§ 113), like a slab of the same
material with plane parallel faces; whereas in the other principal section the effect is the same as that of a plano-spherical
lens of the same radius (r) as that of the cylinder.   If the
axis of the cylinder is parallel to the y-axis, and if the plane
surface is supposed to be the second surface, we shall have
in this case:
$$F_{y,1} = F_{y,2} = F_{z,2} = 0,$$
and, consequently:
$$F_y = 0, \qquad F_z = F_{z,1} = F = (n'-n)R,$$
where F denotes the maximum refracting power of the cylindrical surface, and $R = 1/r$ denotes its curvature.

If M designates the position of an object-point lying on the optical axis (x-axis) of a thin plano-cylindrical lens, and if M_θ' designates the position of the corresponding image-point produced by the refraction through the lens of the rays which lie in the plane of a normal section inclined at an angle θ to the axis of the cylinder; and if we put

$$AM = u, \qquad AM_\theta' = u', \qquad U = n/u, \qquad U_\theta' = n/u_\theta',$$

then

$$U_\theta' = U + F_\theta, \text{ where } F_\theta = F.\sin^2\theta;$$

and for the two principal sections:

$$U_y' = U, \qquad U_z' = U + F.$$

(2) In a *cross-cylindrical lens* the axes of y and z are parallel to the axes of the cylinders. Assuming that the cylindrical axis of the first surface of the lens is parallel to the y-axis, we have for a thin lens of this form:

$$F_{y,1} = F_{z,2} = 0,$$
$$F_y = F_{y,2} = -(n'-n)R_2, \qquad F_z = F_{z,1} = (n'-n)R_1,$$
$$F_\theta = (n'-n)(R_1.\sin^2\theta - R_2.\cos^2\theta);$$

where R_1, R_2 denote the maximum curvatures of the cylinders and F_θ denotes the refracting power in a section inclined at an angle θ to the axis of the first surface.

(3) In a thin *sphero-cylindrical lens*, if we suppose, for example, that the axis of the cylindrical surface is parallel to the y-axis and that this surface is also the first surface of the lens, then

$$F_{y,1} = 0, \qquad F_{y,2} = F_{z,2} = F_2,$$
$$F_y = F_{y,2} = -(n'-n)R_2,$$
$$F_z = F_{z,1} + F_y = (n'-n)(R_1 - R_2),$$
$$F_\theta = (n'-n)(R_1.\sin^2\theta - R_2);$$

where R_1, R_2 denote the maximum curvatures of the cylindrical and spherical faces, respectively, and F_θ denotes the refracting power of the combination in a plane inclined at an angle θ to the axis of the cylinder.

(4) Consider, finally, a thin *toric lens*, whose second face may be supposed to be spherical, so that if r_2 denotes the radius of this surface, its refracting power will be

$F_2 = -(n'-n)R_2$, where $R_2 = 1/r_2$. Then if $R_{y,1}$, $R_{z,1}$ denote the principal curvatures of the toric surface, the refracting powers of the lens will be

$$F_y = (n'-n)(R_{y,1}-R_2), \qquad F_z = (n'-n)(R_{z,1}-R_2),$$
$$F_\theta = (n'-n)(R_{y,1}.\cos^2\theta + R_{z,1}.\sin^2\theta - R_2).$$

115. Transposing of Cylindrical Lenses.—The orientation of a cylindrical refracting surface is described by assigning the value of the angle φ which the axis of the cylinder makes with a fixed line of reference. In a cylindrical spectacle glass this line of reference is a horizontal line usually imagined as drawn from a point opposite the center of the patient's eye either towards his temple or towards his nose;

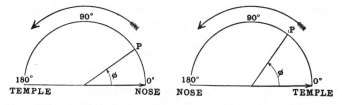

Fig. 154.—Mode of reckoning axis of cylindrical eye-glass.

and the angle through which this line has to be rotated in a vertical plane in order for it to be parallel to the axis of the cylinder is the angle denoted by φ. In England and America it is customary to imagine the horizontal line of reference as drawn *from the center of the glass towards that temple of the patient which is on the right-hand side of an observer* supposed to be adjusting the glass on the patient's eye; so that for a glass in front of either eye the radius vector is supposed to rotate in a counter-clockwise sense from $0°$ to $180°$, as represented in Fig. 154. A different plan was recommended by the international ophthalmological congress which met in Naples in 1909, whereby the angle φ was to be reckoned from an initial position of the radius vector drawn horizontally from a point opposite the center of the eye *towards the nose*. According to this plan, the sense of rotation will be clockwise for one eye and counter-clockwise for the other eye, as represented in Fig. 155.

A sphero-cylindrical glass is described in an ophthalmological prescription by giving the refracting power P of the cylindrical component and the refracting power Q of the spherical component, together with the slope φ of the axis of the cylinder, in a formula which is usually written as follows:

$$Q \text{ sph. } \supset P \text{ cyl., ax.} \varphi,$$

where the symbol $\supset$ means "combined with."

Opticians speak of *transposing* a lens when they substitute a glass of one form for an equivalent glass of another

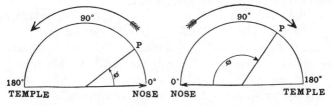

Fig. 155.—Mode of reckoning axis of cylindrical eye-glass.

form. All that is necessary for this purpose is to see that the powers of the lens in the two principal sections remain the same as before. The following *rules for transposing cylindrical lenses* may be useful:

(1) *To transpose a sphero-cylindrical lens into another sphero-cylindrical lens or into a cross-cylindrical lens:*

A lens given by the formula Q sph. $\supset P$ cyl., ax. φ is equivalent to either of the following combinations:

    a. Sphero-cylinder: $(P+Q)$ sph. $\supset -P$ cyl., ax. $(\varphi \pm 90°)$

    b. Cross-cylinder: $(P+Q)$ cyl., ax. $\varphi \supset Q$ cyl., ax. $(\varphi \pm 90°)$.

The power of the spherical component in the original combination is Q dptr. in both principal sections, and the power of the cylindrical component is P dptr. in the section which is inclined to the line of reference at an angle $(\varphi \pm 90°)$; so that the combined power in this latter section is $(P+Q)$ dptr.

Accordingly, a spherical surface of power $(P+Q)$ dptr. must be combined with a cylindrical surface of power $-P$ dptr. and of axis-slope $(\varphi \pm 90°)$. With respect to the double sign in the expression $(\varphi \pm 90°)$, the rule is to select always that one of the two signs which will make the slope of the cylinder-axis positive and less than 180°. Thus, for example, $+8$ dptr. sph. $\supset +2$ dptr. cyl., ax. 20° is equivalent to $+10$ dptr. sph. $\supset -2$ dptr. cyl., ax. 110° or to $+10$ dptr. cyl., ax. 20° $\supset +8$ dptr. cyl., ax. 110°.

(2) *To transpose a cross-cylindrical lens into a spherocylindrical lens:*

The combination P cyl., ax. $\varphi \supset R$ cyl., ax. $(\varphi \pm 90°)$ is equivalent to either of the following:

   a. Sphero-cylinder: P sph. $\supset (R-P)$ cyl., ax. $(\varphi \pm 90°)$, or
   b. Sphero-cylinder: R sph. $\supset (P-R)$ cyl., ax. φ.
Thus, $+2$ cyl., ax. 80° $\supset +3$ cyl., ax. 170° may be replaced by either $+2$ sph. $\supset +1$ cyl., ax. 170° or $+3$ sph. $\supset -1$ cyl., ax. 80°.

(3) *To transpose a spherical lens into a cross-cylinder:*

Q sph. is equivalent to Q cyl., ax. $\varphi \supset Q$ cyl., ax. $(\varphi \pm 90°)$, where the angle φ may have any value between 0° and 180°. For example, $+5$ sph. is equivalent to $+5$ cyl., ax. 10° $\supset +5$ cyl., ax. 100°.

(4) The refracting powers of a *toric* surface in the principal sections are $F_y = (n'-n)/r_y$ and $F_z = (n'-n)/r_z$. Let us suppose that the axis of revolution is parallel to the y-axis. The toric refracting surface may be replaced by a sphero-cylindrical lens in either of two ways, as follows:

   a. F_z sph. $\supset (F_y - F_z)$ cyl., axis parallel to y-axis.
   b. F_y sph. $\supset (F_z - F_y)$ cyl., axis parallel to z-axis.

116. Obliquely Crossed Cylinders.—Oculists and optometrists sometimes prescribe a bi-cylindrical spectacle-glass with the axes of the cylinders crossed, not at right angles (as in the so-called cross-cylinder), but at an acute or obtuse angle γ; and as it is not easy to grind a lens of this form, the optician prefers to make an equivalent sphero-cylinder or a cross-cylinder, which will have precisely the same optical effect as the prescribed combination of obliquely crossed cylinders. His problem may be stated thus:

Being given the refracting powers F_1, F_2 of the two surfaces of the bi-cylindrical lens, and the angle γ between the directions of the axes of the cylinders, it is required to calculate the refracting powers P and Q of the cylindrical and spherical components, respectively, of the equivalent sphero-cylindrical combination, together with the direction of the axis of the cylinder; that is, it is required to transpose

$$F_1 \text{ cyl., ax.} \varphi \subset F_2 \text{ cyl., ax. } (\varphi + \gamma)$$

into

$$Q \text{ sph.} \subset P \text{ cyl., ax. } (\varphi + a).$$

Simple working formulæ for converting one of these lenses into the other were developed first by Mr. CHARLES F. PRENTICE. The following method is based on an article " On obliquely crossed cylinders" by Professor S. P. THOMPSON published in the *Philosophical Magazine* (series 5, xlix., 1900, pp. 316–324).

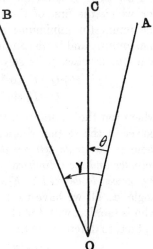

FIG. 156.—Axes of obliquely crossed cylinders.

In Fig. 156 the straight lines OA and OB are drawn parallel to the cylindrical axes of the bi-cylindrical lens, so that $\angle AOB = \gamma$. Through O draw another straight line OC, and let $\angle AOC$ be denoted by θ. In the section of the lens at right angles to OC the total refracting power will be (see § 112):

$$F_1 . \cos^2 \theta + F_2 . \cos^2(\gamma - \theta);$$

and in the section containing OC:

$$F_1.\sin^2\theta + F_2.\sin^2(\gamma-\theta).$$

The sum of these two expressions is equal to (F_1+F_2); and according to the theory of curved surfaces (§ 111), this sum must also be equal to the sum of the maximum and minimum refracting powers of the equivalent sphero-cylindrical lens. Now, obviously, $(P+Q)$ will be the maximum (or minimum) refracting power in a section of the latter lens at right angles to the axis of the cylinder, whereas Q will be the minimum (or maximum) refracting power in the section containing the axis of the cylinder; accordingly, first of all, we find that we must have:

$$2Q+P=F_1+F_2.$$

Now there is a certain value of the angle θ, say, $\theta=\alpha$, for which the first of the two expressions above will be a maximum (or minimum) and the second a minimum (or maximum); and if we can determine this angle α, the problem will practically be solved, because then we shall have:

$$P+Q=F_1.\cos^2\alpha + F_2.\cos^2(\gamma-\alpha),$$
$$Q=F_1.\sin^2\alpha + F_2.\sin^2(\gamma-\alpha);$$

where (on the assumption that Q is the *minimum* refracting power in the section containing the axis of the cylinder) α denotes *the angle between the cylindrical axis of the sphero-cylinder and the cylindrical axis of the cylinder whose refracting power is denoted by F_1.* Now in order to ascertain this angle α, all we have to do (as will be obvious to any one who is familiar with the elements of the differential calculus) is, first, to differentiate the expression

$$F_1.\cos^2\theta + F_2.\cos^2(\gamma-\theta)$$

with respect to θ, and then, after writing α in place of θ, to put the resultant expression equal to zero. Thus we obtain the following equation for finding the angle α in terms of the known magnitudes F_1, F_2 and γ:

$$-2F_1.\sin\alpha\ .\cos\alpha + 2F_2.\sin(\gamma-\alpha).\cos(\gamma-\alpha)=0;$$

which may also be put in the following form:

$$\frac{F_1}{\sin 2(\gamma - a)} = \frac{F_2}{\sin 2 a}.$$

Moreover, since $P = (P+Q) - Q$, we find:

$$P = F_1(\cos^2 a - \sin^2 a) + F_2 \{ \cos^2(\gamma - a) - \sin^2(\gamma - a) \}$$
$$= F_1.\cos 2 a + F_2.\cos 2(\gamma - a);$$

and if in this formula we substitute the value

$$F_2 = \frac{\sin 2 a}{\sin 2(\gamma - a)} F_1,$$

we shall find:

$$P = \frac{\sin 2\gamma}{\sin 2(\gamma - a)} F_1.$$

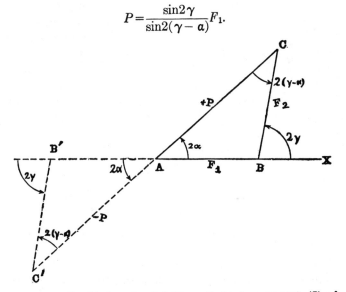

Fig. 157.—Graphical mode of finding cylindrical component (P) of sphero-cylinder equivalent to two obliquely crossed cylinders of powers F_1 and F_2.

Hence,

$$\frac{F_1}{\sin 2(\gamma - a)} = \frac{F_2}{\sin 2 a} = \frac{P}{\sin 2\gamma};$$

which at once suggests an elegant and simple graphical solution of the problem. For, evidently, according to the above relations, the magnitudes denoted by F_1, F_2 and P may be represented in a diagram (Fig. 157) by the sides of a triangle whose opposite angles are $2(\gamma - a)$, $2a$ and $(180° - 2\gamma)$, respectively. Hence the rule is as follows:

On any straight line lay off a segment AB to represent, according to a certain scale, the magnitude of the refracting power F_1; and let X designate the position of a point on AB produced beyond B. Construct the $\angle$XBC equal to *twice* the angle between the axes of the two given cylindrical components ($\angle$XBC$=2\gamma$); and along the side BC of this angle lay off the length BC to represent the magnitude of the refracting power F_2. Then the straight line AC will represent on the same scale the magnitude of the refracting power P of the cylindrical member of the equivalent spherocylindrical lens, and the $\angle$BAC$=2a$ will be equal to *twice* the angle between the cylindrical axes of the surfaces whose powers are denoted by F_1 and P. For calculating the values of P, Q and a, we have by trigonometry the following system of formulæ:

$$P = +\sqrt{F_1^2 + F_2^2 + 2F_1.F_2.\cos 2\gamma},$$
$$Q = \frac{F_1 + F_2 - P}{2},$$
$$\tan 2a = \frac{F_2.\sin 2\gamma}{F_1 + F_2.\cos 2\gamma};$$

which will be found to be applicable in all cases, whether the signs of F_1, F_2 are like or unlike.

There is, to be sure, another solution also, in which the cylindrical axis of the sphero-cylindrical lens is inclined to the cylindrical axis of the cylinder of power F_1 at the angle $(90° + a)$. For if the refracting power Q of the spherical member is assumed to be the maximum (instead of the minimum) refracting power of the sphero-cylindrical combination, then $(P+Q)$ will be the minimum power in a section at right angles to the axis of the cylinder; and in this case the refracting power of the cylindrical component will be represented by the dotted line AC′ in Fig. 157 which is equal to AC in length but opposite to it in direction. In fact, in this case the formulæ for P and Q will be as follows:

$$P = -\sqrt{F_1^2 + F_2^2 + 2F_1.F_2.\cos 2\gamma},$$
$$Q = \frac{F_1 + F_2 + P}{2}.$$

This result could have been obtained from the first result by transposing; for, according to § 115, Q sph. $\supset$ P cyl., ax. ϕ is equivalent to $(P+Q)$ sph. $\supset$ $-P$ cyl. ax. $(\phi \pm 90°)$, where the symbols P and Q denote here the powers of the first combination.

Moreover, since Q sph. $\supset$ P cyl., ax. ϕ is equivalent also to $(P+Q)$ cyl., ax. ϕ $\supset$ Q cyl., ax. $(\phi \pm 90°)$, two obliquely crossed cylinders may be replaced by a cross-cylinder of powers $(P+Q)$ and Q. In fact, since

$$(P+Q) + Q = F_1 + F_2,$$
$$(P+Q) - Q = \sqrt{F_1^2 + F_2^2 + 2F_1.F_2.\cos 2\gamma},$$

it follows that:

$$(P+Q)Q = F_1.F_2.\sin^2\gamma;$$

so that this formula will give us the product of the powers of the equivalent cross-cylinder, and since their sum $P+2Q = F_1 + F_2$, the values of $(P+Q)$ and Q may be obtained independently, without first finding the value of P.

The following numerical example will serve to illustrate the use of the formulæ:

Given a combination of obliquely crossed cylinders as follows:

$$+4 \text{ cyl., ax. } 20° \supset -2.75 \text{ cyl., ax. } 65°;$$

let it be required to find the equivalent sphero-cylinder and also the equivalent cross-cylinder.

We must put $F_1 = +4$, because F_1 denotes the power of the cylinder whose axis-slope is the smaller of the two. Then $F_2 = -2.75$ and $\gamma = (65° - 20°) = 45°$. Substituting these values, we find:

$$P = +4.85, \qquad Q = -1.8, \qquad a = -17°16'.$$

Accordingly, the given combination is equivalent to one of the three following:

$$+4.85 \text{ cyl., ax. } 2° 44' \supset -1.8 \text{ sph.};$$
$$-4.85 \text{ cyl., ax. } 92° 44' \supset +3.05 \text{ sph.};$$
$$+3.05 \text{ cyl., ax. } 2° 44' \supset -1.8 \text{ cyl., ax. } 92° 44'.$$

If $\gamma = 90°$, then $P = F_1 - F_2$, $Q = F_2$ and $a = 0°$, or $P = F_2 - F_1$, $Q = F_1$ and $a = 0°$; so that we can write:

$$F_1 \text{ cyl., ax. } \phi \supset F_2 \text{ cyl., ax. } (\phi \pm 90°)$$

is equivalent to

$$F_1 \text{ sph. } \supset (F_2 - F_1) \text{ cyl., ax. } (\phi \pm 90°)$$

or

$$F_2 \text{ sph. } \supset (F_1 - F_2) \text{ cyl., ax. } \phi;$$

exactly as found in § 115.

PROBLEMS

1. The radius of a convex cylindrical refracting surface separating air from glass $(n = 1.5)$ is $8\frac{1}{3}$ cm. What is its refracting power in a normal section inclined to the axis of the cylinder at an angle of 60°?   Ans. $+4.5$ dptr.

2. A curved refracting surface separates air and glass $(n' : n = 3 : 2)$, and the radii of greatest and least curvature at a point A on the surface are $r_y = +10$ cm. and $r_z = +5$ cm. Find the interval between the two principal image-points corresponding to an object-point lying on the normal to the surface at A in front of the surface and at a distance of 30 cm. from it.   Ans. 67.5 cm.

3. The principal refracting powers of a thin astigmatic lens surrounded by air are denoted by F_y and F_z. The principal image-points corresponding to an axial object-point M are designated by M_y' and M_z'. If the optical center of the lens is designated by A, and if we put $U = 1/u$, where $u = AM$, then

$$M_y'M_z' = \frac{F_y - F_z}{(F_y + U)(F_z + U)}.$$

4. The refracting powers of a thin astigmatic lens in the two principal sections are +3 and +5 dptr. The lens is made of glass of index 1.5. Find the radii of the two surfaces for each of the following forms: (a) Cross-cylinder; (b) Sphero-cylinder; c) Plano-toric.

Ans. (a) Double convex cross-cylinder, radii 10 and 16 $\frac{2}{3}$ cm.; (b) Double convex sphero-cylinder, radius of sphere 16 $\frac{2}{3}$ cm., radius of cylinder 25 cm.; or convex meniscus sphero-cylinder, radius of sphere 10 cm., radius of cylinder 25 cm.; (c) Radii of toric surface 10 and 16 $\frac{2}{3}$ cm.

5 The principal refracting powers of a thin lens are +4 and −5 dptr. If the refracting power in an oblique normal section is +2 dptr., what will be its refracting power in a normal section at right angles to the first? and what is the angle of inclination of the +2 section to the +4 section?

Ans. −3 dptr.; 28° 7′ 32″.

6. Two cylinders each of power +1.18 dptr. are combined with their axes inclined to each other at an angle of 32° 3′ 50″. Show that the combination is equivalent to +0.18 sph. $\subset$ +2 cyl., axis midway between the axes of the two given cylinders.

7. Show that

$$+2 \text{ cyl., ax. } 0° \subset -3 \text{ cyl., ax. } 53° 26′ 14″$$

is equivalent to

$$-2.53 \text{ sph. } \subset +4.06 \text{ cyl., ax. } -22° 30′.$$

8. Transpose

$$-1.25 \text{ cyl., ax. } 20° \subset +3.25 \text{ cyl., ax. } 53° 41′ 24.25″$$

into the equivalent sphero-cylinder.

Ans. −0.5 sph. $\subset$ + 3 cyl., ax. 65°,
or + 2.5 sph. $\subset$ −3 cyl., ax. 155°.

9. Transpose

$$+9.5 \text{ cyl., ax. } 0° \subset +10 \text{ cyl., ax. } 57° 40′ 45″$$

into the equivalent sphero-cylinder.

Ans. +4.53 sph. $\subset$ +10.43 cyl., ax. 30°,
or +14.96 sph. $\subset$ −10.43 cyl., ax. 120°.

10. Find the sphero-cylindrical equivalent of
$$+2 \text{ cyl., ax. } 20° \smile +3 \text{ cyl., ax. } 70°.$$
Ans. $+0.85$ sph. $\smile +3.3$ cyl., ax. $51° 42'$,
or $+4.15$ sph. $\smile -3.3$ cyl., ax. $141° 42'$.

11. Transpose
$$-1.75 \text{ cyl., ax. } 120° \smile +1.25 \text{ cyl., ax. } 135°$$
into the equivalent cross-cylinder.

Ans. $+0.207$ cyl., ax. $98° 30' \smile -0.707$ cyl., ax. $8° 30'$.

12. Transpose $+4$ cyl., ax. $80° \smile -2$ cyl., ax. $120°$ into the equivalent cross-cylinder.

Ans. $+3.075$ cyl., ax. $65° 50' \smile -1.075$ cyl., ax. $155° 50'$.

13. Find the equivalent combinations of the following:
$$+2.25 \text{ cyl., ax. } 40° \smile -4.00 \text{ cyl., ax. } 115°.$$
Ans. (1) $+6.05$ cyl., ax. $30° 21' 20'' \smile -3.90$ sph.

(2) -6.05 cyl., ax. $120° 21' 20'' \smile +2.15$ sph.

(3) $+2.15$ cyl., ax. $30° 21' 20'' \smile -3.90$ cyl.,
ax. $120° 21' 20''$.

CHAPTER X

117. Graphical Method of tracing the Path of a Paraxial Ray through a Centered System of Spherical Refracting Surfaces.—Nearly all optical instruments consist of a combination of transparent, isotropic media, each separated from the next by a spherical (or plane) surface; the centers of these surfaces lying all on one and the same straight line called the *optical axis* of the centered system of spherical surfaces, which is an axis of symmetry. In a symmetrical optical instrument of this kind it is sufficient to investigate the procedure of paraxial rays in any meridian plane containing the axis.

The indices of refraction of the media will be denoted by n_1, n_2, etc., named in the order in which they are traversed by the light; so that if m denotes the number of refracting surfaces, the index of refraction of the last medium into which the rays emerge after refraction at the mth surface will be n_{m+1}. The indices of refraction of the two media which are separated by the kth surface (where k denotes any integer between 1 and m, inclusive) will be n_k and n_{k+1}. The vertex and center of the kth surface will be designated by A_k and C_k, respectively; and the radius of this surface will be denoted by $r_k = A_k C_k$. Moreover, if M_k, M_{k+1} designate the positions of the points where a paraxial ray crosses the axis before and after refraction, respectively, at the kth surface, these points will be a pair of conjugate axial points with respect to this surface; and the points M_1, M_{m+1} will, therefore, be a pair of conjugate axial points with respect

329

to the entire centered system of m spherical refracting surfaces.

The accompanying diagram (Fig. 158) represents a meridian section of an optical system of this kind. The straight line M_1B_1 represents the path of a paraxial ray in the first medium (n_1) which crossing the axis at M_1 meets the first surface (y_1) in the point marked B_1. Similarly, the path

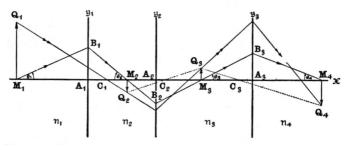

Fig. 158.—Path of paraxial ray through centered system of spherical refracting surfaces.

of the ray from the first surface to the second surface is shown by the straight line B_1B_2 which crosses the axis at M_2. Thus, the entire course of the ray is shown by the broken line $M_1B_1B_2B_3M_4$ which is bent in succession at each of the incidence-points B_1, B_2, B_3 (supposing that $m=3$, as represented in the diagram).

The figure shows also the path of another paraxial ray, emanating from an object-point Q_1 near the optical axis but not on it and represented here as lying perpendicularly above M_1. This ray is the ray which leaves Q_1 along a straight line which passes through the center C_1 of the first refracting surface and also through the point Q_2 which is conjugate to Q_1 with respect to this surface. This point Q_2 can be located by determining the point of intersection of the straight line Q_1C_1 with the straight line M_2Q_2 drawn perpendicular to the axis at M_2. Similarly, the point Q_3 conjugate to Q_2 with respect to the second refracting surface will be at the point of intersection of the straight line Q_2C_2 with the straight line drawn perpendicular to the axis at M_3; and so on from one surface to the next. Provided, therefore, we know the path of one paraxial ray through the system, it is easy to construct the path of a second ray.

But the best graphical method of tracing the path of a paraxial ray through a centered system of spherical refracting surfaces consists in applying the construction described

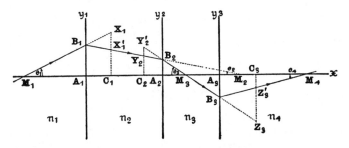

FIG. 159.—Graphical method of tracing path of paraxial ray through centered system of spherical refracting surfaces.

in § 76, as follows: If the straight line M_1B_1 (Fig. 159) representing the path of the ray in the first medium meets the perpendicular erected to the optical axis at the center C_1 in the point X_1, and if on this perpendicular a second point X_1' is taken such that $C_1X_1 : C_1X_1' = n_2 : n_1$, then the straight line B_1X_1' will determine the path B_1B_2 of the ray in the second medium. Draw C_2Y_2 parallel to C_1X_1, and let Y_2 designate the point of intersection of the straight lines B_1B_2 and C_2Y_2; and on C_2Y_2 take a point Y_2' such that $C_2Y_2 : C_2Y_2' = n_3 : n_2$, and draw the straight line $Y_2'B_2$ meeting the third refracting surface in B_3 and intersecting in Z_3 the straight line drawn through C_3 parallel to C_2Y_2. If on C_3Z_3 a point Z_3' is taken such that $C_3Z_3 : C_3Z_3' = n_4 : n_3$, then the straight line B_3Z_3' will determine the path of the ray after refraction at the third surface. This process is to be repeated until the ray has been traced into the last medium.

118. Calculation of the Path of a Paraxial Ray through a Centered System of Spherical Refracting Surfaces.—Obviously, just as in the case of a single spherical refracting surface (§ 80), any figure lying in a plane in the object-space perpendicular to the optical axis of a centered system of spherical refracting surfaces will be reproduced by means of paraxial rays by a similar figure in the image-space also lying in a plane perpendicular to the optical axis.

Moreover, if we put

$$A_k M_k = u_k, \qquad A_k M_{k+1} = u_k',$$

the abscissa-formula (§ 78) for the kth surface may be written:

$$\frac{n_{k+1}}{u_k'} = \frac{n_k}{u_k} + \frac{n_{k+1} - n_k}{r_k}.$$

If also we employ the symbol

$$d_k = A_k A_{k+1}$$

to denote the distance of the vertex of the $(k+1)$th surface from that of the kth surface or the so-called *axial thickness* of the $(k+1)$th medium, then, evidently:

$$u_{k+1} = u_k' - d_k;$$

which enables us to pass from one surface to the next.

If in these so-called recurrent formulæ we give k in succession the values $k = 1, 2, \ldots , (m-1)$, and if also in the first formula we put finally $k = m$, we shall obtain $(2m-1)$ equations; and if the constants of the system are all known, that is, if the values of all the magnitudes denoted by n, r and d are given, together with the initial value u_1, which denotes the abscissa of the axial object-point, these $(2m-1)$ equations will enable us to determine the value of each of the u's in succession. The position of the image point M_{m+1} conjugate to the axial object-point M_1 will have been ascertained when we have found the value of the abscissa u_m'.

The *secondary focal point* of the system is the point F' where a paraxial ray which is parallel to the axis in the first medium crosses the axis in the last medium; and if we put $u_1 = \infty$, then $u_m' = A_m F'$ will be the abscissa of the second-

·ary focal point with respect to the vertex of the last surface. Similarly, the *primary focal point* is the point F where a paraxial ray must cross the axis in the first medium if it is to emerge in the last medium in a direction parallel to the axis. In this case, therefore, we must put $u_m' = \infty$ and solve for $u_1 = A_1F$ in order to obtain the abscissa of the focal point F with respect to the vertex of the first surface of the system.

The *focal planes* are the planes at right angles to the axis at the focal points F, F'.

Moreover, if we put $y_k = M_kQ_k$, then according to the formula for the *lateral magnification* in a spherical refracting surface (§ 82), we can write for the *k*th surface:

$$\frac{y_{k+1}}{y_k} = \frac{n_k}{n_{k+1}} \cdot \frac{u_k'}{u_k} ;$$

and if we give *k* all integral values from $k=1$ to $k=m$, we shall obtain *m* equations, one for each surface, wherein the denominator of the ratio on the left-hand side of each of these proportions will be the same as the numerator of the corresponding ratio in the preceding one of the series. Hence, if we multiply together all of these equations, and if, finally, we put

$$y = y_1, \qquad y' = y_{m+1}, \qquad n = n_1, \qquad n' = n_{m+1},$$

we shall obtain:

$$\frac{y'}{y} = \frac{n}{n'} \frac{u_1'.u_2' \ldots u_m'}{u_1.u_2 \ldots u_m};$$

which may be written also:

$$\frac{y'}{y} = \frac{n}{n'} \prod_{k=1}^{k=m} \frac{u_k'}{u_k},$$

where the symbol Π placed in front of an expression in this way means merely that the continued product of all terms of that type is to be taken. Thus having found the values of all the *u*'s, both primed and unprimed, we can calculate by this formula the *lateral magnification* produced by the entire centered system of spherical refracting surfaces for any given position of the object-point.

Moreover, for the kth surface the so-called SMITH-HELMHOLTZ formula (§ 86) will have the form:

$$n_k.y_k.\ \theta_k = n_{k+1}.y_{k+1}.\ \theta_{k+1},$$

where $\theta_k = \angle A_k M_k B_k$; and if here also we give k all values in succession from $k=1$ to $k=m$, we shall obtain:

$$n_1.y_1.\ \theta_1 = n_2.y_2.\ \theta_2 = \ \ldots\ = n_{m+1}.y_{m+1}.\ \theta_{m+1};$$

and finally:

$$n'.y'.\ \theta' = n.y.\ \theta,$$

where n, n' and y, y' have the same meanings as above, and

$$\theta = \theta_1, \qquad \theta' = \theta_{m+1}.$$

119. The so-called Cardinal Points of an Optical System. The methods which have just been explained, although perfectly simple in principle, involve a more or less tedious process of tracing the path of a paraxial ray from one surface to the next throughout the entire system. We have now to explain the celebrated theory of GAUSS (1777–1855) which was developed (1841) in order to avoid as much of this labor as possible, by keeping steadily in view the fundamental relations between the object-space and the image-space. It is easy to show that the imagery produced by a symmetrical optical instrument in the vicinity of the axis is completely determined so soon as we know the positions of the focal points and one pair of conjugate points on the axis, together with the ratio of the indices of refraction of the first and last media of the system. However, for this purpose certain pairs of conjugate axial points are distinguished above others on account of their simple geometrical relations; and of these the most important are the *principal points* and the *nodal points*. These two pairs of conjugate points, together with the focal points, are sometimes called the *cardinal points* of the optical system. We shall explain now how these points are defined.

(1) *The Focal Planes and the Focal Points.*—In every centered system of spherical refracting surfaces there are

two (and only two) transversal planes at right angles to the axis which are characterized by the following properties:

A bundle of paraxial object-rays which all meet in a point in one of these planes (called the primary focal plane) will emerge from the system as a cylindrical bundle of parallel image-rays; and, similarly, *a cylindrical bundle of parallel object-rays will emerge from the system as a bundle of image-rays which all meet in a point in the other one of these planes (called the secondary focal plane).* The points in which these focal planes are pierced by the axis are *the primary and secondary focal points* F and F', respectively.

(2) *The Principal Planes and the Principal Points.*—Again, in every symmetrical optical system there is one (and only one) pair of conjugate transversal planes characterized by the property, that *in these planes object and image are congruent;* and, therefore, *any straight line drawn parallel to the axis will intersect these planes in a pair of conjugate points.* These are the so-called *principal planes,* one belonging to the object-space (*the primary principal plane*) and the other belonging to the image-space (*the secondary principal plane*). The points H, H' where the optical axis crosses the principal planes are the *principal points* of the system. Attention was first directed to these points by MOEBIUS in 1829, but it was GAUSS who recognized their significance for the development of simple and convenient general formulæ in the theory of optical imagery.

In the principal planes the lateral magnification is unity, that is, $y'=y$. (And hence the principal planes and principal points are called also, especially by English writers, the *unit planes* and the *unit points*.) Consider, for example, the case of a single spherical refracting surface, for which we found (§ 85)

$$\frac{y'}{y}=\frac{f}{f+u}=\frac{f'+u'}{f'}.$$

If we put $y'=y$, we find $u'=u=0$; which means that *the principal points of a spherical refracting surface coincide with each other at the vertex of the surface* (§ 81). We saw likewise that these points coincided with each other at the optical center of an infinitely thin lens (§ 94).

A useful rule is as follows:

To any ray in one region (object-space or image-space) which goes through the focal point belonging to that region,

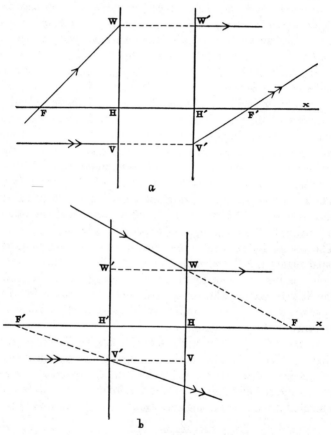

Fig. 160, *a* and *b*.—Focal points (F,F′) and principal points (H, H′) of (*a*) convergent and (*b*) divergent optical system.

there will correspond a ray in the other region which is parallel to the axis, and the rectilinear portions of the path of the ray in these two regions will intersect in a point lying in the principal plane of that region to which the focal point in question belongs; as is illustrated in the accompanying diagrams at W and at V' (Fig. 160, *a* and *b*).

(3) *The Nodal Planes and the Nodal Points.*—Finally, in every centered system of spherical refracting surfaces there is also a pair of conjugate transversal planes characterized by the property, that *the angle between any pair of object-*

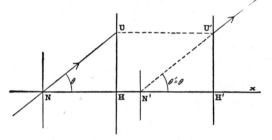

FIG. 161.—Principal points (H, H') and nodal points (N, N').

rays which intersect in a point lying in the so-called primary nodal plane will be exactly equal to the angle between the corresponding pair of image-rays which meet in the conjugate point of the secondary nodal plane. The *nodal points* N, N' where the axis meets these planes were remarked first by MOSER in 1844, but they were brought into prominence through the work of LISTING (1845) with whose name therefore they are generally associated. The distinguishing feature of this pair of conjugate axial points is that *object-ray and image-ray cross the axis at the nodal points at exactly the same slope.* For example, if the straight line NU (Fig. 161) represents the path of an object-ray which crosses the axis at the primary nodal point and meets the primary principal plane in the point marked U, the path of the corresponding image-ray will be represented by a straight line N'U' which is drawn parallel to NU and which meets the secondary principal plane in the point marked U', so that if $\angle HNU = \theta$, $\angle H'N'U' = \theta'$, then $\theta' = \theta$.

Obviously, the quadrilateral NUU'N' is a parallelogram, and hence $H'N' = HN$; that is, *the step from one of the principal points to the corresponding nodal point is identical with the step from the other principal point to its corresponding nodal point.* The nodal points, therefore, lie always on the same side of the corresponding principal points and at equal distances from them. If the primary nodal point and principal point coincide, the same will be true of the secondary nodal point and principal point. Moreover, since $NN' = UU' = HH'$, the interval between the nodal planes is precisely the same as the interval between the principal planes.

If in the SMITH-HELMHOLTZ formula (§ 118) we put $\theta' = \theta$, we find for the lateral magnification in the nodal planes of a centered system of spherical refracting surfaces

$$\frac{y'}{y} = \frac{n}{n'},$$

where n and n' denote the indices of refraction of the first and last media, respectively. Applying this result to the case of a single spherical refracting surface, we obtain for the nodal points N, N' the conditions $u' = u = r$, that is, $AN' = AN = AC$. Consequently, the nodal points of a spherical refracting surface coincide with each other at the center C of the surface; as might have been inferred at once from the fact that a central ray is not deviated by refraction at a spherical surface.

(4) Various writers on optics have distinguished other pairs of conjugate axial points besides the principal points and nodal points, but none of these can be said to have achieved a permanent place in the literature of the subject. We may mention the so-called *negative principal points*, introduced by TOEPLER in 1871, which are characterized by the fact that *for this pair of points the lateral magnification is equal to* -1; that is, $y' = -y$, so that the image is inverted and of same size as object. Professor S. P. THOMPSON, hav-

ing this property in view, has re-named them much more happily the *symmetric points* of the optical system.

120. Construction of the Image-Point Q′ conjugate to an Extra-axial Object-Point Q.—If the principal planes and focal planes have been determined, it will not be necessary to trace the path of a ray in the interior of the system. Sup-

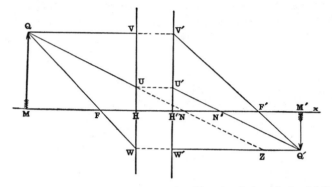

Fig. 162.—Construction of image-point Q′ conjugate to object-point Q in an optical system.

pose, for example, that Q (Fig. 162) designates the position of an object-point not on the axis; the position of the point Q′ conjugate to Q may be constructed as follows:

Through Q draw a straight line QV parallel to the axis meeting the secondary principal plane in the point marked V′ and also another straight line QF meeting the primary principal plane in the point marked W. The required point Q′ will be found at the point of intersection of the straight line V′F′ with the straight line WQ′ drawn parallel to the axis. The feet of the perpendiculars let fall from Q, Q′ on to the axis will locate also a pair of conjugate axial points M, M′. The construction is seen to be entirely similar to that given in §§ 71, 81 and 92. The case represented in the figure is that of a *convergent optical system*, in which parallel object rays are converged to a real focus at a point in the secondary focal plane. The student should draw for himself the corresponding diagram for the case of a *divergent optical system.*

121. Construction of the Nodal Points N, N'.—Having determined the position of the point Q' conjugate to Q, we can easily locate the positions of the nodal points N, N'. For example, on the straight line WQ' (Fig. 162) take a point Z such that ZQ'=HH', and draw the straight line QZ meeting the primary principal plane in the point U. Draw UU' parallel to the axis meeting the secondary principal plane in the point U'. Evidently, the straight lines QU and Q'U' will

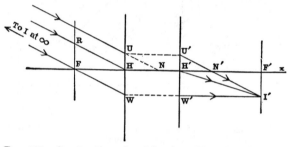

Fig. 163.—Construction of nodal points (N, N'), and proof of relation I' F' = FR.

be parallel, and the points where they cross the axis will be the nodal points N, N' (§ 119).

A simpler way of constructing the nodal points N, N' is as follows:

Through the primary focal point F draw a straight line FW meeting the primary principal plane in the point marked W, and through W draw a straight line parallel to the axis meeting the secondary focal plane in a point marked I' in Fig. 163. This point I' is the image-point of the infinitely distant point I of the straight line FW. The straight line drawn through I' parallel to FW will meet the axis in the secondary nodal point N'; and the position of the other nodal point N can be found immediately.

The diagram shows also that
$$FH = N'F';$$

whence it follows (§ 119) that
$$F'H' = NF.$$
Accordingly, *the step from one nodal point to the corresponding focal point is identical with the step from the other focal
point to its corresponding principal point.* In fact, the three
segments of the axis FF', HN' and H'N all have a common
half-way point.

Incidentally, another useful relation may be seen at a
glance in Fig. 163. Let R designate the point where the ray
IH which passes through the primary principal point crosses

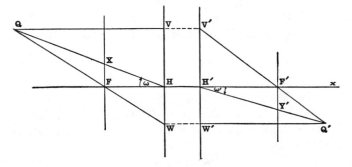

Fig. 164.—Construction of image-point Q' conjugate to object-point Q in
an optical system.

the primary focal plane; the corresponding image-ray will
pass through the secondary principal point H' and cross the
secondary focal plane at I'; and, obviously, since FRHW
and HWI'F' are both parallelograms,
$$I'F' = FR;$$
Consequently, *a pair of conjugate rays passing through the
principal points* H, H' *will cross the focal planes at equal distances from the axis, but on opposite sides thereof.*

This result may be utilized in the construction of the
point Q' (Fig. 164) conjugate to the object-point Q. Let
X designate the point where the straight line QH crosses
the primary focal plane; and take a point Y' in the secondary
focal plane such that F'Y' = XF. Then the required point Q'

will be at the point of intersection of the straight line H'Y'
with either of the straight lines W'Q' or V'F' shown in the
figure.

122. The Focal Lengths f, f'.—Let us employ the symbols
ω, ω' to denote the slopes of a pair of conjugate rays which
pass through the principal points H, H'; thus, in Fig. 164
$\angle$ FHX $= \omega$, $\angle$ F'H'Y' $= \omega'$; and since in the case of paraxial
rays we may write ω and ω' in place of $\tan \omega$ and $\tan \omega'$
(see § 63), we have:

$$\frac{FX}{FH} = -\omega, \qquad \frac{F'Y'}{F'H'} = -\omega'.$$

Accordingly, dividing one of these equations by the other,
and taking account of the fact that F'Y'=XF (§ 121), we
obtain:

$$\frac{FH}{F'H'} = -\frac{\omega'}{\omega}.$$

Since the lateral magnification in the principal planes is
equal to +1, that is, since $y'=y$ (§ 119), the SMITH-HELM-
HOLTZ formula (§ 118) for the pair of conjugate points
H,H' takes the form:

$$n'.\omega' = n.\omega,$$

where n and n' denote the indices of refraction of the first
and last media of the optical system.

If, therefore, *the focal lengths of the optical system are defined as the abscissæ of the principal points with respect to their
corresponding focal points*, that is, if we put $f=$FH, $f'=$F'H',
where f and f' denote the primary and secondary focal lengths,
respectively, then combining the relations found above so
as to eliminate the angles ω and ω', we find:

$$\frac{f}{f'} = -\frac{n}{n'};$$

which may be put in words as follows: *The focal lengths of
a centered system of spherical refracting surfaces are propro-
tional to the indices of refraction of the first and last media,
and are opposite in sign;* except in the single case when the
optical system includes *an odd number of reflecting surfaces,*

in which case *the focal lengths will have the same sign* (that is, in this exceptional case, $f/f' = +n/n'$).

It appears, therefore, that the formula,
$$n'.f + n.f' = 0,$$
which was found (§§ 79 and 96) to hold for a single spherical refracting surface and for an infinitely thin lens, expresses, in fact, a perfectly general relation which is true of any centered system of spherical refracting surfaces. Consider, for example, the optical system of the human eye in which the first medium is air ($n = 1$) and the last medium is the

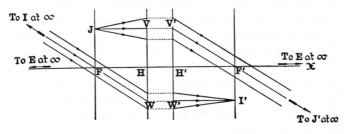

FIG. 165.—Focal lengths (f, f') of an optical system.

so-called vitreous humor whose index of refraction is $n' = 1.336$. In GULLSTRAND's schematic eye (see § 130) the primary focal length is found to be $f = +17.055$ mm., whence, according to the above formula, the secondary focal length is $f' = -22.785$ mm.

In particular, *when the media of object-space and image-space are identical* ($n' = n$), *the focal lengths are equal in magnitude, but opposite in sign* ($f' = -f$). This is the case with most optical systems, since they are usually surrounded by air. According to the definitions of the focal lengths given above, it follows from § 121 that
$$FH = N'F' = f, \qquad F'H' = NF = f';$$
and hence we see that *the nodal points* (N, N') *of an optical system surrounded by the same medium on both sides coincide with the principal points* (H, H'); for when $n' = n$, then
$$FH = f = -f' = FN, \qquad F'H' = f' = -f = F'N'.$$

The focal lengths of a centered system of spherical refracting surfaces may be defined also exactly as in §§ 83 and 95. If in Fig. 165 we put $\angle\,\mathrm{HFW} = \theta, \angle\,\mathrm{H'F'V'} = \theta'$, we can write:

$$f = \mathrm{FH} = \frac{\mathrm{HW}}{\tan\,\theta}, \quad f' = \mathrm{F'H'} = \frac{\mathrm{H'V'}}{\tan\,\theta'}\,;$$

and since $\mathrm{HW} = \mathrm{F'I'}$, $\mathrm{H'V'} = \mathrm{FJ}$, $\tan\,\theta = \theta$, $\tan\,\theta' = \theta'$, we have:

$$f = \frac{\mathrm{F'I'}}{\theta}, \quad f' = \frac{\mathrm{FJ}}{\theta'}\,.$$

Accordingly, we may also define the focal lengths as follows: *The focal length of the object-space (f) is equal to the ratio of the linear magnitude of an image formed in the focal plane of the image-space to the apparent (or angular) magnitude of the correspondingly infinitely distant object;* and, similarly, *the focal length of the image-space (f') is equal to the ratio of the linear magnitude of an object lying in the focal plane of the object-space to the apparent (or angular) magnitude of its infinitely distant image.*

The focal lengths may be said, therefore, to measure the *magnifying power* of the optical instrument, for if the apparatus is adapted to an emmetropic eye (§ 153), the image will be formed at infinity, and the magnifying power will be determined by the ratio of the apparent size of the image to the actual size of the object (see Chapter XIII).

123. The Image-Equations in the case of a Symmetrical Optical System.—The image-equations are a system of relations which enable us to find the position of an image-point Q′ (Fig. 162) conjugate to a given object-point Q. The position of the point Q will be given by its two coordinates referred to a system of rectangular axes in the object-space in the meridian plane in which the point Q lies. Naturally, the optical axis will be selected as the axis of abscissæ and either the primary focal point F or the primary principal point H as the origin. Thus, if we put

$$\mathrm{FM} = x, \qquad \mathrm{HM} = u, \qquad \mathrm{MQ} = y,$$

the object-point Q will be the point (x, y) or the point (u, y), according as we take the origin at F or H, respectively. Similarly, in the image-space, if we put

$$F'M' = x', \qquad H'M' = u', \qquad M'Q' = y',$$

the coördinates of Q' will be denoted by (x', y') or (u', y') according as the origin of this system of axes is at F' or H', respectively.

a. The image-equations referred to the focal points F, F'.—
The following proportions are obtained from the two pairs of similar triangles FHW, FMQ and F'H'V', F'M'Q':

$$\frac{HW}{MQ} = \frac{FH}{FM}, \qquad \frac{M'Q'}{H'V'} = \frac{F'M'}{F'H'} ;$$

and since

$$HW = M'Q' = y', \quad H'V' = MQ = y, \quad FH = f, \quad F'H' = f',$$

we find immediately:

$$\frac{y'}{y} = \frac{f}{x} = \frac{x'}{f'} ;$$

whence the coördinates x', y' can be found in terms of the given coördinates x, y and the focal lengths f, f'.

These formulæ, which were obtained formerly for certain simple special cases (§§ 69, 85 and 93) are seen, therefore, to be entirely general and applicable always to any symmetrical optical system. The so-called Newtonian form of the abscissa-relation, viz.,

$$x.x' = f.f',$$

shows that the product of the focal-point abscissæ is constant.

b. The image-equations referred to the principal points H, H'.—Again, the following proportions are derived from the two pairs of similar triangles FHW, QVW and F'H'V', Q'W'V':

$$\frac{WV}{HW} = \frac{VQ}{FH} = \frac{HM}{FH}, \qquad \frac{V'W'}{H'V'} = \frac{W'Q'}{F'H'} = \frac{H'M'}{F'H'} ;$$

and since $WV = WH + HV = Q'M' + MQ = -(y' - y)$ and $V'W' = V'H' + H'W' = QM + M'Q' = (y' - y)$, we find:

$$\frac{y' - y}{y'} = -\frac{u}{f}, \qquad \frac{y' - y}{y} = \frac{u'}{f'} .$$

These relations give the following expressions for the lateral magnification:

$$\frac{y'}{y} = \frac{f}{f+u} = \frac{f'+u'}{f'} = -\frac{f}{f'}\cdot\frac{u'}{u}.$$

Clearing fractions, we obtain:

$$f.u' + f'.u + u.u' = 0,$$

and dividing through by $u.u'$, we have the well-known abscissa-relation:

$$\frac{f}{u} + \frac{f'}{u'} + 1 = 0;$$

which may also be obtained directly by substituting $x = f+u$, $x' = f'+u'$ in the equation $x.x' = f.f'$.

By means of these formulæ, the coördinates u', y' may be found in terms of the given coördinates u, y and the focal lengths f, f'.

Since $n'.f + n.f' = 0$ (§ 122), we have also another expression for the lateral magnification, viz.,

$$\frac{y'}{y} = \frac{n.u'}{n'.u};$$

which has likewise been obtained already in the special case of a single spherical refracting surface (§ 82).

A simple and convenient method of locating the positions of pairs of conjugate axial points is suggested by the abscissa-relation

$$\frac{f}{u} + \frac{f'}{u'} + 1 = 0;$$

which may be put in the following form:

$$\frac{HF}{u} + \frac{H'F'}{u'} = 1.$$

Suppose, therefore, that the axial line segment H'F' is shoved along the optical axis until the secondary principal point H' is brought into coincidence with the primary principal point H, and that then the optical axis in the image-space (x') is turned about H until it makes a finite angle with the optical axis in the object-space (x), as represented, for example, in Fig. 166. Through the focal points F and F' draw the

straight lines FS and F'S parallel to H'F' and HF, respectively, and let S designate their point of intersection. Then
any straight line drawn through S will intersect x and x' in
a pair of conjugate axial points M, M'; for if we put $u = $ HM
and $u' = $ H'M' in the equation above, the equation will

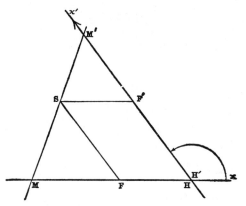

Fɪɢ. 166.—Construction of point M' conjugate to
axial object-point M in an optical system.

evidently be satisfied. The vertex S of the parallelogram
HF'SF is the center of perspective of the two point-ranges
x and x'.

*c. The image-equations referred to any pair of conjugate
axial points O, O'.*

If the origins of the two systems of rectangular axes are
a pair of conjugate axial points O, O' whose distances from
the focal points F, F' are denoted by a, a', respectively, so
that FO $= a$, F'O' $= a'$; and if we put

$$OM = z, \qquad O'M' = z',$$

then

$$x = a + z, \qquad x' = a' + z';$$

and if these values of x and x' are substituted in the equations

$$\frac{y'}{y} = \frac{f}{x} = \frac{x'}{f'},$$

we obtain:

$$\frac{y'}{y} = \frac{f}{a+z} = \frac{a'+z'}{f'}.$$

Since $a.a' = f.f'$, the relation between z and z' may be put in the form:

$$\frac{a}{z} + \frac{a'}{z'} + 1 = 0,$$

where the constants are now a and a' instead of f and f'.

Suppose, for example, that the pair of conjugate axial points O, O' is identical with the pair of nodal points N, N'; then

$$a = \mathrm{FO} = \mathrm{FN} = -f', \qquad a' = \mathrm{F'O'} = \mathrm{F'N'} = -f;$$

so that *the image-equations referred to the nodal points* will have the following forms:

$$\frac{f'}{z} + \frac{f}{z'} - 1 = 0, \qquad \frac{y'}{y} = \frac{f}{z-f'} = \frac{z'-f}{f'},$$

where $z = \mathrm{NM}, \qquad z' = \mathrm{N'M'}$.

d. The image-equations in terms of the refracting power and the reduced vergences (see §§ 105 and 106).

The refracting power of the optical system is defined (§ 105) by the relations:

$$F = \frac{n}{f} = -\frac{n'}{f'}$$

where n, n' denote the indices of refraction of the first and last media. Similarly, the reduced vergences (§ 106) with respect to the principal points are:

$$U = \frac{n}{u} \qquad U' = \frac{n'}{u'}.$$

If, therefore, in the image-equations referred to the principal points we eliminate f, f' and u, u' by means of these two pairs of formulæ, we obtain the image-equations in the following exceedingly useful and convenient form:

$$U' = U + F, \qquad \frac{y'}{y} = \frac{U}{U'}.$$

If the linear magnitudes are measured in terms of the meter

as unit of length, the magnitudes denoted here by U, U' and F will all be expressed in dioptries (§ 107).

124. The Magnification-Ratios and their Mutual Relations.—(a) *The lateral magnification* ***y***. This has already been defined as the ratio of conjugate line-segments lying in planes at right angles to the optical axis. The following expressions were obtained for this ratio in § 123:

$$y = \frac{y'}{y} = \frac{f}{x} = \frac{x'}{f'} = \frac{f}{f+u} = \frac{f'+u'}{f'} = -\frac{f.u'}{f'.u} = \frac{n.u'}{n'.u} = \frac{U}{U'} \; ;$$

whence we see that the lateral magnification is a function of the abscissa of the object-point, and that in any optical system it may have any value from $-\infty$ to $+\infty$ depending on the position of the object.

(b) *The axial magnification or depth-ratio* ***x***. If x, x' denote the abscissæ with respect to the focal points of a pair of conjugate axial points, and if $x+c$, $x'+c'$ denote the abscissæ of another pair of such points immediately adjacent to the former, then, since

$$x.x' = f \cdot f' = (x+c) \; (x'+c'),$$

and since moreover the product $c.c'$ is a small magnitude of the second order as compared with either of the small factors c or c', and is therefore negligible, we find:

$$c.x' + c'.x = 0.$$

The ratio $c' : c$ of small conjugate segments of the axis is called the *axial* or *depth-magnification*. If this ratio is denoted by the symbol ***x***, then, according to the equation above:

$$x = \frac{c'}{c} = -\frac{x'}{x} = -\frac{f.f'}{x^2} \; ;$$

so that, whereas *the lateral magnification is inversely proportional to the abscissa* x, *the depth-magnification is inversely proportional to the square of* x. In fact, the relation between the axial magnification and the lateral magnification may be expressed as follows:

$$\frac{x}{y^2} = -\frac{f'}{f} = \frac{n'}{n} \; .$$

The axial magnification or "depth-elongation" of a small object is proportional to the square of its lateral magnification. If, therefore, we take a series of ordinates, 1, 2, 3, 4, etc. (Fig. 167), all of equal height and at equal intervals apart

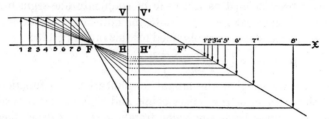

Fig. 167.—Relation between axial or depth-magnification and lateral magnification.

(like a row of telegraph poles), their images will be of unequal heights and at unequal distances apart; but the intervals between the successive images will increase or diminish far more rapidly than the corresponding changes in their heights. Accordingly, the image of a solid object cannot, in general, be similar to the object, but will be distorted, since the dimension parallel to the axis of the optical system is altered very much more than the dimensions at right angles to the axis. This uneven distribution of the images of ob-

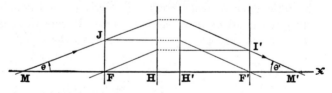

Fig. 168.—Angular magnification or convergence-ratio.

jects at different distances explains "the curious effect noticeable in modern binocular field-glasses of high power, but seen also in opera-glasses and telescopes, in which the successive planes of landscapes seem exaggerated, and flattened almost like the flat scenery of the theater. Thin trees and hedges, for example, seem to occupy definite planes; and the more distant objects appear to be compressed up toward those in front of them" (Professor S. P. Thompson).

(c) *The angular magnification or so-called convergence-ratio z.* If the slopes of conjugate rays are denoted by θ, θ', that is, if we put $\theta = \angle \mathrm{FMJ}$, $\theta' = \angle \mathrm{F'M'I'}$ (Fig. 168), where M, M' designate the points where the ray crosses the axis in the object-space and image-space, respectively, and J and I' designate the points where it crosses the primary and secondary focal planes, then evidently:

$$\tan \theta = \frac{\mathrm{FJ}}{\mathrm{MF}}, \quad \tan \theta' = \frac{\mathrm{F'I'}}{\mathrm{M'F'}}.$$

But the focal lengths are defined by the equations (§ 122):

$$f = \frac{\mathrm{F'I'}}{\tan \theta}, \quad f' = \frac{\mathrm{FJ}}{\tan \theta'};$$

and therefore:

$$\tan \theta = \frac{\mathrm{F'I'}}{f}, \quad \tan \theta' = \frac{\mathrm{FJ}}{f'}.$$

Eliminating the intercepts FJ and F'I', we obtain:

$$z = \frac{\tan \theta'}{\tan \theta} = -\frac{x}{f'} = -\frac{f}{x'},$$

where the ratio $z = \tan \theta' : \tan \theta$ (or $\theta' : \theta$) is called the *angular magnification* or the *convergence-ratio*. It is directly proportional to the abscissa x of the object-point M.

The three magnification-ratios x, y and z are connected by the following relation:

$$\frac{y}{x \, z} = 1.$$

PROBLEMS

1. Taking the index of refraction of water $= \frac{4}{3}$, show that the sun's rays passing through a globe of water, 6 inches in diameter, will be converged to a focus 6 inches from the center of the sphere.

2. A small object is placed at a distance u from the nearer side of a solid refracting sphere of radius r and of refractive

index n. Show that the distance of the image from the other side of the sphere is

$$u' = \frac{2r(u-r) - n.u.r}{2(n-1)u - (n-2)r},$$

and find the lateral magnification.

3. A luminous point is situated at the first focal point of an infinitely thin symmetric double convex lens made of glass (of index 1.5) and surrounded by air. The radius of each surface is 15 cm. Show that the image formed by rays which have been twice reflected in the interior of the lens before emerging again into the air will be on the other side of the lens at a distance of 2.5 cm. from it.

4. An optical system is composed of two equal double convex lenses. The index of refraction of the glass is $n = 1.6202$, and the radii, thicknesses, etc., are as follows:

$$r_1 = -r_4 = 47.92243; \qquad r_3 = -r_2 = 9.39617;$$
$$d_1 = d_3 = 0.2; \qquad d_2 = 2.4287.$$

If an incident paraxial ray crosses the axis at a distance $u_1 = -7.31101$ from the vertex of the first surface, show that the emergent ray will cross the axis at a distance $u'_4 = 33.65725$ from the vertex of the last surface.

5. A. GLEICHEN in his *Lehrbuch der geometrischen Optik* gives the following data of P. GOERZ's "double anastigmat" photographic objective, composed of three cemented lenses, the first being a positive meniscus of crown glass, the second a double concave flint glass lens, and the third a double convex crown glass lens:

Indices of refraction:

$$n_1 = n_5 = 1; \quad n_2 = 1.5117; \quad n_3 = 1.5478; \quad n_4 = 1.6125$$

Radii:

$$r_1 = -0.128965; \qquad r_2 = -0.049597; \qquad r_3 = +0.196423;$$
$$r_4 = -0.1266629$$

Thicknesses:

$$d_1 = +0.01277; \quad d_2 = +0.00664; \quad d_3 = +0.02114.$$

Show that the second focal point of this system is at a distance of $+1.111095$ from the vertex of the last surface. (See scheme for calculation of paraxial ray through a centered system of spherical refracting surfaces, § 181).

6. Define the nodal points N, N' and show that $FN = -f'$, $F'N' = -f$, where F, F' designate the positions of the focal points and f, f' denote the focal lengths of the optical system. Under what circumstances are the nodal points identical with the principal points?

7. Derive the image-equations referred to the principal points.

8. Given the positions on the optical axis of the principal points and of the focal points; construct the nodal points. Also, construct the point Q' conjugate to a given object-point Q. Draw diagrams for convergent and divergent systems.

9. Prove that

$$n'.f + n.f' = 0,$$

where f and f' denote the focal lengths of the optical system, and n and n' denote the indices of refraction of the first and last media.

10. A small cube is placed on the axis of a symmetrical optical instrument with one pair of its faces perpendicular to the axis. Find the two places where the image of the cube will also be a cube. (Assume that the instrument is surrounded by the same medium on both sides.)

Ans. At the points for which the lateral magnification is $+1$ or -1.

11. An object is placed 3 inches in front of the primary focal plane of a convergent optical system. Show that the image will be one-and-a-half times as large as it was at first if a plate of glass ($n = 1.5$) of thickness 3 inches is interposed between the object and the instrument.

12. Show that the axial magnification at the nodal points has the same value as the lateral magnification in the nodal planes.

13. A symmetrical optical instrument is surrounded by the same medium on both sides. If the images of two small

objects A and B on the axis are formed at A′ and B′, show that the ratio of A′B′ to AB is equal to the product of the lateral magnifications for the pairs of conjugate points A, A′ and B, B′.

14. Show that in a symmetrical optical instrument there are two pairs of conjugate points on the axis for which an infinitely small axial displacement of the object will correspond to an equal displacement of the image; and that the focal points are midway between these points.

15. Show that in a symmetrical optical instrument surrounded by the same medium on both sides there are two points on the axis where object and image will be in the same plane; and that if a denotes the distance between the principal planes, the distance between these two points will be

$$\sqrt{a(a+4f)}.$$

16. In a centered system of m spherical refracting surfaces the vertex of the kth surface is designated by A_k. A paraxial ray crosses the axis before refraction at the first surface at a point M_1 which coincides with the primary focal point F of the optical system. Before and after refraction at the kth surface this ray crosses the axis at M_k and M_{k+1}, respectively. If we put $u_k = A_k M_k$, $u_k' = A_k M_{k+1}$, show that

$$f = \frac{u_2.u_3. \ . \ . \ u_m}{u_1'.u_2'. \ . \ . \ u_{m-1}'} .FA_1,$$

where f denotes the primary focal length of the optical system.

17. If the symbols u_k, u_k', employed in the same sense as in the preceding problem, refer to a paraxial ray which is incident on the first surface of the system in a direction parallel to the optical axis, show that

$$f = \frac{n}{n'} \frac{u_1'.u_2'. \ . \ . \ u_m'}{u_2.u_3. \ . \ . \ u_m}, \qquad f' = -\frac{u_1'.u_2'. \ . \ . \ u_m'}{u_2.u_3. \ . \ . \ u_m},$$

where f, f' denote the focal lengths of the system and n, n' denote the indices of refraction of the first and last media.

18. Employing the formulæ of No. 17, determine the focal lengths of a hemispherical lens of glass of refractive index

1.5; and find the positions of the principal planes and the focal planes.

Ans. If r denotes the radius of the curved surface, and if distances are measured from the vertex of this surface, the distances of the focal points are $-2r$ and $+7r/3$, and the distances of the principal points are 0 and $+r/3$. The focal length is twice the length of the radius.

19. If a paraxial ray, proceeding originally in a direction parallel to the axis of a centered system of spherical refracting surfaces (as in No. 17), crosses the axis in the medium of index n_k at a point M_k whose distance from the vertex of the kth surface is $u_k = A_k M_k$ $(U_k = n_k/u_k)$, show that

$$F_{1,k} = F_{1,k-1} \, (U_k + F_k) \left(\frac{1}{U_{k-1} + F_{k-1}} - \frac{d_{k-1}}{n_k} \right),$$

where F_k denotes the refracting power of the kth surface, $F_{1,k}$ denotes the refracting power of the system of surfaces bounded by the 1st and kth inclusive $(F_{1,1} = F_1$ and $F_{1,0} = 0)$, and $d_{k-1} = A_{k-1} A_k$ denotes the axial thickness between the surfaces bounding the medium of index n_k.

20. In any optical system surrounded by the same medium on both sides, the product of the lateral magnification and the angular magnification (§ 124) for a given position of the object is equal to unity.

21. The principal points of an optical system are designated by H, H', and M, M' designate another pair of conjugate points. Moreover, the first focal point and the first nodal point are designated by F and N, respectively. Show that

$$\frac{MF}{MH} = \frac{MN}{MM' - HH'}.$$

How is this formula modified for the case of a single spherical refracting surface? and for the case of an infinitely thin lens?

CHAPTER XI

COMPOUND SYSTEMS.   THICK LENSES AND COMBINATIONS
OF LENSES AND MIRRORS

125. Formulæ for Combination of Two Optical Systems in terms of the Focal Lengths.—Suppose that the optical system consists of two parts I and II, each composed of a centered system of spherical refracting surfaces with their optical axes in the same straight line. On a straight line parallel to this common optical axis take two points P, P′ (Fig. 169), which we shall assume to be a pair of conjugate points with respect to the compound system (I+II); and

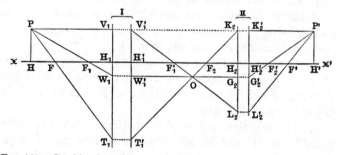

Fig. 169.—Combination of two optical systems. Letters with subscripts refer to component systems; letters without subscripts refer to compound or resultant system.

since these points are on the same side of the optical axis and at equal distances from it, evidently, they must lie in the principal planes of the compound system (§ 119). Accordingly, the feet of the perpendiculars drawn from P, P′ to the optical axis will be the pair of principal points H, H′ of the compound system.

On the optical axis select a point F_1 for the position of

356

the primary focal point of system I; and select also the positions of the principal points H_1, H_1' and H_2, H_2' of systems I and II, respectively. Through F_1 draw the straight line PW_1 meeting the primary principal plane of system I in the point W_1; take $H_1'W_1' = H_1W_1$, and draw the straight line $W_1'G_2$ parallel to the axis meeting the primary principal plane of system II in the point G_2; take $H_2'G_2' = H_2G_2$, and draw the straight line $G_2'P'$, which must necessarily cross the optical axis at the secondary focal point F_2' of system II.

Let the straight line drawn through P parallel to the optical axis meet the primary and secondary principal planes of system I in the points designated by V_1 and V_1', respectively; and select a point on the optical axis for the position of the secondary focal point F_1' of system I. Through F_1' draw the straight line $V_1'F_1'$ meeting the primary principal plane of system II in L_2; take $H_2'L_2' = H_2L_2$, and draw the straight line $L_2'P'$, which will cross the optical axis in the secondary focal point F' of the compound system.

Let the straight line drawn through P' parallel to the optical axis meet the primary and secondary principal planes of system II in the points K_2 and K_2', respectively; and let O designate the point of intersection of the pair of straight lines $W_1'G_2$ and $V_1'L_2$. The point where the straight line K_2O crosses the optical axis will be the position of the primary focal point F_2 of system II. Let the straight line K_2F_2 meet the secondary principal plane of system I in the point T_1', and take $H_1T_1 = H_1'T_1'$; then the straight line PT_1 will cross the optical axis at the primary focal point F of the compound system.

The diagram constructed according to the above directions represents a perfectly general case. The focal lengths of the component systems are: $f_1 = F_1H_1$, $f_1' = F_1'H_1'$ and $f_2 = F_2H_2$, $f_2' = F_2'H_2'$; and the focal lengths of the compound system are: $f = FH$, $f' = F'H'$. The step from the secondary focal point of the first system to the primary focal point of the second system will be denoted by the symbol Δ; thus, $\Delta = F_1'F_2$.

Now if we know the positions on the optical axis of the focal points F_1, F_1' and F_2, F_2' of the two component systems, together with the values of the focal lengths f_1, f_1' and f_2, f_2', it is easy to calculate the positions of the focal points F, F' and the values of the focal lengths f, f' of the compound system; as will now be shown.

The position of the primary focal point F of the compound system may be found from the fact that F and F_2 are a pair of conjugate axial points with respect to system I, and hence (§ 123, a):

$$F_1F. \; F_1'F_2 = f_1.f_1'.$$

And, similarly, the position of the secondary focal point F' may be found from the fact that F_1' and F' are a pair of conjugate points with respect to system II, so that

$$F_2'F'.F_2F_1' = f_2.f_2'.$$

Accordingly, the positions of the focal points F, F' with respect to the known points F_1, F_2', respectively, are given by the following formulæ:

$$F_1F = \frac{f_1.f_1'}{\Delta}, \quad F_2'F' = -\frac{f_2.f_2'}{\Delta}.$$

In order to find the focal lengths f, f', we may proceed as follows:

In the similar triangles FHP, FH_1T_1 we have:

$$\frac{FH}{FH_1} = \frac{H\,P}{H_1T_1};$$

and since

$$HP = H_2K_2, \quad H_1T_1 = H_1'T_1',$$

the proportion above may be written:

$$\frac{FH}{FH_1} = \frac{H_2K_2}{H_1'T_1'}.$$

Now from the similar triangles $F_2H_2K_2$, $F_2H_1'T_1'$ we have also:

$$\frac{H_2K_2}{H_1'T_1'} = \frac{F_2H_2}{F_2H_1'};$$

and hence:

$$FH = \frac{F_2 H_2}{F_2 H_1'} \cdot FH_1.$$

Now $FH_1 = FF_1 + F_1 H_1 = -\dfrac{f_1 . f_1'}{\Delta} + f_1 = -\dfrac{f_1}{\Delta}(f_1' - \Delta)$;

and $F_2 H_1' = F_2 F_1' + F_1' H_1' = f_1' - \Delta$.

Accordingly, putting $FH = f$, $F_2 H_2 = f_2$, we obtain:

$$f = -\frac{f_1 . f_2}{\Delta},$$

whereby the primary focal length of the compound system may be calculated.

Similarly, from the figure we obtain the relations:

$$\frac{F'H'}{F'H_2'} = \frac{H'P'}{H_2'L_2'} = \frac{H_1'V_1'}{H_2 L_2} = \frac{F_1'H_1'}{F_1'H_2} \; ;$$

and since $F'H' = f'$, $F_1'H_1' = f_1'$,

$$F'H_2' = F'F_2' + F_2'H_2' = \frac{f_2 . f_2'}{\Delta} + f_2' = \frac{f_2'}{\Delta}(f_2 + \Delta),$$

$$F_1'H_2 = F_1'F_2 + F_2 H_2 = f_2 + \Delta,$$

we obtain an analogous expression for the secondary focal length of the compound system, as follows:

$$f' = \frac{f_1' f_2'}{\Delta} .$$

By varying the interval Δ, which is the common denominator of all these expressions, it is obvious that it is possible with two given component systems to obtain combinations of widely different optical effects. In particular, when F_1' coincides with F_2, so that the interval Δ vanishes, the focal points F, F' will be situated both at infinity, so that the focal lengths f, f' will be infinite also. This is the case, for example, with the optical instrument known as the telescope; and, accordingly, any optical system which transforms a cylindrical bundle of parallel rays into another cylindrical bundle of parallel rays is called a *telescopic* (or *afocal*) *system*. The simplest illustration of such a system is afforded by a single plane refracting surface or by a plane mirror.

126. Formulæ for Combination of Two Optical Systems in terms of the Refracting Powers.—Although the formulæ derived in the preceding section are very simple and convenient, GULLSTRAND's system of formulæ in terms of the refracting powers possesses certain advantages and is even more useful. The latter formulæ may be derived immediately from the former, as will now be shown.

In GULLSTRAND's system the interval between the two component optical systems is expressed, not by Δ, but by the *reduced distance* (§ 104) c of the primary principal point H_2 of system II from the secondary principal point H_1' of system I. Thus, if n_1, n_2 and n_2, n_3 denote the indices of refraction of the first and last media of systems I and II, respectively, then

$$c = \frac{H_1'H_2}{n_2} .$$

The connection between the two magnitudes c and Δ is easily obtained; for since

$$F_1'F_2 = F_1'H_1' + H_1'H_2 + H_2F_2,$$

we find immediately:

$$\Delta = f_1' + n_2.c - f_2.$$

Now let us introduce the following symbols:

$$F_1 = \frac{n_1}{f_1} = -\frac{n_2}{f_1'}, \quad F_2 = \frac{n_2}{f_2} = -\frac{n_3}{f_2'}, \quad F = \frac{n_1}{f} = -\frac{n_3}{f'},$$

where F_1, F_2 denote, therefore, the refracting powers of the component systems and F denotes the refracting power of the compound system (§§ 105 and 123, d). Hence, since

$$f_1' = -\frac{n_2}{F_1}, \quad f_2 = \frac{n_2}{F_2},$$

we may write:

$$\Delta = -\frac{n_2}{F_1.F_2}(F_1 + F_2 - c.F_1.F_2).$$

Now if this value of Δ is substituted in either of the formulæ

$$f = -\frac{f_1.f_2}{\Delta}, \quad f' = \frac{f_1'.f_2'}{\Delta},$$

and if the focal lengths are expressed in terms of the refracting powers, we find:

$$F = F_1 + F_2 - c.F_1.F_2;$$

which is GULLSTRAND's formula for the refracting power of the compound system in terms of the refracting powers of the two component systems and of the interval c between them.

Likewise, if in the formulæ

$$F_1F = \frac{f_1.f_1'}{\Delta}, \qquad F_2'F' = -\frac{f_2.f_2'}{\Delta}$$

we eliminate f_1, f_1' and f_2, f_2' and put $\Delta = -n_2\dfrac{F}{F_1.F_2}$, we obtain for the reduced steps F_1F and $F_2'F'$ the following expressions:

$$\frac{F_1F}{n_1} = \frac{F_2}{F.F_1}, \qquad \frac{F_2'F'}{n_3} = -\frac{F_1}{F.F_2}.$$

The positions of the focal points F, F' of the compound system with respect to H_1, H_2', respectively are obtained as follows:

$$H_1F = H_1F_1 + F_1F = F_1F - n_1/F_1,$$
$$H_2'F' = H_2'F_2' + F_2'F' = F_2'F' + n_3/F_2;$$

and if herein the values of F_1F and $F_2'F'$ are substituted, and if also we note that

$$F - F_1 = F_2(1 - c.F_1), \qquad F - F_2 = F_1(1 - c.F_2),$$

we obtain finally:

$$\frac{H_1F}{n_1} = -\frac{1 - c.F_2}{F}, \qquad \frac{H_2'F'}{n_3} = \frac{1 - c.F_1}{F}.$$

Moreover, since

$$H_1H = H_1F + FH = H_1F + n_1/F,$$
$$H_2'H' = H_2'F' + F'H' = H_2'F' - n_3/F,$$

the GULLSTRAND system of formulæ for the combination of two optical systems may be written as follows:

$$\frac{H_1H}{n_1} = \frac{F_2}{F}.c, \qquad \frac{H_2'H'}{n_3} = -\frac{F_1}{F}.c,$$
$$F = F_1 + F_2 - c.F_1.F_2.$$

Accordingly, if the positions of the principal points H_1, H_1'

and H_2, H_2' of the two component systems, the refracting powers F_1, F_2 and the indices of refraction n_1, n_2 and n_3 are known, we can calculate the reduced interval c and find the refracting power F of the compound system and the positions of the principal points H, H'. We shall see numerous applications of these formulæ in the succeeding sections of this chapter.

127. Thick Lenses Bounded by Spherical Surfaces.— When a centered system of spherical refracting surfaces consists of two surfaces, it constitutes a spherical lens involving three media, viz., the medium of the incident rays (n_1), the medium comprised between the two spherical surfaces, sometimes called the lens-medium (n_2), and the medium of the emergent rays (n_3), which is generally but not necessarily the same as that of the incident rays. Usually, a lens is described by assigning the values of the three indices of refraction and the positions of the centers C_1, C_2 and the vertices A_1, A_2 on the optical axis; the usual data being the radii $r_1 = A_1C_1$, $r_2 = A_2C_2$ and the thickness $d = A_1A_2$. The lens may be regarded, therefore, as a combination of two spherical refracting surfaces whose refracting powers F_1, F_2 are given by the formulæ (§ 105)

$$F_1 = \frac{n_2 - n_1}{r_1}, \quad F_2 = \frac{n_3 - n_2}{r_2}.$$

Since the principal points of a spherical refracting surface coincide with each other at the vertex of the surface (§§ 81 and 119), the interval $c = \dfrac{H_1'H_2}{n_2} = \dfrac{A_1A_2}{n_2}$, and therefore

$$c = \frac{d}{n_2}.$$

Accordingly, if, by way of abbreviation, we introduce the special symbol

$$N = n_2\big\{ (n_2 - n_1)r_2 - (n_2 - n_3)r_1 \big\} + (n_2 - n_3)(n_2 - n_1)d$$

to denote a constant of the lens, we obtain, by substituting the values of F_1, F_2 and c in the formula $F = F_1 + F_2 - c.F_1.F_2$, the following expression for *the refracting power F of a lens:*

$$F = \frac{N}{n_2.r_1.r_2},$$

where the value of F will be given in dioptries in case the distances r_1, r_2 and d are all measured in meters (§ 107).

The *positions of the principal points* (H, H') *of a lens* are determined in the same way by the formulæ:

$$\frac{A_1H}{n_1} = -\frac{n_2 - n_3}{N} r_1.d, \qquad \frac{A_2H'}{n_3} = -\frac{n_2 - n_1}{N} r_2.d;$$

and the *positions of the focal points* (F, F') may likewise be calculated from the following expressions:

$$\frac{A_1F}{n_1} = -\frac{r_1}{N}\left\{n_2.r_2 + (n_2 - n_3)d\right\}, \quad \frac{A_2F'}{n_3} = \frac{r_2}{N}\left\{n_2.r_1 - (n_2 - n_1)d\right\}.$$

When, as is usually the case, *the lens is surrounded by the same medium on both sides,* we may put

$$n_1 = n_3 = n, \qquad n_2 = n';$$

and then the above formulæ become:

$$N = (n' - n)\left\{n'(r_2 - r_1) + (n' - n)d\right\};$$

$$F = \frac{N}{n'.r_1.r_2};$$

$$\frac{A_1H}{n} = -\frac{n' - n}{N} r_1.d, \qquad \frac{A_2H'}{n} = -\frac{n' - n}{N} r_2.d;$$

$$\frac{A_1F}{n} = -\frac{r_1}{N}\left\{n'.r_2 + (n' - n)d\right\}, \quad \frac{A_2F'}{n} = \frac{r_2}{N}\left\{n'.r_1 - (n' - n)d\right\}.$$

The *nodal points* (N, N') *of a lens* surrounded by the same medium on both sides coincide with the principal points (§ 122).

The positions of the focal points and principal points may be exhibited in the case of a thick convergent lens in the following manner, as described in GRIMSEHL's *Handbuch der Physik:*

Two thin plano-lenses, each 4 cm. in diameter, are cemented with Canada balsam to the opposite faces of a glass

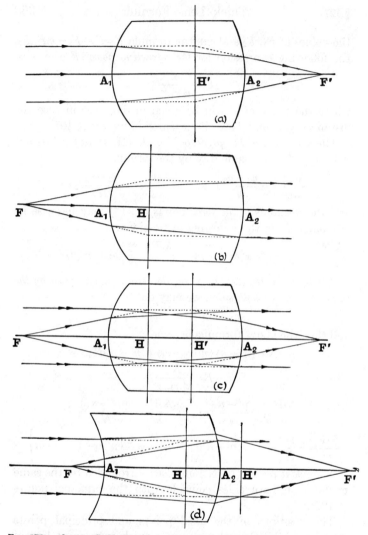

Fig. 170, *a, b, c,* and *d.*—Double convex lens: (*a*) Location of second focal point (F′) and principal point (H′); (*b*) Location of first focal point (F) and principal point (H); (*c*) Location of focal points (F, F′) and principal points (H, H′). (*d*) Meniscus convex lens: location of principal points and focal points, showing their unsymmetrical positions with respect to the surfaces of the lens.

cube of edge 4 cm. and made of the same glass, so as to form
a thick symmetric double convex lens, as represented in
Fig. 170, a, b and c. A diaphragm with three parallel horizontal slits is placed in the path of a cylindrical beam of parallel
rays so as to separate it into three smaller beams, and the
lens is adjusted so that the middle beam proceeds along
the axis of the lens. The paths of the rays in air can be
rendered visible by tobacco-smoke and may be photo-
graphed. In this way figures will be obtained similar to
those shown in the diagrams. The position of the secondary focal point F′ is shown by the point of convergence of
the rays on emergence (Fig. 170, a). A point in the second
principal plane of the lens may be located by finding the
point of intersection of an incident ray parallel to the axis
with the corresponding emergent ray (§ 119), as indicated
by the dotted lines in the figure; and the second principal
point H′ will be at the foot of the perpendicular dropped
from this point on to the axis. If the rays are sent through
the lens from the opposite side (that is, from right to left in
the drawing, Fig. 170, b), they will intersect on emergence
in the primary focal point F; and the position of the primary
principal point H may be found in exactly the same way
as above. The two diagrams Figs. 170, a and b, are combined in one in Fig. 170, c. In Fig. 170, d, the lens is concave towards the incident light and convex when viewed
from the other side; and this figure shows very clearly how
the focal points F, F′ and the principal points H, H′ may be
both unsymmetrically placed with respect to the lens, although here also we have, as before, $FH = H'F'$.

128. So-called " Vertex Refraction " of a Thick Lens.—
The step from the second vertex (A_2) of a lens to the second
focal point (F′), which may be denoted by v, is sometimes
called the "back focus" of the lens; that is, $v = A_2F'$. If
the lens is surrounded by the same medium (n) on both
sides, then $v/n = (1 - c.F_1)/F$, where F denotes the refracting power of the lens, F_1 denotes the refracting power of

the first surface, and $c=d/n'$ denotes the reduced thickness. The reciprocal of this magnitude v/n is called the *vertex refraction* of the lens $\left(\dfrac{n}{v}=V\right)$ and its relation to the refracting power is given by the formula:

$$V=\frac{F}{1-c.F_1}=\frac{F}{1-\dfrac{n'-n}{r_1}\cdot\dfrac{d}{n'}}.$$

If F is given in dioptries, the values of d and r_1 must be expressed in meters; and then the expression above will give the value of V in dioptries. The importance of this function V in the theory of modern spectacle lenses has been pointed out by Von Rohr; it is measured from the second face of the lens because that is the side next the eye. When a lens (with spherical surfaces) is reversed by turning it through 180° around any line perpendicular to its axis, the refracting power F remains the same, whereas the vertex refraction V will be different unless the lens is a symmetric lens or infinitely thin, in which latter case $d=0$ and $V=F$. Thus, whereas the refracting power of a lens is the same whether the light traverses it from one side or the other, the vertex refraction depends essentially on which side of the lens is presented to the incident rays.

129. Combination of Two Lenses.—Let us take the simplest case, and suppose that the system is composed of *two infinitely thin co-axial lenses*, each surrounded by air. Let A_1 and A_2 designate the points where the optical axis meets the two lenses, and let the interval between them be denoted by c; that is, put $c=A_1A_2$. Since the principal points of an infinitely thin lens coincide with each other at the point A where the axis crosses the lens, and since the intervening medium is assumed to be air of index unity, this distance c has here the same meaning as the reduced interval $c=H_1'H_2/n_2$ in the general formulæ of § 126. Accordingly, we may write immediately the following system of formulæ for a combination of two thin lenses of refracting powers F_1, F_2, surrounded on both sides by air and separated by the distance c:

$$F = F_1 + F_2 - c.F_1.F_2;$$

$$A_1H = \frac{c.F_2}{F}, \qquad A_2H' = -\frac{c.F_1}{F};$$

$$A_1F = -\frac{1-c.F_2}{F}, \qquad A_2F' = \frac{1-c.F_1}{F}.$$

These formulæ may also be expressed in terms of the focal lengths f_1 and f_2, as follows:

$$f = \frac{f_1.f_2}{f_1+f_2-c},$$

$$A_1H = \frac{f}{f_2}.c, \quad A_2H' = -\frac{f}{f_1}.c, \quad A_1F = -\frac{f(f_2-c)}{f_2}, \quad A_2F' = \frac{f(f_1-c)}{f_1}.$$

The positions of the focal points F, F' and the princi-

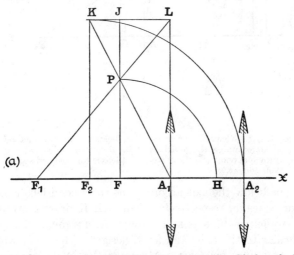

FIG. 171, a.—Combination of two thin lenses. Graphical method of determining the positions of the first focal point (F) and principal point (H): Case when both lenses are convex.

pal points H, H' of a combination of two infinitely thin lenses surrounded by air may be constructed geometrically as follows:

Draw a straight line to represent the common axis of the pair of thin lenses, and mark the points A_1 and A_2 (Fig. 171, a, b, and c) where the axis crosses the lenses, and also the positions of the primary focal points F_1 and F_2. Through F_2 draw a straight line perpendicular to the axis, and take on it a point K such that $F_2K = F_2A_2 = f_2$; this point K lying

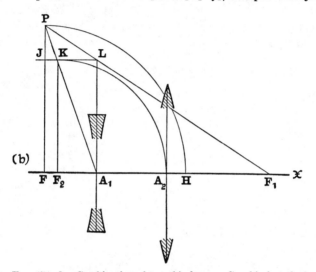

Fig. 171, b.—Combination of two thin lenses. Graphical method of determining the positions of the first focal point (F) and principal point (H): Case when first lens is concave and second lens convex.

above or below the axis according as the second lens is convex or concave, respectively. Through K draw a straight line parallel to the axis and through A_1 a straight line perpendicular to the axis; and let L designate the point where these two lines intersect. Moreover, let P designate the point of intersection of the pair of straight lines LF_1 and KA_1. The foot of the perpendicular let fall from P on to the axis will be the primary focal point F of the compound system; and the ordinate FP will be equal to the primary focal length f of the compound system; and hence if the quadrant of a circle is described around F as center with radius FP, it will cut the axis at the primary principal point H, which lies to the right or left of F according as the point P falls above or below the axis.

According to this construction, the points P and K are a pair of conjugate extra-axial points with respect to the

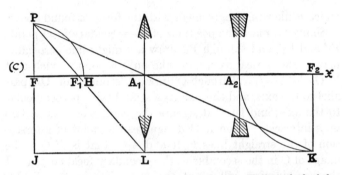

Fig. 171, *c.*—Combination of two thin lenses. Graphical method of determining the positions of the first focal point (F) and principal point (H): Case when first lens is convex and second lens concave.

first lens; so that the construction really consists in locating the object-point P which is imaged by the first lens in the point K. This will help the student to remember the construction.

In order to show that the construction is correct, let J designate the point of intersection of the pair of straight lines FP and LK. Then since JP and FP are corresponding altitudes of the similar triangles PLK and PF_1A_1, we have:

$$\frac{JP}{FP} = \frac{LK}{F_1A_1} = \frac{A_1F_2}{F_1A_1} = \frac{A_1A_2 + A_2F_2}{F_1A_1} = \frac{c - f_2}{f_1}.$$

Now $JP = JF + FP = KF_2 + FP = FP - f_2$, and therefore:

$$\frac{FP - f_2}{FP} = \frac{c - f_2}{f_1},$$

and if this equation is solved for FP, we find:

$$FP = \frac{f_1 \cdot f_2}{f_1 + f_2 - c} = f,$$

in agreement with the formula found above. Moreover, in the similar triangles A_1FP and A_1F_2K,

$$\frac{A_1F}{FP} = \frac{A_1F_2}{F_2K};$$

and since $A_1F_2 = c - f_2$, $F_2K = f_2$, $FP = f$, we find:

$$A_1F = -\frac{f(f_2 - c)}{f_2},$$

which is likewise in agreement with the formula found above.

Similarly, mark the positions of the secondary focal points F_1' and F_2', and through F_1' draw a straight line perpendicular to the optical axis, and take on it a point O such that $F_1'O = F_1'A_1 = f_1'$. Through O draw the straight line OR parallel to the axis, and through A_2 a straight line perpendicular to the axis; and let R designate the point where these two lines intersect. Then if Q designates the point of intersection of the straight lines $F_2'R$ and A_2O, that is, if Q is the image of O in the second lens, the secondary focal point F' of the combination will be at the foot of the perpendicular drawn from Q to the optical axis, and the secondary principal point H' will lie on the axis at a distance $F'H' = F'Q$. This construction may be proved in a manner entirely analogous to the proof given above.

130. Optical Constants of Gullstrand's Schematic Eye.— As a further illustration of the use of the formulæ for the

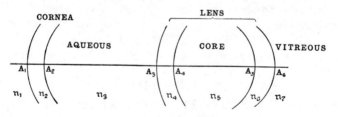

Fig. 172.—Schematic eye.

combination of two optical systems, let us apply them to the calculations of the refracting power (F) of the human eye, together with the positions of the principal points (H,H') and the focal points (F, F'). For this purpose we shall use the data of GULLSTRAND's schematic eye (in its passive state, accommodation entirely relaxed) which are given in the third edition of HELMHOLTZ's *Handbuch der physiologischen Optik*, Bd. I (Hamburg u. Leipzig, 1909), pages 300 and 301, as follows (see Fig. 172):

Indices of refraction:

Cornea......................... $n_2 = 1.376$
Aqueous and vitreous humors $n_3 = n_7 = 1.336$
Lens........................ $n_4 = n_6 = 1.386$
Lens-core .... $n_5 = 1.406$

Position of surfaces:

Posterior surface of cornea:	$A_1A_2 = 0.5$	mm.
Anterior surface of lens:	$A_1A_3 = 3.6$	"
" " " lens-core:	$A_1A_4 = 4.146$	"
Posterior " " lens-core:	$A_1A_5 = 6.565$	"
" " " lens:	$A_1A_6 = 7.2$	"

Radii of surfaces:

Anterior surface of cornea:	$r_1 = + 7.7$	mm.
Posterior " " "	$r_2 = + 6.8$	"
Anterior " " lens:	$r_3 = +10.0$	"
" " " lens-core:	$r_4 = + 7.911$	"
Posterior " " " "	$r_5 = - 5.76$	"
" " " lens:	$r_6 = - 6.0$	"

Consider, first, the cornea-system composed of the anterior and posterior surfaces of the cornea. The refracting power of the anterior surface is:

$$F_1 = \frac{n_2 - n_1}{r_1} = +48.831 \text{ dptr.};$$

and that of the posterior surface is:

$$F_2 = \frac{n_3 - n_2}{r_2} = -5.882 \text{ dptr.}$$

The reduced interval between the two surfaces is:

$$c_1 = \frac{A_1A_2}{n_2} = \frac{0.0005}{1.376}.$$

Hence, if F_{12} denotes the refracting power of the cornea-system, where

$$F_{12} = F_1 + F_2 - c_1.F_1.F_2,$$

we find:

$$F_{12} = +43.053 \text{ dptr.}$$

The positions of the principal points of the cornea-system are given by the formulæ:

$$\frac{A_1H_{12}}{n_1} = \frac{c_1.F_2}{F_{12}}, \qquad \frac{A_2H_{12}'}{n_3} = -\frac{c_1.F_1}{F_{12}};$$

whence we find:

$$A_1H_{12} = -0.0496 \text{ mm.}, \qquad A_1H_{12}' = -0.0506 \text{ mm.}$$

The lens-system is composed of four refracting surfaces. The first two surfaces form the so-called anterior cortex and the last two surfaces the posterior cortex. The refracting power of the anterior surface of the lens is:

$$F_3 = \frac{n_4 - n_3}{r_3} = +5 \text{ dptr.};$$

and that of the anterior surface of the lens-core is:

$$F_4 = \frac{n_5 - n_4}{r_4} = +2.528 \text{ dptr.}$$

The reduced interval between these two surfaces is

$$c_3 = \frac{A_3A_4}{n_4} = \frac{0.000546}{1.386}.$$

Hence, if F_{34} denotes the refracting power of the combination, that is, if

$$F_{34} = F_3 + F_4 - c_3.F_3.F_4,$$

we find: $F_{34} = +7.523$ dptr.

If the principal points of the anterior cortex are designated by H_{34}, H_{34}', then

$$\frac{A_3H_{34}}{n_3} = \frac{c_3.F_4}{F_{34}}, \qquad \frac{A_4H_{34}'}{n_5} = -\frac{c_3.F_3}{F_{34}};$$

whence we obtain:

$$A_1H_{34} = +3.777 \text{ mm.}, \qquad A_1H_{34}' = +3.778 \text{ mm.}$$

so that the principal points of the anterior cortex are coincident with each other.

Proceeding in the same way with the posterior cortex, we have:

$$F_5 = \frac{n_6 - n_5}{r_5} = +3.472 \text{ dptr.,} \quad F_6 = \frac{n_7 - n_6}{r_6} = +8.333 \text{ dptr.,}$$

$$c_5 = \frac{A_5 A_6}{n_6} = \frac{0.000635}{1.386} \; ;$$

and hence if

$$F_{56} = F_5 + F_6 - c_5.F_5.F_6,$$

we find: $F_{56} = +11.792$ dptr.

Moreover, since

$$\frac{A_5 H_{56}}{n_5} = \frac{c_5.F_6}{F_{56}}, \qquad \frac{A_6 H_{56}'}{n_7} = -\frac{c_5.F_5}{F_{56}},$$

we have finally for the positions of the principal points of the posterior cortex:

$$A_1 H_{56} = +7.0202 \text{ mm.,} \quad A_1 H_{56}' = +7.0198 \text{ mm.;}$$

so that H_{56} and H_{56}' may also be regarded as coincident.

If the refracting power of the lens-system as a whole is denoted by L, then

$$L = F_{34} + F_{56} - s.F_{34}.F_{56},$$

where

$$s = \frac{H_{34}' H_{56}}{n_5} = \frac{0.0032422}{1.406} \; ;$$

and if P, P' designate the principal points of the lens-system, then

$$\frac{H_{34}P}{n_3} = \frac{s.F_{56}}{L}, \qquad \frac{H_{56}'P'}{n_7} = -\frac{s.F_{34}}{L} \, .$$

Accordingly, we find:

$$L = +19.110 \text{ dptr.;}$$

$$A_1 P = +5.6780 \text{ mm.,} \quad A_1 P' = +5.8070 \text{ mm.}$$

Lastly, combining the cornea-system and the lens-system, we obtain for the refracting power of the entire optical system of the eye:

$$F = F_{12} + L - c.F_{12}.L,$$

where

$$c = \frac{H_{12}'P}{n_3} = \frac{0.0057285}{1.336} \, .$$

Also,

$$\frac{H_{12}H}{n_1} = \frac{c.L}{F} \qquad \frac{P'H'}{n_7} = -\frac{c.F_{12}}{F},$$

where H, H′ designate the positions of the principal points of the eye. Thus, we find:

$$F = +58.64 \text{ dptr.;}$$
$$A_1H = +1.348 \text{ mm.}, \qquad A_1H' = +1.602 \text{ mm.}$$

If the focal lengths of the eye are denoted by f and f', then, since $f = n_1/F$ and $f' = -n_7/F$, we obtain:

$$f = +17.055 \text{ mm.}, \qquad f' = -22.785 \text{ mm.}$$

The focal points F, F′ are located as follows:

$$A_1F = -15.707 \text{ mm.}, \qquad A_1F' = +24.387 \text{ mm.}$$

In GULLSTRAND's schematic eye the length of the eyeball is taken as 24 mm., and therefore the second focal point F′ is not on the retina but 0.387 mm. beyond it; so that the schematic eye is not emmetropic but hypermetropic (see § 153) to the extent of 1 dptr.

131. Combination of Three Optical Systems.—It is frequently the case, especially in problems connected with physiological optics, that we desire to find the resultant of three co-axial optical systems of known refracting powers F_1, F_2 and F_3 separated by given intervals c_1, c_2, where

$$c_1 = \frac{H_1'H_2}{n_2}, \qquad c_2 = \frac{H_2'H_3}{n_3},$$

the principal points of the component systems being designated by H_1, H_1'; H_2, H_2'; and H_3, H_3'. The indices of refraction of the first and last media of system I are denoted by n_1, n_2; of system II by n_2, n_3; and of system III by n_3, n_4.

Here let us employ the symbol D to denote the refracting power of the compound system (I+II), and the letters G, G′ to designate the positions of the principal points of this partial combination. Evidently, according to the formulæ derived in § 126, we may write:

$$D = F_1 + F_2 - c_1.F_1.F_2 \text{ ;}$$
$$\frac{H_1G}{n_1} = \frac{c_1.F_2}{D}, \qquad \frac{H_2'G'}{n_3} = -\frac{c_1.F_1}{D}.$$

Now let F denote the refracting power of the combination of systems I, II and III, and let H, H′ designate the positions of the principal points of this compound system. Then if the reduced interval between (I+II) and III is denoted by k, that is, if

$$k = \frac{G'H_3}{n_3} ,$$

then also:

$$F = D + F_3 - k.D.F_3,$$
$$\frac{GH}{n_1} = \frac{k.F_3}{F} , \qquad \frac{H_3'H'}{n_4} = -\frac{k.D}{F} .$$

Since

$$\frac{G'H_3}{n_3} = \frac{G'H_2'}{n_3} + \frac{H_2'H_3}{n_3} ,$$

we find:

$$k = \frac{c_1.F_1 + c_2.D}{D} .$$

If now these equations are combined so as to eliminate D and k, the following *system of formulæ for the combination of three optical systems* will be obtained finally:

$$F = F_1(1 - c_2.F_3) + F_2(1 - c_1.F_1)(1 - c_2F_3) + F_3(1 - c_1.F_1);$$
$$\frac{H_1H}{n_1} = -\frac{c_1}{1 - c_1.F_1} + \frac{c_2.F_3 - c_1.F_1}{F(1 - c_1.F_1)};$$
$$\frac{H_3'H'}{n_4} = -\frac{c_2}{1 - c_2.F_3} + \frac{c_2.F_3 - c_1.F_1}{F(1 - c_2.F_3)} .$$

In the special case when the *compound system is symmetrical with respect to system II*, that is, when $n_3 = n_2$ and $n_4 = n_1$ and $c_2 = c_1 = c$ and $F_3 = F_1$, the formulæ above will be simplified as follows:

$$F = (1 - c.F_1)(2F_1 + F_2 - c.F_1.F_2),$$
$$\frac{H_1H}{n_1} = \frac{H'H_3'}{n_1} = \frac{c}{1 - c.F_1} .$$

Thus, if an optical system is symmetrical with respect to a middle component part of the system, the principal points (H, H′) will be symmetrically placed, and their positions will be independent of the refracting power F_2 of the middle system. These latter formulæ should be compared with the formulæ for a "thick mirror" to be developed in the following section.

132. " Thick Mirror."—The general formulæ which have been derived in this chapter are applicable also when the centered system of spherical surfaces includes one or more reflecting surfaces, provided that reflection is treated as a special case of refraction, according to the method explained in § 75. Thus, for example, if the rays are reflected at the kth surface of the system, we must put $n_{k+1} = -n_k$; and, consequently, if the reflecting power of this surface is denoted by F_k, we shall have $F_k = n_k/f_k = n_k/f'_k$, in accordance with the characteristic requirement that the focal lengths of a spherical mirror are identical, that is, $f = f'$ (see § 77).

A special case of much interest and practical importance occurs when *the last surface of the system acts as a mirror*, the rays of light arriving there being reflected back through the system as so to emerge finally at the first surface into the medium of index n_1 where they originated. For example, this happens always in the case of an ordinary glass mirror which is silvered at the back. The rays return into the air in front of a mirror of this kind after having twice traversed the thickness of the glass, and the failure to take account of the refractions from air to glass and from glass to air is sometimes responsible for serious errors in the measurement of the focal length of a glass mirror silvered at the back. The image produced by rays which have been partially reflected from the second surface of an ordinary lens is often very disturbing, although the intensity of the reflected light is usually comparatively feeble unless the second surface of the lens has been silvered.

The name *"thick mirror"* has been applied by Dr. SEARLE* to any combination of centered spherical refracting surfaces

* G. F. C. SEARLE: The determination of the focal length of a thick mirror. *Proc. Cambr. Phil. Soc.*, xviii, Part iii, 1915, 115–126.

wherein the rays are supposed to be reflected at the last surface and to return through the system in the opposite sense.
It may easily be shown that a "thick mirror" as thus defined acts exactly like a single spherical reflecting surface
(or "thin mirror," as we may call it, having in mind a certain analogy which exists here between lenses and mirrors),
whose vertex and center have perfectly definite and calcu-
lable positions depending on the constants of the "thick
mirror." This is proved by Dr. SEARLE in a simple manner
as follows:

In Fig. 173 the system is represented as consisting of
three spherical surfaces, the first two forming a thick lens

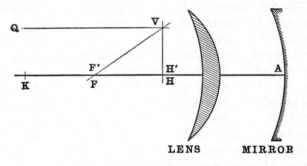

Fig. 173.—Diagram of "thick mirror" system.

and the last surface being a spherical mirror with its vertex
at a point A on the axis of the lens. Draw the straight line
QV parallel to the axis of the system to represent the path of
an incident ray; which after traversing the lens and being
reflected at the mirror will again emerge from the lens and
cross the axis at the secondary focal point (F') of the system.
The point V designates the point of intersection of the incident ray QV and the corresponding emergent ray VF',
and hence this point must lie in the secondary principal
plane of the system (§ 119). Consequently, the foot of the
perpendicular let fall from V on to the axis will be the secondary principal point H'. But by the principle of the re-

versibility of the light-path (§ 29), if the straight line F'V is regarded as an incident ray, then VQ will be the path of the corresponding emergent ray, and since in this case the emergent ray is parallel to the axis, the corresponding incident ray F'V must cross the axis at the primary focal point F, so that the two focal points F and F' will be coincident. Moreover, the point V must lie in the primary principal plane, and hence the two principal planes are coincident. But these are the characteristics of a spherical mirror, and it is evident that the "thick mirror" is equivalent to a "thin mirror" with its vertex at H (or H') and its center at a point K such that HK=2HF.

The four images of PURKINJE are the catoptric images formed in the eye by reflection at the anterior and posterior surfaces of the cornea and the crystalline lens; which are of fundamental importance in determining the curvatures and positions of the refracting surfaces in the optical system of the eye. The first image is produced by direct reflection at the anterior surface of the cornea, but the optical systems which give rise to the three other images are more or less complicated. However, according to the above explanation, each of these systems may be reduced to a single reflecting surface of appropriate radius with its center at a certain definite place to be ascertained by the conditions of the problem. One of these cases will be investigated presently, as soon as the formulæ for a thick mirror have been developed.

The radius and positions of the vertex and center of the equivalent "thin mirror" may easily be calculated by means of the general formulæ which were obtained in the preceding section for a combination of three optical systems. Here the first system (I) of refracting power F_1 may be regarded as composed of the entire lens-system lying in front of the reflecting surface; while the mirror itself of reflecting power F_2 may be regarded as the second system (II). In this case the third system (III) will be the lens-system reversed, and its refracting power will be the same as that of system I, that is, $F_3 = F_1$; but the principal points H_3 and $H_3{}'$ of system III will coincide with the principal points $H_1{}'$ and H_1, respectively, of system I. Above all we must impose here the conditions that

$$n_3 = -n_2 = -n', \qquad n_4 = -n_1 = -n,$$

where n denotes the index of refraction of the medium of the object-space and n' denotes the index of refraction of the medium in contact with the reflecting surface. These conditions take account of the fundamental fact that the sense of propagation of the light is reversed by the mirror. The principal points H_2, $H_2{}'$ of the mirror coincide with each other at its vertex which will be designated here by the letter A'. If therefore c_1, c_2 denote the reduced intervals between the first system and the mirror and between the mirror and the third system, we have:

$$c_1 = \frac{H_1{}'A'}{n'}, \quad c_2 = \frac{A'H_3}{n_3} = \frac{H_1{}'A'}{n'},$$

and hence

$$c_1 = c_2 = c, \text{ say.}$$

Moreover, if the radius of the reflecting surface is denoted by r', then $F_2 = -\dfrac{2n'}{r'}$. Introducing these relations in the general formulæ for the combination of three optical systems (§ 131), we obtain the following expressions for finding *the reflecting power* (F_{13}) *and the positions of the principal points* H_{13}, $H_{13}{}'$ *of a "thick mirror"*:

$$F_{13} = (1 - c.F_1)\,(2F_1 + F_2 - c.F_1.F_2)$$

$$= (1 - c.F_1)\left\{ 2F_1 - \frac{2n'}{r'}\,(1 - c.F_1) \right\};$$

$$\frac{H_1H_{13}}{n} = \frac{H_1H_{13}{}'}{n} = \frac{c}{1 - c.F_1}.$$

Accordingly, we see not only that the principal points of a "thick mirror" are coincident with each other, but that the position of the vertex H_{13} of the equivalent "thin mirror" is entirely independent of the power F_2 or the curvature of the actual mirror. The position of H_{13} does depend on the position of the vertex A' of the actual mirror; but for any mirror placed at A' the vertex of the equivalent "thin mirror" will be at the same point H_{13}. It may be noted that the formula for the reflecting power of a "thick mirror" is identical in form with the expression for the refracting power of a compound system which is symmetric with respect to a middle member (see end of § 131).

If the center of the equivalent "thin mirror" is designated by K, then its radius will be

$$H_{13}K = -\frac{2n}{F_{13}},$$

and hence

$$\frac{H_1K}{n} = \frac{c.F_2 - 2}{2F_1 + F_2 - c.F_1.F_2}.$$

If the surface of the mirror (II) is *plane*, then $F_2 = 0$, and in this case the formulæ for the equivalent "thin mirror" become:

$$F_{13} = 2F_1(1 - c.F_1), \quad \frac{H_1H_{13}}{n} = \frac{H_1H_{13}'}{n} = \frac{c}{1 - c.F_1}, \quad \frac{H_1K}{n} = -\frac{1}{F_1}.$$

The distinguishing characteristic of the imagery in a spherical mirror is that a pair of conjugate axial points M, M' is harmonically separated by the vertex H and the center K of the mirror, that is, $(KHMM') = -1 (\S 68)$. An interesting special case occurs when *one of the points* K *or* H *is at infinity;* for in that case the reflecting power of the mirror vanishes $(F = 0)$. When the center of the mirror is at an infinite distance from it, the mirror lies midway between object and image $(MH = HM')$ and the lateral magnification is equal to $+1$ $(y' = y)$; which is the case of an ordinary plane mirror. But, on the other hand, if the mirror itself is at an infinite distance, while the center K remains in the region of finite space, it is the center of the mirror in this case that is always midway between object and image, that is, $MK = KM'$, and now the lateral magnification will be equal to -1, that is, the image will be of the same size as the object but inverted $(y' = -y)$. Both of these special cases may be realized by a "thick mirror"; for the condition that the reflecting power of the equivalent "thin mirror" shall vanish $(F_{13} = 0)$ requires that either

$$2F_1 + F_2 - c.F_1.F_2 = 0,$$

or

$$1 - c.F_1 = 0.$$

In the former case the center of the mirror (K) is at infinity, and in the latter case the vertex of the mirror (H_{13}) is at infinity. If therefore the distance between the anterior lens-system and the final reflecting surface of a "thick mirror" is $c = 1/F_1$, the system will produce an inverted image of the same size as the object, no matter where the object is placed.

As an illustration of the use of the formulæ for a "thick mirror," consider the optical system in the eye which produces the third of the so-called PURKINJE images, to which allusion was made earlier in this section. The third image is formed by rays which coming from an external source enter the eye, and after having traversed the cornea system and the aqueous humor are reflected at the anterior surface of the crystalline lens; whence returning through the same media in the reverse order they issue again into the air. In order to find the "thin mirror" which is equivalent to this system, we shall employ the constants of GULLSTRAND's schematic eye as given in § 130. The vertex of the anterior surface of the cornea will be designated by A_1 and the principal points of the cornea-system by H_1 and H_1'. We found that $A_1H_1 = -0.0496$ mm. and $A_1H_1' = -0.0506$ mm.; also, $F_1 = +43.05$ dptr., where F_1 denotes the refracting power of the cornea-system. The reflecting power of the anterior surface of the lens is given by the formula:

$$F_2 = -\frac{2n_3}{r_3},$$

where $n_3 = 1.336$ and $r_3 = +0.010$ m.; accordingly, we find:

$$F_2 = -267.2 \text{ dptr.}$$

The reduced distance between the cornea-system and the first surface of the lens is:

$$c = \frac{H_1'A_3}{n_3},$$

where A_3 designates the vertex of this surface; $A_1A_3 =$ 0.0036 m. Thus, we obtain:

$$c = 0.0027325.$$

Substituting these numerical values in the system of formulæ for a "thick mirror," we find for the reflecting power of the equivalent "thin mirror" in this case:

$$F_{13} = -132.062 \text{ dptr.};$$

and for the positions of its vertex H_{13} and its center K:

$$H_1H_{13} = +3.0968 \text{ mm.}, \quad H_1K = +18.2412 \text{ mm.}$$

Accordingly, the system that produces the third of the PURKINJE images in GULLSTRAND's passive schematic eye is equivalent to a convex mirror of radius 15.14 mm. with its vertex at a distance of 3.047 mm. from the vertex of the anterior surface of the cornea.

Formulæ for calculating the reflecting power F_{13} of a "thick mirror" may also be obtained in terms of different data from those employed in the expressions which have been deduced above. Suppose, for example, that we are given the refracting power (F) of a centered system of spherical refracting surfaces, the positions of the principal points of the system (H, H'), and the indices of refraction of the first and last media (n, n'); together with the radius (r') and the position of the vertex (A') of the last surface; and that it is required to determine in terms of these data the characteristics of the imagery produced by light which proceeding from the object-space through the system is partially reflected at the last surface and again partially refracted at the first surface into the original medium. In order to solve this problem in the simplest way, it is convenient to employ a mathematical artifice which will be found to be serviceable in other optical problems. The refracting power of an infinitely thin concentric lens is equal to zero, and it is easy to

show that such a lens may be inserted anywhere in an optical system without affecting at all the resultant imagery
(see § 90). Let us suppose, therefore, that the given optical
system is terminated by an infinitely thin layer of material of
index n', bounded by two concentric spherical surfaces, the
first of which coincides with the last surface of the given
system. Under these circumstances the resultant system may
be considered as compounded of three component systems,
namely, (1) the given system of refracting power $F_1 = F$,
(2) a mirror of reflecting power $F_2 = -\dfrac{2n'}{r'}$, and (3) the given
system reversed ($F_3 = F$). Hence, if

$$c = \frac{H'A'}{n'} ,$$

the following formulæ will be obtained in the same way as
above:

$$F_{13} = (1 - c.F) \left\{ 2F - \frac{2n'}{r'}(1 - c.F) \right\} ,$$

$$\frac{HH_{13}}{n} = \frac{HH_{13}'}{n} = \frac{c}{1 - c.F} ;$$

which are similar in form to the previous expressions, but
c here has a different meaning and F denotes the refracting
power of the entire lens-system and not merely of that part
of the system which is in front of the reflecting surface.

A problem of considerable interest, especially in connection with the optical system of the human eye, is the investigation of the procedure of the light which after being partially reflected at the last surface of the system (as in the
case above) is also partially reflected at the first surface, so
that it emerges finally into the last medium of index n'. The
imagery in this case may be determined by adding a second
infinitely thin concentric lens, which is assumed to be made
of material of index n and whose second surface coincides
with that of the first surface of the system. Accordingly,
now we shall have five systems in all, namely, the first three
systems whose reflecting power F_{13} was obtained above,

a fourth system consisting of the first surface of the lens-system acting as a mirror, whose reflecting power is $F_4 = \dfrac{2n}{r}$, where r denotes the radius of this surface, and a fifth system of refracting power $F_5 = F$. The entire system, whose refracting power may be denoted by F_{15}, and whose principal points may be designated by H_{15}, H_{15}', may, therefore, be considered as compounded of 3 systems of powers F_{13}, $2n/r$ and F, separated by the intervals c_1 and c_2, where (if A designates the vertex of the first surface of the lens-system)

$$c_1 = \frac{AH_{13}}{n}, \qquad c_2 = \frac{AH}{n}.$$

Accordingly, by substituting F_{13} in place of F_1, $2n/r$ in place of F_2, and F in place of F_3 in the formulæ of § 131 for the combination of three optical systems, we obtain here:

$$F_{15} = F_{13}\,(1 - c_2.F) + \frac{2n}{r}\,(1 - c_1.F_{13})\,(1 - c_2.F) + F\,(1 - c_1.F_{13});$$

$$\frac{H_{13}H_{15}}{n} = \frac{c_1}{1 - c_1.F_{13}} + \frac{c_2.F - c_1.F_{13}}{F_{15}\,(1 - c_1.F_{13})};$$

$$\frac{H'H_{15}'}{n'} = -\frac{c_2}{1 - c_2.F} + \frac{c_2.F - c_1.F_{13}}{F_{15}\,(1 - c_2.F)}.$$

Being given the magnitudes denoted by n, n', r, r', and F and the positions of the points designated by A, A′ and H, H′, and having found by means of the previous formulæ the magnitude denoted by F_{13} and the position of the point designated by H_{13} (or H_{13}'), we can introduce these data and results in the expressions above and thus determine the refracting power F_{15} and the distances AH_{15}, $A'H_{15}'$ of the principal points H_{15}, H_{15}' from the vertices A, A′ of the first and last surfaces, respectively.

PROBLEMS

1. Find the refracting power and the positions of the focal points and principal points of each of the following glass lenses surrounded by air ($n = 1$, $n' = 1.5$); and make an ac-

curate sketch of each lens, marking the positions of the points mentioned.

(a) Double convex lens of radii 10 cm. and 15 cm. and of thickness 3 cm.

(b) Double concave lens with same data as above.

(c) Meniscus lens for which $r_1 = +5$ cm., $r_2 = +10$ cm., and $d = +3$ cm.

(d) Meniscus lens for which $r_1 = +6$ cm., $r_2 = +3$ cm., and $d = +2.52$ cm.

(e) A plano-convex lens with its curved surface, of radius 5 cm., turned towards the incident light; $d = +0.5$ cm.

(f) Symmetric convex lens, the radius of each surface being 5 cm.; $d = +0.5$ cm.

(g) Symmetric concave lens with same data as above.

(h) A meniscus lens with radii $r_1 = +5$ cm., $r_2 = +8$ cm., and thickness $d = +0.5$ cm.

(i) A meniscus lens with radii $r_1 = +8$ cm., $r_2 = +5$ cm., and thickness $d = +0.5$ cm.

(j) A meniscus lens with radii $r_1 = +8$ cm., $r_2 = +7$ cm., and thickness $d = +3$ cm.

(k) A plano-convex lens with its curved surface, of radius 5 cm., turned towards the incident light; $d = +5$ cm.

Answers:

	F in dptr.	A_1F in cm	A_2F' in cm.	A_1H in cm.	A_2H' in cm.
(a)	+ 8.000	−11.667	+11.250	+0.833	− 1.250
(b)	− 8.667	+12.307	−12.692	+0.769	− 1.154
(c)	+ 6.000	−18.333	+13.333	−1.667	− 3.333
(d)	− 6.000	+21.333	−14.333	+4.667	+2.333
(e)	+10.000	−10.000	+ 9.667	0.000	− 0.333
(f)	+19.666	− 4.915	+ 4.915	+0.170	− 0.170
(g)	−20.335	+ 5.082	− 5.082	+0.164	− 0.164
(h)	+ 3.959	−25.789	+24.421	−0.526	− 0.842
(i)	− 3.542	+29.176	−27.647	+0.941	+0.588
(j)	0.000	∞	∞	∞	∞
(k)	+10.000	−10.000	+ 6.667	0.000	−3.333

2. In a symmetric lens ($r_1 = -r_2 = r$) surrounded by the

same medium (index n) on both sides, show that we have the following system of formulæ:

$$N = (n'-n)\left\{(n'-n)\ d - 2n'.r\right\};$$

$$F = -\frac{N}{n'r^2}\ ;\quad \frac{A_1F}{n} = -\frac{A_2F'}{n} = -\frac{r}{N}\left\{(n'-n)\ d - n'.r\right\}\ ;$$

$$\frac{A_1H}{n} = -\frac{A_2H'}{n} = -\frac{n'-n}{N}r.d.$$

3. If the first face of a lens is plane, and if the radius of the curved face is denoted by r, show that

$$F = -\frac{n'-n}{r}\ ;\quad \frac{A_1H}{n} = \frac{d}{n'}\ ;\quad A_2H' = 0;$$

$$\frac{A_1F}{n} = \frac{r}{n'-n} + \frac{d}{n'}\ ;\quad \frac{A_2F'}{n} = -\frac{r}{n'-n}\ .$$

And if the second face of the lens is plane,

$$F = \frac{n'-n}{r}\ ;\quad A_1H = 0;\quad \frac{A_2H'}{n} = -\frac{d}{n'}\ ;\quad \text{etc.}$$

If either face of a lens is plane, the refracting power of the lens is equal to that of the curved surface and is entirely independent of the thickness of the lens; and, moreover, one of the principal points coincides with the vertex of the curved face.

4. If the radii r_1 and r_2 of the two surfaces of a lens are both positive, and if r_2 is greater than r_1, show that the lens is convergent, provided the lens-medium is more highly refracting than the surrounding medium.

5. A "lens of zero-curvature" is a crescent-shaped meniscus for which $r_2 = r_1 = r$. Show that such a lens is always convergent unless it is infinitely thin; and that this is the case whether the lens-medium is more or less highly refracting than the surrounding medium.

6. Show that a meniscus lens for which

$$r_1 > r_2 > 0\quad \text{and}\quad n' > n$$

is divergent provided its thickness is less than

$$\frac{n'(r_1-r_2)}{n'-n}\ .$$

7. Show that in any meniscus lens surrounded by air at least one of the principal points must lie outside the lens.

8. A so-called *concentric lens* is one for which the centers of curvature of the two faces are coincident $(d = r_1 - r_2)$. It may be double convex or meniscus. Show that the refracting power of a concentric lens surrounded by the same medium on both sides is

$$F = \frac{n(n'-n)}{n'} \left(\frac{1}{r_1} - \frac{1}{r_2} \right),$$

and that the principal points coincide at the common center of the two surfaces.

9. Find the refracting power and the positions of the focal points and principal points of each of the following concentric glass lenses $(n' = 1.5)$ surrounded by air $(n = 1)$; and draw accurate sketch of each lens showing the positions of the points named:

   (a) Double convex lens with radii $r_1 = +10$ cm., $r_2 = -2$ cm.

   (b) Meniscus lens with radii $r_1 = +5$ cm., $r_2 = +2$ cm.

   Ans. (a) $F = +20$ dptr., $A_1F = +5$ cm., $A_2F' = +3$ cm., $A_1H = +10$ cm., $A_2H' = -2$ cm.; (b) $F = -10$ dptr., $A_1F = +15$ cm., $A_2F' = -8$ cm., $A_1H = +5$ cm., $A_2H' = +2$ cm.

10. Find the focal length and the positions of the principal points of a concentric glass lens surrounded by air $(n = 1, \ n' = 1.5)$, with radii $r_1 = +8$ cm., $r_2 = +5$ cm.

   Ans. $f = -40$ cm., $A_1H = +8$ cm., $A_2H' = +5$ cm.

11. What is the refracting power of a concentric glass meniscus lens surrounded by air $(n = 1, \ n' = 1.5)$, the radii being 5 cm. and 3 cm.?   Ans. $F = -4.44$ dptr.

12. The radius of the second surface of a concentric glass lens surrounded by air $(n = 1, n' = 1.5)$ is $+3$ cm., and its refracting power is -2 dptr. Determine its thickness.

   Ans. 6.59 mm. If it were not too heavy, this would be a fairly good form of spectacle glass for a near-sighted person.

13. If the two principal points of a lens surrounded by the same medium on both sides coincide with each other at

a point midway between the two vertices, what is the form of the lens?   Ans. A solid sphere.

14. The refracting power of a symmetric glass lens surrounded by air $(n=1, n'=1.5)$ is $+10$ dptr., and its thickness is 0.5 cm. Determine the radius of the first surface.

Ans. $+9.916$ cm.

15. A solid sphere is a symmetric concentric lens. If the radius is denoted by r $(r=A_1C)$, show that we have the following system of formulæ for a solid sphere surrounded by the same medium (n) on both sides:

$$F=\frac{2n(n'-n)}{n'.r}\ ;\quad A_1H=H'A_2=r\ ;\quad A_2F'=FA_1=\frac{(2n-n')r}{2(n'-n)}\ .$$

16. If the plane surface of a glass hemisphere, of index n' and surrounded on both sides by a medium of index n, is turned towards the incident light, and if r denotes the radius of the curved surface, show that

$$F=-\frac{n'-n}{r},\quad A_1H=-\frac{n.r}{n'},\quad A_2H'=0,\quad A_1F=\frac{n^2r}{n'(n'-n)},$$

$$A_2F'=-\frac{n.r}{n'-n}\ .$$

17. An object is placed in front of the plane surface of a glass hemisphere, of index 1.5 and radius 3 inches, at a distance of 10 inches from this surface. Find the position, nature and size of the image.

Ans. A real, inverted image, of same size as object, will be formed at a distance of 25 inches from the object.

18. What is the refracting power of a glass sphere $(n'=1.5)$, $16\frac{2}{3}$ cm. in diameter, (a) surrounded by air $(n=1)$, and (b) surrounded by water $(n=\frac{4}{3})$?

Ans. (a) $+8$ dptr.; (b) $+3\frac{5}{9}$ dptr.

19. The radius of each surface of a symmetric convex glass lens $(n'=1.5)$ is 10 cm., and the thickness of the lens is 5 mm. What is its refracting power (a) when the thickness is neglected, and (b) when the thickness is taken into account?   Ans. (a) $+10$ dptr.; (b) $+9\frac{11}{12}$ dptr.

20. The radii of a convex meniscus glass lens $(n'=1.5)$

surrounded by air ($n=1$) are 2.5 cm. and 5 cm. (a) If the lens is infinitely thin, what is its refracting power? (b) If the thickness of the lens is 1 cm., what is its refracting power?

Ans. (a) $F = +10$ dptr.; (b) $F = +11\frac{1}{3}$ dptr.

21. Determine the focal length (f) of a glass lens of index 1.5 surrounded by air for which $r_1 = +10$, $r_2 = +9$, (1) when thickness $d=0$, and (2) when thickness $d=+1$.

Ans. (1) $f = -180$; (2) $f = -270$.

22. A plane object is placed at right angles to the axis of a plano-convex lens at a distance of 8.77 cm. in front of its curved surface. The lens is made of glass of index 1.52, and the thickness of the lens is 0.5 cm. The radius of the curved surface is 4.56 cm. Show that the image will be at infinity, and that, in order to see distinctly the image of a point in the object which is 2 cm. from the axis, an eye behind the lens must look in a direction inclined to the axis of the lens at an angle of nearly 12° 51′.

23. The refracting power of a meniscus spectacle glass is $+6$ dptr., and $r_2 = 2r_1$, $d=6$ mm. The index of refraction is 1.5. Find the radii r_1 and r_2 and the vertex refraction V.

Ans. $r_1 = +4.36$ cm., $r_2 = +8.72$ cm., $V = +6.29$ dptr.

24. The thickness of a spectacle glass is 4.75 mm., and the index of refraction is 1.5. The refracting power of the first surface is $+15.4$ dptr., and that of the second surface is -9.1 dptr. Find the refracting power of the lens and its vertex refraction.   Ans. $F = +6.74$ dptr.; $V = +7.09$ dptr.

25. A paraxial ray is incident on the cornea of GULL-STRAND's schematic eye (§ 130) in a direction parallel to the axis. Trace the path of this ray through the eye and determine the position of the secondary focal point F′ (see calculation-scheme, § 181); and calculate the focal lengths f, $f′$ according to the formulæ derived in problem No. 17 at the end of Chapter X.

Ans. Distance of F′ from the vertex of the cornea is 24.387 mm.; $f = +17.055$ mm., $f′ = -22.785$ mm.

26. The reduced thickness of a symmetric spectacle glass is denoted by c. If V denotes its vertex refraction, show that

$$F = \frac{V(\sqrt{4+c^2.V^2}-c.V)}{2}.$$

27. A hollow globe of glass is filled with water. The diameter of the water sphere is 8.5 inches and the thickness of the glass shell is 0.25 inch. Show that a narrow beam of parallel rays directed towards the center of the globe will be converged to a point 4.68 inches from the outside surface, the indices of refraction of glass and water being $\frac{3}{2}$ and $\frac{4}{3}$, respectively.

28. What is the focal length of a combination of two thin convex lenses, each of focal length f, placed at a distance apart equal to $2f/3$?   Ans. $3f/4$.

29. An optical system is composed of two thin convex lenses of refracting powers $+10$ dptr. and $+6\frac{2}{3}$ dptr., the stronger lens being towards the incident light. Find the refracting power of the combination and the positions of the principal points and focal points when the distance between the lenses is: (a) 5 cm.; (b) 25 cm.; and (c) 40 cm.

Ans. (a) Convergent system: $F=13\frac{1}{3}$ dptr.; $A_1H = +2.5$ cm.; $A_2H' = -3.75$ cm.; $A_1F = -5$ cm.; $A_2F' = +3.75$ cm.; (b) Telescopic system: $F=0$; focal and principal points all at infinity; (c) Divergent system: $F = -10$ dptr.; $A_1H = -26\frac{2}{3}$ cm.; $A_2H' = +40$ cm.; $A_1F = -16\frac{2}{3}$ cm.; $A_2F' = +30$ cm.

30. An optical system is composed of two thin lenses, namely, a front concave lens of power -10 dptr. and a rear convex lens of power $+6\frac{2}{3}$ dptr. Find the refracting power of the combination and the positions of the focal points and principal points, when the interval between the lenses is: (a) 2.5 cm.; (b) 5 cm.; (c) 6.25 cm.; (d) 20 cm.

Ans. (a) Divergent system: $F = -1\frac{2}{3}$ dptr.; $A_1H = -10$ cm.; $A_2H' = -15$ cm.; $A_1F = +50$ cm.; $A_2F' = -75$ cm.; (b) Telescopic system: $F = 0$, focal and principal points all at infinity; (c) $F = +\frac{5}{8}$ dptr.; $A_1 H = +50$ cm.; $A_2H' = +75$ cm.; $A_1F = -70$ cm.; $A_2F' = +195$ cm.; (d) Convergent system: $F = +10$ dptr.; $A_1H = +13\frac{1}{3}$ cm.; $A_2H' = +20$ cm.; $A_1F = +3\frac{1}{3}$ cm.; $A_2F' = +30$ cm.

31. Two thin convex lenses of focal lengths f_1 and f_2 are separated by an interval equal to $2f_2$. If $f_1 = 3f_2$, what is the focal length of the combination?

Ans. Convergent system of focal length $3f_2/2$.

32. Two lenses, one convex and the other concave, are separated by an interval $2a$. The convex lens is the front lens, and its focal length is a, while that of the concave lens is $-a$. Find the focal length of the combination and the positions of the principal points and focal points.

Ans. $f = a/2$; $A_1H = A_2H' = -a$; $A_1F = 3A_2F' = -3a/2$.

33. Where are the principal planes of a system of two thin convex lenses of focal lengths 2 inches and 6 inches, separated by an interval of 4 inches?

Ans. The principal planes coincide with the focal planes of the stronger lens.

34. The objective of a compound microscope may be regarded as a thin convex lens of focal length 0.5. inch. The ocular may also be regarded as a thin convex lens of focal length 1 inch. The distance between the two lenses is 6 inches. Where must an object be placed in order that its image may be seen distinctly by a person whose distance of distinct vision is 8 inches?

Ans. $\frac{46}{83}$ inch in front of the objective.

35. The focal lengths of the objective and ocular of a compound microscope are 0.5 inch and 1 inch, respectively. If the distance of distinct vision is 12 inches, find the distance between the objective and ocular when the object viewed is 0.75 inch from the objective.   Ans. 2.42 inches.

36. A thin convex lens, of focal length 5 inches, is placed midway between two thin convex lenses each of focal length 10 inches. The distance between the first lens and the second

is 5 inches.   Find the focal length of the system and the positions of the principal points.

Ans. $f = +6\frac{2}{3}$ inches;   the   principal   points   are   at   the vertices of the outside lenses.

37. In the preceding problem, suppose that the two outside lenses are concave, everything else remaining the same.

Ans. $f = +6\frac{2}{3}$ inches.   The principal points are on opposite sides of the middle lens and $1\frac{2}{3}$ inches from it.

38. A thin convex lens, of focal length 10 inches, is placed in front of a concave mirror of focal length 5 inches, the distance between them being 5 inches.   The light traverses the lens, is reflected at the mirror, and again passes through the lens.   Find the focal length of this so-called "thick mirror" and the positions of the principal points.

Ans. $f = +6\frac{2}{3}$ inches; the principal points coincide with each other at a point 5 inches behind the vertex of the mirror.

39. In the preceding problem, suppose that the lens is concave, everything else remaining the same.

Ans. $f = +6\frac{2}{3}$ inches; the principal points coincide with each other at a point between the lens and the mirror and $3\frac{1}{3}$ inches from the former.

40. In front of each of the systems described in Nos. 36, 37, 38, and 39, an object, one inch high, is placed at a distance of 5 inches from the first member of the system.   Find the position, size and nature of the image in each case.

Ans. In No. 36: A real, inverted image, 2 inches beyond the third lens and 0.8 in. high.   In No. 37: A real, inverted image, 30 inches beyond the third lens and 4 inches high. In No. 38: A real, inverted image, 2 inches in front of the lens and 0.8 in. high.   In No. 39: A real, inverted image, 30 inches in front of the lens and 4 inches high.

41. The center of a concave mirror, of radius r, coincides with the optical center of a thin lens, of focal length f, and the axes of lens and mirror are in the same straight line.   The light traverses the lens, is reflected at the mirror, and again

traverses the lens. Show that the system is equivalent to a thin mirror of radius $r.f/(r+f)$, with its center at the same place as the center of the given mirror.

42. A centered system of lenses (I) is placed in front of a spherical mirror (II), and the whole constitutes a "thick mirror," as explained in § 132. Show that the vertex A and the center C of the actual mirror are the images of the vertex H and the center K, respectively, of the equivalent "thin mirror," which are produced by the lens-system I in the medium of index n_2 between systems I and II.

43. A "thick mirror" consists of a thin lens of focal length f_1 and a spherical mirror of focal length f_2 placed co-axially so that the focal point of the mirror coincides with the optical center A_1 of the thin lens. Show that the focal length of the equivalent "thin mirror" is

$$f = \frac{f_1^2 . f_2}{f_1^2 - f_2^2} \; ;$$

and that the positions of the vertex H and the center K are given by the following expressions:

$$A_1H = \frac{f_1 . f_2}{f_1 - f_2}, \qquad A_1K = -\frac{f_1 . f_2}{f_1 + f_2} .$$

Does it make any difference whether the lens is convex or concave?

44. At each of the focal points of a thin convex lens of focal length f_2 is placed a thin lens of focal length f_1. Find the focal length of the combination of the three lenses and the positions of the principal points. Does it make any difference whether the two equal outside lenses are convex or concave?

$$\text{Ans. } f = \frac{f_1^2 . f_2}{f_1^2 - f_2^2} \; ; \quad A_1H = H'A_3 = \frac{f_1 . f_2}{f_1 - f_2} .$$

45. A thin convex lens of focal length 10 cm. is placed in front of a plane mirror at a distance of 8 cm. from it. Find the radius of the equivalent "thin mirror" and the position of its vertex H.

Ans. The equivalent "thin mirror" is a concave mirror of radius 50 cm. with its vertex 32 cm. behind the plane mirror.

46. The axes of three thin convex lenses are all in the same straight line, the interval between the first and second lenses being one inch and the interval between the second and third lenses being half an inch. The focal lengths of the first, second and third lenses are $\frac{3}{2}$, $\frac{1}{8}$ and $\frac{3}{8}$ inch, respectively. A plane object is placed at right angles to the axis of the lens-system; show that an inverted image of the same size as the object will be formed in the plane of the object.

47. A plano-concave flint glass lens of index 1.618 is cemented to a double convex crown glass lens of index 1.523. The radii and thicknesses are as follows: $r_1 = \infty$, $r_2 = +50.419$ mm., $r_3 = -74.320$ mm.; $d_1 = +2.15$ mm., $d_2 = +4.65$ mm. Find the focal length of the combination and the positions of the principal points.

Ans. $f = +192.552$ mm.; distances of principal points from the plane surface, $+5.466$ and $+7.908$ mm.

48. A plano-concave flint glass lens of index 1.618 is cemented to a double convex crown glass lens of index 1.523. The radii and thicknesses are as follows: $r_1 = +22.00$ mm., $r_2 = -19.65$ mm., $r_3 = \infty$; $d_1 = +2.60$ mm., $d_2 = +2.00$ mm. Find the focal length of the combination and the positions of the principal points.

Ans. $f = +52.26$ mm.; distances of principal points from plane surface, -5.03 and -3.36 mm.

49. The radii and thickness of a symmetric double convex lens are 10 cm. and 1 cm., respectively. The lens is made of glass of index 1.5 and surrounded by air of index unity. A portion of the light which enters the lens will be reflected at the second surface and partially refracted at the first surface from glass back into the air. Find the radius, reflecting power and position of the vertex of the equivalent "thin mirror."

Ans. Concave mirror of radius -53.050 mm., reflecting

power $+37.7$ dptr., with its vertex $+6.90$ mm. from the vertex of the first face of the lens.

50. In the case of the lens in the preceding problem, assume that the light is reflected internally twice in succession and issues finally at the second face into the air. Find the refracting power and the positions of the principal points for the imagery produced by these rays.

Ans. Refracting power, $+58.03$ dptr.; distances of principal points from vertex of first surface of the lens, $+10.94$ and -0.94 mm.

51. In GULLSTRAND's schematic eye in its state of *maximum accommodation* the crystalline lens consists of an outer symmetric double convex lens of index $n_4 = n_6 = 1.386$ (see § 130), enclosing an inner symmetric double convex "core" lens of index $n_5 = 1.406$; the inner portion being symmetrically placed with respect to the surrounding outer part. The radii of the surfaces are as follows:

Outer portion: $r_3 = A_3C_3 = +5.3333$ mm. $= -r_6 = C_6A_6$;
Inner portion: $r_4 = A_4C_4 = +2.6550$ mm. $= -r_5 = C_5A_5$.
Moreover,
$$A_3A_4 = A_3C_5 = A_5A_6 = C_4A_6 = 0.6725 \text{ mm.};$$
$$A_4A_5 = C_5C_4 = A_4C_4 = C_5A_5 = 2.6550 \text{ mm.}$$
The entire lens is surrounded by a medium of index $n_3 = n_7 = 1.336$. Show (1) that the refracting power of the inner portion or "core" lens is $F_{45} = +14.959$ dptr., and that its principal points are 1.9905 mm. from the anterior and posterior surfaces. Moreover, employing the formulæ of § 131, show (2) that the refracting power of the entire lens in case of maximum accommodation is $F_{36} = +33.056$ dptr. and that $A_3H_{36} = H_{36}'A_6 = +1.9449$ mm.

52. Using the data of the preceding problem, find the refracting power (F) and the positions of the principal points (H, H') of GULLSTRAND's schematic eye in its state of maximum accommodation: being given, according to the results of § 130, that the refracting power of the cornea system is $F_{12} = 43.053$ dptr. and that $A_1H_{12} = -0.0496$ mm., $A_1H'_{12} =$

-0.0506 mm., and also that for maximum accommodation $A_1A_3 = +3.2$ mm.

Ans. $F = +70.575$ dptr.; $A_1H = +1.772$ mm.; $A_1H' = +2.086$ mm.

53. Two thin lenses of focal lengths f_1 and f_2 are placed on the same axis with the second focal point (F_1') of the first lens coincident with the first focal point (F_2) of the second lens, so as to form an afocal or telescopic system. Show that the lateral magnification is constant and equal to $-f_2/f_1$, and that the angular magnification is likewise constant and equal to the reciprocal of the lateral magnification.

54. If (as in HUYGENS's ocular) two thin lenses are placed on the same axis with their second focal points in coincidence, show that the second focal point of the combination is midway between this common focal point and the second lens, and that the deviation produced by the second lens is twice that produced by the first (assuming that the angles are small).

55. Show that the optical center (O) of a lens surrounded by the same medium on both sides is the image of the first principal point of the lens (H) in its first surface; and, similarly, that the second principal point (H') is the image of O in the second surface.

56. Magnifying glasses of high power were formerly made in the form of small "spherules" of glass, as suggested first by ROBERT HOOKE in his "Micrographia" (1665). The most powerful "spherules" ever made are said to have been those sent to the Royal Society by DI TORRÉ of Naples, one of which was $\frac{1}{144}$th of an inch in diameter. Assuming that the index of refraction was 1.5, what was its focal length?

Ans. $\frac{1}{192}$ inch.

CHAPTER XII

133. Limitation of Ray-Bundles by Diaphragms or Stops.
—The geometrical theory of optical imagery which has been
developed in Chapter X was based on the assumption of
punctual correspondence between object-space and image-
space, whereby each point of the object is reproduced by
one point, and by one point only, in the image; and on this
hypothesis simple relations in the form of the so-called
image-equations (§ 123) were obtained for determining the
position and size of the image in terms of the focal lengths
of the optical system. When we attempted to realize the
imagery expressed by these equations, we were obliged to
confine ourselves to the so-called paraxial rays comprised
within the narrow cylindrical region immediately surrounding the axis of symmetry or optical axis of the centered system of spherical refracting or reflecting surfaces. Based on
the same assumptions, certain rules were given for constructing the image-point Q' corresponding to a given object-
point Q. For example, a pair of straight lines was drawn
through Q (Fig. 174), one parallel to the optical axis and
meeting the second principal plane of the system in a point
V', and the other going through the primary focal point F
and meeting the first principal plane in a point W. The
required point Q' was shown to lie at the point of intersection of the straight line V'Q', drawn through the second
focal point F', with the straight line WQ' drawn parallel to
the axis. The position of the point Q' having been located,
the problem was considered as solved, and we were not particularly concerned with inquiring whether the straight
lines used in the construction represented the paths of ac-

tual rays that formed the image at Q'. As a matter of fact, the pair of geometrical lines which is employed here will generally not belong to the bundle of optical rays by which the imagery is actually produced; and a glance at the diagram will show how the diameter of the lens and the size of

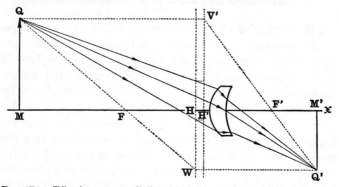

Fig. 174.—Effective rays as distinguished from rays used in making geometrical constructions.

the object control the selection of the rays that are really effective in producing the image.

In Chapter I attention was called to the fact that every optical instrument is provided with some means of cutting out such portions of a bundle of rays as for one reason or another are not desirable; which is usually accomplished, as has been explained, by interposing in the paths of the rays at some convenient place a plane opaque screen at right angles to the axis containing a circular aperture with its center on the axis. There may, indeed, be several such *diaphragms* or *stops* disposed at various places along the axis of the instrument. A perforated screen of this kind is called a *front stop*, a *rear stop* or an *interior stop*, according as it lies in front of, behind or within the system, respectively. The rims and fastenings of the lenses act in the same way as the diaphragms to limit the ray-bundles. The stops have various duties to perform, their chief functions being to cut off the view of indistinct parts of the image (limitation of the field of view), to cut out such rays as would tend to mar the perfection of that part of the image which is to be inspected (limitation of the aperture of the system), and, finally, to nullify injurious reflections from the sides of the tube or other parts of the instrument.

134. The Aperture-Stop and the Pupils of the System.— To an eye looking into the instrument from the side of the object, a front stop (which may be the rim of the first lens of the system) will be the only one that will be visible directly. Any other stop or lens-rim will be seen only by means of the real or virtual image of it that is cast by that part of the optical system which is between it and the eye. Similarly, if the eye is directed towards the instrument from the image-side, an interior stop or a front stop may be seen by means of the image of it that is produced by the part of the system that lies between it and the eye. Now these impalpable stop-images, whether visible or not, are just as effective in cutting out the rays as if they were actual material stops; because, obviously, any ray that goes through an actual stop must necessarily pass either really or virtually through the corresponding point of the stop-image; whereas a ray that is obstructed by a stop will not go through the opening in the stop-image.

That one of the stops which by virtue of its size and position with respect to the radiating object is most effective in cutting out the rays is distinguished as the *aperture-stop* of the system (§ 11), and in order to determine which of the several stops performs this office, it is necessary, first of all, to assign the position of the axial object-point M, without which the aperture of the system can have no meaning. Accordingly, we must suppose that the instrument is focused on some selected point M on the axis, which is reproduced by an image at the conjugate point M'. The transversal planes at right angles to the axis at M and M' will be a pair of conjugate planes, for it is assumed here that the imagery is ideal and of the same character as that produced by par-axial rays. Now this pair of conjugate planes plays a very important *rôle* in the theory of an optical instrument, so that hereafter we shall refer to the object-plane as the *focus-plane* (or the plane which is in focus on the screen) and to the conjugate plane in the image-space as the *screen-plane*.

Now if the eye is supposed to be placed on the axis at the point M and directed towards the instrument, the stop or stop-image whose aperture subtends the smallest angle at M is called the *entrance-pupil* of the system. All the effective rays (§ 11) in the object-space must be directed towards points which lie within the circumference of the circular opening of the entrance-pupil. In general, the entrance-pupil is the image of the aperture-stop as seen by looking into the instrument in the direction of the light coming from the object; but if the aperture-stop is a front stop, it will also be the entrance-pupil.

On the other hand, when the eye is placed on the axis at the point M′ so as to look into the instrument through the other end, the stop or stop-image which subtends the smallest angle at M′ is called the *exit-pupil*, and all the effective rays when they emerge from the instrument must go, really or virtually, through the opening of the exit-pupil. In this statement it is tacitly assumed that M′ is a real image of M; otherwise, it would not be possible for the eye placed at M′ to look into the instrument through the end from which the rays emerge. But in any case the exit-pupil is the stop or stop-image which subtends the smallest angle at M′. Gen-erally, the exit-pupil will be the image of the aperture-stop as seen by looking into the instrument from the image-side; but if the aperture-stop is a rear stop, it will be itself the exit-pupil.

Since the effective rays enter the system through the entrance-pupil in the object-space and leave it through the exit-pupil in the image-space, it is evident that *the exit-pupil is the image of the entrance-pupil, so that the pupil-*

centers, designated by O and O′, *are a pair of conjugate axial points with respect to the entire system.*

The apertures of the ray-bundles in the object-space are determined by the entrance-pupil of the system; and the exit-pupil has a similar office in the image-space. Each of the pupils is the common base of the cones of effective rays in the region to which it belongs.

135. Illustrations.—The name "pupil" applied to these apertures by ABBE was suggested by an analogy with the optical system of the eye. The pupil of the eye is the contractile aperture of the colored iris, the image of which produced by the cornea and the aqueous humor is the entrance-pupil of the eye corresponding to what is popularly called the "black of the eye," because it looks black on the dark background of the posterior chamber of the eye. Since the center O of the entrance-pupil is the image of the center K of the iris-opening formed by rays that are refracted from the aqueous humor through the cornea into the air, then, by the principle of the reversibility of the light-path, we may also regard K as the image of O formed by rays which are refracted from air $(n=1)$ through the cornea into the aqueous humor $(n'=1.336)$. The apparent place of the eye-pupil varies slightly in different individuals and in the same individual at different ages. If we assume that the point O is 3.03 mm. from the vertex (A) of the cornea, that is, if we put $u=0.00303$ m., then $U=n/u=330$ dptr. And if we take the refracting power of the cornea as $F=42$ dptr. (§ 130), then, since $U'=U+F$, we find $U'=372$ dptr. and consequently $u'=AK=n'/U'=0.0036$ m.; so that with these data the plane of the iris is found to be at a distance of 3.6 mm. from the vertex of the cornea. Thus we see that the entrance-pupil of the eye is very nearly 0.6 mm. in front of the iris.

As a simple illustration of these principles, consider an optical system which consists of an infinitely thin convex lens, with a stop placed a little in front of it. In the diagram (Fig. 175) the straight line DG perpendicular to the axis of the lens represents the diameter of the lens which lies in the meridian plane of the paper. The diameter of the stop-opening is shown by the straight line BC parallel to DG. The centers of the lens and stop are designated by

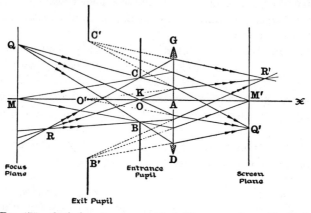

FIG. 175.—Optical system composed of thin convex lens with front stop.

A and K, respectively. The position of the focus-plane is determined by the axial object-point M, which in the figure is represented as lying in front of the lens beyond the primary focal plane. The solid angle subtended at M by the opening in the stop is supposed to be smaller than that subtended by the rim of the lens; that is, as here shown, $\angle$ AMC $<\angle$ AMG; and, consequently, the front stop acts here both as aperture-stop and entrance-pupil, so that the center K of the aperture-stop is likewise the center O of the entrance-pupil. Looking through the lens from the other side, one will see at O′ a virtual, erect image B′C′ of the aperture-stop BC, and hence this image is the exit-pupil of the system. The angle BMC is the aperture-angle of the cone of rays that come from the axial object-point M in the focus-plane; after passing through the system, these rays meet at M′ in the screen-plane, the aperture-angle of the bundle of rays

in the image-space being ∠B'M'C'. The effective rays
coming from a point Q in the focus-plane are comprised
within ∠BQC in the object-space and ∠B'Q'C' in the
image-space. If the object-point does not lie in the
focus-plane, and yet not too far from it, the opening BOC will
act as entrance-pupil for this point also. Thus, for example,
in order to construct the point R' conjugate to an object-
point R which does not lie exactly in the focus-plane, we
have merely to draw the straight lines RB, RO, RC until
they meet the lens, and connect these latter points with B',
O', C', respectively, by straight lines which will intersect in
the image-point R'.

Again, consider a system composed of two equal thin
convex lenses whose centers are at A_1 and A_2 (Fig. 176),

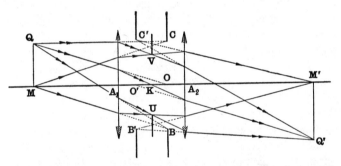

FIG. 176.—Optical system composed of two equal thin convex lenses with
interior stop placed midway between the two lenses.

with a stop UV placed midway between them; if the center
of the stop is designated by K, then $A_1K = KA_2$. The image
of the stop as seen through the front lens is BOC, and its
image as seen by looking through the other lens in the opposite direction is B'O'C'; these images being equal in size
and symmetrically situated with respect to the stop itself.
The image of the rim of each lens cast by the other lens
should also be constructed, but for the sake of simplicity
these images are not drawn in the figure, because the di-

ameters of the lenses are taken sufficiently large as compared with the diameter of the stop interposed between them at K to insure that the latter acts as aperture-stop with respect to the axial object-point M on which the instrument is supposed to be focused. Consequently, since the stop-image BC subtends at M an angle less than that subtended by the rim of the front lens or by the image of the rim of the second lens, it will be the entrance-pupil of the system; and, similarly, B′C′ which is the image of BC formed by the system as a whole will be the exit-pupil. Thus, in order to construct the image-point M′ conjugate to the axial object-point M, we have merely to draw the straight line MC and to determine the point where this line meets the first lens; and from the latter point draw a straight line through the point V in the edge of the stop to meet the second lens; and, finally, draw the straight line which joins this latter point with the point C′ in the edge of the exit-pupil; this line will cross the axis at the required point M′ in the screen-plane. Similarly, drawing from the object-point Q the three rays QB, QO and QC, we can continue the paths of these rays from the first lens to the second through the points U, K and V, respectively, in the stop-opening; and since the rays must issue from the second lens so as to go through B′, O′ and C′, respectively, in the exit-pupil, their common point of intersection in the image-space will be the point Q′ conjugate to Q. In the diagram the point Q is taken in the focus-plane; but the same construction will apply also to determine the position of an image-point R′ conjugate to an object-point R which does not lie in the focus-plane.

136. Aperture-Angle. Case of Two or More Entrance-Pupils.—The angle OMC=η (Figs. 175 and 176) subtended at the axial object-point M by the radius OC of the entrance-pupil is called the *aperture-angle* of the optical system. If we put OC=p (where p is to be reckoned positive or negative according as the point C lies above or below the axis) and $OM = z$, then $\tan \eta = -p/z$. In like manner, if $\eta' = \angle O'M'C'$ denotes the angle subtended at the point M' conjugate to M by the corresponding radius of the exit-pupil $(O'C' = p')$, and if also $O'M' = z'$, then $\tan \eta' = -p'/z'$.

The pupils of an optical system depend essentially, as has been stated, on the position of the axial object-point M on

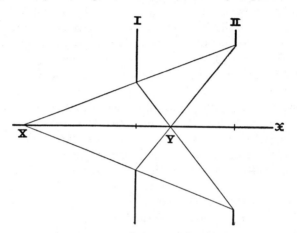

FIG. 177.—Case of two entrance-pupils.

which the instrument is focused. In the diagram (Fig. 177) I and II represent a pair of stops or stop-images as seen by an eye looking into the front end of the instrument. Join one end of the diameter of one of these openings by straight lines with both ends of the diameter of the other opening; and let the points where the straight lines cross the axis be designated by X and Y. The two apertures subtend equal angles at these points, and hence if the object-point M coincides with either X or Y, the entrance-pupil of the system may be either I or II; in fact, for these two special positions of M there will be two entrance-pupils, and, of course, also two exit-pupils. If the object-point M lies between X and Y, then in the case represented in the figure the opening II will subtend a smaller angle at M than the opening I so that the former will act as the entrance-pupil. But for any other position of the axial object-point M besides those above mentioned the opening I will be the entrance-pupil.

137. Field of View.—The limitation of the apertures of the bundles of effective rays is not the only office of the stops and lens fastenings. One of their most important functions is to define the extent of the object that is to be reproduced in the instrument as has been pointed out in several simple illustrations in the earlier pages of this book (see §§ 9, 16, 73 and 98). In the adjoining diagram (Fig. 178), where the entrance-pupil of the system is represented by the opening BC, the other stops or stop-images in the object-space act like circular windows or port-holes through which the rays that are directed from the various parts of the object towards points in the open space of the entrance-pupil will have to pass if they are to succeed in getting through the instrument without being intercepted on the way. Evidently, that one of these openings which subtends the smallest angle at the center O of the entrance-pupil will limit the extent of the field of view in the object-space. This opening which is represented in the figure by GH is called the *entrance-port;* and the material stop or lens-rim which is responsible for it is called the *field-stop* (§ 9).

Let the straight line CH drawn through the upper extremities of the diameters BC and GH of the entrance-pupil and entrance-port meet the optical axis in the point designated by L and the focus-plane in the point designated by U. If this straight line is revolved around the axis of the instrument, the point U will describe a circle in the focus-plane around the axial object-point M as center; and it is obvious that any point in this plane within the circumference of this circle, or, indeed, any object-point contained inside the conical surface generated by the revolution of the straight line passing through C and H, may send rays to all parts of the entrance-pupil which will not be intercepted anywhere in the instrument. Thus, the entire aperture of the entrance-pupil will be the common base of the cones of effective rays emanating from sources which lie within this region of the object-space.

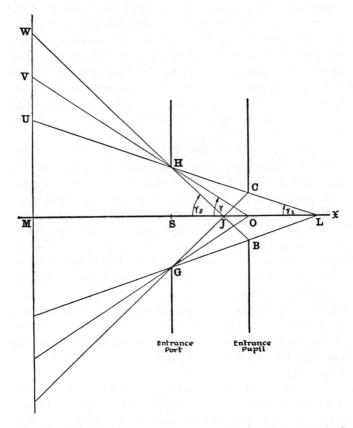

Fig. 178.—Field of view of optical system on side of object, determined by the entrance-pupil and the entrance-port.

Again, the straight line OH drawn through the center of the entrance-pupil and the upper edge of the entrance-port will determine a second limiting point V in the focus-plane which is farther from the optical axis than the first point U;

and in case of object-points lying in the focus-plane between
U and V the sections of the bundles of effective rays made
by the plane of the entrance-pupil will have areas that are
comprised between the entire area of the opening of the
entrance-pupil and half that area; and this will be true likewise with respect to all those points in the object-space that
are contained between the two conical surfaces generated
by the revolution of the straight lines CH and OH around
the axis of symmetry. Such points will not lie outside the
field of view, but although they can utilize more than half
the opening of the entrance-pupil, they are not in a position
to take advantage of the entire opening.

Finally, the straight line BH drawn through the lower
edge of the entrance-pupil and the upper edge of the entrance-
port, which crosses the optical axis at the point marked J,
will determine an extreme point W in the focus-plane which
is more remote from the axis than the point V; and it is evident from the figure that object-points in the focus-plane
which lie in the annular space between the two circles described around M as center with radii MV and MW are
even more unfavorably situated for sending rays into the
entrance-pupil, because they cannot utilize as much as half
of the pupil-opening. In fact, the effective rays which come
from the farthest point W pass through the circumference
of the pupil, and any point lying beyond W will be wholly
invisible, that is, entirely outside the field of view of the
instrument.

Thus, we see that the focus-plane is divided into zones by
three concentric circles of radii MU, MV and MW. Object-
points lying in the interior central zone send their light
through the entrance-pupil without let or hindrance on the
part of the field-stop; so that this is the brightest part of
the field. But in the two outer zones there is a gradual fad-
ing away of light until we reach finally the border of complete
darkness. The three regions of the field of view in the object-
space are usually defined by the angles $2\gamma_1$, 2γ, and $2\gamma_2$

whose vertices are on the optical axis at the points L, O and J, respectively; so that $\gamma_1 = \angle SLH$, $\gamma = \angle SOH$ and $\gamma_2 = \angle SJH$. If the radii of the entrance-pupil and entrance-port are denoted by $p = OC$ and $b = SH$, and if the distance of the entrance-pupil from the entrance-port is denoted by $c = SO$, then

$$\tan\gamma_1 = -\frac{b-p}{c}, \quad \tan\gamma = -\frac{b}{c}, \quad \tan\gamma_2 = -\frac{b+p}{c} \ .$$

The field of view in the image-space is determined in like manner. The image of the entrance-port GH with its center at S, which is produced by the entire optical system, is the exit-port $G'H'$ with its center at S'; and by priming all the letters in the expressions above a similar system of equations will be obtained for defining the three regions, $2\gamma_1'$, $2\gamma'$ and $2\gamma_2'$, of the field of view in the image-space. Generally, the edge of the field is considered as determined by the center of the pupil, that is, by the angle 2γ in the object-space and the angle $2\gamma'$ in the image-space.

138. Field of View of System Consisting of a Thin Lens and the Eye.—A simple but very instructive illustration of the principles explained in the foregoing section is afforded by an ordinary convex lens used as a magnifying glass. In order to obtain a virtual, magnified image with a lens of this kind, the distance of the glass from the object must not exceed the focal length of the lens, and then when the image is viewed through the glass, the iris of the observer's eye will act as the aperture-stop of the system, no matter where the eye is placed, provided the diameter of the pupil of the eye is less than that of the lens, as is practically nearly always the case. Moreover, since the pupil of the eye is the common base of the bundles of rays which come to it from the various parts of the image, it is the exit-pupil of the system, and its image in the glass is, therefore, the entrance-pupil. If the eye is placed on the axis of the lens between the lens and its second focal point (Fig. 179), the entrance-pupil will be a virtual image of the pupil of the eye and will

lie on the same side of the lens as the eye; if the eye is placed
at the second focal point of the glass, the entrance-pupil will
be at infinity (see § 144); and, finally, if, as represented in

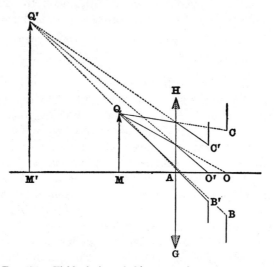

FIG. 179.—Field of view of thin convex lens when the eye
is between the lens and its second focal plane.

Fig. 180, the eye is placed at a point O′ beyond the second
focal point of the convex lens GH, the center of the entrance-
pupil will be at a point O on the same side of the lens as the
object MQ. The distance between the eye and the second
focal point of a convex lens used as a magnifying glass is
never very great, and, consequently, the distance of the center O of the entrance-pupil from the first focal point is relatively always quite large. The rim of the glass acts as the
field-stop, and it is at the same time both the entrance-port
and the exit-port of the system; and hence the field of view
exposed to the eye in the image-space is entirely analogous
to the field which would be seen by an eye looking through
a circular window of the same form, dimensions and position
as the lens. Since the exit-port is represented here as being

at a considerable distance from the exit-pupil, the field of
view will appear vignetted, that is, the border will not be
sharply outlined, but the field will fade out imperceptibly

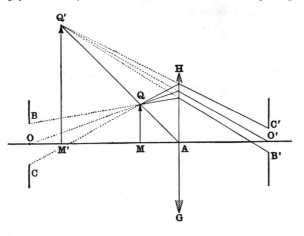

Fig. 180.—Field of view of thin convex lens when the eye is placed
beyond the second focal plane.

towards the edges.   If the diameter of the lens is denoted
by $2b$, and if the distance of the eye from the lens is denoted
by $c = AO'$,   then $\tan\gamma' = -b/c$, where $\gamma' = \angle AO'H$.   The
extent of the field as measured by the angle $2\gamma'$ is independent of the size of the pupil of the eye.   If the focus-plane
coincides with the first focal plane of the magnifying glass,
the diameter of the visible portion of the object will be $2y =
-2f.\tan\gamma'$.

In a compound microscope or in an astronomical telescope
the object-glass produces a real inverted image of the object,
and this image is magnified by the ocular, which is essentially a convergent optical system on the order of a convex
lens used as a magnifying glass.   In the interior of the instrument between the object-glass and the ocular, at the
place where the real image is cast by the object-glass,
there is usually inserted a material stop, which cuts off the

"ragged edge" of the field of view, so that only the central portion which sends complete bundles of rays through the instrument is visible to the eye.

In the Dutch telescope the ocular is a divergent optical system which may be represented in a diagram by a con-

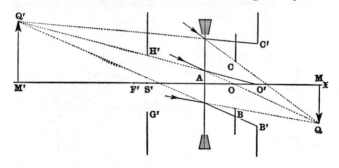

Fig. 181.—Ocular system of Galileo's telescope represented in the diagram by a thin concave lens. Diagram shows how the rays, after having passed through the object-glass, enter the pupil of the observer's eye B'C'. Inverted image of distant object in the object-glass of the telescope is formed at MQ; M'Q' is the image of MQ in the ocular. G'H' is the image of the rim of the object-glass in the ocular. B'C' is the image of BC in the ocular.

cave lens (Fig. 181) which is placed between the object-glass and the real image of the object in the object-glass; so that so far as the ocular is concerned, this image is a virtual object, shown in the figure by the line-segment MQ. The eye in this case is usually adjusted very close to the concave lens. The pupil of the eye is represented in the figure by the opening B'C' with its center on the axis at O'; its image in the lens is BC. Here also, just as in the case of a convergent ocular, the pupil of the eye will act as the exit-pupil unless the diameter of the lens is so small that the lens-rim itself performs this office. The image of MQ is M'Q', which latter will be erect if MQ is inverted, and since MQ is always inverted in the simple telescope, the final image in the Dutch telescope is erect. In the case of the Dutch telescope the rim of the ocular lens does not limit the field of view, but this is limited by the rim of the object-glass, which is the entrance-port of the telescope. Hence, the image of the object-glass in the ocular is the exit-port. This image (called the "eye-ring," § 159) is represented in the diagram by the opening G'H' with its center on the axis at S'. The object-point Q, as shown in the figure, is just at the edge of the field, because the image-ray coming from Q' which is directed towards the center O' of the exit-pupil is made to pass through the edge of the exit-port ($\gamma' = \angle$S'O'H').

139. The Chief Rays.—Every bundle of effective rays emanating from a point of the object contains one ray which in a certain sense is the central or representative ray of the configuration and which may therefore be distinguished as the *chief ray* (see § 11). The ray which is entitled to this preëminence is evidently that one which in traversing the medium in which the aperture-stop lies passes through the center K of this stop. If the optical system is free from the so-called aberrations, both spherical and chromatic (as is assumed in the present discussion), the chief ray of the bundle may also be defined as that ray which in the object-space passes through the center O of the entrance-pupil; but the first definition is preferable because it is applicable to actual as well as to ideal optical systems.

The totality of the chief rays coming from all parts of the object constitute, therefore, a homocentric bundle of rays in the medium where the aperture-stop lies, and these rays proceed exactly as though they had originated from a luminous point at K.

If the aperture-stop is very narrow, comparable, say, with the dimensions of a pin-hole, the apertures of the bundles of effective rays will be correspondingly small; and in the limit when the opening in the stop may be regarded as reduced to a mere point at its center K, the ray-bundles will have collapsed into mere skeletons, so to speak, each one represented by its chief ray. It is because the chief rays are the last

survivors of the ray-bundles that it is particularly important in nearly all optical problems to investigate the procedure of these more or less characteristic rays.

**140. The so-called " Blur-Circles " (or Circles of Dif-
fusion) in the Screen-Plane.**—Now if the cardinal points of
the optical system are assigned, the image-relief corresponding to a three-dimensional object may be constructed point
by point, according to the methods which have been explained. But, as a matter of fact, the image produced by

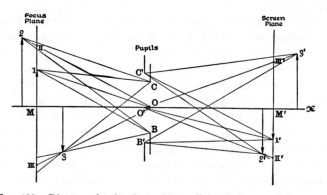

Fig. 182.—Diagram showing how object-relief and image-relief are projected in focus-plane and screen-plane from entrance-pupil and exit-
pupil, respectively; and the "blur circles" in these planes.

an optical instrument, instead of being left, as it were,
floating in space, is almost invariably received on a surface
or screen of some kind, as, for example, the ground-glass
plate of a photographic camera. In case the image is virtual, as in a microscope or telescope, it is intended to be
viewed by the eye looking into the instrument, so that here
also in the last analysis the image is projected on the surface of the retina of the observing eye. This receiving surface is called technically the "screen," which affords also
an explanation of the name screen-plane (§ 134) as applied
to the plane conjugate to the focus-plane.

In the diagram (Fig. 182) the screen-plane is placed at

right angles to the axis at the point marked M′ which is conjugate to the axial object-point M, so that this point is seen sharply focused on the screen. Evidently, however, the optical system cannot be in focus for all the different points of the object-relief at the same time, because the screen-plane is conjugate to only one transversal plane of the object-space, namely, the focus-plane perpendicular to the axis at M. Thus, for example, the reproduction of a solid object such as an extended view of a landscape on the ground-glass plate of a camera is not an image at all in the strict optical sense of the term, inasmuch as it is not conjugate to the entire object with respect to the photographic objective. Only such points of the object as lie in the focus-plane will be reproduced by sharp clear-cut image-points in the screen-plane (as, for example, the point marked 1 in the figure); whereas object-points situated to one side or the other of the focus-plane will be depicted more or less indistinctly on the screen-plane by small luminous areas which are sections cut out by this plane from the cones of image-rays emanating originally from points of the object such as those marked 2, 3 in the diagram. These little patches of light on the screen, which are usually elliptical in form, and whose dimensions depend on obvious geometrical factors, such as the diameter and position of the exit-pupil, etc., are the so-called circles of diffusion or *"blur-circles,"* in consequence of which details of the image as projected on the screen are necessarily impaired to a greater or less degree.

It is a simple matter to reconstruct the object-figure which is optically conjugate to this configuration of image-points and "blur-circles" in the screen-plane, which will obviously be a similar configuration of object-points and "blur-circles" all lying in the focus-plane. Moreover, since the exit-pupil is conjugate to the entrance-pupil, the cones of rays in the object-space corresponding to those in the image-space may be easily constructed by taking the points of the object-relief as vertices and the entrance-pupil as the common base of these cones. The *tout ensemble* of the sections of all these bundles of object-rays made by the focus-plane will evidently be the figure in the object-space that corresponds to the representation on the screen, and according to the theory of optical imagery these two plane configurations will be similar. This "vicarious" object in the focus-plane is sometimes called the *projected copy of the object-relief*, because it is obtained by projecting the points of the object from the entrance-pupil on the focus-plane.

141. The Pupil-Centers as Centers of Perspective of Object-Space and Image-Space.—It hardly needs to be pointed out that the "blur-circles" which arise from this

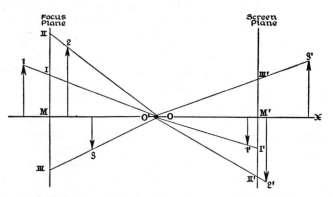

Fig. 183.—Projection of object-relief and image-relief in focus-plane and screen-plane from the centers of entrance-pupil and exit-pupil, respectively.

mode of reproducing a solid object on a plane (or curved) surface are due to no faults of the optical system itself, but are necessary consequences of the mode of representation, having their origin, in fact, in the object-space by virtue of the process employed. The only possible way of diminishing or eliminating the indistinctness or lack of detail in the reproduction of parts of the object that do not lie in the focus-plane consists in reducing the diameter of the aperture-stop, or in "stopping down" the instrument, as it is called.

If the stop-opening is contracted more and more until finally it is no larger than a fine pin-hole, the pupils likewise will tend to become mere points at their centers O, O' (Fig. 183), and the "blur-circles" both in the focus-plane and in the screen-plane will diminish in area *pari passu* and ultimately collapse also into the points where the chief rays cross this pair of conjugate planes. The points marked I, II, III, etc., where the chief rays belonging to the object-points 1, 2, 3, etc., cross the focus-plane, and which are the centers of the so-called "blur-circles" in this plane, are obtained, therefore, by projecting all the points of the object from the center of the entrance-pupil on to the focus-plane. This mode of representing a three-dimensional object is, however, in no wise peculiar to the optical system itself, but is the old familiar process of *perspective reproduction* by central projection on a plane. Thus, the pupil-centers O, O' are to be regarded as the *centers of perspective* of the object-space and image-space, respectively.

142. Proper Distance of Viewing a Photograph.—These principles explain why it is necessary to view a photograph at a certain distance from the eye in order to obtain a correct impression of the object which is depicted. Suppose, for example, that O, O' (Fig. 184) designate the centers of the pupils of a photographic lens, and that an object NR is reproduced in the screen-plane by the perspective copy M'Q' whose size is one kth of that of the projection MQ of the object in the focus-plane. Now if the picture is to produce the same impression as was produced by the original itself on an observer with his eye placed at O, the photograph must be held in front of the eye at a place P such that the visual angle KOP which it subtends at the center of rotation of the eye shall be equal to the angle QOM; that is, the distance PO in the figure must be equal to one kth of the distance of the center of the entrance-pupil from the focus-plane, or $PO = MO/k$. If (as is usually the case with a landscape lens) the focus-plane is at infinity, then PO will be equal to the focal length (f) of the objective. Generally speaking, we may say, therefore, that the correct distance for viewing a photograph of a distant object is equal to the focal length of the objective, this distance being measured

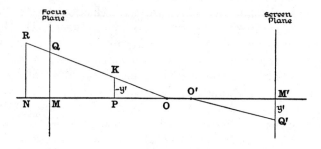

FIG. 184.—Correct distance of viewing photograph.

from the picture to the center of rotation of the observer's eye. Accordingly, if the focal length is less than the distance between the near point of the eye and the center of rotation, which in the case of a normal emmetropic eye of an adolescent is about 10 or 12 cm., it will be impossible to see the picture distinctly with the naked eye and at the same time under the correct visual angle. Moreover, even if the focal length of the photographic lens were not less than this least distance of distinct vision, the effort of accommodation which the eye has to make in order to focus the image sharply on the retina under the correct visual angle will superinduce an illusion which will be different from the impression of reality which it is the purpose of the picture to convey. In the case of a photograph made by an objective of very short focal length it is possible indeed to make an enlarged copy which may be viewed at the correct distance, but this is always more or less troublesome and expensive. Dr. VON ROHR has invented an instrument called a *verant* which is ingeniously designed to overcome as far as possible the difficulties above mentioned; so that viewed through this apparatus the photograph is seen more or less exactly as the object appeared.

143. Perspective Elongation of Image.—If the screen-plane is not focused exactly on the image-point R' (Fig. 185),

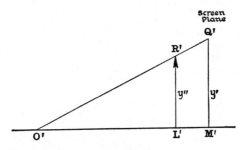

Fig. 185.—Perspective elongation of image.

this point will be shown on the screen by a "blur-circle" whose center will be at the point Q' which is the projection of R' from the center O' of the exit-pupil. Let $e=$L'M' denote the distance of the screen-plane M'Q' from the image-plane L'R', where L', M' designate the feet of the perpendiculars dropped from R', Q', respectively, on the axis. From the diagram we obtain the proportion:

$$\frac{M'Q'}{L'R'}=\frac{O'M'}{O'L'}=\frac{O'M'}{O'M'+M'L'};$$

which may be written:

$$y'/y''=z'/(z'-e),$$

where $y'=$M'Q', $y''=$L'R' and $z'=$O'M'. Moreover, since e may be regarded as small in comparison with z', we obtain:

$$y'-y''=\frac{e}{z'}y'', \text{ approximately.}$$

The difference $(y'-y'')$ is the measure of the *perspective elongation* due to imperfect focusing.

If the exit-pupil is at infinity, then R'Q' will be parallel to the axis and $y'=y''$; and under these circumstances, the perspective reproduction in the screen-plane will be of the same size as the image, no matter how much it is out of focus.

144. Telecentric Systems.—A common laboratory use of an optical instrument is to ascertain the size of an inaccessible or intangible object from the measured dimensions of its image as determined by means of a scale on which the

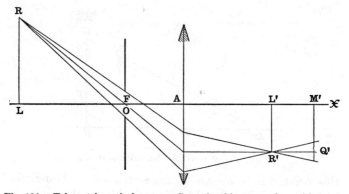

Fig. 186.—Telecentric optical system: Case of a thin convex lens with front stop in first focal plane. Object represented by LR; blurred image M'Q' appears of the same size as sharp image L'R'.

image is projected; but, in general, unless the scale is exactly in the same plane as the image, there will be a parallax error in the measurement of the image due to its perspective elongation. However, if the chief rays in the image-space are parallel to the axis, which may be effected by placing the aperture-stop so that the entrance-pupil lies in the primary focal plane of the instrument, as illustrated in Fig. 186, the perspective elongation vanishes ($y' - y'' = 0$, as explained in § 143); and, consequently, the image $y'' = L'R'$ will appear of the same size as its projection $y' = M'Q'$, no matter whether it lies in the same plane as the scale or not.

Similarly, if the aperture-stop is placed so that the entrance-pupil is at infinity and the exit-pupil lies therefore in the secondary focal plane, the chief rays in the object-space will then all be parallel to the optical axis.

Systems of this description in which one or other of the two projection centers O, O' is at infinity are said to be *telecentric.* This is the principle of nearly all systems for micrometer measurements of optical images.

A simple illustration of a device of this kind that is telecentric on the side next the object is afforded by the ophthalmic instrument called a *keratometer*, which, as the name implies, is intended primarily to measure the diameter of the cornea or the apparent diameter of the eye-pupil. It is used also to measure the distance of a correction-glass (§ 154) from an ametropic eye (§ 153), which is an important factor in the prescription of spectacles. The instrument consists essentially of a long narrow tube, near the middle of which is mounted a convex lens of low power adjusted so that its second focal point F' coincides exactly with the center of a small aperture in a metal disk placed at the end of the tube where the observer puts his eye. At the opposite end of the tube a scale graduated in half-millimeters is mounted so that

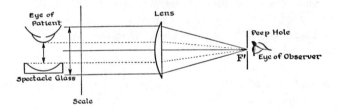

Fig. 187.—Diagram of instrument called keratometer, as used to measure the distance of spectacle glass from the cornea of the eye.

its upper edge coincides with a horizontal diameter of the tube at this place. The upper part of this end of the tube is cut away in order to admit sufficient light to illuminate the scale.

When the keratometer is used to measure the distance between the vertex of the cornea and the vertex of the correction-glass, it is placed with its axis at right-angles to the line of sight of the patient, as represented in the diagram (Fig. 187), the scale being brought as near as possible to the patient between his eye and the spectacle-glass. The distance AB to be measured is projected on the scale by rays that are parallel to the axis of the lens, so that when the observer looks through the instrument he can read off this distance on the image of the scale.

Practically the same principle is employed also in BADAL'S *optometer* for measuring the visual acuity of the eye. It

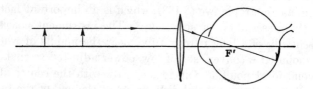

FIG. 188.—BADAL'S optometer, with second focal point (F)′ of convex lens at first nodal point of patient's eye; forming in conjunction with the eye a telecentric system.

consists of a single convex lens mounted at one end of a long graduated bar which is provided with a movable carrier holding a test-chart of some kind. If the lens, which usually has a refracting power of about 10 dioptries, is adjusted about 9 cm. in front of the cornea so that its second focal point F′ coincides with the nodal point of the eye (Fig. 188), a ray meeting the lens in a direction parallel to the axis will emerge from it so as to go through the nodal point of the

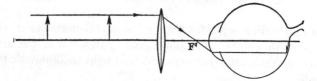

FIG. 189.—BADAL'S optometer, with second focal point (F′) of convex lens at first focal point of patient's eye; forming in conjunction with the eye a telescopic system.

eye and thence to the retina without change of direction. Accordingly, just as though a narrow aperture were placed at the nodal point of the eye, the size of the retinal image will not be altered whether the object or chart on the bar be far or near; whereas the distinctness with which the details of the object are seen, which affords the measure of the visual acuity, will depend on the distance of the object.

Another method of using this optometer is to place the lens about 2 cm. farther from the eye, as shown in Fig. 189, so that now its second focal point lies in the anterior focal plane of the eye. Under these circumstances an incident ray proceeding parallel to the axis will emerge from the lens and cross the axis at the anterior focal point of the eye, so that after traversing the eye-media it will again be parallel to the axis. Consequently, here also the image formed on the retina will be of the same size no matter where the object is placed on the bar in front of the lens, just as if there were a narrow stop at the anterior focal point of the eye. In this latter adjustment the lens and the eye together constitute an optical system which is *telecentric on both* sides, that is, a *telescopic system* (§ 125).

PROBLEMS

1. A cylindrical tube, 2 cm. in diameter and 10 cm. long, is closed at one end by a thin convex lens of focal length 4 cm. If this end of the tube is pointed towards a distant object, what will be the position and diameter of the entrance-pupil?   Ans. $6\frac{2}{3}$ cm. in front of the lens; diameter, $1\frac{1}{3}$ cm.

2. In the preceding problem, where would the object have to be in order that the lens itself might act as entrance-pupil?

Ans. In front of the lens, not more than 20 nor less than 4 cm. away.

3. If in No. 1 the other end of the tube is closed by a thin eye-lens whose focal length is such that when the combination is pointed at an object 24 cm. from the object-glass, the bundles of rays issuing from the eye-lens are cylindrical, find

the positions of the pupils of the system and the focal length of the eye-lens.

Ans. Entrance-pupil $6\frac{2}{3}$ cm. in front of object-glass; exit-pupil coincides with eye-glass; focal length of eye-glass, 5.2 cm.

4. In the preceding problem what will be the answers on the supposition that the object is 12 cm. from the object-glass?

Ans. Entrance-pupil coincides with object-glass; exit-pupil is $6\frac{2}{3}$ cm. beyond eye-glass; focal length of eye-glass, 4 cm.

5. A real inverted image of an extended object is formed by the object-glass of a simple astronomical telescope in the primary focal plane of the eye-glass. The focal lengths of the object-glass and eye-glass are 2 feet and 1.5 inches, respectively, and their diameters are 6 inches and 1 inch, respectively. If the distance of the object from the object-glass is 240 feet, find the position and diameter of the entrance-port and the diameter of the portion of the object that is completely visible through the telescope.

Ans. Entrance-port is 30.21 feet from object-glass, and its diameter is 1.175 feet; diameter of visible portion of object, 5.865 feet.

6. A thin convex lens of focal length 10 cm. and diameter 4 cm. is used as a magnifying glass. If an eye adapted for parallel rays is placed at a distance of 5 cm. from the lens, what will be the diameter of the portion of the object that can be seen distinctly?   Ans. 8 cm.

7. The diameter of a thin convex lens is 1 inch, and its focal length is 10 inches. The lens is placed midway between the eye and a plane object which is 10 inches from the eye. How much of the object is visible through the lens?

Ans. $1\frac{1}{2}$ inch.

CHAPTER XIII

145. The Human Eye.—The organ of vision is composed of the eye-ball, wherein the visual impulses are produced by the impact of light; the optic nerve which transmits these excitations to the brain; and the visual center in the brain where the sensation of vision comes to consciousness.

The eye-ball (Fig. 190) lying in a bony socket on a cushion of fat and connective tissue, in which it is free to turn in all directions with little or no friction, consists of an almost spherical dark chamber, filled with transparent optical media which form the optical system of the eye (Fig. 191).   The outer protecting envelope of the eye-ball is the tough, white membrane called, from its hardness, the *sclerotic coat* or *sclera*, popularly known as the "white of the eye."   This opaque membrane is continued in front by a round opening or window called, on account of its horny texture, the *cornea*.   The cornea is beautifully transparent, and its mirror-like surface forms a slight protuberance shaped something like a watch-glass or a prolate spheroid.   In the interior of the eye the sclerotic coat is overlaid with the dark-colored *choroid* which contains the blood-vessels that nourish the eye and also a layer of brown pigment acting to protect the dark chamber of the eye from diffused light.   Behind the cornea lies the *anterior chamber* filled with transparent fluid called the *aqueous humor*.   This anterior chamber is limited behind by the *iris*, which, rich in blood-vessels, imparts to the eye its characteristic color.   This is an opaque screen or curtain which contains a central hole, the *pupil*, which is circular in the human eye.   The aperture of a bundle of rays entering the eye from a luminous point, in proportion to the dimensions of the eye, is enormous as compared, for example, with the same magnitude in a telescope; and the office of the pupil is

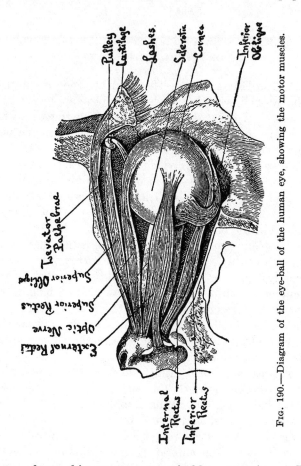

Fig. 190.—Diagram of the eye-ball of the human eye, showing the motor muscles.

to stop down this aperture to suitable proportions. The pupil contracts or dilates involuntarily and regulates the quantity of light that is admitted to the eye. In the structure of the iris there are two sets of fibers, the circular and

the radiating; when the circular fibers contract, the pupil
contracts, and when the radiating fibers contract, the pupil

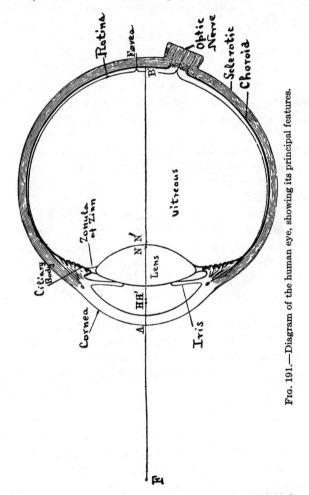

FIG. 191.—Diagram of the human eye, showing its principal features.

dilates. In the front part of the eye the choroid lining is
bordered at the edge of the cornea by a kind of folded drapery
the so-called *ciliary body*, which is hidden from without be-

hind the iris and which contains the delicate system of muscles which control the mechanism of accommodation. The *crystalline lens* composed of a perfectly transparent substance is indirectly attached to the ciliary body by a band which surrounds the edge of the lens like a ring and which is disposed in radial folds somewhat after the manner of a neck-frill. This band is the *suspensory ligament* or *zonule of Zinn*. The lens itself is double convex, the posterior surface being more strongly curved than the anterior surface. The substance of the lens consists of layers of different indices of refraction increasing towards the center or core of the lens. The entire space behind the lens is filled with a transparent jelly-like substance called the *vitreous humor*, which has the same index of refraction as the aqueous humor, namely, 1.336.

The light-sensitive *retina* lying on the inside of the choroid is exceedingly delicate and transparent. In spite of its slight thickness which nowhere exceeds 0.4 mm., the structure of the retina is very complicated, and no less than ten layers have been distinguished (Fig. 192). The layer next the vitreous humor is composed of nerve-fibres spreading out radially from the optic nerve. This layer is connected with the following layer containing the large ganglion or nerve-cells, and this in turn is connected by an apparatus of fibers and cells with the peculiar light-sensitive elements of the retina, the so-called visual cells which form the "bacillary layer." These visual cells consist of characteristic elongated bodies which are distinguished as *rods* and *cones*. The rods are slender cylinders, while the cones or bulbs are somewhat thicker and flask-shaped. They are all disposed perpendicularly to the surface of the retina, closely packed together, so as to form a mosaic layer at the back of the retina.

Near the center of the retina at the back of the eye, a little to the temporal side, is located the *yellow spot* or *macula lutea*, where the visual cells are composed mostly of cones. This is the most sensitive part of the retina, especially the minute pit or depression at the center of this area, called the *fovea centralis*, which consists entirely of cones densely crowded together.

As compared with an artificial optical instrument, the

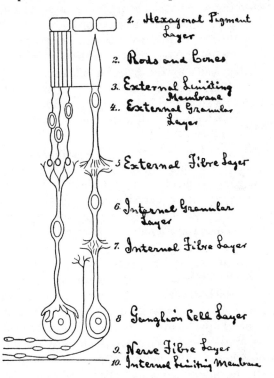

1. Hexagonal Pigment Layer
2. Rods and Cones
3. External Limiting Membrane
4. External Granular Layer
5 External Fibre Layer
6. Internal Granular Layer
7. Internal Fibre Layer
8 Ganglion Cell Layer
9. Nerve Fibre Layer
10. Internal Limiting Membrane

FIG. 192.—Structure of the retina of the human eye.

field of view of the immobile eye is very extensive, amounting to about 150° laterally and 120° vertically. The diameter of the *fovea centralis* corresponds in the field of vision of the eye to an angular space which may be covered by the nail of the fore finger extended at arm's length. In this part of the field vision is so acute that details of an object can be distinguished as separate provided their angular distance is not less than one minute of arc (*cf.* §10). If the apparent size of an object is so small that its image formed on the retina at the *fovea centralis* covers only a single visual cell, the object ceases to have any apparent size at all and cannot be distinguished from a point. The size of the retinal image corresponding to an object whose apparent size is one minute of arc is found by calculation from the known optical constants of the eye to be 0.00487 mm. Anatomical measurements give a similar value for the diameter of a visual cell.

The inverted image cast on the retina of the eye has been compared to a sketch which is roughly outlined in the outer parts, but which is more and more finely executed in towards the center, until at the *fovea centralis* itself the details are exquisitely finished. Thus, only a comparatively small portion of an external object can be seen distinctly by the eye at any one moment. If all the parts of the field of view were portrayed with equal vividness at the same time and came to consciousness at once, the spectator would be completely bewildered and unable to concentrate his attention on a particular spot or phase of the object.

The ends of the rods next the choroid contain a coloring matter which is sensitive to light, the so-called *visual purple*, which is bleached white by exposure to bright light, but which is renewed in darkness by the layer of cells lying between the choroid and the retina. The light-disturbance arriving at the retina penetrates it as far as the bacillary layer of rods and cones, and the stimulus is transmitted back through the interposed apparatus to the layer of nerve-fibers and thence conducted to the *optic nerve* in communication with the brain.

Not far from the center of the retina, a little to the nasal side, the optic nerve pierces the eye-ball through the sclera and choroid. Here the retina is interrupted, so that any light which falls on the optic nerve itself cannot be perceived. This is the place of the so-called *blind-spot* (*punctum cœcum*) of the eye. Corresponding to the area of the blind spot, there is a gap in the field of vision of the eye amounting to about 6° horizontally and 8° vertically. The dimensions of the blind spot are great enough to contain the retinal images of eleven full moons placed side by side. The optic nerve leaves the eyeball through a bony canal and passes thence to the visual center of the brain.

The mobility of the eye is produced by six muscles, the four recti and the two oblique muscles (Fig. 190). The recti originate in the posterior part of the socket and are attached by their tendons to the sclera so as to move the eye up or down and to the right or left. The procedure of the oblique muscles is more complicated. The superior oblique, which also arises in the posterior part of the socket, passes in the front of the eye through a loop or kind of pulley lying on the upper nasal side of the socket and then turns downwards to attach itself to the sclera. The inferior oblique muscle has its origin on the front lower nasal side of the eye-socket, and passes to the posterior surface of the eye-ball, being attached to the sclera on the temporal side. The superior oblique turns the eye downwards and outwards, and the inferior oblique turns it upwards and outwards.

The motor muscles of the two eyes act together so that both eyes turn always in the same sense, to the right or to the left, up or down. It is impossible to turn one eye up and the other down at same time, so as to look up to the sky with one eye and down at the earth with the other.

146. Optical Constants of the Eye.—The *optical axis* of the eye may be defined as the normal to the anterior surface of the cornea which goes through the center of the pupil. This line passes approximately through the centers of curvature of the refracting surfaces. The *schematic eye* (see § 130) is a centered system of spherical refracting surfaces symmetric with respect to the optical axis. The point where the optical axis meets the anterior surface of the cornea is called the *cornea vertex* or *anterior pole* of the eye and is designated by **A**; and the point where the optical axis meets the retina is called the *posterior pole* of the eye and is designated by **B**. In GULLSTRAND'S schematic eye the distance from **A** to **B** is equal to 24 mm., therefore somewhat less than an inch.

The motor muscles of the eye (§ 145), acting in pairs, turn the eye-ball around axes of rotation which all pass through a fixed point or pivot called the *center of rotation* of the eye and designated by **Z**. This point may be considered as lying also on the optical axis in the medium of the vitreous humor about 13 or 14 mm. from the vertex of the cornea or about 10.5 mm behind the pupil. All the excursions of the eye are performed around this point.

The object-point which is sharply imaged on the retina at the *fovea centralis* (§ 145) is called the *point of fixation*, and the straight line which joins the point of fixation with the centre of rotation is called the *line of fixation*. This line indicates the direction in which the eye is looking. The *field of fixation* is measured by the greatest angular distance through which the line of fixation can be turned; which amounts to about a right angle both vertically and horizontally.

In GULLSTRAND'S schematic eye, as was shown in § 130, the primary focal point **F** lies in front of the eye at a distance of 15.707 mm. from the anterior vertex of the cornea, while the secondary focal point **F'** lies on the other side of the cornea at a distance of 24.387 mm. The principal points (**H**, **H'**) lie in the aqueous humor slightly beyond the cornea system at distances $AH = +1.348$ mm., $AH' = +1.602$ mm. Thus the focal lengths are: $f = +17.055$ mm. $f' = -22.785$ mm.; the ratio between them being equal to 1.336, which is therefore the value of the index of refraction (n') of the vitreous humor. Accordingly, the refracting power of GULLSTRAND'S schematic eye is $F = 58.64$ dptr. The nodal points (**N**, **N'**) lie close to the posterior vertex of the crystalline lens, on opposite sides of it, at the following distances from the vertex of the cornea: $AN = +7.078$ mm., $AN' = +7.332$ mm. The straight line which joins the point of fixation with the anterior nodal point of the eye is called the *visual axis*. It is parallel to the straight line which joins the posterior nodal point with the *fovea centralis*. Since the nodal points are so close together, for many problems connected with the eye they may be regarded as coincident; so that then the visual axis may be defined as the line drawn from the point of fixation to the *fovea centralis*. The visual axis meets the cornea a little to the nasal side of the anterior vertex and slightly above it, forming with the optical axis an angle between 3° and 5°.

The above values are all given for the passive, unaccommodated eye. By the act of accommodation the positions of the focal points, principal points and nodal points are all displaced, and accordingly the focal lengths and the refracting power of the eye can be varied within certain limits depending on the power of accommodation, as will be explained in the following section.

147. Accommodation of the Eye.—When the eye is at rest, as when one gazes pensively into space, it is adapted for far

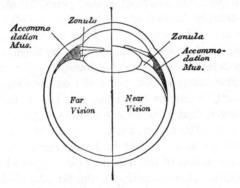

Fig. 193.—Accommodation of the human eye; indicating how the crystalline lens is changed from far vision to near vision.

vision, so that in order to see distinctly objects which are close at hand, an effort has to be made which will be greater in proportion as the object fixed is nearer to the eye. This process whereby the normal eye is enabled to focus on the retina in succession sharp images of objects at different distances is called *accommodation*, and it is this marvelous adaptability of the human eye, together with its mobility, which perhaps more than any other quality entitles it to superiority over the most perfectly constructed artificial optical instruments. The power of accommodation is achieved by changes in the form of the crystalline lens, consisting chiefly in a change in the convexity of the anterior surface, produced through the mechanism of the ciliary muscle. According to the generally accepted theory, so long as the eye is passive, the elastic substance of the lens is held flattened in front by the suspensory ligament; but in the act of accommodation the ciliary muscle contracts, and this is accompanied by a relaxation of the ligament of the lens, which is thereby permitted to bulge forward by virtue of its own elasticity (Fig. 193).

148. Far Point and Near Point of the Eye.—The *far point* of the eye (*punctum remotum*) is that point (**R**) on the axis which is sharply focused at the posterior pole of the eye when the crystalline lens has its least refracting power; it is the point which is seen distinctly when the accommodation is entirely relaxed. On the other hand, the *near point* (or *punctum proximum*) is that point (**P**) on the axis which is seen distinctly when the crystalline lens has its greatest refracting power, that is, when the accommodation is exerted to the utmost. The region of distinct vision within which an object must lie in order that its image can be sharply focused on the retina of the naked eye is comprised between two concentric spherical surfaces, the far point sphere and the near point sphere, described around the center of rotation of the eye (**Z**) with radii equal to **ZR** and **ZP**, respectively. If the far point lies at infinity, as is the case in the normal eye, the far point sphere is identical with the infinitely distant plane of space (*cf.* § 83), as represented in Fig. 194;

whereas the near point sphere will be real and at a finite
distance in front of the eye. In such a case the eye can be
directed towards any point in the field of fixation (§ 146)
lying on or beyond the near point sphere and accommodate

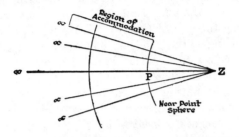

FIG. 194.—Region of accommodation of emmetropic eye.

itself to see this point distinctly.   In a near-sighted eye both
far point and near point are real points lying at finite distances in front of the eye; but the far point of a far-sighted
eye is a "virtual" point lying at a finite distance behind the
eye, and hence an unaided far-sighted eye cannot see distinctly a real object without exerting its accommodation to
a greater or less degree.

**149. Decrease of the Power of Accommodation with
Increasing Age.**—The faculty of accommodation is greatest
in youth and diminishes rapidly with advancing years.
The near point of the eye gradually recedes farther and farther away, which is commonly supposed to be due to a progressive diminution of the elasticity of the crystalline lens.
Thus, at the ages of 10, 20 and 40 years the *punctum proximum* of a normal eye, according to DONDERS, is in front of
the eye at distances from the primary principal point equal
to 7.1, 10 and 22.2 cm., respectively.   When the near point
has retreated to a distance of 22 cm., so that it is no longer
possible to read or write or do "near work" conveniently
without the aid of spectacles, the condition of *presbyopia*
or old-age vision has begun to set in.   Meantime, while the

power of accommodation of the eye thus continually diminishes as the near point recedes farther and farther away,
the position of the far point remains practically fixed until
well after middle life; but between the ages of 55 and 60
years it too begins to separate farther from the eye, and
thereafter both the near point and the far point travel outwards along the axis of the eye, the former, however, constantly gaining on the latter; until at last in extreme old age
the near point actually overtakes the far point, and from
that time until death they remain together, the power of
accommodation having been entirely lost. Both points are
displaced along the axis always in the same direction, that is,
opposite to that of the incident light. For example, the far
point of a normal eye is infinitely distant up to about 55
years of age, whereas ten years later, according to DONDERS,
this point will be about 133 cm. behind the eye, having
moved out through infinity, so to speak, and approached
the eye from behind. At the same age, namely, 65 years,
the near point will also be behind the eye at a distance of
400 cm. At 75 years of age the two points will be together
at a distance of 57.1 cm. behind the eye. Various theories
have been advanced to account for the senile recession of
the far point of the eye. It is probably due to a combination of causes, partly to a change in the form of the lens produced by the increased resistance of the enveloping coat of
the eye-ball and the decreased pressure of the surrounding
tissue, and partly also to senile changes in the lens-substance
itself whereby the "total index" of the lens is lowered in
value.

150. Change of Refracting Power in Accommodation.—
It was remarked above (§ 146) that the positions of the cardinal points of the optical system of the eye are all altered
in the act of accommodation. Thus, for example, in GULL-
STRAND's schematic eye, which is calculated for an adolescent youth, the near point is at a distance $\mathbf{AP} = -10.23$ cm.
from the vertex of the cornea; and for this state of maxi-

mum accommodation the positions of the focal points and principal points are found to be as follows:

$$\mathbf{AF} = -12.397 \text{ mm.}, \quad \mathbf{AF}' = +21.016 \text{ mm.},$$
$$\mathbf{AH} = +\ 1.772 \text{ mm.}, \quad \mathbf{AH}' = +\ 2.086 \text{ mm.};$$

and, accordingly, the focal lengths and the refracting power are:

$$f = +14.169 \text{ mm.}, \quad f' = -18.930 \text{ mm.}, \quad F = +70.57 \text{ dptr.}$$

It will be observed that, whereas the focal points have undergone considerable displacements from their positions in the passive eye, the corresponding displacements of the principal points are less than half a millimeter; and since in most physiological measurements half a millimeter is within the limit of error, we can usually afford to neglect altogether the accommodative displacement of the principal points of the eye, that is, we may regard the positions of the principal points $\mathbf{H}$, $\mathbf{H}'$ as practically fixed and independent of the state of accommodation. This is one reason, among others, why the principal points of the eye have superseded the other cardinal points as points of reference. Their proximity to the cornea is another advantage, inasmuch as measurements referred to them are easily related to an external, visible and tangible point of the eye. In the so-called "reduced eye," which consists of a single spherical refracting surface separating the outside air from the vitreous humor and so placed that its vertex lies at the primary principal point of the schematic eye, the two principal points are, in fact, coincident with each other on the surface of this simplified cornea.

151. Amplitude of Accommodation.—*The far point distance* (a) and the *near point distance* (b) are the distances of the far point and near point, respectively, measured from the primary principal point of the eye; thus, $a = \mathbf{HR}$, $b = \mathbf{HP}$; it being tacitly assumed here that the position of the point $\mathbf{H}$ remains sensibly stationary during accommodation, as was explained above. Each of these distances is to be reckoned negative or positive according as the point in question lies in front of the eye or behind it, respectively. The reciprocals of these magnitudes, namely, $A = 1/a$, $B = 1/b$, are termed the *static refraction* (A), or the refraction of the eye when the accommodation is completely relaxed, and the *dynamic refraction* (B), or the refraction of the eye when the accommodation is exerted to the highest degree. If the distances a and b are given in meters, the reciprocal magnitudes will be expressed in dioptries, as is generally the case.

The *range of accommodation* is defined to be the distance of the near point from the far point, that is, $RP = b - a$; whereas the *amplitude of accommodation* is the value obtained by subtracting algebraically the magnitude of the dynamic refraction from that of the static refraction, thus:

$$\text{Amplitude of Accommodation} = A - B.$$

Imagine a thin convex lens placed in the primary principal plane of the eye with its axis in the same line as the optical axis of the eye, and of such strength that it produces at the far point of the eye an image of the near point; according to the above definition, the amplitude of accommodation of the eye is equal to the refracting power of this lens. For example, in the normal eye at 30 years of age, $a = \infty$, $b = -14.3$ cm., so that the amplitude of accommodation in this case amounts to 7 dptr.; whereas at 60 years of age $a = +200$ cm., $b = -200$ cm., and hence the amplitude of accommodation will have been reduced to 1 dptr.

The distance from the secondary principal point (H') to the posterior pole (B) where the optical axis meets the retina may be regarded as a measure of the length of the eye-axis, especially since the position of H' is sensibly independent of the state of accommodation, as has been explained, (§ 150). If this distance is denoted by a', that is, if we put $a' = H'B$, and if also we put $A' = n'/a'$, where n' denotes the index of refraction of the vitreous humor, then we may write:

$$A' = A + F,$$

where F denotes here the refracting power of the passive, unaccommodated eye. Similarly, if the symbol F_a is employed to denote the refracting power of the eye in its state of maximum accommodation, we shall have:

$$A' = B + F_a.$$

Consequently, we may also say that the power of accommodation $(A - B)$ is equal to the difference $(F_a - F)$ between the greatest and least values of the refracting power of the eye.

152. Various Expressions for the Refraction of the Eye. —The *refraction of the eye* in a given state of accommodation is measured by the reciprocal of the distance from the eye of the axial object-point M for which the eye is accommodated. Thus, if $u = \mathbf{H}M$, $x = \mathbf{F}M$ denote the distances of M from the primary principal point and the primary focal point, respectively, the magnitudes $U = 1/u$ and $X = 1/x$, usually expressed in dioptries, are the measures of the principal point refraction and the focal point refraction. The relation between U and X may be given in terms of the refracting power of the eye (F) when it is accommodated for the object-point M, as follows:

$$U = \frac{F.X}{F - X}, \qquad X = \frac{F.U}{F + U}.$$

If an arbitrary point O on the axis of the eye is selected as the point of reference, and if we put $OM = z$, the refraction of the eye, referred to the point O, will be measured by $Z = 1/z$. If the distances of the points $\mathbf{H}$ and $\mathbf{F}$ from O are denoted by b and g, that is, if $b = O\mathbf{H}$, $g = O\mathbf{F}$, then since $z = u + b = x + g$, we can obtain also the following useful relations between U, X and Z in terms of b and g:

$$U = \frac{Z}{1 - b.Z} = \frac{X}{1 - (b-g)X};$$

$$X = \frac{Z}{1 - g.Z} = \frac{U}{1 + (b-g)U};$$

$$Z = \frac{U}{1 + b.U} = \frac{X}{1 + g.X}.$$

153. Emmetropia and Ametropia.—When the static refraction of the eye is equal to zero $(A = 0)$, that is, when the far point (**R**) is infinitely distant, the eye is said to be *emmetropic*. If in the equation $A'=A+F$, we put $A=0$, we obtain $A'=F$, which therefore may be said to be the condition of emmetropia. Here F denotes the refracting power of the eye when accommodation is entirely relaxed. In emmetropia, therefore, the second focal point (**F'**) of the passive eye lies on the retina at the posterior pole (**B**);

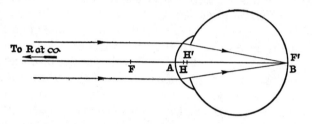

Fig. 195.—Diagram of emmetropic eye.

so that in a passive emmetropic eye incident parallel rays are converged to a focus on the retina, as represented in Fig. 195, and the length of the eye-axis is $a'=-f'$. The normal position of the far point is to be regarded as at infinity; and in this sense an emmetropic eye is a normal eye, although, strictly speaking, an emmetropic eye may at the same time be abnormal in various ways.

On the other hand, if the static refraction of the eye is different from zero $(A{\neq}0)$, that is, when the far point (**R**) is not infinitely distant, the eye is said to be *ametropic* Thus, the condition of *ametropia* may be said to be characterized by the fact that the refracting power (F) of the unaccommodated eye is not equal to A', which is equivalent to saying that the length of the eye-axis (a') is numerically different from the value of the second focal length (f'). In other words, the second focal point (**F'**) of an ametropic eye in a state of repose does not fall on the retina.

Two general divisions of ametropia are distinguished depending, on whether the far point (**R**) lies on one side or the other of the primary principal point (**H**). Thus, if $A<0$, that is, if the far point lies at a finite distance in front of the eye, the ametropia in this case is called *myopia* (Fig. 196). In a myopic eye in a state of repose the second focal point

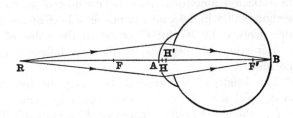

Fig. 196.—Ametropic eye: myopia.

(**F′**) lies in front of the retina (in the vitreous humor), so that parallel incident rays will be brought to a focus before reaching the retina. On the other hand, if $A>0$, the far point will lie at a finite distance beyond (or behind) the

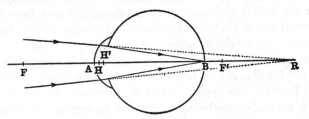

Fig. 197.—Ametropic eye: hypermetropia.

eye, and this form of ametropia is known as *hypermetropia* (Fig. 197). In a hypermetropic eye in a state of repose the second focal point (**F′**) falls beyond the retina, so that incident parallel rays arrive at the retina before coming to a focus. A myopic eye cannot focus for a distant object without the aid of a glass, and it lacks therefore an important part of the capacity of an emmetropic eye. On the other hand, a hypermetropic eye must make an effort of accommodation each time in order to focus on the retina the image of a real object; which frequently produces various troubles, sometimes very annoying. Accordingly, both conditions included under the general name of ametropia are disadvantageous for practical vision.

Theoretically, ametropia may be considered as due to some abnormality in the values of one or of both of the magnitudes denoted by A' and F' on which the value of the static refraction (A) depends; so that the following cases are possible:

(1) The length of the eye-ball (a') may be too great (axial myopia, $a' > -f'$) or too small (axial hypermetropia, $a' < -f'$), whereas the refracting power (F) is normal. This, by far the most common, type is known as *axial ametropia*.

(2) On the other hand, while the length of the eye-ball may be normal, the magnitude of the refracting power (F) may be abnormally great or small. In general, this form of ametropia, which is comparatively rare, is due to abnormal curvatures of the refracting surfaces (*curvature ametropia*). Or the indices of refraction of the eye-media may have abnormal values (*indicial ametropia*). Here also may be mentioned the condition known as *aphakia* produced by the extraction of the crystalline lens in the operation for cataract.

(3) Finally, it may happen that the refracting power and the length of the eye-ball are both abnormal. In fact, these two anomalies might exist together in exactly the degree necessary to counteract each other, so that, in spite of its abnormalities, the eye in such a case would be emmetropic.

In the case of axial ametropia, the relation between the static refraction (A) and the length (l) of the eye-ball is given by the following formula:

$$l = \mathbf{AB} = \mathbf{AH}' + \frac{n'}{A+F} \, ;$$

and if the values for GULLSTRAND's schematic eye (§ 146) are substituted in this formula, it may be written as follows:

$$l = 1.602 + \frac{1336}{A+58.64} \text{ millimeters.}$$

According to this formula, the length of the eye varies from about 21.07 mm. in extreme axial hypermetropia (A = +10 dptr.) to about 36.18 mm. in case of the highest degree of axial myopia (A = −20 dptr.). The length of an axially emmetropic eye (A=0) is 24.38 mm. The length of GULL-

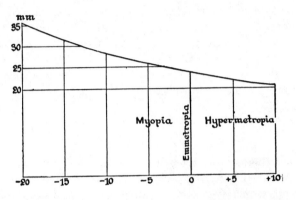

FIG. 198.—Curve showing connection between the length of the eye-axis and the static refraction.

STRAND's schematic eye is 24.01 mm., and hence this eye has 1 dptr. of hypermetropia (A = +1 dptr.). The accompanying diagram (Fig. 198) exhibits graphically the relation between the magnitudes denoted by l and A. The heights of the ordinates indicate the axial length of the eye-ball in millimeters for values of the static refraction of the eye comprised between −20 and +10 dioptries.

154. Correction Eye-Glasses.—When a spherical spectacle lens is placed in front of the passive, unaccommodated eye, with the axis of the lens in the same straight line as the optical axis of the eye, there will be a certain axial point M whose image in the lens will fall at the far point (**R**) of the eye; and hence the eye looking through the lens will see distinctly the image of an object placed at M. If the positions of the principal points of the lens are designated by H_1 and H_1', and if we put

$$u_1 = 1/U_1 = H_1M, \quad u_1' = 1/U_1' = H_1'\mathbf{R},$$

then

$$U_1' = U_1 + F_1,$$

where F_1 denotes the refracting power of the lens. Let the distance of the primary principal point ($\mathbf{H}$) of the eye from the secondary principal point (H_1') of the lens be denoted by c, that is, $c = H_1'\mathbf{H}$; then since $a = u_1' - c$, where a denotes the far point distance of the eye, the following expression for the static refraction ($A = 1/a$) may be derived immediately:

$$A = \frac{U_1 + F_1}{1 - c(U_1 + F_1)}.$$

In case the axial object-point M is infinitely far away, the lens is called a *correction-glass*, because it enables the passive ametropic eye to see distinctly a very distant object on the axis of the lens, so that to this extent the lens interposed in front of the eye endows it with the characteristic faculty of an unaccommodated, naked, emmetropic eye. The condition that M shall be infinitely distant is $U_1 = 0$; and hence the relation between the static refraction of the eye and the refracting power of a correction-glass is given as follows:

$$A = \frac{F_1}{1 - c.F_1} \qquad F_1 = \frac{A}{1 + c.A}.$$

If the distance c between the correction-glass and the eye is neglected entirely, then $F_1 = A$, that is, the power of the correction-glass is approximately equal to the static refraction of the eye. The distance c, which must be expressed in meters in case the magnitudes denoted by F_1 and A are given in dioptries, is always a comparatively small magnitude, which in actual spectacle glasses is comprised between 0.008 and 0.016 m.; so that if, without neglecting c entirely, we neglect only the second and higher powers thereof, the formulæ above may be written in the following convenient approximate forms:

$$A = F_1(1 + c.F_1), \qquad F_1 = A(1 - c.A);$$

which for nearly all practical purposes will be found to be sufficiently accurate.

FIG. 199.—Correction of myopia with concave spectacle-glass.

The condition that a spectacle-lens shall be a correction-glass may be expressed simply by saying that *the second focal point* (F_1') *of the glass must coincide with the far point* (**R**) *of the eye*. Thus, in case of a myopic eye the correction-glass

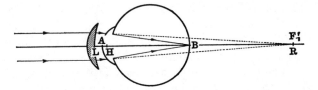

FIG. 200.—Correction of hypermetropia with convex spectacle-glass.

will be concave (Fig. 199) and in case of a hypermetropic eye it will be convex (Fig. 200).

Instead of describing the power of a spectacle glass by means of its refracting power, it is really more convenient and logical to express it in terms of its *vertex refraction* (*V*), as defined in § 128. If the vertex of the lens which lies next the eye is designated by L, and if the distance of the eye from the glass is denoted by *k*, that is, if we put *k* = L**H**, then, since the points designated by F_1' and **R** must be coincident,

$v = a + k$, where v denotes the "back focus" of the lens, that is, $v = 1/V = \mathrm{LF_1'} = \mathrm{LR}$; and hence:

$$A = \frac{V}{1 - k.V}, \qquad V = \frac{A}{1 + k.A},$$

or approximately:

$$A = V(1 + k.V), \qquad V = A(1 - k.A).$$

It may be seen from the above formulæ how the power of a correction-glass depends essentially on the location of the glass in front of the eye. The distance k, being referred to a tangible, external point of the glass, is more easily measured than the interval denoted by c.

155. Visual Angle.—The apparent size of an object, as was explained in § 10, is measured by the visual angle ω which it subtends at the eye; thus, if the vertex of this angle is designated by O and if $y = \mathrm{MQ}$ denotes a diameter of the object at right angles to the line of vision, the apparent size of the object in the direction of this dimension is $\omega = \angle \mathrm{MOQ}$. Accordingly, if the distance of the object from the eye is denoted by z, that is, if $z = \mathrm{OM}$, then $\tan \omega = y/z$. As the immobile eye looking in a fixed direction can see distinctly only that comparatively small portion of the object whose image falls on the sensitive part of the retina in the immediate vicinity of the *fovea centralis* (§ 145), the rays concerned in the production of the retinal image in this so-called case of "indirect vision" may be regarded as paraxial rays. Accordingly, the value of the angle ω in radians may be substituted here for the $\tan \omega$, so that we may write:

$$\omega = y/z = y.Z,$$

where $Z = 1/z$. On the assumption that y is reckoned as positive, a negative value of the angle ω indicates that the object is real and therefore in front of the point O where the eye is supposed to be.

The exact meaning to be attached to the visual angle ω will depend, of course, on the precise location with respect to the eye of the vertex of this angle. To be sure, so long as the object is quite remote from the eye, as is often the case,

it will not generally be necessary to define particularly the
position of the vertex O of the visual angle. For example,
to take a somewhat extreme instance, the apparent size of
the moon will not be sensibly altered by removing the vertex of the visual angle as much as a mile or more away from
the eye. And, in general, provided the object is not less
than, say, 10 meters away, it will be sufficient to know that
the vertex of the visual angle is in the eye without specifying
its position more exactly. On the other hand, especially
when the eye has to exert its power of accommodation in
order to focus the object, it is sometimes a matter of much
importance to define the visual angle with the utmost precision. In such a case several meanings of this term are to
be specially distinguished. For example, when the vertex
of the visual angle is at the primary principal point of the
eye, it is called the *principal point angle* ($\omega_H = \angle \mathbf{MHQ}$), so
that we may write:

$$\omega_H = y/u = y.U,$$

where $u = 1/U = \mathbf{HM}$ denotes the distance of the object from
the primary principal point. Similarly, the so-called *focal
point angle* ($\omega_F = \angle \mathbf{MFQ}$) is the angle subtended by the
object at the primary focal point of the eye; and hence:

$$\omega_F = y/x = y.X,$$

where $x = 1/X = \mathbf{FM}$ denotes the distance of the object from
the primary focal point of the eye.

According to the definitions of these angles and the relations between the magnitudes denoted by X, U and Z, as
given in § 152, we may write therefore:

$$\omega : \omega_H : \omega_F = Z : U : X$$
$$= 1 : (1+b.U) : (1+g.X)$$
$$= (1-b.Z) : 1 : (1-X/\mathbf{F})$$
$$= (1-g.Z) : (1+U/\mathbf{F}) : 1;$$

where $\mathbf{F}$ denotes here the refracting power of the eye when
it is accommodated for the point M.

The apparent size of an object may be measured also at
other points of the eye, for example, at the center of the

entrance-pupil, at the anterior nodal point, at the center of rotation, etc. The center of rotation or eye-pivot is the point of reference in the estimate of the apparent size of an object in the case of ordinary so-called "direct vision" with the mobile eye, when the gaze is directed in quick succession to the different parts of an extended object. Especially, in viewing an image through an optical instrument, it is nearly always desirable, if practicable, to adjust the eye in such a position that the center of rotation coincides with the center of the exit-pupil of the instrument, so as to command as large an extent of the field of view of the image-space as possible. Anyone who has ever tried to look through a key-hole in a door will realize how the field of view would have been widened if the eye could have been placed in the hole itself.

156. Size of Retinal Image.—If the eye is accommodated to see an object y situated at a distance u $(=1/U)$ from its primary principal point, the size of the image (y') formed on the retina is given by the relation:

$$y.U = y'.A',$$

where $A' = n'/a'$ denotes the reciprocal of the reduced length of the eye-axis measured from the secondary principal point of the eye. Since $y.U = \omega_H$ (§ 155), the above equation may be put in the following form:

$$\frac{y'}{\omega_H} = \frac{a'}{n'}.$$

Since the positions of the principal points remain sensibly stationary in the act of accommodation (§ 150), the reduced length of the eye-axis (a'/n') may be considered as constant in the same individual. And hence the peculiar significance of the principal point angle consists in the fact that, according to this formula, this angle (ω_H) may be taken as a measure of the size of the retinal image (y') which is independent of the state of accommodation of the eye. Thus, for a given individual, all objects which have the same apparent size as measured at the principal point of the eye will produce retinal images of equal size.

On the other hand, since $y'.F = y.X = \omega_F$ (§ 155), it appears that, for a given value of the refracting power (F), the size of the image on the retina of the eye is proportional to the focal point angle. And since the variations of the refracting power are, generally speaking, independent of axial ametropia (§ 153), the focal point angle will be particularly useful in comparing the apparent size of an object as seen by different individuals under the same external conditions.

157. Apparent Size of an Object seen Through an Optical Instrument.—Let the principal points of the optical instrument be designated by H, H′ (Fig. 201); and for the

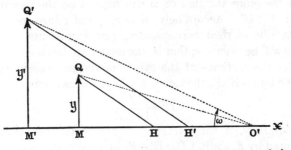
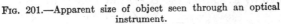

FIG. 201.—Apparent size of object seen through an optical instrument.

sake of simplicity, let us assume that the instrument is surrounded by air so that the straight lines HQ, H′Q′ joining the principal points with corresponding points of object and image will be parallel; and let $y = MQ$, $y' = M'Q'$ denote the linear magnitudes of object and image, respectively. Let the distance of the image from the eye be denoted by $z = O'M'$, where O′ designates the position of the eye on the axis. Then the apparent size of the image will be

$$\omega = y'.Z,$$

where $\omega = \angle M'O'Q'$ (expressed here in radians) and $Z = 1/z$. The angle ω may be increased by reducing the distance between the image and the eye, that is, by increasing Z; but this distance cannot be diminished below the near point distance of the eye, because then distinct vision would not be possible for the naked eye.

If the distances of object and image from the principal points are denoted by u and u', that is, if $u = $ HM, $u' = $ H'M', then

$$y'.U' = y.U,$$

where $U = 1/u$, $U' = 1/u'$; and hence

$$\omega = y.Z.\frac{U}{U'} \,.$$

In general (except when the rays undergo an odd number of reflections), the sign of Z as here defined will be negative, and therefore the sign of ω will depend on the sign of the ratio $U : U'$. Accordingly, if object and image lie on the same side of their corresponding principal points, the sign of ω will be negative, that is, the image will be erect.

Let the distance of the eye from the instrument be denoted by $c = $ H'O'; then since $u' = c + z$, we may write:

$$U' = \frac{Z}{1 + c.Z} \,.$$

Accordingly, if the refracting power of the instrument is denoted by F, so that $U = U' - F$, we may write also:

$$U = -\frac{F - Z(1 - c.F)}{1 + c.Z} \,.$$

Introducing these expressions, we obtain therefore the following formula for the apparent size of the image:

$$\omega = -y\{F - Z(1 - c.F)\} \,.$$

Thus, we see that the apparent size of the image may be varied in one of two ways, either by changing the position of the eye (that is, by varying c) or else by displacing the object so that Z is varied. There are two cases of special practical importance, namely: (1) When the eye is adjusted so that $1 - c.F = 0$, and (2) When the object is focused so that $Z = 0$. In both cases the second term inside the large brackets vanishes, and hence $\omega = -y.F$. The condition

$c = 1/F$ means that the eye is placed at the second focal point (F') of the instrument (which might easily be practicable if the optical system were convergent); so that under such circumstances the apparent size of the image would be the same for all positions of the object, because evidently the highest point (Q') of the image will always lie on the straight line which crosses the axis at the second focal point at the constant angle $\theta = -y.F$. On the other hand, the condition $Z = 0$ means simply that the object lies in the first focal plane of the instrument. Now this is the natural adjustment for a normal, unaccommodated, emmetropic eye, because then the rays flow into the eye in cylindrical bundles. This is the reason why the image produced by the object-glass of a telescope or microscope is usually focused in the primary focal plane of the eye-piece or ocular. Accordingly, when $Z = 0$, the apparent size of the image will be independent of the position of the eye.

An experienced observer who wishes to obtain the best results with an optical instrument will ordinarily adjust it to his eye in such a way that the image can be seen distinctly without his having to make an effort of accommodation. This will be the case if the image is formed at the far point (**R**) of the eye (§ 148). If, therefore, the static refraction of the eye is denoted by A (§ 151), then (assuming that the point O' in Fig. 201 is coincident with the anterior principal point of the eye) we may put $Z = A$; and hence the apparent size of an object as seen in an optical instrument by an eye with relaxed accommodation is given by the expression:

$$\omega_H = -y\left\{ F - A(1 - c.F) \right\}.$$

Thus, it is evident how the apparent size of the image depends not only on the refracting power of the instrument, but essentially also on the adjustment and idiosyncrasies of the eye of the individual who looks through it.

It may be remarked that these formulæ have been derived on the tacit assumption that the eye is at rest, and consequently only a small portion of the external field is sharply in focus at the sensitive part of the retina. Otherwise, we should have had to write tanω instead of ω; nor should we have been justified in assuming that the effective rays were paraxial. If the eye turns in its socket to inspect the image, the apparent size of the image will depend essentially on the angular movement of the eye, and in this case the visual angle must be measured at the center of rotation of the eye. These are considerations that are too often overlooked in discussions of this kind.

158. Magnifying Power of an Optical Instrument Used in Conjunction with the Eye.—An object may be so remote that its details are indistinguishable, or, on the other hand, it may be so close to the eye that not even by the greatest effort of accommodation can a sharp image of it be focused on the retina. Under such circumstances one has recourse to the aid of a suitable optical instrument whereby the object is magnified to such an extent that the parts of it which were obscure or entirely invisible to the naked eye will be revealed to view. The *magnifying power* is usually expressed by an abstract number M, which in the case of an optical instrument on the order of a microscope is defined to be *the ratio of the apparent size of the image as seen in the instrument to the apparent size of the object as it would appear at the so-called "distance of distinct vision."* This latter term is a somewhat unfortunate form of expression for several reasons, not only because the distance at which an object is ordinarily placed in order to be seen distinctly is different for different persons, but because the same person, according to the extent of his power of accommodation, usually possesses the ability of seeing distinctly objects at widely different distances. The expression appears to have arisen from a confusion of ideas, and its origin may probably be traced to the fact that even nowadays many people have difficulty in conceiving how the eye can be "focused for infinity," although, indeed, as has been explained, that is to be regarded as the natural state of the normal eye in repose. However, the phrase has become too deeply rooted in optical literature ever to be eradicated, and no harm will be done by continuing to use it, provided it is not taken literally, but is considered merely as the designation of a more or less arbitrary conventional projection-distance. Accordingly, if the so-called "distance of distinct vision" is denoted by l, the apparent size of the object (y) as seen at this distance from the eye will be $-y/l$, and hence if the apparent size of the image in the instrument is denoted by ω, the magnifying power, as above defined, will be:

$$M = -\frac{\omega}{y} \cdot l .$$

The actual value of this conventional distance l is usually taken as 10 inches or 25 centimeters, which is large enough for the convenient accommodation of most human beings who are not already past the prime of life and yet not so large that the size of the image on the retina differs much from its greatest dimensions. If distances are all measured in meters, the conventional value of the magnifying power will be given, therefore, by the formula:

$$M = -\frac{\omega}{4y} .$$

The explanation of the minus sign in front of the fraction is to be found in the mode of reckoning the visual angle ω, which, as we have pointed out (§ 157), is negative in case the image of the object y is erect, as, for example, with an ordinary convex lens used as a magnifying glass. Thus, according to the above formula, *a positive value of the magnifying power means magnification without inversion.* Ordinarily, what is meant by the magnifying power of an optical instrument is the value of this abstract number M; which gives the ratio of the sizes of the retinal images when an emmetropic eye views one and the same object, first, in the instrument without effort of accommodation, and then without the instrument with an accommodation of four dioptries.

If the expression for the visual angle ω which was obtained in § 157 is introduced here, we shall derive, therefore, the following formula for the magnifying power (M) in terms of the refracting power (F) of the instrument, the distance (c) of the eye from the instrument, and the distance ($z = 1/Z$) of the image (y') from the eye:

$$M = l\{F - Z(1 - c.F)\}.$$

This expression is really a measure of the *individual magnifying power*, since it involves not merely the instrument itself but the characteristic peculiarities of the eye of the observer. In order to obtain a measure of the *absolute magnifying power* of the instrument, the second term inside the large brackets must be made to vanish. Thus, if the object is placed in the primary focal plane, so that the image is infinitely distant, then $Z = 0$, and now $M = l.F$ denotes the absolute magnifying power. If $l = 0.25$ meter, then $F = 4M$; and usually, therefore, when we say that the magnifying power of a lens or microscope is M, this means simply that its refracting power is equal to 4M dioptries.

If the image in the instrument is formed at the "distance of distinct vision" (l), then $Z = -1/l$, and

$$M = 1 + (l - c)F.$$

The distance (c) between the instrument and the eye is usually small in comparison with l, so that it is often entirely neglected. Assuming that ($l - c$) is positive, we may say that in a convergent optical system ($F > 0$), the object will appear magnified ($M > 1$); whereas in a divergent optical system ($F < 0$), the object appears to be diminished in size ($M < 1$).

In order to avoid the use of an arbitrary projection-distance (l), ABBE proposed to define the magnifying power as *the ratio of the apparent size* (ω) *of the image in the instrument to the actual size* (y) *of the object* (compare with ABBE's definition of focal length, § 122); so that if this ratio is denoted by P, then

$$P = -\frac{\omega}{y}.$$

This measure of the magnifying power is not an abstract number like M, but a quantity of the same physical dimensions as the refracting power of the instrument. The two definitions are connected by the simple relation

$$M = l.P;$$

so that if we put $l = 0.25$ m., the value of P will be obtained by multiplying M by the number four ($P = 4M$). Thus, for example, in the case of a convex lens of refracting power F used as a magnifying glass, if the object is placed in the first focal plane, we have $P = F$.

159. Magnifying Power of a Telescope.—In the case of a telescope, which is an instrument for magnifying the apparent size of a distant object, neither of the definitions of magnifying power given in the foregoing section is applicable. An infinitely distant object (like the moon, for example) can be seen distinctly by an emmetropic eye without any effort of accommodation, but its apparent size may be so minute that the distinguishing features cannot be made out by the naked eye. This same eye looking at the object through a telescope will see an infinitely distant image of it, but presented to the eye under a larger visual angle, so that it appears magnified. Essentially, a telescope may be regarded as a combination of two optical systems, one of which—the part pointed towards the object—is a convergent system, generally of relatively long focus and large aperture (so as to intercept a large quantity of light), called the object-glass; while the other, composed of the lenses next the eye, and called therefore the ocular or eye-piece, may be a convergent or divergent system depending on the type of telescope. The object-glass which is at one end of a large tube forms a real inverted image of the object in its second focal plane or not far from it; and this image is inspected through the ocular, which is usually fixed in a smaller tube inserted in the larger one so that the focus can be adjusted to suit different eyes and different circumstances. A simple schematic telescope may be regarded as composed of two thin lenses, one of which, of focal length f_1 (refracting power F_1) acts as the object-glass while the other, of focal length f_2 (refracting power F_2) performs the part of the ocular. When the telescope is adjusted for an emmetropic, unaccommodated eye, *the second focal point* (F_1') *of the object-glass coincides with the first focal point* (F_2) *of the ocular;* and hence the focal length of the entire system is infinite $(f = \infty$ or $F = 0)$, that is, the system is afocal or telescopic (§ 125). In this case the telescope is said to be in normal adjustment.

The first telescope appears to have been invented by one of two Dutch spectacle-makers named ZACHARIAS JANSEN and FRANZ LIPPERSHEY (*circa* 1608). GALILEO (1564–1642), having heard of this Dutch toy, was led to experiment

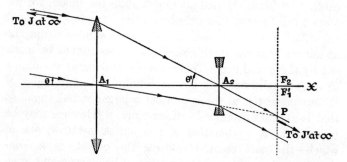

FIG. 202.—Diagram of simple Dutch or Galilean telescope.

with a combination of two lenses and he soon succeeded (1609) in making a telescope with which he made a number of renowned astronomical discoveries. The so-called *Dutch* or *Galilean telescope*, represented schematically in Fig. 202, consists of a large convex object-glass (A_1) combined with a small concave eye-piece (A_2), which intercepts the converging rays before they come to a focus and adapts them to suit the eye of the observer. The other type of telescope (Fig. 203) is composed of two convex lenses. It is called the *astronomical telescope* or *Kepler telescope*, because the idea

occurred first to JOHN KEPLER (1611); but the first instrument of this kind was made by the celebrated Jesuit father,
CHRISTIAN SCHEINER (1615), who also conceived the idea
of using a third lens to erect the image as is done in the so-
called *terrestrial telescope*.

If the telescope is in normal adjustment, then from each
point J of the infinitely distant object there will issue a bundle

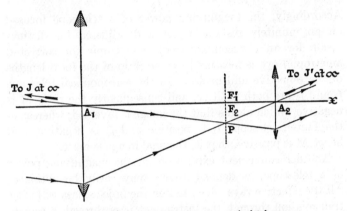

FIG. 203.—Diagram of simple astronomical telescope.

of parallel rays whose inclination to the axis of the telescope
may be denoted by θ.   Falling on the object-glass, these
rays are converged to a focus at a point P lying in the common focal plane of object-glass and eye-piece; and consequently they will emerge from the eye-piece and enter the
eye as a bundle of parallel rays proceeding from the infinitely distant image-point J' in a direction which makes an
angle θ' with the axis. The slope-angles θ and θ' have
a constant relation to each other, as may easily be shown;
for from the right triangles $F_1'A_1P$ and F_2A_2P (Figs. 202
and 203), where $A_1F_1' = A_1F_2 = f_1$, $\angle F_1'A_1P = \theta$, and $F_2A_2 =$
$F_1'A_2 = f_2$, $\angle F_2A_2P = \theta'$, we obtain immediately:

$$\frac{\tan \theta'}{\tan \theta} = -\frac{f_1}{f_2} = \text{constant.}$$

Now the angles denoted here by θ and θ' are the measures of the apparent sizes of corresponding portions of the infinitely distant object and image, and the ratio of these angles (or of their tangents) is defined to be the *magnifying power of the telescope;* so that if this ratio is denoted by M, we shall have:

$$M = -\frac{f_1}{f_2}.$$

Accordingly, the magnifying power of a telescope focused on an infinitely distant object and adjusted for distinct vision for an unaccommodated, emmetropic (or corrected ametropic) eye is measured by the ratio of the focal lengths of the objective and ocular. In the astronomical telescope f_1 and f_2 are both positive, and consequently the ratio M is negative, which means that the image is inverted; whereas in the Dutch telescope f_1 is positive and f_2 is negative, and hence M is positive, that is, the final image is erect.

Another convenient expression for the magnifying power of a telescope, as defined above, may easily be obtained. All the effective rays which fall on the object-glass will after transmission through the instrument pass through a certain circular aperture called the *eye-ring* (or RAMSDEN circle), which is the image of the object-glass in the ocular. If the object-glass is brightly illuminated (for example, if the telescope is pointed towards the bright sky), this image appears as a luminous disk floating in the air not far from the ocular and can easily be perceived by placing the eye at a suitable distance. In the astronomical telescope the eye-ring is a real image which can be received on a screen, and in this instrument it usually acts as the exit-pupil (§ 134). In the case of the Dutch telescope the eye-ring is a virtual image on the other side of the ocular from the eye; and generally its effect is to limit the field of view in the image-space, that is, its office is that of the exit-port of the system (§§ 137, 138). Now if the telescope is in normal adjustment, then the distance of the ocular from the object-glass is equal to the algebraic sum (f_1+f_2) of the focal lengths of the two components; and it may easily be shown that

$$M = -\frac{f_1}{f_2} = \frac{\text{diameter of object-glass}}{\text{diameter of eye-ring}}.$$

The advantage of this latter form of expression is to be found in the fact that even if the telescope is not in normal adjustment, it may still be considered in a certain sense as a measure of the magnifying power of the instrument. Suppose, for example, that the optical system is not telescopic, so that the interval between the second focal point (F_1') of the object-glass and the first focal point (F_2) of the ocular is not negligible, as frequently happens in focusing the eye-piece to suit the eye of the individual, especially if the object itself is not infinitely distant. Consider a ray which is directed originally from the extremity of the object towards a point O on the axis of the telescope and which emerges so as to enter the eye at the conjugate point O'. If the angles which the ray makes with the axis at O and O' are denoted by θ and θ', respectively, then the ratio $\tan\theta' : \tan\theta$ will be a measure of the magnifying power of the telescope for this adjustment and position of the eye. But according to the SMITH-HELMHOLTZ formula (§§ 86 and 118), since the telescope is surrounded by the same medium on both sides, we shall have here:

$$\tan\theta' : \tan\theta = y : y',$$

where y and y' denote the linear magnitudes of an object and its image in conjugate transversal planes at O and O' (the planes of the pupils). Now if the point O' is at the center of the eye-ring, the point O will lie at the center of the object-glass, and the ratio $y : y'$ will be equal to the ratio of the diameters of object-glass and eye-ring. Hence, *provided the eye is placed at the eye-ring*, the magnifying power of the telescope will be

$$M = \frac{\text{diameter of object-glass}}{\text{diameter of eye-ring}}.$$

In an astronomical telescope the best adjustment for commanding a wide extent of the field of view is to place the eye with its center of rotation at the center of the eye-ring, but in a Dutch telescope this is not practicable, because the eye-ring is not accessible.

In order to obtain a general formula for the magnifying power of a telescope, let us fix our attention on the inverted image of the object which is formed by the object-glass. If $u = 1/U$ denotes the distance of the object from the object-glass and if q denotes the linear size of the image, the apparent size of the object as seen from the center of the object-glass will be

$$\tan\theta = q(U + F_1),$$

where F_1 denotes the refracting power of the object-glass. On the other hand, according to the formula deduced in § 157, the apparent size of the image seen in the telescope will be

$$\tan\theta' = -q\{F_2 - Z(1 - c.F_2)\} ,$$

where F_2 denotes the refracting power of the ocular, $z = 1/Z$ denotes the distance of the image in the ocular from the eye, and c denotes the distance of the eye from the ocular itself (or from its second principal point). Accordingly, we obtain the following expression for the magnifying power of the telescope:

$$M = \frac{\tan\theta'}{\tan\theta} = -\frac{F_2 - Z(1 - c.F_2)}{U + F_1} ,$$

which is applicable to all cases. If the object is infinitely distant, then $U = 0$; and if the telescope is in normal adjustment, then the image is also infinitely distant, that is, $Z = 0$, and $M = -F_2/F_1$.

PROBLEMS

1. If the refracting power of a correction spectacle-glass is +10 dptr., and if the distance of the anterior principal point of the eye from the second principal point of the glass is 12 mm., find the static refraction of the eye.

Ans. +11.36 dptr.

2. Take the refracting power of the eye equal to 58.64 dptr., the distances of the principal points from the vertex of the cornea as 1.348 and 1.602 mm., and the index of refraction of the vitreous humor equal to 1.336. If the refracting power of a correction spectacle-glass, whose second principal point is 14 mm. from the anterior principal point of the eye, is −5.37 dptr., show that the total length of the eye-ball is 26.5 mm.

3. In GULLSTRAND's schematic eye, with accommodation relaxed, the distance from the vertex of the cornea to the point where the optical axis meets the retina is 24 mm. The other data are the same as those given in No. 2 above. Find the position of the far point and determine the static refraction.

Ans. The far point is 99.34 cm. from the vertex of the cornea, and the static refraction is +1.008 dptr.

4. In GULLSTRAND's schematic eye in its state of maximum accommodation the distances of the principal points from the vertex of the cornea are 1.7719 and 2.0857 mm., and the refracting power is 70.5747 dptr. The length of the eye-ball is 24 mm., as stated in No. 3. Find the position of the near point and determine the dynamic refraction of the eye.

Ans. The near point is 10.23 cm. from the vertex of the cornea; the dynamic refraction is −9.609 dptr. Accordingly, with the aid of the result obtained in No. 3, we obtain for the amplitude of accommodation 10.62 dptr.

5. Taking the refracting power of the eye as equal to 59 dptr., show that the size of the retinal image of an object

1 meter high at a distance of 10 meters from the eye will be 1.7 mm.

6. The apparent size of a distant air-ship is one minute of arc. Taking the refracting power of the eye as equal to 58.64 dptr., show that the size of the image on the retina will be 0.00495 mm.

7. What is the magnifying power of a convex lens of focal length 5 cm.? Ans. 5.

8. A myope of 10 dptr. uses a convex lens of focal length 5 cm. as a magnifying glass. Find the individual magnifying power, neglecting the distance of the eye from the glass. Ans. $7\frac{1}{2}$.

9. In the preceding example, what will be the individual magnifying power of the same glass in the case of an hypermetrope of 10 dptr.? Ans. $2\frac{1}{2}$.

10. A certain person cannot see distinctly objects which are nearer his eye than 20 cm. or farther than 60 cm. Within what limits of distance from his eye must a concave mirror of focal length 15 cm. be placed in order that he may be able to focus sharply the image of his eye as seen in the mirror?

Ans. In order to see a real image of his eye, the distance of the mirror must be between 43.03 cm. and 78.54 cm.; in order to see a virtual image, the distance of the mirror must be between 6.97 cm. and 11.46 cm.

11. The magnifying power of a telescope 12 inches long is equal to 8: determine the focal lengths of object-glass and eye-glass (1) when it is an astronomical telescope and (2) when it is a GALILEO's telescope.

Ans. (1) $f_1 = +10\frac{2}{3}$, $f_2 = +1\frac{1}{3}$ inches; (2) $f_1 = +13\frac{5}{7}$, $f_2 = -1\frac{5}{7}$ inches.

12. The focal lengths of the object-glass and eye-glass of an astronomical telescope are f_1 and f_2, and their diameters are $2h_1$ and $2h_2$, respectively. Show that the radius of the stop which will cut off the "ragged edge" (§ 138) is equal to

$$\frac{f_1 h_2 - f_2 h_1}{f_1 + f_2}.$$

13. A telescope is pointed at an infinitely distant object, and the eye-piece is focused so that the image is formed at the distance l of distinct vision of the eye. If the distance of the eye from the eye-piece is neglected, show that the magnifying power is $M = -f_1(l+f_2)/l.f_2$, where f_1, f_2 denote the focal lengths of the object-glass and eye-glass.

14. A RAMSDEN ocular consists of two thin convex lenses each of focal length a separated by an interval equal to $2a/3$. Show that the magnifying power of an astronomical telescope furnished with a RAMSDEN ocular is $4f_1/3a$, where f_1 denotes the focal length of the object-glass.

15. The object-glass of an astronomical telescope has a focal length of 50 inches, and the focal length of each lens of the RAMSDEN ocular is 2 inches. The distance between the two lenses in the ocular is $\frac{4}{3}$ inch. Show that the distance between the object-glass and the first lens of the ocular is 50.5 inches, and that the magnifying power is equal to $\frac{100}{3}$.

16. If a GALILEO's telescope is in normal adjustment, show that the angular diameter of the field of the image as measured at the vertex of the concave eye-glass is $2\tan\gamma' = -2h_1/(f_1+f_2)$, where h_1 denotes the radius of the object-glass and f_1, f_2 denote the focal lengths of object-glass and eye-glass.

17. The focal length of the object-glass and eye-glass of an astronomical telescope are 36 and 9 inches, respectively. If the object is infinitely distant and if the eye is placed in the eye-ring at a distance of 9 inches from the image, show that the magnifying power is equal to 3.

18. The magnifying power of a simple astronomical telescope in normal adjustment is M, and the focal length of the object-glass is f_1. Show that if the eye-glass is pushed in a distance x and the eye placed in the eye-ring, the magnifying power will be diminished by $x.M/f_1$.

19. An astronomical telescope is pointed towards the sun, and a real image of the sun is obtained on a screen placed

beyond the eye-lens at a distance d from it. If the diameter of this image is denoted by $2b$, and if the apparent diameter of the sun is denoted by 2θ, show that the magnifying power of the telescope is $M = b.\cot \theta / d$.

20. The eye is placed at a distance c from the eye-glass of a GALILEO's telescope in normal adjustment. The length of the telescope as measured from the object-glass to the eye-glass is denoted by d, the radius of the object-glass is denoted by h_1, and the radius of the pupil of the eye is denoted by g (it being assumed that g is less than the radius of the eye-glass). Show that the semi-angular diameters of the three portions of the field of view on the image-side are given by the following expressions:

$$\tan \gamma_1' = -\frac{h_1 - g.M}{d + c.M}, \quad \tan \gamma' = -\frac{h_1}{d + c.M}, \quad \tan \gamma_2' = -\frac{h_1 + g.M}{d + c.M},$$

where M denotes the magnifying power of the telescope.

CHAPTER XIV

DISPERSION AND ACHROMATISM

160. Dispersion by a Prism.—When a beam of sunlight is admitted into a dark chamber through a small circular hole A (Fig. 204) in the window shutter, a round spot of white light will be formed on a vertical wall or screen opposite the window, which will be, indeed, an image of the sun of the same kind as would be produced by a pinhole camera (§ 3); its

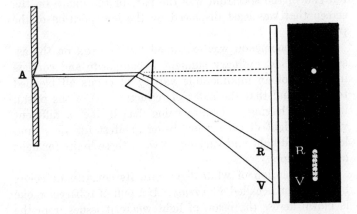

Fig. 204.—Prism dispersion: NEWTON's experiment.

angular diameter, therefore, being equal to that of the sun, namely, about half a degree. In the track of such a beam NEWTON inserted a prism with its refracting edge horizontal and at right angles to the direction of the incident light; whereupon the white spot on the screen vanished and in its stead at a certain vertical distance above or below the place that was first illuminated there was displayed an elongated

465

vertical band or *spectrum*, exhibiting the colors of the rainbow in an endless variety of tints shading into each other by imperceptible gradations. This spectrum was rounded at the ends and its vertical dimension, depending on how the prism was tilted, was about 4 or 5 times as great as its horizontal dimension, the latter being equal to the diameter of the spot of white light that was formed on the screen before the interposition of the prism. For convenience of description, NEWTON distinguished seven principal or "primary" colors arranged in the following order from one end of the spectrum to the other, namely, red, orange, yellow, green, blue, indigo,* and violet; of which the violet portion of the spectrum is the longest and the orange the shortest. The red end of the spectrum was the part of the image on the screen that was least displaced by the interposition of the prism.

This phenomenon was explained by NEWTON on the assumption that ordinary sunlight is composite and consists in reality of an innumerable variety of colors all blended together; and that the index of refraction (n) of the prism, instead of having a definite value, has in fact a different value for light of each color, being greatest for violet and least for red light and varying between these limits for light of other colors.

The resolution of white light into its constituent colors by refraction is called *dispersion*. If a puff of tobacco-smoke is blown across the beam of light where it issues from the prism, only the outer parts of the beam will show any very pronounced color, because the central parts at this place will

---

* There has been much discussion as to what NEWTON understood by the color which he named "indigo" and which lies somewhere between the blue and the violet. Indigo, as we understand it, is more nearly an inky blue rather than a violet blue, more like green than like violet; and hence it has been suggested that NEWTON's color vision may have been slightly abnormal. In this connection see article entitled "Newton and the Colours of the Spectrum" by Dr. R. A. HOUSTOUN, *Science Progress*, Oct. 1917.

not have been sufficiently dispersed to exhibit their individual effects. At some little distance away from the prism the entire section of the beam will be brilliantly colored.

Having pierced a small hole through the screen at that part of it where the spectrum was formed (Fig. 205), NEWTON was able by rotating the prism around an axis parallel to

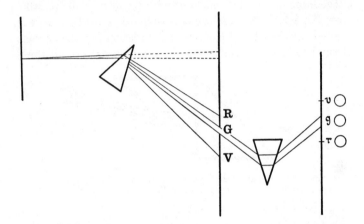

FIG. 205.—NEWTON's experiment with two prisms; showing that light of a definite color traverses the second prism without further dispersion.

its edge to transmit rays of each color in succession through the opening to a second prism placed with its edge parallel to that of the first prism; and, agreeably to his expectations, he found that while these rays were again deviated in traversing the second prism, there was no further dispersion of the light. This experiment demonstrated that the single colors of the spectrum were irreducible or elementary and not a mixture of still simpler colors, and that the light which had been separated in this fashion from the beam of sunlight was *monochromatic light*.

If all the various components of the incident light which has been resolved by the prism are re-united again, the effect will be the same as that of the light before its dispersion.

The simplest way to achieve this result is to cause the rays to traverse a second prism precisely equal to the first, but inverted so that the dihedral angle between the planes of the adjacent faces of the two prisms is equal to 180°, the edges of the prisms being parallel. Indeed, if the two prisms were placed in contact in this way, they would form a slab of the same material throughout with a pair of plane parallel faces, for which the resultant dispersion is zero; because the colored rays would all emerge in a direction parallel to that of the incident ray which was the common path of all these

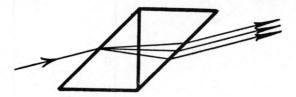

Fig. 206.—Light is not dispersed in traversing a plate with plane parallel faces surrounded by same medium on both sides.

rays before they were separated by refraction at the first face of the plate (Fig. 206).

Another and essentially different way of re-uniting the colored rays is to converge them to a single point by means of a so-called achromatic lens, as represented diagrammatically in the accompanying drawing (Fig. 207); so that the effect at the focus C where the colored rays meet is the same as that of light from the source. Beyond C the rays separate again, so that if they are received on a screen the same succession of colors will be exhibited as before, only in the reverse order. If some of the rays are intercepted before arriving at C, the color at C will be the resultant effect of the residual rays. The point B where the rays are separated on entering the prism and the point C where they are re-united by the lens are a pair of conjugate points with respect to the prism-lens system.

The solar spectrum which NEWTON obtained in his celebrated prism-experiments, described in 1672, had one serious defect, due to the fact that the colors in it were not in reality pure but consisted of a blending of two or more simple colors. When the light passes through a round hole before falling on the prism, the spectrum on the screen will be composed of a series of colored disks, each one overlapping the one next to it. The colors, therefore, are partly superposed on each other, and the eye is so constituted with respect to color vision that it cannot distinguish the separate effects and

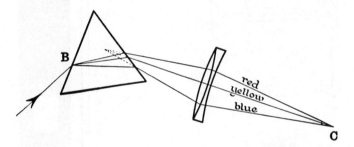

FIG. 207.—Achromatic lens used to re-unite the colored light after it has been dispersed by prism.

analyze them but obtains only a general resultant impression of the whole.

WOLLASTON'S experiments in 1802 differed essentially from NEWTON'S only in the form and dimensions of the beam of sunlight that was dispersed by the prism, but this simple modification represented a distinct advance in the mode of investigation of the spectrum. WOLLASTON admitted the sunlight through a narrow slit * whose length was parallel to

* Dr. HOUSTOUN, in the article already referred to, calls attention to the fact that in some of his prism-experiments NEWTON also employed an opening in the form of a narrow slit, and was aware of its advantages with respect to the purity of the spectrum; for NEWTON states that "instead of the circular hole," "it is better to substitute an oblong hole shaped like a long Parallelogram with its length Parallel to the Prism. For if this hole be an Inch or two long, and but a tenth

the prism-edge; and in order to diminish still more the divergence of the incident beam, a screen with a second slit parallel to the first was interposed in front of the prism, as represented in the accompanying diagram (Fig. 208). The spectrum formed in this way is far purer than that obtained with a round opening in the shutter. But a difficulty that

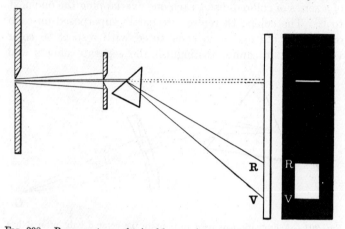

Fig. 208.—Pure spectrum obtained by causing sunlight to pass through two narrow slits before traversing prism.

inheres in both methods arises from the fact that the image formed by a prism is always virtual, and therefore a homocentric bundle of monochromatic divergent rays will necessarily be divergent after traversing a prism, so that if they are received on a screen they will illuminate a certain area on it which is the cross-section of the ray-bundle and not in any strict sense an optical image of the original source.

or twentieth part of an Inch broad or narrower; the Light of the Image, or spectrum, will be as Simple as before or simpler, and the Image will become much broader, and therefore more fit to have Experiments tried in its Light than before." The fact that NEWTON did not discover the FRAUNHOFER lines of the solar spectrum (§ 161) is probably to be explained on the supposition that his prisms were of an inferior quality of glass and that possibly also the surfaces were not as highly polished as they might have been.

Consequently, if the source sends out light of different colors, the effect on the screen will correspond to the sections of all the bundles of colored rays, and since these sections will overlap each other to a greater or less extent, the spectrum will not be pure. The narrower the apertures of the bundles of rays and the farther the screen is from the prism, the less

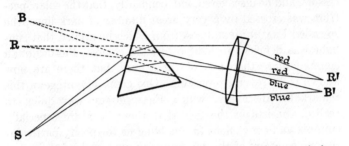

Fig. 209.—Pure spectrum obtained by slit, prism and achromatic lens.

will be the overlapping of the adjacent colors, and therefore the purer the spectrum; but on the other hand, the less also will be the illumination.

A much more satisfactory method consists in making these divergent bundles of rays convergent by means of an achromatic convex lens, as represented in Fig. 209; whereby the blue rays proceeding apparently from a virtual focus at B are brought to a real focus on the screen at B′, and, similarly, the red rays are united at R′. The plane of the diagram represents a principal section of the prism. The light originates in a luminous line or narrow illuminated slit at S parallel to the prism-edge, and the spectrum R′B′ on the screen consists of a series of colored images of this slit and is approximately pure, except in so far as the slit must necessarily have a certain width. Moreover, in the case of a very narrow slit, there are certain so-called diffraction-effects (§ 7) which are indeed of very great importance in any thorough scientific discussion of the condition of the purity of the spectrum.

161. Dark Lines of the Solar Spectrum.—WOLLASTON himself observed that the spectrum of sunlight was not absolutely continuous, but that there were certain narrow gaps or dark bands in it parallel to the slit. FRAUNHOFER (1787–1826), with his rare acumen and experimental skill, was able to obtain spectra of far higher purity than any of his predecessors, and he discovered, independently, that the solar spectrum was crossed by a very great number of dark lines, the so-called FRAUNHOFER lines, from which he argued that sunlight was deficient in light of certain colors. FRAUNHOFER counted more than 600 of these lines, but there are now known to be several thousand. One great advantage of this remarkable discovery, which FRAUNHOFER was quick to realize, consists in the fact that these lines are especially suitable and convenient for enabling us to specify particular regions or colors of the spectrum, because each of them corresponds to a certain degree of refrangibility, that is, to a perfectly definite color of light. An explanation of the origin of the dark lines of the solar spectrum may be found in treatises on physics and physical optics.

The dark lines are distributed very irregularly over the entire extent of the solar spectrum. In some cases they are sharp and fine and isolated; some of them are exceedingly close together so as to be hardly distinguishable apart; others again are quite broad and distinct. In order to describe their positions with respect to each other, FRAUNHOFER selected eight prominent lines distributed in the different regions of the spectrum, which he designated by the capital letters A (dark red), B (bright red), C (orange), D (yellow), E (green), F (dark blue), G (indigo), and H (violet). This notation is still in use, and has since been extended beyond the limits of the visible spectrum.

162. Relation between the Color of the Light and the Frequency of Vibration of the Light-Waves.—According to the undulatory theory of light, a luminous body sets up disturbances or "vibrations" in the ether which are propagated in waves in all directions with prodigious velocities. The velocity of light in the free ether is about 300 million meters per second. When a train of light-waves traverses a rectilinear row of ether-particles all lying in the same medium, the distance between one particle and the nearest one to it that is in precisely the same phase of vibration is called the wave-length; and the number of waves which pass a given point in one second or the *frequency* of the undulation will be equal to the velocity of propagation of the wave divided by the wave-length. The reciprocal of the frequency will be the time taken by a single wave in passing a given point, which is called the *period* of the vibration. If the wave-length is denoted by λ, the velocity of propagation by v, the frequency by N, and the period by $T = 1/N$, the relations between these magnitudes is expressed as follows:

$$\lambda = v/N = v.T.$$

When ether-waves fall on the retina of the eye, they may excite a sensation of light provided their frequencies are neither too small nor too great, the limits of visibility being confined to waves whose frequencies lie between about 392 and 757 million millions of vibrations per second. Just as the pitch of a musical note is determined by its frequency, so also the sensation which we call color appears to be more or less inexplicably associated with the frequency of the vibrations of the luminiferous ether; so that to each frequency between the limits named there corresponds a perfectly definite kind of light or color. Absolutely monochromatic light due to ether-waves of one single frequency of vibration is difficult to obtain. In general, the light which is emitted by a luminous body is more or less complex, and the sensation which it produces in the eye is due to a variety of impulses. The yellow light which is characteristic of the flame of a BUNSEN burner when a trace of common salt is burned in it is a sensation excited by the impact of two kinds of ether-waves corresponding to the double D-line of the solar spectrum which have frequencies of about 509 and 511 million millions of vibrations per second. Red light corresponds to the lowest and violet light to the highest frequency.

It is known that the velocity of light of a given color depends on the medium in which the light is propagated; and it has also been established that the velocity of light in a given medium depends on the color of the light. However, apparently light of all colors is transmitted with equal velocities *in vacuo;* and also in air, on account of its slight dispersion, there is practically no difference in the velocity of propagation of light of different colors.*

One reason for inferring that the frequency of the ether-vibrations is the physical explanation of the phenomenon of

* "When white light enters a transparent medium, the long red waves forge ahead of the green ones, which in their turn get ahead of the blue. If we imagine an instantaneous flash of white light traversing a refracting medium, we must conceive it as drawn out into a sort of linear spectrum in the medium, that is, the red waves lead the train, the orange, yellow, green, blue, and violet following in succession. The length of this train will increase with the length of the medium traversed. On emerging again into the free ether the train will move on without any further alteration of its length.

"We can form some idea of the actual magnitudes involved in the following way. Suppose we have a block of perfectly transparent glass (of ref. index 1.52) twelve miles in thickness. Red light will traverse it in 1/10000 of a second, and on emerging will be about 1.8 miles in advance of the blue light which entered at the same time. If white light were to traverse this mass of glass, the time elapsing between the arrival of the first red and the first blue light at the eye will be less than 1/6000 of a second. MICHELSON's determination of the velocity of light in carbon bisulphide showed that the red rays gained on the blue in their transit through the tube of liquid. The absence of any change of color in the variable star Algol furnished direct evidence that the blue and red rays traverse space with same velocity. In this case the distance is so vast, and the time of transit so long, that the white light coming from the star during one of its periodic increases in brilliancy would arrive at the earth with its red component so far in advance of the blue that the fact could easily be established by the spectro-photometer or even by the eye."—R. W. WOOD: *Physical Optics*, Second Edition (New York, 1911), page 101.

color is found in the fact that the color of monochromatic
light remains unaltered when the light passes from one medium into another; and since the vibrations in the second
medium are excited and forced by those in the first medium,
it is natural to suppose that the vibration-frequency is the
same in both media.

Accordingly, it is the ratio

$$\frac{v}{\lambda} = N$$

that remains constant in the transmission of monochromatic
light through different media. And hence if the velocities of
light in two media are denoted by v, v', and if the wave-lengths
in these two media are denoted by λ, λ', then $v/\lambda = v'/\lambda'$
or $\lambda/\lambda' = v/v'$; that is, *the wave-length of light of a given color
varies from medium to medium, and is proportional to the velocity of propagation of light of that color in the medium in
question.* Thus, the wave-length of yellow light is shorter
in glass than it is in air, because light travels more slowly in
glass than in air.

Generally, therefore, when we speak of the wave-length of
a given kind of light, we mean its wave-length measured *in
vacuo*. The lengths of waves of light are all relatively very
short, the longest, corresponding to the extreme red end of
the spectrum, being less than one 13-thousandth of a centimeter, and the shortest, belonging to the extreme violet end
of the visible spectrum, being less than one 25-thousandth
of a centimeter. These magnitudes are usually expressed in
terms of a special unit called a "tenth-meter" which is one
10-billionth part of a meter (10^{-10} meter) or in terms of a
"micromillimeter" which is equal to the millionth part of
a millimeter and for which the symbol $m\mu$ is employed
($1m\mu = 10^{-6}$ mm.). Thus, the wave-lengths of light corresponding to the red and violet ends of the visible spectrum
are about $767m\mu$ and $397m\mu$, respectively. The FRAUN-
HOFER line A is a broad, indistinct line at the beginning of the
red part of the spectrum, wave-length $759.4m\mu$; the B-line

in the red part corresponds to light of wave-length 686.7mμ; the C-line in the orange corresponds to light of wave-length 656.3mμ; the D-line in the yellow is a double line, corresponding to light of wave-lengths 589.6mμ and 589.0mμ; the E-line in the green corresponds to light of wave-length 527.0mμ; the F-line in the blue corresponds to light of wave-length 486.1mμ; the G-line in the indigo corresponds to light of wave-length 430.8mμ; and the H-line, consisting of two broad lines in the violet, corresponds to light of wave-lengths 396.8mμ and 393.3mμ.

163. Index of Refraction as a Function of the Wave-Length.—Now according to the wave-theory of light, the absolute index of refraction (n) of a medium for light of a definite color is equal to the ratio of the velocity of light *in vacuo* (V) to its velocity (v) in the medium in question (§ 33); that is,

$$n = \frac{V}{v}.$$

Strictly speaking, therefore, the index of refraction of a medium, without further qualification, is a perfectly vague expression, because each medium has as many indices of refraction as there are different kinds of monochromatic light. When the term is used by itself, it is generally understood to mean the index of refraction corresponding to the D-line in the bright yellow part of the solar spectrum, which is characteristic of the light of incandescent sodium vapor. Hence,

$$n_D = \frac{\text{velocity of yellow light } in \ vacuo}{\text{velocity of yellow light in the medium in question}}$$

$$= \frac{\text{wave-length of yellow light } in \ vacuo}{\text{wave-length of yellow light in the given medium}}$$

In the following table the values of the indices of refraction of several transparent liquids are given for light corresponding to the FRAUNHOFER lines A, B, C, D, E, F, G, and H.

	A	B	C	D	E	F	G	H
Wave-length in mμ	759.4	686.7	656.3	589.0	527.0	486.1	430.8	396.8
Alcohol	1.359	1.360	1.361	1.363	1.365	1.367	1.371	1.374
Benzene	1.493	1.495	1.497	1.503	1.507	1.514	1.524	1.536
Sulphuric Acid	1.610	1.616	1.620	1.629	1.642	1.654	1.670	1.702
Water	1.329	1.331	1.332	1.334	1.336	1.338	1.341	1.344

It may be remarked that, in general, the shorter the wave-length, the greater will be the index of refraction of a substance. But the exact relation between the index of refraction and the wave-length of the light has to be determined empirically for each substance. There is, indeed, a certain group of substances which form an exception to the general statement made above, and which yield refraction-spectra with the order of the colors partially or entirely reversed. This phenomenon is called *anomalous dispersion.*

164. Irrationality of Dispersion.—Other things being equal, the length of the spectrum or the interval between

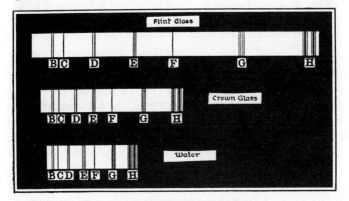

Fig. 210.—Irrationality of dispersion.

a given pair of FRAUNHOFER lines depends essentially on the nature of the refracting medium, so that, in general, as shown by the table in the preceding section, the dispersion of two colors will be found to be different for different substances.

For example, the dispersion of glass is greater than that of water, and the dispersion of so-called flint glass is higher that of so-called crown glass. In Fig. 210 are exhibited the relative lengths of the different regions of the solar spectra cast on the same screen under precisely the same circumstances by prisms of equal refracting angles made of water, crown glass and flint glass. The length of the spectrum may be increased by shifting the screen farther from

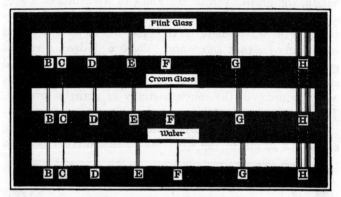

Fig. 211.—Irrationality of dispersion.

the prism, and Fig. 211 shows the relative positions of the FRAUNHOFER lines B, C, D, E, F, G and H, when the lengths of the spectra of the crown glass prism and the water prism have been elongated in this manner until their lengths are both equal to the length of the spectrum of the flint glass prism for the interval between the FRAUNHOFER lines B and H. The other lines in the three spectra do not coincide at all. Moreover, it appears that the dispersion of water for the colors towards the red end of the spectrum is relatively high, whereas the dispersion of the flint glass is relatively high towards the blue end. In the spectrum of flint glass the interval between G and H, and in the spectrum of water the interval between B and F, is greater than it is in either of the other spectra. If the law of the variation of the index of refraction with the color of the light has been found empirically for one substance, this will not afford any clue to the corresponding law in the case of another substance. Diamond, for example, is very highly refracting but shows comparatively little dispersion, whereas flint glass which has a much lower index of refraction gives a much higher dispersion; on the other hand, fluorite has a low index of refraction and at the same time a low dispersion. This phenomenon which is characteristic of refraction-spectra is known as the *irrationality of dispersion*.

165. Dispersive Power of a Medium.—In the case of a prism of small refracting angle β the deviation is given by the formula $\epsilon = (n-1)\beta$, as was explained in § 60. Let the letters P and Q be used to designate two colors, and let n_P and n_Q denote the indices of refraction of the prism-substance for these colors. If the angles of deviation are denoted by ϵ_P and ϵ_Q then $\epsilon_Q - \epsilon_P = (n_Q - n_P)\beta$, and, consequently, for a thin prism the angular magnitude of the interval in the spectrum between the colors P and Q is proportional to the difference of the values of the indices of refraction. This difference $(n_Q - n_P)$ is called the *partial dispersion* of the substance for the spectrum-interval P, Q. Thus, in the brightest part of the spectrum comprised between the FRAUNHOFER lines C and F, the partial dispersion is $(n_F - n_C)$. The deviation of a prism of small refracting angle β for light corresponding to the D-line which lies between C and F is $\epsilon_D = (n_D - 1)\beta$, and since $\epsilon_F - \epsilon_C = (n_F - n_C)\beta$, we obtain:

$$\frac{\epsilon_F - \epsilon_C}{\epsilon_D} = \frac{n_F - n_C}{n_D - 1}.$$

This ratio of the angular dispersion of two colors to their mean dispersion is called the *dispersive power* or the *relative dispersion* of the substance for the two colors, which are usually red (F) and blue (C); so that the dispersive power of an optical medium with respect to the visible spectrum may be defined to be the quotient of the difference $(n_F - n_C)$

between the indices of refraction for red and blue light by $(n_D - 1)$, where n_D denotes the index of refraction for yellow light. The values of the dispersive powers of the various kinds of optical glass that are of chief practical importance in the construction of optical instruments vary from about $\frac{1}{65}$ to about $\frac{1}{34}$; although there are compositions of glass with values of the dispersive power not comprised within these limits. Instead of assigning the value of the dispersive power of a substance, it is more convenient to adopt ABBE's method and employ the reciprocal of this function, which is denoted by the Greek letter ν, and which is known, therefore, as the ν-value of the substance; thus,

$$\nu = \frac{n_D - 1}{n_F - n_C}.$$

If the ν-value of one substance is less than that of another, the dispersive power of the former will be correspondingly greater than that of the latter.

It is this constant ν that is the essential factor to be considered in the selection of different kinds of glass suitable to be used in making a so-called achromatic combination of lenses or prisms. Curiously enough, NEWTON persisted in maintaining that the dispersion of a substance was proportional to the refraction, which is equivalent to saying that the dispersive powers of all optical media are equal; and, consequently, he despaired of constructing an achromatic combination of lenses which would refract the rays without at the same time dispersing the constituent colors. This condition, however, is an essential requirement in the object-glass of a telescope, and it was just because NEWTON and his followers believed that a lens of this kind was in the nature of things unattainable that they expended their efforts in the direction of perfecting the reflecting telescope in which the convex lens was replaced by a concave mirror. On the other hand, from the assumption that the optical system of the human eye is free from color-faults (which is by no means true), it was argued, notably by JAMES GREGORY in England (about 1670) and long afterwards by EULER in Germany (1747), that NEWTON's conclusions as to the impossibility of an achromatic combination of refracting media were erroneous. In fact, an English gentleman named HALL succeeded in 1733 in constructing telescopes which yielded images free from serious color faults. KLINGENSTIERNA in Sweden in 1754 demonstrated the feasibility of combining a pair of prisms of different kinds of glass and of different refracting angles so as to obtain, in one case, deviation without dispersion and, in another case, dispersion without deviation.

But in its practical results the most important advance along this line was achieved by the painstaking and original work of the English optician JOHN DOLLOND. Impressed by the force of KLINGENSTIERNA's demonstration, he carefully repeated NEWTON's crucial experiment in which a glass prism was inclosed in a water prism of variable refracting angle; and having found that the results of this experiment were exactly contrary to those stated by NEWTON, he was led also to the opposite conclusion. After much perseverance DOLLOND had succeeded by 1757 in making achromatic combinations of several different types, which produced a more or less colorless image of a point-source on the axis of the system. In its original form the combination consisted of a double convex "crown glass" lens cemented to a double concave "flint glass" lens. As a rule, the focus of the blue rays will be nearer a convex lens and farther from a concave lens than the focus of the red rays; and hence by combining a convex crown glass lens of relatively lower refractive index (shorter focus) and less dispersive power with a concave flint glass lens of higher refractive index and higher dispersive power, a resultant system may be obtained which still has a certain finite focal length and in which at the same time the opposed color-dispersions for two colors, say, red and blue, are compensated.

166. Optical Glass.—NEWTON's error in supposing that for all substances the dispersion was proportional to the index of refraction retarded the development of technical optics for a long time to come. Although DOLLOND's achievement, mentioned above, was one of far-reaching importance for the practical construction of optical instruments, the great difficulty in the way of utilizing and applying the principle was to be found in the fact that the actual varieties of optical glass at the disposal of the optician were exceedingly limited in number; although from time to time systematic efforts were made, notably by FRAUNHOFER (about 1812) in Germany and by FARADAY (1824), HARCOURT (1834) and STOKES (about 1870) in England, to remedy this deficiency, by discovering and manufacturing new compositions of glass suitable for optical purposes. For a long time after FRAUNHOFER's epoch the art of making optical glass was confined almost exclusively to France and England. It was a fortunate coincidence that just about the time when E. ABBE had reached the conclusion that no further progress in optical construction could be expected unless totally new varieties of optical glass were forthcoming, O. SCHOTT was already beginning to experiment with new chemical combinations and processes of manufacture in his glass works at Jena. Thanks to the systematic and indefatigable efforts of these two collaborators, who were also encouraged by the Prussian government, the obstacle which had stood so long in the way of the improvement and development of optical instruments was at length triumphantly overcome by the successful production of an entire new series of varieties of optical glass with properties in some instances almost beyond the highest expectations. The first catalogue of the *Glastechnisches Laboratorium* at Jena was issued in 1885; which marked the beginning of the manufacture of the renowned Jena glass, to which more than to any other single factor the remarkable development of modern optical instruments is due. From that time to the present the great province of applied optics may almost be said to have become a German territory.

The earlier so-called "ordinary" varieties of optical

glass were silicates in which the basic constituents were lime (crown glass) or lead (flint glass) combined with soda (Na_2CO_3) or potash (K_2CO_3) or both. The newer kinds of optical glass have been produced by employing a much greater variety of chemical substances, including, in addition to those named above, hydrated oxide of aluminum (Al_2O_3,H_2O), barium nitrate (BaN_2O_6), zinc oxide (ZnO), etc., and boric acid (H_3BO_3) or phosphoric acid which to a greater or less extent replace the silica (SiO_2) in the older types. Some of the new compounds have been found to have slight durability, and for this and other reasons certain products formerly listed in the Jena glass catalogue have been discontinued. At present, besides the old "ordinary" silicate crown and flint, the chief varieties are barium and zinc silicate crown, boro-silicate crown, dense baryta crown, baryta flint, antimony flint, borate glass and phosphate glass. The table on the following page contains a list of certain varieties of Jena glass arranged in the order of their ν-values. In the Jena glass catalogue the values of the dispersion are given also for the spectrum-intervals $n_D - n_{A'}$, $n_F - n_D$, $n_{G'} - n_F$ (where A' and G' are the lines corresponding to the wave-lengths 768 and $434\mu\mu$, respectively), together with the values of the so-called relative partial dispersions obtained by dividing each of these numbers by the value of $(n_F - n_C)$.

It has recently been proposed to describe an optical glass by means of two numbers of 3 digits each, separated by an oblique line. The first number gives the first three figures after the decimal point in the value of n_D, while the second number is equal to 10 times the value of ν. Thus, for example, the second glass in the table would be described as crown glass No. 559/669.

SELECTED VARIETIES OF JENA GLASS

Description	Index of Refraction n_D	Mean Dispersion $n_F - n_G$	$\dfrac{n_D - 1}{n_F - n_C} = \nu$
Light phosphate crown	1.5159	0.007 37	70.0
Medium phosphate crown	1.5590	0.008 35	66.9
Boro-silicate crown	1.5141	0.008 02	64.1
Boro-silicate crown	1.5103	0.008 05	63.4
Silicate crown	1.5191	0.008 60	60.4
Silicate crown	1.5215	0.008 75	59.6
Silicate crown	1.5127	0.008 97	57.2
Densest baryta crown	1.6112	0.010 68	57.2
Barium crown	1.5726	0.009 95	57.5
Dense baryta crown	1.6130	0.010 87	56.4
Dense baryta crown	1.6120	0.010 98	55.7
Baryta flint	1.5664	0.010 21	55.5
Borate flint	1.5503	0.009 96	55.2
Baryta flint	1.5489	0.010 25	53.6
Baryta flint	1.5848	0.011 04	53.0
Antimony flint	1.5286	0.010 25	51.6
Boro-silicate flint	1.5503	0.011 14	49.4
Extra light flint	1.5398	0.011 42	47.3
Baryta flint	1.5825	0.012 55	46.4
Ordinary light flint	1.5660	0.013 19	42.9
Silicate flint	1.5794	0.014 09	41.1
Baryta flint	1.6235	0.015 99	39.1
Heavy borate flint	1.6797	0.017 87	38.0
Silicate flint	1.6138	0.016 64	36.9
Silicate flint	1.6489	0.019 19	33.8
Dense silicate flint	1.7174	0.024 34	29.5
Densest silicate flint	1.9626	0.048 82	19.7

In recent years in France, England and the United States much attention has been bestowed on the study of the composition and manufacture of optical glass, and according to the 1916–17 report of the British Committee of the Privy Council for Scientific and Industrial Research (summarized in *Nature*, Vol. 100, pp. 17–20), Professor JACKSON in England "has succeeded in defining the composition of the bath mixtures necessary for the production of several glasses hitherto manufactured exclusively in Jena, including the famous fluor-crown glass," and, moreover, "he has also discovered three completely new glasses with properties hitherto unobtainable." However, it seems improbable

that any essential changes in the optical properties of glass
are to be obtained by the use of materials that have not already been tried.   The index of refraction of all glasses at
present available are comprised between 1.45 and 1.96.   The
mineral fluorite (calcium fluoride), which is used in the best
modern microscope objectives, has an index of refraction of
1.4338 and a ν-value of 95.4, so that in both respects it
lies beyond the limits attainable with glass.   Other crystalline transparent minerals, notably rock crystal or quartz,
have already been employed in lens-systems, and any essential improvement in the range of optical instruments
in the future is more likely to come from an adaptation of
these mineral substances than from the production of new
kinds of glass.

The difficulties involved in the manufacture of high-grade
optical glass are very great, and the utmost care has to be
exercised throughout every stage of the process.   Not only
must the raw materials themselves be free from impurities as
far as possible, but the physical and chemical nature of the
fireclays used in the pots or crucibles also requires the most
painstaking care and preparation.   The empty crucible is
dried slowly and then heated gradually for several days until
it comes to a bright red glow.   Fragments of glass left over
from a previous melting and of the same chemical composition as the glass which is in process of making are introduced
into the pot and melted.   The raw materials, pulverized and
mixed in definite proportions, are placed in the pot in layers
little by little at a time, and the pot, which is covered to
protect the contents from the furnace gases is maintained
at a sufficiently high temperature (between about 800 and
1000° C.) until the contents are all melted together.   The
molten mass is usually full of bubbles of all sizes, and the
temperature must be raised until these are all gotten rid
of as far as possible.   This entire process takes a longer or
shorter time depending on circumstances, say, from 24 to
36 hours or more.   After skimming off the impurities on the

surface, the mixture is allowed to cool gradually, and at the same time it is kept constantly stirred in order to make the glass as homogeneous as possible. This part of the process requires constant care. When the glass in cooling has become quite viscous, so that it is no longer possible to continue the stirring, it is allowed to cool very slowly over a period of days or even weeks. Usually at the end of the cooling process the solid contents of the pot will be found to be broken into irregular fragments of optical glass in the first stage of its manufacture. These fragments are carefully examined to see whether they are homogeneous and above all free from striæ; but the broken surfaces are so irregular that this preliminary examination is necessarily very imperfect. The pieces which pass muster in this way are selected for molding and annealing. The lumps of glass are placed in suitable molds made of iron or fireclay and heated until the glass becomes soft like wax, so that it takes the form of the mold usually with the aid of external pressure. The molded pieces are then annealed by being cooled gradually for a week or longer. They are in the form of disks or rectangular blocks of approximately the right size for being made into lenses and prisms. At this stage the glass has to be subjected to the most rigid testing to see if it is really suitable for optical purposes. Two opposite faces on the narrow sides are ground flat and parallel and polished so that the slab can be inspected in the direction of its greatest diameter. If any striæ or other imperfections are found, the piece will have to be rejected and melted over again. Even in case there are no directly visible defects, there may be internal strains which will be revealed by examination with polarized light. Slight strains are not always serious, but even these will impair the image in a large prism or lens. These strains can be gotten rid of by heating the glass to a temperature between 350 and 480° C., depending on the composition, and then cooling very slowly and uniformly over a period of about six weeks. It is very difficult to obtain pieces of optical glass which do not contain minute bubbles, and indeed they are often to be found in the best kinds of glass.

Of course, the process as above described varies in details according to the special nature of the glass, but enough has been said to enable the reader to form some idea of the patience and skill which are required in the manufacture of optical glass. A yield of 20 per cent. of the total quantity of glass melted is considered good. The glass to be used for photographic lenses has to fulfill the most exact requirements and must be of the highest quality.

167. Chromatic Aberration and Achromatism.—Since the index of refraction varies with the color of the light, and since this function enters in one form or another in all optical calculations, it is obvious, for example, that the positions of the cardinal points of a lens-system will, in general, be different for light of different colors; and that there will be a whole series of colored images of a given object depending on the nature of the light which it radiates, these images being all more or less separated from each other and of varying sizes. This phenomenon is called *chromatic aberration,* and unless it is at least partially corrected, the definition of the resultant image is very seriously impaired. In an optical system which was absolutely free from chromatic aberration all these colored images would coalesce into a single composite image which, so far as the quality of the light was concerned, would be a faithful reproduction of the object. But nothing at all comparable to this ideal condition of *achromatism* can be achieved in the case of any actual lens-system. In fact, the term achromatism by itself and without any further explanation is entirely vague, for an optical system may be achromatic in one sense without being at all so in other senses. For example, the images corresponding to different colors may all be formed in the same plane and yet be of different sizes, or *vice versa.* Fortunately, however, the fact that it is impossible to achieve at best more than a partial achromatism is not such a serious matter after all. The kind of achromat-

ism which is adapted for one type of optical instrument may
be entirely unsuited to another type. Thus, it is absolutely
essential that the colored images formed by the object-glass
of a telescope or microscope shall be produced as nearly as
possible at one and the same place (achromatism with respect to the location of the image), whereas, since the images
in this case do not extend far from the axis, the unequal
color-magnifications are comparatively unimportant. On
the other hand, in the case of the ocular systems of the same
instruments, the main consideration will be a partial achromatism with respect to the magnification or the apparent
sizes of the colored images. The object-glass of a telescope
must be achromatic with respect to the position of its focal
point, and the ocular must be achromatic with respect to its
focal length.

An optical system which produces the same definite effect
for light of two different wave-lengths, no matter what that
special effect may be, is to that extent an *achromatic system*.
A combination which is achromatic, even in its limited sense,
for a certain prescribed distance of the object will, in general,
not be achromatic when the object is placed at a different
distance. No lens composed of two kinds of glass only can
be achromatic for light of all different colors. It can be constructed, for example, so that it will bring the red and violet
rays accurately to the same focus at a prescribed point on
the axis; but then the yellow, green and blue rays will, in
general, all have different foci, some of which will be nearer
the lens than the point of reunion of the red and violet light
while others will lie farther away. Accordingly, when achromatism has been attained in the case of two chosen colors,
there will usually remain an uncorrected residual dispersion
or so-called *secondary spectrum*, which under certain circumstances may impair the definition of the image to such a
degree as to be very injurious and annoying. It is necessary to abolish the secondary spectrum in the object-glass of
a microscope. This may be done by using more than two

kinds of glass. There is also the possibility of diminishing the secondary spectrum by employing two kinds of glass whose relative partial dispersions (§ 166) are very nearly the same for all the spectrum-intervals; and, in fact, one of the principal items in the ABBE-SCHOTT programme for the manufacture of optical glass was the production of various pairs of flint and crown glass suitable for such combinations, so that the dispersions in the different regions of the spectrum should be, for each pair, as nearly as possible proportional. This purpose was satisfactorily accomplished, and we have now achromatic lenses of a far more perfect kind than could be made out of the older kinds of glass. This higher degree of achromatism is called *apochromatism*. An apochromatic photographic lens is absolutely essential in the three-color process of photography in which the three images taken through light-filters on a plate of medium or large size must be superposed as exactly as possible. In most ordinary optical systems, however, the secondary spectrum is relatively unimportant, and achromatism with respect to two principal colors will usually be found to be sufficient.

168. " Optical Achromatism " and " Actinic Achromatism."—The character and extent of the secondary spectrum (§ 167) of an achromatic combination of lenses will evidently depend essentially on the *choice of the two principal colors* for which the achromatism is to be achieved. This choice will be determined by the purpose for which the instrument is intended and the mode of using it. Thus, if the system is to be an *optical* instrument in the strict literal sense of the word, that is, if it is constructed to be used subjectively in conjunction with the eye, we shall be concerned primarily with the physiological action of the rays on the retina of the human eye; whereas in the case of a photographic lens which is used to focus an image on a prepared sensitized plate, it is important to have achromatism with respect to the so-called actinic rays corresponding to the violet and ultra-violet regions of the spectrum, because these are the rays which are most active on the ordinary bromo-silver gelatine plate.

The retina of the human eye is most sensitive to the kind of light which is comprised within the interval between the lines C and F, with a distinct maximum of visual effect corresponding to wave-lengths lying somewhere between the lines D and E. Accordingly, in an optical instrument which is to be applied to the eye, it is usually desirable to unite the red and blue rays as nearly as possible at the focus of the yellow rays. If, for example, the system is assumed to be a convergent combination of two thin lenses in contact (as in the case of the object-glass of a telescope), it will be found that the focal points corresponding to the colors (say, green and yellow) between C and F will lie nearer the lens and the focal points corresponding to the other colors (dark red, dark blue and violet) will lie farther from it than the common focal point of the two principal colors C and F. Moreover, the residual color-error or secondary spectrum in this case will be least for some color very nearly corresponding to the D-line, which is a favorable circumstance, since, as above stated, this is the region of the brightest part of the visible spectrum. Achromatism with respect to the colors C and F $\left(\nu = \dfrac{n_D - 1}{n_F - n_C}\right)$ is sometimes called *optical achromatism*.

On the other hand, in the construction of a photographic lens a kind of compromise must be effected between the convergence of the visual rays and the so-called actinic rays, because the image has to be focused first on the ground glass plate by the eye and afterwards it has to be received on the sensitized plate or film which is inserted for exposure in the camera in the place of the translucent focusing screen. Accordingly, for ordinary photographic practice an exact coincidence of the "optical" and "actinic" images is demanded. Here it is found that the best results are obtained by uniting the colors corresponding to the D-line and the violet band in the spectrum of hydrogen, which, since it is

not far from the G-line, may be designated by G′ (434mμ).
This is sometimes called *actinic* or *photographic achromat-ism* for which the function ν has a special value, namely:

$$\bar{\nu} = \frac{n_{\text{D}} - 1}{n_{\text{G}'} - n_{\text{D}}} \ .$$

If the photographic lens is a combination of two thin lenses in contact, which is achromatic for the colors D and G′, the focus of the rays corresponding to the blue-green region of the spectrum will be nearer the lens than the common focus of the two principal colors and the focus of the bright red rays will be farther from the lens. In an achromat of this kind the residual dispersion will usually be quite large for both the "optical" and the "actinic" image, but for most practical purposes the definition of the image in either case is good enough. In astrophotography the focus of the camera is determined once for all, and a lens for stellar photography is usually designed to have an *entirely actinic achromatism*, the two principal colors in this case correspond-ing to the F-line (486mμ) and the violet line in the mercury-spectrum (405mμ). The rays belonging in these two colors are made to unite as nearly as possible at the focus of the rays corresponding to the G′-line, which is approximately the place of maximum actinic action. In a photographic achromat of this kind the foci of the green, yellow and red rays will lie beyond the actinic focus in the order named.

169. Achromatic Combination of Two Thin Prisms.— Two prisms of different substances may be combined so as to obtain achromatism in the sense that rays of light cor-responding to a definite pair of colors will issue from the system in parallel directions, as represented in Fig. 212. When an object is viewed through the combination, the red and blue rays, for example, will be fused or superposed and the residual color-effect will be comparatively slight. By employing a greater number of prisms a more perfect union of colors could be obtained, but usually two prisms are suf-ficient.

The problem is simplified by assuming that the refracting angles of the prisms, denoted here by β and γ, are both small; so that the deviation produced by each prism may be considered as proportional to its refracting angle, according to the approximate formula deduced in § 60. Usually,

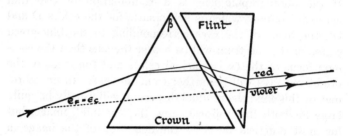

FIG. 212.—Achromatic combination of two thin prisms.

the two prisms are cemented together with their edges parallel but oppositely turned, as shown in the diagram, so that the thicker portions of one prism are adjacent to the thinner portions of the other; accordingly, the total deviation (ϵ) will be equal to the arithmetical difference of the deviations produced by each prism separately.

Let P, Q and R designate three elementary colors, the color Q being supposed to lie between P and R in the spectrum; and let the indices of refraction for these three colors be denoted by n_P', n_Q' and n_R' for the first prism and by n_P'', n_Q'' and n_R'' for the second prism. The total deviations for the three colors will be:

$$\epsilon_P = (n_P' - 1)\beta - (n_P'' - 1)\gamma, \qquad \epsilon_Q = (n_Q' - 1)\beta - (n_Q'' - 1)\gamma,$$
$$\epsilon_R = (n_R' - 1)\beta - (n_R'' - 1)\gamma.$$

Now if the system is to be achromatic with respect to the colors P and R, the condition is that $\epsilon_P = \epsilon_R$, which, therefore, is equivalent to the following:

$$\frac{\beta}{\gamma} = \frac{n_R'' - n_P''}{n_R' - n_P'} ;$$

that is, the refracting angles of the prisms must be inversely proportional to the partial dispersions of the two media for the two given colors.

Moreover, the deviation of the rays of the intermediate color Q will be:

$$\epsilon_Q = (n_R{}' - n_P{}') \left\{ \frac{n_Q{}' - 1}{n_R{}' - n_P{}'} - \frac{n_Q{}'' - 1)}{n_R{}'' - n_P{}''} \right\} \beta.$$

Actually the colors P, Q and R are usually chosen to correspond to the FRAUNHOFER lines C, D and F, respectively, in which case the combination will be achromatic with respect to C (red) and F (blue). Thus, the fractions inside the large brackets are the ν-values of the two kinds of glass. Accordingly, for an achromatic combination of two thin prisms for which the deviation ϵ_D has a finite value, whereas the dispersion ($\epsilon_C - \epsilon_F$) is abolished, we have the following formulæ:

$$\frac{\beta}{\gamma} = \frac{n_F{}'' - n_C{}''}{n_F{}' - n_C{}'}, \qquad \epsilon_D = (n_F{}' - n_C{}') \, (\nu' - \nu'') \, \beta.$$

Consider, for example, a combination of two kinds of Jena glass as follows:

	n_D	$n_F - n_C$	ν
Light Phosphate Crown	1.5159	0.007 37	70.0
Borate Flint	1.5503	0.009 96	55.2

Assuming that the angle of the crown glass prism is $\beta = 20°$, we find: $\gamma = 14.8°$, $\epsilon_D = 2.18°$. Generally speaking, those pairs of glasses in which the partial dispersions are more nearly equal will be found to be best adapted for achromatic combinations.

170. Direct Vision Combination of Two Thin Prisms.— In the case of an ordinary prism-spectroscope the rays are deflected in passing through the system, so that in order to view the spectrum the eye has to be pointed not directly towards the luminous source, but in some oblique direction; which is sometimes inconvenient, especially in astrophysical observations. Accordingly, various prism-systems have been proposed which are designed so that rays corresponding to some definite standard color are finally bent back into their original direction, with the result that there is dispersion without deviation, which is an effect precisely opposite to that which is obtained with an achromatic prism. In these so-called *direct vision prisms* (*prismes à vision directe*)

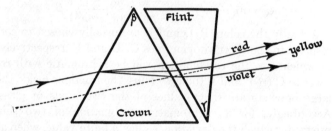

FIG. 213.—Direct vision prism combination (dispersion without deviation).

the spectrum of an illuminated slit will be seen in the same direction as the slit itself. The condition that the light corresponding, say, to the FRAUNHOFER D-line shall emerge from the system in the same direction as it entered is $\epsilon_D = 0$. Assuming that the combination is composed, as before, of two thin prisms juxtaposed in the same way (Fig. 213), and employing the same symbols (§ 169), we derive immediately the following formulæ:

$$\frac{\beta}{\gamma} = \frac{n_D'' - 1}{n_D' - 1},$$

$$\epsilon_C - \epsilon_F = (n_D' - 1)\left(\frac{1}{\nu''} - \frac{1}{\nu'}\right)\beta.$$

Consider, for example, the following combination:

	n_D	ν
Light Phosphate Crown	1.5159	70.0
Heavy Silicate Flint	1.9626	19.7

the difference of the ν-values here being very great. If we put $\beta = 20°$, we find: $\gamma = 10.72°$, $\epsilon_C - \epsilon_F = 22.58'$.

It will be profitable for the student to satisfy himself by several examples that two kinds of glass which are best adapted for a direct vision prism combination are on the contrary not very suitable for an achromatic prism, and *vice versa;* as might naturally be expected, since the effects are opposite in the two cases. Generally speaking, the two kinds of glass used for a direct vision prism should have very different ν-values, as in the illustration given above.

In the case of prisms of large refracting angles, the formulæ here and in § 169 are hardly to be considered as even approximate.

171. Calculation of Amici Prism with Finite Angles.— Accurate formulæ for the calculation of an achromatic or direct vision prism-system may easily be derived when the

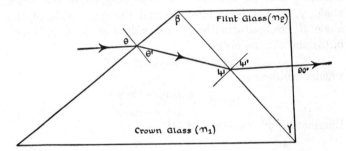

Fɪɢ. 214.—Direct vision prism combination. Diagram represents one-half of so-called Aᴍɪᴄɪ direct vision prism.

system consists of only two prisms. As an illustration of the method in the case of a direct vision prism, let us employ here the symbols n_1 and n_2 to denote the indices of refraction of the crown glass prism and the flint glass prism, respectively, for light of some standard wave-length; and let β and γ denote their refracting angles. We shall suppose also that the two prisms are cemented along a common face, as represented in Fig. 214. A ray of the given wavelength is incident on the crown glass prism at an angle θ and is refracted into this medium at the angle θ', so that

$$n_1.\sin\theta' = \sin\theta. \qquad (1)$$

If the angles of incidence and refraction at the surface of

separation of two kinds of glass are denoted by ψ and ψ', then

$$n_1.\sin\psi = n_2.\sin\psi', \tag{2}$$
$$\theta' = \beta - \psi; \tag{3}$$

the angles here being all reckoned as positive. If, finally, it is assumed that the ray meets the second face of the second prism normally and issues again into the air in the same direction as it had originally, then also:

$$\psi' = \gamma, \quad (4) \quad \text{and} \quad \theta = \beta - \gamma. \tag{5}$$

The problem consists in determining the angle of one of the prisms when the angle of the other is given. Suppose, for example, that an arbitrary value is assigned to the acute angle γ, and it is required to find the magnitude of the angle β. Substituting in (1) the values of θ, θ' as given in (3) and (5), we obtain:

$$n_1.\sin(\beta - \psi) = \sin(\beta - \gamma),$$

whence we derive:

$$\tan\beta = \frac{n_1.\sin\psi - \sin\gamma}{n_1.\cos\psi - \cos\gamma}.$$

Eliminating ψ' from (2) and (4), we find:

$$n_1.\sin\psi = n_2.\sin\gamma,$$

and consequently also:

$$n_1.\cos\psi = \sqrt{n_1^2 - n_2^2.\sin^2\gamma}.$$

Accordingly, the value of β in terms of n_1, n_2 and γ is given by the formula:

$$\tan\beta = \frac{(n_2-1)\sin\gamma}{\sqrt{n_1^2 - n_2^2\sin^2\gamma} - \cos\gamma}.$$

If, on the other hand, the value of the angle β has been chosen arbitrarily, the calculation of γ will be found to be trigonometrically a little more difficult. It is left as an exercise for the student to show that:

$$\tan\gamma = -\frac{n_2-1 + \sqrt{n_1^2(n_2-1)^2 + (n_1^2-1)(n_2^2-n_1^2)\tan^2\beta}}{(n_2^2-n_1^2)\tan^2\beta + (n_2-1)^2}\tan\beta.$$

If it is desired that the emergent ray shall not only be parallel to the incident ray but that its path shall be along the same straight line, it is necessary to add to the above another combination identical with it and placed so that the two flint glass prisms constitute in reality one single prism of refracting angle 2γ inserted between two equal crown glass prisms each of refracting angle β, as shown in Fig. 215; and,

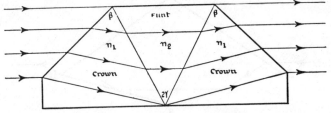

FIG. 215.—AMICI direct vision prism.

in fact, this is the actual construction of the common form of the AMICI prism. Suppose, for example, that the angle $\gamma = 45°$ and that the two kinds of glass are those described in the Jena catalogue as "light phosphate crown" and "heavy silicate flint" with indices $n_1 = 1.5159$ and $n_2 = 1.9626$ corresponding to the D-line; then we find that the angle $\beta = 98° 7.4'$.

172. Kessler Direct Vision Quadrilateral Prism.—One of the principal objections to a train of prisms is the loss of light by reflection at the various surfaces and also by absorption in traversing the successive media. Partly with a view to diminishing these losses and partly also on account of other advantages, many forms of direct vision prism have been proposed which are made of one piece of glass with four or more plane faces; in all of which, however, the principle is the same, namely, by means of a series of total internal reflections to bend the rays corresponding to some standard intermediate color back finally into their original direction. The simplest of all these devices is the four-faced prism ABCD (Fig. 216) proposed by KESSLER, a principal section of which has the form of a quadrilateral with perpendicular diagonals. The ray of standard wave-length enters the prism and leaves it in a direction parallel to the diagonal BD; it is totally reflected twice, first at the face BA and again at the face AD, the path of the ray between these reflections being parallel to its direction at entrance and emergence. More-

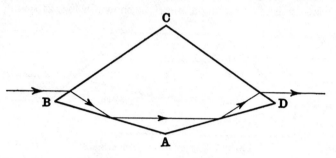

Fig. 216.—Kessler direct vision prism.

over, in virtue of the symmetry of the prism, the path of the emergent ray will be a continuation of the rectilinear path of the incident ray. If the angles at A, B and C are denoted by α, β and γ, respectively, then

$$\alpha + 2\beta + \gamma = 360°; \qquad (1)$$

and if the angles of incidence and refraction at the face BC are denoted by θ, θ', then

$$\theta = \frac{\gamma}{2}, \qquad \theta' = \frac{\alpha}{2} - \beta; \qquad (2)$$

and, finally, if the index of refraction is denoted by n,

$$n.\sin\theta' = \sin\theta. \qquad (3)$$

Consequently, eliminating the angles θ, θ' by means of (2) and (3), we obtain:

$$n.\sin(\frac{\alpha}{2} - \beta) = \sin\frac{\gamma}{2} ; \qquad (4)$$

so that if the value of one of the angles α, β and γ is chosen arbitrarily, the other two angles can be determined by means of equations (1) and (4).

If the principal section of a Kessler prism has the form of a rhombus (Fig. 217), parallel incident rays may be re-

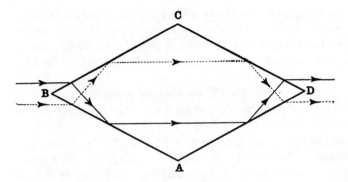

FIG. 217.—Rhomboidal form of KESSLER prism.

ceived on both faces BA and BC. In this case the angles
α and γ are equal, and hence $\beta + \gamma = 180°$, and therefore

$$\theta = \frac{\gamma}{2}, \qquad \theta' = \frac{3\gamma}{2} - 180°,$$

so that

$$n.\sin\left(\frac{3\gamma}{2} - 180°\right) = \sin\frac{\gamma}{2},$$

whence we obtain:

$$\sin\frac{\beta}{2} = \cos\frac{\gamma}{2} = \sqrt{\frac{n-1}{4n}}.$$

For example, if $n = 1.64$, we find $\beta = 36° 24', \gamma = 143° 36'$.

173. Achromatic Combination of Two Thin Lenses.—
The positions of the principal and focal points of a lens-
system vary for light of different colors, and if the system is
to be used as a magnifying glass or as the so-called ocular
of a microscope or telescope, a chief consideration will be
that the apparent sizes of the colored virtual images which
are presented to the eye shall all be the same, that is, that
the red and blue images, for example, shall subtend the
same angle at the eye, no matter whether their actual sizes
and positions are different or not. But the apparent size
of the infinitely distant image of an object lying in the
primary focal plane of the lens-system is measured by the

refracting power of the system (§ 122); and hence the condition of achromatism in this case is that the refracting powers (or focal lengths) of the system shall be equal for the two colors in question. (Achromatism with respect to the focal length; see § 167.)

Let us assume that the system is composed of two thin lenses whose refracting powers for light of a certain definite wave-length λ are denoted by F_1 and F_2; then the refracting power of the combination will be $F = F_1 + F_2 - c.F_1.F_2$, where c denotes the air-interval between the two lenses. For a second color of wave-length $\lambda + \Delta\lambda$ (where $\Delta\lambda$ denotes a small variation in the value of λ), the refracting powers of the lenses will be slightly different, and the refracting power of the combination for this color will be:

$$F + \Delta F = (F_1 + \Delta F_1) + (F_2 + \Delta F_2) - c(F_1 + \Delta F_1)(F_2 + \Delta F_2).$$

Subtracting these two equations, at the same time neglecting the term which involves the product of the small variations ΔF_1 and ΔF_2, we obtain:

$$\Delta F = \Delta F_1 + \Delta F_2 - (F_2.\Delta F_1 + F_1.\Delta F_2)c.$$

Evidently, the condition that the system shall be achromatic with respect to its refracting power is $\Delta F = 0$; which, therefore, is equivalent to the following:

$$\frac{1}{c} = \frac{F_2.\Delta F_1 + F_1.\Delta F_2}{\Delta F_1 + \Delta F_2}.$$

Now if n_1 denotes the index of refraction of the first lens for light of wave-length λ, then

$$F_1 = (n_1 - 1)K_1,$$

where K_1 denotes a constant whose value depends simply on the form of the infinitely thin lens, that is, on the curvatures of its surfaces. Similarly, for light of wave-length $\lambda + \Delta\lambda$, we have:

$$F_1 + \Delta F_1 = (n_1 + \Delta n_1 - 1)K_1;$$

and hence

$$\Delta F_1 = K_1.\Delta n_1 = F_1 \frac{\Delta n_1}{n_1 - 1}.$$

But $\Delta n_1/(n_1-1)=1/\nu_1$ is the expression for the dispersive power of the material of the first lens (§ 165), and accordingly we may write:

$$\Delta F_1 = \frac{F_1}{\nu_1}\ ;$$

and, analogously, for the second lens:

$$\Delta F_2 = \frac{F_2}{\nu_2}.$$

Introducing these expressions for ΔF_1 and ΔF_2 in the equation above, we find, therefore, as the condition that a pair of thin lenses shall be achromatic with respect to the refracting

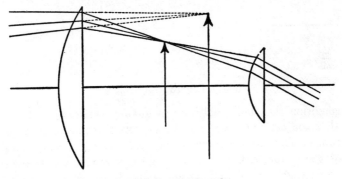

FIG. 218.—HUYGENS's ocular.

power of the system, the requirement that the distance between the two thin lenses shall satisfy the following equation:

$$c = \frac{\nu_2.F_1+\nu_1.F_2}{(\nu_1+\nu_2)F_1.F_2}\ ;$$

or

$$c = \frac{\nu_1.f_1+\nu_2.f_2}{\nu_1+\nu_2}\ ,$$

where $f_1=1/F_1$ and $f_2=1/F_2$ denote the focal lengths of the lenses.

If *both lenses are made of the same glass*, then $v_1 = v_2$, so that in this case the condition of achromatism becomes:

$$c = \frac{f_1 + f_2}{2}.$$

Thus, for example, HUYGENS's ocular (Fig. 218) is composed of two plano-convex lenses made of the same kind of glass, the curved face of each lens being turned away from the eye and towards the incident light. The first lens is called the "field-lens" and the second lens is called the "eye-lens." In this combination $f_1 = 2f_2$ (although in actual systems this

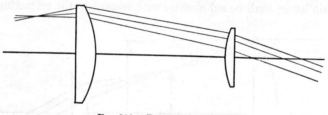

FIG. 219.—RAMSDEN's ocular.

condition is usually only approximately satisfied) and $c = 3f_2/2$, or $f_2 : c : f_1 = 2 : 3 : 4$. RAMSDEN's ocular (Fig. 219) consists likewise of two plano-convex lenses of the same kind of glass, but with their curved faces turned towards each other and in this combination $f_1 = f_2 = f = c$. Both of these types satisfy, therefore, the above condition of achromatism and yield images that are free from color-faults not only in the center but at the border of the field.

174. Achromatic Combination of Two Thin Lenses in Contact.—If the two lenses are in contact $(c = 0)$, the condition of achromatism, as found in the preceding section, becomes:

$$v_1.f_1 + v_2.f_2 = 0,$$

or

$$\frac{F_1}{v_1} + \frac{F_2}{v_2} = 0.$$

The quotient of the refracting power of a lens by the dispersive power of the glass of which it is made, namely, the magnitude F/ν, is sometimes called the *dispersive strength* of the lens; so that according to the above equation we may say that the condition of achromatism of a combination of two thin lenses in contact is that the algebraic sum of their dispersive strengths shall vanish. Accordingly, it appears that such a system can be achromatic only in case the substances of which the two lenses are made are different. Moreover, while one of the lenses must be convex and the other concave, their actual forms are of no consequence so far as the mere correction of the chromatic aberration is concerned. It is to be remarked also that in an achromatic lens of negligible thickness achromatism with respect to the focal lengths implies also achromatism with respect to the positions of the focal points and principal points, so that such a lens will be achromatic for all distances of the object.

If F denotes the prescribed refracting power of the combination then, since,

$$F = F_1 + F_2,$$

we find:

$$F_1 = \frac{\nu_1}{\nu_1 - \nu_2} F, \qquad F_2 = -\frac{\nu_2}{\nu_1 - \nu_2} F.$$

The total refracting power F will have the same sign as that of the lens which has the greater ν-value; for example, the combination will act like a convex lens provided the ν-value of the positive element exceeds that of the negative element.

Thus, being given the values of F, ν_1 and ν_2, we can employ the above relations to determine the required values of F_1 and F_2. Moreover, if K_1 denotes the algebraic difference of the curvatures of the two faces of the first lens, and, similarly, if K_2 denotes the corresponding magnitude for the second lens, then

$$K_1 = \frac{F_1}{n_1 - 1}, \qquad K_2 = \frac{F_2}{n_2 - 1},$$

where n_1, n_2 denote the indices of refraction of the two kinds of glass for some standard wave-length, as already stated, which is usually light corresponding to the FRAUNHOFER D-line. Thus, while the magnitudes denoted by K_1 and K_2 may be computed, the actual curvatures or radii of the lens-surfaces remain indeterminate; so that there are still two

FIG. 220.—DOLLOND's telescope objective.

FIG. 221. — FRAUN-HOFER's telescope objective, No. 1.

FIG. 222. — FRAUN-HOFER's telescope objective, No. 2.

FIG. 223.—HERSCHEL's telescope objective.

FIG. 224.—BARLOW's telescope objective.

FIG. 225. — GAUSS's telescope objective.

other conditions which may be imposed on an achromatic combination of this kind. For example, in some cases it may be convenient to cement the two components together, and then one of the conditions will be that the curvatures of the two surfaces in contact shall be equal. Usually, however, a more important requirement will be the abolition of two of the so-called spherical errors due to the fact that the rays are not paraxial, so that the image will be sharp and distinct, especially at the center.

Some historic types of achromatic object-glasses of a telescope are illustrated in the accompanying diagrams. DOL-LOND's achromatic doublet (Fig. 220) consisted of a double convex crown glass lens combined with a double concave flint glass lens; whereas FRAUNHOFER's constructions show a combination of a double convex and a plano-concave lens (Fig. 221) and of a double convex and a meniscus lens (Fig. 222). J. HERSCHEL's form (1821) is shown in Fig. 223, BARLOW's (1827) in Fig. 224; and, finally, the GAUSS type made by STEINHEIL in 1860 is exhibited in Fig. 225. The newer varieties of Jena glass make it possible to construct an achromatic objective of two lenses which is far superior in achromatism to any of the older types above mentioned.

PROBLEMS

1. Find the values of the reciprocals of the dispersive powers (§ 165) of alcohol and water, using data given in table in § 163.　　　　Ans. Alcohol, 60.5; water, 55.7.

2. The indices of refraction of rock salt for the FRAUN-HOFER lines C, D and F are 1.5404, 1.5441 and 1.5531, respectively. Calculate the value of the reciprocal of the dispersive power.　　　　Ans. 42.84.

3. White light is emitted from a luminous point on the axis of a thin lens. If the yellow rays are brought to a focus at a point whose distance from the lens is denoted by u', show that the distance between the foci of the red and blue rays is approximately equal to $F.u'^2/\nu$, where F denotes the refracting power of the lens for yellow light and ν denotes the reciprocal of the dispersive power of the lens-medium.

4. A lens is made of borate flint glass for which $\nu = 55.2$. The focal length of the lens for sodium light is 30 inches. Find the distance between the red and blue images of the sun formed by the lens.　　　　Ans. 0.54 in.

5. A crown glass prism of refracting angle 20° is to be combined with a flint glass prism so that the combination will be achromatic for the FRAUNHOFER lines C and F. The indices of refraction are as follows:

	n_C	n_D	n_F
Crown	1.526 849	1.529 587	1.536 052
Flint	1.629 681	1.635 036	1.648 260

Using the approximate formulæ for thin prisms, show that the refracting angle of the flint prism will be 9° 54′ 11″, and that the deviation of the rays corresponding to the D-line will be 4° 18′ 7″.

6. A direct vision prism combination is to be made with the same kinds of glass as in the preceding problem; so that rays corresponding to the D-line are to emerge without deviation. If the refracting angle of the crown glass prism is 20°, show that the refracting angle of the flint glass prism will be 16° 40′ 48″, and that the angular dispersion between C and F will be 7′ 33″.

7. An AMICI direct vision prism (§ 171) is to be made of crown glass and flint glass whose indices of refraction for the D-line are 1.5159 and 1.9626, respectively. If the refracting angles of the two equal crown glass prisms are each equal to 45°, show that the refracting angle of the middle flint glass prism will be 98° 7.4′.

8. A KESSLER prism (§ 172) in the form of a rhombus is made of glass of index $n_D = 1.6138$. Find the angles of the prism.   Ans. 35° 5′ and 144° 55′.

9. A thin lens is made of crown glass for which $\nu_1 = 60.2$. Another thin lens is made of flint glass for which $\nu_2 = 36.2$. When the two lenses are placed in contact they form an achromatic combination of focal length 10 cm. Find the focal length of each lens.   Ans. $f_1 = 3.99$ cm.; $f_2 = -6.63$ cm.

10. An achromatic doublet is to be made of two thin lenses cemented together, and the focal length of the combination for the D-line is to be 25 cm. The first lens is a symmetric convex lens of barium silicate glass and the other

lens is a concave lens of sodium lead glass. The indices of refraction are:

	n_D	$n_F - n_C$
Barium silicate	1.6112	0.01747
Sodium lead	1.5205	0.01956

Find the radii of the surfaces on the supposition that the rays corresponding to the lines C and F are united.

Ans. The radii of the first and last surfaces are +7.32 and +9.30 cm., respectively.

11. A symmetric double convex lens is made of rock salt for which $n_C = 1.5404$ and $n_F = 1.5531$. Find the thickness of the lens if the focal lengths for the colors C and F are equal.

Ans. $d = 3.4363.r$, where r denotes the radius of the first surface of the lens.

12. Two thin lenses of the same kind of glass, one convex of focal length 9 inches, the other concave of focal length 4 inches, are separated by an interval of 20 inches. A small white object is placed 36 inches in front of the convex lens. Show that the various colored images are all formed at the same place.

13. Two thin lenses of the same kind of glass, one convex and the other concave, and both of focal length 4 inches, are adjusted on the same axis until the colored images of a white object placed 12 inches in front of the convex lens are formed at the same place. Show that the interval between the lenses must be twelve inches.

14. A lens-system surrounded by air is composed of m spherical refracting surfaces. Assuming that the total thickness of the system is negligible, show that the condition of achromatism is

$$\sum_{k=2}^{k=m} (R_{k-1} - R_k) \, \delta n_k = 0,$$

where R_k denotes the curvature of the kth surface and δn_k denotes the dispersion of the medium included between the $(k-1)$th and kth surfaces for light of the two colors to be compensated.

CHAPTER XV

175. Introduction.—The theory of the symmetrical optical instrument, as it has been developed in the preceding chapters, is based on the assumption that the rays concerned in the formation of the image are entirely confined to the so-called paraxial rays (§ 63) whose paths throughout the system are contained within an exceedingly narrow cylindrical region of space immediately surrounding the axis. With this fundamental restriction it was found that there was perfect collinear correspondence between object-space and image-space; so that a train of spherical waves emanating from an object-point was transformed by the optical system into another train of spherical waves accurately converging to or diverging from a corresponding center called the image-point; and so that, in general, a plane object at right angles to the axis was reproduced point by point by a similar plane image. As a matter of fact, these ideal conditions are never realized in any actual optical system except in the case of a plane mirror or combination of plane mirrors. Moreover, according to the wave-theory of light, a mere homocentric convergence of the rays is not sufficient for obtaining a point-image of a point-source; for this theory lays particular stress on the further essential requirement that the effective portion of the wave-surface which contributes to the production of the image shall be relatively large in comparison with the radius of the surface, if the light-effect is to be concentrated as nearly as possible at a single point and not spread over some considerable area in the vicinity of the point. This condition implies, therefore, that the aperture of the bundle of effective rays must not be below a certain finite limit, in other words we are compelled by a practical necessity, wholly aside from the principles at the basis of geometrical optics, to employ more or less wide-angle bundles of rays. Moreover, if a wide-angle bundle of rays is a requirement of a distinct, clear-cut image, it is also equally essential for a bright image. Thus, on both theoretical and practical grounds, it is found necessary to extend the limits of the effective rays beyond the paraxial region.

Instead, therefore, of the ideal case of collinear correspondence of object-space and image-space, the theory of optical instruments is complicated by numerous practical and, for the most part irreconcilable difficulties, due chiefly to the so-called *aberrations* or failure of the rays to arrive at the places where they might be expected according to the simple theory of collineation or point-to-point correspondence (punctual imagery). In the preceding chapter brief reference was made to the *chromatic aberrations* arising from the differences in the color of the light; but now we have to deal with the *monochromatic aberrations* of rays of light of one definite wave-length which are caused by the peculiarities of the curved surfaces at which the rays are reflected and refracted. These surfaces are nearly always spherical in form, and hence the aberrations of this latter kind are usually called *spherical aberrations*. A complete treatment of this intricate subject lies wholly outside the scope of this volume. In the present chapter it must suffice to point out the general nature of some of the more important of the so-called spherical errors. First, however, we must see how to trace the path of a single ray through a centered system of spherical surfaces before we are in a position to study a bundle of rays.

176. Construction of a Ray Refracted at a Spherical Surface.—In § 34 a method was explained for constructing the path of a ray refracted from one medium into another, which is always applicable to a refracting surface of any form.

The following elegant and useful construction of the path of
a ray refracted at a spherical surface was published in 1807
by THOMAS YOUNG (1773–1829.)

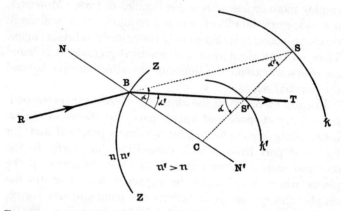

FIG. 226.—Construction of ray refracted at convex spherical surface $(n' > n)$.

In the accompanying diagrams (Figs. 226 to 229) the
center of the spherical refracting surface ZZ is designated
by C. The point R is any point on the path of the incident
ray lying in the first medium of refractive index n. The point

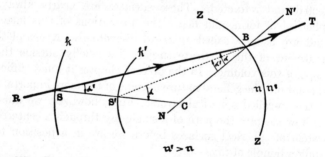

FIG. 227.—Construction of ray refracted at concave spherical surface $(n' > n)$.

where the ray meets the spherical refracting surface is marked
B. The plane of the paper which contains the incident ray
RB and the incidence-normal BC is the plane of incidence.

The index of refraction of the second medium is denoted by
n' and the radius of the spherical refracting surface by r.
Around C as center and with radii equal to $n'.r/n$ and $n.r/n'$

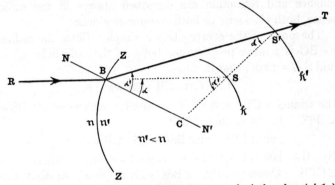

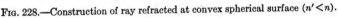

FIG. 228.—Construction of ray refracted at convex spherical surface $(n'<n)$.

describe, in the plane of incidence, the circular arcs k and k',
respectively; and let S designate the point where the straight
line RB, produced if necessary, meets the arc k. Draw the
straight line CS intersecting the arc k' in the point S'. Then

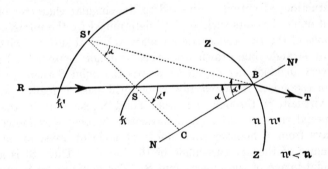

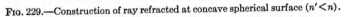

FIG. 229.—Construction of ray refracted at concave spherical surface $(n'<n)$.

the straight line BT drawn from B through S' will represent
the path of the refracted ray. In making this construction,
care must be taken to select for the point S that one of the

two points in which the straight line RB cuts the circle k which will make the segments BS and BS′ both fall on the same side of the incidence-normal, since the angles of incidence and refraction are described always in the same sense, both clockwise or both counter-clockwise.

The proof of the construction is simple. Since the radius $r = BC$ is a mean proportional between the radii $SC = n'.r/n$ and $S\ C = n.r/n'$, that is, since

$$CS : CB = CB : CS' = n' : n,$$

the triangles CBS and CBS′ are similar, and hence $\angle CBS = \angle BS'C$. In the triangle CBS:

$$\sin\angle CBS : \sin\angle BSC = CS : CB = n' : n.$$

By the law of refraction: $n.\sin\alpha = n'.\sin\alpha'$, where $\alpha = \angle CBS$. Consequently, $\angle BSC = \angle CBS' = \alpha'$, so that the straight line BS′ is the path of the refracted ray.

This construction can be employed to trace the path of a ray graphically from one surface to the next through a centered system of spherical refracting surfaces.

177. The Aplanatic Points of a Spherical Refracting Surface.—Incidentally, in connection with the preceding construction, attention is directed to the singular character of all pairs of points such as S, S′ determined by the intersections of the two concentric auxiliary spherical surfaces with any straight line drawn from their common center C. To every incident ray directed towards the point S there will correspond a refracted ray which will pass ("really" or "virtually") through the other point S′; so that in this special case we obtain a homocentric bundle of refracted rays from a homocentric bundle of incident rays, for all values of the aperture-angle of the bundle. Thus, S′ is a point-image of the object-point S. The distances of S and S′ from the center C are connected by the invariant-relation:

$$n'^2.CS' = n^2.CS.$$

That pair of these points which lies on the optical axis is especially distinguished and called the pair of *aplanatic points* of the spherical refracting surface; they are designated by J, J′ (Fig. 230). Thus, we have:

$$CJ : AC = AC : CJ' = n' : n,$$

or

$$CJ.CJ' = r^2, \quad n^2.CJ = n'^2.CJ'.$$

The aplanatic points, therefore, lie always on the same side

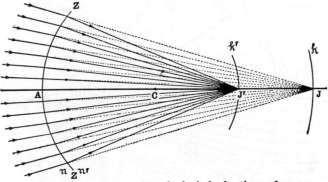

Fig. 230.—Aplanatic points of spherical refracting surface.

of the center C, so that whereas the rays must pass "really" through one of them, they will pass "virtually" through the other. In geometrical language the points J, J′ are said to be harmonically separated (§ 67) by the extremities of the axial diameter of the refracting sphere.

178. Spherical Aberration Along the Axis.—However, in general, a homocentric bundle of rays incident on a spherical refracting surface will not be homocentric after refraction. The diagram (Fig. 231) represents the case of a meridian section of a bundle of incident rays which are all parallel to the axis of a convex spherical refracting surface for which $n' > n$. It will be seen that, whereas the paraxial rays after refraction meet on the axis at the second focal point F′, the outermost or edge rays cross the axis at a point L′ between the vertex A and the focal point F′; and the intermediate rays cross the axis at points lying between F′ and L′. The segment F′L′ is the measure of the *spherical aberration along* *the axis* or the axial aberration of the edge ray of a direct cylindrical bundle of incident rays. (By a "direct" bundle of rays is meant a bundle of rays emanating from a point on the axis.) In the figure this segment is negative, that is, measured in the sense opposite to that of the incident light; and

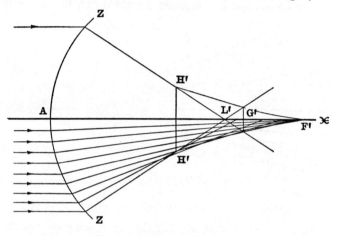

FIG. 231.—Spherical aberration.

this effect is usually described by saying that a convex spherical refracting surface at which light is refracted from air to glass is *spherically under-corrected;* whereas, under the same circumstances, a concave spherical refracting surface will be found to be spherically *over-corrected*, that is, the segment F'L' in this case will be positive. In fact, the points of intersection of pairs of consecutive rays lying in the plane of a meridian section of a spherical refracting surface form a curved line lying symmetrically above and below the axis, if the bundle of incident rays is symmetric with respect to the axis; and this plane curve is the so-called *caustic curve* of the meridian rays. The two branches on opposite sides of the axis unite in a double point or cusp at the point on the axis where the paraxial rays intersect, so that the axis is tangent to both branches at this point, which in the figure is the point F′. The system is said to be spherically over-corrected or under-corrected according as the cusp is turned towards the incident light (<) or away from it (>), respectively; on the supposition that the incident rays are parallel to the axis. Each refracted ray in the meridian plane touches the caustic curve, and hence this curve is said to be the geometrical envelope of the meridian section of the bundle of refracted rays.

If the entire figure is revolved around the optical axis the arc ZZ will generate a zone of the spherical refracting surface containing the vertex A; and each incident ray proceeding parallel to the axis will generate a cylindrical surface, and all the refracted rays corresponding to the incident rays which lie on the surface of one of these cylinders will intersect in one point lying on the axis between F′ and L′. The revolution of the caustic curve will generate a *caustic surface*, which will be the enveloping surface of the bundle of refracted rays (see § 187.)

The caustic curve terminates at the point H′ where the edge ray intersects the next consecutive ray in the meridian section. If a plane screen erected at right angles to the axis so as to catch the light transmitted by the bundle of refracted rays is placed initially in the transversal plane that passes through the extreme point H′ and then gradually shifted parallel to the axis towards the second focal plane, there will appear on the screen at first a circular patch of light surrounded on its outer edge by a brighter ring, which will gradually contract as the screen approaches L′. Between L′ and F′ there will be seen at the center of the circular patch of light an increasingly bright spot. For a certain position G′ where the distance of the screen from F′ is about three-fourths of the length of F′L′ the cross-section of the bundle of refracted rays will have its narrowest contraction. This section is sometimes called the *least circle of aberration*.

179. Spherical Zones.—Since, in general, it is not possible to abolish the spherical aberration of a single spherical refracting surface, the only means available is to try to accomplish this result by distributing the duty of refracting the rays over a series of surfaces whose curvatures and distances apart are so nicely adjusted with respect to each other that when the rays finally emerge they will all unite in one focus on the axis. Thus, for example, if the incident rays are supposed to be parallel to the axis of the system, and if the system has been designed so as to be spherically corrected

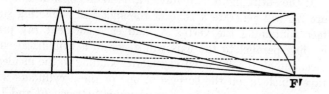

FIG. 232.—Graphical representation of the spherical zones of a lens.

for the edge ray which meets the first surface at the distance h from the axis, it is conceivable that all the intermediate rays of incidence-heights z (where $h > z > 0$) might perchance emerge from the system along paths which all likewise passed through the focal point F′; but practically this never happens. If the edge ray intersects the axis at F′, an intermediate ray of incidence-height z will cross the axis at some other point L′, and the segment F′L′ is called the *spherical aberration of the zone of radius z* or simply the *spherical zone z*. The spherical zones of a lens may be exhibited graphically by plotting a curve whose abscissæ are the values of F′L′ and whose ordinates are the corresponding values of z, as represented in Fig. 232.

180. Trigonometrical Calculation of a Ray Refracted at a Spherical Surface.— The diagram (Fig. 233) represents a meridian section ZZ of a spherical refracting surface of radius r ($=AC$) separating two media of indices of refraction n, n'. A ray RB incident on the surface at B at an angle $\alpha = \angle NBR = \angle CBL$ crosses the axis at L at a slope-angle $\theta = \angle ALB$. If the central angle is denoted by $\phi = \angle BCA$, and if the abscissa of the point L with respect to the center C is denoted by c, that is, if $c = CL$, then in the triangle CBL, we have the relations:

$$a = \theta + \phi, \qquad c.\sin\theta = -r.\sin a.$$

The path of the corresponding refracted ray is shown by the straight line BT which crosses the axis at the point L′; and

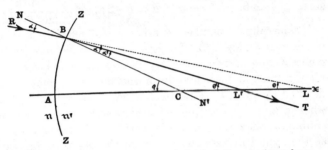

Fig. 233.—Diagram for trigonometrical calculation of refracted ray.

if we put $a' = \angle N'BL'$, $\theta' = \angle AL'B$ and $c' = CL'$, we obtain a similar pair of formulæ from the triangle CBL′, namely:

$$a' = \theta' + \phi, \qquad c'.\sin\theta' = -r.\sin a'.$$

Accordingly, being given the constants denoted by n, n' and r, and the parameters (c, θ) of the incident ray, we can find the parameters (c', θ') of the refracted ray by means of the following system of equations:

$$\sin a = -\frac{c}{r}\sin\theta,$$

$$\sin a' = \frac{n}{n'}\sin a, \qquad \theta' = \theta + a' - a,$$

$$c' = -r\frac{\sin a'}{\sin\theta'}.$$

It is easy to see that if we have given two incident rays which both cross the axis at the same point L, so that the abscissa c has the same value for both rays while the slope-angles θ are different, different values of c' will, in general, be obtained for the abscissæ of the points where the two corresponding refracted rays cross the axis. This is the analytical statement of the fact of spherical aberration (§ 178).

The formulæ for calculating the path of a ray reflected at a *spherical mirror* may be derived immediately by putting $n' = -n$ (§ 75) in the preceding system of equations. Thus we find:

$$\sin a = -\frac{c}{r}\sin\theta, \quad a' = -a, \quad \theta' = \theta - 2a, \quad c' = r\frac{\sin a}{\sin(\theta - 2a)}.$$

Incidentally, a number of other useful relations may be obtained from Fig. 233. For example, if the distances of the points L and L′ where the ray crosses the axis before and after refraction measured from the incidence-point B are denoted by l and l', respectively, that is, if $l = BL$, $l' = BL'$, where l and l' are to be reckoned positive or negative according as these lengths are measured in the same direction as the light traverses the ray or in the opposite direction, respectively; then

$$l'.\sin\theta' = l.\sin\theta;$$

and, since by the law of refraction,

$$n'.c'.\sin\theta' = n.c.\sin\theta,$$

we obtain the useful invariant relation:

$$\frac{n'.c'}{l'} = \frac{n.c}{l}.$$

Moreover, by projecting the two sides c and l of the triangle CBL on the third side r, the following formula is obtained:

$$r = l.\cos a - c.\cos\phi,$$

which may be written:

$$\frac{c}{l} = \frac{r}{\cos\phi}\left(\frac{\cos a}{r} - \frac{1}{l}\right).$$

Similarly, in the triangle CBL′:

$$\frac{c'}{l'} = \frac{r}{\cos\phi}\left(\frac{\cos a'}{r} - \frac{1}{l'}\right).$$

Multiplying the first of these equations by n and the second by n' and equating the resulting expressions, we find:

$$n'\left(\frac{\cos a'}{r} - \frac{1}{l'}\right) = n\left(\frac{\cos a}{r} - \frac{1}{l}\right),$$

which may also be written:

$$\frac{n'}{l'}-\frac{n}{l}=\frac{n'.\cos a'-n.\cos a}{r}=D \text{ (say)};$$

or finally:

$$L'=L+D,$$

where $L=n/l$, $L'=n'/l'$.

If the ray is a *paraxial ray*, we may put $\cos a=\cos a'=1$ (§ 63); and now if we write u, u' in place of l, l', respectively, the formula above will reduce to the abscissa-equation for the refraction of a paraxial ray at a spherical surface (§ 78).

Moreover, if in the last formula we put $n'=-n$ (§ 75), we find the corresponding relation for the *reflection of a ray at a spherical mirror*, namely:

$$\frac{1}{l}+\frac{1}{l'}=\frac{2\cos a}{r}.$$

181. Path of Ray through a Centered System of Spherical Refracting Surfaces.   Numerical Calculation.—Using the same system of notation as in § 118, we may write the formula for the refraction of a paraxial ray at the kth surface of a centered system of spherical refracting surfaces, as follows:

$$U_k'=U_k+F_k,$$

where

$$U_k=n_k/u_k, \quad U_k'=n_{k+1}/u_k', \quad \text{and } F_k=(n_{k+1}-n_k)/r_k;$$
$$u_k=A_kM_k, \quad u_k'=A_kM_{k+1}, \quad r_k=A_kC_k.$$

And if $d_k=A_kA_{k+1}$, then also:

$$1/U_{k+1}=1/U'_k-d_k/n_{k+1}.$$

According to the relations given in § 180, we have the following system of formulæ for the refraction at the kth surface of a ray whose slope-angles before and after refraction have the finite values $\theta_k=\angle A_kL_kB_k$ and $\theta_{k+1}=\angle A_kL_{k+1}B_k$, respectively:

$$\sin a_k=-\frac{c_k}{r_k}.\sin \theta_k, \quad \sin a_k'=\frac{n_k}{n_{k+1}}.\sin a_k,$$
$$\theta_{k+1}=\theta_k+a_k'-a_k, \quad c_k'=-r_k.\frac{\sin a_k'}{\sin \theta_{k+1}},$$

where $c_k = C_k L_k$ and $c_k' = C_k L_{k+1}$. Moreover, if we put
$$a_k = C_k C_{k+1} = d_k + r_{k+1} - r_k,$$
then

$$c_{k+1} = c_k' - a_k.$$

In order to exhibit the methods of calculations by means of these formulæ, a comparatively simple numerical illustration is appended. The actual example here chosen is one given by Dr. MAX LANGE in his paper entitled "Vereinfachte Formeln für die trigonometrische Durchrechnung optischer Systeme" (Leipzig, 1909), pages 24, foll. The optical system is a two-lens object-glass of a telescope for which the data were published by Dr. R. STEINHEIL in the *Zeitschrift für Instrumentenkunde*, xvii (1897), p. 339, as follows:

Indices of refraction (for D-line):
$n_1 = n_3 = n_5 = 1$ (air); $n_2 = 1.614\ 400$ (flint); $n_4 = 1.518\ 564$ (crown).

Thicknesses:
$$d_1 = 2; \quad d_2 = 0.01; \quad d_3 = 5.$$
Radii:

$r_1 = +420;\ r_2 = +181.995;\ r_3 = +178.710;\ r_4 = -40\ 133.8.$
The incident rays are parallel to the axis, so that
$$\theta_1 = 0, \qquad u_1 = c_1 = \infty \quad (U_1 = 0).$$
The calculation is divided into two parts, namely: (1) the calculation of the paraxial ray, and (2) the trigonometric calculation of the edge ray which meets the first surface of the object-glass at the height $h_1 = 33$ above the axis. When $c_1 = \infty$, we find $\sin a_1 = h_1/r_1$, which, according to the above data, gives lg $\sin a_1 = 8.8952646$. This is the starting point of the calculation of the edge ray.

Each vertical column contains the calculation for one spherical refracting surface. The sign written after a logarithm indicates the sign of the number to which the logarithm belongs. Generally the calculations do not have to be performed to the degree of accuracy to which they are carried here.

1. PARAXIAL RAY

	$k=1$	$k=2$	$k=3$	$k=4$
$\lg(n_{k+1}-n_k)$	9.7884512+	9.7884512−	9.7148024+	9.7148024−
clg r_k	7.3767507+	7.7399406+	7.7478511+	5.3964898−
lg F_k	7.1652019+	7.5283918−	7.4626535+	5.1112922+
F_k	+0.00146286	−0.00337592	+0.00290171	+0.00001292
U_k	0.00000000	+0.00146552	−0.00191036	+0.00099459
U_k'	+0.00146286	−0.00191040	+0.00099135	+0.00100751
clg U_k'	2.8347981+	2.7188755−	3.0037761+	2.9967506+
lg d_k	0.3010300+	8.0000000+	0.6989700+	
clg n_{k+1}	9.7919889+	0.0000000+	9.8185669+	
$\lg(d_k/n_{k+1})$	0.0930189+	8.0000000+	0.5175369+	
$-d_k/n_{k+1}$	− 1.2389	− 0.0100	3.2926	
$1/U_k'$	+683.5924	−523.4504	+1008.7327	
$1/U_{k+1}$	+682.3535	−523.4604	+1005.4401	
lg U_{k+1}	7.1659906+	7.2811162−	6.9976438+	

$$\lg u_4' = \text{clg } U_4' = 2.9967506+; \quad u_4' = A_4F' = +992.546$$

$$\text{clg } (U_1'.U_2'.U_3'.U_4') = 1.5541994-$$
$$\lg (U_2.U_3.U_4) = 1.4447506-$$
$$\lg f = 2.9989500+$$
$$f = +997.585$$

2. EDGE RAY

	$k=1$	$k=2$	$k=3$	$k=4$
$-a_{k-1}$		+236.0050	+ 3.2750	+40307.51
$c_k'-1$		+682.2850	− 685.6727	+ 1353.49
c_k		+918.2900	− 682.3977	+41661.00
lg c_k		2.9629799+	2.8340376−	4.6197297+
lg $\sin\theta_k$		8.4765370−	8.8114112+	8.3325613−
clg r_k		7.7399405+	7.7478511+	5.3964898−
lg $\sin\alpha_k$	8.8952646+	9.1794574+	9.3932999+	8.3487808−
lg n_k/n_{k+1}	9.7919889+	0.2080111+	9.8185669+	0.1814331+
lg $\sin\alpha_k'$	8.6872535+	9.3874685+	9.2118668+	8.5302139−
lg r_k	2.6232493+	2.2600595+	2.2521489+	4.6035102−
clg $\sin\theta_{k+1}$	1.5234630−	1.1885888+	1.6674387−	1.4803948−
lg c_k'	2.8339658+	2.8361168−	3.1314544+	4.6141189+

$$-\alpha_1 = -\ 4°\ 30'\ 23.24'' \qquad c_4' = +41126.23$$
$$\alpha_1' = +\ 2°\ 47'\ 22.69'' \qquad r_4 = -40133.80$$
$$\theta_1 = 0,\ \ \alpha_1' - \alpha_1 = \theta_2 = -\ 1°\ 43'\ \ 0.55''\ \mathrm{A}_4\mathrm{L}_5 = +\ \ \ 992.43$$
$$-\alpha_2 = -\ 8°\ 41'\ 40.45'' \quad -u_4' = -\ \ \ 992.55$$
$$\overline{-10°\ 24'\ 41.00''}\ \ \mathrm{F'L}_5 = -\ \ \ \ \ \ 0.12$$
$$\alpha_2' = +14°\ \ 7'\ 31.28''$$
$$\overline{\theta_3 = +\ 3°\ 42'\ 50.28''}$$
$$-\alpha_3 = -14°\ 19'\ 13.26''$$
$$\overline{-10°\ 36'\ 22.98''}$$
$$\alpha_3' = +\ 9°\ 22'\ 26.69''$$
$$\overline{\theta_4 = -\ 1°\ 13'\ 56.29''}$$
$$-\alpha_4 = +\ 1°\ 16'\ 45.13''$$
$$\overline{+\ 0°\ \ 2'\ 48.84''}$$
$$\alpha_4' = -\ 1°\ 56'\ 33.95''$$
$$\overline{\theta_5 = -\ 1°\ 53'\ 45.11''}$$

Thus, we see that this object-glass has a slight spherical aberration of -0.12, that is, it is a little under-corrected (§ 178).

182. The Sine-Condition or Condition of Aplanatism.— Suppose that for a certain object-point M (Fig. 234) on the axis of a symmetrical optical instrument the spherical aberration has been abolished for all the zones of the system, so that rays proceeding from this point will all be accurately focused at the conjugate image-point M'. On a straight line perpendicular to the axis at M take a point Q very close to M; and let $y' = $ M'Q' denote the size of the image of the object $y = $ MQ which is produced by the central zone, that is, by the paraxial rays. Now even though the system is spherically corrected with respect to the pair of axial points M, M', it by no means follows that rays emanating from Q will all meet again in Q'. In order that this shall be the case, the magnification-ratio must be equal to y'/y for all the zones of the system. Draw the object-ray MB₁ and the corresponding image-ray B₂M'; if the slopes of these rays are denoted by θ and θ', it may be shown that for the zone corresponding to the incidence-point B_1 the magnification-ratio is equal to $n.\sin\theta/n'.\sin\theta'$; and if this is equal to y'/y, then the image formed by rays belonging to this zone will be of the same size as the image y' made by the paraxial rays.

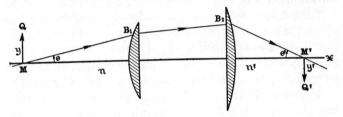

Fig. 234.—Sine-condition.

Thus, in order that with the employment of wide-angle bundles of rays a symmetrical optical instrument may produce a sharp image of a little plane element perpendicular to the axis of the instrument, not only must the system be spherically corrected for the pair of conjugate axial points M, M′, but it must also satisfy the so-called *Sine-Condition*, namely,

$$\frac{n.\sin\theta}{n'.\sin\theta'}=\frac{y'}{y}=\boldsymbol{y}.$$

This celebrated principle was clearly formulated by Abbe in 1873, but it had already been recognized by Seidel, and it may be deduced from a general law of radiant energy which was first given by Clausius (1864). The proof of it must be omitted here. It may be stated in words as follows: The necessary and sufficient condition that all the zones of a spherically corrected system shall produce images of equal size at the point M′ conjugate to the axial point M is that, for all rays proceeding from M, the ratio of the sines of the slope-angles θ, θ' of each pair of corresponding incident and emergent rays shall be constant; that is,

$$\frac{\sin\theta}{\sin\theta'}=\frac{n'}{n}.\boldsymbol{y}=\text{constant}.$$

The sine-condition

$$n.y.\sin\theta = n'.y'.\sin\theta'$$

is essentially different from the SMITH-HELMHOLTZ law for paraxial rays (see § 88 and § 118), namely, $n.y.\tan\theta = n'.y'.\tan\theta'$, although when the angles θ, θ' are small, both conditions may be expressed by the equation $n.y.\ \theta = n'.y'.\ \theta'$.

If the optical system is spherically corrected for the pair of axial points M, M', and if at the same time the sine-condition is satisfied, the points M, M' are called the *aplanatic pair of points* of the system. It may be demonstrated that no optical system can have more than one pair of such aplanatic points. In the case of a single spherical refracting surface the two points J, J' (§ 177) whose distances from the center C are such that

$$CJ.CJ' = r^2, \qquad n^2CJ = n'^2CJ',$$

are a pair of aplanatic points as above defined; for they are free from spherical aberration and if they are joined by straight lines BJ, BJ' with any point B on the spherical refracting surface, and if we put $\theta = \angle CJB$, $\theta' = \angle CJ'B$, we have $\sin\theta/\sin\theta' = n/n' = \text{constant}$. This property of the points J, J' of a refracting sphere has been ingeniously utilized in the construction of the objective of the compound microscope.

If in Fig. 234 we put $l = B_1M$, then $\sin\theta = -h/l$, where h denotes the height of the point B_1 above the axis. Hence, the sine-condition may be written:

$$\frac{h}{l.\sin\theta'} = \frac{n'}{n}\cdot y;$$

or since (§ 124)

$$y = \frac{f}{x} = -\frac{n}{n'}\cdot\frac{f'}{x},$$

where f, f' denote the focal lengths of the system and x denotes the abscissa of M with respect to the primary focal point F ($x = FM$), we obtain also:

$$\frac{h}{\sin\theta'} = \frac{l.f'}{x}.$$

Suppose now that the object-point M is infinitely distant so that $x = l = \infty$; then for a ray parallel to the axis meeting the first surface at the height h, we shall have:

$$\frac{h}{\sin \theta'} = f'.$$

Thus, if the aplanatic points are the infinitely distant point of the axis and the second focal point F', and if around F' as center we describe a sphere of radius equal to f', the parallel object-rays will meet their corresponding image-rays on the surface of this sphere; whereas in the case of collinear imagery with paraxial rays the points of intersection of the incident and emergent rays under the same circumstances will all lie in the secondary principal plane (§ 119), which touches the sphere above mentioned at the point where the axis crosses it.

If therefore we put $h/\sin \theta' = e$, the sine-condition for an infinitely distant object is $e + f = 0$. For example, in the case of the telescope objective calculated in § 181:

$$\begin{aligned}
\lg h_1 &= 1.5185139 + \\
\text{clg } \sin \theta_5 &= \overline{1.4803948 -} \\
\lg e &= 2.9989087 - \quad e = -997.490 \\
&\qquad\qquad\qquad\quad f = +997.585 \\
&\qquad\qquad\quad e + f = +\ \ 0.095
\end{aligned}$$

Accordingly, the sine-condition is very nearly satisfied in the case of this object-glass.

183. Caustic Surfaces.—The characteristic geometrical property of a bundle of light-rays emanating originally from a point-source is expressed in a law announced by MALUS in 1808 (§ 39), which may be stated in terms of the undulatory theory of light as follows: The rays of light are always normal to the wave-surfaces. In fact, what is meant by a wave-surface is any surface which cuts the rays orthogonally. In general, the curvatures of the normal sections at any point of a curved surface will vary from one azimuth to another; but, according to EULER's theorem (§ 111), the normal sections of greatest and least curvature, called the *principal sections* of the surface at the point in question, are always at right angles to each other. It is well known that the normal drawn to any point of a curved surface will not meet the normal at a consecutive point taken arbitrarily. But if the consecutive point is taken in the direction of either of the principal sections, the two consecutive normals will intersect. Thus, along each normal to a curved surface there are two points called the principal centers of curvature (§ 111), where consecutive normals lying in the two principal sections intersect.

Accordingly, if we regard a bundle of rays of light as a system of normals to the wave-surface, we may say that each ray determines two principal sections of the bundle, and that, in general, there will be two points on the ray, the so-called *image-points* (*cf.* § 113), where contiguous rays in each of the two principal sections intersect the ray in question. The assemblage of these pairs of image-points on all the rays of a wide-angle bundle of rays emanating originally from a point-source form a surface of two sheets called the *caustic surface* (*cf.* § 42). Each ray of the bundle is tangent to both sheets of the caustic surface. In the special case when the bundle of rays is symmetrical about an axis, one sheet of the caustic surface will be a surface of revolution, whereas the other sheet will be a portion of the axis of symmetry (see § 178).

184. Meridian and Sagittal Sections of a Narrow Bundle of Rays before and after Refraction at a Spherical Surface. —The apertures of the bundles of effective rays which are transmitted through a symmetrical optical instrument are all limited by the position and dimensions of the aperture-stop (§ 134). For the present it will be assumed that the diameter of the stop is very small. Each point of the object lying in the field of view is the source of a narrow bundle of rays which contains one ray, called the *chief ray* (§ 140), which in traversing the medium where the stop is placed, passes through the center of the stop. Accordingly, the chief ray will lie in the meridian plane determined by the object-

point where the bundle of rays originates. The path of this
chief ray may be traced geometrically by YOUNG's construction (§ 176) or it may be calculated trigonometrically by
means of the system of formulæ given in § 181. We have
now to investigate the positions on this chief ray of the two
image-points produced by the intersections of this ray with
the rays immediately adjacent to it lying in the two principal sections of the bundle as determined by its chief ray
(§ 183). Whenever a narrow bundle of rays has two such
image-points, it is said to be *astigmatic*. Practically, this is
always the case if the chief ray is incident on a refracting
surface at an angle *a* which is not vanishingly small. Under
such conditions the bundle of refracted rays will be astigmatic, and we have the case which some writers call "astigmatism by incidence" but which is better described as the
astigmatism of an oblique bundle of rays, as distinguished from

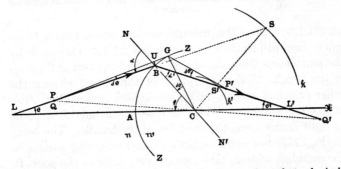

Fig. 235.—Meridian section of narrow bundle of rays refracted at spherical
surface.

the astigmatism produced by direct (normal) incidence on
an astigmatic refracting surface or surface of double curvature (Chapter IX).

In the diagrams (Figs. 235, 236), which show the meridian
section ZZ of a spherical refracting surface whose center is at
C and vertex at A (Fig. 235), the point designated by P (or Q)
represents an object-point which is the source of a narrow

homocentric bundle of rays whose chief ray PB (or QB) is incident on the surface at the point B at the angle of incidence a. This ray crosses the axis at the point màrked L in Fig. 235 and the corresponding refracted ray crosses the

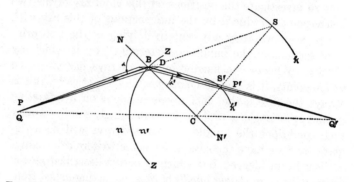

FIG. 236.—Sagittal section of narrow bundle of rays refracted at spherical surface.

axis at L'. One of the principal sections of the bundle of incident rays will be the *meridian section* (§§ 112, 113) made by the plane containing the optical axis and the vertex P (or Q) of the bundle, that is the plane of the paper; whereas the other principal section, called the *sagittal section* (Fig. 236), is made by a plane which intersects the meridian plane at right angles along the chief ray of the bundle. The point G (Fig. 235) is a point on the spherical refracting surface in the meridian section, taken exceedingly close to the point B. Likewise, the point D (Fig. 236) lies on the spherical refracting surface very near to B; but it is contained in the sagittal section and is represented in the diagram as lying slightly above the plane of the paper. The ray PG (Fig. 235) after refraction meets the chief refracted ray at the image-point P' of the narrow pencil of refracted meridian rays. Similarly, the ray QD (Fig. 236) after refraction will meet the chief refracted ray at the image-point Q' where the straight line QC intersects this ray, as will be immediately obvious by supposing that the triangle QBQ' is revolved around the central line QQ' as axis through a small angle out from the plane of the paper. Thus, whereas the meridian section of the bundle of refracted rays is contained in the same plane as the meridian section of the bundle of incident rays, the sagittal sections are in two different planes BDQ and BDQ' (Fig. 236) which intersect each other in a straight line perpendicular to the meridian plane at the point B, that is, in the line BD, which, since the point D is infinitely near to B, may be regarded as a straight line.

185. Formula for Locating the Position of the Image-Point Q' of a Pencil of Sagittal Rays Refracted at a Spherical Surface.—As was explained (§ 184), the image-point Q' (Fig. 236) in the sagittal section corresponding to the object-point Q is at the point of intersection of the straight line QC with the chief ray of the bundle of refracted rays. This construction suggests at once a method of obtaining an analytical relation connecting the points Q and Q'; for if the straight line QQ' is regarded for the time being as the axis of the spherical refracting surface, and if we put $q = BQ$, $q' = BQ'$ (where the distances denoted by q, q' are to be reckoned positive or negative according as they are measured from the incidence-point B in the same direction as the light takes along the chief ray or in the opposite direction, respectively), we have merely to write q, q' in place of the symbols l, l' in the formula derived in § 180 in order to obtain the desired relation, namely,

$$\frac{n'}{q'} - \frac{n}{q} = D,$$

where the function denoted here by D is a constant for a given chief ray and is defined by the following expression:

$$D = \frac{n'.\cos a' - n.\cos a}{r} = \frac{n.\sin(a - a')}{r.\sin a'}.$$

Thus, having ascertained the path of the chief ray, and knowing the position of the object-point Q, that is, being given the value of q, we may calculate the value of q' by means of the above formula and thus locate the position of the image-point Q′ of the sagittal section of the bundle of refracted rays.

186. Position of the Image-Point P′ of a Pencil of Meridian Rays Refracted at a Spherical Surface.—The angles of incidence and refraction of the chief ray are denoted by a, a', respectively. Moreover, let θ, θ' (Fig. 235) denote the angles which the chief ray makes with the axis of the spherical refracting surface before and after refraction, respectively; and also let the central angle BCA be denoted by ϕ. Then for a contiguous ray in the meridian section which is incident at the point G very close to the point B, these angles may be denoted by $a+da$, $a'+da'$; $\theta+d\theta$, $\theta'+d\theta'$; and $\phi+d\phi$, where da, da', etc., denote the little increments in the magnitudes of the angles a, a', etc., in passing from the chief ray to an adjacent ray in the meridian section. Now since for the rays PB and PG these angles are connected by the formulæ (§ 180);

$$a = \theta+\phi, \qquad a+da = \theta+d\theta+\phi+d\phi,$$

we obtain by subtraction:

$$da = d\theta+d\phi.$$

Around P as center and with radius equal to PB describe the small arc BU which subtends $\angle BPG = d\theta$; so that we may write:

$$d\theta = -\frac{\text{arc BU}}{p},$$

where $p=$ BP denotes the distance of the object-point P from the incidence-point B, being reckoned positive or negative exactly in the same way as q in § 185. Now the sides of the little curvilinear triangle BGU may be considered as straight to the degree of approximation with which we are concerned at present, and since the sides of the angle GBU are perpendicular to the sides of the angle of incidence a, so that $\angle GBU = a$, we obtain:

$$\text{arc BU} = \text{arc GB}.\cos a.$$

Combining this relation with the one above, we have therefore:

$$d\theta = -\frac{\text{arc GB.cos } \alpha}{p} .$$

Moreover, since $\angle \text{GCB} = d\phi$,

$$d\phi = \frac{\text{arc GB}}{r} ;$$

and, therefore, by adding this equation to the last and taking account of the relation above, we find:

$$d\alpha = \left(\frac{1}{r} - \frac{\cos \alpha}{p}\right) . \text{arc GB.} \qquad (1)$$

Similarly, for the corresponding refracted rays BP′ and GP′ which intersect at the image-point P′, for which BP′ = p', we can derive the analogous relation:

$$d\alpha' = \left(\frac{1}{r} - \frac{\cos \alpha'}{p'}\right). \text{arc GB.} \qquad (2)$$

Now according to the law of refraction,

$$n.\sin \alpha = n'.\sin \alpha', \qquad n.\sin(\alpha + d\alpha) = n'.\sin(\alpha' + d\alpha'),$$

and if in the expansions of $\sin(\alpha + d\alpha)$ and $\sin(\alpha' + d\alpha')$ we write $d\alpha$ and $d\alpha'$ in place of $\sin d\alpha$ and $\sin d\alpha'$ and put $\cos d\alpha = \cos d\alpha' = 1$, as is permissible on account of the smallness of these angles, we may derive the following relation between $d\alpha$ and $d\alpha'$:

$$n.\cos \alpha.d\alpha = n'.\cos \alpha'.d\alpha'. \qquad (3)$$

Hence, multiplying equation (1) by $n.\cos \alpha$ and equation (2) by $n'.\cos \alpha'$, and equating the two expressions thus obtained, according to equation (3), we find, after removing the common factor, arc GB, the following formula connecting the ray-intercepts p and p':

$$n'.\cos \alpha' \left(\frac{\cos \alpha'}{p'} - \frac{1}{r}\right) = n.\cos \alpha \left(\frac{\cos \alpha}{p} - \frac{1}{r}\right) ;$$

which may also be written thus:

$$\frac{n'.\cos^2 \alpha'}{p'} - \frac{n.\cos^2 \alpha}{p} = D,$$

where the symbol D has the same meaning as before in § 185. If we introduce ABBE's differential notation and use the operator Δ placed in front of a symbol to denote the difference in the value of the magnitude denoted by the symbol before and after refraction, that is, for example, if $\Delta z = z' - z$; then we may write the two formulæ for p and q in the following abbreviated form:

$$\Delta \frac{n}{q} = \Delta \frac{n.\cos^2 a}{p} = D.$$

The position of the image-point P′ of the meridian section of a narrow bundle of rays refracted at a spherical surface may also be quickly ascertained by a simple geometrical

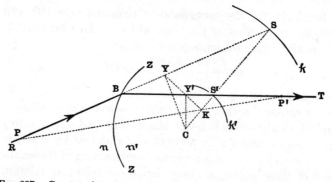

Fig. 237.—Construction of center of perspective (K) with respect to a given ray refracted at a spherical surface.

construction which depends on finding a point K called the *center of perspective*, which bears precisely the same relation to the pair of points P, P′ as the center C of the spherical surface bears to the pair of points Q, Q′ (§ 184); that is, just as the straight line QQ′ must pass through C, so also the straight line PP′ must pass through K. The existence of this point K was first recognized by THOMAS YOUNG (1801). In the diagram (Fig. 237) the chief incident ray is represented by the straight line RB and the chief refracted ray, constructed by the method given in § 175, is represented by the straight line BT. From the center C draw CY and CY′ perpendicular to RB and BT at Y and Y′, respectively. The point K will be found to lie at the point of intersection of the straight lines YY' and SS'; and hence if P designates the position of an object-point lying anywhere on the chief incident ray, the corresponding image-point P' in the meridian section will lie at the point where the straight line PK meets the chief refracted ray. This beautiful construction is exceedingly useful in graphical methods of investigating the imagery in the meridian section along a particular ray. The proof of the construction is not at all difficult, but it cannot be conveniently given here.

187. Measure of the Astigmatism of a Narrow Bundle of Rays.—We have seen that, in general, a narrow homocentric bundle of rays falling obliquely on a spherical refracting surface is transformed into an astigmatic bundle of refracted rays, so that corresponding to a given object-point P (or Q) there will be two so-called image-points P' and Q' lying on the refracted chief ray at the points of intersection of the rays of the meridian and sagittal sections, respectively. The interval between these image-points, that is, the segment $P'Q' = q' - p'$ is called the *astigmatic difference*. However, it is more convenient to measure the astigmatism by the difference between the reciprocals of the linear magnitudes p' and q'. If, for example, according to the system of notation introduced in § 106, we put

$$n/p = P, \quad n'/p' = P', \quad n/q = Q, \quad n'/q' = Q',$$

the formulæ derived in §§ 185, 186 may be written as follows:

$$Q' - Q = P'.\cos^2 \alpha' - P.\cos^2 \alpha = D;$$

where, on the assumption that the meter is taken as the unit of length, the magnitudes denoted by the capital letters will all be expressed in terms of the dioptry. The astigmatism of the bundle of refracted rays is measured by $(P' - Q')$. If the bundle of incident rays is homocentric $(Q = P)$, the astigmatism of the bundle of refracted rays will be:

$$P' - Q' = P'.\sin^2 \alpha' - P.\sin^2 \alpha.$$

Accordingly, we see that the astigmatism of a bundle of rays refracted at a spherical surface will vanish provided

$Q = P$ and $P'.\sin^2 \alpha' - P.\sin^2 \alpha = 0$; which may happen in two ways, as follows:

(1) If $\alpha' = \alpha = 0$, that is, if the chief ray of the narrow bundle meets the refracting surface normally, as, for example, when it is directed along the axis, then no matter where the object-point may lie, the two image-points will coincide. In fact, in case of the axial ray we may put $Q = P = U$, $Q' = P' = U'$, $D = F$, so that the formulæ for the meridian and sagittal sections both reduce in this case to the fundamental equation for the refraction of paraxial rays at a spherical surface, namely, $U' = U + F$.

(2) But for any value of α, we shall have $P' - Q' = 0$, that is, $P'.\sin^2 \alpha' = P.\sin^2 \alpha$, provided $P'/n'^2 = P/n^2$ or $n'.p' = n.p$. In this case the points designated by P, P' (or Q, Q') are identical with the points S, S' in Figs. 226 to 229. If the vertex of the homocentric bundle of incident rays lies at any point S on the surface of the sphere described around C as center with radius equal to $n'.r/n$, the bundle of refracted rays will likewise be homocentric with its vertex at the corresponding point S' on the surface of the concentric sphere of radius $n.r/n'$ (see § 177).

188. Image-Lines (or Focal Lines) of a Narrow Astigmatic Bundle of Rays.—In all the preceding discussion of the properties of an astigmatic bundle of rays, it cannot have escaped notice that only such rays have been considered as are contained in the two principal sections of the bundle. If there were no other rays to be taken into account besides these, we might say that to each point of the object P (or Q) there corresponded two image-points P' and Q'. But this is by no means a complete or even approximately complete statement of the image-phenomenon in this case; for, indeed, the rays which lie in neither of the two principal sections do, as a matter of fact, constitute by far the greater portion of the total number of rays of the bundle. According to the theorem of STURM (1803–1855), the constitution of a narrow bundle of rays is exhibited in the accompanying diagram

(Fig. 238) called STURM'S conoid (§ 113).   All the rays of the
bundle pass through two very short focal lines or *image-lines*
XX and YY which are both perpendicular to the chief ray.
The image-line XX which goes through the point of intersection P' of the meridian rays lies in the plane of the sagittal
section; and, similarly, the image-line YY which goes through
the point of intersection Q' of the sagittal rays lies in the

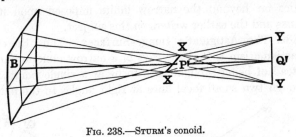

FIG. 238.—STURM'S conoid.

plane of the meridian section.   Strictly speaking, this theorem can be regarded as representing the actual facts only on
the assumption that the bundle of rays is infinitely thin; and
on this assumption the entire bundle may be conceived as
generated by a slight rotation either of the meridian section
around the image-line YY as axis, whereby the point P' will
trace the image-line XX, or of the sagittal section around
the image-line XX as axis, whereby the point Q' will trace
the image-line YY.   Thus, according to STURM'S theorem,
with an object-point P (or Q) lying on the chief ray of an
infinitely narrow bundle of incident rays there are associated
two exceedingly tiny image-lines lying in the principal sections of the bundle of refracted rays at right angles to the
chief ray.   Not only as to the orientation of the image-lines
of STURM, but as to their practical, nay, even as to their
mathematical existence, there has been much controversy,
but we cannot enter into this discussion here.   In spite of
its limitations and admittedly imperfect representation,
STURM'S conoid remains a very useful preliminary mode of
conception of the character of a narrow astigmatic bundle

of rays. The only proper way of arriving at a more accurate knowledge of the constitution of a bundle of light-rays is by the aid of the powerful methods of the infinitesimal geometry. Mathematical investigations of this kind have been pursued with great skill by GULLSTRAND whose writings contained in a series of published papers and treatises dating from about 1890 have extended the domain of theoretical optics far beyond the narrow limits imposed upon it by GAUSS and the earlier writers on this subject.

189. The Astigmatic Image-Surfaces.—Thus, the effect of astigmatism is that the rays of a narrow oblique bundle, instead of being brought to a focus at a single point, pass through two small focal lines at right angles to the path of

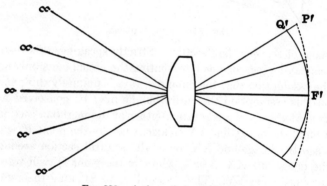

FIG. 239.—Astigmatic image-surfaces.

the chief ray in the image-space. If the chief rays proceeding from the various object-points lying in a meridian plane of a symmetrical optical instrument are constructed, and if along each of these rays the positions of the image-points P', Q' of the pencils of meridian and sagittal rays are determined, the loci of these points will be two curved lines, both symmetrical with respect to the axis, which touch each other at their common vertex on the axis. In the diagram (Fig. 239) the object is supposed to be infinitely distant, as, for example, in the case of a landscape photographic lens. The contin-

uous curved line represents the locus of the points of intersection of the sagittal rays, whereas the dotted curve represents the locus of the points of intersection of the meridian
rays. These curved lines are the traces in the meridian plane
of the two *astigmatic image surfaces* which are generated by
revolving the figure around the axis of symmetry. The two
image-surfaces which correspond to a definite transversal
plane in the object-space, and which are the loci of the most
sharply defined images of object-points lying in this plane, are
not to be confused with the two sheets of the caustic surface
of a wide-angle bundle of rays emanating from a single point
of an object (§ 183). The focal lines of the narrow pencils of
meridian rays lie on one of these surfaces and the focal lines
of the narrow pencils of sagittal rays lie on the other surface.
The positions and forms of the image-surfaces will depend
essentially on the place of the stop; for it is evident that if
the stop is shifted to a different place, the chief ray of each
bundle (§§ 140, 184) will be a different ray, and the points
P' and Q' will all occupy entirely different positions. If a
curved screen could be exactly adjusted to fit one of the
image-surfaces, a fairly sharp image of the object might be
focused on it, but not only would the image be curved instead of flat, but there would also be a certain *astigmatic
deformation* due to the fact that each point of the object
would be reproduced not by a point but by a little focal line,
as has been explained. Between the two image-points P' and
Q' on each chief ray there lies a certain approximately circular cross-section of the narrow astigmatic bundle known
(§ 113) as the "circle of least confusion," and the locus of
the centers of these circles will lie on a third surface intermediate between the other two, which is sometimes taken as a
kind of average or compromise image-surface.

There can be no doubt that astigmatism of oblique bundles
is responsible for serious defects in the image produced by
an optical instrument, and much pains has been bestowed on
trying to remedy this fault as far as possible. Fortunately,

the possibility of abolishing astigmatism of this kind, that is, of making the two image-surfaces coincide in a single surface, is afforded by the fact that the astigmatic difference (§ 187) is opposite in sign according as the refracting surface is convergent or divergent. For example, Fig. 240 shows

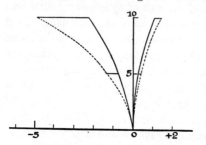

graphically the opposite effects of a convergent and a divergent spherical refracting surface under otherwise equal conditions. The t w o curves on the left-hand side relate to the convergent system, and the two curves on the right-hand side relate to the divergent system; and we see that not only are

Fig. 240.—Astigmatism of convergent spherical refracting surface (plotted on the left) and astigmatism of divergent spherical refracting surface (plotted on the right).

the curvatures opposite in the two cases, but the relative positions of the curves are different. It will not be difficult to understand that it may be possible, by suitable choice of the radii of the refracting surfaces and of their distances apart and also of the position of the stop, to design a system which will be free from astigmatism at any rate for a certain zone of the lens; so that, although we may not be able to make the two astigmatic image-curves coincide absolutely throughout their entire extent, we may contrive so that the two curves are nowhere very far apart, while at one point, corresponding to the corrected zone, they actually intersect each other.

190. Curvature of the Image —Now let us suppose that the astigmatism of oblique bundles has been completely abolished for a certain angular extent of the field of view, so that at last there is strict point-to-point correspondence by means of narrow bundles of rays between object and image. The two image-surfaces have thus been merged into one, and over this surface, within the assigned limits, the definition of the image is clear-cut and distinct. There still remains, however, another trouble due to the fact that the image is curved and not flat; consequently, if the image is received on a plane focusing screen, only those parts of the stigmatic image which lie in the plane of the screen will be in focus (Fig. 241), whereas the rest of the image on the screen will be blurred.

Now this error of the curvature of the image cannot be

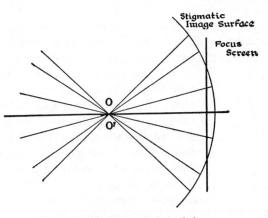

Fig. 241.—Curvature of stigmatic image.

overcome by employing methods similar to those above described for the abolition of astigmatism. For the correction of the latter error the particular kinds of glass of which the lenses were made were not essential; whereas with unsuitable kinds of glass there is no choice of the radii, thicknesses, etc., which will yield an image which is at the same time stigmatic and flat. This fact was well known to PETZVAL (1807–1891). PETZVAL's formula (published in 1843) for the abolition of the curvature of a stigmatic image produced by a system of infinitely thin lenses in contact with each other is

$$\Sigma \frac{F_i}{n_i} = 0,$$

where F_i denotes the refracting power and n_i denotes the index of refraction of the ith lens of the system. This formula is equivalent also to the following statement: The curvature of the stigmatic image of an infinitely distant object in a system of lenses whose total thickness is negligible is equal to

$$\Sigma \left\{ \frac{1}{n} \Sigma \text{ (refracting powers of all lenses of index } n) \right\}$$

The general principal of this equation was discovered by AIRY and was given by CODDINGTON in his treatise published in 1829. SEIDEL pointed out that the two faults of astigmatism and curvature could not both be corrected at the same time unless some of the convex lenses of the system were made of more highly refracting glass than the concave lenses. Now with the varieties of glass which were available before the production of the modern Jena glass, this requirement was directly opposed to the condition of achromatism, and as the latter error was considered more serious than the curvature-error, the earlier lens-designers made no attempt to obtain a flat stigmatic image. But with the new kinds of glass now at our disposal, it is possible to design the optical system so that not only is the astigmatism corrected for a certain zone, as explained in § 189, but the point of intersection of the two image-lines lies in the same transversal plane as the axial point where the two image-lines touch each other (Fig. 242). Accordingly, we may say that for this zone the image is both flat and stigmatic. The construction of modern photographic lenses which are practically free from these spherical errors is an almost unsurpassed triumph of human ingenuity.

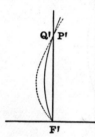

FIG. 242. — Stigmatic image in transversal focal plane for a given zone of optical system.

191. Coma.—Astigmatism implies that the bundles of rays concerned in producing the image are very narrow, and this means that the diameter of the stop is very small. But the validity of the assumptions which are at the foundation of geometrical optics begins to be called in question in the case of narrow bundles of rays, as was pointed out in § 175; so that we must be careful here not to push our conclusions too far. As a matter of fact, in various optical instruments and particularly in some modern types of photographic lenses, the diameter of the stop is by no means small and the

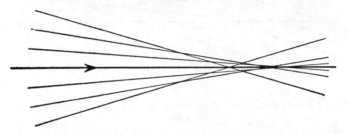

FIG. 243.—Symmetrical character of sagittal section.

field of view is extensive. The spherical aberrations which are encountered in an optical system of this kind are of an exceedingly complicated nature which cannot be described here in detail.

A bundle of rays of finite aperture emanating from a point outside the optical axis will show aberrations of a general character similar to the aberrations along the axis of a direct bundle of rays (§ 178). But the effects in the two principal sections of the bundle will be very different from each other; because, whereas the rays in the sagittal section, being symmetrically situated on opposite sides of the meridian plane, are therefore symmetrical with respect to the chief ray, as represented in Fig. 243, there will, in general, be a complete absence of symmetry in the meridian section (Fig. 244). The image (if indeed we may continue to use this term) of an extra-axial object-point under such circumstances will be at best an element of one or other of the two sheets of the caustic surface. Usually, however, what is called the image is the light-effect as obtained on a focusing screen placed at right angles to the axis at the place where the central parts of the object are best delineated. The appearance on the screen may be described as a kind of balloon-shaped flare of light,

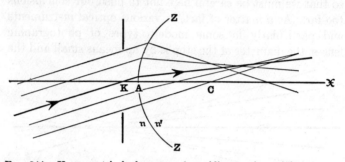

FIG. 244.—Unsymmetrical character of meridian section, giving rise to coma.

with a bright nucleus growing fainter as it expands in some cases towards, in other cases away from, the axis. This defect of the image is known to practical opticians as side-flare or *coma* (from the Greek word meaning "hair" from which the word "comet" is likewise indirectly derived). The definition in the outer parts of the field of the object-glass of a telescope depends on the removal of this error; and this applies also to the case of a wide-angle photographic lens. The only way to obtain a really clear and accurate conception of this important spherical aberration is to study the forms of the two sheets of the caustic surface. Generally speaking, we may say that the convergence of wide-angle bundles of rays will be better in the case of an optical system which has been corrected for astigmatism, but even then there will be lack of symmetry in all the sections of a bundle of rays except in the sagittal section. If the slope of the chief ray is comparatively slight, although not negligible, the condition of a sharp focus is equivalent to ABBE's sine-condition (§ 182). But for greater inclinations of the chief rays, it will generally be necessary to resort to the exact methods of trigonometrical calculation of the ray-paths in order to determine the nature and degree of the convergence.

192. Distortion; Condition of Orthoscopy.—Let us assume that the system has been corrected for both astigmatism and curvature of the image, in the sense explained in § 190; so that by means of narrow bundles of rays a flat stigmatic image is obtained of a plane object placed at right angles to the axis. The next question will be to inquire whether the image is a faithful reproduction of the object or whether it is distorted. If the image in the "screen-plane" (§ 134) is geometrically similar to the object-relief projected from the center of the entrance-pupil on the "focus-plane" (§ 141), then we may say that the optical system is *orthoscopic* or free from distortion.

The dissimilarity which may exist between an object and its image is a fault of an essentially different kind from those which have been previously considered, and there is no in-

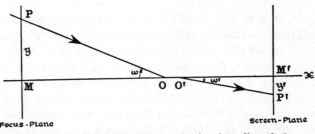

Fig. 245.—Condition of orthoscopy (freedom from distortion).

timate connection between this defect and the others. Here we are not concerned so much with the quality and definition of the image on the screen as with the positions of the points where the chief rays cross the screen-plane. The positions of these representative points will not be altered by reducing the stop-opening (§§ 141, 142); and accordingly the image in the screen-plane is to be regarded merely as a central projection on this plane along the chief rays proceeding from the center of the exit-pupil.

In the diagram (Fig. 245) the centers of the entrance-pupil and exit-pupil of the optical system are designated by O and O'. The straight lines PO, P'O' represent the path of a chief ray which crosses the focus-plane in the object-space at the point P and the screen-plane in the image-space at the point P'. If $y = MP$, $y' = M'P'$ denote the distances of P, P' from the axis, then the condition that the image in the screen-plane shall be similar to the projected object in the focus-

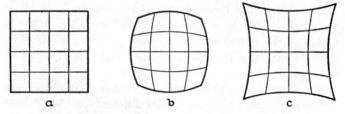

Fig. 246.—Object (a) reproduced by image (b) barrel-shaped distortion or by image (c) cushion-shaped distortion.

plane, that is, the condition of orthoscopy (freedom from distortion) is that the ratio y'/y shall have a constant value for all values of y within the limits of the field of view. If, on the contrary, this is not the case, and if the ratio y'/y is variable for different values of y, then the image will be distorted; and this distortion will be one of two kinds according as the ratio y'/y increases or decreases with increase of y. For example, if the object is in the form of a square, as shown in Fig. 246, a, then, on the supposition that y'/y decreases as y increases the image of the diagonal will be shortened relatively more than the image of a side of the square, and the square will be reproduced by a curvilinear figure with convex sides as shown in Fig. 246, b; this is the case of *barrel-shaped distortion*, as it is called. On the other hand, if the ratio y'/y increases in proportion as the object-point is taken farther and farther from the axis, we have the opposite type known as *cushion-shaped distortion* (Fig. 246, c).

If in Fig. 245 we put $OM = z$, $O'M' = z'$, $\angle MOP = \omega$,

$\angle M'O'P' = \omega'$, the condition of orthoscopy may be expressed
as follows:

$$\frac{y'}{y} = \frac{z'.\tan\omega'}{z.\tan\omega} = \text{constant};$$

and if we assume, as has been tacitly assumed in the preceding discussion, that the chief rays all pass through the
pupil-centers O, O', so that the abscissæ denoted by z, z' have
the same values for all distances of the object-point P from
the axis, then we derive at once Airy's *tangent-condition* of
orthoscopy, namely, $\tan\omega'$: $\tan\omega$ = constant. But although
a chief ray must pass through the center of the aperture-
stop (§ 140), it will not pass through the centers of the pupils
unless the latter are free from spherical aberration. The
constancy of the tangent-ratio by itself is not a sufficient
condition for orthoscopy; in addition, the spherical aberration must be abolished with respect to the centers of the
pupils.

If the optical system is symmetrical with respect to an interior aperture-stop, the tangent-condition will be immediately satisfied, because on account of the symmetry of the
two halves of the system, every chief ray will issue in exactly
the same direction as it had on entering, and therefore
$\tan\theta$: $\tan\theta' = 1$. Accordingly, if a "symmetric doublet"
of this kind is spherically corrected with respect to the center
of the aperture-stop, it will give an image which will be free
from distortion.

193. Seidel's Theory of the Five Aberrations.—In the
theory of optical imagery which was developed according to
general laws first by Gauss (§ 119) in his famous *Dioptrische
Untersuchungen* published in 1841, the fundamental assumption is that the effective rays are all comprised within a narrow cylindrical region of space immediately surrounding the
optical axis; this region being more explicitly defined by the
condition that a paraxial ray is one for which the angle of
incidence (a) and the slope-angle (θ), in the case of each
refraction or reflection, are both relatively so minute that the

powers of these angles higher than the first can be neglected
(§ 63). Evidently, therefore, GAUSS's theory is applicable
only to optical systems of exceedingly small aperture and
limited extent of field of view. But with the development
of modern optical instruments and especially with the increase of both aperture and field demanded for certain types
of photographic lenses, it became necessary to take account
of rays which lie far beyond the narrow confines of the central
or paraxial rays. Long prior to the time of GAUSS important
contributions to the theory of spherical aberrations had been
made in connection with certain more or less special problems;
but the first successful attempt to extend GAUSS's theory in
a general way by taking account of the terms of higher orders
of smallness was made by SEIDEL (1821–1896) in a remarkable series of papers published between the years 1852
and 1856 in the *Astronomische Nachrichten*. SEIDEL's
method consisted in tracing the path of the ray through the
centered system of spherical refracting surfaces and in developing the trigonometrical expressions in series of ascend-
ing powers which were finally simplified by neglecting all
terms above the third order. If the ray-parameters are regarded as magnitudes of the first order of smallness, it is
easy to show that on account of the symmetry around the
optical axis these series-developments can contain only terms
of the odd orders of smallness; so that in SEIDEL's theory
the terms neglected are of the fifth and higher orders. It is
impossible to describe here in detail the elegant mathematical treatment by which SEIDEL was enabled to arrive at
his final results; suffice it to say, that he obtained a system of formulæ from which it was possible to ascertain the
influence both of the aperture and the field of view on the
perfection of the image. In SEIDEL's formulæ the aberrations of the ray, that is, its deviations from the path prescribed by GAUSS's theory, are expressed by five different
sums, denoted by S_1, S_2, S_3, S_4, and S_5, which depend only on
the constants of the optical system and the position of the

object-point, and which are, in fact, the cöefficients of the various terms in the equations. The condition that there shall be no aberration demands that all of these five sums shall vanish simultaneously, that is,

$$S_1 = S_2 = S_3 = S_4 = S_5 = 0.$$

If, on the other hand, these conditions are not satisfied, the image yielded by the lens-system will not be faultless; and therefore it will not be without interest to inquire more particularly into the separate influence of each of these five expressions which occur in SEIDEL's formulæ.

Thus, for example, if the optical system is designed so that $S_1 = 0$, then there will be no spherical aberration at the center of the field (§ 178) for the given position of the axial object-point. And if not only $S_1 = 0$ but also $S_2 = 0$, then there will be no coma (§ 191). The condition $S_2 = 0$ means also that ABBE's sine-condition (§ 182) will also be satisfied, so that the image of the parts of the object in the immediate vicinity of the axis is sharply defined.

But even when we have $S_1 = S_2 = 0$, the optical system will, in general, still be affected by astigmatism of oblique rays (§ 184), so that an object-point lying at some little distance from the axis will not be reproduced by an image-point but at best by two short focal lines at different distances from the lens-system and directed approximately at right angles to each other. Moreover if the distance of the object-point from the axis is varied, the positions of these two focal lines will vary also both with respect to their distance from the lens-system and with respect to their mutual distance apart. In other words, when both S_1 and S_2 vanish, then, in general, there is no unique image of a transversal object-plane, but this latter may be said to be reproduced by two so-called image-surfaces (§ 189) which are surfaces of revolution around the optical axis and which unite and touch each other at the point where the axis crosses them. The expressions for the curvatures of these surfaces at this common point of tangency are given by SEIDEL's sums S_3 and

S_4; so that if also $S_3 - S_4 = 0$, the two image surfaces will coalesce and now the image of the plane object will be sharply defined, that is, stigmatic, although it will usually still be curved. But if also $S_3 = S_4 = 0$, the image will be both plane and stigmatic. However, it may still show unequal magnifications toward the margin, which means that there is distortion (§ 192). This last error will be abolished provided $S_5 = 0$; and now the image may be said to be ideal inasmuch as it is flat and sharply defined not only in the center but out toward the edges and is at the same time a faithful reproduction of the plane object.

To attempt to derive SEIDEL's actual formulæ or even to discuss the equations would be entirely beyond the scope

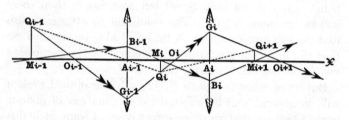

FIG. 247.—Diagram representing the $(i-1)$th and ith lenses of a system of infinitely thin lenses.

of this volume. But it may be convenient to insert here without proof the expressions of SEIDEL's five sums for the comparatively simple case of an optical system considered as composed of a series of m infinitely thin lenses each surrounded by air.

Let A_i (Fig. 247) designate the point where the optical axis crosses the ith lens of the system, the symbol i being employed to denote any integer from 1 to m; and let us consider two paraxial rays which traverse the optical system, one of which emanating from the axial object-point M_1 ($A_1M_1 = u_1$) and meeting the first lens at a point B_1 such that $A_1B_1 = h_1$, crosses the axis after passing through the $(i-1)$th lens at a point M_i ($A_iM_i = u_i$) and meets the ith lens at a point B_i

such that $A_iB_i = h_i$ whereas the other ray, which emanates from an extra-axial object-point and which in the object-space passes through the center O_1 of the entrance-pupil (§ 139) of the system $(A_1O_1 = s_1)$ and meets the first lens at a point G_1 such that $g_1 = A_1G_1$, crosses the axis after passing through the $(i-1)$th lens at a point $O_i(A_iO_i = s_i)$ and meets the ith lens at a point G_i such that $A_iG_i = g_i$. Then if we put

$$U_i = 1/u_i, \qquad S_i = 1/s_i,$$

it may easily be shown that

$$h_i(U_i+F_i) = h_{i+1}.U_{i+1},$$
$$g_i(S_i+F_i) = g_{i+1}.S_{i+1};$$

where F_i denotes the refracting power of the ith lens. Now if n_i denotes the index of refraction of the ith lens and if R_i denotes the curvature of the first surface of this lens; and if, further, for the sake of brevity, the symbols A_i, B_i, C_i, D_i, and E_i are introduced to denote the following functions of n_i, F_i, R_i, U_i and S_i, namely:

$$A_i = \frac{n_i+2}{n_i} F_iR_i^2 - \left\{ \frac{4(n_i+1)}{n_i} U_i + \frac{2n_i+1}{n_i-1} F_i \right\} F_iR_i$$
$$+ \frac{3n_i+2}{n_i} F_iU_i^2 + \frac{3n_i+1}{n_i-1} F_i^2U_i + \left(\frac{n_i}{n_i-1} \right)^2 F_i^3;$$

$$B_i = \frac{n_i+2}{n_i} F_iR_i^2 - \left\{ \frac{n_i+1}{n_i}(3U_i+S_i) + \frac{2n_i+1}{n_i-1} F_i \right\} F_iR_i$$
$$+ \frac{n_i+1}{n_i} F_iU_i^2 + \frac{2n_i+1}{n_i} F_iU_iS_i + \frac{2n_i+1}{n_i-1} F_i^2U_i$$
$$+ \frac{n_i}{n_i-1} F_i^2S_i + \left(\frac{n_i}{n_i-1} \right)^2 F_i^3;$$

$$C_i = \frac{3(n_i+2)}{n_i} F_iR_i^2 - \left\{ \frac{6(n_i+1)}{n_i}(U_i+S_i) + \frac{3(2n_i+1)}{n_i-1} F_i \right\} F_iR_i$$
$$+ \frac{1}{n_i}F_iU_i^2 + \frac{2(3n_i+2)}{n_i}F_iU_iS_i + \frac{3n_i+1}{n_i} F_iS_i^2$$
$$+ \frac{3(n_i+1)}{n_i-1} F_i^2U_i + \frac{6n_i}{n_i-1}F_i^2S_i + 3\left(\frac{n_i}{n_i-1} \right)^2 F_i^3;$$

$$D_i = \frac{n_i+2}{n_i} F_i R_i^2 - \left\{ \frac{2(n_i+1)}{n_i}(U_i+S_i) + \frac{2n_i+1}{n_i-1} F_i \right\} F_i R_i + \frac{1}{n_i} F_i U_i^2$$

$$+ 2F_i U_i S_i + \frac{n_i+1}{n_i} F_i S_i^2 + \frac{n_i+1}{n_i-1} F_i^2 U_i$$

$$+ \frac{2n_i}{n_i-1} F_i^2 S_i + \left(\frac{n_i}{n_i-1} \right)^2 F_i^3;$$

$$E_i = \frac{n_i+2}{n_i} F_i R_i^2 - \left\{ \frac{n_i+1}{n_i}(U_i+3S_i) + \frac{2n_i+1}{n_i-1} F_i \right\} F_i R_i + \frac{3n_i+1}{n_i} F_i S_i^2$$

$$+ \frac{1}{n_i} F_i U_i S_i + \frac{1}{n_i-1} F_i^2 U_i + \frac{3n_i}{n_i-1} F_i^2 S_i + \left(\frac{n_i}{n_i-1} \right)^2 F_i^3;$$

then SEIDEL's formulæ for the spherical errors of a system of m infinitely thin lenses may be expressed as follows:

$$S_1 = \sum_{i=1}^{i=m} \left(\frac{h_i}{h_1} \right)^4 A_i; \qquad\qquad S_2 = \sum_{i=1}^{i=m} \left(\frac{h_i}{h_1} \right)^3 \frac{g_i}{g_1} B_i;$$

$$S_3 = \sum_{i=1}^{i=m} \left(\frac{h_i}{h_1} \cdot \frac{g_i}{g_1} \right)^2 C_i; \qquad\qquad S_4 = \sum_{i=1}^{i=m} \left(\frac{h_i}{h_1} \cdot \frac{g_i}{g_1} \right)^2 D_i;$$

$$S_5 = \sum_{i=1}^{i=m} \frac{h_i}{h_1} \left(\frac{g_i}{g_1} \right)^3 E_i.$$

The greatest practical value of these formulæ is to guide the optician to a correct basis for the design of his instrument and to supply him, so to speak, with a starting point for a trigonometrical calculation of the optical system which he aims to achieve. But the reader who wishes to pursue this subject further will find it necessary to consult the more advanced treatises on applied optics.

PROBLEMS

1. If L, L' designate the points where a ray crosses the axis of a spherical refracting surface before and after refraction, respectively, and if C designates the center of the surface, show that

$$\frac{n}{c'} - \frac{n'}{c} = \frac{n'-n}{r} \frac{\cos\dfrac{\theta+\theta'}{2}}{\cos\dfrac{a+a'}{2}},$$

where $c = CL$, $c' = CL'$, a, a' denote the angles of incidence and refraction, θ, θ' denote the slope-angles of the ray before and after refraction, r denotes the radius of the surface, and n, n' denote the indices of refraction. Also, show that

$$\frac{c'+r}{c+r} = \frac{\sin\theta\cos\dfrac{a'+\theta'}{2}}{\sin\theta'\cos\dfrac{a+\theta}{2}}.$$

2. A ray parallel to the axis meets the first surface of a glass lens (index 1.5) at a height of 5 cm. above the axis, and after emerging from the lens crosses the axis at a point L'. The thickness of the lens is 1 cm. Determine the aberration F'L', where F' designates the position of the second focal point, for each of the following cases: (a) First surface of lens is plane and radius of curved surface is 50 cm.; (b) Second surface of lens is plane and radius of curved surface is 50 cm.; and (c) Lens is symmetric, radius of each surface being 100 cm.

Ans. (a) $f = \pm 100$ cm., $F'L' = \mp 1.13$ cm.; (b) $f = \pm 100$ cm., $F'L' = \mp 0.29$ cm.; (c) $f = \pm 100.17$ cm., $F'L' = \mp 0.42$ cm.; where in each case the upper signs apply to positive lens and the lower signs apply to negative lens.

3. An incident ray crosses the axis of a lens at an angle θ_1 and meets the first surface at a point B_1, the angle of incidence being a_1; the slope of the refracted ray B_1B_2, which meets the second surface at the point B_2 is θ_2, and the angle of incidence at this surface is a_2. If the radii of the surfaces are denoted by r_1 and r_2, show that

$$B_1B_2 = \frac{r_2 . \sin(a_2 - \theta_2) - r_1 . \sin(a_1 - \theta_1)}{\sin \theta_2}.$$

4. The chief ray of a narrow bundle of parallel rays is incident on a spherical mirror of radius 32 cm. at an angle of 60°. Find the distance between the two image-points P' and Q' of the bundle of reflected rays.   Ans. 24 cm.

5. The chief ray of a narrow bundle of parallel rays is incident on a spherical mirror of radius r at a point B, the angle of incidence being 60°. Determine the positions of the image-points P' and Q'.   Ans. $BP' = r/4$, $BQ' = r$.

6. A narrow bundle of parallel rays in air is refracted at a spherical surface of radius r into a medium whose index of refraction is $\sqrt{3}$. If the angle of incidence is 60°, find the positions of the image-points P' and Q'.

Ans. $p' = 3r\sqrt{3}/4$, $q' = r\sqrt{3}$.

7. A narrow bundle of parallel rays is incident on a spherical refracting surface at an angle of 60°. If the meridian rays are converged to a focus at a point P' lying on the surface of the sphere, show that the angle of refraction of the chief ray is equal to the complement of the critical angle of the two media.

8. The radius of each of the two surfaces of an infinitely thin double convex lens is 8 inches, and the index of refraction is equal to $\sqrt{3}$. The chief ray of a narrow bundle of parallel rays inclined to the axis at an angle of 60° passes through the optical center of the lens. Find the positions of the foci of the meridian and sagittal rays.

Ans. The focal point of the meridian rays is 1 inch and that of the sagittal rays is 4 inches from the optical center.

9. If in Young's construction of a ray refracted at a spherical surface (§ 176) a semi-circle is described on the incidence-radius BC as diameter intersecting the incident and refracted rays in the points Y, Y', respectively, show that the straight

line YY′ is perpendicular to the straight line CS. The point K where the straight lines YY′ and CS meet is the center of perspective of the range of object-points lying on the incident ray and the corresponding range of meridian image-points lying on the refracted ray (see § 186). Show that

$$CK = \frac{n.r.\sin^2\alpha}{n'},$$

and that

$$\tan\angle BKC = \tan\alpha + \tan\alpha'.$$

10. If the chief ray of a narrow homocentric bundle of rays is incident on a plane refracting surface at a point B, and if α, α' denote the angles of incidence and refraction, show that

$$BP' = \frac{n'\cos^2\alpha'}{n\cos^2\alpha}.BP, \qquad BQ' = \frac{n'}{n}.BQ,$$

where P (or Q) designates the position of the vertex of the incident rays and P′ and Q′ designate the positions of the image-points of the meridian and sagittal rays, respectively.

11. In the preceding problem show that the straight line QQ′ is perpendicular to the plane refracting surface.

12. The position of the image-point P′ of a pencil of meridian rays refracted at a plane surface may be constructed as follows: Through the object-point P (or Q) draw PQ′ perpendicular to the refracting plane and meeting the chief refracted ray in Q′; and from P and Q′ draw PX and Q′Y perpendicular to the incidence-normal at X and Y, respectively. Draw XG perpendicular to the chief incident ray at G and YG′ perpendicular to the corresponding refracted ray at G′. Then the straight line PP′ drawn parallel to GG′ will intersect the chief refracted ray in the required point P′. Using the result of No. 10 above, show that this construction is correct.

13. The chief ray RB of a narrow pencil of sagittal rays meets a spherical refracting surface at the point B and is refracted in the direction BT. Through the center C draw CV

parallel to BT meeting BR in V and CV' parallel to BR meeting BT in V'. If Q, Q' designate the positions of the points of intersection of the sagittal rays before and after refraction, respectively, and if BQ=q, BQ'=q', show that

$$\frac{BV}{q}+\frac{BV'}{q'}=1,$$

and that

$$VQ.V'Q'=VB.V'B.$$

(Compare this last result with the Newtonian formula for refraction of paraxial rays at a spherical surface, viz., $x.x' = f.f'.$)

14. The chief ray RB of a narrow pencil of meridian rays meets a spherical refracting surface at the point B, and is refracted in the direction BT. Through the center of perspective K (see § 186; see also problem No. 9 above) draw KU parallel to BT meeting BR in U and KU' parallel to BR meeting BT in U'. If the positions of the points of intersection of the meridian rays before and after refraction are designated by P and P', respectively, and if BP=p, BP'=p', show that

$$\frac{BU}{p}+\frac{BU'}{p'}=1,$$

and that

$$UP.U'P'=UB.U'B.$$

(Compare this result with that of the preceding problem.)

15. If J, J' designate the positions of the aplanatic points of a spherical refracting surface, and if θ, θ' denote the slopes of the incident and refracted rays BJ, BJ', respectively, show that

$$\frac{\sin\theta}{\sin\theta'}=\frac{n'}{n}\cdot\boldsymbol{y},$$

where $\boldsymbol{y}$ denotes the magnification-ratio for paraxial rays.

16. A. STEINHEIL's so-called "periscope" photographic lens is composed of two equal simple meniscus lenses, both of crown glass, separated from each other with a small stop midway between. The data of the system, as given in VON

ROHR's *Theorie und Geschichte des photographischen Objektivs* (Berlin, 1899), p. 288, are as follows:

Indices: $n_1 = n_3 = n_5 = 1$; $n_2 = n_4 = 1.5233$

Radii: $r_1 = -r_4 = +17.5$ mm.; $r_2 = -r_3 = +20.8$ mm.

Thicknesses: $d_1 = d_3 = +1.3$ mm.; $d_2 = 12.6$ mm.

Distance of center of stop from second vertex of first lens $= +6.3$ mm.; diameter of stop $= 2.38$ mm.; diameter of each lens $= 11.32$ mm.

Employing the above data, determine (1) the position and size of the entrance-pupil, (2) the angular extent of the field, (3) the position of the second focal point F′; and (4) the point where an edge-ray directed towards a point in the circumference of the entrance-pupil and parallel to the axis crosses the axis after emerging from the system.

Ans. (1) Distance of center of entrance-pupil from second vertex of first lens is $+6.45$ mm.; diameter of entrance-pupil is 2.53 mm. (2) The angular extent of the field is nearly 90°. (3) Distance of F′ from last surface is $A_4F' = +90.946$ mm. (4) The edge-ray crosses the axis at a distance $A_4L_5 = +90.432$ mm.

17. The abscissæ of the points M_k, M_{k+1} where a paraxial ray crosses the axis of a centered system of m spherical refracting surfaces before and after refraction at the kth surface are denoted by $u_k = A_kM_k$, $u_k' = A_kM_{k+1}$. If the ray proceeds in the first medium of index n_1 in a direction parallel to the axis, it may be shown (*cf.* problems Nos. 16 and 17, end of Chapter X) that the primary focal length of the system is given by the formula

$$f = \frac{U_2 . U_3 \ldots U_m}{U_1' . U_2' \ldots U_m'}, (U_1 = 0),$$

where $U_k = n_k/u_k$, $U_k' = n_{k+1}/u_k'$. Having calculated the path of the paraxial ray in the preceding problem, employ the above formula to determine the focal length of STEINHEIL's "periscope."   Ans. $f = +98.696$ mm.

18. The path of a chief ray which in traversing the air-space between the two lenses of STEINHEIL's "periscope"

(see No. 16) goes through the center of the stop will be symmetrical with respect to the two parts of the optical system, so that for such a ray we must have:

$$c_4' = -c_1, \quad c_4 = -c_1', \quad c_3' = -c_2, \quad c_3 = -c_2';$$
$$a_4 = a_1', \quad a_4' = a_1, \quad a_3 = a_2', \quad a_3' = a_2;$$
$$\theta_5 = \theta_1, \quad \theta_4 = \theta_2.$$

Show that if $\theta_3 = -30°$ for a ray which goes through the stop-center, the ray must have been directed initially at a slope-angle $\theta_1 = -28° \; 2' \; 54.43''$ towards a point L_1 on the axis whose distance from the second vertex of the first lens is $A_2L_1 = +6.563$ mm.

19. The astigmatism of a narrow bundle of rays refracted through a centered system of spherical surfaces may be computed logarithmically by means of the following recurrent formulæ:

$$D_k = \frac{n_k.\sin(a_k - a_k')}{r_k.\sin a_k'},$$

$$h_k = r_k.\sin(a_k - \theta_k), \quad t_k = \frac{h_{k+1} - h_k}{n_{k+1}.\sin \theta_{k+1}};$$

Sagittal Section

$$Q_k' = Q_k + D_k, \quad Q_{k+1} = \frac{Q_k'}{1 - t_k.Q_k'};$$

Meridian Section

$$P_k' = \frac{P_k.\cos^2 a_k + D_k}{\cos^2 a_k'}, \quad P_{k+1} = \frac{P_k'}{1 - t_k.P_k'};$$

where the symbols a, a', θ, n and r have their usual meanings and where P, P' and Q, Q' and D are the magnitudes defined in §§ 186 and 184. The calculations according to these formulæ will be considerably simplified in the case of a chief ray which traverses a system like STEINHEIL's "periscope" (see No. 16) which is symmetric with respect to the stop-center. For example, for this particular system we can write for a chief ray:

$$D_4 = D_1, \quad D_3 = D_2, \quad h_4 = -h_1, \quad h_3 = -h_2, \quad t_3 = t_1;$$
$$a_1 - a_1' = -(a_4 - a_4'), \quad a_2 - a_2' = -(a_3 - a_3'),$$
$$a_1 - \theta_1 = a_4' - \theta_5 = a_: - \theta_4, \quad a_2 - \theta_2 = a_3' - \theta_4 = a_3 - \theta_3.$$

Apply the above formulæ to the optical system of problem No. 16 to calculate the astigmatic difference (§ 186) of a narrow bundle of emergent rays whose chief ray is the ray whose path was determined in problem No. 18; assuming that the bundle of incident rays was cylindrical, that is, $P_1 = Q_1 = 0$.

Ans. $p_4' - q_4' = +6.453$ mm.

20. The refracting power of a glass lens of index n, surrounded by air, and of negligible thickness ($d = 0$), is denoted by F. The refracting power of the first surface of the lens is denoted by $F_1 = (n-1)R_1$. The lens is provided with a rear stop whose distance from it is denoted by $z' = 1/Z'$. Using SEIDEL's formulæ for the abolition of astigmatism (§ 193), show that the condition that this system shall give a punctual or stigmatic image of an infinitely distant object ($U_1 = 0$) is given by the following equation arranged as a quadratic in F_1:

$$\alpha F_1^2 + \beta F_1 + \gamma = 0,$$

where the symbols α, β, γ are abbreviations used to denote the following functions of n, F and Z':

$$\alpha = \frac{n+2}{n(n-1)^2} F, \quad \beta = -\left\{ \alpha + \frac{2(n+1)}{n(n-1)} Z' \right\} F,$$

$$\gamma = \left(\frac{F}{n-1} + Z' \right)^2 F.$$

21. A plane object is set up in the primary focal plane of a thin lens ($d = 0$, $U_1 = -F$) which is provided with a rear stop whose distance from the lens is $z' = 1/Z'$, as in the preceding problem, a similar notation being used here. From the formulæ in § 193, show that the condition of the abolition of astigmatism of oblique bundles in case of a single thin lens

with this arrangement of object and stop is given by the following quadratic equation in F_2:

$$\alpha F_2{}^2 + \beta F_2 + \gamma = 0,$$

where $F_2 = -(n-1)R_2$ denotes the refracting power of the second surface of the lens, and the functions denoted by the symbols α, β, γ have here the following meanings:

$$\alpha = \frac{n+2}{n(n-1)^2} F, \quad \beta = -\left\{ \frac{2n+1}{(n-1)^2} F - \frac{2(n+1)}{n(n-1)} Z' \right\} F,$$

$$\gamma = \left(\frac{n}{n-1} F - Z'\right)^2 F.$$

22. If in Problem No. 21 the center of the stop is beyond the lens at a distance of 25 mm., show that for n = 1.52 the extreme limiting values of the refracting power are $F = +7.78$ dptr. and $F = -24.68$ dptr.; and that for higher powers, either positive or negative, it is impossible to satisfy the required condition.

23. If in Problem No. 22 the center of the stop is beyond the lens at a distance of 30 mm., show that for n = 1.52 the maximum value of the refracting power of a convex lens which will give a punctual image of a plane object placed in the primary focal plane is $F = +12.72$ dptr.

CHAPTER XVI

194. Rectilinear Propagation of Light (Historical).—The "motes in the sunbeam" showing the path of sunlight through dust-laden air, the forms of shadows, the passage of sunlight through windows and crevices, all the various processes of sighting and aiming, together with many other common phenomena of similar nature, had satisfied the ancient philosophers that vision was performed in straight lines; and they had fixed their attention upon those straight lines, or *rays*, as the proper object of optics. It was generally supposed at first that light was some sort of fiery substance which had its source in the eye; but the opinions of the early Greek philosophers about all these questions and particularly about form and color are extremely vague. They were fond of speculations but had an aversion, it would almost seem, to making experiments in support of their hypotheses. ARISTOTLE (384–322 B. C.) questioned whether the eye could be considered as the source of light. Geometrical optics can hardly be called a science before the time of EUCLID (330–275 B. C.) and ARCHIMEDES. In the work on Optics attributed to EUCLID it is assumed as an axiom that the so-called rays of light proceed from the eye and are separated by intervals between them, so that if an object lies in a gap where no rays fall on it, it is invisible to the eye in question. The art of perspective which reached a high degree of development among the Greeks is merely a corollary from the doctrine of rectilinear visual rays. This art was reinvented in modern times in the flourishing period of painting in Europe. According to LEONARDO DA VINCI (1452–1519), if rays of light coming through a plate of glass set in a picture-frame could leave their impresses on the glass, each ray making its own characteristic sign or mark on the glass where it passed, the picture of the scene thus produced would appear to the eye in correct perspective.

However, there were some phenomena of common occurrence whose explanation on the hypothesis of the rectilinear propagation of light continued to offer some difficulties. Thus, for example, when sunlight enters a dark chamber through a small aperture in the window-shutter and falls on the opposite vertical wall, it forms there a round spot of light, no matter whether the aperture itself is round or square or any other shape. Moreover, when the sun is partially eclipsed by the moon, the spot of light on the wall will be found to be then more or less crescent-shaped and similar in outline to the exposed segment of the sun's disk, but oppositely turned or inverted. During a partial eclipse these crescent-formed spots of light produced by sunlight shining through the vacant spaces in the foliage of a tree can be seen scattered about on the pavement below. Why is it that the contour of the spot of light is similar in form to that of the light-source and quite independent of the form of the aperture? This was a question that perplexed ARISTOTLE and other natural philosophers for a long time to come. A correct explanation on the hypothesis that light goes in straight lines was given first by MAUROLYCUS (1494–1577) and afterwards by KEPLER (1571–1630). A simple and interesting experiment which KEPLER made to show how the effect on a screen is obtained by rectilinear rays coming from a luminous source through an aperture of any form may be described as follows: He mounted an object, for example, a book, on a high shelf to represent the luminous body; and at one of its corners he attached the end of a long cord which was drawn through an irregular hole cut in the top of the table. The other end of the cord had a crayon attached to it for drawing a figure on a vertical wall or blackboard at some considerable distance in the room beyond the table. Keeping the cord stretched straight to represent a ray of light and guiding it by the edge of the hole with which it was always in contact, KEPLER drew the outline of a closed figure. He constructed a number of such diagrams, partly overlapping each other, for different points of attachment of the string to the object on the shelf; and he found that the contour of the figure which would envelop or circumscribe all these overlapping closed curves was more and more similar to the form of the object on the shelf the farther the blackboard was moved away from it.

In one of the chapters of his famous book called *Magia naturalis* PORTA (1543–1615) describes the arrangement of a *camera obscura*, which he invented; explaining how an inverted image will be cast on the wall of a dark room by admitting the light through a narrow opening in the window-shutter, and how the size of the image depends only on the distance between the aperture and screen. This is the *pinhole camera* (§ 3). With a certain air of mystery as if he were revealing a great secret, the author proceeds then to tell how a brighter and more distinct image will be obtained by inserting a glass lens in the aperture, and adds significantly, "There can be no doubt that the human eye is such a *camera obscura* into which the light comes from outside." It is not without interest to mention here that the eye of the nautilus which is a beautiful little marine animal that is often seen floating on the surface of the sea is of a very primitive type, consisting of a little hollow depression in the head which appears to act like a pinhole camera of large aperture, so that vision by means of this organ is probably blurred and extremely rudimentary in every way.

The theory of shadows was also an object of investigation by the Greek geometers. In the adjoining diagram (Fig. 248) $d = CC'$ denotes the distance of the center C' of an opaque globe or disk from the center C of a similar luminous body, and $2r = BD$, $2r' = B'D'$ denote their diameters. The straight lines BB', DD' and BD', DB' intersecting the line of centers CC′ at A and A′, respectively, determine the limits of the *umbra* and *penumbra* of the shadow cast by the opaque obstacle (§ 4) and l = C′A denotes the length of the *umbra*

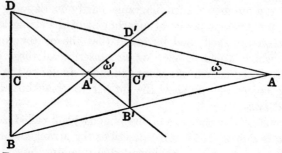

FIG. 248.—Shadow of opaque disk B′D′ illuminated by luminous disk BD.

and l' = A′C′ gives the corresponding dimension of the *penumbra*. From the two pairs of similar right triangles ACD, AC′D′ and A′CD, A′C′D′, the following expressions for l and l' can be readily found:

$$l = \frac{r'}{r-r'}d, \qquad\qquad l' = \frac{r'}{r+r'}d.$$

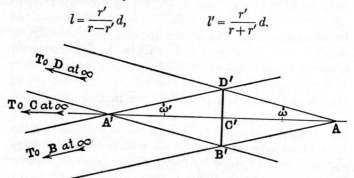

FIG. 249.—Shadow of opaque disk illuminated by infinitely distant luminary.

Moreover, if we put $\angle CAD = \omega$, $\angle C'A'D' = \omega'$, then

$$\tan \omega = \frac{r'-r}{d}, \qquad\qquad \tan \omega' = \frac{r'+r}{d};$$

and hence, taking account of the signs of these angles,

$$\tan \omega - \tan \omega' = -2r/d = 2 \tan \theta,$$

where $\theta = \angle$ CC′D.

When the luminary is infinitely distant ($d = \infty$), DB′ (or A′B′) will be parallel to DD′ (or D′A), and, similarly, BD′ (or A′D′) will be parallel to BB′ (or B′A); and consequently the triangle AA′D′ (Fig. 249) will be isosceles ($\omega = -\omega' = \theta$). However, when the luminary is the sun or moon, its angular diameter 2θ is only about half a degree and therefore the *penumbra* will be scarcely perceptible unless the screen on which the shadow is cast is placed relatively far away from the opaque obstacle. For $d = \infty$, we find the length C′A $= A'C' = r' \cdot \cot \theta$.

195. Reflection of Light; Mirrors.—The law of the reflection of light was probably known in very early times. From the symmetrical congruence of object and image in a plane mirror (§ 15) the fundamental relation of the equality between the angles of incidence and reflection was deduced by EUCLID in the first proposition of his treatise on "Catoptrics" (from the Greek "katoptron" meaning a mirror), which was the name given by the ancients to that part of Optics which treats of the behavior of light when it is reflected from a polished surface of a metal or glass or from the smooth surface of a tranquil liquid. EUCLID's methods and conclusions are not always free from objections by any means; but even so, his investigations of the properties of both plane and curved mirrors were original and remarkable in many ways. Although it is known that ARCHIMEDES (who was born about 287 B. C.) made contributions to the science of Optics as well as to other branches of Physics and Geometry, his writings have not come down to us. The story of his having set fire to the Roman fleet by concentrating the sun's rays on the ships by means of a huge concave mirror is perhaps no more than a fairy tale, and yet it may have a substratum of truth enough to warrant a conjecture whether this renowned philosopher may not have been an optical as well as a mechanical engineer. HERO of Alexandria, with an insight deeper than Euclid's, derived the law of reflection of light from the principle of the shortest path (§ 38) as a striking instance of economy here as in so many other natural processes. The optical theories of Alhazen who lived in the eleventh century at a time when Arabian science was at the zenith of its extraordinary development as contained in his famous treatise on optics were far in advance of those of the Greeks. For example, his notions about the nature of vision, so far from being vague were exceedingly concrete and almost modern in many respects; and he was under no illusion about the rays emanating from the eye instead of from the object. He amplified the statement of the fundamental fact that the reflected ray is contained in the plane of incidence (§ 13); and besides the forms of mirrors treated by earlier geometers he investigated also cylindrical and conical mirrors. Two centuries or more glide by before there is any further progress in Optics worthy to be noted, and here we have to pause to mention at least that extraordinary and eccentric genius Roger Bacon (c. 1294) or "Frier" Bacon, as he was commonly called by his contemporaries in England and by many writers long afterwards. He was undoubtedly a man of prodigious learning and skill, but his scientific imagination was probably greater than his real scientific performance, and when he speaks of the possibility of having locomotives that are propelled by their own power and machines that can make flights in the air, it is not necessary to suppose that he had actually invented the ancestors of the modern automobile and aëroplane. Spectacles appeared in Europe in the thirteenth century, and Bacon was doubtlessly well acquainted with their various uses, just as he was familiar also with ordinary reading glasses and magnifiers; but there is little evidence to show that he invented these things. One item about his work may be mentioned as adding a link to the chain of contributions to this particular branch of Optics and that is a book which he wrote entitled *Tractatus de speculis;* wherein a more complete theory of the concave mirror (see Problem 23, p. 632) is to be found than in the works of any of his predecessors. About the same time VITELLO (c. 1270), a native of Poland, composed a treatise on optics, based in large measure on AL-HAZEN's book, but which contained also some original material. Apparently, he deserves the credit of having been the first to point out the peculiar focal advantages possessed by a parabolic mirror (§ 205). Finally, in order to complete this brief historical survey of the development of the science of Catoptrics it may be added that PORTA's *Magia naturalis* (alluded to in § 194) contains much discussion of the properties of mirrors of various kinds, with perhaps what is the first accurate explanation of the images of an object that are to be seen in a pair of inclined mirrors (§§ 17, foll.).

In connection with the theory of a pair of inclined mirrors, a problem of some practical importance is as follows:

To construct a pair of plane mirrors which will produce a given deviation of a ray which has been reflected once from each mirror (see § 17).

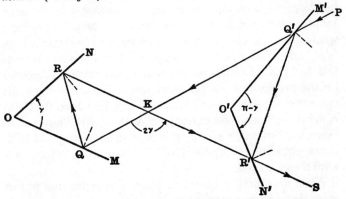

FIG. 250.—Deviation of ray by successive reflections from pair of inclined plane mirrors: deviation is same for pair of mirrors OM, ON and for pair of mirrors O'M' and O'N'.

Draw two straight lines PK and KS (Fig. 250) intersecting in K to represent the paths of the ray before and after the two reflections. Take a point Q anywhere on the straight line PK and through Q draw a straight line QR intersecting the straight line KS in a point R. Draw the straight lines, OM perpendicular to the bisector of the angle PQR and ON perpendicular to the bisector of the angle QRS, intersecting each other at O. Then if OM, ON represent the traces of the planes of the mirrors (both supposed to be perpendicular to the plane of the paper), the broken line PQRS will represent the path of the light in going from P to S after being reflected from OM at Q and from ON at R.

In the diagram the light after being reflected at the second mirror ON is represented as actually, that is, "really" going through the point K; and when this is the case the dihedral angle $\gamma = \angle MON$ between the two mirrors is half the angle PKR. As long as these conditions are satisfied, the mirrors may be placed anywhere, the angle γ being kept always the same; and the only other change in the diagram will be in the path QR which the light takes in going from the first mirror to the second. But it is possible to have also a different combination of plane mirrors which will accomplish the same result, as is shown in the same diagram by the pair of mirrors whose traces in the plane of the paper are the straight lines O'M' and O'N' which are constructed in the same way as OM and ON. In this case the path of the ray is represented by the broken line PQ'R'S, and the difference between the two cases consists essentially in the fact that here the point K is behind the second mirror so that the ray R'S now passes "virtually" through K. In this case also the angle M'O'N' is not equal to γ but to $(180° - \gamma)$, where, as before, $\gamma = \angle MON = \frac{1}{2} \angle PKR$.

When an object is placed in front of a compound mirror consisting of two plane mirrors so adjusted that the angle between them expressed in degrees is an exact multiple of 180°, the last image of one of the two series of images will coincide precisely with the last image of the other series, as explained in § 18; and the position of this final image can be found simply by rotating the object around the common edge or geometrical line of intersection of the planes of the two mirrors through an angle equal to twice the angle made by the mirrors. A special case of much practical importance (for example, in the construction of reflection prisms) is a compound mirror in which the two plane mirrors are at right angles to each other (§ 20), so that the final image formed by rays which have been twice reflected has the same position and appearance as if the object had been rotated bodily around the edge through an angle of 180°, as shown in Fig. 31 and represented also in Fig. 251. Now when a point of this

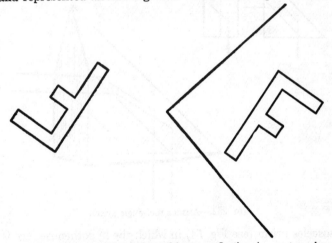

Fig. 251.—Reversal of image formed by two reflections in a rectangular pair of plane mirrors.

image is viewed, the actual rays that enter the eye may indeed be portions of two entirely different bundles, because it is all the same here whether the rays proceeding originally from the corresponding point of the object fall partly on one of the mirrors and partly on the other, because ultimately they will all appear to come from the same point behind the compound rectangular mirror. It is this circumstance that is the essential principle in the *modus operandi* of so-called *roof-angle prisms* such as are employed in parts of various modern optical instruments (particularly in many military fire-control instruments, such as panoramic telescopes, "anti-aircraft fire-control apparatus," etc.)   AMICI's roof-angle prism (Fig. 252) may be considered as an ordinary right angle

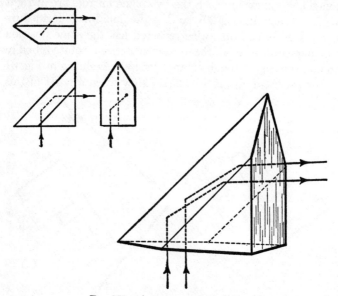

FIG. 252.—AMICI's roof-angle prism.

isosceles prism (see Fig. 54) in which the hypothenuse face is replaced by two plane reflecting surfaces placed at right angles to each other and forming the roof of the prism; the faces of entrance and emergence being the gable-ends of this sloping roof.   The rays suffer two reflections inside the prism first at one side of the roof and then at the other; and, consequently, an object (for example, the portion of a printed page) seen through a roof-angle prism will not appear "per-verted" like the image of the object in a single plane mirror, but merely inverted with respect to the edge of the roof. But if the roof-angle differs ever so little from a right angle, the effect will be a double or overlapping image; and hence such prisms are peculiarly hard to manufacture, because the right angle has to be exceedingly accurate for good results. If the incident rays fall perpendicularly on one of the gable-ends they will emerge perpendicularly to the other one, and the total deviation of the beam will be 90°.

196. Dioptrics. (Historical).—The science of Dioptrics which is concerned with the behavior of light when it passes from one transparent optical medium to another made slow progress among the ancients; and although many of the phenomena of refraction were too striking not to be recognized and described, it is not until after the first century of the Christian Era that we find in such writings of the Greek philosophers as have survived any well-directed efforts to find an explanation of these effects. In fact, the law of refraction itself remained to be discovered until after the invention of the telescope. The first data on the subject are to be found in the *Optics* of CLAUDIUS PTOLEMY, the great Greek astronomer and geographer who flourished in Alexandria (138 A. D.) and whose epicyclic theory of the mechanism of the solar system is still given in modern text-books on celestial mechanics. One of the divisions of this work is on Dioptrics. The experiment with a coin in a basin of water (§ 26) is described there and explained; and the fact that a ray of light is bent in towards the normal to the refracting surface when the ray passes from one medium into a denser one, and away from the normal when the second medium is less dense than the first, is specifically stated perhaps for the first time. But unlike his predecessors, PTOLEMY was not content with mere qualitative results, and a noteworthy thing about this work is that here we find almost the first attempt among the Greek scientists at making physical measurements.* He actually measured the refraction at different

---

* R. A. HOUSTOUN, "The Law of Refraction." *Science Progress*, XVI (1922), pp. 397–407. The quotations in the text are from this valuable paper.

angles for at least three different pairs of substances, and although we do not know the kind of glass he used, some idea of the degree of precision of his experimental methods can be obtained by calculating "the numerical values of the indices of refraction from PTOLEMY's data" which "give means of 1.311 for air to water, 1.485 for air to glass, and 1.109 for water to glass." "PTOLEMY, of course," as DR. HOUSTOUN adds, "did not discover the law of refraction, and knew nothing of the index of refraction. He merely left his results in the form of tables. But he applied them correctly to the explanation of astronomical refraction, *i. e.*, the apparent displacement of a star towards the zenith by the refraction of its rays in its passage through the earth's atmosphere."

ALHAZEN (§ 195) was well aware that the density of the atmosphere diminishes with increase of altitude above the earth's surface and, consequently, he inferred that the path of a ray of light proceeding from a star not directly overhead must be curvilinear after it entered the earth's atmosphere (§ 3). He argued also that on account of atmospheric refraction the disks of the sun and moon near the horizon must appear oval instead of circular, and likewise that a star would be visible a short time after it had actually set below the horizon or before it had actually risen (§ 8). He investigated also the deviation of the refracted rays by making measurements similar to those of PTOLEMY, and he noted the fact that the refracted ray, like the reflected ray, lies in the plane of incidence.

VITELLO   (§ 195) published tables of corresponding values of the angles of incidence and refraction from air to both water and glass, from water and glass to air, from water to glass, and from glass to water, which agree very closely with PTOLEMY's results. About this time spectacles began to be used in Europe and magnifying glasses also. Several centuries later we find PORTA (§§ 3, 194, 195) and MAUROLYCUS (§ 194) studying the properties of lenses. In one of his writings MAUROLYCUS shows that a ray of light issues from a transparent plate bounded by two parallel plane faces in the same direction it had originally (§ 44).

The beginning of the seventeenth century marks a notable epoch in the history of optical science. Already in 1604 KEPLER (1571–1630) had published in Latin a small volume on geometrical optics called "Supplements to VITELLO's Optics" which, together with his subsequent work on "Dioptrics" (1611), was by far the most original and systematic treatise on the subject that had been composed up to that time.* Meanwhile the invention of the telescope in 1609 and the extraordinary discoveries which GALILEO (1564–1642) had made with his new instrument stimulated the imagination and added a practical motive to the cultivation of optics as an applied science. In MILTON's famous lines in which he compares the shield of Satan to the moon

> " Whose orb
> Through optic glass the Tuscan artist views
> At ev'ning from the top of Fesole
> Or in Valdarno, to descry new lands
> Rivers or mountains in her spotty globe,"

we catch even now an echo of the universal acclaim that greeted the celestial discoveries of GALILEO and his successors. Taking VITELLO's numerical data for air and water as the basis of investigation, KEPLER attacked anew the problem of refraction in his peculiar thoroughgoing fashion and sought to discover a general relation connecting the angles of incidence and refraction which would be satisfied, approximately at least, by each of the pairs of corresponding values as given in the table. The nearest he could come to finding a law was to say that the deviation of the ray was apparently proportional both to the angle of incidence (a) and to the secant of the angle of refraction (a'); which is equivalent to the following formula:

$$a - a' = C. a.\sec a',$$

---

* Both of these works have been published in German in Ostwald's "Klassiker der exakten Wissenschaften."

where C denotes a certain constant characteristic of the two media. The smaller the angles the better the agreement was found to be between the values as calculated by the formula and those obtained by actual measurement; but when the angles were comparatively large, the discrepancy was more and more marked. For very small values of a', there is no great error in putting $\sec a' = 1$, and then the formula becomes: $a - a' = C.a$ or $a' = (1 - C) a$. Now both PTOLEMY and ALHAZEN had observed long before that so long as a and a' were small angles, they were in a constant ratio to each other, that is, $a = na'$ or $a' = \dfrac{a}{n}$, where n denotes the constant which is now known as the relative index of refraction of the two media (§ 27). Comparing the two expressions for a', we are able to translate KEPLER's constant C into the following function of n, namely:

$$C = \frac{n-1}{n}.$$

Although KEPLER did not succeed in ascertaining the true law of refraction, it is little short of astonishing to read his writings and see what an insight he somehow contrived to get into the essential nature of this phenomenon and how surely and accurately he perceived the characteristic effects of prisms and lenses and optical combinations. He understood clearly the principle of total reflection (§ 36) and knew how to determine the so-called "critical angle"; and with unerring genius he conceived the combination of two convex lenses which constitutes the astronomical telescope (§ 159) and which enabled SCHEINER afterwards (c. 1614) to construct an instrument according to this theory.

SCHEINER had a remarkable talent for experimenting together with an extraordinary grasp of optical laws. His famous book on the eye and vision called "Oculus sive fundamentum opticum" published first in 1619 is extremely valuable and interesting even to this day. In trying to trace the paths of the visual rays through the various ocular media, he was confronted always with the difficulty of not knowing precisely how the rays were bent so as to form finally an image on the retina. He spared no pains to discover the exact law of refraction; and a book called "Ars magna" published by a Jesuit writer named KIRCHER in 1646 contains SCHEINER's table of the corresponding values of the angles of incidence and refraction for air and water.

The law of refraction, however, was at last discovered about 1621 by W. SNELLIUS (§ 27), a professor of mathematics at Leyden, who died without publishing his manuscript on the subject. HUYGENS states that he had seen this manuscript, in which the correct geometrical construction is given for drawing the refracted ray. The modern form of stating the law in terms of the ratio of the sines of the angles of incidence and refraction (p. 66) was given first by DESCARTES (§ 28) in his *Dioptrique* published in 1637.

197. Reflection Prisms.—In modern optical instruments glass "reflection prisms" in which the light is reflected internally at one or more of the plane faces are employed for manifold purposes, sometimes, for example, to erect an image which would otherwise appear inverted (as in the PORRO prism-system, § 20), and sometimes also merely to change the directions of the rays so that the eyepiece of the instrument can be inserted at a more convenient place, etc. Particularly in the case of a prism of this type, a very considerable portion of the light path lies in the glass medium, and hence to minimize as far as possible losses of light by absorption the optical glass used in the manufacture of these parts must be of the highest quality, that is, as transparent and uniform as possible, and at the same time in order to reduce losses by reflection and also in order to obtain the requisite effects with the necessary precision the surfaces and edges of the prism must be executed by the optician with the greatest mechanical skill (§ 37). The reflecting faces are sometimes silvered.

A plane perpendicular to the parallel edges of a prism will cut it in a principal section (*cf.* § 48), which usually has the form of a polygon of three or more sides. Some of the faces of a prism may be "idle" in the sense that they have absolutely no duty to perform so far as light is concerned, and their only *raison d'être* is that sometimes by shaping the prism in this way it is possible to use a smaller piece of glass which is not only economical of the material but also makes the prism as a whole take up less space in the optical instrument.

According as the light in transit through the prism undergoes one or two or more reflections, the prism is called a "single reflection," "double reflection," "triple reflection"

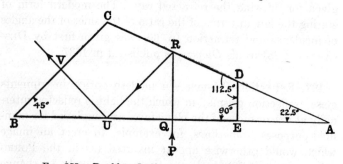

Fig. 253.—Double reflection prism BCDE: deviation 45°.

prism, etc. In the ordinary form of prism (Chapter V) where internal reflections are not considered at all but merely the refractions which the rays undergo on entering and leaving the prism, only these two refracting surfaces are concerned in producing the deviation of the light; but a reflection prism usually has at least as many as three active faces where the rays are deviated either by refraction or by reflection. However, even in a reflection prism only two of the faces may be involved, for the rays can have two adventures at the same face; as, for example, in the prism illustrated by the section BCDE in the above diagram (Fig. 253), which shows the case of a double reflection prism where the ray is transmitted

into the prism across the first face BE and then after being
reflected from the second face CD is reflected again at the
first face. In the diagram the ray is represented as crossing
the first face perpendicularly and leaving the prism at right
angles to the face BC. The two reflecting faces are inclined
at an angle of 22° 30'. The actual form of a principal section
is that of the quadrilateral BCDE with a right angle at E and
an angle of 45° at B. The ray is deviated through 45° which
is twice the angle between the reflecting faces (§ 17).

Thus, in a reflection prism a ray must have at least three
"adventures" (as we called them above), one of refraction
when the ray enters the prism, and two others consisting of
an internal reflection and another refraction on leaving the
prism (single reflection prism) or of two internal reflections
(double reflection prism), in which latter case there will have
to be another refraction also if the ray is to emerge back into
the air again. And generally (as has been stated) these three
first "adventures" or deviations will occur at *three different
faces*, which are the important faces so far as the geometry
of the prism and its optical effects are concerned. In a diagram of a principal section of the prism these three active
faces will be shown as straight lines whose points of intersection A, B, C determine a triangle ABC.

198. Single Reflection Prism.—Consider, first, the case of
a single reflection prism as represented by the triangle ABC in
Fig. 254; and suppose that a ray of light whose path in air is
along the straight line PQ meets the side AB at Q; where it
is refracted into the glass along the straight line QR meeting the side AC in R; reflected thence it falls on the side BC
at S and emerges finally back into the air along the straight
line ST. We proceed to show that the problem of tracing the
path PQRST of a ray through a single reflection prism can be
reduced to that of constructing the path of a ray through an
ordinary prism, as shown in § 49.

Locate the point B' which is symmetrical to B with respect

to the opposite side of the triangle ABC, and construct the triangle AB'C, which, obviously, is not only congruent with the triangle ABC but is in fact the image of the latter tri-

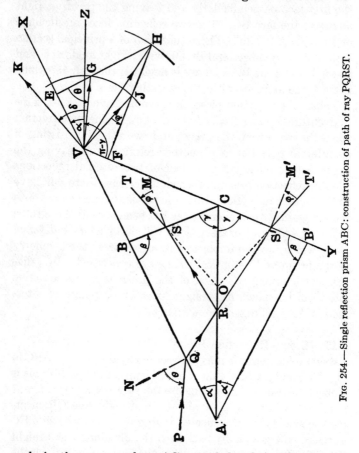

Fig. 254.—Single reflection prism ABC: construction of path of ray PQRST.

angle in the common base AC regarded as being the trace of a plane mirror. Now if the quadrilateral ABCB' were the section of a glass prism, the ray after entering the prism would proceed along the straight line QRS' to the point S' in the side B'C and would emerge into the air in the direction

S′T′; and it is quite a simple matter to construct the path PQS″T′, as follows:

Take a point V anywhere in the plane of the drawing; which, if convenient, may be (as in Fig. 254) the point of intersection of the straight lines AB and B′C. Draw VX, VY and VZ parallel to, and co-directional with, the straight lines AB, CB′ and AC, respectively. Around V as center describe the arcs of two concentric circles with radii in the

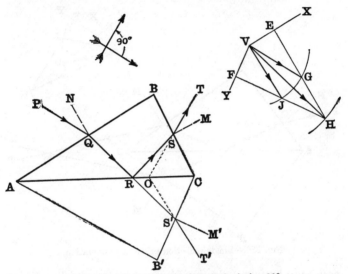

Fig. 255.—Single reflection prism: deviation 90°.

ratio 1 : n, where n denotes the index of refraction of the glass; and draw the straight line VG in the same direction as that of the given incident ray PQ, marking the point G where VG meets the inner arc. Draw GE perpendicular to VX at E and meeting the outer arc at H. Draw HF perpendicular to VY at F and meeting the inner arc at J. Draw QS′ parallel to VH and S′T′ parallel to VJ.

As a matter of fact, however, the glass body does not extend below the line AC; and the light, on arriving at the point R is reflected (partially or totally, as the case may be) along RS to a point S in the side CB which is symmetrical to S' with respect to the straight line AC. Thus, by taking the point C as center and striking an arc with radius equal to CS', the point S can be located and the straight line RS can be drawn. Determine the point O at the intersection of the straight lines S'T' and AC and draw the straight line OS which determines the path ST of the emergent ray. This

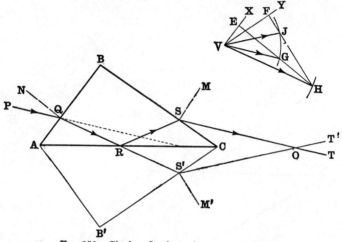

Fig. 256.—Single reflection prism: zero deviation.

path may be found also by drawing the straight line VK so that ∠JVZ = ∠ZVK; because ST is parallel to VK.

Conversely, being given two of the sides of the prism together with the index of refraction of the glass, it is easy to construct the third side of the triangle ABC when the directions VG and VK of the incident and emergent rays are prescribed in advance.

Several special cases are shown in the accompanying diagrams. For example, Fig. 255 is drawn for the case when the ray ST emerges in a direction perpendicular to that of the incident ray PQ, whereas in Fig. 256 ST is parallel to PQ.

that is, the total deviation is zero. If the triangle ABC is isosceles (BA = BC), the quadrilateral ABCB' is a rhomb; and if also PQ is parallel to AC, ST will likewise be parallel to AC (Fig. 257).

The total deviation of a single reflection prism is measured by the angle $\delta = \angle GVK$ (Fig. 254) through which the direction of the incident ray has to be turned in order to bring it into the direction of the emergent ray. The internal angles at the vertices of the triangle ABC are denoted in the following discussion by α, β, γ, thus: $\alpha = \angle CAB$, $\beta = \angle ABC$,

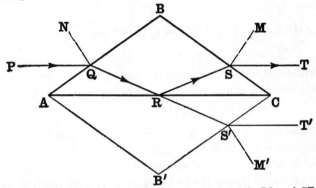

Fig. 257.—Isosceles single reflection prism: AB = BC; PQ and ST both parallel to the base AC.

$\gamma = \angle BCA$, so that if these angles (which are expressly defined so that they all have the same sense of rotation and are reckoned as positive) are given in radians, then $\alpha + \beta + \gamma = \pi$. Evidently, also $\angle ZVK = \alpha$, $\angle YVZ = \pi - \gamma$. Draw NQ perpendicular to AB at Q, MS perpendicular to BC at S, and M'S' perpendicular to B'C at S', the points designated by N, M and M' being all outside the glass. The angles of incidence and emergence, denoted here by the symbols θ and φ, respectively (neither of which is ever more than a right angle), are defined thus:

$$\theta = \angle NQP = \angle EGV, \quad \varphi = \angle MST = \angle T'S'M' = \angle VJF;$$

and are reckoned positive or negative according as the

sense of rotation is the same as that of the angles a, β, γ or in the opposite sense, respectively.

Now from the diagram it is evident that

$$\angle GVK = \angle GVX + \angle XVZ + \angle ZVK;$$

and since

$$\angle ZVK = \angle JVZ = \angle JVY + \angle YVZ,$$

it follows that

$$\angle GVK = \angle GVX + \angle XVZ + \angle JVY + \angle YVZ.$$

If in this equation the symbols are introduced as defined above, noting that

$$\angle GVX = \frac{\pi}{2} - \theta, \ \angle XVZ = -a, \ \angle JVY = \varphi - \frac{\pi}{2},$$
$$\angle YVZ = \pi - \gamma, \ \beta = \pi - a - \gamma;$$

we find the following convenient expression for the angle of deviation of a single reflection prism, namely:

$$\delta = \varphi - \theta + \beta. \tag{1}$$

This formula might have been obtained also by considering the total deviation δ as the algebraic sum of the separate deviations produced at each of the three active faces of the prism. Thus, if the angle of refraction at the first face AB of the prism is denoted by θ', so that according to the law of refraction,

$$n. \ \sin \theta' = \sin \theta; \tag{2}$$

and if the angle of incidence at the emergent face BC is denoted by ψ, so that in the same way

$$n. \ \sin \psi = \sin \varphi; \tag{3}$$

then evidently $\theta' = \angle EHV$, $\psi = \angle VHF$ and

$$\gamma - a = \theta' + \psi. \tag{4}$$

Moreover, if $\left(\frac{\pi}{2} - \eta\right)$ denotes the angle of incidence of the ray when it falls on the reflecting face AC, that is if

$$\eta = \angle QRA = \angle CRS = \angle S'RC = \angle HVZ,$$

then

$$\eta = \frac{\pi}{2} - (a + \theta') = \frac{\pi}{2} - (\gamma - \psi). \qquad (5)$$

The deviations of the ray at each of the three faces in succession are $(\theta' - \theta)$, 2η and $(\varphi - \psi)$; and hence the total deviation is

$$\delta = \theta' - \theta + 2\eta + \varphi - \psi;$$

which after elimination of θ', η and ψ by means of equations (4) and (5) reduces immediately to formula (1) obtained above.

Combining (3) and (4) so as to eliminate ψ, we obtain a very useful formula for calculating the angle of emergence φ in terms of n, a, γ and θ', as follows:

$$\sin \varphi = n.\sin (\gamma - a - \theta'). \qquad (6)$$

This formula not only enables us to see clearly what we must know in order to determine the angle φ; but, taken in connection with (2), it shows also that for a given set of values of n, θ and $(\gamma - a)$ the angle φ has a perfectly definite value; and it should not be difficult for the student to show that this value of φ is precisely equal to the angle of emergence of a ray which traverses an ordinary prism whose refracting angle is equal to $(a - \gamma)$, provided it meets the first face of this prism at an angle of incidence equal to $-\theta$. In Fig. 258 PQRST shows the path of a ray which traverses the single reflection prism whose section is ABC; and P'Q'RST shows the path of a ray which traverses an ordinary prism AV'B whose refracting angle AV'C $= a - \gamma$. If the angles of incidence of the two rays are equal but opposite in sign, the angle of emergence from each of the prisms will be the same.

More important still is another conclusion which can be derived immediately from formula (6), namely: If for a given direction of the incident ray PQ, that is, for a given value of the angle θ, the direction of the emergent ray is to be independent of the value of the index of refraction n, we must have

$$\gamma - a = 0;$$

and this means that *a single reflection prism will be achromatic* (*cf.* § 169), *that is, the deviation will be the same for all colors*

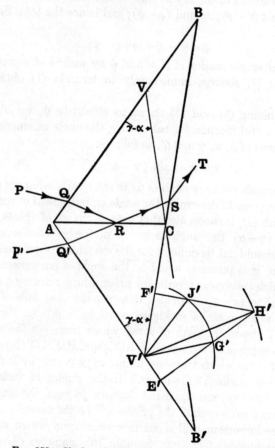

Fig. 258.—Single reflection prism ABC: construction of path of ray.

(*no matter how* n *varies for different colors, p. 466*), *provided the triangle ABC is isosceles* (BA = BC). For example, a ray of white light PQ entering an isosceles single reflection triangular glass prism ABC, as represented in Fig. 259, will be split, say, into a red ray and a blue ray which will have differ-

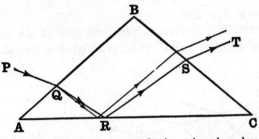

Fig. 259.—Isosceles single reflection triangular glass prism ABC: showing how red and blue rays emerge from the prism parallel to each other.

ent paths inside the prism but will emerge in the same direction. In this case

$$\varphi = -\theta, \quad \delta = \beta - 2\theta, \quad (\gamma = a).$$

When the incident rays are parallel to the base AC of an isosceles single reflection triangular prism ABC, as shown in Fig. 260, that is, when $\theta = \beta/2$, the deviation vanishes ($\delta = 0$).

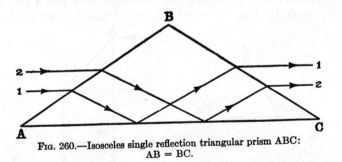

Fig. 260.—Isosceles single reflection triangular prism ABC: AB = BC.

The so-called "reversion prism" of Dove is an isosceles single reflection triangular prism with the faces of entrance and emergence perpendicular to each other ($\beta = \pi/2, \delta = \theta - \varphi + \pi/2$).

The condition that a ray shall traverse a single reflection prism without deviation is

$$\theta - \varphi = \beta, \quad (\delta = 0);$$

as shown in Fig. 256.

A particularly important practical type is the so-called *"constant deviation prism"* which is designed so that the angle

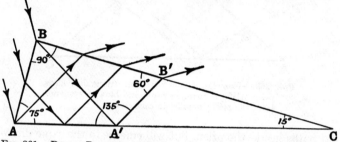

FIG. 261.—PELLIN-BROCA constant deviation prism ABB'A': deviation 90°.

of deviation is equal to the angle β between the two refracting faces; and for which, therefore, we have the following relations:

$$\theta = \varphi, \quad \theta' = \psi = \frac{\gamma - a}{2}, \quad \eta = \frac{\beta}{2}, \quad (\delta = \beta).$$

It appears from the above that the angles θ', ψ and η which are made by the ray inside a prism of this description de-

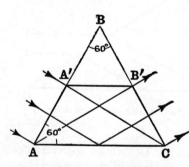

FIG. 262.—Single reflection constant deviation prism: $\delta = a = \beta = \gamma = 60°$.

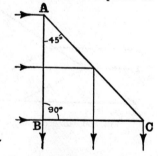

FIG. 263.—Single reflection constant deviation prism: isosceles right angle prism: $\delta = \beta = 90°$.

pend entirely on the geometrical form of the prism and are
wholly independent of the optical material of which the prism
is made, since the expressions for
these angles do not involve the index
of refraction (n). The PELLIN-BROCA
constant deviation prism which has
the form of a quadrilateral ABB'A'
(Fig. 261) has a right angle at B and
hence the deviation is 90°. The interior angles at A, B' and A' are 75°,
60° and 135°, respectively. Figs. 262,
263 and 264 show principal sections
of several common constructions of
single reflection constant deviation
prisms ($\delta = \beta$) designed for rays
which enter and leave the glass
body at right angles to two of the

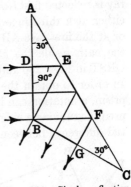

FIG. 264.—Single reflection
constant deviation
prism BDEFG: $\delta = \beta =$
120°.

faces ($\theta = \theta' = \varphi = \psi = 0$, $\gamma = \alpha$). In order to utilize completely all the material of a single reflection constant de-
viation prism, the design should be such that after refraction

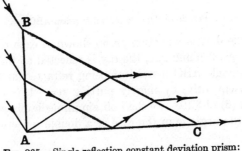

FIG. 265.—Single reflection constant deviation prism:
$\delta = \theta = 2\gamma$.

at the first face AB the rays should go over to the reflecting
face AC in lines parallel to the emergent face BC, as shown
in Fig. 265; which means that here

$$\eta = \gamma, \quad \delta = \beta = 2\gamma = \frac{2(\pi - \alpha)}{3}.$$

199. Double Reflection Prism.—After entering a double reflection prism across the face AB (Figs. 266 and 267), the ray is reflected first from the face AC and then reflected again either at a third face BC (as represented in both diagrams) or at the first face AB (as represented in Figs. 253 and 270); the path inside the glass being shown by the broken line QRST in Figs. 266 and 267, and QRUV in Figs. 253 and 270. In order to obtain the angle relations for a double reflection prism, a notation can be employed almost identical with that used in studying a single reflection prism (§ 198). The essential difference between the two types of prism is that in the

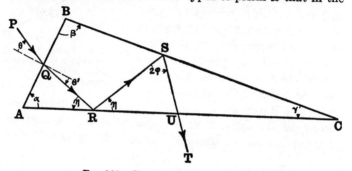

Fig. 266.—Double reflection prism ABC.

case of the double reflection prism shown in each of the diagrams, Figs. 266 and 267, the ray is reflected at the side BC of the triangle ABC instead of being refracted at this side; and, consequently, by merely putting $n = -1$ (see § 75) in equation (6) of § 198, we shall obtain immediately an expression for the angle φ in the case of a double reflection prism, namely,

$$\varphi = a - \gamma + \theta';$$

as can be also obtained immediately from a consideration of either of the two diagrams, since $\angle QRA = \angle CRS = \eta$, $\angle RST = 2\varphi$ and evidently

$$a + \theta' = \frac{\pi}{2} - \eta = \gamma + \varphi.$$

The deviations at each face in succession are $(\theta' - \theta)$, 2η and $(\pi + 2\varphi)$; and hence the total deviation δ which is the algebraic sum of these partial deviations will be found, after eliminating η and θ', to be given by the following expression:

$$\delta = \pi + \varphi - \theta + \beta.$$

This may be written also:

$$\delta = \theta' - \theta - 2\gamma + 2\pi,$$

from which, however, the last term can be dropped because 2π is merely equivalent to a complete revolution of 360°.

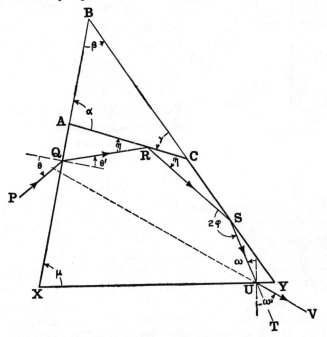

Fig. 267.—Double reflection prism ACYX.

The term 2γ in this expression is due to the two reflecting surfaces which are inclined to each other at the angle γ (see § 17).

The ray ST which marks the path of the light after it has been reflected at the face BC is still inside the prism, and if the light is to emerge into the air, it must be refracted from glass to air at one of the plane faces. Suppose, for example, that the face of emergence is represented by the straight line XY (Fig. 267) which intersects the straight lines BA and BC in the points designated here by X and Y, respectively. If

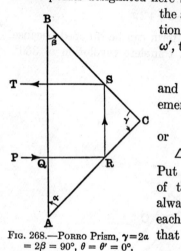

the angles of incidence and refraction at this face are denoted by ω, ω', then, by the law of refraction,

$$n \sin \omega = \sin \omega';$$

and the total deviation of the emergent ray UV will be:

$$\triangle = \delta + \omega' - \omega,$$

or

$$\triangle = (\theta' - \theta) + (\omega' - \omega) - 2\gamma.$$

Put $\mu = \angle\, YXB$, and an inspection of the diagram (taking account always of the sense of rotation of each angle as defined) will show that

FIG. 268.—PORRO Prism, $\gamma = 2\alpha$
$= 2\beta = 90°$, $\theta = \theta' = 0°$.

$$\mu = 2\gamma + \omega - \theta'.$$

Hence, in the special case when $\omega = \theta'$, we must have $\mu = 2\gamma$; and since also in this case $\omega' = \theta$, it follows that the total deviation $\triangle$ will be $\triangle = -2\gamma$. Accordingly, if the straight line XY is drawn so as to make with the side AB an angle twice the given angle γ between the two reflecting sides AC and BC of the triangle ABC, the deviation $\triangle$ will be constant for all rays that traverse the prism. A good example of a *constant deviation* double reflection prism is the quadrilateral prism ACYX shown in Fig. 269, a so-called WOLLASTON prism, in which the angle denoted by μ is a right angle (and hence angle $\gamma = 45°$) so that the total deviation is 90°. Another illustration is the well known *penta prism* (see Problem 43, p. 148) the principal section of which has the form of a pentagon BXA′C′B′ with the sides BX and XA′ equal in length and also the sides A′C′ and BB′, ∠BXA′ = 90°, ∠XA′C′ = ∠B′BX = 112° 30′. The ray is refracted into the prism across the face BX and reflected first from A′C′ and then from B′B and finally emerges across the face A′X in a direction which makes a right angle with the direction

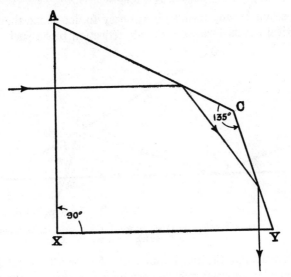

FIG. 269.—WOLLASTON Prism: deviation 90°.

of the incident ray. The side B′C′ is an "idle" face. (The diagram can be readily drawn from the description.)

Allusion was made to another type of double reflection prism in which the ray is reflected back from the second face AC to the first face AB where it is again reflected; so that including the refraction on entering the prism across AB, the ray suffers three deviations at the two faces AB and AC, as represented in Fig. 270 where the broken line PQRUV shows the route the ray pursues. If ∠CAB = α, ∠QRA = η, ∠RUV = 2σ, the following relations between these angles are obvious from the figure:

$$a + \theta' = \frac{\pi}{2} - \eta = \sigma - a;$$

and the deviation is:

$$\delta = (\theta' - \theta) + 2\eta + (2\sigma - \pi) = \sigma - a,$$

or

$$\delta = \theta' - \theta + 2a.$$

It is not by any means always easy to determine the best practical actual form of a double reflection prism such that

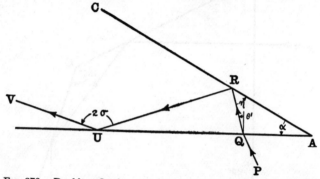

Fig. 270.—Double reflection prism in which ray is reflected internally from the face at which it entered the prism.

it will transmit the maximum part of a bundle of parallel rays incident normally on the entrance-face AB. If the two reflections take place at the faces AC and BC in succession, then, since $\theta = \theta' = 0$, the deviation will be $\delta = -2\gamma$. Consider the ray which enters the prism at the corner A (Fig. 271) and proceeds inside the prism along the path shown by the broken line AEZ, where Z designates the point of intersection of the straight lines EZ and AC. Draw ZD perpendicular to AB at D; then AD is the part of the side AB which is actually utilized in the transmission of light through the prism; and accordingly the triangular portion of glass DBE, having no part in the optical performance, may be removed. Draw the straight line ZF meeting the side BC at F; and draw FG parallel to EZ, and ZG perpendicular to FG at

G. It can easily be shown that ZG=AD. The most economical and efficient shape of the prism is represented by
one whose principal section has the form of the polygon
ADEFGZA. The emergent face ZG will be a continuation of

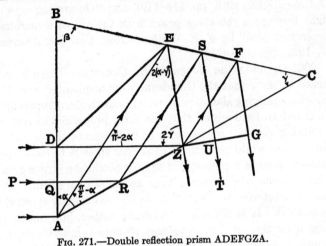

FIG. 271.—Double reflection prism ADEFGZA.

the face AZ when the angle α is equal to twice the angle
γ $(\alpha=2\gamma)$.

The more complicated forms of optical prisms hardly need
to be described in this book, especially as their effects can
nearly always be ascertained by application of the same general methods as have been employed in the above analysis.
The orientation of the image in a reflection prism is the same
as the problem of an image in a plane mirror or in a combination of such mirrors and involves the same questions as are
treated in §§ 15, foll.; although it must be admitted that it is
not always easy to keep in mind the various rotations of the
image that take place in a prism-system where there are numerous reflections. An excellent description of certain special types of prisms which are essential parts of optical apparatus that is extensively used in modern warfare, in both army
and navy, is to be found in a serviceable little volume on

"Elementary optics and applications to fire control instruments" published by the Ordnance Bureau in Washington, 1922. The following papers may be recommended to the student: "Reflecting Prisms" by T. Y. BAKER (*Trans. Opt. Soc.*, XIX, 1918, pp. 113–119), and "On tracing rays of light through a reflecting prism with the aid of a meridian projection plot" by F. E. WRIGHT (*Jour. Opt. Soc. America*, V, 1921, pp. 410–419).

200. Optics in the Seventeenth Century.—There is evidence to show that the Chaldeans were acquainted with the use of magnifying glasses perhaps some six thousand years ago. It is not to be doubted that the focal properties of convex "burning glasses" were known in very remote times; but in the ancient world generally a glass lens appears to have been treated more as a philosophic toy for producing striking and often curious effects rather than as an aid to vision. The use of spectacles in Europe probably dates from about the year 1300. It is difficult to estimate either how much or how little the early investigators of optics, individuals, for example, as widely separated as ROGER BACON (§ 195) and LEONARDO DA VINCI (§ 194), knew about the theory of lenses and their combinations. We do know that MAUROLYCUS (§ 194) sought to explain the action of the crystalline lens in the human eye by analogy with a double convex glass lens and was acquainted with the use of spectacles for both near sightedness and far sightedness. An idea of the originality and extent of his researches is afforded by the fact that he investigated the caustic surface (§ 178) which arises when a cylindrical bundle of incident rays is refracted through a glass sphere. With the invention of the telescope and the compound microscope probably about ten years later, the hope of bringing these instruments to greater perfection was perhaps the impelling motive that directed men's minds more and more to the study of optical laws. Even before the discovery of the law of refraction, both KEPLER and SCHEINER (§§ 194, 196) had succeeded in gaining clear conceptions of the fundamental actions of lens-systems so that they were able to design and construct quite complicated optical combinations. One of the problems in KEPLER's *Dioptrics* is "to show objects distinct, erect, and magnified by a system composed of three convex lenses," which is the principle of the so-called "terrestrial telescope" (§ 159) which was afterwards constructed by SCHEINER for his patron Duke MAXIMILIAN of Tirol. Another one of KEPLER's problems is to combine a concave lens with a convex lens so as to produce an enlarged image on a screen which will be greater than the image made by the convex lens alone; which has been pointed out to be the essential feature in the construction of the modern telephoto-objective. Far more clearly and accurately than MAUROLYCUS had done, KEPLER also compared the crystalline lens in the human eye to a double convex glass lens whose posterior surface he imagined to be hyperbolic (instead of spherical) for the sake of giving better definition to the image. The image itself was real and inverted and focused on the retina; an hypothesis which SCHEINER subsequently verified by experiments made with freshly enucleated eyes of sheep and oxen and in 1625 with a human eye.

The law of refraction, as has been previously stated (§§ 27, 196), was announced first by DESCARTES who belonged to the next generation after KEPLER and SCHEINER, although the latter died in the same year (1650) as DESCARTES. Notable contributions to the science of Dioptrics were made by DESCARTES. He investigated mathematically the form which a curve must have in order that rays of light emanating from a point in one medium shall be refracted at the curve accurately to a point focus in another medium which is the remarkable property possessed by the famous "ovals" which ever since have been called after the name of their discoverer. As a result of these studies he was led to try to manufacture certain special forms of aspherical lenses based on these curves, particularly lenses with elliptic and hyperbolic surfaces, in the expectation that such types would prove vastly superior to the ordinary forms of lenses (see § 205). KEPLER had already discovered (see § 205) that a hyperbolic refracting surface under certain conditions was free from spherical aberration along the axis (§ 178). DESCARTES is to be considered also as the genuine author of the explanation of the rainbow which for many generations had been one of the fascinating problems in optics and had exercised the ingenuities of MAUROLYCUS, KEPLER and ANTONIUS DE DOMINIS (about 1600) each of whom made some contributions towards the final solution. In trying to find a philosophical explanation of reflection and refraction as a general principle of mechanics, DESCARTES was not so successful. This achievement remained to be accomplished by FERMAT (1601–1665) who formulated the "principle of least time" (§ 38) which may be considered as an extension of the principle of the shortest path employed by HERO of Alexandria in the deduction of the law of reflection (§ 195).

As far as known, the first definite rule for calculating the focal length of a thin glass lens was given by CAVALERI in 1647 and was equivalent to the formula:

$$f = \frac{2r_1.r_2}{r_2 - r_1}, \quad (n = 1.5);$$

but he did not know the so-called abscissa-relation between conjugate foci $(1/u' = 1/u + 1/f$; see § 89), although equivalent formulæ were now soon to be discovered almost simultaneously in various quarters, as we shall see.

HUYGENS (§ 6) and NEWTON, who was the younger, are the two most illustrious names in the annals of natural philosophy in the generation succeeding that of DESCARTES. Optics was only one of the rapidly expanding territories of science which was enriched by their powerful labors. At intervals during nearly the whole of his busy life HUYGENS was at work on a treatise on *Dioptrics* which he died without ever completing and which in its unfinished form was published in 1703 in the first posthumous edition of his voluminous writings. It has been republished recently (1916) by the Dutch Society of Sciences. Unfortunately, not a few of HUYGENS' original and sometimes most valuable theorems in optics did not come to light until long after they were first obtained, and, consequently, he lost the priority of a number of important discoveries. The problem of conjugate foci both for a single spherical refracting surface and for an infinitely thin lens is contained in the following proportion which HUYGENS obtains in the first part of his *Dioptrics*, namely:

$$MF : MA = MC : MM',$$

where the letters used here have the same meanings as in Chapter VI on the "Reflection and Refraction of Paraxial Rays at a Spherical Surface"; and if in this formula A is written in place of C, the equation is equivalent to the abscissa-relation for the case of an infinitely thin lens as given on p. 229. HUYGENS obtained these results about 1653, and communicated them to the Royal Society of London in the form of an anagram in 1669. Meantime, in that same year, Dr. ISAAC BARROW (1630–1677), a professor in Cambridge University when NEWTON was a student in Trinity College, had just published his "Lectures on Optics" in which were to be found essentially the same theorems derived in a different way. BARROW's methods are long and involved as compared with the simple proportion by which HUYGENS summarized his results, but they are applicable to thick lenses also. On the other hand, HUYGENS had the idea of equivalent lenses which BARROW did not have. When HUYGENS' *Dioptrics* was finally published in 1703, other writers, notably WILLIAM MOLYNEUX (1692) and EDMUND HALLEY (1693) had given rules which were practically the same as those of HUYGENS.

HUYGENS had the clearest ideas of the action of optical systems, nor did he ever lose sight of the essential fact that all instruments of this kind were intended to aid vision and therefore were to be used in conjunction with the eye. He treats of magnifying power and field of view, and he was fundamentally aware of the nature and importance of the so-called "pupils" of the instrument (§ 134). His theory of the telescope is in every way quite as modern and complete as if it were embodied in an elementary text-book of to-day. There can be no question that the beautiful theorem which states that the apparent size of an object as seen through a lens-system (*cf.* § 157) will not be altered when the positions of the eye and object are mutually interchanged, and which is generally attributed to ROBERT SMITH, had been discovered by HUYGENS a century before the publication of SMITH's "Compleat System of Opticks" in 1738. The construction that HUYGENS gives for the path of a ray refracted at a spherical surface (see Fig. 274) is practically identical with YOUNG's construction as given in § 176. HUYGENS was certainly the discoverer of the pair of so-called "aplanatic points" of a spherical refracting surface (§ 177). A large part of the *Dioptrics* is devoted to an investigation of spherical aberration of lenses, and the results in many respects are in complete agreement with the modern theory of this complicated subject. The famous "Treatise on Light" in which HUYGENS espouses the wave-theory and shows how the wavefront is constructed (§ 6) was written in 1678 but not published until 1690. In this work is contained also his theory of double refraction in Iceland spar, which had been described first by ERASMUS BARTHOLINUS in 1669. Another strange phenomenon which was soon noticed in this same substance and which belongs to the class of facts known as the polarization of light was discovered and investigated by HUYGENS. But it would take too long to enumerate in detail all the advances in optical theory which we owe to this original and penetrating philosopher.

Certain curious and obscure phenomena of light had been observed and investigated by F. M. GRIMALDI (1613–1663), a Jesuit professor of mathematics in Bologna, which led him to infer that light does not travel only by straight lines and by reflection and refraction but may have also under some circumstances a fourth method of procedure which he called *diffraction* (p. 14) and which NEWTON discusses in his "Opticks" (1704) under the name of "inflexion" of the rays of light. Similar observations were communicated to the Royal Society independently in 1672 by ROBERT HOOKE (1635–1703), who in his "Micrographia" (1664) had already described another series of remarkable investigations concerning the "fantastical colors" seen in thin transparent plates and films. It was these observations that led to NEWTON's experiments with the phenomena of the rainbow-colored rings which are produced when two glass lenses are pressed together in close contact so as to enclose between them a film of air of varying thickness, and which are described in NEWTON's "Discourse on Light and Colours" (1675). HOOKE's optical researches and his own explanations were an anticipation of the doctrine of interference which was destined to become famous long afterwards by the epoch-making work of YOUNG and FRESNEL (§ 7) and inclined him to adopt in an imperfect form the undulatory theory of light. According to ROBERT SMITH it is to HOOKE that we owe the famous datum about the resolving power of the human eye which states "that the sharpest eye cannot well distinguish any distance in the heavens, suppose a spot of the moon's body, or the distance of two stars, which subtends a less angle at the eye than half a minute; and that hardly one of a hundred men can distinguish it when it subtends a minute" (§ 10).

Sir ISAAC NEWTON (1642–1727) was born the same year that GALILEO died and lived well into the eighteenth century. His lectures on optics in Cambridge University in 1669–1671 (published in 1728) and his first communication to the Royal Society in 1672 show that he was the real discoverer of the laws of astigmatism of oblique bundles of rays (§§ 184, foll.), which had been previously investigated also by BARROW with

a certain measure of success. In the same year (1672) NEW-
TON sent another communication to the Royal Society describing the celebrated experiments on dispersion of light
(Chapter XIV) which were begun as early as 1666 and among
other notable results had led to the invention of the reflecting
telescope (*cf*. p. 480). A whole series of hitherto puzzling
phenomena concerning light and color were capable of satisfactory explanation on the assumption that there was an
endless variety of light of different kinds or colors each having its own peculiar refrangibility or index of refraction for a
given pair of media (see § 163). It is usually stated that
NEWTON was the first to distinguish seven colors in the prismatic spectrum (§ 160), but MAUROLYCUS in the explanation
which he gave of the circular arc of the rainbow (1575) calls
attention to the "four principal colors" in it, namely, *croceus*
(yellowish like saffron), *viridis* (green), *cœruleus* (sky-blue),
and *purpureus* (purple) together with three other colors
which he regards as transitions or *connexiones*. NEWTON'S
investigations ranged over all the known phenomena of light
including double refraction, polarization, etc.; but these are
intricate questions and beyond the scope of this volume. In
fact, the most notable advance in optics that marks the close
of the seventeenth century (as the invention of the telescope
and the microscope and the discovery of the law of refraction
may be said to have given birth to the science of Geometrical
Optics in the early part of this century) is the growth and
development of theories as to the nature of light itself leading
to bigger views and wider generalizations which belong rather
to the more modern province of Physical Optics. The era
made illustrious by the achievements of HUYGENS and HOOKE
and NEWTON a hundred years later was to be followed by the
epoch of YOUNG and FRESNEL and FRAUNHOFER. But now
the story becomes too complicated to be told in detail; and
the student must consult special works on the history of
modern optics in all its manifold developments in both theory
and practice.

201. Combination of Two Thin Lenses.—The formula for the focal length of a combination of two thin lenses, as given on page 367, is:

$$f = \frac{f_1 f_2}{f_1 + f_2 - c},$$

where f_1, f_2 denote the focal lengths of the separate lenses and $c = A_1 A_2$ denotes the length of the air-interval between them. As long as the only condition imposed is that the focal length of the system shall have a certain prescribed value, this requirement can manifestly be satisfied by an endless variety of possible combinations in which two of the arbitrary variables f_1, f_2 and c may be treated as independent while the third depends on the other two according to the above equation. In the following discussion in order to keep clearly in mind the variable character of these magnitudes, it may be helpful to substitute x, y and z in place of the symbols used above, and put

$$f_1 = x, \quad f_2 = y, \quad c = z.$$

Any constant value may be chosen for the focal length of the combination; for example, it is convenient to put $f = 1$, in which case all the other linear magnitudes will be expressed in terms of f as the unit of length. The results thus obtained can be applied immediately to any other case when f has a value greater or less than unity and is positive or negative; because all that is necessary is to multiply each linear magnitude by this new value of f. The preceding formula may therefore be written:

$$\frac{xy}{x+y-z} = 1, \quad (f=1). \tag{1}$$

Incidentally, it may be remarked that this equation is symmetrical with respect to x and y, as shown by the fact that it is not altered when these letters are interchanged; and hence the focal length of a combination of two lenses remains unchanged when the system as a whole is reversed so that the light goes through it from the opposite end. Now according as x, y or z is regarded as the dependent variable, equation (1) may be written in three different ways, thus:

$$x = \frac{y-z}{y-1}, \quad y = \frac{x-z}{x-1}, \quad z = x+y-xy. \qquad (2)$$

But, in general, the optical system will have to fulfill some other requirement in addition to the condition of having a given focal length. Thus, for example, it may be demanded that the distance (a) of the second focal point (F′) from the second lens, that is, the so-called "back focus" (§ 128) of the combination ($a = A_2F'$) shall have a certain value as compared with the focal length. This second condition leads to another equation which is obtained from the expression for A_2F' given on page 367, and which in terms of the new symbols will appear here as follows:

$$\frac{x-z}{x} = a, \quad (f=1). \qquad (3)$$

The variables x and z are therefore connected by the linear relation

$$z = (1-a)\, x,$$

which referred to a system of rectangular axes x, z represents a straight line going through the origin. If x and z are regarded as the independent variables, the second of equations (2) gives the expression for the dependent variable y in terms of the other two variables.

On the other hand, regarding x and y as the two independent variables, we can combine equations (1) and (3) so as to eliminate the dependent variable z, thus obtaining the following relation:

$$xy - ax - y = 0; \qquad (4)$$

which when plotted with reference to a pair of rectangular axes x, y will be found to represent a curve known as an equilateral hyperbola, one of whose branches goes through the origin of the system of coördinates. The asymptotes of the hyperbola are parallel to the axes of x and y, and the center of the curve is at the point $x=1$, $y=a$. The third of equations 2) gives the expression for the dependent variable z in this case.

Finally, if y and z are treated as independent variables, and accordingly if x is eliminated from equations (1) and (3), the following result will be obtained:

$$yz+(a-1)y-az=0; \qquad (5)$$

which, referred to axes y, z, likewise represents an equilateral hyperbola which goes through the origin and has its center at the point $y=a$, $z=1-a$. The first of equations (2) gives the corresponding expression for the dependent variable x.

Thus three pairs of equations may be derived, which, although they are in fact identical with each other, having all been obtained from the same two original equations (1) and (3), are useful in these various forms depending on which two of the three variables x, y, and z it is convenient to choose as independent variables to which more or less arbitrary values can be assigned. Each of equations (3), (4) and (5) represents a family of curves, the differences between the curves in any one family being due to differences in the value of a.

In the particular illustration which is used here, the "back focus" a expressed in terms of the focal length of the combination is an arbitrary constant or "parameter," the actual value of which has to be selected with reference to each peculiar problem as being the best value for that purpose. If, for example, we choose $a=f=1$, then according to equation (3), either $z = 0$, which means that the two thin lenses must be placed in contact and that their focal lengths x, y may have any finite values provided their product is equal to their algebraic sum $(xy=x+y)$; or, else, we must have x infinite and $y=a=1$, that is, the first lens must be afocal (like a plate of glass with plane parallel faces), whereas the focal length of the second lens, which may be placed anywhere beyond it, must be unity.

A telephoto-lens for photographing far distant objects consists essentially of a combination of a positive front lens with a stronger negative rear lens, placed at such a distance apart that the "back focus" of the system is much shorter than the focal length; so that the parameter a in this case is a proper fraction. For example, suppose $f = 1$ and $a = 0.2$; and hence according to equation (3), $z = 0.8\,x$. If from practical considerations it is found that the best value to give z is $z = 0.16$, we must have $x = +0.2$. Thus if the focal length of the combination is to be one meter, the two lenses must have focal lengths of $+20$ and -5 cm. and must be separated by an interval of 16 cm. This simple example may serve to illustrate how the formulæ and particularly the graphs obtained by plotting these equations will help us to make the best choice of values for a practical solution of a problem of this kind; which is a process that has nearly always to be carried out in the preliminary design of an optical system, even if these values may subsequently require to be modified to a greater or less extent in virtue of other conditions.

202. Types of Optical Instruments.—Optical instruments are usually classified as convergent or divergent (§ 120) according as the focal length of the system is positive ($f > 0$) or negative ($f < 0$); and the system is said to be "afocal" when the focal length is infinite, as in the case of a telescope when the instrument is in what is called sometimes normal adjustment. In a recent paper entitled "The classification of optical instruments" (*Jour. Opt. Soc. America and Rev. Sci. Instr.*, VI, 1922, pp. 682–687) Mr. T. Smith has proposed a new method of "division comprising five classes," which certainly has much to be said in its favor from the point of view of the practical designer of optical instruments, even if it should never be generally adopted. The basis of the new method depends essentially on the fundamental constants

which according to GAUSS's theory (§§ 119, foll.) determine
the character of the imagery produced by an optical system
which is symmetrical around an axis.

Let the positions of the focal points of a centered system
of spherical refracting surfaces surrounded by air on both
sides be designated by F, F'; and let the vertex of the first
surface be designated by A and the vertex of the last surface
by B; and, moreover, let the point conjugate to A be designated by A'. Put AF=a, BF=b and BA'=k. Finally, if
M, M' designate the positions of a pair of conjugate points
on the axis, and if we put x=AM, x'=BM', then, since
(§ 123)

$$FM \cdot F'M' = FA \cdot F'A' = -f^2,$$

where f ($=-f'$) denotes the focal length of the system, the
following equations may easily be derived:

$$xx' - ax' - bx + ak = 0,$$

and

$$ab - ak + f^2 = 0.$$

Accordingly, when three of the steps denoted by a, b, k and f
are known, the other one can be found, and hence also the
value of x' corresponding to any assigned value of x. Thus,
for example, if the focal length of the system is given together
with the positions of the three points designated by A', B and
F', the character of the imagery can be completely ascertained.

Mr. SMITH's method of classifying optical systems is based
therefore on the order of arrangement of the points A', B and
F'. When an object-point starting at an infinite distance in
front of the instrument moves along the axis steadily in the
same direction as that of the incident light until it arrives at
the vertex A of the first surface, the conjugate image-point
starting at F' and moving always in one constant direction
will finally reach the point A' conjugate to A. But this journey must be performed in one direction only, that is, in the
direction along the axis in which the image-point is compelled

to go by the nature of the imagery in each special case; and hence when A' is at a finite distance from F' in the direction of motion of the image, the distance which the image goes will be finite, otherwise it will be infinite because it has to pass through the infinitely distant point of the axis before it can reach its final destination at A'. For example, in the accompanying diagrams (Figs. 272 and 273) the direction of the incident light, the so-called positive direction, is that indicated by the arrow; and here not only the object but the image also is supposed to move in this same direction; but no matter how the diagrams are drawn the statements below will be found to be perfectly general and applicable to all cases. The horizontal line representing the axis must be thought of as extending to infinity in both directions, and that part of it which is drawn thicker than the other represents the portion of the axis which is traversed by the image when the object progresses from an infinite distance to the vertex of the first surface. In Fig. 272, the distance from F' to A' in the sense of the motion is a finite interval, and when this is the case, the points A', B, F' may be ranged along the axis in three possible orders as shown; on the other hand in Fig. 273, the image point has to pass through the infinitely distant point of the axis in order to go from F' to A', and again there are three possible orders of arrangement of the points A', B, F' as shown.

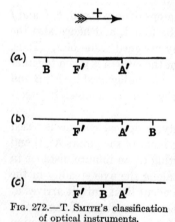

Fig. 272.—T. Smith's classification of optical instruments.

Accordingly, optical systems may all be grouped under one or other of two main divisions, which in turn may be subdivided as follows:

The first group includes those optical systems for which

the part of the axis traversed by the image is finite (Fig. 272) and in this case:

1. If the step BF' is in the same direction as that of the incident light ($b>0$), the order in which the points occur is B, F', A', as in Fig. 272 (*a*); whereas

2. If the step BF' is in the opposite direction to that of the incident light ($b<0$), the order in which the points occur may be either F', A', B (when $k=$BA' is negative), as in Fig. 272 (*b*), or F', B, A' (when $k=$BA' is positive), as in Fig. 272 (*c*).

The second group includes those optical systems for which *the part of the axis traversed by the image is infinite* (Fig. 273); and in this case:

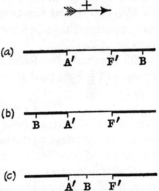

1. If the step BF' is in the opposite direction to that of the incident light ($b<0$), the order in which the points occur is A', F', B, as shown in Fig. 273 (*a*); whereas

2. If the step BF' is in the same direction as that of the incident light ($b>0$), the order in which the points occur may be either B, A', F' (when $k=$BA' is positive), as in

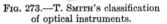

Fig. 273.—T. Smith's classification of optical instruments.

Fig. 273 (*b*), or A', B, F' (when $k=$BA' is negative), as in Fig. 273, (*c*).

If the optical system is a single infinitely thin lens, the points A' and B coincide with each other and lie both on the same side of F'; so that an infinitely thin convex lens belongs to the second division of the second group and an infinitely thin concave lens to the second division of the first group. An ordinary concave thick lens will have the arrangement F', A', B as represented in Fig. 272 (*b*); and (to quote from Mr. Smith's original paper) it is because the negative lenses ordinarily used belong to this class, and not because the power is negative, that all the images they form are virtual.

An optical instrument on the order of a telescope, that is, an afocal instrument ($f=\infty$) constitutes a special case, because in this case the focal point F′ is itself the infinitely distant point of the axis, and consequently the segment F′A′ is necessarily infinite in this case. In the KEPLER type of telescope (p. 456), prism binoculars, etc., A′ lies beyond B in the direction of the incident light, so that all such instruments have either the arrangement F′, B, A′ (Fig. 272, c) or B, A′, F′ (Fig. 273, b); whereas in the Dutch telescope (p. 456) and similar constructions the order of these points is just opposite, that is, either A′, B, F′ (Fig. 273, c) or F′, A′, B (Fig. 272, b).

203. Formula for Refracting Power ($F_{1, k}$) of Centered System of k Spherical Refracting Surfaces.

Let

$$F_k = (n_{k+1} - n_k) R_k$$

denote the refracting power of the kth surface of a centered system of spherical refracting surfaces, where R_k denotes the curvature of the surface and n_k, n_{k+1} denote the indices of refraction of the two media on opposite sides of it. Moreover, let $F_{1, k}$ denote the refracting power of the entire system from the first to the kth surface, inclusive. This system may be considered as a compound system composed of two partial systems, one of refracting power $F_{1, k-1}$ consisting of all the members except the kth surface and the other being the kth surface itself; and the formulæ of § 126 may be applied to obtain an expression for the refracting power $F_{1, k}$ of the resultant system together with expressions for the positions of the principal points $H_{1, k}$, $H_{1, k}'$; provided the corresponding data in the case of each of the two component systems may be assumed as known. The principal points of the kth surface coincide with each other at the vertex A_k of this surface (§ 119); and hence if the reduced interval (§ 126) between the two systems is denoted here by s_{k-1}, that is, if

$$s_{k-1} = \frac{H_{1,\,k-1}'A_k}{n_k},$$

then according to the formula for the refracting power of a combination of two optical systems, the following equation may be written immediately:

$$F_{1,\,k} = F_{1,\,k-1} + F_k - s_{k-1}.F_{1,\,k-1}.F_k; \qquad (1)$$

and the position of the second principal point of the centered system of k spherical refracting surfaces will be given by the following expression:

$$\frac{A_k H_{1,\,k}'}{n_{k+1}} = -\frac{s_{k-1}.F_{1,\,k-1}}{F_{1,\,k}}. \qquad (2)$$

However, this latter formula can be put in a more convenient form; for, since

$$A_k H_{1,\,k}' = A_k A_{k+1} + A_{k+1} H_{1,\,k}',$$

it follows that

$$\frac{A_k H_{1,\,k}'}{n_{k+1}} = c_k - s_k,$$

where $n_{k+1}.c_k = d_k = A_k A_{k+1}$ denotes the axial thickness of the medium comprised between the kth and the (k+1)th surfaces. If this value is substituted in (2) above, the following recurrent formula will be obtained:

$$s_k.F_{1,\,k} = s_{k-1}.F_{1,\,k-1} + c_k.F_{1,\,k}. \qquad (3)$$

In formulæ (1) and (3) we may give k in succession all integral values from k=1 to k=m, where m denotes the total number of surfaces. Here a difficulty will arise as to the meaning of the symbols $F_{1,\,1}$ and $F_{1,\,0}$ which may occur when k is put equal to 1 or 2 in the formulæ referred to; because without special explanation these symbols can have no meaning of themselves. It appears that in order that the formulæ may be true for all the values of k above mentioned, we must put

$$F_{1,\,1} = F_1, \quad F_{1,\,0} = 0.$$

Thus, for example, if the values 1, 2, 3 are assigned to k in succession and the three equations obtained in this way from equation (3) are combined, we find:

$$s_3.F_{1,\,3} = c_1.F_{1,\,1} + c_2.F_{1,\,2} + c_3.F_{1,\,3};$$

which is sufficient to indicate the general rule as contained in the following formula:

$$s_{k-1}.F_{1,\,k-1} = \sum_{p=1}^{p=k-1} c_p.F_{1,\,p}, \qquad (4)$$

where the expression on the right-hand side of the equation means that we must take the algebraic sum of all the products obtained by putting p in succession equal to all whole numbers from p = 1 to p = k–1, inclusive. And if now this equation (4) is combined with equation (1), the following recurrent formula will be obtained finally for the refracting power of a centered system of k spherical refracting surfaces, in terms of the refracting powers of the single surfaces and the reduced intervals between them:

$$F_{1,\,k} = F_{1,\,k-1} + F_k \left\{ 1 - \sum_{p=1}^{p=k-1} c_p.F_{1,\,p} \right\}, \qquad (5)$$

where k is to be given in succession all integral values from k = 2 to k = k. This elegant and useful formula was communicated to the writer in 1920 by Professor C. W. WOOD-WORTH of the University of California.

These results can be expressed also in a different form by introducing the symbol $X_{1,\,k}$ as a convenient abbreviation for the following function:

$$X_{1,\,k} = 1 - s_{k-1}.F_{1,\,k-1}; \qquad (6)$$

whereby formulæ (1) and (3) may now be written:

$$F_{1,\,k} = F_{1,\,k-1} + F_k.X_{1,\,k},$$
$$X_{1,\,k} = X_{1,\,k-1} - c_{k-1}.F_{1,\,k-1}. \qquad (7)$$

For the value k=1, we must put $X_{1,\,1} = 1$. These formulæ (7), in a different system of notation, were given first by Mr. T. SMITH in a "Note on Optical Imagery" published in *Proc. Phys. Soc. of London*, XXV (1912–13), pp. 239–244. Practically, they are equivalent to formula (5), so that if the value of F is known for each surface and the value of c for each medium, the refracting power of the system can be calculated.

Incidentally it may readily be shown that the position of the second focal point (F') of a centered system of m spherical refracting surfaces is given by the following expression:

$$\frac{A_m F'}{n_{m+1}} = -\frac{X_{1,m}}{F_{1,m}}. \tag{8}$$

If the light is supposed to traverse the system in the reverse sense (that is, to proceed through it from the opposite end), and if, corresponding to the symbols s and X, two new symbols t and Y are introduced, which are defined as follows:

$$t_{k-1} = \frac{A_{k-1} H_{k,m}}{n_k}, \tag{9}$$

$$Y_{k-1,m} = -(1 - t_{k-1}.F_{k,m}), \tag{10}$$

evidently, another pair of formulæ, similar to (7), can be obtained, namely:

$$\begin{aligned} F_{k-1,m} &= F_{k,m} + F_{k-1}.Y_{k-1,m}, \\ Y_{k-1,m} &= Y_{k,m} - c_{k-1}.F_{k,m}. \end{aligned} \tag{11}$$

Here it should be noted that $Y_{m,m} = 1$. Equations (11) are useful, partly because they afford a check on the calculation of $F_{1,m}$ as obtained by equations (7), but especially also because by means of them the position of the first focal point (F) can be found, since we have here a relation analogous to (8), namely:

$$\frac{A_1 F}{n_1} = \frac{Y_{1,m}}{F_{1,m}}. \tag{12}$$

The convenience and utility of these formulæ will be perceived best by performing an actual numerical calculation to determine the refracting power $F_{1,m}$ and the positions of the focal points F, F' of a special system. For this purpose let us take the object-glass of a telescope in the form of a triple cemented lens (m=4) made of two kinds of glass. The indices of refraction of the media (for light corresponding to the D-line in the solar spectrum) are given as follows: $n_1=n_5=1$ (air); $n_2=n_4=1.61358$ (flint); $n_3=1.51806$ (crown). The radii of the surfaces are:

$$r_1 = +45.382; \; r_2 = +24.243; \; r_3 = -86.932; \; r_4 = -406.245;$$

and the thicknesses and corresponding reduced thicknesses are:

$$d_1=d_3 = +0.500290, \; d_2 = +1.005820;$$
$$c_1=c_3 = +0.310050, \quad c_2 = +0.662569.$$

(As a matter of fact, the precision indicated by using six places of decimals is far more than would probably be required in practice; but for purposes of the present illustration it is desirable to retain these figures just as they were originally obtained in the theoretical design of the object-glass.)

The refracting powers of each of the surfaces must be calculated by the formula $F_k = (n_{k+1} - n_k)R_k$, $(R_k = 1/r_k)$; and thus the following values are found:

$$F_1 = +0.013520; \; F_2 = -0.003940; \; F_3 = -0.001099;$$

$F_4 = +0.001510$. The calculation proceeds then by means of formulæ (7) as indicated in the following scheme:

	$X_{1,k}$	$F_k \cdot X_{1,k}$	$F_{1,k}$	$-c_k \cdot F_{1,k}$
k = 1.....	+ 1.000000	+ 0.013520	+ 0.013520	− 0.004192
k = 2.....	+ 0.995808	− 0.003923	+ 0.009597	− 0.006359
k = 3.....	+ 0.989449	− 0.001087	+ 0.008510	− 0.002639
k = 4.....	+ 0.986810	+ 0.001490	+ 0.010000	

Each horizontal line in this table is the calculation of one surface as indicated by the value of k on the left-hand side. Each number in the first column (except the first number of all) is obtained by algebraic addition of the two numbers in the preceding line in the first and last columns; and, similarly, each number in the third column (except the first) is obtained by algebraic addition of the preceding number on the same line and the preceding number in the same column. The last number in this column gives the value of the refracting power of the system, which here is found to be $F_{1,4}=0.01$, so that the focal length of the object-glass is equal to 100.

The scheme for the calculation of the system in the reverse sense, according to formulæ (11), is as follows:

	$Y_{k,4}$	$F_k Y_{k,4}$	$F_{k,4}$	$-c_{k-1}.F_{k,4}$
k = 4.....	+ 1.000000	+ 0.001510	+ 0.001510	− 0.000468
k = 3.....	+ 0.999532	− 0.001099	+ 0.000411	− 0.000272
k = 2.....	+ 0.999260	− 0.003937	− 0.003526	+ 0.001093
k = 1.....	+ 1.000353	+ 0.013526	+ 0.010000	

The same value is obtained as before, viz. $F_{1,4}=0.01$. The positions of the focal points are calculated by means of formulæ (8) and (12), which give:

$$A_1F = -100.0353, \quad A_4F' = +98.6810.$$

A good exercise for the student would be to calculate by this method the focal length, etc., of the object-glass given in § 181. He may also repeat the calculations in § 130 of GULLSTRAND's schematic eye in this way.

204. Trigonometrical Calculation of Ray Refracted at a Spherical Surface.—Instead of using the abscissa $c=$CL for one of the ray-coördinates, as in § 180, any other convenient linear parameter may be chosen for this purpose; and thus various systems of formulæ may be obtained similar to that given on page 517 for the trigonometrical calculation of a ray refracted at a spherical surface. Suppose, for example, that the ray is determined by the angle θ which it makes with the axis and the length of the central perpendicular CY (Fig. 237) let fall from the center C on the ray RB. If the length of this perpendicular is denoted here by p, that is, if $p=$CY (where this symbol must not be confounded with the same symbol p used in § 186), the exact definition of this new linear parameter is contained in the formula:

$$p = -c.\sin\theta;$$

and if p' has the corresponding meaning with reference to the refracted ray, it may easily be shown that the following relations are true:

$$\sin a = p.R, \; \sin a' = p'.R, \; n'.p' = n.p;$$

where $R = 1/r$ denotes the curvature of the surface and n, n', a and a' have the same meanings as in § 180. Accordingly, knowing the values of p, θ for the ray before refraction, we can obtain the corresponding values of p', θ' from the above equations taken in connection with the invariants relation between the angles, namely: $a' - \theta' = a - \theta$.

When the path of a ray has to be traced through a centered system of spherical refracting surfaces, the value of p_{k+1} before refraction at the $(k+1)$th surface can be obtained from the value of p'_k after refraction at the kth surface, by means of the following evident relation between these perpendiculars:

$$p_{k+1} = p'_k + a_k.\sin \theta_{k+1},$$

where $a_k = C_k C_{k+1}$ denotes the distance between the centers of the kth and $(k+1)$th surfaces and is given in terms of the radii and the axial thickness by means of the following formula:

$$a_k = d_k + r_{k+1} - r_k.$$

If the ray incident on the first surface is given by the two linear parameters (c_1, h_1), as is frequently the case (see p. 520), where $c_1 = C_1 L_1$ and h_1 denotes the distance of the incidence-point B_1 from the axis, the slope (θ_1) which has to be found in order to begin the calculation can be ascertained by means of the following formula:

$$\tan \theta_1 = -\frac{h_1}{c_1 \pm \sqrt{r_1^2 - h_1^2}},$$

where the upper sign in front of the radical must be used if the first surface is convex and the lower sign if it is concave. This angle having been found, the length of the central perpendicular on the incident ray can be computed by means of the relation

$$p_1 = -c_1 . \sin \theta_1;$$

and then we may proceed to trace the ray from one surface to the next by the system of formulæ given above.

Nearly always a numerical calculation of this kind involves tracing the paths of several rays through the system and at least one paraxial ray in order to obtain the magnitude of the spherical aberration along the axis, as, for example, in the calculation given on pages 521, 522; which is usually a very satisfactory mode of calculation. However, there is a certain obvious advantage and convenience in calculating the paraxial ray and the so-called edge-ray side by side in parallel vertical columns, so that corresponding magnitudes for the two rays (particularly their intercepts on the optical axis) may be constantly compared with each other during the progress of the calculation as some kind of a check against *gross* errors which can easily be made by some inadvertence or by an oversight perhaps in respect to an algebraic sign. Now any system of formulæ for computing the path of an edge-ray can be used also for computing the path of the corresponding paraxial ray, because all that is necessary for this purpose is to substitute the angles θ, θ' and a, a' in these formulæ in place of the sines and tangents of the angles. So far as the paraxial ray is concerned, the actual numerical values which are assigned to these angles at the outset of the calculation are of no consequence whatever; just as in drawing diagrams to show the optical effects of paraxial rays, the actual slopes of the rays and the angles which they make with each other and with the other lines in the figures were of no importance and may indeed be wholly incorrect, so long as the points where these lines intersect the axis are all shown correctly; as was explained in § 70.

If, therefore, the calculations of the paraxial ray and the edge-ray are to be made side by side for the sake of comparison with each other, and if it is true that it makes no differ-

ence what initial value is assigned to the slope θ_1 in case of
the paraxial ray, then in order that the numerical results in
the two columns may agree as nearly as possible, the value of
θ_1 which is chosen for starting the calculation of the paraxial
ray should be put equal to the value of $\sin \theta_1$ for the edge-
ray.

If the formulæ given above are to be used, the scheme will
be as follows:

Paraxial Ray	Edge-Ray
$p'=\dfrac{n}{n'}p;$	$p'=\dfrac{n}{n'}p;$
$a=p.R,\ a'=p'.R;$	$\sin a=p.R,\ \sin a'=p'.R;$
$\theta' = \theta+a'-a;$	$\theta' = \theta+a'-a;$
$p_{k+1}=p_k'+a_k.\theta_{k+1};$	$p_{k+1}=p_k'+a_k.\sin \theta_{k+1}.$

In the special case when the incident ray is parallel to the
optical axis ($\theta_1=0$, $c_1=\infty$), the calculation starts with:

Paraxial Ray	Edge-Ray
$a_1 =h_1.R_1;$	$\sin a_1 =h_1.R_1.$

If a plane refracting (or reflecting) surface is included in
the system of surfaces, then for this surface $R=0$, p, p'
become infinite, and the formulæ given above cannot therefore be employed. Suppose the kth surface is plane, and that
before refraction at this surface the edge-ray crosses the optical axis at L_k and the corresponding paraxial ray crosses the
optical axis at M_k; then the calculation here may proceed
according to the following scheme:

Plane Surface $(R_k=0)$:

Paraxial Ray   *Edge-Ray*

Symbols:

$z_{k-1}' = C_{k-1}M_k;$ $c_{k-1}' = C_{k-1}L_k;$

$u_k = A_kM_k,\ u_k' = A_kM_{k+1};\ v_k = A_kL_k,\ v_k' = A_kL_{k+1}.$

Formulæ:

$$z_{k-1}' = -\frac{p_{k-1}'}{\theta_k};$$ $$c_{k-1}' = -\frac{p_{k-1}'}{\sin \theta_k};$$

$$u_k = z_{k-1}' + r_{k-1} - d_{k-1};$$ $$v_k = c_{k-1}' + r_{k-1} - d_{k-1};$$

$$\sin \theta_{k+1} = \frac{n_k}{n_{k+1}} \sin \theta_k;$$

$$u_k' = \frac{n_{k+1}}{n_k}\ u_k;$$ $$v_k' = \frac{\tan \theta_k}{\tan \theta_{k+1}}\ v_k.$$

A numerical example will illustrate more clearly the process of calculation in parallel columns which has been described above. A comparatively simple optical system will suffice for this purpose, consisting, let us say, of a single double convex lens surrounded by air $(n_1=n_3=1;\ n_2=1.5)$, with dimensions as follows:

$$r_1 = -r_2 = +40;\ d_1 = +4.$$

Assume that the rays emanate from a luminous point on the axis at a distance of 100 from the lens $(u_1=v_1=A_1L_1= A_1M_1=-100)$; and hence $z_1=c_1=u_1-r_1=-140$. Assume also that the edge-ray meets the first surface at a point whose height above the axis is equal to 10 $(h_1=+10)$. We find then that lg tan $\theta_1=8.994\ 5185+$; and thereafter the calculation proceeds as follows:

	Paraxial Ray		*Edge-Ray*
		Logarithmic Calculation	
$\lg \theta_1$	8.992 4114+	$\lg \sin\theta_1$	8.992 4114 +
		$\lg c_1$	2.146 1280 −
		$\lg p_1$	1.138 5394 +
		$\lg n_1/n_2$	9.823 9087 +
		$\lg p_1'$	0.962 4481 +
		$\lg R_1$	8.397 9400 +
$\lg a_1'$	9.360 3881 +	$\lg \sin a_1'$	9.360 3881 +
$\lg a_1$	9.536 4794 +	$\lg \sin a_1$	9.536 4794 +
$\lg a_1$	1.880 8136 −	$\lg a_1$	1.880 8136 −
$\lg \theta_2$	8.214 2609 −	$\lg \sin\theta_2$	8.328 9660 −
	0.095 0745 +		0.209 7796 +
$a_1 \theta_2$	+ 1.244728	$a_1.\sin\theta_2$	+1.620987
p_1'	+ 9.171664	p_1'	+9.171664
p_2	+ 10.416392	p_2	+10.792651
$\lg p_2$	1.017 7173 +	$\lg p_2'$	1.033 1281 +
$\lg n_2/n_3$	0.176 0913 +	$\lg n_2/n_3$	0.176 0913 +
$\lg p_2'$	1.193 8086 +	$\lg p_2'$	1.209 2194 +
$\lg R_2$	8.397 9400 −	$\lg R_2$	8.397 9400 −
$\lg a_2'$	9.591 7486 −	$\lg \sin a_2'$	9.607 1594 −
$\lg a_2$	9.415 6573 −	$\lg \sin a_2$	9.431 0681 −
$\lg p_2'$	1.193 8086 +	$\lg p_2'$	1.209 2194 +
$\text{clg } \theta_3$	0.833 9167 −	$\text{clg } \sin\theta_3$	0.784 9957 −
$\lg z_2'$	2.027 7253 +	$\lg c_2'$	1.994 2151 +
		Angle Computation	
θ_1	+0.098 2678	θ_1	+ 5° 38′ 21.96″
a_1'	+0.229 2916	a_1'	+13° 15′ 19.32″
	+0.327 5594		+ 18° 53′ 41.28″
$-a_1$	−0.343 9374	$-a_1$	− 20° 7′ 0.99″
θ_2	−0.016 3780	θ_2	− 1° 13′ 19.71″
a_2'	−0.390 6147	a_2'	− 23° 52′ 25.89″
	−0.406 9927		− 25° 5′ 45.60″
$-a_2$	+0.260 4098	$-a_2$	+ 15° 39′ 12.00″
θ_3	−0.146 5829	θ_3	− 9° 26′ 33.60″

$$z_2' = +106.5922$$
$$-c_2' = -\ \ 98.6768$$
$$L_3M_3 = z_2' - c_2' = +7.9154$$

The example in § 181 should be calculated by the above method also.

205. Cartesian Optical Surfaces (or Surfaces which are free from Spherical Aberration along the axis).—An ordinary spherical refracting surface or spherical mirror exhibits the phenomenon of spherical aberration (§ 178) in case of a monocentric bundle of incident rays which all intersect in one point on the axis of symmetry of the system. It is doubtful whether DESCARTES was aware of the existence of the pair of so-called aplanatic points J, J′ on the axis of a spherical refracting surface (§ 177), for which the spherical aberration vanishes. They were certainly discovered independently by HUYGENS prior to 1653 who constantly alludes to them in his Dioptrics (see Fig. 274) and at least once in his "Treatise on Light." He showed how these points could be utilized in designing the form of a lens with spherical surfaces which would convert a wide-angle bundle of

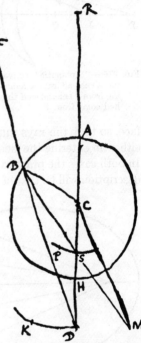

FIG. 274.—HUYGENS' diagram for showing construction of ray refracted at a spherical surface, by aid of aplanatic points D, S; reproduced from Fig. 27, Vol. XIII of HUYGENS' Œuvres complétes, p. 63.

incident rays diverging from a point J on the optical axis in front of the lens into another monocentric bundle of emergent rays diverging also from an axial point J′ on the same side of the lens as J, where J, J′ are the positions of the pair of aplanatic points of one of the spherical refracting surfaces, and either J or J′ is the center of curvature of the other sur-

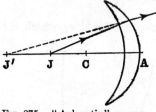 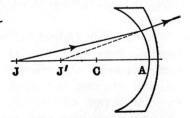

FIG. 275.—"Aplanatic" convex meniscus: all rays emanating from J emerge as if they had come from J′.

FIG. 276.—"Aplanatic" concave meniscus: all rays emanating from J emerge as if they had come from J′.

face, so that the rays must meet this latter surface normally either on entering the lens or on leaving it, as the case may be. In both cases the practical form of an "aplanatic lens" of this description will be that of a meniscus, either convex (Fig. 275)

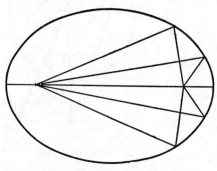

FIG. 277.—Ellipsoidal mirror.

with the center of the less curved face at J, or concave (Fig. 276) with the center of the less curved face at J′.

A *plane mirror* is unique among optical contrivances by reason of the fact that no matter where the object lies, or whether it is "real" or "virtual," its image in a

plane mirror is completely free from the so-called spherical aberrations (and from chromatic aberrations also). But one or two special forms of curved mirrors possess a property akin to this in a restricted way inasmuch as they are free from spherical aberration along the axis for a single object-point in a certain definite position with respect to the curved surface; namely, an *ellipsoidal mirror* (Fig. 277), whose surface is a prolate spheroid generated by the revolution of a portion of an ellipse about its major axis, and a *paraboloidal mirror* (which may be considered as an ellipsoidal mirror with its center of symmetry at infinity) generated by the revolution of a parabola about its axis. It can be shown that all rays emanating from one of the two foci of the generating ellipse of an ellipsoidal mirror will be reflected accurately to the other focus; and, similarly, rays emanating from the

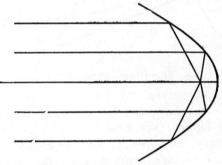

Fig. 278.—Parabolic mirror.

focus of the generating parabola of a paraboloidal mirror (Fig. 278) will be reflected in a cylindrical bundle of rays all parallel to the axis of revolution, or, conversely, incident rays parallel to the axis will be reflected to the focus. Paraboloidal mirrors are much employed in searchlights, locomotive and automobile headlights and in some of the more expensive models of flashlights.

Even before the law of refraction itself had been accurately ascertained, KEPLER with his remarkable scientific instinct had discovered the form of a *curved refracting surface* which produced an effect not unlike that obtained with a paraboloidal mirror. This surface was that of an hyperboloid generated by the revolution of an hyperbola about its transverse axis; and is such that, when the relative index of refraction of the two media has a certain value greater than unity, incident rays emanating from the farther focus of the hyperbola and falling on the convex side of the surface will be refracted into the denser medium in a direction parallel to the

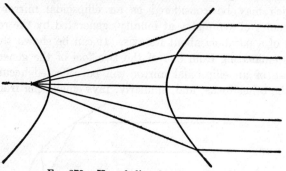

Fig. 279.—Hyperbolic refracting surface.

optical axis as represented in Fig. 279. It can be shown also that a concave refracting surface having the form of a prolate spheroid (ellipsoid) will bend incident rays emanating at the far focus of the ellipse in the denser medium into a cylindrical bundle of rays in the rarer medium proceeding in a

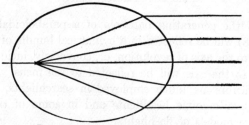

Fig. 280.—Elliptical refracting surface.

direction parallel to the major axis (Fig. 280). In each of these cases the actual dimensions of the surface and therefore the distance of the focus from the vertex will depend on the value of the relative index of refraction of the two media.

The several examples of reflecting and refracting surfaces of revolution which have been instanced above and all of which are characterized by having the power, under certain conditions, of transforming a monocentric or stigmatic bundle of incident rays into a similar bundle of emergent rays are merely particular cases of the so-called *Cartesian Optical Surface* called after DESCARTES who first discovered the gen-

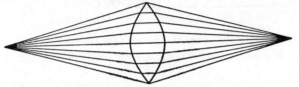

FIG. 281.—Double convex hyperbolic lens.

eral equation applicable to all such surfaces and investigated their mathematical properties (§ 200). DESCARTES himself expended much effort in trying to devise convenient mechanical appliances for successfully grinding hyperboloidal and other aspherical optical surfaces, but even with the help of the best opticians of that day in both France and Holland he never practically succeeded with this task. He even im-

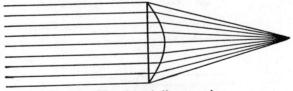

FIG. 282.—Plano-hyperbolic convex lens.

agined that lenses with hyperbolic surfaces combined in a telescope would enable him to perceive the very details on the surfaces of the moon and other celestial objects; but he would have been disappointed in this expectation, because a good optical image involves many other factors besides mere sharpness at one particular mathematical point. Fig. 281 shows a double convex hyperboloidal lens such as DESCARTES probably had in mind which is designed to unite rays, emanating originally from a certain point on the axis, at another point equally distant on the other side of the lens.

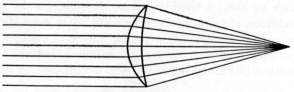

FIG. 283.—Sphero-elliptic convex lens.

Figs. 282 and 283 show the forms of a plano-hyperbolic convex lens and a sphero-elliptic convex lens, respectively, which

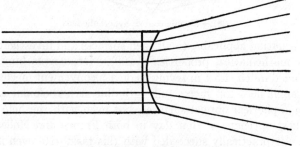

FIG. 284.—Plano-hyperbolic concave lens.

will converge parallel incident rays to a real focus; and Figs. 284 and 285 show the corresponding forms of concave lenses

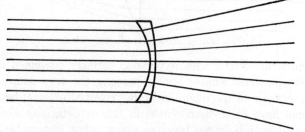

FIG. 285.—Sphero-elliptic concave lens.

each of which will make a beam of parallel incident rays diverge from a virtual focus after traversing the lens.

The problem of finding the form of "a surface CDE (Fig. 286) which shall reassemble at a point B, rays coming from another point A", the "summit of the surface" being at "a given point D in the straight line AB," is treated with great skill and thoroughness by HUYGENS in the last chapter of his famous *Traité de la lumière* (composed by HUYGENS in 1678 and translated into English by Professor S. P. THOMPSON, London 1912); although HUYGENS himself realized that there was much difficulty in manufacturing aspherical surfaces and doubted whether it was worth while to take the trouble, notwithstanding (as he says) that "it may occur that

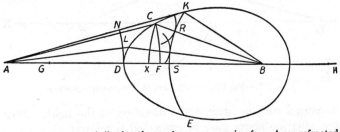

FIG. 286.—"Aplanatic" refracting surface: rays coming from A are refracted at the surface to B.

some one in the future will discover in it [that is, in "the invention" of such surfaces] utilities which at present are not seen."

The problem, as above stated, consists in ascertaining the form of a surface of revolution which will bend rays, either by refraction or by reflection, from a given point L on the axis to another given point L′ also on the axis (Fig. 287), when the position of the straight line LL′ is known, the value of the relative index of refraction (n) of the two media being given also. Since the time taken by light to go from L to L′ is the same by all the actual paths between these points, according to FERMAT's Law (§ 38), the *optical length* (§ 39) from L to L′ along the path LPL′ is the same as that along the axis LAL′; that is,

$$LP + n.PL = LA + n.AL'.$$

Using the same symbols as are employed in Chapter XV for the corresponding linear magnitudes in case of a spherical refracting surface, let us write therefore:

$$v = AL, \quad v' = AL', \quad l = PL, \quad l' = PL',$$

with the understanding that these distances along the rays are to be reckoned positive or negative according as they are

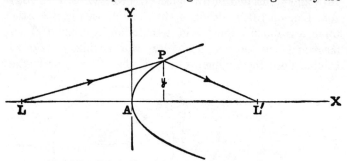

Fig. 287.—For finding the form of " aplanatic " surface.

measured with or against the direction of the light. Then the equation above may be expressed as follows:

$$nl' - l = nv' - v = a,$$

where a denotes the constant value of the optical length between the two terminal points L and L'. This is the focal form of the equation of the famous "ovals of DESCARTES", which is the name given to these curves in honor of their discoverer and on account of their oval forms. The actual form and dimensions of the curve in any given case will depend on the value of the constant a. Thus, for example, when $a = 0$, the curve reduces to a circle ($nl' - l = 0$) and the corresponding Cartesian surface will be a spherical refracting surface for which the pair of points L, L' are identical with the aplanatic points J, J'. Or, again, by putting $n = -1$ (§ 75), we find that the equation of the generating curve of a mirror which will reflect rays from L to L' is $l' + l = a$ constant, which is the characteristic property of an ellipse.

If the vertex A is taken as the origin of a system of rectangular coördinates whose abscissa-axis is the straight line joining L and L' and if x, y denote the coördinates of the point P, then

$$l^2 = y^2 + (v-x)^2, \quad l'^2 = y^2 + (v'-x)^2;$$

and if l and l' are eliminated from the equation $nl' - l = nv' - v$, the following equation of the fourth degree in x, y is obtained as the general equation of the meridian section of the Cartesian Surface:

$$\left\{ (n^2-1)(x^2+y^2) - 2(n^2 v' - v)x \right\}^2$$
$$+ 4n(v-nv') \left\{ (v'-nv)(x^2+y^2) + 2(n-1)vv'x \right\} = 0$$

In a paper by the writer entitled "Aplanatic (or Cartesian) Optical Surfaces" (*Journ. Franklin Inst.*, 193 (1922), pp., 609-626; also, 194 (1922), pp. 69-73) this equation is discussed in some detail and a method is given for making a simple geometrical construction of the required curve for any special case.

With improvements in processes and machinery for manufacturing optical surfaces, it is by no means unlikely that these Cartesian Curves will have a utility in certain specialized forms of modern optical contrivances (condenser lenses, etc.). Real progress in optical instruments is certainly to be gained by the possibility of using aspherical surfaces of some kind, although these surfaces will be quite different from the Cartesian surfaces which have been described above. Several years ago GULLSTRAND published a monograph entitled "Ueber asphaerische Flaechen in optischen Instrumenten" (Stockholm, 1919, 155 pages) which is a masterly treatment of the entire subject from every point of view and contains both theoretical and practical suggestions which will undoubtedly have much influence on the future of optical design and construction.

MISCELLANEOUS PROBLEMS

1. KEPLER gave an approximate formula for the law of refraction which may be written as follows (§ 200):

$$a = \frac{a'}{1 - C.\sec a'}, \qquad C = \frac{n-1}{n};$$

whereas the true law as found afterwards is $\sin a = n.\sin a'$. Give a' a series of values (say, 5°, 10°, 15°, etc.) and calculate by each of these formulæ the corresponding values of the angle of incidence (a) for $n = \frac{4}{3}$: and plot two curves on a sheet of coördinate paper with same set of axes exhibiting the results.

2. The principal section of a single reflection glass prism has the form of a triangle ABC, the rays entering and leaving the prism at the sides AB and BC, respectively, having been reflected meantime from the side AC. (1) Construct the path of a ray through the prism for which the total deviation is a right angle; and (2) construct the path of a ray which leaves the prism parallel to the side AC.

3. The principal section of a double reflection glass prism has the form of a quadrilateral ABCD and is so designed that rays entering the prism across the face AD and being internally reflected, first, at the face AB and then at the face BC, emerge across the face CD into the surrounding medium with a constant total deviation δ. Show that the angle CDA $=\delta$ and angle ABC $= 180° - \delta/2$.

4. The principal section of a double reflection glass prism has the form of a triangle ABC, the angle at A being twice that at C. Rays refracted into the prism across the side AB are reflected internally at the sides AC and BC in succession, and emerge finally into the surrounding medium across the side AC. Show that the total deviation is equal to twice the angle at C.

5. Show that the distance between the two principal points

of a thick lens of index n surrounded by air is $(n-1)^2\, ad/N$, where a and d denote the distances between the centers and between the vertices of the two surfaces $(a = C_1 C_2,\ d = A_1 A_2)$ and $N = (n-1)\,(na - d)$.

6. Show that the greatest possible diameter of a convex lens of radii r_1, r_2 and thickness d is equal to

$$\frac{\sqrt{(2r_1 - d)\,(2r_2 + d)\,(2r_2 - 2r_1 + d)\,d}}{r_2 - r_1 + d}$$

7. The crystalline lens of GULLSTRAND's schematic eye is a double convex lens of radii 10 mm. and 6 mm. surrounded by a medium of index 1.336. The thickness of the lens is 3.6 mm. and its refracting power as found on p. 373 is 19.110 dptr. Find the index of refraction of the equivalent lens of the same external form and of equal refracting power, but homogeneous in substance.

Ans. 1.4087 (whereas the index of the lens-core in the schematic eye is 1.406).

8. Let O, O' and M, M' designate the positions of two pairs of conjugate points on the axis of a centered system of spherical refracting surfaces; and put $z = $ OM, $z' = $ O'M', $Z = n/z$, $Z' = n'/z'$ where n, n' denote the indices of refraction of the first and last media. If m denotes the lateral magnification ratio (§ 124) for the pair of conjugate points O, O' ,and if y'/y is the value of this same ratio for M, M', where y, y' denote the heights of object and image at M, M'; show that the image-equations may be expressed in the following form:

$$m^2.Z' = Z + m.F, \quad m.y'.Z' = y.Z,$$

where F denotes the refracting power of the system. And in the special case when the points designated by O, O' are identical with the nodal points N, N', show that the image-equations referred to the nodal points may be written as follows:

$$\frac{Z'}{n'^2} = \frac{Z}{n^2} + \frac{F}{n.n'}, \quad \frac{y'.Z'}{n'} = \frac{y.Z}{n}.$$

9. Find the positions of the nodal points of GULLSTRAND's schematic eye, employing data in § 130. What is the distance between them? Ans. 7.078 and 7.332 mm. from the vertex of cornea.

10. WOLLASTON's doublet is an eyepiece consisting of two thin planoconvex lenses with their plane faces towards the incident light. The focal length of the second lens is 3 times that of the first and the interval between them is 1.5 times the focal length of the first lens. Find the focal length of the combination. Draw a diagram of the system showing where an object must be placed in order that rays coming from any point in it will issue from the system all in the same direction.

11. An automobile headlight is made by silvering the rear surface of a concave meniscus glass lens so as to make a "thick" concave mirror. The radii and axial thickness of the lens are:

$$A_1C_1 = r_1 = -6.317 \text{ cm}; \; A_2C_2 = r_2 = -8.440 \text{cm.};$$
$$A_1A_2 = d = +0.676 \text{ cm.}$$

The index of refraction of the glass is 1.5. Find the positions of the vertex H and the center K of the equivalent "thin" mirror (§ 132).

Ans. $A_1H = +0.435$ cm.; $A_1K = -8.768$ cm.

12. An eye is accommodated to see distinctly an object placed at a point M' on the optical axis. A thin spectacle glass is placed in front of the eye at a point L; and now the eye without changing its accommodation can see an object at a point M. Show that FM : LM = LM : MM', where F designates the position of the first focal point of the interposed lens. What is the condition that the point F shall coincide with M'? and what is the condition that the point M' shall coincide with the second focal point of the lens?

13. A man begins to be presbyopic (§ 149) when his near point distance (§ 151) is equal, say, to 22 cm. When he wears a certain thin spectacle lens at a distance of 12 mm. from the

first principal point of his eye, he can just see an object 10 cm. away. What is the refracting power of the lens?

Ans. About +6.56 dptr.

14. Using the numerical data of GULLSTRAND's schematic eye (§ 130), and supposing the crystalline lens has been extracted (as in the operation for cataract), find the position on the axis of this so-called "aphakic" eye of the point which is focused sharply on the retina. And find also the refracting power of a lens which placed with its second principal point 12 mm. from the vertex of the cornea will enable an aphakic eye to see distinctly an infinitely distant object like a star.

Ans. 8 cm. beyond the vertex of the cornea towards which incident rays must converge in order to be united on the retina; refracting power of lens is +10.9 dptr.

15. The following construction of the path of a ray refracted at a spherical surface is given in ISAAC BARROW's Lectures on Optics (1669): Draw a straight line RB to represent the path of a ray incident on a spherical surface at B; and draw the normal NN′ passing through B and the center C. Through C draw a straight line parallel to RB meeting the surface in A, and on this line take two points X, Y such that AY : CY = XY : CX = n : 1, where n denotes the relative index of refraction of the two media. (If the construction here indicated is made correctly, the points X, Y will be found to lie both on the same side of C, and X will be between C and Y.) Describe the arc of a circle around X as center which goes through Y and meets NN′ in a point G. On the straight line CY find the point K such that CK=CG. The straight line BS which goes through K will be the refracted ray corresponding to the incident ray RB. Prove that this construction is correct; and draw four diagrams for cases when the surface is convex and concave and for n greater and less than unity.

16. If the aplanatic points of the first surface of a glass lens surrounded by air are designated by J, J′, and if the center of the second surface is at J′, the lens will be a convex

meniscus (Fig. 275) or a very thick double convex lens and will be free from spherical aberration with respect to the points J, J'.

17. In trigonometrical calculations of the path of a ray refracted at a spherical surface (§§ 180, 204) a certain expression connecting the sines of the angles a, θ and a', θ' occurs so frequently that it is convenient to employ a special symbol E by way of abbreviation, which is therefore defined as follows:

$$E = (\sin\theta' - \sin a') - (\sin\theta - \sin a).$$

Show that E may also be expressed in the following form which is more convenient for logarithmic computation:

$$E = 4 \sin \frac{a-\theta}{2} . \sin \frac{a'+\theta}{2} . \sin \frac{a'-a}{2}.$$

18. If the lengths of the perpendiculars let fall from the center of a spherical refracting surface on a ray before and after refraction are denoted by p and p', respectively, show that $n' . p' = n.p$, where n, n' denote the indices of refraction of the two media.

19. The points where a ray crosses the axis of a spherical refracting surface before and after refraction are designated by L, L', and $c = CL$, $c' = CL'$ denote the abscissæ of these points with respect to the center C. The refracting power of the surface is denoted by F. Show that

$$\frac{C'}{n'^2} = \frac{C}{n^2} + \frac{F}{n.n'} - \frac{E}{n.p},$$

where the symbols n, n', E and p have the same meanings as in Nos. 17 and 18 above, and $C = n/c$, $C' = n'/c'$.

20. A paraxial ray and an edge-ray emanate from the same point on the axis of a centered system of spherical refracting surfaces. The paraxial ray crosses the axis at M and M' before and after refraction, respectively, at one of the surfaces;

the corresponding points for the edge-ray are designated by L, L'. The center of this surface is designated by C, and the indices of refraction of the two media separated by this surface are denoted by n, n'. Put z = CM, z' = CM'; c = CL, c' = CL'; and Z = n/z, Z' = n'/z', C = n/c, C' =n'/c'. By the aid of the formula found in the preceding problem, show that

$$\frac{C'-Z'}{n'^2} = \frac{C-Z}{n^2} - \frac{E}{n.p}.$$

($C -\cdot Z$ and $C' - Z'$ in this formula are measures of the spherical aberration along the axis before and after refraction at the surface in question, so that if one of these magnitudes is known the other can be found.)

21. The points where a ray crosses the axis before and after reflection at a spherical mirror are designated by L, L'; the tangent to the surface at the point of incidence intersects the axis in a point designated by T; and the center of the mirror is designated by C. Show that

$$\frac{1}{TL} + \frac{1}{TL'} = \frac{2}{TC},$$

and therefore that the spherical aberration along the axis is proportional to the distance of T from the vertex of the mirror. In case of a paraxial ray how will the formula apply?

22. A ray of light falls on a spherical mirror at a point B ($\angle BCA = \varphi$), where A and C designate vertex and center of the mirror. A straight line is drawn through C perpendicular to the axis of the mirror, and the points where the incident ray and the corresponding reflected ray intersect this line are designated by K and K'. If the angle of incidence is denoted by a, show that

$$\frac{CK'}{CK} = -\frac{\cos (a-\varphi)}{\cos (a+\varphi)}.$$

23. The radius of a spherical mirror is $r = AC$. A ray crosses the axis before and after reflection at L and L′ ($c = CL$, $c' = CL'$). Show that

$$c' = - \frac{c.r}{2c.\cos\varphi + r},$$

where $\varphi = \angle BCA$, as in preceding problem. How will this formula be modified when the incident ray is parallel to the axis? In this latter case show that the point L′ will lie farther from C than halfway between C and A, except when the ray is a paraxial ray when L′ will be exactly midway between C and A. When the incident ray is parallel to the axis, can the reflected ray cross the axis at the vertex of the mirror? can it cross the axis at a point on the other side of the vertex from the center? Explain. (The answers to all these questions had been found by ROGER BACON in the thirteenth century; see § 195).

24. Employing the formula obtained in the preceding problem, show that the spherical aberration along the axis of the mirror is given by the following expression:

$$\frac{4 \; c^2 r.\sin^2 \dfrac{\varphi}{2}}{(2c + r) \; (2c.\cos \varphi + r)}.$$

Under what conditions will the aberration vanish?

25. A cemented glass lens surrounded by air is composed of three different kinds of glass of indices n_2, n_3 and n_4 ($n_1 = n_5 = 1$) such that the value of n_3 is the geometrical mean between the values of n_2 and n_4. The two outside surfaces are plane ($R_1 = R_4 = 0$); whereas the two inner surfaces are concentric with each other with their curvatures in the ratio of the indices n_2 and n_3, or more accurately:

$$\frac{R_2}{R_3} = -\frac{n_2}{n_3}.$$

Show that a bundle of incident rays parallel to the axis will issue from the lens in the same direction, and that under the given conditions this lens is entirely free from spherical aberration.

26. A ray is refracted at a curved surface separating two media whose indices of refraction are denoted by n, n'. If the normal to the surface is drawn through the point of incidence P, and if a straight line is drawn intersecting the normal at G and the incident and refracted rays at L and L', respectively, show that

$$n' \frac{GL'}{PL'} = n \frac{GL}{PL}.$$

27. A ray crosses the axis at an angle θ and is incident on a spherical refracting surface at an angle α. If the curvature of the surface is denoted by R, and if the length of the perpendicular from the vertex on the ray is denoted by e, show that $\sin\alpha = \sin\theta + e.R$. Write the corresponding formula for the refracted ray; and show also that

$$\frac{e'}{e} = \frac{\cos\alpha' + \cos\theta'}{\cos\alpha + \cos\theta}.$$

28. The radii and thickness of a meniscus lens made of glass of index 1.51 and surrounded by air are : $r_1 = -10$, $r_2 = -8.4$, $d = +1$. The lens is provided with a front stop with its center at a distance equal to 1 from the vertex of the first surface. The chief ray coming from an infinitely distant point crosses the axis at an angle of 35°. Find the astigmatic difference (§ 187) along this ray.

Ans. $P_3Q_3 = -1.306$.

29. In the preceding problem, suppose the thickness of the lens is changed to $d = +1.5$, everything else remaining the same as before. Find the astigmatic difference now.

Ans. $P_3Q_3 = -11.333$.

30. In No. 28, suppose the stop is 5 times as far away, everything else remaining the same as before. What effect is produced on the astigmatism?   Ans. $P_3Q_3 = -17.013$.

31. In No. 28, suppose the index of the glass is changed to

1.61; everything else remaining the same as before. What effect is produced on the astigmatism? Ans. $P_3Q_3 = +1.506$.

32. The data of PETZVAL's famous photographic portrait objective, as given by VON ROHR, are:

(Distances expressed in mm.)

Radii:

$$r_1 = +52.9; \ r_2 = -41.4; \ r_3 = +436.2; \ r_4 = +194.8;$$
$$r_5 = +36.8; \ r_6 = +45.5; \ r_7 = -149.5.$$

Thicknesses:

$$d_1 = +5.8; \ d_2 = +1.5; \ d_3 = +46.6; \ d_4 = +2.2;$$
$$d_5 = +0.7; \ d_6 = +3.6.$$

Indices of Refraction (n_D):

$$n_1 = n_4 = n_6 = n_8 = 1 \text{ (air)}; \ n_2 = n_7 = 1.517;$$
$$n_3 = n_5 = 1.575.$$

Find the focal length of the lens and the positions of the focal points.   Ans. $f = 100$; $A_1 F = -74.5$; $A_2 F' = +58.6$.

CHAPTER XVII

THE MICROSCOPE

206. Introduction.—Modern optical instruments date back to the nearly simultaneous inventions of the telescope and the microscope by spectacle-opticians early in the seventeenth century. The magic lantern which at first was little more than an ingenious and entertaining toy was invented not long afterwards. A new era began with the discovery of photography in the first half of the nineteenth century which was soon followed by the invention of the daguerreotype process and the development of the photographic negative less than a hundred years ago. The art of photography gave an entirely new incentive to the design and construction of optical instruments for all kinds of pictorial representations and reproductions. So various and manifold are the uses of optical instruments today in all the arts and industries as well as in scientific investigations that it would be difficult to enumerate them and still more difficult to classify them. Besides microscopes, telescopes and photographic lenses, there are all kinds of special appliances such as lanterns, search-lights, field-glasses, range-finders, periscopes, stereoscopes, ophthalmometers, ophthalmoscopes, moving-picture apparatus, etc., and almost innumerable scientific instruments (refractometers, spectroscopes, photometers, spectrophotometers, interferometers, polariscopes, etc.). It would take a separate volume to give anything like an adequate description of the principal types of optical instruments. For a general survey of the subject no better book can be recommended than Professor M. v. Rohr's admirable compendium on *Die optischen Instrumente* (4th ed., Berlin, 1930), although this slender volume is by no means intended to cover the whole field. Each form of optical instrument is designed for a special purpose, and so a photographic lens, for example, that is intended to project an image on a flat surface for reproduction has little in common with a telescope or a microscope that has to be applied to the eye of the observer. No one optical instrument is typical of all the others. In order to show how the general principles of geometrical optics as explained in the preceding chapters of this book are applicable to the theory of optical instruments, the microscope has been selected for treatment in this chapter as being perhaps as good a single example as could be taken for that purpose.

I. *The Magnifying Glass (or Simple Microscope)*

207. The Purpose of a Microscope.—Everybody is aware that the coarser details of an object can be perceived more clearly when it is close to the eye because then the various parts of the object subtend larger angles than they do when the object is far away. In order to discern minute details, a near-sighted person will sometimes remove his spectacles and hold the object so close to his eye that one wonders how he can see it distinctly at all; but as a matter of fact for this particular purpose his eyesight is superior to that of an individual whose vision is normal or emmetropic. For while it is true that the nearer the object is to the eye, the larger the angle it subtends, yet if the object is closer than the near point of accommodation (§ 148), the eye cannot be focused to see it distinctly. To a certain extent the visual acuity under these circumstances can be enhanced by viewing the object through a narrow hole or slit whose width is less than the diameter of the pupil of the eye; which has the effect of diminishing the size of the blur circles on the retina and is therefore practically equivalent to shifting the near point a little closer to the eye than it really is. But this device is a rather poor makeshift at best, not only because the image is dim and the field contracted, but chiefly because if the width of the aperture is less than a millimeter, the resolving power of the eye is lowered to such an extent by the diffraction-pattern which is always obtained with a narrow aperture that the purpose is entirely defeated.

The experiment of trying to read the letters on a printed page through a small aperture made by piercing a hole with a fine needle in a sheet of dark paper is very instructive. As the size of the hole is reduced by using smaller and smaller needles, the illumination of the printed page should be steadily increased to compensate for the narrower beam of light that is admitted through the hole. When the diameter of the latter is below one millimeter, the outlines of the letters begin to be less and less sharp; until when the diameter is no more than one-fifth of a millimeter, they will be too blurred to be distinguished distinctly at all, and when the aperture is still further reduced, the entire page assumes a uniform grayish complexion. The appearance of an intensely bright source of light, for example, a star, as seen through a tiny round hole is that of a disk with a bright spot in the center surrounded by a series of concentric colored rings, each of which is blue or green on its inner margin and red or orange on the outer side (§ 230). In the theory of the compound microscope, as we shall see (§ 216), these diffraction-effects have a very important bearing on the resolving power of the microscope.

The magnifying power of a transparent body with convex curved surfaces must have been known from very ancient times; otherwise, it is difficult to account for the numerous specimens of fine handiwork (engraving, gem-cutting, etc.) that are found in museums of the arts of ancient civilization. The cuneiform characters on the tablets found by LAYARD in the ruins of Nineveh are so minute in some instances as to be illegible to the naked eye, and they must have been engraved with the help of a magnifier.

An optical instrument which, being focused on a tiny object, produces a magnified virtual image at a convenient distance for distinct vision is called a microscope. The object will always be close to the microscope and therefore not far from the observer's eye at the other end of the instrument; whereas the image subtending a large angle (ω') will be formed at a comparatively great distance, preferably infinitely far away if the observer is emmetropic.

208. Simple Microscope; Magnifying Power.

—A simple microscope or magnifying glass of low power often consists of

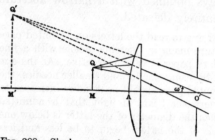

a single convex lens, which is sometimes mounted in a little circular frame or rim to protect it from being broken and in order that it may be carried conveniently in the pocket like a watch. The small object MQ (Fig. 288; *cf.* also Fig. 180, p. 411), placed between the lens and its anterior

Fig. 288.—Single convex lens used as magnifying glass. Object $MQ = y$ placed between lens and its anterior focal plane; virtual, erect, magnified image $M'Q' = y'$; O' center of pupil of observer's eye; $\angle AO'Q' = \omega'$; $O'M' = z'$.

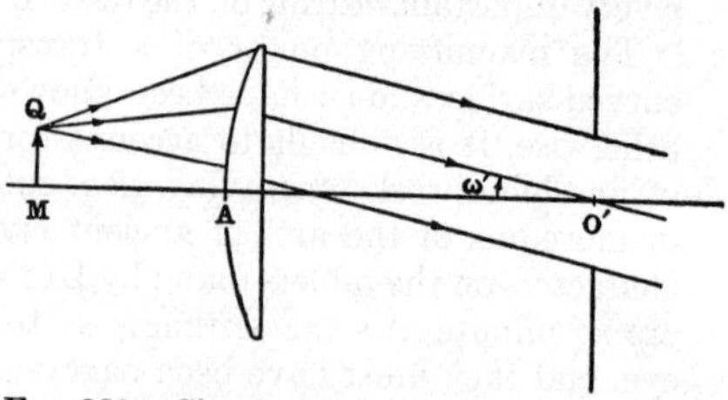

focal plane, is reproduced by a virtual, erect and magnified image $M'Q'$, which will be farther away the nearer the object is to the focal plane. The observer, looking through the glass, adjusts it with reference to the object to suit his convenience, that is, so as to see the image distinctly and with as little effort as possible. The pupil of his eye with its center on the optical axis at O' is the common base of the narrow cones of

Fig. 289.—Simple convex lens used as magnifying glass. Object MQ in anterior focal plane of lens, image at infinity. Diameter of lens exceeds diameter of pupil of eye $(h > p')$.

rays which proceed from the points of the virtual image. If the object lies in the anterior focal plane, as represented in Figs. 289 and 290, the image will be infinitely far away, and the bundles of rays entering the eye will be cylindrical.

The visual angle ($\omega' = \angle AO'Q'$) subtended at the eye by the image $M'Q' = y'$ in the magnifying glass will be generally much greater than the angle that would be subtended by the object $MQ = y$ at the conventional "distance of distinct vision" denoted by l (p. 452), that is, by the angle whose tangent is $-y : l$. The magnifying power (§ 158), being de-

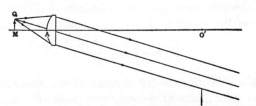

Fig. 290.—Simple convex lens used as magnifying glass. Object MQ in anterior focal plane of lens, image at infinity. Diameter of pupil of eye exceeds diameter of lens $(p' > h)$.

fined as the ratio between (the tangents of) these two angles, is given therefore by the formula:

$$M = -\frac{\omega'}{y},$$

which, as we have seen (p. 454), may be put in the more convenient form:

$$M = l\{F - Z'(1 - e.F)\},$$

where $F = 1/f$ denotes the refracting power of the glass, Z' denotes the reciprocal of the distance $z' = O'M'$ of the image from the eye, and e denotes the distance of the eye from the lens or rather from the second principal point (H') of the lens $(e = H'O')$. The image, as stated above, is usually far from the eye, and hence the magnitude denoted by Z' is correspondingly small and generally negligible; so that the absolute magnifying power of the glass, as distinguished from the individual magnifying power which depends on the state of accommodation of the eye (p. 454), is given by the simple formula:

$$M = l.F, \qquad (Z' = 0);$$

that is, the absolute magnifying power is directly proportional to the refracting power of the microscope. Hereafter when the term magnifying power is used without qualification, it should be understood to mean the absolute magnifying power as thus defined.

If m denotes the lateral magnification (§ 124) or ratio of the size of the image to that of the object ($m = y' : y$), then

$$m = \frac{x'}{f'} = -\frac{x'}{f},$$

where $x' = F'M'$ denotes the distance of the image from the posterior focal plane or second focal point (F') of the lens and f, f' denote the focal lengths of the lens ($f + f' = 0$). Since $x' = z' + s'$, where $s' = F'O'$ denotes the distance of the eye from the second focal point of the lens, the formula above may be written:

$$m = -\frac{z' + s'}{f} = -\frac{z'}{f}, \text{ approximately,}$$

since s', being usually very small, may generally be neglected in comparison with z'. In the special case when the distance of the eye from the image is equal to the distance denoted by l, that is, for the condition $z' = -l$, the magnification-ratio may be denoted by $\bar{m}$, and accordingly

$$\bar{m} = \frac{l}{f} = l.F = M.$$

In other words, the magnifying power of the glass is equal to the magnification-ratio when the distance of the eye from the image is equal to the conventional distance denoted by l; the usual value of which is $l = 250$ mm.

The diameter ($2h$) of an ordinary magnifying glass of low power usually exceeds the diameter ($2p'$) of the pupil of the eye; and in this case $(p' < h)$ the pupil of the eye is the aperture-stop of the system, and the lens itself acts as field-stop, and therefore the observer views the image just as if he were looking at it through a round hole whose contour was the same as that of the rim of the lens (Figs. 288, 289 and 291). On the assumption that the object is uniformly illuminated, only the central portion of the image will appear uniformly bright, and the brightness gradually fades from

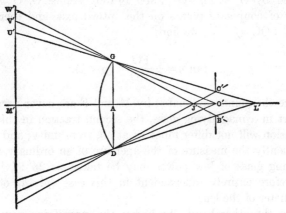

Fig. 291.—Field of view of magnifying glass. Diameter of pupil $= 2p'$; diameter of glass $= 2h$. Case when $p' > h$.

U' to W' (Fig. 291) in case the image extends that far from the axis. If $\gamma = \angle AO'G$ is the semiangular diameter of the central part of the field of view of the image-space corresponding to the region of maximum brightness, and, similarly, if $\gamma_1 = \angle AL'G$, $\gamma_2 = \angle AJ'G$ are the semiangular diameters of the regions corresponding to the points in the image-plane marked V' and W', respectively, evidently

$$\tan \gamma_1 = -\frac{h-p'}{e}, \quad \tan \gamma = -\frac{h}{e}, \quad \tan \gamma_2 = -\frac{h+p'}{e}, \quad (p' < h),$$

where $p' = O'C'$, $h = AG$ and $e = AO'$. The smaller the pupil of the eye, the less the distinction between these three regions; and if the eye could be considered as a mere point ($p'=0$), there would be no difference between them at all, and the points U′ and W′ would coincide with each other at the intermediate point V′.

The aperture of the cone of effective rays proceeding from the axial object-point M is measured by the angle (2η) subtended at M by the diameter BC of the entrance-pupil; and hence if the center of the entrance-pupil is designated by O, $\tan \eta = \text{OC} : \text{MO}$ (§ 136). Since O, O′ are a pair of conjugate points on the optical axis, and therefore $\text{O}'\text{C}' : \text{OC} = f : \text{FO}$, we find:

$$\tan \eta = \frac{p'}{f} \cdot \frac{\text{FO}}{\text{MO}}, \quad (p' < h).$$

Since the points designated by M and F are never very far apart in a magnifying glass, the second fraction in this expression will not differ much, if at all, from unity; and consequently the measure of the aperture of an ordinary magnifying glass of low power may be taken as $2p' : f$, being therefore entirely independent in this case ($p' < h$) of the diameter of the lens.

On the other hand, the higher the magnifying power of the glass, that is, the shorter its focus, the smaller will be its diameter; and so with a high power glass for which the diameter of the pupil exceeds that of the glass ($p' > h$), the case is just the reverse of that described above, that is, the glass acts as the aperture-stop and the pupil of the eye as the field-stop (Figs. 290 and 292). Using the same notation as before, we find now:

$$\tan \gamma_1 = \frac{p'-h}{e}, \quad \tan \gamma = \frac{p'}{e}, \quad \tan \gamma_2 = \frac{p'+h}{e}, \quad (p' > h)$$

where $\gamma_1 = \angle \text{O}'\text{L}'\text{C}'$, $\gamma = \angle \text{O}'\text{AC}'$ and $\gamma_2 = \angle \text{O}'\text{J}'\text{C}'$ (Fig. 292). For a lens of very small diameter there is hardly any difference between these three regions of the field of view.

The aperture in this case is the angle (2η) subtended at M by the diameter of the lens, that is, $\eta = \angle \, \text{AMG}$, and on the

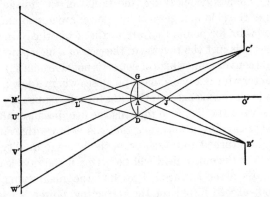

FIG. 292.—Field of view of magnifying glass. Diameter of pupil $= 2p'$; diameter of glass $= 2h$. Case when $p' > h$.

supposition that M lies nearly, if not exactly, in the anterior focal plane (as must be the case), we find that

$$\tan \eta = \frac{h}{f}, \quad (p' > h);$$

that is, the aperture here is entirely independent of the width of the pupil of the eye.

The above formulæ may be easily modified for the case when the magnifying glass has a special field-stop. The mobility of the eye in its socket (p. 452) can increase considerably the extent of the field of view of a simple microscope of low power; and when this important factor is taken into account the chief rays of the bundles entering the eye will be those rays that are directed, not to the center O' of the pupil, but to the point which with respect to the glass is conjugate to the center of rotation of the eye. On the supposition that the air-interval between glass and eye as measured along the axis is, say, one centimeter in length, the eye-pivot (Z) will be about 25 mm. from the vertex of the last surface of the glass.

209. Useful Forms of Magnifying Glass.—The require-ments for a good magnifying glass depend essentially on its power. Generally speaking, the faults of the image in the center of the field in a glass of low power are not so important as the faults for points that are farther from the optical axis; whereas it is just the reverse in the case of a high power glass. A single convex lens (which of course is not achromatic) is quite satisfactory for many ordinary purposes where a low magnifi-cation is all that is needed; the best form being usually plano-convex with the flat face towards the eye, because, although the spherical aberration along the axis is more than it is for such a lens turned the other way, the average quality of the image over the entire field will be better if the rays leave the lens at its plane surface. Provided the magnifying power does not exceed 8-fold (or the refracting power is less than 32 dptr.), a plano-convex lens used in this fashion will give a fairly good image over a field of about 12° in angular diameter; but for a larger field both the astigmatism and the distortion would prove objectionable. A magnifying glass consisting of a single lens may be "bent" (exactly as in the case of a modern meniscus spectacle lens which is free from astigmatism over a comparatively wide field) into a form that will practically abolish astigmatism, provided the center of rotation of the eye (Z) is placed at the point on the axis beyond the lens for which the curvatures of the two surfaces have been computed. This particular problem was investigated by CODDINGTON more than a century ago (1829).

A glass for reading conveniently the small divisions of a vernier scale is placed usually so close to the scale that the slightly magnified image is not far enough from the eye to be seen distinctly unless the eye is at quite a little distance from the glass; and for this particular purpose the best form of the lens will be either double convex or plano-convex with the flat surface next the scale.

With higher powers the optical and mechanical difficulties

in the way of making a magnifying glass consisting of a single lens are soon found to be almost insurmountable, although up to about a hundred years ago much ingenuity was expended in this direction. Not only are such lenses necessarily very minute in size, and the field of view very narrow, but the faults of the image even on the axis are apt to be exceedingly confusing and annoying.

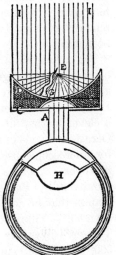

In his *Dioptrice et meteora* DESCARTES describes a form of magnifying glass which was very popular in his day. It consisted of a single lens and was called a "flea glass" ("perspicilia pulicaria ex uno vitro," Fig. 293). The small plano-convex lens (A) with its plane face towards the observer's eye (H) was mounted in a little case. The other side of the case turned towards the light formed a concave mirror which was intended to converge the light to its focus at E and thus to illuminate the microscopic object that was fastened on the point of the needle or peg G. Although this little piece of apparatus was not much more than an optical toy, many interesting observations of insects and tiny structures were made with it. The celebrated Father SCHEINER had one of these "flea glasses" which he carried about with him to use as a mag-

FIG. 293.—Early form of magnifying glass, so-called "flea glass" as described by DES-CARTES in his *Dis-cours de la méthode*, section entitled *La dioptrique*. (Diagram is reproduced from picture on page 126 of edition published in Leyden in 1637.)

nifying glass; and when he died in a little village where he had rested on a journey, the peasants believed he was a sor-cerer because the image of the flea in his "flea glass" ap-peared to them to be a devil or evil genius of some kind.

Nearly three centuries ago ANTON VAN LEEUWENHOEK (1632–1723), a man of extraordinary scientific ability and

practical ingenuity, by far the greatest amateur micro-
scopist of his day, succeeded in grinding and polishing glass
lenses of such short focus that the microscopic discoveries he
made with them seem now almost incredible. By the fine
observations he made as well as by the praise of his contemporaries we know that the lenses and mechanical appliances of VAN LEEUWENHOEK'S microscopes must have
been excellent.

For a long time the solid sphere was the favorite form
of high power magnifying glass; but as it is very hard to
grind a glass sphere of exceedingly small diameter, ROBERT
HOOKE, whose ingenuity was never at a loss, devised (1665)
a clever method of obtaining tiny globules of molten glass.
Occasionally one of these molten drops proves to be excellent
for microscopic use, and HOOKE'S method was soon much
in vogue. About a hundred years later the process was so
improved by Father GIOVANNI MARIA DELLA TORRE of
Naples that he succeeded in obtaining globules of glass less
than half a millimeter in diameter in some instances (p. 396).
Theoretically, their magnifying power was between 400 and
500, but, aside from the faults of the image, it is hard to
comprehend how anything can be seen distinctly through
such a tiny bit of glass. Drops of liquid (water) were likewise
used for magnifying purposes. Sir DAVID BREWSTER (1781–
1868), pointing out the high index of refraction of certain
precious stones, recommended the manufacture of small
lenses of garnet or diamond; but the high cost of these gems
and the difficulty of grinding and polishing them were sufficient reasons against using such material.

However, the notion of a lens in the form of a glass sphere
was based on a sound principle, for on the assumption that
the diameter of the sphere is less than that of the pupil of
the eye, entrance-pupil and exit-pupil both lie in the central
transversal plane, and consequently all faults for points of
the image that are not on the axis (astigmatism, distortion,
chromatic difference of magnification, etc.) will be auto-

matically corrected. Moreover, for reducing the spherical aberration along the axis a solid sphere has much in its favor as compared with other forms. On the other hand, with a solid sphere the so-called "working distance" or interval between the object and the glass is very slight and inconvenient, never exceeding a quarter of the diameter of the sphere for $n = 1.5$, and being still less for a higher value of the index of refraction. Early in the eighteenth century simple microscopes, which had magnifying powers as high as 400 and which in some instances were provided with special illumination devices, were made with a single small glass sphere and used to advantage.

Dr. WOLLASTON (1766–1828), who was quick to perceive the advantages of a glass sphere above mentioned, conceived the simple and ingenious idea of dividing it into two hemispheres separated by a plate of metal with a circular hole in it, whereby the angular diameter of the field was increased to about 20°. Commenting on this construction, BREWSTER suggested that it could be improved "by filling up the central aperture with a cement of the same refractive power of the lenses, or what is far better, by taking a sphere of glass and grinding away the equatorial parts," that is, by cutting a deep groove in the sphere so as to limit the central aperture. CODDINGTON proposed what was practically the same idea perhaps a little earlier than BREWSTER, namely, a lens in the form of a narrow glass cylinder the curved ends of which were the two opposite portions of one and the same spherical surface. The so-called STANHOPE lens was outwardly similar to CODDINGTON's construction, except that the curvature of the surface next the object was less than that of the surface next the eye; the result of this difference of curvature being that the working distance was so small that the glass was practically in actual contact with the object.

210. Practical Types of Simple Microscope.—For convenience of description the term "simple microscope" may be used to apply to those forms of magnifying glass that are composed of more than one single lens; although ordinarily this distinction is not observed. In some respects a simple microscope consisting of two or more lenses has decided advantages, first, because for a given power the curvatures of the surfaces do not have to be so great as in a single lens, and this circumstance alone tends to reduce the spherical aberration along the axis; second, because the astigmatism for points off the axis can be largely compensated by a suitable choice of the curvatures of the several surfaces; and, lastly, because by regulating the interval between the lenses and also by using different varieties of optical glass an achromatic combination is possible.

Like HUYGENS's ocular (p. 502), WOLLASTON's doublet (1821) is a combination of two separated plano-convex lenses whose plane faces are both turned towards the object. The focal lengths of the lenses are in the ratio of 1 : 3, the stronger lens being the one nearer the object. Both the WILSON doublet and the FRAUNHOFER doublet were likewise composed of two separated plano-convex lenses, but with their curved faces towards each other. In the WILSON type, which resembles RAMSDEN's ocular (p. 502), the interval between the lenses is greater than it is in FRAUNHOFER's construction, but the working distance is not so great in the former as in the latter. Various other special forms of simple microscope were made by ZEISS, STEINHEIL and other opticians not only in Germany but especially in England. Until about the middle of the last century nearly all microscopic research and investigation were carried on by means of simple microscopes which in some instances had a power of 200.

FIG. 294.—STEINHEIL's aplanatic magnifying glass.

STEINHEIL's aplanatic magnifying glass (Fig. 294) consists of a middle symmetric double convex crown glass lens cemented between two equal flint glass lenses, the data for which (as given in

A. GLEICHEN's *Lehrbuch der geometrischen Optik*, Leipzig & Berlin, 1902, S. 365) are as follows:

$$n_1 = n_5 = 1; \quad n_2 = n_4 = 1.61440; \quad n_3 = 1.51856$$
(these values being for the FRAUNHOFER D-line);
$$radii: \quad r_1 = -r_4 = 0.762; \quad r_2 = -r_3 = 0.339;$$
$$thicknesses: \quad d_1 = d_3 = 0.056; \quad d_2 = 0.185;$$
focal length equal to unity.

For $M = 10$ the working distance of this glass is 21 mm., and the diameter of the object may be as much as 15 mm.

A peculiar type of simple microscope, invented first by CH. CHEVALIER (1839) and afterwards in a modified form by BRÜCKE, consists essentially of an anterior convergent system with a divergent system next the eye (Fig. 295).

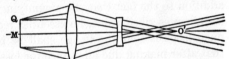

FIG. 295.—CHEVALIER-BRÜCKE type of simple microscope (compound system).

Before the inverted image is formed by the convergent system, the rays are intercepted by the divergent lens; and the final image, much magnified by the latter lens, is formed at a convenient distance for observation. As compared with an ordinary magnifying glass of the same power, the working distance is much increased. Thus for moderate powers, between, say, $M = 6$ and $M = 10$, this interval may amount to between 7 and 3 cm. The CHEVALIER-BRÜCKE microscope really is a small compound microscope with a negative ocular, a sort of "Dutch" microscope as it might be called by analogy with the Dutch telescope (p. 456).

No matter how admirable and ingenious a simple microscope may be, its range and efficiency are necessarily much restricted, if for no other reason merely by the fact that it is essentially a single compact optical system with little or no flexibility, and this is especially true of the higher magnifying powers. A limit is soon reached in this direction on account of the impracticably small dimensions of the lenses. Another obvious disadvantage is the steady diminution of the working distance of the magnifying glass with increase of power. This unavoidable proximity of the object is not only very inconvenient, but may sometimes damage the glass and perhaps be dangerous also to the observer's eye, because the illuminated object under a microscope is not always harmless. A simple microscope also has other very definite optical limitations, as will be explained in the following section.

II. *The Compound Microscope*

211. General Characteristics of the Instrument.—In addition to the fact that the magnifying power must have a certain prescribed value, an essential requirement of a good microscope is that the image shall be bright; which means that after making due allowance for losses of light by reflection and absorption a sufficient amount of radiation must be transmitted from the object at one end of the instrument to the eye at the other end. In order to insure that there shall be no lack of light to start with, the object itself is often highly illuminated by an auxiliary illumination-system specially made for this purpose; but even so, to be really efficient, the microscope should have a large aperture so as to admit freely wide-angle bundles of rays coming from all parts of the object. On the other hand, tiny as the microscopic object usually is, its dimensions are not inconsiderable as compared with the short focus of a microscope of high power, and therefore, instead of the field of view being narrow and contracted as it might be natural to suppose, it is really comparatively quite extensive. Now a simple microscope cannot be made to satisfy both of these requirements, wide aperture and broad field, at the same time. In fact, in accordance with the fundamental laws of optical imagery, there is no way of accomplishing this double result except

Fig. 296.—Early compound microscope, reproduced from frontispiece of 1926 Oxford edition of Robert Hooke's *Micrographia* (by kind permission of Dr. R. T. Gunther, editor, "Old Ashmolean Reprints," No. VI).

by resorting to a compound optical system composed of at least two separate and distinct members each of which has a special dioptric duty to perform. The great superiority of the so-called compound microscope over even the best simple microscope of equal magnifying power is due mainly to this "team work" or efficient coöperation and division of duty between its component parts, namely, the *objective* or anterior group of lenses at the end of the tube next the object and the *ocular* consisting of a series of lenses at the other end of the tube next the eye. Besides the other advantages an incidental convenience of this arrangement is that the same objective can be combined with a different ocular to obtain an entirely different magnifying power, as is sometimes much to be desired. Moreover, to a limited extent the magnifying power can be altered by merely altering the interval between the objective and the ocular, although in high power instruments this interval is generally fixed. Not only is the compound microscope more flexible or adaptable than a simple microscope, but since the optician has so many more factors at his disposal, the quality of the image obtained with a compound microscope can be enormously improved with respect to the correction of chromatic and monochromatic aberrations for both the central and the peripheral parts of the field of view. In fact the extraordinary development and improvement of the compound microscope mainly during the last century,* which is due especially to the efforts of Fraunhofer (1787–1826), Amici (1786–1864),

---

* Like the telescope, the compound microscope was invented by spectacle-makers during the early part of the seventeenth century, but it made very little progress at first. According to the data of J. Chr. Sturm (1676) a compound microscope which he used had a double convex lens of focal length 23.7 mm. for objective and an ocular of two plano-convex lenses with a focal length of 47.4 mm.; the optical tube-length was $\Delta = 216$ mm., so that the magnifying power was $M = 48$ (A. König, *Geometrische Optik*, Leipzig, 1929, p. 390). Fig. 296 is an illustration of a compound microscope used by Robert Hooke, probably made about 1667.

J. J. LISTER (1786–1869) and ABBE (1840–1905), is certainly
one of the most successful and remarkable achievements of
applied optics. Its characteristic feature as compared with
other optical instruments is its unusually large aperture.
Thus for instance the relative aperture $(2h : f)$ of the objective of an astronomical telescope, as measured by the
ratio between its diameter and its focal length, seldom ever
exceeds about 1–15th; the objective of a small Dutch telescope may have a relative aperture equal to 1–3rd; and
some modern photographic objectives often have very large
relative apertures, perhaps never as much as one-half. On
the other hand, the diameter of the effective aperture of the
objective of a compound microscope of high power often
exceeds its focal length, that is, $2p : f$ is greater than unity;
the angular diameter (2η) of the aperture being about 180°
in some remarkable instances.

The working distance between the object and the objective
depends on the type of construction of the latter as well as
on its focal length. With a low power objective the working
distance may be a little in excess of the focal length, but as
a rule when the objective has a high power, the working
distance is a smaller and smaller fraction of the focal length
as the latter is more and more reduced, and for the strongest
objectives it is hardly ever more than 0.1 mm.

The tube of the microscope containing the objective and
the ocular is ordinarily mounted on a firm iron stand and
pointed vertically downwards at the object, which is supported on a little horizontal bracket or platform just below
the objective. The preliminary preparation of the microscopic object or specimen for examination under the microscope is often a matter of much importance in the art of
microscopy, requiring both patience and skill. For instance,
it may be a section of a bit of animal tissue so thin that it is
translucent and can therefore be illuminated from below
by transmitted light, as is often the case. The texture or
structure of the object under the microscope is apt to be so

fine and delicate that diffraction-patterns are produced in the image; and these diffraction-effects, as we shall see (§ 216), are of fundamental importance in determining the resolving power of the microscope as distinguished from its magnifying power. In order to protect the fragile specimen as much as possible, it is inserted ordinarily between two thin strips of glass, the lower one with the tiny object on it being called the "slide." The upper strip or "cover glass" may not be more than 0.2 mm. thick, but thin as it is, the optical effect of this little interposed plate of glass must be taken in account in the painstaking computation of a high power microscope objective. Sometimes the object is immersed in a layer of water or glycerine, and sometimes it is embedded or "frozen" in a hard transparent substance such as Canada balsam. ABBE regarded the object under the microscope as being resolved by the instrument into "optical cross-sections," only one of which could be exactly in focus at a time; because the depth of focus of a compound microscope in the object-space is so very slight that those parts of the object that do not lie exactly in the focus-plane (p. 400) will be so blurred and out of focus in the image-space that they cannot be perceived at all.

The objective of a compound microscope is a convergent optical system of comparatively short focus whose duty it is to project a sharply defined and faithful image of the object by means of wide-angle bundles of rays. Incidentally, this is not an easy task to perform, and it means that the objective must be very carefully designed for this purpose. In the weaker types the objective may be a simple achromatic combination, but a high power microscope objective is a complicated system composed of a number of lenses. In consequence of the small dimensions of the object, the slopes of the chief rays that go through the center of the aperture-stop (§ 139) are comparatively slight before entering the objective. The image-rays issue from the objective in bundles of much narrower aperture and form a real inverted image at a relatively great distance from the objective. The rays may be intercepted by the first lens of the ocular system before this intermediate image is actually formed; but whether this is the case or not, this image serves as the object with respect to the ocular which acts like a magnifying glass and forms a bright virtual image, much magnified and far enough away to be convenient for observation. The exit-pupil of the microscope, which can generally be seen as a small round disk floating in the air just above the ocular, is the common base of the very narrow cones of image-rays that issue from the ocular as if they had actually come from the distant points of the virtual image. The observer should place his eye at the exit-pupil of the microscope and focus the instrument to suit his vision, which is accomplished by shifting the entire tube up or down until the interval between the object and the objective is exactly right for clear and convenient vision. The instrument is provided with a special fine-screw adjustment for this purpose. If the observer's eye is emmetropic, he probably will not wish to exert his power of accommodation, and in that case the instrument will be focused so that the image is infinitely far away and the object lies therefore in the anterior focal plane of the microscope. Under such circumstances the narrow bundles of rays entering the eye will be cylindrical; and the real image formed by the objective which serves as object for the ocular will lie in the anterior focal plane of the ocular.

In the ordinary form of compound microscope, such as that above described, the ocular is convergent, and in all that follows we shall assume that this is the case.* One advantage of a convergent or positive ocular is that the intermediate real image is formed in the tube of the instrument where it is accessible and where, for example, a scale

---

* However, in some special types the ocular of a compound microscope is negative. As was noted above, the peculiar CHEVALIER-BRÜCKE type of simple microscope may be considered as a compound microscope with a negative ocular.

can be inserted for measurements. The ocular in this case, as we have said, acts just like a simple magnifying glass, and the field of the ocular usually has an angular diameter of from 30° to 40°.

The astronomical telescope (p. 456) is likewise a combination of an objective with a positive ocular, which however differs essentially from the compound microscope with respect to the interval $\Delta = F_1'F_2$ between the posterior focal point (F_1) of the objective and the anterior focal point (F_2) of the ocular; for when a telescope is in normal adjustment, these two focal points are coincident $(\Delta = 0)$, whereas in the compound microscope the interval Δ, called the "optical tube-length," is usually between 6 and 10 inches. The objective is screwed to the tube at its lower end, and the actual tube-length as measured from the shoulder of this screw to the draw-tube for the ocular at the upper end is somewhat longer than Δ. Ordinarily it is 16 cm. or over 6 inches, although English microscopes are longer and have a tube-length of about 10 inches.

212. The Ray-Procedure in the Compound Microscope.— A general idea of the *modus operandi* and procedure of the rays in a compound microscope can be derived from Fig. 297 in which objective and ocular are each represented as consisting of a combination of two thin lenses. Inside the objective between the optical centers A_1 and A_2 of the two lenses, a stop is inserted with its center on the axis at the point designated by K, which acts as the aperture-stop (p. 399). The diameter DKE of this stop is the image of COB in the first lens of the objective, and therefore COB is the diameter of the entrance-pupil (p. 400) of the microscope. Similarly, if $D'K'E'$ is the image of DKE in the second lens of the objective, it will be the image of COB in the combination of the two lenses; that is, $D'K'E'$ is the diameter of the exit-pupil of the objective. Finally, the image of $D'K'E'$ formed by the ocular, which will be the image of COB formed by the entire microscope, will be the corresponding diameter

C'O'B' of the exit-pupil of the microscope. With a positive ocular this will be a real inverted image whose center O' lies on the axis a short distance beyond the optical center (A_4) of the eye-lens.

In the diagram a single cone of rays is shown which emanates from a point Q at a little distance from the axis ($y = MQ$) and very close to the front lens of the objective (MA_1 working distance). The slope of the chief ray QO is measured by the angle $\omega = \angle MOQ$, which is a comparatively small angle; whereas the aperture-angle ($\angle CQB$) is under the circumstances a very large angle. This wide-angle cone of rays is transformed by the objective into a much narrower bundle converging to a distant point R on the other side of the axis; but before the rays actually meet in this image-point, they are intercepted by the first lens of the ocular, the so-called "field-lens" whose optical center is the point on the axis designated by A_3, and diverted to a nearer point R' lying closer to the axis, where a real image is formed inside the ocular between the field-lens and the eye-lens. In fact, as shown in the diagram, the point R' lies in the anterior focal plane of the eye-lens, and consequently the bundle of rays diverging from R' finally issues from the eye-lens as a narrow cylindrical bundle of rays coming from the infinitely distant image-point Q' and passing through the exit-pupil B'O'C' into the eye of the observer looking at this image through the microscope; the apparent size of the image being measured by the angle $\omega' = \angle M'O'Q'$, which is the angle made with the axis by the chief ray passing through O'.

In the diagram it is assumed, of course, that the imagery is ideal and that there is perfect collineation or point-to-point correspondence between object-space and image-space such as cannot be realized by any actual optical instrument. It is merely accidental that the entrance-pupil in Fig. 297 lies a short distance beyond the objective, because it was convenient to make the drawing that way. The size and position of the aperture-stop which controls the pupils are

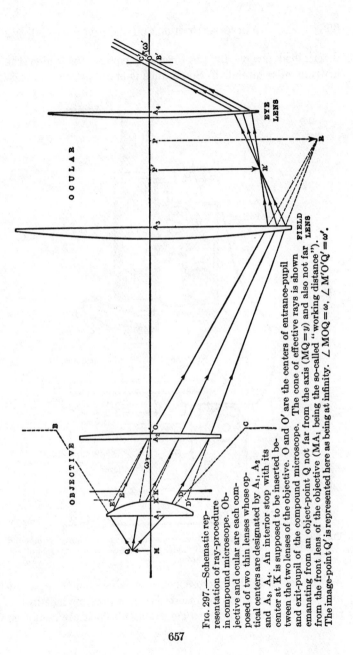

Fig. 297.—Schematic representation of ray-procedure in compound microscope. Objective and ocular are each composed of two thin lenses whose optical centers are designated by A_1, A_2 and A_3, A_4. An interior stop with its center at K is supposed to be inserted between the two lenses of the objective. O and O' are the centers of entrance-pupil and exit-pupil of the compound microscope. The cone of effective rays is shown emanating from an object-point Q not far from the axis ($MQ = y$) and also not far from the front lens of the objective (MA_1 being the so-called "working distance"). The image-point Q' is represented here as being at infinity. $\angle MOQ = \omega$, $\angle M'O'Q' = \omega'$.

657

determined always by the special purposes for which the instrument is intended. Sometimes it is important to meas-

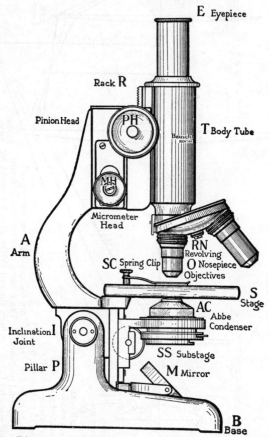

FIG. 298.—Diagram of mechanical construction of ordinary compound microscope, Bausch & Lomb model (reproduced from catalogue of the Bausch & Lomb Optical Company).

ure the image in the microscope, in which case a transparent micrometer-scale may be inserted at the proper place in the tube; and then in order to get a reliable measurement free

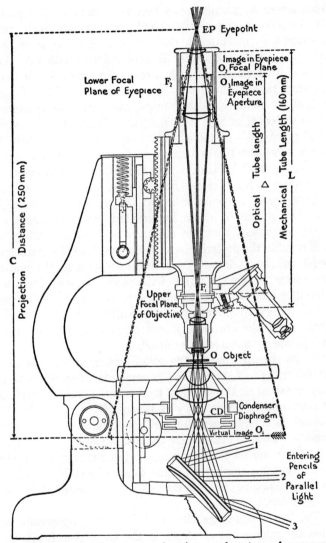

FIG. 299.—Chart showing ray-procedure in a modern type of compound microscope (reproduced from catalogue of Bausch & Lomb Optical Company).

from errors of parallax, the objective must be *telecentric* on the side of the object (§ 144), and consequently the aperture-stop must be in the posterior focal plane of the objective, that is, its center K must coincide with F_1'. An incidental advantage of such a telecentric objective is that the chief rays coming from the various points of the object will all be parallel to the optical axis, and the apertures of all the cones of rays will be equal. Usually the posterior focal point (F_1') of the objective of a microscope of high power falls inside this system not far from one of the posterior lenses, so that the rim of this lens automatically acts as aperture-stop for a telecentric objective, and it is not necessary to insert a special stop for the purpose. Generally therefore it can be taken for granted, without danger of being far wrong, that the objective is telecentric with its exit-pupil in the posterior focal plane; and then the entrance-pupil will be at infinity, and the exit-pupil of the entire microscope, where the pupil of the observer's eye should be placed, will lie in the posterior focal plane, that is, the center O' of the exit-pupil will coincide with the focal point F'. Even when the objective is not exactly telecentric, these two points are never very far apart.

While the aperture of the compound microscope is controlled by the objective, and is sometimes dependent to a certain extent on the source of light and the auxiliary system of illumination, the field of view is generally regulated by the ocular. It is customary to insert a stop in the ocular (or in front of it) at the place where the real image $P'R'$ (Fig. 297) is formed; and then the entrance-port of the microscope will lie in the same transversal plane as the object MQ, that is, in the focus-plane; whereas the exit-port will be in the distant image-plane.

The two charts (Figs. 298 and 299), copied by permission from the microscope catalogue of the BAUSCH & LOMB Optical Company, show the mechanical construction of a modern laboratory microscope, and the procedure of the light through it in the formation of the virtual inverted image. The latter is here represented as being at the conventional distance $l = 250$ mm. (instead of at an infinite distance, as in the schematic diagram Fig. 297); and consequently for this particular focusing of the instrument the observer's eye must be accommodated for this distance in order to see the image distinctly.

213. Metric Relations in the Compound Microscope.— The formulæ for a combination of two optical systems as given in § 125 are applicable immediately to the compound microscope composed of a convergent objective and a convergent ocular. The ocular is always surrounded by air on both sides, but the first medium of the objective (whose index of refraction will be denoted by n) is sometimes different from air (in the so-called "immersion systems" as distinguished from the "dry systems" for which n = 1); and hence if f_1, f_1', f_2, f_2' and f, f' denote the focal lengths of objective, ocular and compound microscope, respectively, then by § 122 these magnitudes have the following relations:

$$f_1 + n'.f_1' = f_2 + f_2' = f + n.f' = 0.$$

If therefore the positions of the various focal points are designated similarly by F_1, F_1', F_2, F_2' and F, F', and if, as above, the optical tube-length is denoted by $\Delta = F_1'F_2$, the general formulæ for a compound microscope may be written:

$$n.F_1F = -\frac{f_1^2}{\Delta}, \quad F_2F' = \frac{f_2^2}{\Delta}, \quad f = -n.f' = -\frac{f_1.f_2}{\Delta}.$$

For a dry system (n = 1) in which the objective is surrounded by air on both sides, we have:

$$F_1F = -\frac{f_1^2}{\Delta}, \quad F_2F' = \frac{f_2^2}{\Delta}, \quad f = -f' = -\frac{f_1.f_2}{\Delta}.$$

If we bear in mind that the focal length (f_1) of the objective is comparatively small while the interval Δ is essentially positive in sign and very large, the first of these formulæ shows that the two focal points F_1 and F are always close together, although F is a little farther from the objective than F_1, which is never very far from the front lens. In Fig. 297 the axial object-point M coincides with F, and it is never more than a short distance from it, usually between F and F_1. The posterior focal point (F') of the microscope lies always a little distance beyond the posterior focal point (F_2') of the ocular, as shown by the second formula. The third formula shows that the focal length (f) of the microscope is never large, and always negative for a positive ocular.

On the assumption that the real image PR (Fig. 297) formed by the objective lies in the anterior focal plane of the ocular, and therefore that $F_1'P = F_1'F_2 = \Delta$, the lateral magnification of this image, that is, the ratio $m_1 = PR : MQ$, will be directly proportional to Δ, since

$$m_1 = \frac{\Delta}{f_1'};$$

and since in a high power microscope the objective must be calculated for a given value of Δ in order to obtain a satisfactory image, the value of m_1 will likewise be fixed and invariable.

If the magnifying power, as defined in § 158, is denoted by

$$M = -\frac{\tan \omega'}{y} \cdot l,$$

where (as above stated) $\omega' = \angle M'O'Q'$ denotes the visual angle subtended by the image at the center of the exit-pupil, the absolute magnifying power (as distinguished from the so-called individual magnifying power, p. 454), or the value of M for the case when the image is infinitely distant will be $M = -l/f'$. The fact that when f is negative, as it is in a compound microscope with a positive ocular, the value of M is negative also, has no significance except to indicate that the virtual image here is inverted. Ordinarily the negative sign is omitted, although it is important to keep it in mind when the numerical value of M has to be inserted in an algebraic formula for purposes of calculation. Obviously the absolute magnifying power of a compound microscope is given by the formula:

$$M = -\frac{l \cdot \Delta}{f_1 \cdot f_2};$$

which may also be expressed in terms of m_1 as follows:

$$M = \frac{m_1}{n} \cdot \frac{l}{f_2},$$

where for a dry system $n = 1$. Since m_1 is usually constant, as above stated, this latter formula shows how the magnifying power of the microscope will be changed simply by using an ocular of different focal length (f_2).

The diameter ($2y$) of the field of view as measured in the focus-plane diminishes as the magnifying power (M) increases, for

$$2y = -\frac{2l \cdot \tan \omega'}{M}.$$

An ordinary HUYGENS's ocular has an angular field of view of about 30°, that is, $\omega' = 15°$, say; consequently, putting $l = 250$ mm. and discarding the minus sign, we find that $2y = (134/M)$ mm., approximately. Of course, for a larger value of ω' the field will be correspondingly increased.

214. The Numerical Aperture.—The efficiency of an optical instrument is closely connected with the aperture-angle (2η) subtended by the entrance-pupil at the axial object-point M, because in a certain sense this angle is a measure of the quantity of radiation that is transmitted through the instrument from M to the conjugate point M' (neglecting losses of light by reflection and absorption). If $z = $ OM denotes the distance of the object from the center O of the entrance-pupil, and if $p = $ BO $=$ OC denotes the distance of the object from the center O of the entrance-pupil, then (§ 136)

$$p = -z.\tan \eta,$$

where $\eta = \angle \, OMC = \angle \, BMO$; and hence we see that the magnitude of the aperture-angle depends on the diameter of the entrance-pupil and on the interval between it and the object.

However, there are two principal reasons why the aperture-angle alone is not sufficient as a measure of the quantity of radiation that is transmitted through the instrument. In the first place, according to LAMBERT's (1728–1777) cosine-law of radiation, on the assumption that the luminous object is a small plane element (MQ) perpendicular to the optical axis, the intensity at a point Y in the plane of the entrance-pupil is less than the intensity (I) at the center, being equal to $I.\cos \theta$, where $\theta = \angle \, OMY$; in other words, the quantities of light delivered at the different points of the entrance-pupil are not all equal, but diminish with the increase of the distance from the axis. The other reason why the aperture-angle by itself is not a measure of the amount of radiation is because, other things being equal, the amount of radiation is proportional to the index of refraction (n) of the medium in which the luminous object is situated; as we shall now proceed to show.

There is a fundamental difference between the so-called GAUSSIAN imagery by means of narrow bundles of paraxial rays, for which the SMITH-HELMHOLTZ equation (§ 118) must be satisfied, namely,

$$n'.y'.\tan \, \theta' = n.y.\tan \, \theta,$$

and the imagery produced by wide-angle bundles of rays which must satisfy ABBE's sine-condition (§ 182), namely,

$$n'.y'.\sin \, \theta' = n.y.\sin \, \theta,$$

as was pointed out on p. 524. In both of these formulæ y, y' denote corresponding dimensions of object and image; θ, θ'

the slopes of a pair of conjugate rays crossing the axis at
M, M′, respectively; and n, n′ the indices of refraction of
the first and last media. A preliminary requirement or *sine
qua non* to the fulfilment of the sine-condition is that all
rays coming from the axial object-point M shall be re-united
at the conjugate image-point M′; in other words, with respect
to this pair of points—the so-called pair of aplanatic points—
the optical system must, first of all, be free from spherical
aberration along the axis (§§ 178, 179). Soon after ABBE
began to study the theory of the microscope with a view to
improving the optical design, he found that in order for any
optical instrument of wide aperture to produce a sharply
defined image even of a tiny object lying in a transversal
plane, the system must comply with the sine-condition or
condition of aplanatism as formulated above; and that consequently a good microscope, and above all the objective, is
subject to this fundamental law.

The aperture-angles $\eta = \angle\,\mathrm{OMC}$, $\eta' = \angle\,\mathrm{O'M'C'}$ subtended
at M, M′ by the semidiameters of the two pupils are the maxi-
mum values of the slope-angles denoted by θ, θ'; and if they
are substituted for θ, θ', and if at the same time the image
$(\mathrm{M'Q'} = y')$ is supposed to be formed in air, as is always the
case in a microscope $(\mathrm{n'} = 1)$, the formula for the sine-
condition becomes:

$$\sin \eta' = \frac{1}{\mathrm{m}} \cdot \mathrm{n.sin}\ \eta,$$

where $\mathrm{m} = y' : y$ denotes the (constant) value of the magnification-ratio for the pair of aplanatic points. Now while
the angle η is generally a large angle in a microscope, the
angle η' is always very small so that we may put $\sin \eta' = \eta'$;
and consequently

$$\eta' = \frac{\mathrm{n.sin}\ \eta}{\mathrm{m}}.$$

This formula shows that the quantity of radiation conveyed
in any meridian plane of the symmetrical instrument through

the exit-pupil to the image-point—or, rather let us say, into the observer's eye supposed to be placed at the exit-pupil—is proportional, not simply to the sine of the aperture-angle in the object-space, but to the product n.sin η, which ABBE called the *numerical aperture* (A). So far as the concentration of rays is concerned, two optical systems whose numerical apertures, according to the definition

$$A = n.\sin \eta,$$

have the same value for both systems will be equivalent to each other. On the supposition that the microscopic object is surrounded by air ($n = 1$, $A = \sin \eta$), the greatest possible value of the numerical aperture would be unity ($\eta = 90°$). On the other hand, if the object were immersed in a liquid medium, for example, in water ($n = 1.33$, $A = 1.33.\sin \eta$), and if the aperture-angle in this case were equal to the critical angle of the liquid (p. 80), that is, equal to 48° 35' in the case of water, the numerical aperture would also be equal to unity, although the aperture-angle itself would not be much more than half of what it was in the other case. The value of A cannot exceed that of n.

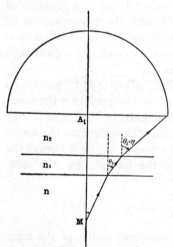

FIG. 300.—Numerical aperture of microscope objective. Diagram shows path of ray traversing several intervening media before entering objective.

The objective of a microscope is called a "dry system" when the medium between the object and the first lens is air. In a so-called "immersion system" the interval between the cover-glass and the objective is filled with a transparent liquid. In the accompanying diagram (Fig. 300), if M designates the position

of the object on the optical axis of the front hemispherical lens of a microscope objective, embedded perhaps in
some medium like Canada balsam of index n, and if θ denotes the slope of a ray proceeding from M in this medium, the subsequent path of the ray in traversing the
cover-glass (n_1) and the intervening medium (n_2) between
it and the first lens of the objective is shown by the broken
line, the successive portions of which are inclined to the
axis at the angles denoted by θ, θ_1 and θ_2 ($=\eta$); and since
the refracting surfaces are a series of parallel transversal
planes (§ 44), evidently the numerical aperture is

$$A = n.\sin\theta = n_1.\sin\theta_1 = n_2.\sin\theta_2.$$

If the index of refraction of any one of these media is equal
to unity, that is, if there is a layer of air between the object
and the objective, the objective is a dry system whose
numerical aperture cannot possibly exceed the value unity.
On the other hand, if there is no intervening medium whose
index of refraction does not exceed that of air, the objective
is an immersion system, and the numerical aperture may be
greater than unity. In the special case when $n = n_1 = n_2 = n_3$,
where n_3 denotes the index of refraction of the front lens,
the objective is a "homogeneous immersion system."—ABBE
designed a simple contrivance called an apertometer for
finding directly the numerical aperture of the objective.

215. Brightness of the Image.—If the distance of the
image from the exit-pupil of the microscope is denoted by
$z' = O'M'$ and the radius of the exit-pupil by $p' = B'O' = O'C'$,
then $p' = -z'.\tan\eta'$, or $p' = -z'.\eta'$, since we may put
$\tan\eta' = \eta'$. Consequently, if A denotes the numerical aperture and m the magnification-ratio, then

$$\eta' = -\frac{p'}{z'} = \frac{A}{m}.$$

Now $m = x' : f'$, where $x' = F'M'$ denotes the distance of the
image from the posterior focal plane of the optical instru-

ment, and since the latter is never far from the exit-pupil of a compound microscope, we are justified here in substituting z' in place of x'; and thus we find that

$$p' = A.f', \text{ approximately;}$$

in other words, for a given magnifying power $(M = -l/f')$, the diameter of the exit-pupil $(2p')$ is directly proportional to the numerical aperture of the microscope.

In ROBERT SMITH's *Compleat System of Opticks* published in Cambridge nearly two centuries ago (1738) the general law was enunciated that the apparent brightness of an object (or image) as seen by the eye depends essentially on the area of the pupil that is filled with light. Now on the assumption that the pupil of the observer's eye is placed in the exit-pupil of the microscope, only part of the pupil will be filled with light, because the diameter $(2p_0)$ of the latter cannot possibly be greater than $2p'$; and hence if B denotes the brightness of the image in the microscope, and B_0 denotes the brightness of the object as seen directly without the interposition of the instrument, then

$$\frac{B}{B_0} = \left(\frac{p'}{p_0}\right)^2,$$

or

$$B = \beta^2 . B_0,$$

where $\beta = p' : p_0$ is a proper fraction $(\beta \leqq 1)$ denoting the ratio between the diameters of the exit-pupil of the microscope and the pupil of the eye. Obviously, therefore, the brightness of the image in the microscope can never surpass the natural brightness of the object itself; which is a general law applicable to all optical instruments.

Since $p' = \beta . p_0 = A.f'$, as was found above, the absolute magnifying power of the microscope as defined in terms of the conventional distance (l) of distinct vision, may evidently be expressed in the following form:

$$M = -\frac{l.A}{\beta.p_0},$$

which shows how, other things being equal, the magnifying power is proportional to the reciprocal of the fraction denoted by β; in other words, magnifying power and brightness of image (as measured by β^2) vary inversely, so that in order to get brightness, we must sacrifice magnifying power, and *vice versa*. Suppose, for example, that the diameter of the pupil of the eye is $2p_0 = 4$ mm. (which may be taken as the average size of the pupil in ordinary daylight vision), and put $l = 250$ mm. as usual; and, finally, assume that the numerical aperture of the objective of the microscope is $A = 1.25$. Substituting these values in the above formula (and discarding the minus sign as being of no importance so far as the numerical calculation is concerned), we find under these circumstances that $M = 625 : 4\beta$. Accordingly, if the brightness of the image is to be equal to that of the object (on the assumption that none of the light is lost *en route* through the instrument), we must put $\beta^2 = 1$, which gives $M = 156.25$, as the highest power we can use; but if we are satisfied with a brightness that is one-fourth that of the object ($\beta^2 = \frac{1}{4}$), the magnifying power may be double as much as it was before, namely, $M = 312.5$. In order to increase the magnifying power, it is possible that we shall be content with a much less brightness of image, say, only one-sixteenth the brightness of the object ($\beta^2 = \frac{1}{16}$), and then $M = 625$.

216. Resolving Power of a Microscope.—It must be kept constantly in mind that the so-called rays of light (§ 5) have no real physical existence, being merely the directions in which the luminous radiation is propagated. Geometrical optics takes for granted the common notion of every-day experience that light travels in straight lines, without stopping to inquire how this happens and without raising any question as to the nature of light; it clings to a few fundamental facts as its basis and leaves all theories of light (corpuscular, undulatory, electromagnetic, quantum theories) severely alone. Thus it asserts that rectilinear rays proceed independently from a luminous point in all directions in a homogeneous, isotropic medium. But as a matter of fact, according to the wave-theory of light and HUYGENS's construction of the wave-front (§ 6), each point on a ray may be considered as a new source sending out rays in every direction; and consequently every point on the wave-front must contribute its quota to the luminous effect that is produced at any specified place lying in the path of the advancing wave. All the phenomena of interference and diffraction that are studied in such detail in physical optics are deliberately ignored in geometrical optics, and therefore the conclusions of the latter may sometimes be very misleading to a student who is not at the same time familiar with the other domains of the science of optics.

A traveller at night looking at an arc-light through the wire screen in the window of a Pullman railway-coach perceives a luminous rectangular cross which is due to diffraction of light through the tiny intervals in the wire-mesh. Similar phenomena, sometimes including striking color-effects, will invariably be noticed whenever the details (narrow slits, grating spaces, etc.) that are responsible for diffraction have dimensions of the same order of magnitude as the wave-lengths of light. Now the illuminated object that is examined under a microscope often has an exceedingly fine texture, so that all the conditions are present for the production of diffraction-spectra or colored patterns. Accordingly, ABBE's theory of the formation of the image in a microscope rests on a broader foundation than that of the rectilinear rays of geometrical optics and takes account of the fundamental conceptions of interference and diffraction. Without attempting to discuss these questions here, we must call attention to a formula which is of special importance because it affords a measure of the *resolving power* of a microscope in terms of the numerical aperture (A) and the wave-length (λ) of the light by which the object under the microscope is illuminated. Resolving power must not be confused with magnifying power, for it may be possible to see more through a microscope of moderate magnifying power than through one of higher magnifying power, simply because the resolving power of the former exceeds that of the latter. The resolving power of an optical instrument is measured by the smallest interval (d) between two details of an object that can be just detected as separate from each other in the image. In order that the diffraction-disks due to such a pair of closely adjacent structural elements in the object shall not overlap each other and be confounded together in the image, the interval between the elements may not be less than

$$d = \frac{\lambda}{2A}.$$

The general validity of this formula which is a simple consequence of the theory of diffraction will be assumed here without proof. If for convenience of calculation the maximum value of the numerical aperture of a microscope is taken as 1.5 (although in some oil-immersion systems the value of A may be a little in excess of this number), we may say that no microscope, no matter how powerful, can resolve details in an object that are closer together than about one-third of a wave-length of light; and consequently no microscope will ever reveal to the eye the ultimate particles of matter that are ever so much smaller than this limit. In ordinary daylight vision the brightest part of the spectrum is the yellow-green light corresponding to a wave-length of about 570 mμ; and if we put $\lambda = 0.00057$ mm. and A $= 1.5$, according to the above formula $d = 0.00019$ mm., which may therefore be regarded as about the smallest interval that can possibly be seen in a microscope by ordinary daylight illumination. Mere increase of magnifying power will not reveal any finer details simply because they are not there to be seen, the image itself is "empty."

If the angle subtended at the center of the exit-pupil by the image of the least perceptible interval d in the object is denoted by ϵ, the magnifying power of the microscope, as defined on p. 453, evidently is

$$M = \frac{\epsilon}{d} \cdot l,$$

the minus sign being omitted as being irrelevant for the purpose of the present discussion. After substituting for d its value in terms of A and λ, we obtain therefore

$$M = \frac{2A.l.\epsilon}{\lambda}$$

as the critical value of M for the given resolving power. The minimum value of the angle ϵ to be used in this formula depends on the keenness of vision of the observer whose eye is supposed to be placed at the exit-pupil of the microscope. The conventional value for an eye with so-called normal visual acuity that is generally adopted is $\epsilon = 1'$ (p. 21), but as this value is much too small for the tiniest details that can be readily detected in the image in the microscope by the average individual, it is better to err on the safe side and give ϵ a value from two to four times as large as the conventional value. Accordingly, let us put $\epsilon = 2'$, that is, $\epsilon = 0.00058178$ radian, $l = 250$ mm., and $\lambda = 0.00057$ mm. (yellow-green light); in which case a perfectly simple and definite numerical relation must exist between the magnifying power of the microscope and its numerical aperture for a given resolving power, namely, $M = 510.A$, approximately. If for a given numerical aperture the magnifying power is below the value of M as obtained by this formula, the microscope will not reveal the finest details of the object that can possibly be seen; and on the other hand, if the magnifying power exceeds this value of M, nothing is gained by it. Thus on the assumption that the extreme maximum value of the numerical aperture of a microscope is $A = 1.6$, the limit of resolution (for $\epsilon = 2'$) will be reached when the magnifying power is around 800.

Beyond that limit it is useless to try to increase the magnifying power unless we resort to light of shorter wave-length; as is actually done in microphotography in which ultraviolet light is used of wave-length less than $\lambda = 0.0003$ mm. Although these waves are too short to affect the eye, they act more powerfully on the sensitive surface of a photographic plate than the longer waves corresponding to the visible region of the spectrum; the chief difficulty about using them being that ultraviolet light is strongly absorbed by nearly all kinds of optical glass. This difficulty can be overcome by making the lenses of the microscope out of quartz, especially as the objective is designed in this case for monochromatic light and does not have to be achromatic. With a glycerine immersion-system of numerical aperture 1.3, the resolving power as measured by the least perceptible interval is found to be $d = 0.000106$ mm. for $\lambda = 0.000275$ mm.

Before leaving the subject of the resolving power, it may be recalled that the brightness of the image in a microscope is dependent on the size of the exit-pupil, whose diameter is

$$2p' = 2\mathrm{A}.f' = \frac{2\mathrm{A}.l}{\mathrm{M}}$$

(neglecting the minus sign as usual). Thus for a given numerical aperture, the brightness of the image diminishes as the magnifying power is increased; which is an additional reason for not using a higher magnifying power than is actually needed. When the magnifying power has the proper value corresponding to the numerical aperture, the diameter of the exit-pupil will be

$$2p' = \frac{\lambda}{\epsilon};$$

that is, it depends simply on the wave-length of the light and the value of the angle ϵ. Thus for $\lambda = 0.00057$ mm. and $\epsilon = 2'$, the diameter of the exit-pupil turns out to be very little less than one millimeter.

217. Optical Requirements of the Objective of a Microscope.—The real (intermediate) image formed by the objective of a high power microscope of large aperture should be as nearly faultless as it is possible for human ingenuity to contrive, not simply because it is primarily intended to be an accurate and faithful picture of the object, but because any blemishes in it are likely to be accentuated by the magnification of the ocular. The construction of a microscope-objective that fulfils this severe requirement with a reasonable degree of perfection is a task of much difficulty and demands the highest skill both on the part of the engineer who conceives and designs the complicated optical system and on the part of the optician who executes it. Let us try to obtain a clear idea of the optical problem in its various aspects.

For simplicity, we shall begin by supposing that the light used in forming the image made by the objective is strictly monochromatic light corresponding to a definite wave-length, for example, yellow sodium light. Then the first requirement is that, with respect to the prescribed position of the object, the objective must be an aplanatic optical system in the strict sense of that term (§ 182); which embraces two conditions, namely, first, that the system must be free from spherical aberration along the axis so that rays emanating from the axial point of the object shall all intersect puntually at the corresponding place in the image, and, second, that ABBE's sine-condition shall be rigorously fulfilled, which means literally that all the images made by rays coming from each separate zone of the objective must coincide exactly with the image made by the paraxial rays coming from the central zone. Without pausing to discuss this requirement further, suffice it to say that it is quite impossible to make an objective that is perfectly aplanatic even for light of one single wave-length.

However, as a matter of fact, instead of being illuminated by monochromatic light, the object under the microscope will generally be illuminated by daylight or artificial light comprising a vast number of different wave-lengths. Consequently, if the colors in the image are to duplicate those in

the object as closely as possible, and above all not show any
colors that are not in the original, the objective must certainly be free from chromatic aberrations; that is, besides
fulfilling the condition of *aplanatism* above mentioned, it
must likewise fulfil the condition of *achromatism*. Let us
analyze exactly what this involves. In the first place, a
definite pair of colors or wave-lengths must be carefully
selected with a view to the purpose for which the microscope
is to be used, so that the system will be achromatic with
respect to these two colors, for example, red and blue not far
from the two ends of the visible region of the spectrum; on
the assumption that the instrument is to be used in conjunction with the eye and that therefore so-called optical
achromatism (§ 168) is desirable. Accordingly, the first
requisite in this case is that the objective shall focus at the
same point in the image all the red and blue paraxial rays
issuing from the axial point of the object. Under these
circumstances, provided the several lenses in the objective
are made of suitable kinds of optical glass, that is, glass
that has been judiciously selected from the numerous varieties
that are available at present (p. 484), paraxial rays of other
colors (yellow, green, violet) will cross the optical axis very
nearly at the same place as the point of intersection of the
red and blue rays. However, in spite of the utmost pains to
prevent it, a so-called *secondary spectrum* is almost certain
to be left uncompensated, which, small as this error usually
is, may prove very annoying in an objective of wide aperture.

We have still to consider the color-faults of the image
due to rays that lie outside the narrow region of the paraxial
rays. When we supposed at first that the spherical aberration
along the axis was abolished for some intermediate color
(yellow) between red and blue, it did not follow that the
optical system would therefore be free from spherical aberration for light of other colors; on the contrary, in this case
the system would most likely be spherically under-corrected
(p. 514) for the (red) rays of longer wave-lengths and spher-

ically over-corrected for the (blue) rays of shorter wave-lengths. Consequently, the objective must be corrected also for the fault of *chromatic difference of spherical aberration,* as ABBE termed it. Even then one last error remains to be eliminated, for although all the different colored images of the object should lie now in one and the same transversal plane, there will still be overlapping of one image by another unless they are all of precisely the same size. This so-called *chromatic difference of magnification* cannot be perfectly corrected even if the sine-condition were satisfied for light of each separate wave-length, because the value of the magnification-ratio itself is different for different wave-lengths.

It is, therefore, idle to suppose that a microscope-objective could be designed to be completely free from all error; and if it could be done, it would be beyond the power of any optician to grind the lenses and adjust and center them exactly according to the most rigid specifications. The best we can hope for in such a case is a compromise that will be reasonably satisfactory for all practical requirements. The small residual errors that cannot possibly be eliminated are blemishes in the image, aberration-disks or spots where the rays have failed to meet exactly in the ideal image-point; but if their dimensions are less than the width of the image of the least perceptible detail (d) in the object (§ 216), the imperfections of the image will be, so to speak, beneath notice and therefore practically non-existent. Thus according to v. ROHR, these aberration-disks in the image made by the objective of a fine microscope may be compared to the tiny pebbles in a piece of mosaic-work in which the details of the pattern cannot be recognized unless the pebbles themselves are comparatively much smaller than the dimensions of the details.

Since no optical system can have more than one pair of aplanatic points (p. 524), the optical tube-length (Δ) of a microscope with a high power objective cannot be varied, and consequently the actual dimensions of the aberration-disks or faults in the intermediate image projected by the objective in (or near) the anterior focal plane of the ocular will depend simply on the objective, not on its focal length (f_1'). On the other hand, the dimensions of the least perceptible details in this image, being equal to $\Delta.d/f_1'$, are inversely proportional to the focal length of the objective and can therefore be made to have a prescribed value by giving the objective the proper focal length. Thus with a given type of objective, the focal length can be reduced until the perceptible details in the image are made to appear decidedly larger than the aberration-disks that are inherent in this type of construction. Accordingly, when the image is viewed by an ocular of the proper power, the details of the object will come out distinctly, while the aberration-disks will still be below the limit of visibility. A convenient way of testing the degree of perfection of the optical construction of a given type of objective consists in ascertaining the ocular magnification or additional magnifying power that the image will bear.

218. Types of Microscope Objectives.—The early forms of high power objectives in the compound microscope were generally the result of the practical experience of skillful opticians without much aid from theory. From about 1820 AMICI's objectives were made by careful optical computations. In his objectives, as is usually the case today in all high power microscopes, the front lens was a small glass hemisphere with its plane face close to the object. In order to utilize as much as possible the property of the pair of aplanatic points of the spherical surface (§ 177), the hemisphere was sometimes augmented by the addition of a thin glass plate which was cemented to the plane face, or a lens of this form was made all out of one piece of glass. It was customary to correct the spherical aberration at the plane surface and the chromatic under-correction of the front lens by a pair of doublets each composed of a plano-concave flint glass lens cemented to a double convex crown glass lens, as represented in Fig. 301; and with constructions of this kind AMICI obtained (about 1830) objectives with apertures of $2\eta = 100°$. One of his minor difficulties was to make objectives compensate for the aberration which is due to the cover-glass (§ 211) that is interposed between the object and the microscope and which depends on the thickness of the cover-glass.

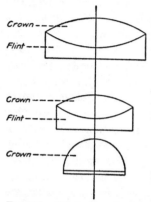

Crown

Flint

Crown

Flint

Crown

FIG. 301.—Illustration of a simple form of microscope objective.

The influence of the cover-glass was ingeniously counteracted by a simple device invented by the English optician A. Ross in 1838 which consisted of a screw-collar attached to the tube of the microscope, whereby the upper part of the objective can be slightly shifted and adjusted enough to allow for the aberration due to the thickness of the particular cover-glass that happens to be in use.

The principle on which objectives of wide aperture are constructed is to offset the unavoidable errors of both spherical and chromatic aberration in one part of the system by deliberately introducing opposite compensating errors in the other part; and, consequently, as has been stated before, the objective as a whole is usually a complex optical system composed of several groups of lenses which have to be ground, adjusted and centered with extraordinary care and precision.

In the most powerful modern microscopes a drop of liquid is inserted to span the narrow interval between the cover-glass and the plane surface of the small front lens of the objective. Thus instead of the two focal lengths being equal and opposite ($f_1' = -f_1$), as in the so-called dry objectives, the focal lengths of an immersion objective are unequal ($f_1 = -n.f_1'$, where n denotes the index of refraction of the liquid). In the first immersion systems made by AMICI about the middle of the last century the liquid used was water, but other liquids (oils) are used more frequently nowadays. One obvious effect of the interposition of the liquid medium is to annul or at least partly overcome the injurious influence of the cover-glass and also at the same time to reduce the losses of light by reflection; but the main advantage consists in the increase of the numerical aperture and the accompanying increase of the resolving power.

The efficiency of the microscope was improved in many ways by ABBE. He found that oil of cedar wood had an index of refraction (n = 1.51414) and a dispersive power ($\nu = 49.0$) very nearly the same as for glass, and in 1879 he designed for CARL ZEISS an objective with a focal length of one-twelfth of an inch and a numerical aperture of 1.25, in which by using homogeneous immersion the object was to all intents and purposes optically in the same medium as that of the front lens of the objective; and consequently the property of the aplanatic points of the hemispherical surface could now be utilized for the widest possible aperture. Moreover, if the hemispherical front lens was succeeded by an aplanatic meniscus lens of the type shown in Fig. 275 or perhaps by a series of such lenses, the angular aperture of the bundle of rays coming from the axial object-point could be successively reduced. The effect of this arrangement is to convert the wide-angle bundle of incident rays into a much narrower monocentric bundle, thereby making it much easier for the last lenses of the objective to produce the required spherical and chromatic corrections.

The new varieties of Jena optical glass (p. 482) were advertised in 1885; and the following year new types of objectives called *apochromats*, both dry systems and immersion systems, were brought out by the firm of CARL ZEISS. Designed and computed by ABBE, and executed with the greatest pains and ingenuity, these objectives not only showed no secondary spectrum but were spherically corrected for two

or three different wave-lengths. Fig. 302 represents the type
of construction of an oil-immersion apochromat. Subsequently, ABBE utilized the remarkable optical properties of
the mineral fluospar (p. 485), for which n = 1.43391 and

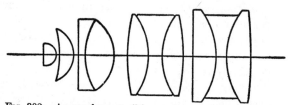

FIG. 302.—An apochromat oil-immersion microscope objective.

$\nu = 95.4$ (low refraction with high dispersion) to construct a
series of objectives which were called semiapochromats.

219. The Ocular.—On the assumption that the image
made by the objective is a faithful reproduction of the object,
the task that remains to be performed by the ocular system
is a comparatively simple one. Generally (as has been previously stated) the ocular is composed of two parts, namely,
the field-lens towards the objective, which acts like a condenser and increases the field of view of the instrument, and
the eye-lens next the eye at some little distance from the
field-lens. On account of the feeble divergence of the bundles
of rays, the spherical aberrations along the axis are of such
minor importance that they can be ignored entirely, and
errors of astigmatism and distortion can be easily reduced to
such a degree that they will not be noticeable. On the other
hand, achromatism with respect to the focal length (f_2) of
the ocular (see p. 488 and § 173) is an essential requirement,
because, while it does not make much difference whether the
various colored images seen through the ocular all lie exactly
in the same far off transversal plane, it is very important that
these images should all have the same apparent size, that is,
subtend the same angle ω' at the center O' of the small exit-
pupil where the observer views the image as through a little
round hole or window. On the assumption that field-lens

and eye-lens are both single thin lenses made of one kind of glass, the condition of achromatism in this sense of the term is that the interval (c) between the two components shall be equal to the arithmetical mean of their focal lengths (p. 502); that is, $c = (a+b)/2$, where a and b denote the focal lengths of field-lens and eye-lens, respectively.

The two historic types of ocular that are still used today with various modifications are HUYGENS's ocular (Fig. 218), which is the older type and goes back to the beginning of the eighteenth century (1703), and RAMSDEN's ocular (Fig. 219), which was introduced about eighty years later. (The so-called "RAMSDEN circle" or "eye-circle" is the exit-pupil of the microscope.) In each of these typical constructions both lenses are plano-convex and made of the same kind of glass. In HUYGENS's ocular the curved surfaces are both turned the same way towards the objective, whereas in RAMSDEN's ocular the curved surfaces are opposite each other.

In the original form of HUYGENS's ocular the relations between the focal lengths a, b and f_2 and the distance c between the two lenses were expressed by the following proportions: $b : f_2 : c : a = 2 : 3 : 4 : 6$. In the modern form of this ocular the numerical ratios are different, namely, $b : f_2 : c : a = 6 : 8 : 9 : 12$, so that here the distances of the focal points (F_2, F_2') of the ocular from field-lens and eye-lens are $\frac{4}{9} c$ and $\frac{2}{9} c$, respectively; as may be easily verified. Since the real image made by the objective falls inside HUYGENS's ocular between the field-lens and the eye-lens, this image is a virtual object with respect to the ocular, and consequently this type of ocular is not suitable for the insertion of cross-hairs and scale for measurements of the image, because the image of the scale and accessories would be formed by the eye-lens alone and not by the ocular as a whole.

In RAMSDEN's ocular, where $a = b = c = f_2$, the thin plano-convex lenses are in the focal planes of the combination;

and one trouble, therefore, about this arrangement is that the image made by the objective falls so close to the field-lens that particles of dust on the surface of this lens or flaws in the glass itself will be magnified by the eye-lens and confused with the image as seen in the microscope. This difficulty is remedied in practice by reducing the interval between the two lenses so that as a matter of fact c is a little less than the focal length of each of the two equal lenses, and although the condition of achromatism is no longer satisfied exactly, the error is not serious. For example, if $c = \frac{2}{3} a$, the real image made by the objective will be formed in front of the field-lens at the distance $-\frac{1}{4} a$ from it, and accordingly with this arrangement there is no difficulty (as there is in HUYGENS's ocular) about inserting cross-hairs and scale in the tube at the place where this image is formed.

KELLNER's so-called orthoscopic ocular (1849) is an improved form of RAMSDEN's ocular ($a = b = c = f_2$) in which the eye-lens is an achromatic doublet and the field-lens is a thin double convex lens. GUNDLACH's "periscopic" ocular is also of the RAMSDEN type, in which the eye-lens is a triplet and the field-lens is a doublet.

The simple chromatic correction obtained with oculars of these types is ample unless the objective is of high power, and then the unavoidable chromatic difference of magnification inherent in the objective itself must be taken in account. In other words, if the image presented to the ocular for magnification has color-faults in it, it is incumbent on the ocular to correct them if possible, otherwise the faults will be merely accentuated. This trouble is encountered even with apochromatic objectives that are as achromatic as it is possible to make them; and in order to overcome it, ABBE calculated a special form of *compensation ocular* essentially more complicated than the simple types of ocular that are generally used. Intentionally designed to have a certain chromatic difference of magnification opposite to that of the objective, this type of ocular has a shorter focal length for

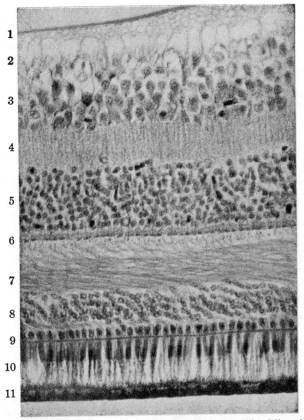

Fig. 303.—Human retina, whorl fibers, magnified 300-fold. Microphotograph of section of retina of human eye, reproduced by courtesy of Mr. Max Poser.

1. Internal limiting membrane
2. Layers of fibers of optic nerve
3. Layer of ganglion cells
4. Inner reticular layer
5. Inner nuclear layer
6. Outer reticular layer
7. Henle's fiber layer
8. Outer nuclear layer
9. External limiting membrane
10. Layer of rods and cones
11. Pigmentary epithelium

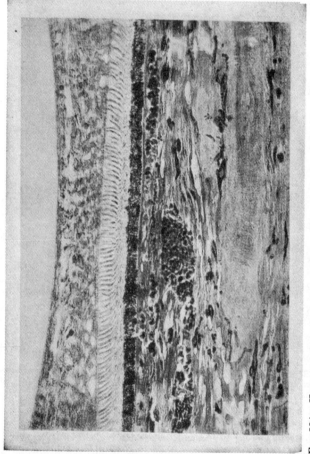

Fig. 304.—Human retina, fovea centralis, magnified 300-fold. Microphotograph of section of retina of human eye (fovea centralis), reproduced by courtesy of Mr. MAX POSER.

red light than for blue light. The principle of the method
can easily be illustrated by a numerical example by the aid
of the formula for the magnifying power of the microscope,
namely,

$$M = m_1 \cdot \frac{l}{f_2},$$

where $m_1 = \Delta / f_1'$ denotes the value of the magnification-ratio
for the image made by the objective and $l = 250$ mm. If, for
example, $m_1 = 50$ for red light and $= 52$ for blue light, and
if the focal length (f_2) of the compensation ocular is 25 mm.
for red light and 26 mm. for blue light, evidently the magnifying power of the microscope will have the same value
$M = 500$ for both red and blue light.

**220. Microphotography and Other Applications of the
Microscope.**—Concerning the mechanical construction of the
compound microscope and its adjuncts (stand and accessory
contrivances for convenience of manipulation and focusing),
and especially concerning the various illumination-devices
(for transparent and opaque objects) that have an important
bearing on the theory of the formation of the image, the
student must be referred to books and special articles on
the microscope where these subjects are treated in more or
less detail. For lack of space it is impossible to give here
any description of the many applications of the microscope
(binocular microscope, polarization microscope, etc.) and of
the special constructions for mineralogy and other fields
of scientific research. For lecturing purposes and demon-
strations the objective may be used in conjunction with an
ordinary ocular or preferably with a special type of ocular
for projecting the magnified image on a transparent or
opaque screen where it will be visible to an assembly of
spectators. The efficiency and usefulness of the microscope
have been enormously extended in recent years by the
applications of photography. In microphotography where
it is very important to have a flat image focused on the
sensitive plate, it is better to use a special concave (negative)

ocular. For ultraviolet light ($\lambda = 275$ mμ) the ZEISS mono-chromatic objectives (1904) made of amorphous quartz ($n_D = 1.45846$, $\nu = 67.7$), which does not absorb these short waves as ordinary glass does, bring out details in the photo-graph that could never be seen at all in looking through a high power microscope; because on account of the short wave-length of the light used for obtaining the photograph the resolving power is between two and three times as great as it can possibly be for direct vision with the eye.

No better illustration of the extraordinary possibilities and usefulness of the photographic process can be given than the reproductions (Figs. 303 and 304) of two beautiful micro-photographs of parts of the retina of a human eye which were made by Mr. MAX POSER of the BAUSCH & LOMB Optical Company of Rochester, N. Y., with one of their apochromats of focal length 4 mm. and numerical aperture 0.85.

In conclusion, we can merely allude to the method of *dark-yield illumination* whereby it is possible to perceive de-tails even below the limit of the resolving power of the microscope, just as the motes in a sunbeam that are invisible by ordinary illumination can be made perceptible by dif-fraction. We cannot discern the forms of these excessively minute objects, all we can do is to detect their presence in the field. This method of illumination was utilized by H. SIEDENTOPF in his *ultramicroscope*, in which the image is a diffraction-pattern whose form and size enable the observer to make certain inferences as to the dimensions of the object. With sunlight illuminations the presence of particles in colloidal solutions as small as four-millionths of a millimeter has been detected by this instrument.

CHAPTER XVIII

NOTES ON PHYSICAL OPTICS AND PHYSIOLOGICAL OPTICS

221. Index of Refraction.—Instead of referring to the velocity of light (v) in an optical medium, it is customary in geometrical optics to use a number (n) called the *index of refraction* which is inversely proportional to v and is defined as follows:

$$n = \frac{c}{v},$$

where c denotes the velocity of light *in vacuo* and is equal in round numbers to 3.10^{10} cm./sec (see § 33). On the supposition that the light is *monochromatic* (corresponding to a definite place in the spectrum), the value of n depends only on the medium; but in general the medium itself is variable and consequently the value of n may not only be different at different places in the same medium, but at any given point it may be different in different directions. Thus, for example, consider a point P whose position in the medium is defined by its Cartesian coördinates (x, y, z), and also a certain direction from P defined by its direction-cosines (α, β, γ); then in the most general case the index of refraction at the point P is a function not only of (x, y, z) but also of (α, β, γ). The medium is said to be *homogeneous* when the value of n does not depend on the position of the point P, that is, when n is independent of x, y and z; and it is said to be *isotropic* when the value of n at any point in the medium is the same in all directions, that is, when n is independent of α, β and γ. For example, the earth's atmosphere is an isotropic medium, but it is not homogeneous, because the index of refraction diminishes as we ascend from sea-level

685

to the higher levels of the atmosphere. On the other hand, crystalline media are examples of homogeneous media that are not isotropic. Finally, ordinary optical glass is a medium that is both homogeneous and isotropic.

The index of refraction depends also on the color of the light or its wave-length *in vacuo*. The accompanying table taken from a recent paper on "Modern optical glass" by T. SMITH (*Trans. Opt. Soc.*, XXXII, 89) gives the wave-lengths of the spectral lines used in the 1926 List of the PARSONS Optical Glass Company (1 mμ = 10^{-6} mm.).

NOTATION	COLOR	SPECTRUM	WAVE-LENGTH IN mμ
b	Red	Helium	706.519
C	Red	Hydrogen	656.279 ± 6
D	Yellow	Sodium	589.295 ± 298
d	Yellow	Helium	587.562
e	Green	Mercury	546.073
F	Blue	Hydrogen	486.133
g	Blue	Mercury	435.834
G'	Violet	Hydrogen	434.046
h	Violet	Mercury	404.656

I. *Double Refraction*

222. Double Refraction in Iceland Spar.—In most of the problems of geometrical optics it is generally taken for granted that the optical media are not only homogeneous but isotropic, and that therefore the index of refraction has the same value at all points of a medium and for all directions of the rays, depending only on the wave-length of the light. Thus when light is refracted across a boundary surface between two such media we need only to know the direction of the incident ray in order to tell that of the refracted ray, in accordance with the law of refraction (n'.sin α' = n.sin α). The restriction imposed by this underlying assumption is indeed so rigorous and narrow that in order to comply with it in practice the optician is obliged to make his lenses and prisms almost exclusively of a purely artificial material known as optical glass which, as has been explained (§ 166), is manufactured for the purpose with the utmost patience and skill. The transparent solids found in nature are mostly gems and precious stones of comparatively few varieties, none of them very abundant, as is implied by the designation we have just used; and in most instances they are not suitable for optical instruments. Almost without exception they have a crystalline structure, more or less homogeneous but anisotropic; and generally when a ray of monochromatic light falls on one of these crystals, there will be two refracted rays instead of one. This phenomenon known as *double refraction* was noticed first (1669) by ERASMUS BARTHOLINUS, who observed it in the case of the mineral called Iceland spar which exhibits the effect beautifully. Not long afterwards HUYGENS began to investigate the new phenomenon and brought his great genius to bear on all its curious and interesting relations; and one of the most famous chapters in his *Traité de la lumière* (1690) is devoted to the description and explanation of his experiments on the passage of light through Iceland spar. It is a masterly treatment of the whole subject as far as the facts had been ascertained at that time, and the construction of the wave-surface in the crystal as HUYGENS originally proposed it nearly two hundred and fifty years ago is given in all the elementary text-books of optics today. As one of the two refracted rays was found to obey the ordinary law of refraction, it was called the *ordinary ray*, to distinguish it from the other or *extraordinary ray* which follows an entirely different law. Knowing already that the form of the wave in an isotropic medium like glass was spherical, HUYGENS naturally assumed that the ordinary wave in the crystal was spherical also and therefore propagated with the same speed in all directions. The extraordinary wave certainly was not spherical, and HUYGENS assumed that it was spheroidal and had the form of an ellipsoid of revolution. If it is merely a question of the directions of the two rays in Iceland spar, this theory that the refracted wave consists of two concentric sheets, a sphere and a spheroid, affords a complete and satisfactory explanation of

all the observed effects; but it leaves us entirely in the dark
as to *why* the incident ray undergoes double refraction at all,
and why one of the two rays follows the ordinary law.
HUYGENS's ingenious and careful experiments led him
strongly to suspect that the light that had passed through
the crystal was somehow strangely different from the incident light because, although in general both rays were
again doubly refracted when they traversed a second rhomb
of Iceland spar, yet for certain special positions of the second
rhomb with respect to the first, this was not the case, and
neither of the two rays was doubly refracted the second time.
At the conclusion of his treatise on light HUYGENS tells us
that he was much perplexed by this truly "marvellous phenomenon," as he calls it. It would be entirely beyond the
scope of this book to describe here these interesting experiments or to discuss the important bearing they have on the
wave-theory of light. Both HUYGENS and NEWTON seem
to have been more or less dimly aware of the fact of the
polarization of light which was discovered long afterwards
by MALUS in 1810 and led FRESNEL in 1821 to adopt the
far-reaching hypothesis of transverse vibrations in the
luminiferous ether.

**223. Huygens's Construction of the Wave-Surface in
Iceland Spar.**—Iceland spar, which is a clear transparent
form of calcite ($CaCO_3$) belonging to the rhombohedral system, is said to be a *uniaxial crystal* because there is a certain
specific direction in it called the *optic axis* that is distinguished
from all the other directions by the fact that when a beam
of light traverses the crystal in this unique direction, the
two waves, ordinary and extraordinary, proceed with equal
speed, and consequently if a ray of light is transmitted
through the crystal parallel to the optic axis, it will not be
divided into two rays, as is otherwise the case, because in
any other direction the speeds of the two waves are different.
The optic axis is not a fixed line, it is merely a fixed direction
in the crystal. Uniaxial crystals are classified as positive or

negative, according as the extraordinary ray is bent towards
the axis or away from it; thus quartz, which is likewise a
uniaxial crystal, is positive, while Iceland spar is negative.
Many crystals have two optic axes and are therefore *biaxial;*
and in these crystals neither of the two rays obeys the ordinary law of refraction. The two sheets of the wave-surface
in a biaxial crystal are in fact more complicated than the
sphere and spheroid that are characteristic of a uniaxial
crystal; and the student who desires to pursue the subject
further must consult special treatises on physical optics
where FRESNEL's wave-surface in a double refracting medium
is fully described and explained by mathematical analysis.
In the following description of HUYGENS's method the
crystal always has reference to Iceland spar.

When the advancing wave reaches a point on the surface
or in the interior of the crystal, this point straightway becomes a new center of disturb-
ance from which two waves
are propagated onwards in
all directions. One of these
waves, being spherical,
spreads out with constant
speed just as if the double
refracting medium were isotropic, as was stated before;
whereas the other wave, being spheroidal, proceeds with
different speeds in different
directions. In Iceland spar
(and all other negative uniaxial crystals) the sphere is in-

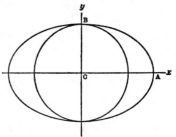

FIG. 305.—Form of wave-surface in
principal section of a negative uniaxial crystal, such as Iceland spar.
Circle inscribed in ellipse, optic
axis of crystal being parallel to
principal axis minor of ellipse,
Semiaxes of ellipse: CA = a,
CB = b, a > b.

scribed in a prolate spheroid generated by the revolution of an
ellipse around its shorter principal axis which is parallel to the
optic axis of the crystal. Thus if the equation to the ellipse is

$$\frac{x^2}{a^2} + \frac{y^2}{b^2} = 1, \qquad (a > b),$$

the sphere may be considered as generated by the revolution
of the circle

$$x^2 + y^2 = b^2$$

around the diameter that coincides with the shorter axis of
the ellipse (Fig. 305). The semiaxes of the ellipse denoted

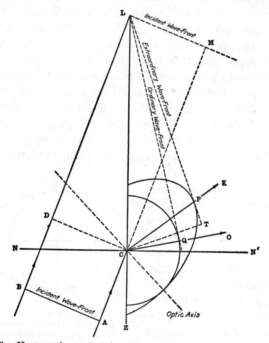

FIG. 306.—HUYGENS's construction of wave-front in Iceland spar. The plane
wave AB is incident on the plane surface ZL of the crystal; the optic
axis of the crystal being in the plane of incidence (plane of diagram).
AC is the incident ray; CO is the ordinary refracted ray and CE the
extraordinary refracted ray. CQ and CT are the normals to the ordinary and extraordinary wave-fronts within the crystal.

here by a and b are proportional to the greatest and least
velocities of light in the crystal.

If the surface of the crystal is a smooth, polished, plane
refracting surface, and if the incident wave is plane also

(p. 13), the construction is very simple. The straight line AC (Fig. 306) represents the path of a ray that is incident on the surface at the point C in the straight line ZZ which is the trace of the surface in the plane of the diagram; and, similarly, the straight line BL drawn parallel to AC represents the path of another incident ray in the same plane of incidence, which intersects ZZ at a point L some distance beyond C. Thus at the instant when the incident wave arrives at C, its position is shown by the straight line CD perpendicular to AC at C and to BL at D. From this moment C is the center of two disturbances in the crystal, and during the time the wave takes to travel *in vacuo* a distance equal to DL, the disturbances spreading out from C in all directions in the crystal will have been propagated to all points lying on two concentric surfaces of revolution whose traces in the plane of the diagram are the two generating curves, namely, the portions of circle and ellipse as shown in the drawing. The line perpendicular to the plane of the diagram at the point L is the line of intersection of two planes, one of which is tangent to the sphere and the other tangent to the spheroid; and these planes are the planes of the two refracted waves in the crystal at the moment when the incident wave arrives at the point L on the refracting surface. The traces of the planes are the straight lines LQ and LP tangent to the curves at Q and P. The two refracted rays corresponding to the incident ray AC are shown by the straight lines joining C with the point Q on the sphere and the point P on the spheroid.

The diagram is drawn for a special case, for the point P where the tangent-plane touches the spheroid generally does not lie in the plane of incidence (plane of the diagram); whereas the point Q where the other tangent-plane touches the sphere is always in the plane of incidence. In other words, the ordinary ray CQ lies in the plane of incidence, but the extraordinary ray CP as a rule does not lie in this plane. The plane of incidence in the diagram coincides with a *principal section* of the crystal made by a plane containing the optic axis; and when the optic axis lies in the plane of incidence, the section of the spheroidal sheet of the wave-surface is the generating ellipse, and in that case the incident ray AC and the two refracted rays CQ and CP all lie in the same plane, that is, in a principal section of the crystal.

In Fig. 307 (which is merely a particular case of the preceding diagram) the incident rays are normal to the surface

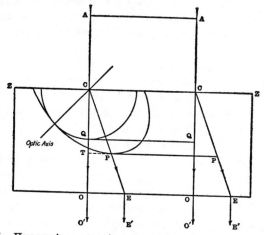

FIG. 307.—HUYGENS's construction of wave-front in Iceland spar: for the special case when the plane wave AA is incident normally on the plane surface ZZ of the crystal; the optic axis of crystal being in the plane of incidence (plane of diagram). AC is the incident ray (perpendicular to ZZ); CO is the ordinary refracted ray (undeviated) and CE the extraordinary refracted ray (deviated). CQ and CT, both perpendicular to ZZ, are the normals to the ordinary and extraordinary wave-fronts QQ and PP within the crystal.

of the crystal, and therefore the ordinary wave QQ and the extraordinary wave PP are both parallel to the incident wave; but although the ordinary ray CQ continues in the crystal along the same straight line as the incident ray AC, the extraordinary ray CQ generally pursues a different direction and will not even lie in the plane of incidence unless this plane happens to be in a principal section of the crystal, as shown in the drawing. The figure brings out clearly another striking difference between the attitudes of the two rays with respect to the wave-surface, which should be carefully noted. As is the case always in an isotropic medium (p. 91), the direction of the ordinary ray CQ is along the normal to the wave-front QQ; but, as a rule, the direction of the extraordinary ray CP is not the same as that of the normal CT to the wave-front PP. Accordingly while the ordinary wave advances in the direction of the normal CQ, the extraordinary wave appears to be jerked to one side and proceeds through the crystal, not in the direction of the normal CT, but in the direction of the ray CP.

The student is advised to draw similar diagrams for other special cases besides those shown in Figs. 306 and 307; particularly for the case when the optic axis of the crystal is parallel to the refracting surface and also for the case when it is perpendicular to this surface.

224. The Variable Index of Refraction of the Extraordinary Ray in Iceland Spar.—From what was said above concerning the attitude of the two rays with respect to the wave-surface in the crystal, it follows that a distinction must be made in the case of the extraordinary wave between the *ray-velocity* along the ray CP and the *wave-velocity* along the normal CT (Figs. 306 and 307). The index of refraction is defined to be the number given by the ratio $n = c/v$, where c denotes the velocity of light *in vacuo* and v denotes the velocity in the medium in question (§ 221). So far as the ordinary wave is concerned, this definition is perfectly simple, because the velocity of this wave is constant and equal to the least velocity of light in the crystal; and consequently n is constant also. But in the case of the extraordinary wave, the question arises as to what is meant by v in the formula $n = c/v$; does v here denote the ray-velocity or the wave-velocity?

This point can easily be settled by reference to Fig. 306. Evidently if α denotes the angle of incidence of the incident ray AC and α' the angle of refraction of the extraordinary ray CP, then $\angle\,\mathrm{LCD}=\alpha$ and $\angle\,\mathrm{CLP}=\alpha'$; and since the two right triangles CDL and CTL have the same hypothenuse CL, we obtain:

$$\frac{\sin \alpha}{\sin \alpha'}=\frac{\mathrm{DL}}{\mathrm{CT}}=\frac{c}{v}=\mathrm{n}.$$

This result shows that v, which is proportional to CT, denotes the wave-velocity.

When *the plane of incidence coincides with a principal section* of a uniaxial crystal like Iceland spar, the velocity (v) of the extraordinary wave in any particular direction is found to be a comparatively simple function of the angle φ between this direction and the fixed direction of the optic axis. If indeed we put $v=\mathrm{CT}$, the angle φ is the angle between the axis minor of the ellipse and the central perpendicular on the tangent; and consequently by the well-known properties of this curve,

$$v^2=a^2.\sin^2 \varphi+b^2.\cos^2 \varphi, \ \ (a>b),$$

where (in accordance with our previous notation) a and b denote the two principal semidiameters of the generating ellipse of the spheroidal sheet of the wave-surface. For example, in the direction parallel to the optic axis ($\varphi=0$), the velocity of propagation of the extraordinary wave is least and equal to that of the ordinary wave ($v=b$), as has been pointed out before; whereas in the direction perpendicular to the optic axis ($\varphi=90°$), the velocity is greatest ($v=a$). The maximum and minimum values of the index of refraction of Iceland spar for sodium light are found to be 1.6584 and 1.4864 corresponding to $v=b$ and $v=a$, respectively.

225. Wollaston's Prism.—When a plane wave is incident normally on a plate of Iceland spar with plane parallel faces, and the plane of incidence is in a principal section of the crystal, the ordinary and extraordinary waves will be separated by a parallel displacement, and will emerge in the same direction. Sometimes it is desirable for the emergent beams to be far apart, but this involves a fairly long path inside the crystal, and large pieces of Iceland spar suitable for optical use are hard to obtain and are expensive. In WOLLASTON'S prism the two waves undergo an angular displacement and emerge therefore in different directions; which has obvious advantages for some purposes. This prism (Fig. 308) consists of two equal right-triangle prisms made

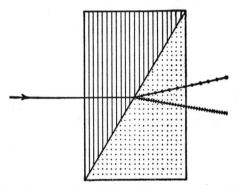

FIG. 308.—WOLLASTON'S prism which produces an angular separation between the ordinary and extraordinary rays. The shading of the drawing indicates the directions of the optic axes in the two halves of the prism, the optic axis in the left-hand portion being in the plane of the diagram and the optic axis in the right-hand portion being perpendicular to that plane. The directions of the vibrations (planes of polarization) are also indicated on the emergent rays.

of Iceland spar and united along the common hypotenuse face into a single block which does not have to be very thick. The refracting edge of the first prism is perpendicular to the optic axis of the crystal, whereas the refracting edge of the other prism is parallel to the optic axis. Thus in the drawing, where the direction of the optic axis is indicated by the shading in the usual way, the optic axis of the first prism is in the plane of the paper, and that of the second prism is perpendicular to this plane. The two waves traverse the first prism along exactly the same path, only the ordinary wave, being slower, is retarded behind the extraordinary wave. According to the theory of the polarization of light, the vibrations in the ordinary wave are parallel to the optic axis of the crystal, while those of the extraordinary wave are perpendicular to this direction; and consequently on entering the second prism, the *rôles* are reversed; that is, the ordinary wave in the first prism becomes the extraordinary wave in the second prism, and *vice versa*. Therefore the wave that was faster in the first prism will be slowed down on being refracted into the second prism, and so in this case the rays will be bent towards the normal; whereas in the other case which is exactly opposite the rays will be bent away from the normal. Accordingly, the two waves will emerge from the WOLLASTON prism in divergent directions, and so may be widely separated. This is an exceedingly convenient device for this purpose and is utilized, for example, in the modern clinical form of HELMHOLTZ's ophthalmometer, in which the essential feature is a so-called "doubling" system for splitting a beam of light into two portions so as to obtain a double image of an object (§ 227).

II. *The Ophthalmometer*

226. The External Surface of the Cornea of the Human Eye.—Practically the only scientific method of accurately measuring the linear dimensions of the dioptric system of the living eye (curvatures of cornea and crystalline lens, positions of the vertices of the refracting surfaces, etc.) is by means of precise observations of the catoptric or so-called PURKINJE images (p. 378) reflected in the eye by an external object. The most important of all the ocular refracting surfaces is the external (anterior) surface of the cornea, not merely because its refracting power is about four-fifths of the total refracting power of the unaccommodated eye, but also because all the other measurements in the interior of the eye, where the reflex images are generally much more difficult to locate and determine, are necessarily based on careful preliminary measurements of the cornea, which is, so to speak, the window of the eye. C. SCHEINER (1573–1650), one of the pioneers in physiological optics, made rough measurements of the cornea by comparing the reflex image in the anterior surface of this membrane with that of the same object reflected in the convex surface of a small glass marble or agate of approximately the same dimensions. Having near at hand a series of marbles of different sizes, he placed the individual whose eye was to be measured opposite a bright window where the reflected image of the cross-bars of the sash could be plainly discerned in the cornea; and then after a number of trials a marble was found which, on being inserted in one corner of the eye, gave a reflex image of the same size as the image in the cornea as nearly as could be determined by visual comparison.

The beautifully clear and transparent membrane of the cornea is not as regular and symmetrical in curvature as it seems to outward appearance, although in the central or optical zone extending two or three millimeters out from the vertex of the cornea (somewhat farther horizontally than vertically) the curvature is approximately regular for a normal eye. Towards the margin of the cornea the surface becomes flatter, more so in some meridians than in others, and not to the same extent in opposite directions from the center along the same meridian. The shape of the cornea is also different for different individuals. However, so far as vision is concerned, the really important area is the small optical zone around the vertex of the cornea; and here the radius of curvature is found to vary for different individuals (even when they are of the same age and sex) between the limits of 7.03 and 8.88 mm., although in the great majority of cases this value is comprised between 7.80 and 7.89 mm. The optical zone of the cornea is hardly ever truly spherical but nearly always astigmatic to a greater or less degree; and generally the refracting power is found to be between 0.5 and 1.25 dptr. higher in the vertical than in the horizontal meridian. This is the so-called normal or *physiological* astig-

matism "with the rule," which is apparently compensated
by a lenticular astigmatism of the crystalline lens in the
opposite sense, that is, "against the rule," so that it causes
no annoyance of vision. On the other hand, if the difference
of refracting power in the horizontal and vertical meridians of
the optical zone of the cornea amounts to less than 0.25 dptr.
or more than between 1.00 and 1.25 dptr., the astigmatism is considered to be *pathological;* and in that case cylindrical or toric spectacle lenses (§ 114) will generally be needed
to correct this error; which may be a source of continual,
perhaps unconscious irritation that can have serious consequences in one way and another.

Although ocular astigmatism is one of the most prevalent
so-called errors of refraction of the human eye, this trouble
was apparently not definitely noticed until THOMAS YOUNG
called attention to it about the beginning of the last century.
The fault was corrected by the celebrated astronomer,
Sir G. B. AIRY, by using a cylindrical lens (1827) for one of
his eyes; but not much progress could be made in this direction before the invention of the ophthalmometer by HELM-
HOLTZ in 1854 which has proved to be an almost inestimable
boon to mankind. Much important pioneer work in this
field was accomplished soon afterwards by DONDERS in Holland and KNAPP in Germany and the United States; and
the fact was established beyond question that the seat of
ocular astigmatism was in the cornea of the eye. Although
HELMHOLTZ's ophthalmometer gives the most accurate and
reliable measurements of the cornea, and has never been
improved in this respect, it was essentially a laboratory type
of instrument, not only demanding skill on the part of the
observer, but also involving somewhat tedious and complicated computations before the findings could be interpreted.
The difficulties of manipulation and other inconveniences
were triumphantly overcome by the clinical ophthalmometer
that was perfected in 1881 by JAVAL and SCHIÖTZ. Essentially the same in principle as the HELMHOLTZ instrument,

this new construction was incomparably more convenient for the ophthalmologist to use in his ordinary practice. Of all the measurements made by the oculist or optometrist in the routine of an eye-examination, the measurement of the cornea with the ophthalmometer is the most precise and trustworthy; and it has the advantage of being independent of the state of accommodation of the eye and also of the psychology of the patient.

227. The Optical Theory of the Ophthalmometer.—As is invariably the case whenever a real object is portrayed in a convex mirror, the reflex image in the anterior surface of the cornea is erect and virtual and smaller than the object. If the distance (a) of the eye from the object is known and likewise the size of the latter (y), the radius of curvature (r) of the convex surface may be considered as being simply proportional to the size of the image (y'), provided (as is always the case in measurements made with the ophthalmometer) the distance denoted by a is many times greater than r. For under such circumstances the ordinary magnification-formula, on being solved for r, is approximately:

$$r = \frac{2a}{y} \cdot y'.$$

Accordingly the determination of the value of r amounts simply to our being able to measure accurately the size of the virtual image y'.

The peculiar feature of the ophthalmometer is an optical mechanism called the *doubling device* which is based essentially on the same principle as that used in the astronomical heliometer. Inserted in the optical system, this mechanism automatically divides each bundle of rays reflected from the cornea into two bundles; and consequently when the observer looks through the instrument, instead of seeing a single image as he would do ordinarily, he sees two images usually separated from each other by a certain interval; which can be varied within fixed limits in one of two ways depending on the collimating mechanism. Not only the doubling mechanism itself but also the collimating mechanism connected with it is apt to be of different design and construction in different types of ophthalmometers. For example, in the original form of the instrument as devised by HELMHOLTZ the interval between the two images could be altered by making a delicate adjustment in the doubling system itself; whereas, on the other hand, in the ophthalmometer of JAVAL and SCHIÖTZ the doubling mechanism was rigid and invariable, and the collimation of the two images was accomplished by a device that changed the size of the object symmetrically at both ends by reducing or increasing the distance between two illuminated mires, which will be described presently (§ 228). In any case when the two images are collimated so that the end of one image is exactly in contact with the adjacent end of the other image, the instrument is set for reading the scale and thereby obtaining the measurement of the curvature of the cornea. Exactly how the doubling mechanism serves the purpose, has now to be explained; and the simplest explanation will be to describe the method used by HELMHOLTZ.

A bright window with cross-bars in the sash is a very convenient object for the HELMHOLTZ instrument. The image reflected in the cornea is viewed by the observer through a short-focus telescope mounted a few inches in front of the patient's eye and pointed horizontally at the place on the cornea where the curvature is to be measured; the total distance between the observing eye and the observed eye being usually not more than about 25 inches. The telescope being sharply focused on the image in the cornea, it is this image therefore that constitutes the object with respect to the telescope itself.

In HELMHOLTZ's ophthalmometer the combined doubling mechanism and collimating mechanism, contained in a small rectangular box attached to the end of the tube of the telescope, consisted simply of two little glass plates with

parallel plane faces placed symmetrically with respect to
the axis of the telescope, side by side in vertical planes; so
that each bundle of rays reflected from the cornea was
divided by the plates in two parts and transmitted through
them to opposite sides of the objective of the telescope. By
means of a thumb-screw the two plates could be turned
simultaneously and precisely, each around a vertical axis,
through equal angles in opposite directions, the angle between the plates being registered on a scale provided for
that purpose. In the initial or zero position when both plates

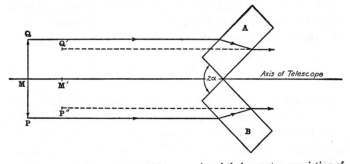

Fig. 309.—Doubling system in Helmholtz's ophthalmometer, consisting of
pair of plane parallel glass plates A and B inclined to each other at
variable angle 2α.

are in the same vertical plane perpendicular to the horizontal axis of the telescope, they unite into a single continuous plate, and with this setting only one image is seen
through the telescope. If the plates A and B (Fig. 309) are
rotated outwardly from this position each through an angle α,
the single image divides into two images separated by an
interval that increases with increase of the angle 2α between
the adjacent end-sides of the plates. In the diagram the
straight line $PQ = y'$, which is bisected perpendicularly at M
by the axis of the telescope, represents the image reflected in
the convex surface of the cornea. The image of the point Q
in plate A is designated by Q' and that of the point P in
plate B by P''; and if d denotes the thickness of each plate

and n the index of refraction of the glass, evidently (p. 102) the displacement of either P'' or Q' towards the axis can be computed by the following expression:

$$\frac{\sin (a - a')}{\cos a'} \cdot d, \qquad \left(\sin a' = \frac{\sin a}{n} \right).$$

Accordingly the difference $(PQ - P''Q')$ is equal to twice this displacement. When $a = 0°$, the two plates form a single plate and then $P''Q' = PQ = y'$; and in the other limiting case when $a = 90°$, $P''Q' = y' - 2d$. Obviously for a certain value of a ($a = \varphi$) between $0°$ and $90°$, $P''Q' = 0$, and then when Q' and P'' coincide with each other at the axial point M', the total displacement will be:

$$y' = \frac{2 \sin (\varphi - \varphi')}{\cos \varphi} \cdot d, \qquad \left(\sin \varphi' = \frac{\sin \varphi}{n} \right).$$

Consequently, by collimating the plates until the two images $P'Q'$ and $P''Q''$ are in contact with each other at Q' and P'', and then reading the angle φ as given by the scale, the value of y' may be computed, from which the radius of curvature of the measured meridian of the cornea can be derived immediately.

Obviously, the same result can likewise be obtained with a pair of fixed plates inclined to each other at a constant angle $2a$, by using a different collimating mechanism in which the interval between P and Q is altered until, as before, contact is obtained between Q' and P''. This could be accomplished by varying the size of the object (y) until the size of the image in the cornea had a certain fixed value, namely,

$$y' = \frac{2 \sin (a - a')}{\cos a} \cdot d.$$

Thus no matter whether the curvature of the cornea is much or little, with a fixed doubling mechanism, the reflex image in the cornea always has the same size, so that in this case the value of y' is a constant of the instrument which may be calculated once for all, and the radius of curvature (r) will be inversely proportional to y. In the JAVAL-SHIÖTZ type of ophthalmometer in which the doubling mechanism consists of a WOLLASTON quartz or calc-spar prism (§ 225) inserted in the tube of the telescope between the two lenses of the objective the constant value of y' is generally slightly less than 3 mm.

Each ray in traversing the WOLLASTON prism is automatically separated into two rays diverging from each other at a constant angle; and thus two images of PQ (Fig. 310)

FIG. 310.—Constant doubling system of ophthalmometer, consisting of a WOLLASTON's prism. P'Q' and P''Q'' are the double images of the image PQ reflected in the anterior surface of the cornea of the eye.

are formed by the objective, namely, P'Q' and P''Q''. Contact is obtained between Q' and P'' by means of the collimation mechanism that varies the size of the object (y) until the size of the image (y') has the requisite constant value.

These two forms of variable and constant doubling mechanism are typical of the different constructions of ophthalmometer or keratometer, as the instrument is sometimes called; but the actual optical system itself by which the doubling is produced may be totally different from that of either of those which have been described above.

228. Clinical Ophthalmometer.—As has been already intimated, the measurement of the cornea of the human eye has been enormously facilitated by the compactness and convenience of the modern clinical forms of the ophthalmometer. Under ordinary circumstances a skillful operator requires only a few minutes to adjust the instrument and obtain the readings for the two principal meridians of each of the two eyes of the patient. A characteristic feature of all the new constructions is the fact that the object which is reflected in the cornea is a part of the instrument itself, the distance between it and the eye to be measured being made as short as possible so that it seldom exceeds about 25 cm. The size of the object (y) is the distance between two brightly illuminated areas called mires, which are a pair of rectangular or circular plates made of some translucent material, white or colored, and lighted from behind by small electric lamps. The mires are mounted symmetrically with respect to the axis of the telescope on a circular arc which is bisected by the axis of the telescope; the eye of the patient being at the center of the arc. This circular arc can be rotated around the axis of the telescope so as to bring the mires opposite each other into any desired meridian, and the angle which this meridian makes with the horizontal or vertical meridian may be read on a special scale for this purpose. When the collimation mechanism is connected with the mires, the latter can be finely adjusted on the circular arc by a single screw which causes them to approach each other or recede from each other; the interval between them being indicated by a scale which usually gives the refracting power of the cornea in dioptries and perhaps also the equivalent radius of curvature in millimeters. A sharp black line is marked on the surface of each mire in a plane containing the axis of the telescope; and on one of the mires two series of equal steps are marked on opposite sides of the middle line as shown in Figs. 311, 312 and 313. The telescope being focused on the image reflected in the cornea of the patient's eye, the observer will see two images of each mire, but his attention is concentrated on the two adjacent central images, which will usually be separated by an interval, as in Fig. 311. The edges of these images can be brought in contact by turning the dial that regulates the equal and opposite movements of the mires along the circular arc; and then if the cornea is spherical, the two middle black lines will appear united in a single continuous line, as in Fig. 312; and contact will be steadily maintained as the circular arc is revolved slowly from one meridian to another. On the other hand, if, as is usually the case, the cornea

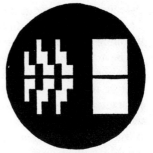

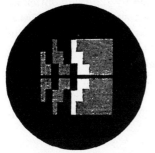

FIG. 312.—Ophthalmometer mires, overlapping.

FIG. 311.—Ophthalmometer mires, separated. (This illustration and the illustrations in Figs. 312, 313 and 314 are copied from a descriptive circular published by the manufacturers of the so-called "genothalmic" ophthalmometer.)

is astigmatic, the two black lines will not join together except in the two principal meridians which are always perpendicular to each other (p. 302), unless the astigmatism of the cornea is irregular (as, for example, in keratoconus or "conical cornea"). Accordingly the first thing to be done in this case is to locate one of the two principal meridians if it is possible to do so, by revolving the arc with the mires around the axis of the telescope until the two black lines of the partly overlapping central images are united as in Fig. 312; and then the mires must be adjusted until the images are in contact as in Fig. 313. This being done, suppose

FIG. 313.—Ophthalmometer mires, contact.

the readings give a refracting power of 44.25 dptr. for a principal meridian at angle of 75°. The circular arc must then be turned through an angle of 90° into the other principal meridian at 165°; and contact being made as before, suppose that the refracting power in this meridian is found to be 45.50 dptr. According to these readings, the astigmatic difference amounts therefore to 1.25 dptr.

The actual manipulation and procedure will not be exactly the same for ophthalmometers made by different opticians, because each instrument has its own special peculiarities of construction which can only be learned by using it. The accompanying illustration (Fig. 314) is made from a picture of the so-called "genothalmic universal ophthalmometer" which is widely used in the United States and in which the doubling system is a WOLLASTON prism as described above.

The readings (F) given on the scale in dioptries are computed by the formula

$$F = \frac{1000(n-1)}{r},$$

where r denotes the radius of curvature in millimeters and $n = 1.3375$. This latter number is not the index of refraction of the cornea, as might naturally be supposed, but is a purely instrumental number which has this particular value in order to make the reading 45 dptr. correspond to a radius of curvature of 7.7 mm. If we put

$$k = \frac{1000(n-1)}{2ay'} = \frac{3375}{2ay'},$$

where a denotes the radius of the circular arc that carries the mires and y' denotes the size of the reflex image in the cornea (or the "amount of doubling" when the instrument is collimated), the ophthalmometric formula is simply

$$F = k.y,$$

where y denotes the size of the object or the linear separation of the mires as measured by the chord of the circular arc.

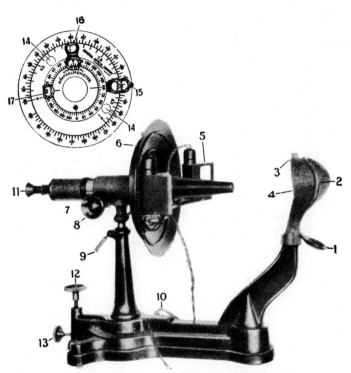

FIG. 314.—So-called "genothalmic" ophthalmometer.

1. Chin rest	10. Light switch
2. Head rest	11. Eyepiece
3. Eye blinder	12. Large raising and lowering screw
4. White dots on head rest	(for telescope)
5. Mire boxes	13. Small raising and lowering screw
6. Pegs for rotating disk	(for chin rest)
7. Rough grip section of telescope	14. Sight holes
8. Focusing wheel	15. Red marker
9. Locking handle	16. White double pointer

17. Green marker

III. *Visual Acuity in Daylight Vision*

229. Size of Retinal Image of Distant Object.—The size of the retinal image of a distant object on which the eye is focused may easily be calculated in terms of the apparent size of the object and the refracting power of the eye. The problem is simplified by supposing that the eye in question is a normal emmetropic eye (§ 153), for in that case the image will be sharply focused on the retina without any effort of accommodation, and the refracting power of the eye will have its minimum value $F = 58.64$ dptr. (if we use

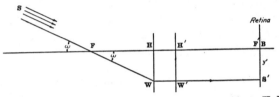

FIG. 315.—Visual acuity: size of retinal image of distant object. H, H' and F, F' are principal and focal points of ocular optical system; S' is image on retina of distant object-point S (a star, for example) whose angular distance from the optic axis is $\angle$ HFW $= \omega$; and B designates the point where optic axis meets the retina (BS' $= y'$).

the numerical value of GULLSTRAND's schematic eye, § 146). The geometrical relations are obvious from Fig. 315, where the pairs of cardinal points of the optical system are designated as usual by H, H' and F, F'. In this case it will be noticed that the posterior focal point (F') coincides with the point **B** where the optical axis meets the retina, and the retina itself may be considered as lying in the posterior focal plane. The problem consists merely in locating the position in this plane of the point S' that is conjugate to a distant object-point S, for example, a star whose angular distance from the axis may be denoted by ω. The direction of the cylindrical bundle of rays proceeding from S will be parallel to the straight line FW drawn through the anterior focal point which meets the anterior principal plane at a point W such that $\angle$ HFW $= \omega$. The straight line drawn through W parallel to the optical axis will intersect the posterior focal plane in the point S′ conjugate to S. If we put F′S′=y′, and if f=FH denotes the focal length, then since BS′=HW,

$$y' = \frac{\tan \omega}{F},$$

where $F=1/f$ denotes the refracting power. This simple relation (which should be compared with the more general formula given near the top of p. 449) has been obtained on the tacit assumption that the rays concerned in the imagery are paraxial rays; and consequently we may put $\tan \omega = \omega$, provided the value of ω is given in circular measure (radians). However, since it is more convenient to express this small angle in minutes of arc $(1' = 0.000291$ radian), the formula may be modified as follows:

$$y' = 0.291 \frac{\omega}{F},$$

which gives the value of y' in millimeters when ω denotes the angle in minutes subtended by a distant object and F is the value of the refracting power of the passive emmetropic eye in dioptries. For example, the retinal image of the full moon whose angular diameter is little more than 30′ is found by this formula to be a disk of about 0.15 mm. in diameter.

If the eye is not emmetropic, the ametropia (A) may be supposed to be corrected by a suitable correction-glass placed in front of the eye at a distance c from it, the refracting power of the glass (p. 444) being

$$F_1 = \frac{A}{1 + c.A},$$

and then

$$y' = 0.291 \frac{\omega}{F},$$

where

$$F = F_1 + F - c.F_1.F$$

denotes the refracting power of the compound system

(glass+eye). Strictly speaking, c denotes the distance of the anterior principal point of the eye from the posterior principal point of the glass; and since the anterior principal point of the schematic eye with relaxed accommodation is 1.348 mm. beyond the vertex of the cornea (p. 432), and since the distance between the glass and the cornea is usually about 12 mm., for ordinary calculations we may generally put $c = 0.01335$ m. It will be found that the size of the retinal image of a distant object as seen by a corrected ametropic eye does not differ much, certainly as a rule not appreciably, from that of the retinal image of the same object as seen by an emmetropic eye. The image is slightly larger for a myopic eye and slightly smaller for a hypermetropic eye than it is for an emmetropic eye under the same conditions.

230. Diffraction Disk due to a Small Round Aperture.— As a matter of fact when the eye looks at a star or at any so-called point-source of light, the image never appears to be a point or even a smooth round spot but a kind of irregular star-pointed pattern with a bright central nucleus surrounded by several luminous offshoots or patches of light, generally as many as four and perhaps as many as eight, more or less symmetrically disposed. The actual appearances are different for different individuals and for the same individual under different circumstances, nor are they at all the same for both eyes. These singular effects are undoubtedly due mainly to aberrations of one sort and another and to idiosyncrasies in the eye itself, perhaps also to habits of vision, because one has to learn to see just as he learns to walk and talk. In any case the image on the retina is the cross-section of a complicated bundle of refracted rays that has issued into the vitreous humor after having traversed the heterogeneous medium of the crystalline lens. The effect of the contraction of the pupil of the eye, which always accompanies accommodation and the effort to see distinctly, is to cut out some of these rays and thereby to obtain a sharper image.

However, entirely aside from all questions of geometrical optics (caustic surfaces, astigmatic bundles of rays, etc.), and on the supposition that the optical system of the eye were wholly free from both chromatic and monochromatic aberrations, we ought not to expect a punctual image of a point-source of light, for the simple reason that in passing through a small circular opening like the pupil the luminous radiation must necessarily be deflected or *diffracted* around the edge (p. 14). The truth is that point-to-point correspondence between object and image such as we are supposed to attain by means of paraxial rays and with homogeneous or monochromatic light is only a convenient fiction of geometrical optics, in many ways very useful to be sure, but not to be taken too seriously if we do not wish to run into difficulties of which we may be unaware. On the contrary, when the aperture of the system is reduced beyond a certain limit, the definition of the image, instead of getting better, actually gets worse, paradoxical as this seems at first. The explanation is that geometrical optics from the outset deliberately ignored a whole class of luminous phenomena that under ordinary circumstances are inconspicuous and not of much consequence but that upset all our nice calculations and demand recognition when the apertures and other material parts of the optical system are of such fine dimensions that they are comparable in size with the lengths of the waves of light.

In general the phenomena of diffraction through narrow apertures (pinholes, slits, etc.) are so complicated even in the simpler cases that the analytical investigations are far beyond the compass and plan of this book. Here we shall allude therefore to only one instance that happens to be of special importance with respect to the resolving power of an optical instrument, namely, the case when *a cylindrical bundle of rays is incident normally on a plane screen which is perforated by a small circular aperture.* According to HUYGENS's principle (§ 6), from each point of the aperture as from a new source rays proceed beyond the screen in all directions; and therefore in any single direction making an angle φ with the normal to the screen a cylindrical bundle of so-called diffracted rays issues from the aperture, one ray in this direction from each point in it. Accordingly if a convex lens is placed fairly close to the aperture on the far side of the screen so as to intercept these cylindrical bundles, each bundle of parallel rays will be converged to a point in the focal plane of the lens, the resultant effect at that place being due to the mutual interference of all the disturbances

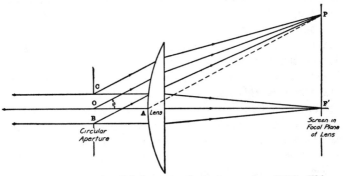

Fig. 316.—Diffraction disk due to small circular aperture BOC. This disk is projected on a screen by a lens. ∠ F′AP = φ.

that arrive there along these different routes. The position of the point of convergence corresponding to one of these bundles of rays depends simply on the direction in which the rays leave the aperture, that is, on the angle of diffraction (φ); and it may therefore be located by drawing a straight line through the optical center of the lens in this direction and determining the point where this line crosses the focal plane; as represented in the accompanying diagram (Fig. 316), which is purely schematic. If a second screen is erected parallel to the aperture-screen in the posterior focal plane of the lens, the diffraction-pattern as seen on this screen (assuming that the light is monochromatic) is found to consist of a bright central disk surrounded by a series of alternately dark and bright rings, which however are hardly perceptible beyond the first two or three, because even the first bright ring is dim as compared with the illumination at the center of the disk. Indeed the main phenomenon is the central disk itself, and the concentric rings are not of much importance and need not concern us at all at present. The center of the disk is on the optical axis of the lens directly opposite the center of the aperture, and the brightness falls off rapidly from the center towards the circumference, but it is hard to say exactly where it ends and the first dark ring begins.

The mathematical theory of this effect was thoroughly investigated by G. B. AIRY (1801–1892) in a paper published by him nearly a century ago (1834) in the *Cambridge Philosophical Transactions*. So far as the central disk is concerned, the result of this analysis may be stated very simply by reference to Fig. 316, in which the centers of the circular aperture BC and the central luminous disk in the focal plane of the lens are designated by O and F', respectively, and the optical center of the lens by A. The first completely dark place on the screen in the focal plane of the lens is supposed to occur at the point marked P, which is the point of convergence of the rays that are diffracted by the aperture in the direction parallel to AP. Accordingly to AIRY's calculations the angle $\varphi = \angle F'AP$ corresponding to the first minimum of brightness or place of zero ilumination is given by the formula

$$\sin \varphi = 1.22\frac{\lambda}{2p},$$

where $2p = BC$ denotes the diameter of the circular aperture and λ denotes the wave-length of the light. Thus it will be seen that the angle φ diminishes with increase of the size of the aperture, and *vice versa*. On the supposition that the lens is aplanatic, the central disk shrinks in diameter with increase in the size of the stop, until when the latter is fairly large, the luminous disk will not be appreciably different from a point. In any case the angle φ is invariably so small that no sensible error is involved by putting sin $\varphi =$ tan $\varphi = \varphi$; and consequently the formula is usually written

$$\varphi = 1.22\frac{\lambda}{2p},$$

where the angle φ is expressed now in circular measure. If $b = \mathrm{F'P}$ (Fig. 316) denotes the radius of the central disk on the screen, then since $b = f.$tan $\varphi = f.\varphi$, the diameter of the disk is

$$2b = 1.22\frac{\lambda.f}{p}.$$

For example, if $\lambda = 0.000589$ mm. (for sodium light), $2p = 2$ mm., and $f = 1000$ mm., the theoretical value of the diameter of the central disk is found to be about 0.72 mm. In practice, however, the eye is unable to discern the outermost border of the disk where the illumination fades out entirely and the edge of the dark ring begins; and consequently the observed value is generally only about half of the calculated value.

231. Resolving Power of the Eye in Central Daylight Vision.—Airy's formula for the semiangular diameter (φ) of the diffraction-disk as given above is applicable to any aplanatic optical system, provided the circular stop lies in front of the first refracting surface. Strictly speaking, therefore, it does not apply without reservations to the optical system of the human eye in which the pupil is interposed between the cornea and the crystalline lens; but nevertheless it may be used to obtain an approximate value at least of the size of the luminous disk on the retina when the eye is focused for a distant point-source of light, on the supposition that the diameter of the pupil is so small that the monochromatic aberrations along the axis are practically of no importance. The *resolving power* of the eye or its *visual* *acuity* is measured by the reciprocal of the angle ϵ, whose value, expressed in minutes of arc, is determined by AIRY's formula as follows:

$$\epsilon = 4194\frac{\lambda}{2p},$$

where $2p$ denotes the diameter of the entrance-pupil of the eye and λ denotes the wave-length of the light. This angle is the theoretical measure of the angular interval between two distant point-like objects that are just far enough apart for the eye to distinguish them as being separate and distinct. It is doubtless much smaller than the actual value of ϵ as obtained by direct measurements of the visual acuity, because it is based on the doubtful assumption that the eye can distinguish the two points as separate provided the edge of one diffraction-disk passes through the center of the other diffraction-disk; which is obviously a rather severe test. The value of ϵ, as above stated, is given in angular minutes, and that is the explanation of the change of the numerical coefficient in AIRY's formula from 1.22 to 4194.

The minimum diameter of the pupil of the eye is about 2 mm., the maximum being about 8 mm. If we put $2p = 3$ mm. (say) and $\lambda = 0.000589$ mm. (sodium light, corresponding nearly to the brightest part of the spectrum for daylight vision which is actually in the yellow-green close to $\lambda = 570$ mμ), the approximate value of ϵ as found by the above formula is $\epsilon = 0.82'$; that is, less than the conventional value of one minute of arc (p. 21), as might have been expected. If this value of ϵ is substituted in the formula

$$y' = 0.291\frac{\epsilon}{F},$$

where y' denotes the size of the retinal image in millimeters and $F = 58.64$ dptr. denotes the refracting power of the schematic eye, we obtain $y' = 0.0041$ mm.

This value is so nearly the same as that of the diameter of the smallest visual element of the retina (0.0045 mm.) as found by the early measurements of KOELLIKER that it was natural to jump to the conclusion that in order for the eye to distinguish two points as separate their retinal images must be at least as far apart as the interval between two adjacent cones in the *fovea centralis*. One trouble about this theory is that more recent measurements give much smaller values for the diameter of the macular cones, perhaps less than half the value found by KOELLIKER.

According to the formula, the angle ϵ, being inversely proportional to the diameter of the pupil, should be less for a dilated pupil than for a contracted pupil, and hence the resolving power or visual acuity should be greater with a large aperture; but the monochromatic aberrations likewise increase with increase of aperture, and this effect offsets the advantage of a wide pupil. Thus actual measurements seem to show that for values of $2p$ between 3 and 5 mm. the resolving power of the eye is fairly constant, and that it is lowered for values of $2p$ exceeding 5 mm.

The conception of the visual acuity of the eye as being measured by the smallest interval between two points that can be discerned as separate may be used to explain the doctrine of a mathematical limit. For example, suppose that u denotes the limit of a convergent series of numbers u_1, u_2, u_3, etc. A convenient way of picturing the series is to imagine a variable number x traversing it and assuming the value of each number in succession, so that the limit of x is the number u. If the numbers u_1, u_2, u_3, etc. are represented by points lying on a straight line, then the number x will be a variable point which leaps from one point on the line to the next point in the number series. At first these leaps may occur in all sorts of ways depending on the law of the series, but after a while the leaps begin to get shorter and shorter until at last the variable point becomes so "tame" that it settles down in an interval comprised between $(u+e)$ and $(u-e)$, where e denotes a positive number of any magnitude; and it is just this fact, that the variable x can be reduced to any desired degree of "tameness," that is the essence of the conception of a mathematical limit. Suppose that the eyesight of a spectator who is watching the career of x is just keen enough to tell that two points are separate provided the interval between them is greater than e. The smaller this "threshold" value of e is, the finer and more exact his observations will be; but no matter how small the threshold value becomes that is denoted here by e, a time will come when he will insist that there is no longer any difference between x and u.

232. Snellen's Sight-Test Charts.—Apparently the visual acuity of the human eye has not altered much over long centuries of time, and from references in the Bible and other ancient records it may be inferred that the seven stars of the Pleiades appeared just the same to former generations as they do to us today. According to v. ROHR, EUCLID (who flourished about 300 B. C.) estimated the limit of the average resolving power of the eye to be measured by an angle of one minute of arc ($\epsilon = 1'$), which is the conventional scientific value in use at present, the so-called *minimum visible* of PORTERFIELD (1759) or the *minimum separabile* of GIRAUD TEULON. However, it should be remarked that the apparent size of the test-object is not the only factor concerned in the determination of acuity of vision, for illumination and contrast both enter into the question. For instance, a dark object exposed against the bright background of the sky may be perceived even when its angular diameter is hardly more than about $4''$. The *aligning power* of the eye or width-perception is considerably greater than the resolving power as determined by the ability of telling whether two adjacent points are separate and distinct. Sir JOHN PARSONS thinks it was "a sheer piece of luck" on the part of the physicists to have "hit upon the finest of all forms of sensory discrimination, viz. contour discrimination" and to have "applied it in the form of the vernier to their instruments" of precision. The reading of a vernier consists in finding the mark that is as nearly as possible the exact prolongation of an opposite mark on the main scale; and while an accuracy of $10''$ or $12''$ may be considered high for such a setting, a practised observer under the most favorable conditions may attain a precision in which the error is not more than $3''$.

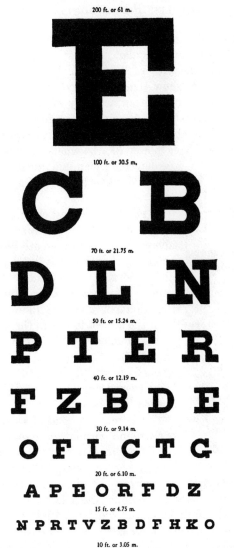

FIG. 317.—Visual acuity: SNELLEN's sight-test chart (about one-third actual size). This chart has nine rows of letters and the distances are given in whole numbers of feet above each row of letters (the equivalent distances in meters being also given).

In the coincidence-type of range-finder in which the two half-images in the binocular field have to be adjusted in correct alignment with each other across a fine separating line, actual tests show that under good conditions the unaided eye can align with an accuracy of less than 4″; and the normal value of the aligning power for settings of this kind is considered to be about 12″. Thus with a range-finder of magnifying power M, the smallest angle that can be detected by an individual with normal vision is taken to be (12 : M) seconds of arc.

FIG. 318.—Visual acuity: example of SNELLEN-test letter showing its construction. The letter is inscribed in a square whose sides are divided into five equal parts, as shown. When the square subtends an angle of 5′, the letter is at the proper distance from the eye.

SNELLEN's sight-test charts, which have been in use for seventy years (that is, since about 1862), and which are based on the value $\epsilon = 1'$ as a purely arbitrary standard of normal visual acuity, consist generally of seven rows of capital letters of the alphabet arranged in order of size from the largest letters in the highest line to the smallest letters in the lowest line (Fig. 317). The chart is hung on a wall where it is well illuminated, the patient being placed opposite it at a distance of about 6 meters or 20 feet.

The letters are dead black on a white background without glare or luster. All the letters in one row are of exactly the same size in the sense that each of them can be inscribed in a certain square, as illustrated in Fig. 318. The inscribed letter is constructed by dividing the side of the square into 5 equal parts and making the width of each line of the letter exactly equal to one of these parts. Opposite (or above) each row a number D is printed in type too small for the patient to see from the place where he is, which means that if this row of letters was at the distance D meters (or feet), the total height or width of each letter would subtend an angle of exactly 5', and the width of each line in the letter an angle of 1'. Thus if a denotes the length of the side of the square in which the letter is inscribed, $a/D = \tan 5'$ and therefore $D/a = 687.55$.

If d denotes the distance of the patient from the chart, and if D is the number opposite the row of the smallest letters that he is able to see distinctly, his visual acuity is $d : D$. For example, if $d = 6$ meters (as is usually the case for distance-test of vision), and if the patient can see distinctly the letters on the lowest row for which $D = 6$ meters, his visual acuity is six-sixths or unity, that is, he has normal vision according to this rating. If, on the other hand, he cannot do better than make out the large letters on the top row ($D = 60$ m.) and cannot distinguish the letters below that row, his visual acuity is $6 : 60$ or only one-tenth of normal visual acuity. The value of D in meters for the seven rows from the lowest to the top are 6, 8, 12, 18, 24, 36 and 60, corresponding for $d = 6$ m. to the following series of values of the visual acuity: $1, \frac{3}{4}, \frac{1}{2}, \frac{1}{3}, \frac{1}{4}, \frac{1}{6}$ and $\frac{1}{10}$. In the chart illustrated in Fig. 317 there are nine rows of letters instead of seven rows, and the values of D are given for the distance of the chart in whole numbers of feet.

It is easy to criticize SNELLEN's charts on various accounts, and numerous improvements of one kind and another have been proposed from time to time; but on the whole the SNELLEN letters seem to answer the purpose and to be satisfactory for ordinary eye-examinations as made by oculists and optometrists.

Normal visual acuity is hard to define, and when we speak of unit visual acuity as found by SNELLEN's test as being normal, all that is meant is that every normal eye should have a visual acuity of at least unity. Many persons that are perfectly normal in every way have a visual acuity that is higher than unity, for example, 1.25 or 1.50; and 1.75 is not uncommon. Occasionally we find individuals whose visual acuity is as high as 2.0 or even 3.0.

IV. *The Color Sensations*

233. Color Vision.—The only way we can discern the form and outlines of objects on the visual globe is by gradations of light and shade and differences of color. If the word color is used in a broad sense to include brightness or luminosity as well as hue or chroma (§ 238), then all vision may be said to be color vision. Strictly speaking, light itself is nothing but a visual sensation, the quality of which is described by its color. Ordinarily, it is true, the words light and color are both used loosely, sometimes with reference to the external cause of the sensation and sometimes to denote the sensation itself; and this unscientific mode of speech is often a source of much confusion in serious discussions of the subject. If we were careful and accurate in the use of language, we should avoid saying that a rose is red or that a frock is lavender, since colors are not the properties of objects but characteristics of our own visual sensations, and the same objects that look red or blue by daylight may look entirely differently by artificial illumination and under different conditions, as everybody knows. Obviously, it is not the same thing to say that sugar *tastes* sweet as to say that sugar *is* sweet; and there is exactly a similar difference between saying that a rose looks red and that a rose is red. The special color names, red, yellow, brown, green, blue, purple, pink, etc., also, black, white and gray, are far too few in number to describe all the hues and gradations of color that the eye can perceive; and so many colors are called by the names of flowers, fruits, precious stones, pigments, etc., as rose, orange, olive, emerald, vermilion, buff, cream, golden-yellow, sea-green, sky-blue, chalk-white, etc.

As a matter of fact, the actual color seen by the eye depends on a number of factors, above all on the physical character of the luminous radiation by which the organ of vision is stimulated, not only as to the wave-length distribution of this radiation but as to its intensity also; and unless

the intensity exceeds a certain "threshold" limit, there is
no visible response at all. Moreover, the concentric contraction and dilatation of the pupil automatically regulates
to a certain extent the quantity of radiant energy that is
admitted to pass the portal of the eye. In addition to these
obvious factors, the nature of the perception depends also
on the state of adaptation of the organ of vision itself and
on how it is attuned; for the visual mechanism in daylight
vision (cone-vision) is essentially different from the mechanism in twilight vision (rod-vision). Thus when the shadows
of evening fall, all the brilliant colors of the variegated landscape fade out gradually, and where a little while before red,
yellow, green and blue in all their mingled varieties enlivened
the scene, all now is somber gray relieved only by being
brighter in some places and darker in others. Even under
daylight illumination the color evoked depends too on the
part of the retina that is stimulated. In the central fovea
where the cones are most numerous and where vision is
most distinct, color discrimination is keenest also; whereas
in the peripheral parts of the retina where the rods pre-
dominate, vision is almost if not entirely achromatic or
colorless in the ordinary sense, as in twilight vision. Psychological factors also have much to do with our color percep-
tions as is manifested very strikingly in many contrast phenomena in which, for example, the background of the field
may exert a very decided influence on the appearance of an
object in the center. Lastly, all individuals do not see alike,
and although most persons have what is called normal color
vision, now and then we find a man or woman who varies
from the type and is perhaps partially or even totally color-
blind or who, without being color-blind, exhibits certain
peculiarities or anomalies of the color sense. Interesting and
exceedingly important for scientific study as these abnormal
forms of color vision are, we can only allude to them here;
and in the following discussion of the color sensations (which
is necessarily very inadequate) it will be tacitly assumed that

the eye is normal and bright-adapted for ordinary daylight illumination and foveal vision.

234. Elementary Facts of Color Mixing.—When two lights of different colors are directed into the eye at the same time, the color impression will be different from that which would be made by either of the lights separately and is a sensational mixture of the two. Here we are not speaking of a mixture of pigments or anything of that nature, but of a combination

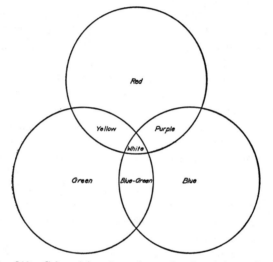

Fig. 319.—Color mixing, shown by overlapping of three colored disks projected on screen, as represented in the diagram.

of two simultaneous color sensations. The simple facts of color mixing may be readily demonstrated by means of an ordinary projection-lantern with the addition of an inexpensive attachment in the form of a round metal cap that can be fitted in the nozzle. This cap contains three small glass lenses all exactly alike except that they are colored red, green and blue. The lenses are mounted symmetrically around the center of the cap all in one plane, so that when the attachment is in place, none of the light from the lamp can issue from the nozzle of the lantern without first being filtered through one of the three colored lenses. Accordingly, on a screen placed at a suitable distance in front of the lantern, three colored disks will be projected partly overlapping each other in the central part of the screen, as shown in Fig. 319, the color of each disk being the same as that of the lens that formed it. Wherever a pair of disks overlaps, there will be a mixture of two of the three colors, red, green and blue; and in the most central part of the field where all three colors are superposed, the curious fact will be noticed that here the screen appears white or colorless. The observed appearances may be summarized in the following color equations:

$$\text{Green} + \text{Blue} = \text{Green-blue};$$
$$\text{Blue} + \text{Red} = \text{Purple};$$
$$\text{Red} + \text{Green} = \text{Yellow};$$
$$\text{Red} + \text{Green} + \text{Blue} = \text{White}.$$

When a narrow opaque object as, for example, an ordinary lead-pencil is held close in front of one of the colored lenses so as to intercept some of the rays coming through that glass, the strip of shadow across the white patch in the center of the screen will be colored green-blue, purple or yellow according as the intercepted rays are red, green or blue, respectively.

Green and blue being adjacent colors in the spectrum, it is natural to expect that their combination would give a *color-blend*, blue-green or green-blue, because we always find color-blends between two adjacent principal colors in the spectrum.

On the other hand, red and green which are far apart in the spectrum combine to give an intermediate yellow, which is not a color-blend at all, but a *color-fusion*, as Mrs. LADD-FRANKLIN termed it. Here we have a very striking distinction. There are no reddish greens or greenish reds, and when we see yellow, there is no trace in our consciousness of either red or green, but a totally new and distinct impression; nor have we any way of telling by the eye alone whether this yellow came directly from the middle of the spectrum or was a mixture of the red and green colors near the two ends of the spectrum. This fact is so characteristic of the nature of vision as distinguished especially from the sense of hearing that it needs to be emphasized.

When luminous radiation of two entirely different kinds is focused at one place on the retina, the color impression is unitary, whether it be a color-blend or a color-fusion. In the latter case the color bears no resemblance to that produced by either component acting separately, although it may be quite similar to the color produced by homogeneous radiation of a wave-length different from that of either of the two components. Thus as a means of analyzing the physical composition of the radiation, the eye is extremely inadequate, entirely unlike the organ of hearing in this respect. The ear differentiates and analyzes; the eye, on the contrary, integrates and synthesizes. Consequently, to quote Mrs. LADD-FRANKLIN, "we can never have, in the play of colors, intricate æsthetic combinations and involutions corresponding to musical compositions in tones"; and therefore a term like "color music," which one sometimes hears, generally implies a misconception of the fundamental difference between the two organs of sense, the eye and the ear.

Returning to the color equations above, let us merely notice the perfectly natural fact that blue and red blend into purple; although, strange to say, the spectrum itself does not contain any of the color blends intermediate between blue and red, a circumstance to which we shall recur (§ 237).

By a simple transposition of the four color equations which we obtained by mixing red, green and blue, we discover also several pairs of so-called *complementary colors*, each pair arousing the perfectly neutral, hueless sensation of *white*; namely,

$$\text{Red} + \text{Blue-green} = \text{Yellow} + \text{Blue} = \text{Green} + \text{Purple} = \text{White}.$$

We shall speak presently of the pairs of complementary colors in the spectrum (§ 236).

To the average person who is aware that a mixture of yellow and blue pigments is a green pigment, the fact that yellow and blue are complementary is a puzzle. Perhaps the simplest way of explaining the reason why yellow and blue pigments mix into green is by means of the following illustration:

Suppose that a continuous spectrum has been projected on a screen by a lantern in the usual way by interposing slit, prism and lens in the path of a beam of parallel rays; and that then a blue glass or celluloid filter is held in front of the slit so that most of the red, all of the yellow and some of the green light is absorbed from the beam, and consequently the continuous spectrum on the screen is changed into a narrow strip of red separated by a dark interval from a long colored band beginning somewhere in the green and extending to the extreme violet end of the spectrum. If now the blue filter is replaced by a yellow filter, the absorption spectrum is found to consist of a continuous band that stretches from the red to the border between green and bright blue. Consequently when the rays are filtered through both the yellow and the blue glass in succession, nothing but the green portion of the spectrum remains, because the green light is the only light that succeeds in getting through both filters. Obviously, green obtained in this way cannot be said to be the result of the addition of yellow to blue, but is due to the subtraction of everything except green. Now that is exactly what happens when blue and yellow pigments are mixed: all the light falling on a surface that is painted with a mixture of this kind is sifted out and absorbed except green which, being reflected by each of the pigments, escapes and so lends its color to the appearance of the mixture (p. 2). "It is a striking illustration of our mental processes," says MAXWELL, "that many persons have not only gone on believing, on the evidence of the mixture of pigments, that blue and yellow make green, but they have even persuaded themselves that they could detect the separate sensations of blueness and yellowness in the sensation of green."

235. Character and Distribution of the Spectral Colors.— The visible spectrum corresponding to luminous radiant energy is a comparatively insignificant interval of the entire spectrum, being comprised, in round numbers, between the limiting wave-lengths $\lambda = 700$ mμ and $\lambda = 400$ mμ, which is less than a whole octave. Under ordinary circumstances it appears to the normal eye as a continuous series of vivid hues or chromata, each of which is characterized, physically, by the fact that it is produced by homogeneous radiation of a single definite wave-length or frequency, that is, by so-called monochromatic light.

Because the spectral colors correspond to homogeneous radiations they are sometimes called "simple colors," as opposed to "compound colors" that are due to a mixture of lights of different wave-lengths. HELMHOLTZ himself used this terminology which has been a source of much confusion ever since. "Simple" and "compound" are relative terms of course, and just because a conception happens to be simple from one point of view is no reason why it may not be very complex from a wholly different point of view. Nothing is simple about the spectral colors themselves except the physical composition of the radiant energy that produces each of them. We have just seen that white can be obtained by mixing yellow and blue or, what is the same thing, by mixing red, green and blue, but it would be wrong to infer that white was a compound color or a complex sensation. On the contrary, there is every reason to suppose that the achromatic sensation of white is the simplest and most primitive of all the visual sensations; and in twilight vision white in different degrees of luminosity is the only response to luminous radiation of all kinds.

The expression monochromatic light, used regularly by writers on optics and by physicists generally to designate homogeneous radiation belonging to a definite part of the spectrum and characterized by a certain value of the wave-length, is likewise open to objection, inasmuch as it seems literally to imply a unitary color sensation, whereas that is not its meaning at all.

Ever since NEWTON's discovery and explanation of the phenomenon of the dispersion of light, the incidental connection between color and refrangibility or wave-length, two entirely separate affairs, one mental and the other physical, has been a source of much confusion of phraseology, as in the instances above mentioned.

The visible spectrum may be divided naturally into four intervals, namely, (1) a yellowish red section where the wave-lengths are longest, which begins, not with pure unadulterated red, but with a red at about $\lambda = 700$ mμ that is already appreciably a little yellow and blends gradually through the intervening yellowish reds and reddish yellows (orange colors) into pure yellow at, say, $\lambda = 570$ mμ; (2) a yellow-green section extending from pure yellow through greenish yellow and yellowish green to pure green lying between $\lambda = 530$ mμ and $\lambda = 500$ mμ; (3) a green-blue section from pure green through bluish green and greenish blue to pure blue at about $\lambda = 470$ mμ; and, finally, (4) a short incomplete blue-red section comprising the shortest wave-lengths between pure blue and violet ($\lambda = 400$ mμ), where the visible spectrum ends abruptly. The distribution of the colors as compared with the wave-lengths is seen, therefore, to be quite irregular. For a given change of wave-length change of hue occurs far more rapidly in the middle of the yellow-green section.

236. Complementary Spectral Colors.—Painstaking experiments have been carried out in various laboratories to determine as accurately as possible the wave-lengths (λ, λ') of pairs of complementary colors in the spectrum. Owing to the vagueness of what is meant by white, a certain standard white for ordinary daylight vision must be adopted as a basis of comparison in careful measurements of this kind, for example, the appearance of a particular kind of white paper under a certain degree of illumination. The complementary colors for the long waves from red at $\lambda = 671$ to yellow at $\lambda = 570$ mμ are found to lie at the other end of the spectrum in the interval from blue-green at $\lambda' = 492$ to violet at $\lambda' = 430$ mμ; whereas there are no spectral colors that are complementary to the greenish hues in the spectrum in the interval between $\lambda = 570$ and $\lambda = 492$ mμ. From a careful compilation of the best measurements GRÜNBERG has derived the following purely empirical formula for computing the wave-length (λ') of the spectral color that is complementary to a spectral color of given wave-length (λ):

$$(\lambda - 559)\ (498 - \lambda') = 424,$$

where λ, λ' are expressed in mμ. If the values of λ are taken as abscissæ and those of λ' as ordinates and plotted with respect to a pair of rectangular axes, the equation is found to

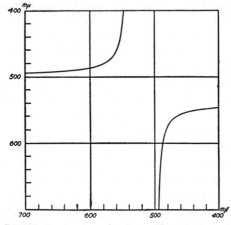

Fig. 320.—Complementary spectral colors. The curve represents the two branches of a rectangular hyperbola and shows the complementary color as a function of the wave-length for the spectral colors from 400 to 700 mμ.

represent an equilateral hyperbola whose asymptotes are $\lambda = 559$ and $\lambda' = 498$ (Fig. 320).

237. The Gap in the Visible Spectrum.—As above stated, there are no spectral colors that are complementary to the greens in the interval 570–492 mμ; for the simple reason that purple and green make white, and purple which is a color-blend of blue and red is not in the spectrum at all. This is a singular fact. The physical spectrum, ending as it does abruptly in red and violet, has a gap in it from the physiological point of view, inasmuch as it does not contain all the hues that can be perceived by the eye. When this gap is filled in by the purples, the physiological spectrum forms a closed series of hues which, starting, say, with red, blend gradually into yellow, green and blue in succession and through the purples back to red again, without the slightest break anywhere in the closely linked chain.

Accordingly if the colors of the visible spectrum are disposed in order around the circumference of a circle as represented in Fig. 321, where a single point corresponds to each wave-length from $\lambda = 700$ to $\lambda = 400$ mμ, and the op-

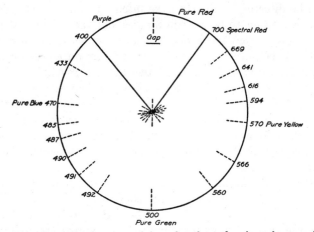

Fig. 321.—Spectral colors ranged in order along the circumference of a circle (color circle), each pair of complementary colors being at opposite ends of a diameter. The gap in the visible spectrum is represented by the (shorter) arc from 400 to 700 mμ. Pure red occurs in this gap complementary to pure green (500 mμ).

posite ends of each diameter are the positions of a pair of complementary colors, an arc of the circle will be left to be filled in by the purple blends that have no corresponding wave-numbers, simply because there are no homogeneous radiations that excite these sensations.

If the short waves in the ultraviolet region excited the purple sensations or if the long waves in the infrared region excited them, the physical spectrum would be a closed series; but neither of these kinds of waves affects the organ of vision at all so far as sensation is concerned. The only physical analogy to a closed spectrum is supplied in a case where, as in dispersion by means of a grating, the red end of a spectrum of one order partly overlaps the blue end of a spectrum of the next higher order, thereby giving the transition purples from blue back to red.

It should be noticed that pure red is not in the visible spectrum itself but in the physiological gap. The yellowishness of spectral red can be made manifest in several ways, for example, by the plainly increasing yellowishness that can be discerned in it when the intensity is increased. The important fact to be kept in mind about the colors that lie in the gap is that the perfectly elementary sensation of pure red and the purple sensations cannot be produced except by a physical mixture of at least two lights. Psychologically, there is nothing peculiar about these so-called extra-spectral hues, which are color-blends exactly in the same way as the hues between two adjacent pure colors in the visible spectrum; and the only extraordinary thing about them is the physical complexity of the mixture that is needed to evoke these color sensations.

238. Hue, Saturation and Luminosity.—Looking at a wide expanse of uniform color, we are conscious of a visual sensation without being able adequately to describe it; but if we analyze it as best we can and try to express the quality of it in scientific language, we find (as all artists know instinctively) that it involves three, and only three, independent variables, namely, *hue, saturation* and *luminosity* or brightness; and that if the values of each of these three factors can be assigned, the color in question will be uniquely and completely determined.

Hue or color-tone is color in the narrow sense as implied by such terms as redness, yellowness, blueness, etc. The colors of the spectrum, for example, are a continuous series of different hues, although it does not contain all possible hues because the purples, as we have just seen, for some reason or other are not in the visible spectrum. The human eye can distinguish perhaps not more than 130 different hues in the spectrum.

Saturation is the degree of purity of the color; the paler

it is, the less saturated. Sometimes we have special names for these pale colors; thus pink is an unsaturated or pale purple. If a series of colors all of the same hue is arranged in order of saturation, the last member of such a series is invariably a toneless white without any trace of the original hue. The most saturated natural colors are the spectral colors themselves.

Luminosity is the brilliance of a color and depends on the illumination. Colors of low luminosity are said to be dark. The difference of color between the bright-green grass of a sun-lit lawn and the dark-green grass under the shade of a tree is a difference of brightness only. Brown, olive-green and gray are merely low luminosities of orange, green and white. In an orderly sequence of colors differing in luminosity only the series invariably ends in black or entire absence of luminosity. Black is a real, positive sensation, just as much so as any other visual sensation. It is true that the "perfectly black body" in the theory of radiation does not send any stimulus to the retina of the eye, but absence of radiation does not necessarily imply lack of sensation. If blackness were simply absence of all sensation, that is, a purely negative thing, the objects behind our eyes ought to look black; which is absurd of course. The darkest night is not black but only a very dark gray, and it is not until light dawns that we begin to distinguish black in contrast with white.

Thus the totality of all the colors that can possibly be seen is a 3-dimensional manifold; which accordingly might be represented geometrically by any solid body, for example, by a pyramid or perhaps more conveniently by a cone in which the apex O was the point of total darkness or absence of luminosity. Each position of the generating line on the surface of the cone might correspond to one of the spectral or purple hues in every degree of luminosity along this line; whereas a line drawn from the apex into the interior of the cone would correspond then to a more or less pale variety of a saturated hue, and the axis of the cone would represent white in all degrees of brightness. Thus every possible color would be represented by a point on the surface of the cone or in the interior; and the vector OP drawn from the apex to the point P in question would be perfectly unique. Obviously, three points A, B, C on the surface of the cone may be taken in countless ways so that the sum of the vectors OA, OB and OC is equal to OP; and consequently the color P may be considered as a mixture of three saturated colors A, B, C in proper proportions.

In NEWTON's color chart the saturated hues were ranged in order around the circumference of a circle with white at the center, in a manner similar to Fig. 321. In effect this color circle is nothing more nor less than a section of the color cone. A plane chart is useful and convenient, but it necessarily leaves out one of the three dimensions, as, for example, the luminosity. YOUNG's triangle of colors, which is the best of all these devices, must be described in more detail.

239. The Color Triangle.—If three standard colors are chosen such that no mixture of two of them together is equivalent to the third, in general any fourth color (C) may be obtained by mixing them in proper proportions. This is a well-established experimental fact; which, if the standard colors are, let us say, red (R), green (G), and blue or violet (V), may be expressed in the form of a color equation as follows:

$$C = x_1\ R + x_2\ G + x_3\ V,$$

where the numbers denoted by x_1, x_2, x_3, called the color valences or color coördinates of C, are the relative amounts of R, G and V in the mixture. The absolute values of these numbers are immaterial; it is the ratios $x_1 : x_2 : x_3$ that are important. If the equation is to be perfectly general, negative values of the coördinates must not be excluded; and in fact if the four colors concerned are all spectral colors, one of the three color coördinates will always be found to be negative, and in that case the corresponding term must be transposed to the other side of the equation. For example, when x_3 is negative, the interpretation is that, in order to make a perfect color match with the color obtained by a mixture of spectral red and green in certain proportions, a definite amount of spectral violet must be added to the spectral color C (which in this case would be yellow). However, it is always possible, theoretically at any rate, to choose the standard colors so that x_1, x_2, x_3 will invariably be all positive.

These relations may be exhibited graphically in various ways, most simply and naturally by means of the color cone, but perhaps most conveniently by means of the *color triangle* (Fig. 322), in which the standard colors R, G, V are placed at the corners of a triangle, an equilateral triangle being best, although a triangle of any form will serve the purpose. So far as hue and saturation are concerned, any color (C) may be represented by a point P lying in the plane of the triangle, provided its trilinear coördinates as measured by the perpendicular distances of P from the sides of the triangle GV, VR, RG are equal or proportional to the color coördinates x_1, x_2, x_3, respectively. If the point P lies inside the triangle, x_1, x_2, x_3 are all positive, and conversely. If one of the coördinates vanishes, the point P will be found on one of the sides of the triangle, namely, in GV when $x_1 = 0$, in VR when $x_2 = 0$, and in RG when $x_3 = 0$. Obviously, all three of the coördinates cannot vanish at the same time. In the special case when $x_1 = x_2 = x_3$, that is, when $x_1 : x_2 : x_3 = 1 : 1 : 1$, the color is white (W). Thus the amounts of R, G, V that are required to make standard white will determine the unit quantum of each of these colors.

On the assumption that the three component colors R, G, V have been chosen so as to exclude negative values of any one of the color coördinates, all possible colors (so far as hue and saturation are concerned) will be contained within the border of the triangle, and the spectral colors will be ranged in sequence along a curved line, as shown in the case represented in Fig. 322. A short portion of this line corresponding to the red end of the spectrum lies along the side RG. The point W corresponding to white is in the center

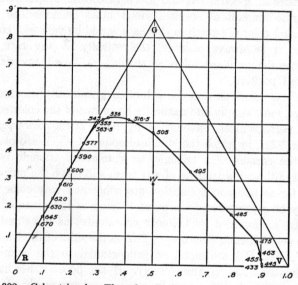

Fig. 322.—Color triangle. The colors R, G, V at the three corners of the triangle are so-called fundamental red, green and violet (hypothetical colors). The curved line is the locus of the spectral colors and in the red portion it follows closely part of the side RG of the triangle. The white point W lies in the center of the equilateral triangle RGV. A straight line drawn through W will intersect the spectral curve or the side of the triangle RV (where the purples lie) in two points corresponding to pairs of complementary colors. The part of such a straight line comprised between the point W and the spectral color corresponds to the different degrees of saturation of the spectral hue.

of the equilateral triangle between the spectral curve and the side RV on which the saturated purples lie. The saturation of a color is measured by its distance from W; and since the spectral colors are the most saturated of all real colors, all degrees of saturation of a given spectral hue will be shown by points on a straight line drawn from W to the corresponding point on the spectral curve. If this straight line extended in the opposite direction meets the spectral curve in another point, the two spectral colors determined by this chord are complementary.

On the other hand, if the three standard colors are spectral red, spectral green and spectral violet, the curve of spectral colors RGV will lie outside the color triangle RGV, with white again in the center of the equilateral triangle. If we mix spectral red and spectral green so as to obtain yellow lying on the side RG, this yellow will not be quite as saturated as the same hue of spectral yellow; and, generally, the colors along the two sides RG and GV will be paler than the spectral colors of the same hues.

240. Note concerning Homogeneous Projective Coördinates.—The color coördinates x_1, x_2, x_3 used to determine the position of a point in the color triangle are indeed a system of homogeneous projective coördinates, as they are called in geometry. The absolute values of these numbers are of no importance, and they may all be multiplied by any common factor, because this will not affect the ratios $x_1 : x_2 : x_3$, and the position of the point P is determined, not by the numbers themselves, but by their mutual ratios. A brief explanation may help the student to form a clear notion of what is meant by the homogeneous projective coördinates of a point in a plane.

In the accompanying diagram (Fig. 323) the letters A, B, C and W designate four fixed points all in one plane no three of which are on one straight line; and accordingly the straight lines CW, AW and BW will determine three fixed points D, E and F lying on the sides AB, BC and CA, respectively, of the triangle ABC. Through any other point P in the plane of the triangle draw CP, AP and BP meeting AB, BC and CA in the points X, Y and Z, respectively. Thus each side of the triangle ABC contains four points, three of which are fixed, whereas the fourth depending on the position of P is variable. Consequently the three double ratios (§ 65)

$$(ABDX) = \frac{AD}{BD} : \frac{AX}{BX}, \ (BCEY) = \frac{BE}{CE} : \frac{BY}{CY}, \ (CAFZ) = \frac{CF}{AF} : \frac{CZ}{AZ},$$

will be variable likewise.

According to a famous theorem of plane geometry known as CEVA's law, the segments into which the sides of the

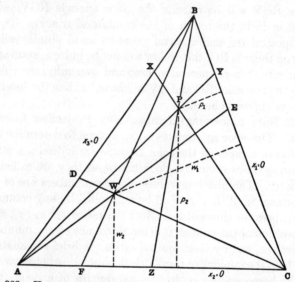

FIG. 323.—Homogeneous projective coördinates (trilinear coördinates). ABC is triangle of reference with a fixed point W (so-called unit-point) inside the triangle. P marks the position of any other point in the plane of the diagram. The dotted lines p_1, p_2 and w_1, w_2 drawn from P and W are perpendicular to the sides BC ($x_1 = 0$) and AC ($x_2 = 0$).

triangle ABC are divided in one case by the points D, E and F and in the other case by the points X, Y and Z are connected by the following simple relations:

$$\frac{AD}{BD} \cdot \frac{BE}{EC} \cdot \frac{CF}{FA} = \frac{AX}{XB} \cdot \frac{BY}{YC} \cdot \frac{CZ}{ZA} = 1;$$

and consequently, no matter where the point P happens to be located in the plane of the triangle ABC, the product of the three double ratios above mentioned will invariably be equal to unity, and therefore all we need to know in order to determine the position of P in any particular case are the values of two of the double ratios. Thus we may put

$$x_1 : x_2 = (\text{ABDX}), \quad x_2 : x_3 = (\text{BCEY}), \quad x_3 : x_1 = (\text{CAFZ}),$$

where x_1, x_2, x_3 are any three numbers whose ratios are thus defined; the only condition being that all three of these numbers cannot be equal to zero at the same time, and therefore at least two of the ratios $x_1 : x_2$, $x_2 : x_3$, $x_3 : x_1$ must have finite values for every possible position of the point P. Thus being given the fixed points of reference A, B, C and W and the three numbers x_1, x_2, x_3, two of the points X, Y and Z can certainly be located, and so the point P can be found as the point of intersection of one pair of the concurrent lines AX, BY and CZ. The three numbers x_1, x_2, x_3 are called the homogeneous projective coördinates of the point P with respect to the triangle of reference ABC and the so-called unit-point W. The fixed point W is called the unit-point of the system of coördinates, because when P coincides with W, $(\text{ABDX}) = (\text{BCEY}) = (\text{CAFZ}) = 1$, that is, $x_1 : x_2 : x_3 = 1 : 1 : 1$. The coördinates of W are therefore all equal $(x_1 = x_2 = x_3)$.

If one of the coördinates (x_1, x_2, x_3) is equal to zero, the point P will lie on one of the sides of the triangle of reference; on BC if $x_1 = 0$, on CA if $x_2 = 0$, and on AB if $x_3 = 0$. The coördinates of the vertices of the triangle are A $(x_1, 0, 0)$, B $(0, x_2, 0)$ and C $(0, 0, x_3)$ or $(1, 0, 0)$, $(0, 1, 0)$ and $(0, 0, 1)$, respectively, since the numerical value of the coördinate that does not vanish at one of the vertices of the triangle may be put equal to any number as unity, for instance.

We proceed now to show that the homogeneous projective coördinates x_1, x_2, x_3 are in fact equivalent to the so-called *trilinear coördinates* (x_1', x_2', x_3') of the point P. If w_1, w_2, w_3 and p_1, p_2, p_3 are the lengths of the perpendiculars let fall from W and P on the sides of the triangle BC, CA and AB, respectively, the trilinear coördinates of P are defined as follows:

$$x_1' = \frac{p_1}{w_1}, \qquad x_2' = \frac{p_2}{w_2}, \qquad x_3' = \frac{p_3}{w_3}.$$

Evidently (Fig. 323),

$$\frac{p_2}{p_1} = \frac{\sin \angle \text{XCA}}{\sin \angle \text{BCX}}, \qquad \frac{w_2}{w_1} = \frac{\sin \angle \text{DCA}}{\sin \angle \text{BCD}}.$$

Now if we put $k = \sin B : \sin A$, then (as may also be easily obtained from the diagram by the law of sines)

$$\frac{\text{AD}}{\text{BD}} = k.\frac{\sin \angle \text{DCA}}{\sin \angle \text{BCD}} = k.\frac{w_2}{w_1},$$

$$\frac{\text{AX}}{\text{BX}} = k.\frac{\sin \angle \text{XCA}}{\sin \angle \text{BCX}} = k.\frac{p_2}{p_1};$$

and hence

$$\frac{\text{AD}}{\text{BD}} : \frac{\text{AX}}{\text{BX}} = \frac{w_2}{w_1} : \frac{p_2}{p_1},$$

or

$$(\text{ABDX}) = \frac{p_1}{w_1} : \frac{p_2}{w_2}.$$

Similarly, we find:

$$(\text{BCEY}) = \frac{p_2}{w_2} : \frac{p_3}{w_3}, \qquad (\text{CAFZ}) = \frac{p_3}{w_3} : \frac{p_1}{w_1}.$$

Consequently,

$$x_1 : x_2 : x_3 = \frac{p_1}{w_1} : \frac{p_2}{w_2} : \frac{p_3}{w_3} = x_1' : x_2' : x_3';$$

and therefore the homogeneous projective coördinates of P are shown to be perfectly equivalent to the trilinear coordinates.

241. The Young-Helmholtz Three-Components Color Theory.—In 1807 (three years before GOETHE published his *Farbenlehre* or "doctrine of colors" in which he ridiculed NEWTON's conception of white as the combination of all the colors of the spectrum and even disputed some of the ex-

perimental facts), THOMAS YOUNG (1773–1829) tentatively
proposed an original theory of color vision * which, however,
attracted little notice at the time and might have been almost
forgotten if it had not been revived many years later by
MAXWELL (1831–1879) in England and adopted by HELM-
HOLTZ (1822–1894) in Germany. Today it is generally known
as the YOUNG-HELMHOLTZ theory. It is sometimes called
a trichromatic theory of vision because it is based on the
assumption that the eye is capable of feeling directly three,
and only three, independent elementary or fundamental
color sensations, namely, red, green and violet (or blue); and
consequently that all the visible colors are merely combinations in varying proportions of these essential constituent
elements. Each one of the visual cells of the color mechanism
of the retina or, to be specific, let us say each of the cones
(although in reality we know little or nothing of their *modus
operandi*) is supposed to contain three nerve-receptors or
fibers; which, on being stimulated by the impact of homogeneous radiation, arouse the three fundamental color sensations in different degrees depending primarily on the wave-
length of the light. In general, the red-sensitive mechanism
is affected most by the longer waves, comparatively little by
the shorter waves; whereas it is just the reverse with the
violet-sensitive mechanism which responds most to the
shorter waves and not much or hardly at all to the longer
waves; while the green-sensitive mechanism, being intermediate between the other two, is not affected much by
either the long or the short waves but responds most to the

---

* "As a matter of fact, YOUNG's contributions to the theory of color
vision are limited to two or three short paragraphs in his voluminous
writings, and there is no evidence that he attached very much importance to them himself." See THOMAS YOUNG Oration on "YOUNG's
theory of color vision (1801–1931)" by Sir JOHN H. PARSONS, *Trans.
Opt. Soc.*, XXXII, 165–185. This is an excellent critique of the present
status (1932) of the three-components theory and should be consulted
by all who wish to obtain a clear idea of the arguments for and against
the theory.

middle of the spectrum. According to the best determinations by the method of "gauging the spectrum," the maxima of the red-sensitive, green-sensitive and violet-sensitive receptors apparently correspond to wave-lengths of about 570, 550 and 455 mμ, respectively; as shown by the so-called "fundamental-sensation curves" (Fig. 324) derived from ex-

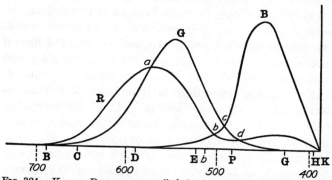

Fig. 324.—KOENIG-DIETERICI so-called fundamental-sensation curves R, G and B (as corrected by EXNER), which are supposed to give the spectral distribution of the three so-called fundamental color sensations. The actual forms of these curves are really quite arbitrary depending on the way the experimental determinations are evaluated numerically. These curves have been a subject of much controversy, and they have been given greater significance than was attached to them by the original investigators themselves.

perimental data obtained by matching the spectral colors with mixtures of red, green and blue.* But no matter what the wave-length of the homogeneous radiation is, each mechanism makes some response, strong, moderate or feeble

---

* These much discussed curves which seem to lend support to the three-components theory should not be taken too seriously. They are derived from the experimental data by perfectly legitimate mathematical transformations, but the interpretation of the data is open to question, and according to the assumptions that are made at the outset the forms of the curves will be quite different. KOENIG and DIETERICI who were the first to obtain curves of this kind were careful not to attach too much importance to them. The name "fundamental-sensation" curves begs the whole question.

as the case may be, the total sensation being the resultant of these three components. Thus according to the theory the only way that an eye can ever see one of the fundamental colors themselves would be when for some reason two of the three receptors of normal color vision were lacking or atrophied, and then everything would be seen in one color only, more dimly in some cases than in others, and the vision would be monochromatic in the literal sense.

The solid basis of the theory consists in the incontrovertible experimental facts of color-mixing; and so far as this part of the theory is concerned, it is hardly to be considered a theory at all, but rather a formulation of the observed facts. If the three standard colors of the color triangle RGV are the hypothetical colors, fundamental red (R), fundamental green (G) and fundamental violet (V), all real colors will be contained within the triangle (Fig. 322).

We have seen that there are three, and only three, different and independent ways in which a sensation of color can be modified and that therefore if two colors have the same hue, saturation and luminosity, it is impossible to tell them apart. In this case both colors will correspond to the same point P of the color cone and will be represented by the same vector OP drawn from the apex of the cone at O to the point P. Since the vector OP is a function of three variables, it seems logical to conclude that the physiological process set in motion by the stimulation of the organ of vision by external radiant energy must itself be a complex of not more than three essential characteristics that determine the nature of the resultant sensation; and that each of these characteristics must in some way be a definite function of the color coördinates as ascertained by careful and precise measurements in which practically the same results are obtained by different practised observers. Moreover, the ascertained facts concerning congenital partial color-blindness (dichromatic vision as distinguished from normal or trichromatic vision) may apparently be explained to a large extent

in accordance with the YOUNG-HELMHOLTZ theory simply
by assuming that the so-called anopic eye is lacking in one
of the three hypothetical fundamental-sensation receptors,
and that consequently the color-manifold of partially color-
blind vision has only two dimensions.   Actually, we do find
just three types of anopes, red-blind, green-blind and blue-
blind (although the last mentioned is such an exceedingly
rare and unusual type that its occurrence is open to doubt).
On the other hand, there are many outstanding problems
in connection with dichromatic vision that have still to be
solved before we are in a position to say that the facts
unequivocally lend support to the YOUNG-HELMHOLTZ theory.

When we come to consider the actual tri-receptor mechanism itself, the ground of the theory is far less secure. Various
conjectures and physiological hypotheses have been offered
to account for the three-components processes, some of them
highly ingenious in conception but none of them deserving
to be taken too seriously. Thus, for example, we may mention the following suggestions: (1) three different nerve-
terminals or even three types of nerve-cells whose maxima
of excitation correspond to three places in the spectrum;
(2) three kinds of resonators tuned to respond to three
different wave-lengths of light; and (3) photo-electric or
photo-chemical processes of one kind or another. Not the
slightest positive evidence can be adduced for any of this
elaborate apparatus in the living eye, and so far as this part
of the YOUNG-HELMHOLTZ theory is concerned, it lacks
confirmation.

What is considered by the opponents of the theory to
be an insuperable objection is that it asks us to believe that
the sensation of white which contains no trace of redness,
greenness or blueness is in fact a mixture of red, green and
blue in equal proportions; whereas according to these critics
white is to be considered as the simplest and most primitive
form of visual sensation (§ 235). If white is a mixture of red,

green and blue, they ask how can we account for the achromatic vision of twilight illumination, for colorless rod
vision in the outer parts of the retina, and for totally color-
blind vision. In spite of the experimental facts of color-
mixing, it must be admitted it is difficult to find a satisfactory reply to this objection.

242. Hering's Opponent-Colors Theory. The rival theory
of E. HERING (1834–1918) is diametrically opposed to HELM-
HOLTZ's theory of vision at all points, owing to the fact that
the mental attitudes of these two philosophers towards the
phenomena were radically divergent from the start. Whereas
"HELMHOLTZ deemed it illegitimate or at least untrustworthy
to draw conclusions as to physiological processes from the
direct psychological character of the sensations" (v. KRIES)
and preferred therefore to rely as far as possible on the concrete facts of color-mixing, etc., for HERING it was the actual
sensations themselves, not so much their physical or physiological antecedents, that constituted the real facts and the
immediate data. Accordingly HERING stoutly insisted that
the sensation of light was not just merely a function of the
external stimulus and of the adaptation of the organ of vision
for the time being, but that it was also linked with the visual
center of the brain where the optical experiences of many
years were recorded and, so to speak, systematized and co-
ordinated. The tone of a violin depends not only on the
vibrations of the bowed string but on the resonance and
mellowness of the whole instrument; and so likewise in
HERING's view the impression of color is not just an affair
of the impact of luminous radiation and the stimulation of
certain sensitive cells in the retina but is the concomitant
result of the reverberations of the whole sensorium. From
the psychological point of view color is neither the property
of an external object nor of the radiation that proceeds from
it, but is a content of consciousness, an aspect of vision, not
determined by the external surroundings merely or chiefly
or by the nervous mechanism itself, but consisting of the

reproductions of former experiences awakened by a host of concurrent circumstances.

In HERING's theory a quite special importance is attached to the gray series of *toneless or hueless sensations* ranging all the way from black to white. Nobody with normal color sense can deny that, psychologically, the number of so-called pure, simple or primary chromata (toned colors) is four, and not three, namely, red and green, yellow and blue. Whatever may be true of yellow in a physical sense, mentally it certainly is not a mixture of red and green any more than white is a mixture of red and bluish-green. A red may be yellowish but never greenish; and similarly a yellow may be greenish but never bluish. Thus according to HERING red and green, yellow and blue are two pairs of incompatibles or opponent-colors (*Gegenfarben*).

From the standpoint of physiology the essential characteristic of living tissue is constant replenishment and change of organic substance; some substances being taken in and incorporated by a process of assimilation on the one hand, foreign substances arising and being thrown off by a process of dissimilation on the other hand. The two processes, always intimately interconnected, occur simultaneously even in the smallest subdivisions of the organism. Thus in the nervous mechanism of the visual organ, either in the retina itself or possibly somewhere nearer the brain (zonal theory of vision), HERING's theory assumes that there are three kinds of 2-way processes, namely, the black-white, the red-green and the yellow-blue, generally occurring simultaneously in opposite directions. In one direction the process is *assimilative* (A-effect) and is accompanied by renewal and regeneration of the nervous substance; in the other direction it is *dissimilative* (D-effect) involving decomposition and breaking down of this substance. The ratios between A and D in each of the processes are the factors that determine the resultant sensation.

The black-white process is peculiar as compared with

the other two. Stimulated by luminous radiation of any kind, this process invariably acts in one direction only, D-effect (whiteness); but if no luminous energy enters the eye, the process acts automatically in the reverse direction, A-effect (darkness).

Luminous radiation of any kind promotes the red-green and yellow-blue processes in definite degrees or *valences* in

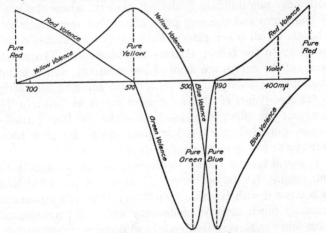

FIG. 325.—HERING'S valence spectral curves.

one direction or the other, depending on the nature of the radiation. Thus the long waves from red to pure yellow have a D-effect (red) on the red-green process, and from red to pure green a D-effect (yellow) on the yellow-blue process; whereas the short waves from pure yellow to pure blue have an A-effect (green) on the red-green process, but from pure blue to violet a D-effect (red); and the short waves from pure green to violet have an A-effect (blue) on the yellow-blue process. The red-green process remains in equilibrium $(A = D)$ under the action of pure yellow or of pure blue, the resultant sensation being neither red nor green; and, similarly, the yellow-blue process is unaffected by either pure red or pure green, the resultant sensation being neither yellow nor blue.

When $A = D$ for both processes, an achromatic sensation is the result.

The accompanying diagram (Fig. 325) is a purely schematic representation of the red-green and yellow-blue valence curves according to HERING's opponent-colors theory. Within the interval from $\lambda = 700$ to $\lambda = 400$ mμ corresponding to the series of hues in the visible spectrum, there are three places with only one ordinate (valence), namely, where the peak of one curve and the zero-point of another occur together; whereas at all other places there are two ordinates corresponding to the binary mixture of two colors. The actual forms of the curves are more or less arbitrary, and it is not absolutely necessary for the peak of one curve to be exactly at the zero-points of two of the other curves as shown in the diagram; the effect of which is to make the four turning-points, pure red, pure yellow, pure green and pure blue, correspond to the maxima of the valence curves.

It would take us too far to discuss here the arguments for and against HERING's theory. It should be admitted that as compared with HELMHOLTZ's theory HERING's attitude is certainly much more in conformity with the psychological color-order as perceived directly, and perhaps for that reason his theory is better adapted for a survey of the sensations that come to the consciousness of anybody who has normal color sense. Thus, for example, artists generally are disposed to be in agreement with HERING's mode of explanation. In the main his theory accounts quite satisfactorily for the facts of color-mixing and for many other color phenomena; but where it seems to be weakest is in its wholly unsatisfactory explanations of the anomalies of the color sense and especially the disorders of partial color-blindness; and here at least the HELMHOLTZ theory certainly offers a more natural and consistent explanation. Some of the main objections to HERING's original theory were overcome by G. E. MÜLLER's modification and extension of it. HERING's conceptions and ideas are still very much alive and current especially among psychologists and physiologists; whereas physicists are apt to prefer the HELMHOLTZ theory. Unfortunately, the adherents of one theory do not always seem to appreciate the objections that are urged against their view by the other side, and so in a discussion of color theories there is sometimes much misapprehension and misrepresentation of the opposite point of view. Until we know much more than we know at present about the morphological and chemical subdivisions of the retina and about the action of luminous radiation, no color theory, trichromatic (HELMHOLTZ) or tetrachromatic (HERING), can be said to have any really firm basis.

V. *Perception of Depth in Binocular (Stereoscopic) Vision*

243. Monocular Field of View (Eye at Rest).—In ordinary daylight vision when the gaze is fixed intently on a small luminous area in the field of view, this spot is sharply focused on the retina in a tiny oval depression not far from the center called the yellow spot or *macula lutea* (p. 428) where the cones are greatly in excess of the rods and where the keenest visual discriminations are possible. This most sensitive part of the retina in bright illumination, which is not more than about one or two millimeters in diameter and corresponds therefore to an angular width of less than 7° in the external field of view, lies a little to the temporal side of the point where the optical axis meets the retina and also slightly below this point. The place of most distinct vision is at the very center of the little depression in the *fovea centralis* or *foveola*, which corresponds to the *point of fixation* in the field of view where the spectator's attention is riveted for the time being.

As compared with almost any artificial optical instrument, the field of view of the motionless human eye is unusually large, having a horizontal extent of about 160° (considerably more outwards than inwards where the field is curtailed by the protrusion of the nose) and a vertical range of 70° downwards and 50° upwards. However, the excentric and peripheral parts of the field corresponding to the outer and less sensitive regions of the retina are perceived more or less vaguely and indistinctly; and hence, so far as the visual impression is concerned, the field of view of the stationary eye may be compared to a perspective picture in which the details in the center are very accurately and finely executed as in a steel engraving, whereas the surroundings have been left unfinished and roughly sketched as in a charcoal drawing. Accordingly when the gaze is kept steady, a distinction must be made between central or *direct vision* and peripheral or *indirect vision*, that is, between "cone vision" and "rod vision" under conditions of ordinary daylight illumination.

244. Field of Fixation of the Mobile Eye.—As a matter of fact the gaze is seldom kept riveted on one spot for any long interval of time, but the eye roams from place to place in quick succession and scans the entire *field of fixation*, which is considerably more extensive than the visual globe of the passive eye. In executing these movements the eye-ball turns readily in its socket under the control of a mechanism of three pairs of motor muscles (p. 431) that are extraordinarily efficient for the purpose. Acting in perfect harmony and with the utmost precision, these muscles turn the eye-ball around a fixed (geometrical) pivot called the *center of rotation* of the eye which may be considered as lying on the optical axis about 13 mm. beyond the vertex of the cornea and therefore not far from the geometrical center of the eye-ball (p. 432). A *line of fixation* is a straight line drawn through the center of rotation of the eye to the point of fixation at the time. The field of fixation of the mobile eye has a horizontal range of about 180°, that is, about 135° outwardly from the median plane which divides the face symmetrically in two opposite halves, and about 45° inwardly on the other side of this plane.

Just as we imagine the vault of the starry sky overhead, so also we naturally think of the field of fixation as being part of a globe surrounding the center of the eye with the objects of vision distributed over its surface. Inasmuch as distance cannot be discerned by monocular vision alone, the radius of this imaginary globe is entirely indefinite and unimportant. In the natural consciousness of the spectator the retina of his eye has no existence whatever. It is none of his business if the image on the retina is inverted, because he is not even so much as aware that any image has been formed or what an optical image is. All that he sees and appreciates are the outward tokens of these inner relations, that is, the superficial projections of the retinal images in his field of view. Ever since he can first remember, these have been familiar appearances, mental pictures which by long and varied experience he has learned to associate with actual things, solid material objects, in the external world. Yet after years of daily observations and almost incessant training, he is liable still to optical illusions and sometimes discovers, much to his bewilderment, that his eyes have deceived him and that what he took to be real is only a mirage.

245. Field of Binocular Fixation.—But man is not dependent on one eye alone; like all other animals, he has two eyes which can be moved in unison without turning the head and directed voluntarily towards any desired point in the field of binocular fixation. The team-work between the two eyes is as precise and admirable as everything else in the complex mechanism of vision. When both eyes are concentrated on a single point of fixation, an image of it is focused on the retina of each eye in the *fovea centralis*, and the two images are *fused* in one mental impression, exactly how nobody can tell. One eye never turns by itself, but the two always move in concert, in one of two ways or usually in a combination of both ways (p. 431). When the eyes turn from looking at one place to look at another place at the same distance but in a different direction, they are said to execute *associated movements;* that is, both eyes turn the same way, sideways to the right or to the left, vertically up or down, or one way or the other in some oblique meridian. On the other hand, when, gazing steadily in a certain direction, the eyes turn to look at another point at a different distance, they execute *movements of convergence;* that is, the two eyes turn in opposite directions, either towards each other when the second point of fixation is nearer than the first or away from each other when the second point of fixation is farther than the first. In general, when the point of fixation is displaced, the variation involves change of both distance and direction, and in that case the movements of the two eyes are convergent and associated at the same time.

The fields of fixation of the two eyes overlap to a certain extent in a common *binocular field* that lies directly in front of the face. This is the region where the two hands come into play in nearly all ordinary human occupations, and here perhaps the sense of touch can aid and corroborate the indications of the sense of sight. Nearly all our judgments and conclusions are the result of a coöperation of this kind between several modes of sensation. In a human being the two eyes are located just below the forehead on either side of the bridge of the nose, and the horizontal extent of the binocular field is about 90°, that is, 45° on each side of the median plane of the face. In most other animals the two eyes are not so much in front but more over on the two sides of the head, and consequently the binocular field is much more restricted, although it always lies in the region in front of the face. Apparently the overlapping binocular field of a dog does not exceed 34° horizontally; that of a chicken is perhaps less than half as much, say 15°; and that of a fish in water probably cannot be more than about 5°. The optic axis of the eye of a goose is normally nearly perpendicular to the median plane, and doubtless with one eye or the other this fowl can command a total field of 360° without turning its head, but its binocular field must be exceedingly narrow.

A striking optical illusion of binocular double vision, described first by W. B. ROGERS (1805–1882), can be obtained by holding a tube of black paper (about 12 inches long and 2 inches in diameter) close in front of the right eye and looking through the tube at a lighted lamp in the opposite corner of the room. If under these circumstances the spectator screens his left eye from the light by interposing a sheet of paper near the far end of the tube between this eye and the light that is seen through the tube by the right eye, he gets the illusion of looking at a light through a round hole in the paper where there is no hole at all.

246. Binocular Perception of Depth.—Each eye separately affords a perspective view of an object in front of it, but since the two eyes do not occupy exactly the same place but are on opposite sides of the face, the two copies of the object projected from these different points of view will be slightly different also, unless the object is exactly alike no matter how it is presented to the eye. We need not linger to inquire how the two images are fused mentally into a single stereoscopic impression; it is a fact of experience well known to everybody. That the images in the two eyes are really different, can be easily verified by holding a pencil at arm's length and looking at it with one eye at a time, alternately. If it is viewed first by the right eye with the left eye closed, and then by the left eye with the right eye closed, the image will be very perceptibly displaced to the right.

Without moving the head, all that we can tell by monocular vision is the *direction* in which the point of fixation lies, just as we can point to a star and, if necessary, give its right ascension and declination, that is, two dimensions in space; but binocular vision affords at least a possibility of determining the third dimension also, that is, the *distance* of the point of fixation, provided the requisite data are sufficiently accurate and can be conveniently employed. Long ago LEONARDO DA VINCI (1452–1519) in his treatise on painting remarked that not even the most perfect pictorial representation on canvas can give a plastic impression similar to that of the original objects themselves, because the two retinal images of the flat picture are exactly alike, whereas the perspective view of the natural objects as seen by one eye is not quite the same as that presented to the other eye. Of course if the objects are all very far away, there is practically no difference whatever between their appearances in the two eyes. Thus the accuracy of binocular judgment of distance diminishes with increase of distance.

247. Stereoscopic Vision.—The keenness and accuracy of binocular perception of solidity or depth is shown very

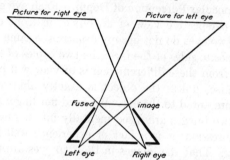

Fig. 326.—Depth perception: simple stereoscope without mirrors or lenses.

convincingly by so-called stereoscopic views or double pictures of an object representing it in somewhat different aspects. If the two pictures are mounted side by side on one card so as to form a stereogram, as it is sometimes called, generally they will be so much alike that on being viewed in the ordinary way it is doubtful whether the differences will be noticed at all; but if a small screen is held in the median plane between the two eyes so that each eye can see only the picture that is intended for it, then almost immediately the two pictures will be fused into a single plastic impression from which all the flatness has disappeared, and the effect of the third dimension (depth) is so vivid in some instances as to be almost startling. The plan of a simple device for viewing stereograms, involving nothing but a box of peculiar shape with two peep-holes for the eyes, is shown in Fig. 326. This is the principle of the *mirror stereo-scope* first invented by WHEATSTONE (1802–1875) nearly a century ago (1838), which is shown diagrammatically in Fig. 327. The simple apparatus consists essentially of a pair of plane mirrors, one in front of each eye, which are inclined to each other at an angle of 270°. The two halves of the stereogram are separated and placed opposite each other so that the line joining the centers of the two pictures is bisected

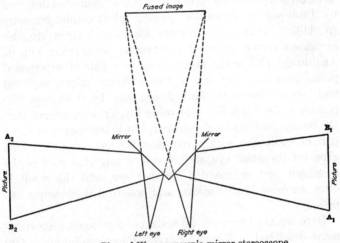

FIG. 327.—Plan of WHEATSTONE's mirror stereoscope.

perpendicularly by the median plane between the two eyes. When the spectator looks in the instrument, he sees with his right eye an image AB of the picture A_1B_1 in the mirror on that side, and with his left eye an overlapping image AB of the picture A_2B_2 in the mirror opposite that eye. In order for the two images to be fused properly so as to give a correct stereoscopic impression, the pictures must be inserted in the frames reversed with respect to each other, that is, so that the two corresponding horizontal lines A_1B_1, A_2B_2 are in opposite directions. Even so, the fused stereoscopic image will be "perverted" (p. 39) as compared with the original

object itself, as is always the case with an image in a single
plane mirror; but this disadvantage of a mirror stereoscope
can be compensated without much difficulty, either by first
"perverting" the pictures themselves or by suitably inserting a second mirror on each side of the instrument.

The *lens stereoscope* of BREWSTER (1781–1868), which came
into general use about 1850, is a more convenient type, especially in its modern form in which the prismatic lenses
have been replaced by so-called "Verant" lenses as designed
by Professor v. ROHR for viewing photographs correctly
(p. 418). Besides the ordinary stereoscope there are also
numerous clever devices for obtaining stereoscopic effects.
An "anaglyph" is the name given to a pair of superposed
prints reproduced in ink of two different colors, say, red
and blue. Viewed in the ordinary way by both eyes, the
picture looks much like any other line-drawing except that
the outlines are curiously colored; but if the spectator has a
pair of spectacles with a red glass for one eye and a blue
glass for the other eye, each eye sees only that part of the
anaglyph that is intended for that eye, and the result is
often an exceedingly striking and beautiful stereoscopic impression.

Here we may mention an instructive stereoscopic experiment described in ROBERT SMITH's *Compleat System of Opticks*, § 977, which requires no apparatus except an ordinary
pair of compasses. The latter should be held at some little
distance in front of the face, pointed vertically upward at
first, and then opened until the interval between the tips
of the two legs is about equal to the interpupillary distance
between the eyes. If the spectator gazes past this interval
at a point on the opposite wall of the room (or through a
window at a distant object outside), he will see at first two
images of each prong forming a figure like the old-fashioned
capital letter W; then as the angular opening between the
two legs is gradually reduced, the two inner points will
approach each other, and at the instant when they unite,

"the two inner legs will also entirely coincide and bisect the angle under the outward ones; and will appear more vivid, thicker and longer than they do, so as to reach from your hand to the remotest object in view, even in the horizon itself, if the points be exactly coincident." The reader should not be satisfied until he has performed the experiment for himself and can explain it.

248. Simple Laws of Stereoscopic Projection.—If the point of fixation is very far away, the angle of convergence

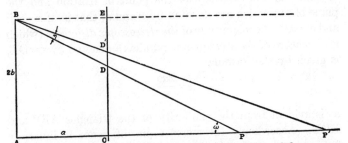

FIG. 328.—Stereoscopic projection. The centers of rotation of the two eyes are designated by A and B; interpupillary distance, $AB = 2b$. CE drawn parallel to AB is trace of the plane of projection (plane of stereogram); AC is perpendicular to AB; $AC = a$. P, P' designate positions of two luminous points (shown here as lying on prolongation of AC); $AP = x$, $AP' = x'$. $\angle APB = \omega$, $\angle PBP' = \eta$. Dotted line BE is drawn parallel to AC; $BE = AC$. Lines BP, BP' intersect CE in D, D', respectively.

of the two eyes will be zero, that is, the two lines of fixation will be parallel. The nearer the point of fixation, the greater the angle of convergence, until finally the limit is reached at the near point of convergence which for most individuals is only several inches in front of the face. In the accompanying diagram (Fig. 328) the centers of rotation of the two eyes are designated by the letters A and B, and the point of fixation by the letter P. The plane of the drawing determined by these three points is the so-called visual plane. The angle at A in the figure is a right angle, but this is merely a matter of convenience and is of no importance, as all the results can be obtained just as well with a triangle ABP of

any form. The straight line CD parallel to the *base-line* AB
is the trace of the plane of projection which is perpendicular
to the visual plane and which coincides with the plane of the
stereogram in a stereoscope. The projections of the point of
fixation P in this plane are the points designated by C and D;
and E is the foot of the perpendicular drawn from B to the
straight line CD. The length of the base-line $2b = $ AB varies
for different individuals (men, women and children) between
the limits of 58 and 72 mm., the average value being about
65 mm. If the distances of the point of fixation and the
plane of projection are denoted by x and a, that is, if $x = $ AP
and $a = $ AC, the magnitude of the *stereoscopic difference* (which
is a measure of the stereoscopic parallax), denoted by $s = $ DE,
is given by the formula

$$s = \frac{2ab}{x},$$

as is evident from the similarity of the triangles ABP and
EDB. Accordingly the stereoscopic difference is inversely
proportional to the distance of the point of fixation. For
example, when P is infinitely far away, D coincides with E
$(x = \infty,\ s = 0)$; when P coincides with C, D also coincides
with C $(x = a,\ s = 2b)$; and when P is nearer than C, the point
D, which was above C in the diagram as long as P was beyond C, now lies below C $(x < a,\ s > 2b)$.

For another point P′ at the distance $x' = $ AP′, the stereoscopic difference $(s' = $ D′E) is $s' = 2ab/x'$; and consequently

$$DD' = s - s' = 2ab\left(\frac{1}{x} - \frac{1}{x'}\right);$$

and therefore if we put

$$r = \frac{2ab}{s - s'},$$

we obtain:

$$\frac{1}{x} - \frac{1}{x'} = \frac{1}{r};$$

a formula which, it may be noted, is similar to the abscissa-formula of a thin lens (p. 229). Accordingly the magnitude r, which is inversely proportional to the difference $(s-s')$, is itself a certain distance, because it is the value of x when x' is infinite $(x'=\infty,\ x=r)$. In other words, when the point P' is infinitely far away, the point P is at the distance denoted by r.

If we put $\omega=\angle\,\text{BPA}$ and $\eta=\angle\,\text{PBP}'$, the angles of convergence at P and P' will be equal to ω and $(\omega-\eta)$, respectively; and on the assumption that these angles are so small that $\tan\omega=\omega$ and $\tan\eta=\eta$, evidently

$$\omega=\frac{2b}{x},\ \omega-\eta=\frac{2b}{x'};$$

and consequently

$$\eta=2b\left(\frac{1}{x}-\frac{1}{x'}\right)=\frac{2b}{r}.$$

Now there is necessarily a limit to the binocular perception of difference of distance, and unless the difference of distance between P and P' exceeds this limit, the two eyes cannot discern that P' is farther (or nearer) than P. Let us suppose therefore that the interval between P and P' is this minimum perceptible distance measured by the angle η (or, what is the same thing, measured by the interval DD' in the plane of projection), and that the two eyes can just detect that P and P' are at unequal distances. The conventional value of the angular measure of the limit of binocular perception of depth as determined by tests of a large number of individuals is taken to be one-half minute of arc; that is,

$$\eta=30''=0.000145\text{ radian}.$$

If this value of η is substituted in the formula $r=2b/\eta$ (in which case r denotes the so-called *radius of stereoscopic vision*), and if the distance between the centers of rotation of the two eyes is put equal to 65.25 mm. $(2b=0.06525\text{ m.})$, we obtain $r=450$ m. This result simply means that ordinary stereoscopic vision does not extend beyond a distance of about

450 m. or not much over a quarter of a mile; in other words, the differences between the two retinal images of an object more than 450 meters away are, as a rule, too slight to be appreciable.

249. Telestereoscope and Binocular Telescopes.—Since the limiting angle of binocular perception of depth is 30″ or one 6,876th part of a radian, the radius of stereoscopic vision in round numbers may be said to be about 7,000 times the length of the base-line connecting the two different points of view. Consequently if the separation of the

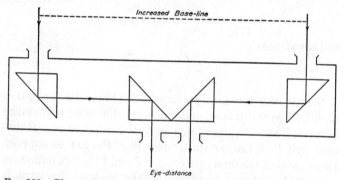

Fig. 329.—Plan of simple telestereoscope without lenses (object-glasses and oculars). The right triangles represent principal sections of total-reflecting glass prisms.

two eyes were, let us say, ten times as much as it really is or 65 cm. instead of only 65 mm., the radius of stereoscopic vision would be extended in the same proportion from 450 m. to 4.5 Km. Obviously, this raises the question as to whether the base-line might not be artificially magnified by a suitable optical device; a problem which HELMHOLTZ solved by the invention of the *telestereoscope* in 1857. Essentially, this instrument (Fig. 329) consists of a long narrow box or tube containing two pairs of round apertures symmetrically situated on the two opposite sides, namely, one pair on the front side towards the object, near the ends of the box and therefore far apart, and another pair on the rear surface close together near the middle, for the two eyes to look through. Consequently when the light entering the box by the front apertures is reflected by a system of mirrors or right-angle prisms in the interior so as to emerge finally through the rear apertures into the observer's eyes, the effect produced is just the same as if the two eyes were separated by a distance equal to that between the centers of the two apertures where the light entered the instrument; and so this simple optical device enables the observer to obtain two perspective views of the object that are far more different than the views he would obtain by his two eyes alone.

It is scarcely necessary to say that the telestereoscope as above described can easily be converted into a binocular telescope by simply inserting the object-glasses of the two telescopes in the apertures where the light enters and the oculars in the other pair of apertures where the eyes are applied to the instrument. The centers of the two objectives in a relief-telescope of this kind may be as much as a meter apart, and for this reason alone the radius of stereoscopic vision is extended much farther.

Prism binocular field-glasses (see Fig. 33) are constructed on exactly the same principle so as to give a greatly enhanced stereoscopic impression. The separation of the centers of the object-glasses of the pair of telescopes is sometimes nearly double the interpupillary distance for which the oculars are adjusted.

Even if the base-line of a binocular telescope is no greater than the interpupillary distance, the magnifying power (M) of the instrument alone will bring out differences between the two views of the objects that could never be detected by the naked eyes. In other words, the angle η which is the measure of the limit of binocular perception of depth is M times as small with the telescope as without it. Consequently if $r = 2b/\eta$ denotes the radius of stereoscopic vision with the naked eyes, and if M denotes the magnifying power of a binocular telescope for which the base-line is k times the interval between the centers of the eye-pieces, the radius of stereoscopic vision with the instrument will be k.M.r. For example, in the case of an ordinary pair of prism field-glasses of, say, 8-fold power, the average value of k is perhaps about 1.75; and therefore on the assumption that $r=450$ m., the field of stereoscopic vision of these glasses will be over a range of more than 6 Km. With a relief-telescope of power $M=10$, in which the two object-glasses are a half-meter apart, that is, $k=500 : 65=7.7$, the range of stereoscopic vision will be 77 times 450 m. or nearly 35 Km.

However, there is a practical limit to the extension of the stereoscopic field by means of a binocular telescope, partly because the magnifying power cannot exceed a limit imposed on all optical instruments by the nature of light (*cf.* § 216) and also partly because the difficulties of mechanical construction are enormously increased by a very long base-line.

On the other hand, the stereoscope itself used in conjunction with photography seems to afford almost endless possibilities of increasing the range of binocular perception of depth; for two photographs of the same scene taken from widely separated standpoints and fused in a stereoscope can give very extraordinary impressions of distance. The amateur photographer has here a fine opportunity of obtaining beautiful telestereoscopic pictures by photographing some prominent feature of a landscape from two stations perhaps as much as a mile or more apart and making a stereogram which as seen in a stereoscope will produce an impression similar to that which the original scene might make on an imaginary giant whose eyes were as far apart in his forehead as the two stations from which the pictures were taken. Photographs of cloud formations in the sky taken from points not more than 10 or 12 yards apart and viewed in a stereoscope bring out all the details of depth and illumination in striking relief; although, of course, such pictures must be taken in

quick succession before the evanescent shapes have had time
to be much altered. Two photographs of the moon taken
months apart and made into a stereogram may have an
equivalent base-line as long as one-fourth of the distance
between the earth and the moon; and thus a relief-view may
be obtained of that satellite such as mortal man could hardly
have expected ever to see. Professor MAX WOLF of Heidel-
berg has made a series of beautiful stellar stereograms, one
of which, for example, consisted of two photographs of the
planet Saturn made on two successive evenings. In this
particular instance the base-line in space between the two
points of view, taking into account the relative movements
of the earth and Saturn and also the drift of the solar system,
was estimated to be more than a million miles. Viewed in
the stereoscope, Saturn can be seen with his moons standing
out from the starry dome and floating in the great void of
space. Remarkable relief-maps of extensive terrain can be
made from stereograms in which the original photographs
were taken from air-planes.

VI. *Concerning the Nature of Light*

250. Fresnel's Wave-Theory.—Consistently throughout
this volume the language and methods of the wave-theory
of light have been employed without considering the need of
explanation or apology, perhaps mainly because it was the
path of least resistance and easiest to be followed without
distracting attention too much from the topic immediately
under discussion. While this plan seemed to be justified in an
elementary text-book of geometrical optics, it is scarcely to
be expected that the reader will be satisfied to be left entirely
in the dark as to the new era in physics which has been
crowded with such great achievements in every direction.
Accordingly it is not out of place to append here a brief,
necessarily wholly inadequate, historical outline of the main
points of view concerning the real nature of light from NEW-
TON's time down to our own day when almost before a new

theory has had time to gain a hearing it is apt to be modified or perhaps abandoned to be superseded by another that is still more up to date.

It is well known that NEWTON himself, not without obvious misgivings, was disposed to favor the *corpuscular or emission theory of light*, although his observations of the colored rings of thin films required him to endow the corpuscles of light with periodic dispositions or "fits" (as NEWTON called them) "of easy reflexion" and "fits of easy transmission," whereby sometimes they were in the mood to be reflected at the boundary between two optical media and at other times in the mood to be refracted. On the other hand, NEWTON's great contemporary HUYGENS, with even greater ardor, espoused the *undulatory or wave-theory of light* in spite of the difficulty of accounting for the rectilinear propagation of light and also in spite of the fact that apparently a necessary hypothesis of this theory was an omnipresent, all-pervading, universal medium to be the vehicle of the light waves, the so-called *luminiferous ether*. According to HUYGENS's conception the ether was composed structurally of tiny elastic particles whose mutual impacts transmitted from one particle to the next in continuous succession were propagated with prodigious speed from the source where the disturbance originated to far distant parts of space provided the waves of light were not intercepted and absorbed or diverted by some intervening obstacle. Although the ether penetrated and permeated ordinary matter with the utmost ease and freedom, nevertheless it was more or less affected by it depending on the nature of the substance; which explained why some bodies were transparent and others opaque, not to mention various other differences of behavior with respect to light. Obviously, the wave-theory with its ether vibrations was better adapted to explain the *periodicity* or *frequency* which is such an essential characteristic of the beautiful optical effects that are embraced under the names of interference, diffraction and polarization of light. But it was not until early in the nineteenth century, thanks chiefly to THOMAS YOUNG in England and above all to AUGUSTIN FRESNEL in France (who died in 1827 one hundred years after NEWTON's death), that the wave-theory finally triumphed over the rival corpuscular theory; although by this time the ether had to be radically renovated to accommodate as far as possible all the new facts that had accumulated meanwhile. Subtle and rarefied as the ether was assumed to be, it was compelled more and more to take on structural properties analogous to those of ordinary matter until at length in 1821 FRESNEL, without mincing matters, startled the scientific world of that day by boldly asserting that the luminiferous ether behaved as if it were a perfectly elastic solid! Strange to say, this extraordinary theory stood the test for a long time to come. It made predictions which were verified experimentally with the most perfect precision, perhaps the most notable instance of all being Sir W. R. HAMILTON's prediction in 1832 of internal conical refraction which was actually demonstrated experimentally the next year by LLOYD. Nevertheless, FRESNEL's elastic solid ether continued to be a paradoxical conception hard to comprehend, being non-resistant like a perfect fluid and at the same time more elastic than solid steel. Whether it corresponded to reality or not, the scientific power of FRESNEL's hypothesis lay in the fact that it afforded a consistent and comparatively simple explanation of the facts as far as they were then known. All during the latter half of the nineteenth century one of the most constant and persistent objects of experimental investigation was to detect the presence of the ether and to establish the fact of its existence by some mechanical effect if possible. The most crucial and painstaking of all these projects was the famous MICHELSON-MORLEY experiment which was first carefully performed in 1887 and which has been subsequently repeated from time to time, notably only a few years ago (1928) under the direction of the late Professor ALBERT A. MICHELSON (1852–1931) himself on an elaborate scale with every possible precaution against error. The purpose of this method was to ascertain whether the velocity of light was affected by the velocity of the earth's motion in its orbit around the sun. Without exception all these attempts to come to actual grips with the ether have uniformly ended in failure, insomuch that as long ago as 1894 Lord SALISBURY in his inaugural address at the Oxford meeting of the British Association for the Advancement of Science remarked that "for more than two generations the main, if not the only function of the word ether has been to furnish a nominative case to the verb 'to undulate.' " In that same year H. POINCARÉ pointed out that "even if the assumption of the ether should ever be discarded as of no use, the laws of optics and the analytical equations by which they are formulated will continue to be valid as a first approximation at least, and therefore it will always be worth while to consider and investigate the theories of an elastic ether"; and if POINCARÉ were alive today, perhaps he might still subscribe to this opinion expressed nearly forty years ago.

251. Maxwell's Electromagnetic Theory.—However, the physics of the nineteenth century was concerned far more with the progress and development of the new science of electricity and magnetism than with the elaboration of the wave-theory of light which after FRESNEL's penetrating mathematical analysis came to be regarded almost like a closed chapter, *une chose jugée.* With the discoveries of OERSTED and AMPÈRE in 1820 of the mutual interactions between currents of electricity and magnetic needles a systematic investigation was begun of the laws of electrodynamics and electromagnetism, that is, of all those phenomena in which the motion of electricity was an essential factor involving therefore the element of time. A way out of the difficulties presented by this host of new facts could have been found only by a genius who came to the study of them with a mind not only vigorous but fresh and untrammelled, and MICHAEL FARADAY (1791–1867) was the man that was needed for this work. Without ever losing sight of

the experimental facts themselves, at the same time FARADAY
penetrated them with his keen scientific insight, above all
with that faculty of scientific imagination which TYNDALL
so greatly extolled, thus combining qualities of mind and
judgment that do not always or often go together in the same
individual.   Heedless of the prevailing theories, FARADAY
fastened his attention not on the charged conductor itself
but on the dielectric medium surrounding it which he conceived to be permeated by lines of force due to the strains
and tensions in it. He demonstrated the existence of the lines
of magnetic force and mapped the field by means of iron
filings sprinkled on a sheet of paper on which a magnet was
placed.   With great acumen he conjectured that possibly
there was some intimate connection between the waves of
light in the ether and the electromagnetic phenomena in the
dielectric medium, and he sought to obtain direct experimental evidence of such a connection.   This is not the
place to tell of FARADAY's contributions and discoveries,
and all we need to say at present is that he established
the fact that electromagnetic forces were transmitted with
finite speed and also the fact that electromagnetic waves
were produced by an electric spark.   His revolutionary
conceptions together with his extraordinary experiments
tended to upset the current theories of both light and electricity, although not all of his scientific contemporaries were
aware of this by any means. All the more credit is due to his
younger contemporary JAMES CLERK MAXWELL (1831-1879)
for discerning and appreciating the significance of FARADAY's
innovations and the implications of his theory of the dielectric
polarization of the ether. Fortunately, MAXWELL had the
advantage of being a great mathematician as well as a
trained and acute observer, and nobody was better equipped
for translating FARADAY's thought into the precise and lofty
language of mathematical physics. MAXWELL's truly epoch-
making treatise on *Electricity and Magnetism*, published
first in 1867, is still today an unfailing source of knowledge

and inspiration to all who can see the significance of it and
the far-reaching bearing of MAXWELL's equations. Here also
appeared for the first time an entirely new theory of luminous
phenomena known ever since as the *electromagnetic theory of
light*. According to this theory, it could be inferred that the
waves of light were essentially electromagnetic, in other
words, that light itself was simply an electromagnetic phenomenon.

A generation later HELMHOLTZ's brilliant pupil HEINRICH
HERTZ (1857–1894) confirmed MAXWELL's predictions by
detecting (1887) electromagnetic waves in space generated
by the spark of an electric coil and demonstrating that these
waves could be reflected and refracted and that they exhibited properties similar to those of ordinary waves of light.
Moreover, these electrical waves were found to be propagated
with precisely the same velocity as the velocity of light. Of
course, their real nature was still just as much a puzzle as the
real nature of the waves in FRESNEL's elastic solid ether, but
the advantage of the electromagnetic theory was that the
results obtained by it were equally valid for both light and
electricity. Thus while it was extremely difficult to make
optics conform to the notions of ordinary mechanics, as
NEWTON and all his successors had tried to do down to the
era of FARADAY and MAXWELL, the electromagnetic theory
could at least boast of having found, so to speak, a common
denominator for optics and electricity. It still remained to
discover, if possible, a bond of union between electrodynamics
and ordinary mechanics in order to consolidate and unify the
scientific structure of the universe in a single consistent
scheme.

Instead of an ether that was at once fluid and solid, the
particles of which executed mechanical vibrations, MAX-
WELL's ether was to be conceived as the substratum for the
transmission of periodic fluctuations of intensity of electromagnetic fields of force. Luminous radiation was only one of
many varieties of radiation that utilized this universal me-

dium as the vehicle of propagation of waves. FRESNEL'S equations were not invalidated in the least, only now they had to be interpreted not in terms of mechanics but in terms of electro-dynamics.

252. Modern Theories.—The fundamental and necessary factors of a periodic phenomenon being time and space, instead of mentioning the ether by name, it has become the fashion nowadays to speak of

"space-time as the representative of the ancient void or vacuum, without," says Sir OLIVER LODGE, "necessarily supposing it to be a substantial reality, and yet admitting that it has physical properties which we can hope to investigate by experiment."

In spite of the fact that undoubtedly MAXWELL himself had endeavored at first to reduce the physics of electricity to a mechanical scheme, he and his successors were gradually forced by the irrefutable logic of their own deductions to change their point of view entirely; and thus towards the end of the last century electric theories of matter began to be prevalent. It is certainly very remarkable, as MAX PLANCK has pointed out, "how easily and, so to speak, noiselessly the transition in physics was accomplished from the mechanical to the electromagnetic conception"; and indeed in retrospect it seems to those who are old enough to remember almost as if a whole army had quietly decamped by night leaving behind all its baggage and equipment and taken up a new position and an entirely new strategy next day. Thus without flourish or commotion the new physics full of confidence and vigor calmly and resolutely superseded the old classical physics that traced back to GALILEO, DESCARTES, NEWTON and HUYGENS.

The lucky, perhaps not wholly accidental, discovery of X-rays by W. C. RÖNTGEN (1845–1923) in 1895 was the culmination of a long series of noteworthy experiments on electrical discharge in rarefied gases which had been made by numerous investigators. It threw open immediately another great field of research called radioactivity, and here one of the first rewards was the revelation of ultra-atomic corpuscles or electrons, which in turn paved the way for the *electron theory* of H. A. LORENTZ (1853–1928). Ultimately this theory too led to new conceptions of the ether, pushing it still further into the background; for although the electron theory did not dispense with the ether entirely, it left it little to do and denied it any vestige of materiality.

Finally ALBERT EINSTEIN's *special relativity theory* announced in 1905 seemed to remove the last prop from under the ether, for since according to this theory all natural phenomena are dependent simply on the relative motions of bodies and since the most searching experiments failed to reveal the faintest evidence of so-called "ether drift" due to the orbital motion of the earth, the hypothesis of the ether was simply superfluous and no longer necessary. And yet before dismissing it from the stage, one may pause here to recall again its strange eventful history. Borrowed no doubt from the ancient Greek cosmogonies and invented expressly to satisfy the needs of the wave-theory of light, the luminiferous ether had been conceived at first as a fluid such as never was on sea or land, the primordial essence of which all things consist; then gradually it assumed the nature of an elastic solid comparable with no earthly substance that could be imagined; and next it was metamorphosed into the web or garment, as it were, in which the concepts of the electromagnetic theory were clothed—to dissolve at last at the hands of LORENTZ and EINSTEIN into "such stuff as dreams are made of," a mere nonentity!

However, the last word on the subject has not yet been spoken, and since the appearance of the *general relativity theory* in 1915 the ether has showed faint signs of coming to life again, although it will certainly never enjoy the prestige it once had. In this new theory EINSTEIN showed that NEWTON's assumption of a gravitational action between two bodies may also be unnecessary, since the motions of falling bodies and of the planets in their orbits can be explained as being simply the natural geometrical consequences of the "curvature of space-time." Thus according to the theory of relativity space is no longer what the spontaneous perception of common sense supposes it to be, because now it has a property, namely curvature, no trace of which is revealed to us by our ordinary senses.

Difficult as it is to adapt the wave-theory to the abstruse geometrical and philosophical conceptions that have thus been merely alluded to above, it is harder still to reconcile it with the great array of new experimental evidence which has been steadily accumulating year by year in the vast territory of radioactivity. More than thirty years ago the *quantum theory* (1901) was devised by MAX PLANCK to take account of the observed phenomena in this special field of physics. Briefly this bold conception amounts simply to an atomic theory of radiant energy. In other words, instead of being steady and continuous, radiation is intermittent and spasmodic and operates by definite quanta or units of energy in the case of both emission and absorption. PLANCK's constant denoted by h, being the quotient of the energy ($h\nu$) divided by the frequency of oscillation (ν), is a natural unit of energy or activity, just as the electron is a natural unit of matter and electricity. Thus according to the quantum theory the emission of light by a luminous source is not a steady, uninterrupted, continuous flow of energy as is supposed by the wave-theory, but consists rather in a constant stream of tiny parcels of energy (which perhaps might be compared roughly to the separate drops as revealed in a jet of water when it is illuminated by a flash of lightning); in other words we must think of a luminous body as sending out, so to speak, "atoms of light" analogous to NEWTON's corpuscles in the old emission theory of light. From this point of view therefore our modern ideas of the nature of light prove to be after all not unlike those that were prevalent two centuries ago.

"The whirligig of time brings in his revenges."

The dilemma that has now to be faced is, How are the incontrovertible facts of the quantum theory to be reconciled with the fundamentally periodic phenomena of light (interference, diffraction, polarization, etc.) for the explanation of which the wave-theory was specially devised and was indeed specially competent?

"And here," says Sir OLIVER LODGE in the same article from which we have quoted already (*Hibbert Journal*, XXIX, 1931, p. 396), "we have to make use of the wave theory of matter. Modern physics has shown that, like the corpuscles of NEWTON, every particle has associated with it something periodic. The electron does not now appeal to us as a minute spherical charge and nothing else, it has been found to have something associated with it, a series of waves. In fact it is found that many of the properties of a particle of matter can be possessed by what is known as a 'group wave'; in other words that the energy of a particle can be expressed as the energy of a set of group waves, and that these, strangely enough, obey the laws of dynamics. Consequently it is realised that the particle and the wave are much more united than ever they have been before. A wave may exist without a particle. A particle can hardly exist without a wave. The waves seem the most fundamental things."

This is the brilliant *theory of wave mechanics* as proposed and developed in the last few years by DE BROGLIE and SCHRÖDINGER which is indeed a triumph of mathematical power and ingenuity, not easy however for the uninitiated to understand and entirely beyond the scope of this book.

Between atomic physics on the one hand and cosmic physics on the other hand, what may be called mundane physics (for lack of a better word), which to a great extent is governed still by NEWTON's laws of motion, occupies somewhat the same position as geometrical optics in its special field, being good and trustworthy as far as it goes but at best only superficial in the eyes of those who seek to penetrate nature's deepest secrets. An intelligent layman listening to a discussion of modern theories in physics with its curious notions of space, time and matter might perhaps be provoked to say as the learned SCALIGER said wittily concerning the Basque language: "*Les Basques se parlent comme s'ils se comprenaient entre eux; quant à moi, je n'en crois rien.*" Yet after all it is experimental physics of the present day with its steady accumulation of new and as it were mutinous phenomena that makes it necessary to resort to entirely different modes of explanation in natural philosophy from those that seemed reasonably satisfactory a generation or more ago.

INDEX

The numbers refer to the pages.

A

ABBE, E.: Apertometer, 667; apochromats and semiapochromats, 679, 680; chromatic difference of spherical aberration, 676; compensation ocular, 682; definition of focal length, 344; differential notation, 531; homogeneous immersion system, 679; magnifying power, 454; v-value of optical medium, 480; numerical aperture, 666; optical glass, 482, 489; PORRO prism system, 50; pupils, 401; refractometer, 128; sine-condition, 523, 542, 547, 665, 674; theory of microscope, 652, 653, 665, 670, 679.

Aberration, Chromatic: see *Chromatic aberration, Achromatism*, etc.

Aberration-disks, 676, 677. See also *Blur circles*.

Aberration, Least circle of, 515.

Aberration, Spherical: see *Spherical aberration*.

Aberrations, Chromatic and monochromatic, 509; SEIDEL's five sums, 545–550, 557.

Aberrations, Monochromatic: see *Spherical (monochromatic) aberrations*.

Aberrations, Ocular, 710.

ABNEY's formula for diameter of aperture of pinhole camera, 5, 26.

Abscissa formula for centered system, 332, 519; infinitely thin lens, 228, 229, 279, 285; plane refracting surface, 97, 191, 269; spherical mirror, 154, 155, 191, 276, 285; spherical refracting surface, 191, 193, 200, 274, 285. See also *Image equations*.

Absorption of light, 2; absorption spectrum, 725.

Accommodation: Concomitant contraction of pupil, 709.

Accommodation of eye, 433–439; amplitude, 437–439; range, 438; diminishes with age, 435, 436; effected by changes in crystalline lens, 434; refracting power of eye in accommodation, 436, 437.

Achromatic (colorless) vision, 721, 743.

Achromatic combinations: Prisms, 480, 481, 491–493; lenses 480, 481, 499–505.

Achromatic optical system, 488.

Achromatic sensation, 726. See also *Whiteness, Blackness sensation*.

Achromatic single reflection prism, 582.

Achromatic telescope, 480, 481, 505.

Achromatism, 480, 481, 487 and foll.; optical and actinic or photographic, 489–491, 675.

Achromatism of microscope-objective, 675, 676; of microscope-ocular, 680, 681–683.

Adaptation of eye, 721, 743.

AIRY, Sir G. B.: Cylindrical lens, 315, 698; tangent-condition of orthoscopy, 545; curvature of image, 540; diffraction-formula, 712, 713, 714.

ALHAZEN, 564, 565, 570, 572.

Aligning power of eye, 716, 718. See also *Visual acuity, Resolving power*.

Ametropia, 439 and foll.; axial, curvature and indicial ametropia, 442.

Ametropic eye, 440 and foll.; distance of correction-glass, 445, 446.

AMICI, G. B.: Direct vision prism system, 495, 497, 506; roof-angle prism, 568; compound microscope, 651, 677, 678, 679.

AMPÈRE, A. M., 764.

Amplitude of accommodation, 437–439.

Anaglyph, 754.

Anastigmatic (or stigmatic) lenses, 314.

Angle, Central, 152, 516.

Angle, Critical: see *Critical angle of refraction, Total reflection*.

Angle of deviation: In case of inclined mirrors, 43, 565; in case of refraction, 78; in prism, 50, 51, 125; in lens, 293. See also *Prism, Thin prism, Prism-dioptry, Prismatic power of lens, Double reflection prism, Single reflection prism*.

Angle, Slope, 151, 334, 516.

Angle, Visual: see *Visual angle, Apparent size*.

Angles, Measurement of, by mirror and scale, 56.

Angles of incidence, reflection and refraction, 30, 31, 65.

ÅNGSTROM unit of wave-length, 10. See also *Tenth-meter*.

Angular magnification (or convergence-ratio), 351.

Anisotropic optical medium, 687.

Anopic eye, 742. See also *Color blindness*.

Anterior and posterior poles of eye, 431, 432.

Anterior chamber of eye, 425.

Apertometer, 667.

Aperture angle, 404, 663, 665, 666; microscope, 656, 665–667, 678.

Aperture, compound microscope, 652, 660, 663 and foll. See also *Numerical aperture*.

Aperture, Magnifying effect of narrow, 636–637.

Aperture of optical system: see Chap. XII.

Aperture stop, 399; of magnifying glass, 641; of microscope objective, 655, 656, 660.

Aphakia, 213, 442, 629.

Aplanatic lens, 618, 621, 622, 629, 679. See also *Aspherical lenses.*

Aplanatic points of optical system, 524, 665, 676; of spherical refracting surface (J, J'), 512, 513, 554, 596, 617, 618, 624, 628, 677, 679.

Aplanatism, 524, 665, 674, 675. See also *Sine-condition.*

Apochromatism, 489; apochromats, 679, 680, 682, 684; semiapochromats, 680.

Apparent place and direction of point-source, 15–18. See also *Monocular vision.*

Apparent place of object viewed through plate of glass, 102, 103, 105, 106.

Apparent size, 20–22, 446 and foll.; in optical instrument, 449 and foll.

Aqueous humor, 213, 371, 425.

ARCHIMEDES, 559, 563.

ARISTOTLE, 559, 560.

Aspherical lenses, 593. See also *Aplanatic lenses.*

Assimilation and dissimilation, 744. See also HERING'S *opponent-colors theory.*

Associated movements of two eyes, 431, 749.

Astigmatic bundle of rays, 25, 310–314, 526–538, 552 and foll.; image-lines, 100, 312, 313, 534–536, 547; image-points, 312, 526, 527, 529–534; principal sections 311, 528, 704. See also *Meridian rays, Sagittal rays, Image-points, Image-lines,* STURM'S *conoid, Astigmatism.*

Astigmatic difference, 533, 706.

Astigmatic image-surfaces, 536–538, 547.

Astigmatic lenses, Chap. IX, 300 and foll., 314.

Astigmatism by incidence, 527.

Astigmatism, Measure of, 533.

Astigmatism, Ocular, 697, 698, 699, 706; irregular, 705; lenticular, 698; pathological and physiological, 697, 698; with and against the rule, 698. See also *Cornea, Ophthalmometer.*

Astigmatism of oblique bundles, 527, 547, 597.

Astigmatism, STURM'S theory, 313, 534.

Astronomical telescope, 411, 456, 572, 606, 655; field of view, 411, 412; magnifying power, 454–460.

Atmospheric refraction, 4, 570, 685.

Axial ametropia, 442; static refraction and length of eye-ball, 442, 443.

Axial (or depth) magnification, 351.

Axis: see *Optic axis, Optical axis.*

Axis of collineation, 243.

Axis of lens, 217; spherical refracting surface, 149. See also *Optical axis.*

Axis, Visual, 433.

B

Back focus: Of combination of two lenses, 600; of single lens, 365.

BACON, R.: Lenses, 592; scientific achievements, 564; spherical mirror, 632.

BADAL's optometer, 422, 423.

BAKER, T. Y.: Reflection prisms, 592.

BARLOW's achromatic object-glass, 504, 505.

Barrel-shaped distortion, 544.

BARROW, I.: Lectures on optics, 595, 629; theory of astigmatism, 597.

BARTHOLINUS, E.: Double refraction, 596, 687.

Base-line (binocular vision), 756, 758–761.

BAUSCH & LOMB Optical Company: Microscope, 658, 659, 684.

Bending of lens, 284, 644.

Biaxial crystals, 689.

Binocular depth-perception, 751 and foll.; limits of, 757 and foll.

Binocular double vision, 749.

Binocular field of view of various animals, 750.

Binocular fusion, 749, 751.

Binocular microscope, 683.

Binocular telescope, 51, 606, 759–760. See also *Relief-telescope*.

Binocular vision, 747, 749–761. See also *Depth perception, Stereoscopic vision*.

Black, 720, 731, 744.

Black body, 731.

Blackness sensation, 731.

Black-white process in HERING's color theory, 744, 745.

Blind spot of retina, 430, 431.

Blue-blindness: see *Color blindness, partial*.

Blur circles, 414–417, 419. See also *Aberration-disks*.

BREWSTER, Sir D.: Kaleidoscope, 47; magnifying glass, 646, 647; stereoscope, 754.

Brightness of point-source, 23; image in microscope, 667–669, 673.

Brightness (or luminosity), 720, 730–732.

Brilliance, 731. See also *Luminosity*.

DE BROGLIE, M.: Theory of wave mechanics, 770.

Brown color, 720, 731.

BRÜCKE: see CHEVALIER-BRÜCKE microscope.

Bundle of rays: Character of, 24, 25, 508, 509, 525; "direct," 514; homocentric (or monocentric), 25; limitation by means of stops, 397–399. See also *Astigmatic bundle of rays*.

BUNSEN burner, 66, 473.

BURNETT, S. M.: Prism-dioptry, 135.

C

Calcite: see *Iceland spar, Double refraction.*

Calculation of GULLSTRAND's schematic eye, 371–376; of PURKINJE reflex images, 381–384.

Calculation of path of ray: Refracted at spherical surface, 516–519, 611–617; reflected at spherical mirror, 518; refracted through prism, 124, 125; refracted through centered system, 332, 519–522; numerical examples for paraxial and edge rays, 520–522, 615–617.

Calculation of refracting power and of positions of focal points of centered system, 606–611.

Camera obscura, 561.

Camera: see *Pinhole camera, Camera obscura.*

Cardinal points of optical system, 334–339.

Cartesian optical surfaces, 593, 617–625; hyperbolic refracting surface, 593, 594, 619, 620; elliptic refracting surface, 593, 620; parabolic mirror, 565, 619.

Cataract: see *Aphakia.*

Catoptrics, 563; catoptric (reflex) images in eye: see PURKINJE, J.; SCHEINER, C.; *Ophthalmometer.*

Caustic curve, 514.

Caustic surface, in general, 526, 592; by refraction at plane surface, 98, 99; by refraction at spherical surface, 515.

CAVALERI, 594.

Centered system of spherical refracting surfaces: Optical axis, 329; construction of paraxial ray, 330, 331; calculation of path of paraxial ray, 332, 520–522, 615–617; conjugate axial points (M, M'), 346, 347; extra-axial conjugate points (Q, Q'), 339–342; lateral magnification, 333, 349; SMITH-HELMHOLTZ formula, 334; focal planes, 333–335; focal points, 332–335; ray of finite slope, 519–522, 611–617.

Center: Of collineation, 243; of curvature, 260, 526; of perspective (K), 532, 554; of rotation of eye, 432, 434, 448, 452, 748.

Centers of perspective of object-space and image-space, 416, 417.

Centrad, 134, 294.

Central angle (φ), 152, 516.

Central collineation, 242–247.

Central (direct) vision, 448, 748. See also *Daylight vision, Cone vision.*

Central ray, 243.

CEVA's law (geometry), 736.

CHEVALIER-BRÜCKE microscope, 649, 655.

Chief rays, 24, 413, 420, 526.

Choroid, 425.

Chroma (hue, color-tone), 720, 726, 744. See also *Hue.*

Chromatic aberration, 487–489, 509, 674, 675, 677, 678.

Chromatic difference of spherical aberration and of magnification, 676, 682.

Ciliary body, 427; mechanism of accommodation, 434.

Circle of aberration, Least, 515.

Circle of curvature, 260.

Circle of least confusion, 314, 537.

Circles of diffusion: see *Blur circles*.

Classification of optical instruments (according to T. SMITH), 602–606.

CLAUSIUS, R.: Sine-condition, 523.

Clinical ophthalmometer, 698, 699, 703–706. See also *Ophthalmometer*.

CODDINGTON, H.: Curvature of image, 540; magnifying glass, 644, 647.

Collimating mechanism of ophthalmometer, 700, 702, 704.

Collinear correspondence, 242, 508. See also *Punctual imagery*.

Collineation: Central, 242–247; center of, 243; axis of, 243; invariant of, 246.

Color and frequency of vibration, 472–476; and wave-length, 475; and refrangibility, 726.

Color blends, 723, 724, 728–730.

Color blindness, partial, 721, 741, 742; total, 721, 743, 746.

Color chart, 732.

Color circle, 729, 732.

Color cone (or pyramid), 731–732, 733, 741.

Color coördinates, 732, 733, 735, 741.

Color equations, 723, 724, 732.

Color fusions, 723, 724.

Color manifold, 731–732.

Color match: see *Color mixing*.

Color mixing, 722–725, 732–735, 740, 741, 743, 746. See also *Color cone, Color chart, Color circle, Color triangle, Pigments*.

Color music, 724.

Color names, 720, 731.

Color of a body, 2, 720.

Color, quality of visual sensation, 720.

Color sensations, 720–747. See also *Hue, saturation and luminosity*.

Color sense: Anomalies, 721, 746; normal, 721, 744, 746.

Color theory: YOUNG-HELMHOLTZ trichromatic, 738–743; HERING tetrachromatic, 743–747.

Color tone: see *Hue*.

Color triangle, 732 and foll., 733, 741.

Color valences (HERING's theory), 732, 745, 746.

Color vision, 720–722; normal, 721, 744, 746; anomalous, 721, 746. See also *Color sensations, Hue, Saturation, Luminosity, Color blindness,* etc.

Colors, dark, 731; pale, 731; pure, 726–727, 729, 730, 744, 746; simple and compound, 726, 744; standard, 732 and foll.; spectral, 466, 469, 472, 598, 724, 725–727, 728–730, 730, 731, 732, 733, 734, 735. See also *Spectral colors, Complementary colors.*

Colors of spectrum: see *Spectral colors.*

Colors of thin plates and films, 597, 762.

Coma, 542, 547.

Combination of three optical systems, 374–376.

Combination of two lenses, 366–370, 599–602; achromatic, 499 and foll.

Combination of two optical systems, 356–362; focal lengths, 359; focal and principal points, 358, 361; refracting power, 361.

Compensation ocular, 682, 683.

Complementary colors, 724; spectral colors, 725, 727–728, 729, 734, 735.

Complete quadrilateral, 162.

Compound colors, 726.

Compound microscope, 650–684; general characteristics, 650–655; laboratory form, 660–661. See *Microscope, Ultramicroscope.*

Compound microscope: Achromatism of objective, 675; aplanatism of objective, 674, 675; aperture, 652, 660, 663 and foll.; aperture-angle, 656, 665–667; brightness of image, 667–669, 673; dry system, 661, 666, 667, 678; field of view, 660, 663; immersion system, 661, 666, 667, 671, 673, 678, 679, 680; invention 635, 651; illumination system, 650, 683; numerical aperture, 663–673; objective, 651, 653, 673–680; ocular, 651, 680–683; magnifying power, 651, 662–663, 668, 669, 671, 672, 673, 683; metric relations, 661–663; numerical aperture, 663–669, 670–673, 679; optical tube length, 652-653, 655, 661, 676; pupils, 655, 667, 668, 671, 672, 673, 680; ray-procedure, 655–661; resolving power, 669–673, 679, 684, 710.

Compound optical systems, Chap. XI, 356 and foll.

Concave, convex: Lens, 221; surface, 150.

Concentric lens, 221, 232, 387, 388.

Cone vision: see *Daylight vision.*

Cones and rods of retina, 428, 429, 714–715, 721, 739, 747. See also *Daylight vision, Twilight vision.*

Conjugate planes, 172, 194, 236.

Conjugate points off axis (Q, Q′): Centered system of spherical refracting surfaces, 339–342; infinitely thin lens, 234–236; spherical mirror, 171–175; spherical refracting surface, 193–196.

Conjugate points on axis (M, M′): Centered system of spherical refracting surfaces, 346, 347; infinitely thin lens, 227–229, 232, 595;

plane refracting surface, 97; plate with parallel faces, 105; spherical mirror, 154, 164; spherical refracting surface, 181, 183, 595.

Conoid, STURM's, 313, 314, 535.

Contrast and visual acuity, 716.

Contrast phenomena, 721.

Convergence angle, 755.

Convergence movements of two eyes, 750.

Convergence, Near point of, 755.

Convergence-ratio: see *Angular magnification*.

Convergent and divergent optical systems, 186, 339, 340.

Convergent lens, 221.

Convergent series of numbers, Limit of, 715–716.

Convex, concave: see *Concave, convex*.

Coördinates: see *Color coördinates, Trilinear coördinates*.

Cornea of human eye, 425, 696–699; measurement of curvature, 696, 697, 699; optical constants, 371, 372, 401; optical zone, 697, 698; principal meridians, 704–706; seat of ocular astigmatism, 698; shape of, 697; vertex, 431. See also *Ophthalmometer*.

Corneal astigmatism, 697 and foll. See also *Ophthalmometer*.

Corpuscles of light, 762, 769.

Corpuscular or emission theory of light, 669, 762, 763, 769, 770.

Correction glass for ametropia: Refracting power and vertex-refraction, 443–446, 708; second focal point of glass at far point of eye, 445.

Correction glass for aphakic eye, 629.

Cover glass for microscopic object, 653, 666, 678, 679.

CREW, H.: "Dioptric," 287.

Critical angle of refraction, 80, 572.

Cross-cylindrical lens, 315, 317, 319, 320, 325.

Crystalline lens of human eye, 213, 371, 372, 373, 378, 381, 395, 428, 592, 593, 627; astigmatism, 698; changes in accommodation, 395, 434; optical constants, 371–373, 395, 434; "total index," 436. See also *Aphakia*.

Crystalline optical media, 686, 687. See also *Iceland spar, Quartz, Fluorite, Diamond*, etc.

Crystals, Optic axis, 688 and foll.; positive and negative, 688, 689; principal section, 692 and foll.; uniaxial and biaxial, 688, 689.

CULMANN, P.: SMITH-HELMHOLTZ formula, 202.

Curvature ametropia, 442.

Curvature-method in geometrical optics, 282.

Curvature of anterior surface of cornea of eye, 697 and foll. See also *Ophthalmometer, Schematic eye*, etc.

Curvature of arc: Total, 258; mean, 259; center of, 260; circle of, 260;

sign (plus or minus), 260; measure, 260–264. See also *Lens-gauge, Spherometer.*

Curvature of image, 538–540, 547, 548.

Curvature of normal sections of surface, 300–303; principal sections, 302, 303, 525.

Curvature, Unit of, 286–288. See also *Dioptry.*

Cushion-shaped distortion, 544.

Cylindrical lenses, 217, 310, 314–317; types, 315–317; combinations, 318–326; transposition, 318–320.

Cylindrical spectacle glasses, 314 and foll., 698.

Cylindrical surface, 265, 305–308, 310–313; refracting power, 307, 308.

D

Daguerreotype process, 635.

Dark colors, 731.

Dark-field illumination, 684. See also *Ultramicroscope.*

Daylight vision (cone vision), 707, 713, 714, 721, 747, 748.

DENNETT: Centrad, 134.

Depth-magnification, 351.

Depth perception (binocular vision), 747, 751–761; limiting angle of binocular depth perception, 757 and foll. See also *Radius of stereoscopic vision.*

DESCARTES, R.: Law of refraction, 67, 573, 593, 594; ovals, 593, 624; aspherical optical surfaces and lenses, 593, 621; aplanatic points, 617; magnifying glass, 645; philosophy, 767.

Deviation by prism: see *Prism.*

Deviation of ray: see *Angle of deviation, Minimum deviation.*

Deviation without dispersion, 481, 491–493.

Diamond, 70, 479, 646.

Diaphragms or stops for cutting out rays, 397–399. See also *Aperture stop, Field stop,* etc.

Dichromatic vision, 741, 742; see also *Color blindness, partial.*

Dielectric medium, 764. See also *Ether.*

DIETERICI, C.: Fundamental-sensation curves, 740.

Diffraction of light, 14, 597, 637, 670, 671, 684, 709–713, 762, 770; diffraction disk due to small round aperture, 637, 709–713; diffraction effects in microscope, 637, 670, 671; diffraction spectra, 670; diffraction through pupil of eye, 710.

Dioptrics, 569 and foll.

Dioptry, 286–288; "dioptrie," "dioptre," etc., 286, 287; Hecto-, Kilo-, millidioptry, etc., 287.

Direct and indirect vision, 448, 748.

"Direct" bundle of rays, 514.

Direct vision prism-systems (*prismes à vision directe*), 493–499.

Direction along ray or straight line: see *Positive direction.*

Direction of point of fixation, 751.

Direction of point-source, 15–18. See also *Monocular vision.*

Dispersion of light, Chromatic: Chap. XIV, 465 and foll., 598, 726; anomalous, 477; irrationality of, 477–479; partial, 479, 483; relative, 479, 483.

Dispersion without deviation, 481, 493–499.

Dispersive power (or strength), 479–481; dispersive power of lens, 503.

Dissimilation and assimilation, 744. See HERING, E.

Distinct vision, Distance of, 452, 453.

Distortion, 543–545.

Divergent lens, 221; divergent and convergent optical systems, 339, 340.

DOLLAND, J.: Achromatic object-glass, 481, 482, 504, 505.

DOMINIS, ANTONIUS DE, 594.

DONDERS, F. C.: Astigmatism of eye corrected by cylindrical glasses, 316, 698; loss of accommodation with increasing age, 435, 436; reduced eye, 214.

Double concave lens, 219; double convex lens, 217.

Double (cross) ratio, 156–164, 735, 736, 737, 738.

Double reflection prism, 574, 586–592; deviation, 587.

Double refraction, 596, 598, 686–696; ordinary and extraordinary rays, 687, 691 and foll.

Doubling system in ophthalmometer: see *Ophthalmometer*, WOLLASTON'S *prism.*

DOVE, H. W.: "Reversion" prism, 583.

DRYSDALE, C. V.: Curvature-method, 287.

Dry system microscope objective, 661, 666, 667, 678, 679.

Dutch telescope, 456, 571, 606; field of view, 412, 413; "eye-ring," 413, 458; magnifying power, 455–460.

Dynamic refraction of eye, 438.

E

Ear and eye, 724.

Effective rays, 23.

EINSTEIN, A.: Special relativity theory, 768; general relativity theory, 768.

Electricity and magnetism, 764 and foll.

Electromagnetic theory of light, 669, 764–767, 768.

Electron, 768, 769, 770; electron theory, 768.

Ellipsoidal mirror, 618, 619; refracting surface, 620, 622.

Emergent rays, 24.

Emmetropia and ametropia, 439–443.

Emmetropic eye, 440.

Entrance-port, 406–409, 410, 413.

Entrance-pupil, 43, 179, 400 and foll., 543, 596; two or more entrance-pupils, 405, 406; of eye, 401, 448, 714; of microscope, 655, 656, 660.

Ether, Luminiferous, 10, 472–476, 688, 762 and foll.; according to electron theory, 768; according to relativity theory, 768; ether drift, 768; experiments concerning, 10, 763, 764; electromagnetic ether, 765, 766, 768; FRESNEL's elastic solid ether, 763, 766, 768; HUYGENS's ether, 762, 768; nominative of verb "to undulate," 764; equivalent to space-time, 767.

EUCLID, 559, 563, 564, 716.

EULER, L.: Theory of curved surfaces, 303, 306, 525; achromatism, 481.

Exit-port, 409, 410, 413.

Exit-pupil, 400–405, 411–413, 415, 417, 419, 420, 448, 543, 596; of microscope objective, 655, 660; of microscope, 654, 656, 660, 666, 667, 668, 671, 672, 673, 680.

EXNER, F.: "Fundamental-sensation" curves, 740.

Extraordinary ray in double refraction, 687, 691, 692, 693; variable index of refraction, 693–694. See also Double refraction.

Extraordinary wave: see Double refraction.

Eye: Adaptation, 721, 743; accommodation, 433–439; anterior chamber, 425; aqueous humor, 371, 425; bacillary layer of rods and cones, 428; "black of the eye," 401; blind spot, 430; center of rotation, 432, 434, 448, 452, 643, 748; change of refracting power in accommodation, 436, 437; choroid, 425; ciliary body, 427; cornea, 371, 372, 401, 425, 696–699; cornea-vertex, 431; crystalline lens, 371–373, 428, 698; decrease of accommodation with age, 435, 436; description of human eye, 425–431; entrance-pupil, 401, 448, 714; expressions for refraction of eye, 439; far and near points, 434, 435; field of fixation, 432, 435, 748–750; focal lengths, 343, 374, 389, 432; focal lengths for maximum accommodation, 437; focal points, 374, 389, 423, 432; fovea centralis, 429, 432, 433, 446, 715, 721, 747, 749; iris, 401, 425; line of fixation, 432, 748; motor muscles, 431, 432, 748; nodal points, 422, 432; optical axis, 431; optic nerve, 430; point of fixation, 432, 747; positions of cardinal points for maximum accommodation, 437; posterior pole, 432, 438; principal points, 374, 432; pupil, 23, 401, 409–413, 421, 425, 710, 714, 715, 721; refracting power, 374, 432; resolving power, 21, 22, 597, 672, 713–716; retina, 428, 684, 747, 748, 749; static and dynamic refraction, 438 and foll.; variation of principal points in accommodation, 437; visual axis, 433; visual purple, 430; white of the eye, 425; yellow spot (macula lutea), 428, 747; zonule of ZINN, 428, 434.

Eye: see also Ametropic eye, Emmetropic eye, Hypermetropic eye, Mobile eye, Myopic eye, Reduced eye, Schematic eye, etc.

Eye and ear, 724.

Eye-axis, Length of, 438, 440–443, 448.

Eye-ball, 426, 431, 748. See also *Center of rotation of eye.*

Eye-glasses: see *Correction-glass, Astigmatic lenses, Cylindrical lenses, Ophthalmic prisms,* etc.

Eye-lens of ocular, 656, 680, 681, 682.

Eye-ring (or eye-circle) of telescope, 413, 458, 459; of microscope, 681.

F

FARADAY, M.: 482, 764, 765, 766; optical glass, 482; theory of dielectric polarization, 764–766.

Far point, 434, 438, 440, 442; coincides with second focal point of correction glass, 445; of schematic eye, 461; senile recession of, 436.

Far point distance, 437, 444.

Far point sphere, 434.

Far sighted eye, 435. See also *Hypermetropia.*

FERMAT, P.: Principle of least time, 86, 594, 623.

Field-glasses: see *Binocular telescope.*

Field-lens of ocular, 656, 680, 681, 682.

Field of fixation of mobile eye, 432, 435, 748–749; field of binocular fixation, 749–751.

Field of stereoscopic vision, 760.

Field of view, 18, 19, 406–409, 448, 596; of plane mirror, 40–43; of spherical mirror, 176–179; of infinitely thin lens, 247–249, 409–411; of Dutch telescope, 412, 413; of astronomical telescope, 411, 412; of compound microscope, 660, 663; of simple microscope, 640–643; monocular field of view, 747–748; "ragged edge," 412.

Field stop, 19, 178, 249, 406, 410; of magnifying glass, 641, 643.

Fish-eye camera, 81.

Fixation: Field of, 432, 435, 748–749; field of binocular, 749–751; line of, 432, 748, 755; point of, 432, 747, 749, 750, 751, 755, 756.

Flat image, 539, 540, 548.

Fluorite (fluorspar), 479, 485, 680.

Focal lengths of centered system, 354, 355, 521, 606–611.

Focal lengths of combination of two lenses, 367.

Focal lengths of compound system, 359.

Focal lengths of infinitely thin lens, 229, 240–242.

Focal lengths of optical system in general, 342–344.

Focal lengths of schematic eye, 343, 374, 389, 432; for maximum accommodation, 437.

Focal lengths of spherical mirror, 167; of spherical refracting surface, 191, 192, 193, 199, 281; of thick lens, 363.

Focal planes of centered system of spherical refracting surfaces, 333;

of infinitely thin lens, 232; of optical system, 334, 335, 341; of spherical refracting surface, 197–199.

Focal point angle, 447; as measure of size of retinal image, 449.

Focal points of centered system of spherical refracting surfaces, 332, 333, 521, 609; of combination of two lenses, 367; of compound system, 358, 361; of infinitely thin lens, 229–232; of optical system, 334, 335; of spherical mirror, 166, 189; of spherical refracting surface, 186–189; of thick lens, 363.

Focal points of schematic eye, 374, 389, 423, 432.

Focus plane, 400, 402–404, 406–408, 414–417, 543.

Fovea centralis, 429, 432, 433, 446, 715, 721, 747, 749.

Foveal vision: see *Daylight vision*.

Foveola, 747. See also *Fovea centralis*.

FRAUNHOFER, J.: 145, 479, 493, 494, 506, 597, 598; dark lines of solar spectrum, 470, 472, 475, 476, 477, 649; measurement of index of refraction, 129; notation of dark lines, 472; production of optical glass, 482; achromatic object-glass, 504, 505; magnifying glass, 648; microscope, 651.

Frequency of vibration and color, 472–476, 726, 762; connection with wave-length, 475.

FRESNEL, A. J.: Principle of interference, 14, 598; use of cylindrical lens, 315; wave-surface, 689; wave-theory, 688, 761, 763, 764, 766, 767.

Fundamental-color sensations, 734, 739; KOENIG-DIETERICI curves, 740, 741. See also YOUNG-HELMHOLTZ *color theory*.

Fusion, Binocular, 749, 751.

G

GALILEO: Telescope and astronomical discoveries, 456, 462, 463, 464, 571, 597; mechanics, 767.

Gap in visible spectrum, 728–730.

Gauging of visible spectrum, 740. See also *Color mixing*.

GAUSS, K. F.: Reduced distance, 279, 280; theory of optical imagery, 334, 536, 545, 546, 603, 664; principal points, 335; achromatic object-glass, 504, 505.

Geometrical optics, its limitations, 669, 670, 686, 710, 761, 770.

GIRAUD TEULON: *Minimum separabile*, 716.

Glass, Optical: see *Optical* glass.

GLEICHEN, A., *Lehrbuch der geometrischen Optik*, 352, 649.

Glycerine immersion-system, 673.

GOERZ, P.: "Double anastigmat" photographic lens, 352.

GOETHE, J. W.: Doctrine of colors, 738.

Graphical methods: Paraxial ray diagrams, 168–171; path of paraxial ray through centered system, 331; YOUNG'S construction, 509–511, 509–511. See also *Color chart, Color circle, Color cone, Color triangle.*

Grating spectrum, 729.

Gray color, 720, 731, 744.

Green-blindness: see *Color blindness, partial.*

GREGORY, J.: Achromatism, 480.

GRIMALDI, F. M., 596.

GRIMSEHL, E., *Lehrbuch der Physik,* 363.

Group wave, 770.

GRÜNBERG, complementary spectral colors, 727.

GULLSTRAND, A.: Reduced distance, 280; schematic eye, 343, 370, 371, 374, 381, 382, 389, 395, 432, 436, 442, 443, 461, 611, 627, 628, 629, 707; formulæ for compound systems, 360, 361; schematic eye in state of maximum accommodation, 395, 436, 461; writings, 536, 625.

GUNDLACH, E.: Periscopic ocular, 682.

GUNTHER, R. T.: see caption of Fig. 296.

H

HADLEY'S sextant, 58–60.

HALL, C. M.: Achromatic telescope, 481.

HALLEY, E., 595.

HAMILTON, Sir W. R.: Internal conical refraction, 763.

HARCOURT, W. V.: Optical glass, 482.

Harmonic range of points, 161–164.

Heliometer, 699.

Heliostat, 54, 55.

HELMHOLTZ, H. v.: Color theory, 726, 739, 742, 743, 746, 747; electro-dynamics, 766; *Handbuch der physiolog. Optik,* 371; ophthal-mometer, 103, 696, 698, 700, 701; SMITH-HELMHOLTZ equation, 201, 202, 214, 215, 334, 338, 342, 459, 524, 664; telestereoscope, 758.

HERING, E.: *Opponent-colors theory,* 743, 744, 745, 746, 747.

HERO of Alexandria, 87, 563, 594.

HERSCHEL, Sir J. F. W.: Achromatic object-glass of telescope, 504, 505.

HERTZ, H.: Electromagnetic waves, 766.

Homocentric (or monocentric) bundle of rays, 25.

Homogeneous immersion microscope objective, 679.

Homogeneous medium, 685, 686.

Homogeneous projective coördinates, 735–738. See also *Trilinear coördinates.*

Homogeneous radiation: see *Monochromatic light.*

HOOKE, R., 598; magnifying glass, 396, 646, 651; resolving power of eye, 597.

HOUSTOUN, R. A.: NEWTON and colors of spectrum; 466, 469; law of refraction (history), 569, 570.

Hue, 720, 726, 727, 728, 746; hue discrimination, 731; hue, saturation and luminosity, 730–732, 741.

Hueless (toneless) sensations, 744. See also *Gray, Achromatic vision.*

HUYGENS, C.: Aplanatic lenses, 618; aplanatic points of spherical refracting surface, 596, 617; aplanatic surfaces, 623.

HUYGENS, C.: Construction of wave-front in general, 10–13, 123, 670, 710; in case of reflection at plane mirror, 33–37, 61; in case of refraction at plane surface, 70–72; for double refraction in Iceland spar, 688–693.

HUYGENS, C.: Construction of ray refracted at spherical surface, 596, 617.

HUYGENS, C.: Law of conjugate points, 595; law of refraction, 573.

HUYGENS, C.: Loss of priority, 595; notion of equivalent lenses, 595.

HUYGENS, C.: Ocular, 396, 501, 502, 648, 663, 681, 682.

HUYGENS, C.: Polarization of light, 596, 688; pupils of optical system, 596; spherical aberration, 596; theorem about apparent size, 596; theory of telescope, 596.

HUYGENS, C.: Theory of double refraction in Iceland spar, 596, 687, 688, 689, 690, 692.

HUYGENS, C.: Treatise on dioptrics, 594, 595, 596, 617; treatise on light, 596, 617, 623, 687, 688; wave-theory of light, 762, 767.

Hyperbolic refracting surface, 593, 594, 619, 620, 621.

Hyperboloidal lens, 621, 622.

Hypermetropia, 441, 443, 445.

Hypermetropic eye, 441; correction glass, 445.

I

Iceland spar, 687, 688, 689, 690, 692, 694, 695; index of refraction, 693–694. See also *Double refraction.*

Image, 5, 17, 18, 25; ideal, 25, 506, 548; real and virtual, 17, 18.

Image-equations of optical system: Referred to focal points, 345; referred to principal points, 345–347; referred to pair of conjugate points, 347, 348, 627; referred to nodal points, 348, 627; in terms of refracting power and reduced "vergences," 348.

Image-equations of spherical refracting surface, 200, 201.

Image-lines of narrow astigmatic bundle of rays, 100, 312, 313, 534–536, 547; for plane refracting surface, 100.

Image-point, 25.

Image-points of narrow astigmatic bundle of rays, 312, 526, 527, 529–534.

Image-rays, 24.

Image, Rectification of, by successive reflections, 50, 51. See also *Mirror stereoscope.*

Image, Retinal, inverted, 749.

Image, Size of retinal, 448, 449, 707–709.

Image-space and object-space, 242, 243.

Image-surfaces, Astigmatic, 536–538, 547.

Images in inclined mirrors, 43–51.

Immersion system: see *Compound microscope*.

Incidence: Angle of, 30; height, 151; normal, 30; plane of, 30.

Incident rays, 24, 30.

Inclined mirrors, 43–51, 565–567.

Index of refraction: Absolute, 74, 685–686, 693; limiting value of, 70; relative, 66; measurement of, 106, 107, 128, 129; function of wave-length, 476, 477; in Iceland spar, 693–694.

Indicial ametropia, 442.

Indirect vision, 446, 721, 743, 748. See also *Vision*.

Infinitely distant plane of space, 197, 434.

Infinitely distant point of straight line, 158.

Infinitely thin lens, central collineation, 246.

Infinitely thin lens, conventional representation, 226.

Infinitely thin lens: Paraxial rays, 217–257, 276–279, 285; abscissa-formula, 226–229, 285; character of imagery, 237–240; conjugate axial points, 227–229, 232–234, 595; construction of image, 236; extra-axial conjugate points, 234–236; field of view, 247–249, 409, 411; focal lengths, 229, 240–242, 594; focal planes, 232; focal points, 229–232; lateral magnification, 236, 237; principal planes, 239; prismatic power, 291–295; refracting power, 283, 284.

Infinitely thin lens, Refraction of spherical wave through, 276–279.

Infinitely thin lens-system, 289–291, 599–602; formulæ for spherical aberrations, 548–550. See also *Achromatic combinations, Combination of two lenses*.

Infrared region of spectrum, 729.

Interference of light, 14, 597, 670, 762, 770.

Interpupillary distance, 756.

Invariant: of refraction, 76; of central collineation, 246; in case of re-fraction of paraxial rays at spherical surface, 191.

Iris of eye, 401, 425.

Isotropic medium, 3, 4, 685, 686.

J

JACKSON, Professor: New optical glass, 484.

JANSEN, Z.: Reputed inventor of telescope, 456.

JAVAL, E., 698, 700, 703. See also *Ophthalmometer*.

Jena glass, 482–485, 540, 679.

K

Kaleidoscope, 47.
KELLNER, C.: Ocular, 682.
KEPLER, J.: Astronomical telescope, 455, 456, 606; sagitta, 202; formula for law of refraction, 571, 572, 626; works on optics, 571; rectilinear propagation of light, 560, 561; lens combinations (terrestrial telescope, etc.), 593; hyperbolic refracting surface, 593, 594, 619; crystalline lens, 593.
Keratoconus, 705.
Keratometer, 421, 422; another name of ophthalmometer, 703.
KESSLER, F.: Direct vision prism, 497, 498, 499, 506.
KIRCHER, A.: Jesuit writer, 573.
KLINGENSTIERNA, S.: Achromatic prism combination, 481.
KNAPP, J. H.: Ophthalmologist, 698.
KOELLIKER, A. v.: Dimensions of retinal cones, 715.
KOENIG, A.: Author, 651.
KOENIG, ARTHUR: KOENIG and DIETERICI fundamental-sensation curves, 740.
KOHLRAUSCH, F.: Measurement of index of refraction, 128.
KRIES, J. v.: Physiologist, 743.

L

LADD-FRANKLIN, C.: Color terminology, 723; "color music," 724.
LAGRANGE, J. L.: SMITH-HELMHOLTZ formula, 202.
LAMBERT, J. H.: Cosine-law of radiation, 664.
LANDOLT, E.: Ophthalmologist, 287.
LANGE, M.: Calculation-system, 520.
Lateral magnification: Centered system, 333, 349; infinitely thin lens, 236, 237; spherical mirror, 176; spherical refracting surface, 196.
Law: Of independence of light-rays, 15; of rectilinear propagation, 3, 4, 559 and foll.; of reflection, 31; of refraction, 66; of MALUS, 89–91, 525.
Least circle of aberration, 515.
Least confusion, Circle of, 314.
Least deviation: see *Prism*.
Least perceptible details, 671–673, 676, 677.
Least time, Principle of, 86–89, 594, 623.
LEEUWENHOEK, A. v.: Microscope, 645, 646.
Lens: Axis, 217; bending, 284; concentric, 221, 232, 387, 388; concave and convex, 222; convergent or positive and divergent or negative, 223; definition, 217; dispersive strength, 503; double convex and double concave, 217, 219; meniscus, 219, 226, 385, 386, 387; of zero curvature, 221, 386; optical center, 223–226; plano-convex

and plano-concave, 219; refracting power, 283, 363; symmetric, 217, 385, 388; thickness, 219.

Lens: see *Astigmatic lens, Cylindrical lens, Infinitely thin lens, Thick lens, Toric lens*, etc.

Lens, Crystalline: see *Crystalline lens*.

Lenses, Forms of, 217–223.

Lens-gauge, 263–265, 288, 289.

Lens stereoscope, 754.

Lens-system: see *Combination of two lenses*.

Lens-system, Thin, 289–291; achromatic combination, 502–505.

Lens-system (thin lenses), Spherical aberrations, 545 and foll.

Lenticular astigmatism, 698.

Light: Nature of, 9–10, 669, 761–771.

Light: Rectilinear propagation, Chap. I and 559–563; sensation, 720, 743; wave-theory, 9, 10, 472 and foll., 508, 596, 597, 669, 688, 760–767, 768, 769, 770; corpuscular theory, 669, 762, 763, 769, 770; electromagnetic theory, 669, 764–767, 768; velocity, 10, 72, 75, 474, 475, 685, 693, 764, 766.

Light: see also *Diffraction, Interference, Polarization*, etc.

Limit, Mathematical, 715–716.

Limit of binocular depth perception, 757, 759.

Line of fixation, 432, 748, 755.

LIPPERSHEY, F.: Reputed inventor of telescope, 456.

LISTER, J. L.: Microscope, 652.

LISTING, J. B.: Reduced eye, 214; nodal points, 337.

LLOYD, H.: Internal conical refraction, 763.

LODGE, Sir O.: Space-time, 767; wave-theory of matter, 770.

LORENTZ, H. A.: Electron theory, 768.

Luminiferous ether: see *Ether*.

Luminosity, 720, 726, 730, 731, 732, 741.

Luminous bodies, 1.

Luminous point, direction and location, 15–18. See also *Monocular vision*.

Luminous radiation, 1 and foll., 720, 726. See also *Light*.

M

Macula lutea or yellow spot, 428, 747. See also *Fovea centralis*.

Macular cones, diameter, 714–715.

Magic lantern, invention, 635.

Magnification, Chromatic difference of, 676.

Magnification-ratios, 349–351.

Magnification: see *Angular magnification, Axial magnification, Lateral magnification, Magnification-ratios, Magnifying power*.

Magnifying glass, 636 and foll.; antiquity of, 637; aperture-stop and field-stop, 640–643; magnifying power, 638–640; useful forms, 644–650. See also *Microscope, Simple microscope.*

Magnifying power, 199, 344, 452 and foll., 596; ABBE's definition, 454; absolute, 454; individual, 454.

Magnifying power of compound microscope, 454, 651, 662–663, 668, 669, 671, 672, 673, 683; of magnifying glass, 453, 638–640; of telescope, 455–460; of binocular telescope, 760.

MALUS, E. L.: Law, 89–91, 525; polarization, 688.

Mathematical limit, 715–716.

MAUROLYCUS, F., 560, 570, 592, 593, 594, 598.

MAXIMILIAN, Duke, 593.

MAXWELL, J. C.: Color sensations, 725; color theory, 739; electromagnetic theory of light, 764, 765, 766.

Medium: see *Dielectric medium, Homogeneous medium, Isotropic medium, Optical medium.*

Meniscus lens, 219, 226, 385, 386, 387.

Meridian rays, 311. See also *Meridian section of narrow bundle of rays.*

Meridian section of narrow bundle of rays, 311, 528, 530–533, 535, 552, 553, 554, 556; lack of symmetry in, 541.

Meridian section of surface of revolution, 305.

Metric relations in compound microscope, 661–663.

MICHELSON, A. A.: Velocity of light, 474; MICHELSON-MORLEY experiment, 763.

Microphotography, 673, 683–684.

Microscope, Chap. XVII. See also *Compound microscope, Magnifying glass, Simple microscope.*

Microscope: Cover glass, 653, 666, 678, 679; definition, 637; immersion system, 661, 666, 667, 671, 673, 678, 679, 680; invention, 635, 651; magnifying power, 452 and foll., 638 and foll., 651, 662–663, 668, 669, 671, 672, 673, 683; numerical aperture, 663–673; optical cross-sections of object, 653; pupils, 642–643, 654, 655, 656, 660, 666, 667, 668, 671, 672, 673, 680; purpose of, 636–637; resolving power, 669–673; slide, 653; tube, 652, 655, 661, 676; working distance, 647, 650, 652.

Millimicron or micromillimeter, 475, 686.

MILTON, J., reference to GALILEO, 571.

Minimum deviation of prism: see *Prism.*

Minimum separabile and minimum visible, 716.

Mires of ophthalmometer, 700, 704–706.

Mirror and scale for angle measurement, 56–58.

Mirror stereoscope, 753–754.

Mirrors: see *Plane mirror, Spherical mirror, Thick mirror, Thin mirror, Inclined mirrors, Ellipsoidal mirror, Parabolic mirror,* etc.

Mobile eye, 431–432, 452, 643; field of fixation, 748–749.

MOEBIUS, A. F.: Principal points, 335.

MOLYNEUX, W., 595.

Monocentric bundle of rays, 25.

Monochromatic aberrations, 509, 715. See also *Spherical aberration.*

Monochromatic light (homogeneous radiation), 66, 467, 473–477, 673, 674, 685, 710, 724, 726.

Monochromatic microscope objective, 684.

Monochromatic vision, 741.

Monocular field of view, 747–749.

Monocular vision, 747–749, 751.

MONOYER, F.: "Dioptrie," 286.

MORLEY, E. W.: MICHELSON-MORLEY experiment, 763.

MOSER, C.: Nodal points 337.

MÜELLER, G. E.: Theory of vision, 746.

Muscles, Ocular motor, 431, 432, 748. See also *Center of rotation of eye.*

Myopia, 441, 443, 445.

Myopic eye, 441; correction-glass, 445.

N

Near point distance, 437.

Near point of accommodation, 434, 435, 438, 636; near point sphere, 434, 435; near point recedes from eye with increase of age, 435, 436; near point of schematic eye, 436, 461.

Near point of convergence, 755.

Near-sighted eye, 435. See also *Myopic eye.*

Negative lens, 223.

Negative principal points, 338.

Neutralization of lenses, 291.

NEWTON, Sir ISAAC: 11, 594, 595, 597, 598, 766, 767, 768, 770; astigmatism of oblique bundles, 597; color chart, 732; corpuscular or emission theory of light, 669, 761, 762, 763, 769, 770; diffraction, 597; double refraction and polarization, 598, 688; NEWTON's rings (interference), 597; "Opticks," 597; prism experiments and dispersion, 66, 465, 466, 467, 469, 470, 480, 481, 597, 598, 726, 738.

Newtonian formula $(x.x' = f.f')$, 168, 201, 237, 345, 554.

Nodal planes, 337.

Nodal points, 337, 338; construction, 340; relation between nodal points and principal points, 341, 343; image-equations referred to, 348; of lens, 226, 363; of eye, 422, 432, 628.

Normal sections of curved surfaces, 300–305, 525, 526; cylindrical surface, 306.

Normal vision: see *Color vision, Resolving power of eye, Visual acuity,* SNELLEN, H., etc.

Numerical aperture of microscope, 663–669, 670–673, 679.

O

Object-glass: see *Objective.*

Objective of compound microscope, 651, 653, 673–680; aperture-stop, 655; apochromats, 489, 679; different types, 677–680; optical requirements, 673–677; pupils, 655; telecentric system, 660. See also *Compound microscope.*

Objective of telescope: see *Telescope.*

Object-point, 25.

Object-rays, 24.

Object-space and image-space, 242, 243.

Obliquely crossed cylinders, 320–326.

Ocular: Achromatism, 502, 680; of compound microscope, 651, 654, 680–683; field-lens and eye-lens, 656.

Ocular astigmatism, 698. See also *Corneal astigmatism, Ophthalmometer,* etc.

Ocular: Compensation, 682, 683; GUNDLACH's periscopic ocular, 682; HUYGENS's ocular, 396, 501, 502, 648, 663, 681, 682; KELLNER's ocular, 682; RAMSDEN's ocular, 463, 502, 681, 682.

Ocular movements, Convergent and associated, 431, 749–750. See also *Center of rotation of eye, Mobile eye, Muscles.*

OERSTED, H. C., 764.

Oil-immersion objectives, 671, 679, 680.

Olive color, 720, 731.

Opaque bodies, 2, 762.

Ophthalmic lenses: see *Astigmatic lenses, Cylindrical lenses, Correction-glass, Toric lenses,* etc.

Ophthalmic prism: Base-apex line, 135; combination of two ophthalmic prisms, 138–142; deviation, 133, power, 134; rotary prism, 141.

Ophthalmometer, 103, 696–706; clinical, 698, 699, 703–706; doubling device, 696, 699–703; invention, 698; mires, 700, 704–706; optical theory, 699–703.

Opponent-colors, 744.

Opponent-colors theory of E. HERING, 743–747.

Optic axis of crystals, 688, 689, 690, 692, 693, 694, 695, 696.

Optic nerve, 430.

Optical achromatism, 489, 490, 675.

Optical axis: Axis of symmetry, 23; of centered system, 329; of lens, 217.

Optical axis of eye, 431.
Optical center of lens, 223–226.
Optical cross-sections of object under microscope, 653.
Optical disk for verifying laws of reflection and refraction, 32, 67, 68; total reflection, 83, 84.
Optical glass, 481 and foll., 673, 675, 679, 686; process of manufacture, 485–487.
Optical illusions, 749, 750–751, 754–755.
Optical image, 5, 17, 18, 25. See also *Image.*
Optical image on retina, 749.
Optical instruments, 23, 635–636; types of, 602–606. See also *Microscope, Telescope,* etc.
Optical invariant of refraction, 76.
Optical length, 89–91, 278, 279, 623.
Optical medium, 3; homogeneous, 669, 685, 686; isotropic, 3, 4, 670, 685, 686.
Optical system, 23.
Optical tube length of microscope, 655, 661, 676.
Optical zone of cornea of eye, 697, 698.
Optometer of BADAL, 422, 423.
Orange color, 720, 731.
Ordinary ray in double refraction, 687, 691, 692, 693. See also *Double refraction.*
Ordinary wave: see *Double refraction.*
Origin of coördinates, 149. See also *Image-equations.*
Orthoscopy, Conditions of, 543–545.

P

Pale colors, 731.
Parabolic mirror, 565, 619.
Paraxial ray, Calculation of, 519–521, 606–617.
Paraxial ray, definition, 152.
Paraxial ray diagrams, 168–171.
Paraxial rays: Centered system, 329–334, 519–521; infinitely thin lens, 217–257, 276–279, 285; plane refracting surface, 96–98, 191, 265–269, 615; plate with parallel faces, 105–107; spherical mirror, 153–179, 189, 274–276, 285; spherical refracting surface, 179–202, 269–274, 285, 519, 534, 614; thin lens-system, 289–291.
PARSONS Optical Glass Company, 686.
PARSONS, Sir JOHN H., 716, 739.
Pathological astigmatism, 698.
PELLIN-BROCA constant deviation prism, 584, 585.
Pencil of rays, 24.

PENDLEBURY, C.: "Lenses and systems of lenses," 280.

Pentaprism, 148, 588.

Penumbra, 7, 562, 563.

Period of vibration, 473.

Periodic character of luminous phenomena, 762, 770.

Peripheral (indirect) vision, 446, 721, 743, 748. See also *Rod vision, Twilight vision.*

Perspective, Center of, 159; so-called center (K), 532; pupil-centers as centers of perspective, 416, 417.

Perspective elongation of image, 419, 420.

Perspective in art, 22, 559.

Perspective ranges of points, 159–161.

Perspective reproduction in screen-plane, 417.

Perversion of image in plane mirror, 39–40, 753.

PETZVAL, J.: Curvature of image, 539; portrait lens, 634.

Photograph, Correct distance of viewing, 417–419, 754.

Photographic negative, 635.

Photography, Discovery of, 635. See also *Microphotography.*

Physical optics, 598, 670. See also Chap. XVIII.

Physiological astigmatism, 697.

Physiological optics: see Chap. XVIII.

Pigments, Mixing of, 722, 725.

Pinhole camera, 5, 561. See also *Fish eye camera.*

Pink color, 720, 731.

PLANCK, MAX: Quantum theory, 769; transition from classical physics to new physics, 767.

Plane image, Conditions of, 538–540, 548.

Plane mirror: Conjugate points, 38; reflection of plane and spherical waves at, 33–37; image of extended object in, 37–40; perversion of image, 39–40, 753; uses of, 52; rotation of, 32, 56; field of view, 40–43; punctual imagery, 508, 618; reflecting power, 380, 381. See also *Inclined mirrors, Mirror and scale, Thick mirror, Sextant, Heliostat,* etc.

Plane mirrors, Inclined, 43–51, 565–569; rectangular combinations, for rectifying image, 50, 51, 566–568.

Plane refracting surface: Caustic surface, 98, 99; narrow astigmatic bundle of rays, 98–100, 553; paraxial rays, 96–98, 191, 265–269; plane wave, 70–72; spherical wave, 265–269; principle of least time, 87–89.

Plane wave, 13; reflection at plane mirror, 33–35; refraction at plane surface, 70–72; refraction through prism, 123, 124; mechanical illustration, 72, 73.

Plano-convex and plano-concave lenses, 219, 225.

Plano-cylindrical lenses, 315–317.

Plastic impression, 751. See also *Depth perception.*

Plate (or slab) with plane parallel faces: Path of ray through, 101–103, 570, 571; refraction of paraxial rays, 105–107; apparent position of object when plate is perpendicular to line of sight, 102, 103, and when plate is inclined to line of sight, 105–107; multiple images by reflection and refraction, 107–110; parallel plate micrometer, 103.

POINCARÉ, H.: Ether, 764.

Point of fixation, 432, 747, 749, 750, 751, 755, 756.

Point-source of light, 1; apparent place and direction, 15–18; appearance of, 709.

Polarization microscope, 683.

Polarization of light, 596, 598, 688, 695, 696, 762, 770.

PORRO, I.: Prism system for rectification of image, 50, 51, 573, 588.

PORTA's pinhole camera, 5, 561; *camera obscura,* 561; inclined mirrors, etc., 565; properties of lenses, 570.

Porte lumière, 53.

PORTERFIELD, W.: *Minimum visibile,* 716.

Ports: see *Entrance-port, Exit-port.*

POSER, M.: Microphotographs of retina, 684.

Positive and negative directions along a straight line, 104; positive direction along the axis, 149, 219.

Positive lens, 223.

Posterior pole of eye, 432, 438.

Power of accommodation: see *Accommodation.*

Power of lens or prism: see *Prism, Prismatic power of lens, Reflecting power, Refracting power.*

PRENTICE, C. F.: Crossed cylinders, 321; diagrams, 308, 309, 310; power of ophthalmic prism, 135.

Presbyopia, 435, 628.

Primary colors, 744. See also *Simple colors, Pure colors.*

Principal planes, 335; of a thin lens, 239; of a spherical refracting surface, 196, 335.

Principal point angle, 447; as measure of size of retinal image, 448.

Principal points, 334, 335; relation to nodal points, 341, 343; image equations referred to, 345–347; of combination of two lenses, 367, 369, 370; of compound system, 361; of compound system of three members, 375; of infinitely thin lens, 239; of "thick" mirror, 377–379, 383; of thick lens, 363.

Principal points of schematic eye, 374, 432; of eye in state of maximum accommodation, 437; as points of reference, 437.

Principal section of crystal, 692 and foll.

Principal section of prism, 113.

Principal sections: Of curved surfaces, 302, 525; of surface of revolution,

305; of cylindrical surface, 306; of toric surface, 309; of toric lenses, 310; of a bundle of rays, 304, 311–314, 528, 535; of cornea, 704–706.

Prism, 85, 86, 113 and foll.; base-apex line, 134; edge, 113; refracting angle, 113; and its measurement, 55; principal section, 113. See also *Thin prism, Ophthalmic prism, Roof-angle prism, Reflection prisms.*

Prismatic power of infinitely thin lens, 291–295.

Prism binoculars, 51, 606, 759–760. See also *Binocular telescope.*

Prism, Constant deviation, 584, 585, 588.

Prism-dioptry, 135, 294.

Prism, Dispersion by, 465 and foll.

Prism, DOVE's reversion prism, 583.

Prism, Path of ray through a: Calculation, 124, 125, and construction of, 113–116; deviation, 116, 148; deviation away from edge, 122; "grazing" incidence and emergence, 117, 118; limiting incident ray, 118; minimum deviation, 119–122, 128–133; normal emergence, 129; symmetrical ray, 119–122, 129–133.

Prism, Refraction of plane wave through, 123, 124.

Prism-system: Achromatic combination of two thin prisms, 491–493; direct vision prism combinations, 493 and foll.; direct vision prism of AMICI, 495–497, and of KESSLER, 497–499.

Prism, WOLLASTON: see WOLLASTON, W. H.

Problems, 25–27, 60–63, 92–94, 110–112, 142–148, 203–216, 249–257, 295–299, 326–328, 351–355, 384–396, 423–424, 461–464, 505–507, 551–557, 626–634.

Projected image and object, 415, 416.

PTOLEMY, C.: "Optics," 569; law of refraction, 570, 572.

PULFRICH, C.: Refractometer, 128.

Punctual imagery, 313, 314, 397, 508, 509, 710; in plane mirror, 508.

Punctum cæcum (blind spot), 430.

Punctum proximum (near point), 434, 435.

Punctum remotum (far point), 434.

Pupil of eye, 23, 401, 409–413, 421, 425; contraction and dilatation of, 426, 709, 715, 721; diameter of, 714; size of pupil and resolving power, 715; diffraction, 710.

Pupils of microscope-objective, 655, 660.

Pupils of optical system, 399 and foll. See also *Entrance-pupil, Exit-pupil, Microscope, Telescope,* etc.

Pure colors, 726–727, 729, 730, 744, 746.

Pure red, not in visible spectrum, 726, 727, 729, 730.

Purity of spectrum, 469–471.

PURKINJE, J.: Reflex images in the eye, 378, 696; calculation of equivalent optical system, 381, 382.

Purple, 720, 723, 724, 728–730, 730, 734.

Q

Quantum theory of radiation, 669, 769, 770.

Quartz, 485; quartz lenses for microphotography, 673, 684; uniaxial crystal, 689.

R

Radiation, cosine law, 664.

Radioactivity, 768, 769.

Radius: Of curvature, 260; of spherical reflecting or refracting surface, 150.

Radius of stereoscopic vision, 757 and foll.

Rainbow, 594, 598.

RAMSDEN, J.: Eye-circle, 458, 681; ocular, 463, 502, 681, 682.

Range-finder, Coincidence type, 718.

Range of accommodation, 438.

Ray-coördinates (or ray-parameters), 95, 517.

Ray-procedure in compound microscope, 655–661.

Rays, Chief: see *Chief rays.*

Rays of finite slope, Chap. XV, 508 and foll.

Rays of light, 9, 669; mutual independence, 15; meet wave-surface normally, 13, 14, 89–91. See also *Bundle of rays, Effective rays, Emergent rays, Image-rays, Incident rays, Object-rays, Paraxial rays, Pencil of rays,* etc.

Ray-velocity and wave-velocity, 693–694.

Real and virtual, 17; images, 17, 18.

Rectangular combinations of plane mirrors, 50, 51.

Rectilinear propagation of light, 3–5, 559–563, 669, 762.

Red-blindness: see *Color blindness, partial.*

Red-green process, 745. See also HERING's *opponent-colors theory.*

Reduced abscissa and "vergence," 284–286, 348.

Reduced distance, 279–281; reduced distance (c) between two optical systems, 360.

Reduced eye, 214, 437.

Reduced focal lengths, 281; focal point "vergences," 284–286.

Reflecting power of mirror, 283; plane mirror, 380, 381; "thick" mirror, 379.

Reflecting surface, Quality of, 29, 30.

Reflecting telescope, 480, 598.

Reflection and refraction, Generalization of laws of, 86–89.

Reflection, Angle of, 31; and laws of, 31, 563, 564.

Reflection as special case of refraction, 182, 183, 189, 518.

Reflection prisms, 573 and foll.; and single reflection prism, 574, 575–585; double reflection prism, 586–592; triple reflection prism, 574.

Reflection, Regular and irregular (or diffuse), 28–30.

Reflex (catoptric) images in eye.

Refracted ray, Construction of, 76–78; deviation, 78. See also *Plane refracting surface, Spherical refracting surface,* etc.

Refracting angle of prism, 113; measurement of, 55.

Refracting power, 281–284; in normal section of refracting surface, 303; of spherical refracting surface, 282, 300; of compound system of two members, 361, and of three members, 375; of thick lens, 363; of thin lens, 283, 284; of thin lens-system, 290; of combination of two lenses, 367; of centered system of spherical refracting surfaces, 606–611.

Refracting power of correction-glass, 444.

Refracting power of schematic eye, 374, 432; in state of maximum accommodation, 437, 438, 439.

Refraction, Internal conical, 763.

Refraction of eye, 438, 439; dynamic, 438, and static refraction, 438.

Refraction of light, 64, 65, 599 and foll.; angle of, 65; laws of, 66, 569 and foll., 592, 685–686; experimental proofs, 67–69; mechanical illustration, 72, 73; early experiments on, 569 and foll. See also *Double refraction, Index of refraction, Total reflection,* etc.

Refrangibility and color, 726. See also *Color, Dispersion,* etc.

Relativity: see EINSTEIN, A.

Relief-telescope, 759, 760.

Resolving power of eye, 21, 22, 597, 672, 713–716; effect of size of pupil, 715; normal, 672, 716, 718, 719. See also *Visual acuity, Aligning power of eye.*

Resolving power of microscope, 669–673, 679, 684, 710.

Resultant of combination of two thin prisms, 138–142.

Retina, 428, 749; microphotographs of human retina, 684; sensitivity, 747, 748. See also *Cones and rods of retina, Fovea centralis, Daylight vision, Twilight vision, Peripheral vision,* etc.

Retinal image, 593; of distant object, 707–709; inversion of, 749. See also *Point-source of light, appearance of, Resolving power of eye,* etc.

Retinal image, Size of, 448, 449, 707–709.

Reversibility of light-path, 69.

Rod vision: see *Twilight vision, Peripheral vision, Color blindness.*

Rods and cones: see *Cones and rods of retina.*

ROENTGEN, W. C.: Discovery of X-rays, 767.

ROGERS, W. B.: Optical illusion, 750.

ROHR, M. v.: Abbreviation "dptr," 287; aberration-disks in microscope image, 676; data of PETZVAL lens, 634; resolving power of eye, 716; *Theorie u. Geschichte d. photograph. Objektivs,* 555; verant lens, 418, 754; vertex refraction, 366.

Roof-angle prism, 568.

Ross, A.: Microscope-tube adjustment, 678.

Rotary prism, 141.

S

Sagittal rays, 311. See also *Sagittal section of narrow bundle of rays.*

Sagittal section of narrow bundle of rays, 311–314, 528–530; symmetry in, 541.

Sagitta of arc, 262.

SALISBURY, Lord: Ether, 764.

Saturation (color), 730, 731, 732, 734, 741.

SCALIGER, J., 770.

SCHEINER, C.: Astronomical and terrestrial telescopes, 456, 572, 592, 593; corneal curvature, 697; experiments on refraction, 573; magnifying glass, 645; retinal image, 593; treatise on the eye and vision, 572.

Schematic eye: Far point, 461; focal lengths, 343, 374, 389, 432; focal points, 374, 389, 423, 432; in state of maximum accommodation, 395, 436, 437, 461; length of eye-axis, 432, 442, 443; near point, 436, 461; nodal points, 432, 628; optical constants, 370–374, 389, 432, 436, 437, 443, 461, 627, 628; principal points, 374, 432, 709.

SCHIÖTZ (JAVAL-SCHIÖTZ): Clinical ophthalmometer, 698, 700, 703.

SCHOTT, O.: Optical glass, 482, 489.

SCHRÖDINGER, E.: Theory of wave mechanics, 770.

Sclerotic coat (*sclera*), 425.

Screen-plane, 400, 402, 414–417, 419, 543.

SEARLE, G. F. C.: "Thick" mirror, 376, 377.

Secondary spectrum, 488, 675, 679.

Segments of straight line, 104, 105.

SEIDEL, L. v.: Theory of the five spherical aberrations, 545, 546, 547, 548, 550, 557; curvature of image, 540; sine-condition, 523.

Self-conjugate point, 243.

Self-conjugate ray, 243.

Sensations, Visual: see *Color sensations, Light.*

Sensitivity of retina, 747–748. See also *Retina.*

Sextant, 58–60.

Shadows, 6–9, 561–563.

SIEDENTOPF, H.: Ultramicroscope, 684.

Sight-test charts, 716–719. See also *Resolving power of eye.*

Simple colors, 726, 744.

Simple microscope: Field of view, 640–643; field-stop and aperture-stop, 640–643; limitations of, 649–651; magnifying power, 638–640; practical types, 644–650. See also *Magnifying glass.*

Sine-condition, 522–525, 547, 664, 665, 674, 676.

Single reflection prism, 574, 575–585; deviation, 579 and foll.; achromatic, 582, 583.

Slab with plane parallel faces: see *Plate*.

Slope of ray, 151, 334, 516.

SMITH, R.: Resolving power of eye, 597; apparent brightness of object, 668; SMITH-HELMHOLTZ formula, 201, 202, 214, 215, 334, 338, 342, 459, 524, 664; stereoscopic vision, 754; theorem of apparent size, 596.

SMITH, T.: Classification of optical instruments, 602, 603, 604, 605; formulæ for calculating refracting power of centered system, 608; wave-length values, 686.

SNELL (or SNELLIUS), W.: Law of refraction, 67, 72, 573.

SNELLEN, H.: Sight-test charts, 716, 717, 718, 719.

Space-time, 767; curvature, 769.

Spectacle glasses, 564, 592. See also *Correction-glass, Ophthalmic lenses, Ophthalmic prism*.

Spectral colors, Character and distribution, 466, 469, 472, 598, 724, 725–727, 728–730, 730, 731, 732, 733, 734, 735; complementary, 725, 727–728, 729, 734, 735, 746.

Spectrum, 466 and foll.; purity of, 469–471.

Spectrum: Absorption, 725; grating (diffraction), 729; prismatic (dispersion), 465 and foll.; physical and physiological, 728, 729; infrared and ultraviolet regions, 729.

Spectrum, Solar, 466 and foll.; NEWTON's experiments, 465 and foll., 598; WOLLASTON's experiments, 469, 470; FRAUNHOFER's dark lines, 472.

Spectrum, Visible: 724, 725–727; brightest region, 671; complementary colors, 727–728, 729, 735; gap in, 728–730; gauging of, 740. See also *Spectral colors*.

Spherical aberration, Chap. XV, 509, 513 and foll., 596; along the axis, 513–516, 518, 522, 547, 631, 632, 674, 675, 677, 678; chromatic difference of, 676.

Spherical lens, 217.

Spherical mirror, Ray reflected at, 518, 519, 631, 632.

Spherical mirror: Paraxial rays, 153–179, 189, 274–276, 285; abscissa-formula, 154, 285; construction of conjugate axial points, 164–166; focal points, 166, 189; focal length, 167; Newtonian formula, 168; extra-axial conjugate points, 171–173; construction of image, 173; imagery, 174, 175; lateral magnification, 176; field of view, 176–179; reflecting power, 283; spherical wave reflected at spherical mirror, 274–276.

Spherical mirror, spherical aberration, 631, 632.

Spherical mirror; see *Thick mirror*.

Spherical (monochromatic) aberrations, Chap. XV, 508–550, 715.

Spherical over- and under-correction, 514, 515, 675, 676.

Spherical refracting (or reflecting) surface: Axis, 149; convex and concave, 150; convergent and divergent, 186; magnifying power, 199; radius, 150; vertex, 149.

Spherical refracting surface: Aplanatic points, 512, 513, 524, 554, 596, 617, 618, 624, 628, 677, 679; calculation of refracted ray, 516–519, 611–617; construction of refracted ray, 509–512, 596, 617, 629; formulæ for refracted ray, 517–519, 614, 615, 630.

Spherical refracting surface, astigmatism of oblique bundle of rays, 526–534, 553, 554, 556.

Spherical refracting surface: Paraxial rays, 179–202, 269–274, 285, 519, 534; abscissa formula, 191, 193, 285; conjugate axial points, 179–186, 191, 192, 595; conjugate extra-axial points, 193–196; conjugate planes, 193, 194; construction of image, 194–196; construction of refracted ray, 199, 200; focal lengths, 191–193, 199; focal planes, 197–199; focal points, 186–189; image-equations, 200, 201; lateral magnification, 196; principal planes, 196, 335; nodal points, 338; refracting power, 179–202; refraction of spherical wave, 269–276.

Spherical wave reflected at plane mirror, 35–37, and at spherical mirror, 274–276.

Spherical wave refracted at plane surface, 265–269; at spherical surface, 269–274; through infinitely thin lens, 276–279.

Spherical zones, 515, 516, 674.

Sphero-cylindrical lens, 217, 315, 317.

Spherometer, 263.

STANHOPE magnifying glass, 647.

Static refraction of eye, 438.

STEINHEIL, H. A.: Aplanatic magnifying glass, 648; data of "periscope" photographic lens, 554, 555, 556.

STEINHEIL, R.: Achromatic object-glass, 505; calculation of object-glass, 520.

Stereogram, 752; stellar stereograms, 760–761.

Stereoscope, 752–754, 760–761; lens stereoscope, 754; mirror stereoscope, 753.

Stereoscopic difference (or parallax), 756.

Stereoscopic projection, Laws of, 755–758.

Stereoscopic views, 752.

Stereoscopic vision, 752–761; radius of, 757 and foll. See also *Depth perception.*

Stigmatic (or anastigmatic) lenses, 314.

STOKES, Sir. G. G.: Optical glass, 482.

Stop: Effect of, 398, 399; front stop, rear stop, interior stop, 398. See also *Aperture stop*, *Field stop*, etc.

STURM, J. C. F.: Conoid (theory of astigmatism), 310, 313, 534, 535.

STURM, J. CHR. (1676), 651.

Surface of revolution, 305; meridian section, 305; principal sections, 305.

Surfaces, Theory of curved, 300–303, 525, 526; normal sections, 300–303, 525, 526; principal sections, 302, 525.

Suspensory ligament of crystalline lens, 428, 434.

Symmetric lens, 217, 385, 388.

Symmetric points, 339.

T

Tangent-condition of orthoscopy, 545.

Telecentric optical system, 420–423; microscope objective, 660.

Telephoto-lens, 593, 602.

Telescope: see *Astronomical telescope*, *Dutch telescope*, *Terrestrial telescope*, *Reflecting telescope*, *Binocular telescope*, *Relief-telescope*.

Telescope: Eye-ring or RAMSDEN circle, 413, 458, 459; magnifying power, 445–460, 596; invention, 456, 457, 571, 572, 592, 593, 598, 635; object-glass and ocular, 455; simple schematic telescope, 455.

Telescopic imagery, 359.

Telescopic system, 359.

Telestereoscope, 758–759.

Tenth-meter, 10, 475.

Terrestrial telescope, 457, 593.

Tetrachromatic vision, 744, 747. See also HERING's *opponent-colors theory*.

Thick lens, 361–366; focal points, nodal points, principal points and refracting power, 363; vertex refraction, 365, 366.

"Thick mirror," 376–384, 392, 393; principal points, 377–379, 383; reflecting power, 379.

Thin lens: see *Infinitely thin lens*, *Infinitely thin lens-system*.

"Thin mirror," 377.

Thin prism: Deviation, 133, 134, and power, 134–138. See also *Ophthalmic prism*.

Thin prisms: Achromatic combination, 491–493; combination of two thin prisms, 138–142; direct-vision combination, 493–495.

THOMPSON, S. P.: Axial (or depth) magnification, 351; English translation of HUYGENS's treatise on light, 623; image in plane mirror, 38; obliquely crossed cylindrical lenses, 321; "prismoptrie," 135; symmetric points of optical system, 338.

Three-components color theory: see YOUNG-HELMHOLTZ *color theory*.

Threshold value, 716, 721, 757.

TOEPLER, A.: Negative principal points of optical system, 338.

Toric lens, 310, 314, 316, 317, 698.

Toric surface, 265, 305, 306, 308–310, 320.

TORRE, G. M. DELLA: Minute globules of glass, 396, 646.

Total reflection, 79–86, 572; experimental illustrations, 83–89. See also *Prism.*

Total reflection prism, 85, 86, 125, 127.

Translucent and transparent, 2, 3, 762.

Transposing of cylindrical lenses, 318–320.

Trichromatic (normal color) vision, 741, 747.

Trichromatic theory of vision: see YOUNG-HELMHOLTZ *color theory.*

Trilinear coördinates, 733, 736, 737, 738.

Tri-receptor mechanism of trichromatic theory, 740, 741, 742.

TSCHERNING, M.: *Physiological Optics,* 287.

Tube of microscope, 652–653, 655, 661, 676, 678.

Twilight vision, 721, 726.

TYNDALL, J., natural philosopher, 765.

U

Ultramicroscope, 684.

Ultraviolet light in microphotography, 673, 684; ultraviolet radiation, 729.

Umbra, 7, 562, 563.

Undulatory theory of light: see *Wave-theory.*

Uniaxial crystals, 688, 689, 694.

Unit planes and points of optical system, 335. See also *Principal planes, Principal points.*

Unit point of projective coördinates, 737.

V

Valences: see *Color coördinates, Color valences.*

Velocity of light in different media, 72–75, 475, 685, 693; varies with color or frequency of vibration, 474.

Velocity of light *in vacuo,* 10, 75, 474, 476, 685, 693, 764, 766.

Velocity of light: Ray-velocity and wave-velocity, 693–694.

Verant lens, 418, 754.

Vernier readings, 716. See also *Aligning power.*

Vertex-depth of concave surface of meniscus lens, 298.

Vertex of spherical surface, 149; of cornea of eye, 431.

Vertex refraction (vertex power) of lens, 365, 366; of correction-glass, 445, 446.

Vertices of lens, 219.

Vibration frequency and color, 472 and foll., 726; and wave-length, 473 and foll.

Vibrations of ether: see *Ether, Polarization of light.*

VINCI, LEONARDO DA, 559, 592, 751.

Virtual and real, 17; images, 17, 18.

Virtual object in case of plane mirror, 38.

Visible spectrum: see *Spectrum, visible.*

Vision: Achromatic, 721, 743; central or direct, 448, 748; peripheral or indirect, 446, 721, 743, 748.

Vision, Binocular and monocular: see *Binocular vision, Monocular vision.*

Vision, Distance of distinct, 452, 453.

Vision, Organ of: Adaptation, 721, 743. See also *Eye, Adaptation of eye,* etc.

Vision, Place of most distinct, 429, 446, 747. See also *Fovea centralis.*

Vision: see *Color vision, Daylight vision, Twilight vision,* etc.

Visual acuity affected by illumination and contrast, 716.

Visual acuity, Conventional value, 21, 22, 597, 672, 714, 716, 718.

Visual acuity, normal, 21, 22, 597, 672, 716, 718, 719; in daylight vision, 707–719; measure, 713, 714, 715, 716. See also *Resolving power of eye,* SNELLEN's *sight-test charts.*

Visual angle, 20, 446 and foll.; principal point angle, 447, 448; focal point angle, 447, 449. See also *Apparent size.*

Visual axis, 433.

Visual globe, 720, 748, 749.

Visual plane, 755.

Visual purple, 430.

Visual sensations: see *Color sensations, Light.*

VITELLO, 565, 570, 571.

Vitreous humor, 213, 371, 428.

W

Wave-front, Plane, 13, and spherical, 11. See also *Double refraction,* HUYGENS, MALUS, *Plane wave, Spherical wave.*

Wave-length *in vacuo*, 5, 475, 686; wave-length and frequency, 475; wave-length and index of refraction, 476, 477; wave-length and color, 474–477, 686, 726.

Wave-mechanics, 770.

Wave-surface in double-refracting medium, 687, 688–693.

Wave-surface, Rays normal to, 13, 14, 89–91, 525.

Wave-theory of light, 9, 10, 472 and foll., 508, 596, 597, 669, 688, 761–767, 768, 769, 770.

Wave-theory of matter, 770.

Wave-velocity and ray-velocity, 693–694.

WHEATSTONE, C.: Mirror stereoscope, 753.

Whiteness, 720, 723, 724, 726, 727, 731, 732, 733, 734, 738, 742, 744, 745. See also *Complementary colors.*

WILSON doublet magnifying glass, 648.

WOLF, M.: Stellar stereograms, 761.

WOLLASTON, W. H.: Dark lines of solar spectrum, 472; dispersion experiments, 469; doublet (magnifying glass), 113; double reflection prism, 588, 589; eyepiece, 628; magnifying glass, 647; prism (double refraction), 694–696, 703, 706.

WOOD, R. W.: Fish-eye camera, 81; velocity of light of different colors, 474.

WOODWORTH, C. W.: Formula for refracting power, 608.

WRIGHT, F. E.: Reflection prisms, 592.

Y

Yellow-blue process, 745. See also HERING's *opponent-colors theory.*

Yellow spot (*macula lutea*), 428, 747. See also *Fovea centralis.*

YOUNG-HELMHOLTZ three-components color theory, 738–743, 743, 746–747.

YOUNG, T.: Astigmatism of eye, 698; center of perspective (K) of spherical refracting surface, 532; color theory, 739, 742; color triangle, 732; construction of ray refracted at spherical surface, 509, 510, 511, 527, 552, 596; principle of interference, 14, 597; wave-theory, 598, 763.

Z

ZEISS, C., 648, 679, 684.

ZINN's zonule (suspensory ligament of crystalline lens), 428.

Zonal theory of vision, 744.

Zones, Spherical: see *Spherical zones.*

CATALOGUE OF DOVER BOOKS

BOOKS EXPLAINING SCIENCE AND MATHEMATICS
General

WHAT IS SCIENCE?, Norman Campbell. This excellent introduction explains scientific method, role of mathematics, types of scientific laws. Contents: 2 aspects of science, science & nature, laws of science, discovery of laws, explanation of laws, measurement & numerical laws, applications of science. 192pp. 5⅜ x 8.
S43 Paperbound **$1.25**

THE COMMON SENSE OF THE EXACT SCIENCES, W. K. Clifford. Introduction by James Newman, edited by Karl Pearson. For 70 years this has been a guide to classical scientific and mathematical thought. Explains with unusual clarity basic concepts, such as extension of meaning of symbols, characteristics of surface boundaries, properties of plane figures, vectors, Cartesian method of determining position, etc. Long preface by Bertrand Russell. Bibliography of Clifford. Corrected, 130 diagrams redrawn. 249pp. 5⅜ x 8.
T61 Paperbound **$1.60**

SCIENCE THEORY AND MAN, Erwin Schrödinger. This is a complete and unabridged reissue of SCIENCE AND THE HUMAN TEMPERAMENT plus an additional essay: "What is an Elementary Particle?" Nobel laureate Schrödinger discusses such topics as nature of scientific method, the nature of science, chance and determinism, science and society, conceptual models for physical entities, elementary particles and wave mechanics. Presentation is popular and may be followed by most people with little or no scientific training. "Fine practical preparation for a time when laws of nature, human institutions . . . are undergoing a critical examination without parallel," Waldemar Kaempffert, N. Y. TIMES. 192pp. 5⅜ x 8.
T428 Paperbound **$1.35**

FADS AND FALLACIES IN THE NAME OF SCIENCE, Martin Gardner. Examines various cults, quack systems, frauds, delusions which at various times have masqueraded as science. Accounts of hollow-earth fanatics like Symmes; Velikovsky and wandering planets; Hoerbiger; Bellamy and the theory of multiple moons; Charles Fort; dowsing, pseudoscientific methods for finding water, ores, oil. Sections on naturopathy, iridiagnosis, zone therapy, food fads, etc. Analytical accounts of Wilhelm Reich and orgone sex energy; L. Ron Hubbard and Dianetics; A. Korzybski and General Semantics; many others. Brought up to date to include Bridey Murphy, others. Not just a collection of anecdotes, but a fair, reasoned appraisal of eccentric theory. Formerly titled IN THE NAME OF SCIENCE. Preface. Index. x + 384pp. 5⅜ x 8.
T394 Paperbound **$1.50**

A DOVER SCIENCE SAMPLER, edited by George Barkin. 64-page book, sturdily bound, containing excerpts from over 20 Dover books, explaining science. Edwin Hubble, George Sarton, Ernst Mach, A. d'Abro, Galileo, Newton, others, discussing island universes, scientific truth, biological phenomena, stability in bridges, etc. Copies limited; no more than 1 to a customer,
FREE

POPULAR SCIENTIFIC LECTURES, Hermann von Helmholtz. Helmholtz was a superb expositor as well as a scientist of genius in many areas. The seven essays in this volume are models of clarity, and even today they rank among the best general descriptions of their subjects ever written. "The Physiological Causes of Harmony in Music" was the first significant physiological explanation of musical consonance and dissonance. Two essays, "On the Interaction of Natural Forces" and "On the Conservation of Force," were of great importance in the history of science, for they firmly established the principle of the conservation of energy. Other lectures include "On the Relation of Optics to Painting," "On Recent Progress in the Theory of Vision," "On Goethe's Scientific Researches," and "On the Origin and Significance of Geometrical Axioms." Selected and edited with an introduction by Professor Morris Kline. xii + 286pp. 5⅜ x 8½.
T799 Paperbound **$1.45**

BOOKS EXPLAINING SCIENCE AND MATHEMATICS
Physics

CONCERNING THE NATURE OF THINGS, Sir William Bragg. Christmas lectures delivered at the Royal Society by Nobel laureate. Why a spinning ball travels in a curved track; how uranium is transmuted to lead, etc. Partial contents: atoms, gases, liquids, crystals, metals, etc. No scientific background needed; wonderful for intelligent child. 32pp. of photos, 57 figures. xii + 232pp. 5⅜ x 8.
T31 Paperbound **$1.50**

THE RESTLESS UNIVERSE, Max Born. New enlarged version of this remarkably readable account by a Nobel laureate. Moving from sub-atomic particles to universe, the author explains in very simple terms the latest theories of wave mechanics. Partial contents: air and its relatives, electrons & ions, waves & particles, electronic structure of the atom, nuclear physics. Nearly 1000 illustrations, including 7 animated sequences. 325pp. 6 x 9.
T412 Paperbound **$2.00**

FROM EUCLID TO EDDINGTON: A STUDY OF THE CONCEPTIONS OF THE EXTERNAL WORLD, Sir Edmund Whittaker. A foremost British scientist traces the development of theories of natural philosophy from the western rediscovery of Euclid to Eddington, Einstein, Dirac, etc. The inadequacy of classical physics is contrasted with present day attempts to understand the physical world through relativity, non-Euclidean geometry, space curvature, wave mechanics, etc. 5 major divisions of examination: Space; Time and Movement; the Concepts of Classical Physics; the Concepts of Quantum Mechanics; the Eddington Universe. 212pp. 5⅜ x 8.   T491 Paperbound **$1.35**

PHYSICS, THE PIONEER SCIENCE, L. W. Taylor. First thorough text to place all important physical phenomena in cultural-historical framework; remains best work of its kind. Exposition of physical laws, theories· developed chronologically, with great historical, illustrative experiments diagrammed, described, worked out mathematically. Excellent physics text for self-study as well as class work. Vol. 1: Heat, Sound: motion, acceleration, gravitation, conservation of energy, heat engines, rotation, heat, mechanical energy, etc. 211 illus. 407pp. 5⅜ x 8. Vol. 2: Light, Electricity: images, lenses, prisms, magnetism, Ohm's law, dynamos, telegraph, quantum theory, decline of mechanical view of nature, etc. Bibliography. 13 table appendix. Index. 551 illus. 2 color plates. 508pp. 5⅜ x 8.
Vol. 1 S565 Paperbound **$2.25**
Vol. 2 S566 Paperbound **$2.25**
The set **$4.50**

A SURVEY OF PHYSICAL THEORY, Max Planck. One of the greatest scientists of all time, creator of the quantum revolution in physics, writes in non-technical terms of his own discoveries and those of other outstanding creators of modern physics. Planck wrote this book when science had just crossed the threshold of the new physics, and he communicates the excitement felt then as he discusses electromagnetic theories, statistical methods, evolution of the concept of light, a step-by-step description of how he developed his own momentous theory, and many more of the basic ideas behind modern physics. Formerly "A Survey of Physics." Bibliography. Index. 128pp. 5⅜ x 8.   S650 Paperbound **$1.15**

THE ATOMIC NUCLEUS, M. Korsunsky. The only non-technical comprehensive account of the atomic nucleus in English. For college physics students, etc. Chapters cover: Radioactivity, the Nuclear Model of the Atom, the Mass of Atomic Nuclei, the Disintegration of Atomic Nuclei, the Discovery of the Positron, the Artificial Transformation of Atomic Nuclei, Artificial Radioactivity, Mesons, the Neutrino, the Structure of Atomic Nuclei and Forces Acting Between Nuclear Particles, Nuclear Fission, Chain Reaction, Peaceful Uses, Thermonuclear Reactions. Slightly abridged edition. Translated by G. Yankovsky. 65 figures. Appendix includes 45 photographic illustrations. 413 pp. 5⅜ x 8.   S1052 Paperbound **$2.00**

PRINCIPLES OF MECHANICS SIMPLY EXPLAINED, Morton Mott-Smith. Excellent, highly readable introduction to the theories and discoveries of classical physics. Ideal for the layman who desires a foundation which will enable him to understand and appreciate contemporary developments in the physical sciences. Discusses: Density, The Law of Gravitation, Mass and Weight, Action and Reaction, Kinetic and Potential Energy, The Law of Inertia, Effects of Acceleration, The Independence of Motions, Galileo and the New Science of Dynamics, Newton and the New Cosmos, The Conservation of Momentum, and other topics. Revised edition of "This Mechanical World." Illustrated by E. Kosa, Jr. Bibliography and Chronology. Index. xiv + 171pp. 5⅜ x 8½.   T1067 Paperbound **$1.35**

THE CONCEPT OF ENERGY SIMPLY EXPLAINED, Morton Mott-Smith. Elementary, non-technical exposition which traces the story of man's conquest of energy, with particular emphasis on the developments during the nineteenth century and the first three decades of our own century. Discusses man's earlier efforts to harness energy, more recent experiments and discoveries relating to the steam engine, the engine indicator, the motive power of heat, the principle of excluded perpetual motion, the bases of the conservation of energy, the concept of entropy, the internal combustion engine, mechanical refrigeration, and many other related topics. Also much biographical material. Index. Bibliography. 33 illustrations. ix + 215pp. 5⅜ x 8½.   T1071 Paperbound **$1.25**

HEAT AND ITS WORKINGS, Morton Mott-Smith. One of the best elementary introductions to the theory and attributes of heat, covering such matters as the laws governing the effect of heat on solids, liquids and gases, the methods by which heat is measured, the conversion of a substance from one form to another through heating and cooling, evaporation, the effects of pressure on boiling and freezing points, and the three ways in which heat is transmitted (conduction, convection, radiation). Also brief notes on major experiments and discoveries. Concise, but complete, it presents all the essential facts about the subject in readable style. Will give the layman and beginning student a first-rate background in this major topic in physics. Index. Bibliography. 50 illustrations. x + 165pp. 5⅜ x 8½. T978 Paperbound **$1.15**

THE STORY OF ATOMIC THEORY AND ATOMIC ENERGY, J. G. Feinberg. Wider range of facts on physical theory, cultural implications, than any other similar source. Completely non-technical. Begins with first atomic theory, 600 B.C., goes through A-bomb, developments to 1959. Avogadro, Rutherford, Bohr, Einstein, radioactive decay, binding energy, radiation danger, future benefits of nuclear power, dozens of other topics, told in lively, related, informal manner. Particular stress on European atomic research. "Deserves special mention . . . authoritative," Saturday Review. Formerly "The Atom Story." New chapter to 1959. Index. 34 illustrations. 251pp. 5⅜ x 8.   T625 Paperbound **$1.60**

THE STRANGE STORY OF THE QUANTUM, AN ACCOUNT FOR THE GENERAL READER OF THE GROWTH OF IDEAS UNDERLYING OUR PRESENT ATOMIC KNOWLEDGE, B. Hoffmann. Presents lucidly and expertly, with barest amount of mathematics, the problems and theories which led to modern quantum physics. Dr. Hoffmann begins with the closing years of the 19th century, when certain trifling discrepancies were noticed, and with illuminating analogies and examples takes you through the brilliant concepts of Planck, Einstein, Pauli, de Broglie, Bohr, Schroedinger, Heisenberg, Dirac, Sommerfeld, Feynman, etc. This edition includes a new, long postscript carrying the story through 1958. "Of the books attempting an account of the history and contents of our modern atomic physics which have come to my attention, this is the best," H. Margenau, Yale University, in "American Journal of Physics." 32 tables and line illustrations. Index. 275pp. 5⅜ x 8. **T518 Paperbound $1.75**

THE EVOLUTION OF SCIENTIFIC THOUGHT FROM NEWTON TO EINSTEIN, A. d'Abro. Einstein's special and general theories of relativity, with their historical implications, are analyzed in non-technical terms. Excellent accounts of the contributions of Newton, Riemann, Weyl, Planck, Eddington, Maxwell, Lorentz and others are treated in terms of space and time, equations of electromagnetics, finiteness of the universe, methodology of science. 21 diagrams. 482pp. 5⅜ x 8. **T2 Paperound $2.25**

THE RISE OF THE NEW PHYSICS, A. d'Abro. A half-million word exposition, formerly titled THE DECLINE OF MECHANISM, for readers not versed in higher mathematics. The only thorough explanation, in everyday language, of the central core of modern mathematical physical theory, treating both classical and modern theoretical physics, and presenting in terms almost anyone can understand the equivalent of 5 years of study of mathematical physics. Scientifically impeccable coverage of mathematical-physical thought from the Newtonian system up through the electronic theories of Dirac and Heisenberg and Fermi's statistics. Combines both history and exposition; provides a broad yet unified and detailed view, with constant comparison of classical and modern views on phenomena and theories. "A must for anyone doing serious study in the physical sciences," JOURNAL OF THE FRANKLIN INSTITUTE. "Extraordinary faculty . . . to explain ideas and theories of theoretical physics in the language of daily life," ISIS. First part of set covers philosophy of science, drawing upon the practice of Newton, Maxwell, Poincaré, Einstein, others, discussing modes of thought, experiment, interpretations of causality, etc. In the second part, 100 pages explain grammar and vocabulary of mathematics, with discussions of functions, groups, series, Fourier series, etc. The remainder is devoted to concrete, detailed coverage of both classical and quantum physics, explaining such topics as analytic mechanics, Hamilton's principle, wave theory of light, electromagnetic waves, groups of transformations, thermodynamics, phase rule, Brownian movement, kinetics, special relativity, Planck's original quantum theory, Bohr's atom, Zeeman effect, Broglie's wave mechanics, Heisenberg's uncertainty, Eigen-values, matrices, scores of other important topics. Discoveries and theories are covered for such men as Alembert, Born, Cantor, Debye, Euler, Foucault, Galois, Gauss, Hadamard, Kelvin, Kepler, Laplace, Maxwell, Pauli, Rayleigh, Volterra, Weyl, Young, more than 180 others. Indexed. 97 illustrations. ix + 982pp. 5⅜ x 8.
T3 Volume 1, Paperbound $2.25
T4 Volume 2, Paperbound $2.25

SPINNING TOPS AND GYROSCOPIC MOTION, John Perry. Well-known classic of science still unsurpassed for lucid, accurate, delightful exposition. How quasi-rigidity is induced in flexible and fluid bodies by rapid motions; why gyrostat falls, top rises; nature and effect on climatic conditions of earth's precessional movement; effect of internal fluidity on rotating bodies, etc. Appendixes describe practical uses to which gyroscopes have been put in ships, compasses, monorail transportation. 62 figures. 128pp. 5⅜ x 8. **T416 Paperbound $1.25**

THE UNIVERSE OF LIGHT, Sir William Bragg. No scientific training needed to read Nobel Prize winner's expansion of his Royal Institute Christmas Lectures. Insight into nature of light, methods and philosophy of science. Explains lenses, reflection, color, resonance, polarization, x-rays, the spectrum, Newton's work with prisms, Huygens' with polarization, Crookes' with cathode ray, etc. Leads into clear statement of 2 major historical theories of light, corpuscle and wave. Dozens of experiments you can do. 199 illus., including 2 full-page color plates. 293pp. 5⅜ x 8. **S538 Paperbound $1.85**

THE STORY OF X-RAYS FROM RÖNTGEN TO ISOTOPES, A. R. Bleich. Non-technical history of x-rays, their scientific explanation, their applications in medicine, industry, research, and art, and their effect on the individual and his descendants. Includes amusing early reactions to Röntgen's discovery, cancer therapy, detections of art and stamp forgeries, potential risks to patient and operator, etc. Illustrations show x-rays of flower structure, the gall bladder, gears with hidden defects, etc. Original Dover publication. Glossary. Bibliography. Index. 55 photos and figures. xiv + 186pp. 5⅜ x 8. **T662 Paperbound $1.50**

ELECTRONS, ATOMS, METALS AND ALLOYS, Wm. Hume-Rothery. An introductory-level explanation of the application of the electronic theory to the structure and properties of metals and alloys, taking into account the new theoretical work done by mathematical physicists. Material presented in dialogue-form between an "Old Metallurgist" and a "Young Scientist." Their discussion falls into 4 main parts: the nature of an atom, the nature of a metal, the nature of an alloy, and the structure of the nucleus. They cover such topics as the hydrogen atom, electron waves, wave mechanics, Brillouin zones, co-valent bonds, radioactivity and natural disintegration, fundamental particles, structure and fission of the nucleus, etc. Revised, enlarged edition. 177 illustrations. Subject and name indexes. 407pp. 5⅜ x 8½. **S1046 Paperbound $2.25**

TEACH YOURSELF MECHANICS, P. Abbott. The lever, centre of gravity, parallelogram of force, friction, acceleration, Newton's laws of motion, machines, specific gravity, gas, liquid pressure, much more. 280 problems, solutions. Tables. 163 illus. 271pp. 6⅞ x 4¼.
Clothbound **$2.00**

MATTER & MOTION, James Clerk Maxwell, This excellent exposition begins with simple particles and proceeds gradually to physical systems beyond complete analysis: motion, force, properties of centre of mass of material system, work, energy, gravitation, etc. Written with all Maxwell's original insights and clarity. Notes by E. Larmor. 17 diagrams. 178pp. 5⅜ x 8.
S188 Paperbound **$1.35**

SOAP BUBBLES, THEIR COLOURS AND THE FORCES WHICH MOULD THEM, C. V. Boys. Only complete edition, half again as much material as any other. Includes Boys' hints on performing his experiments, sources of supply. Dozens of lucid experiments show complexities of liquid films, surface tension, etc. Best treatment ever written. Introduction. 83 illustrations. Color plate. 202pp. 5⅜ x 8.
T542 Paperbound **95¢**

MATTER & LIGHT, THE NEW PHYSICS, L. de Broglie. Non-technical papers by a Nobel laureate explain electromagnetic theory, relativity, matter, light and radiation, wave mechanics, quantum physics, philosophy of science. Einstein, Planck, Bohr, others explained so easily that no mathematical training is needed for all but 2 of the 21 chapters. Unabridged. Index. 300pp. 5⅜ x 8.
T35 Paperbound **$1.85**

SPACE AND TIME, Emile Borel. An entirely non-technical introduction to relativity, by world-renowned mathematician, Sorbonne professor. (Notes on basic mathematics are included separately.) This book has never been surpassed for insight, and extraordinary clarity of thought, as it presents scores of examples, analogies, arguments, illustrations, which explain such topics as: difficulties due to motion; gravitation a force of inertia; geodesic lines; wave-length and difference of phase; x-rays and crystal structure; the special theory of relativity; and much more. Indexes. 4 appendixes. 15 figures. xvi + 243pp. 5⅜ x 8.
T592 Paperbound **$1.45**

BOOKS EXPLAINING SCIENCE AND MATHEMATICS

Astronomy

THE FRIENDLY STARS, Martha Evans Martin. This engaging survey of stellar lore and science is a well-known classic, which has introduced thousands to the fascinating world of stars and other celestial bodies. Descriptions of Capella, Sirius, Arcturus, Vega, Polaris, etc.—all the important stars, with informative discussions of rising and setting of stars, their number, names, brightness, distances, etc. in a non-technical, highly readable style. Also: double stars, constellations, clusters—concentrating on stars and formations visible to the naked eye. New edition, revised (1963) by D. H. Menzel, Director Harvard Observatory. 23 diagrams by Prof. Ching-Sung Yu. Foreword by D. H. Menzel and W. W. Morgan. 2 Star Charts. Index. xii + 147pp. 5⅜ x 8½.
T1099 Paperbound **$1.00**

AN ELEMENTARY SURVEY OF CELESTIAL MECHANICS, Y. Ryabov. Elementary exposition of gravitational theory and celestial mechanics. Historical introduction and coverage of basic principles, including: the elliptic, the orbital plane, the 2- and 3-body problems, the discovery of Neptune, planetary rotation, the length of the day, the shapes of galaxies, satellites (detailed treatment of Sputnik I), etc. First American reprinting of successful Russian popular exposition. Elementary algebra and trigonometry helpful, but not necessary; presentation chiefly verbal. Appendix of theorem proofs. 58 figures. 165pp. 5⅜ x 8.
T756 Paperbound **$1.25**

THE SKY AND ITS MYSTERIES, E. A. Beet. One of most lucid books on mysteries of universe; deals with astronomy from earliest observations to latest theories of expansion of universe, source of stellar energy, birth of planets, origin of moon craters, possibility of life on other planets. Discusses effects of sunspots on weather; distances, ages of several stars; master plan of universe; methods and tools of astronomers; much more. "Eminently readable book," London Times. Extensive bibliography. Over 50 diagrams. 12 full-page plates, fold-out star map. Introduction. Index. 5¼ x 7½.
T627 Clothbound **$3.50**

THE REALM OF THE NEBULAE, E. Hubble. One of the great astronomers of our time records his formulation of the concept of "island universes," and its impact on astronomy. Such topics are covered as the velocity-distance relation; classification, nature, distances, general field of nebulae; cosmological theories; nebulae in the neighborhood of the Milky Way. 39 photos of nebulae, nebulae clusters, spectra of nebulae, and velocity distance relations shown by spectrum comparison. "One of the most progressive lines of astronomical research," The Times (London). New introduction by A. Sandage. 55 illustrations. Index. iv + 201pp. 5⅜ x 8.
S455 Paperbound **$1.50**

OUT OF THE SKY, H. H. Nininger. A non-technical but comprehensive introduction to "meteoritics", the young science concerned with all aspects of the arrival of matter from outer space. Written by one of the world's experts on meteorites, this work shows how, despite difficulties of observation and sparseness of data, a considerable body of knowledge has arisen. It defines meteors and meteorites; studies fireball clusters and processions, meteorite composition, size, distribution, showers, explosions, origins, craters, and much more. A true connecting link between astronomy and geology. More than 175 photos, 22 other illustrations. References. Bibliography of author's publications on meteorites. Index. viii + 336pp. 5⅜ x 8.
                                                                          T519 Paperbound **$1.85**

SATELLITES AND SCIENTIFIC RESEARCH, D. King-Hele. Non-technical account of the manmade satellites and the discoveries they have yielded up to the autumn of 1961. Brings together information hitherto published only in hard-to-get scientific journals. Includes the life history of a typical satellite, methods of tracking, new information on the shape of the earth, zones of radiation, etc. Over 60 diagrams and 6 photographs. Mathematical appendix. Bibliography of over 100 items. Index. xii + 180pp. 5⅜ x 8½.
                                                                          T703 Paperbound **$2.00**

BOOKS EXPLAINING SCIENCE AND MATHEMATICS

Mathematics

CHANCE, LUCK AND STATISTICS: THE SCIENCE OF CHANCE, Horace C. Levinson. Theory of probability and science of statistics in simple, non-technical language. Part I deals with theory of probability, covering odd superstitions in regard to "luck," the meaning of betting odds, the law of mathematical expectation, gambling, and applications in poker, roulette, lotteries, dice, bridge, and other games of chance. Part II discusses the misuse of statistics, the concept of statistical probabilities, normal and skew frequency distributions, and statistics applied to various fields—birth rates, stock speculation, insurance rates, advertising, etc. "Presented in an easy humorous style which I consider the best kind of expository writing," Prof. A. C. Cohen, Industry Quality Control. Enlarged revised edition. Formerly titled "The Science of Chance." Preface and two new appendices by the author. Index. xiv + 365pp. 5⅜ x 8.
                                                                          T1007 Paperbound **$1.85**

PROBABILITIES AND LIFE, Emile Borel. Translated by M. Baudin. Non-technical, highly readable introduction to the results of probability as applied to everyday situations. Partial contents: Fallacies About Probabilities Concerning Life After Death; Negligible Probabilities and the Probabilities of Everyday Life; Events of Small Probability; Application of Probabilities to Certain Problems of Heredity; Probabilities of Deaths, Diseases, and Accidents; On Poisson's Formula. Index. 3 Appendices of statistical studies and tables. vi + 87pp. 5⅜ x 8½.
                                                                          T121 Paperbound **$1.00**

GREAT IDEAS OF MODERN MATHEMATICS: THEIR NATURE AND USE, Jagjit Singh. Reader with only high school math will understand main mathematical ideas of modern physics, astronomy, genetics, psychology, evolution, etc., better than many who use them as tools, but comprehend little of their basic structure. Author uses his wide knowledge of non-mathematical fields in brilliant exposition of differential equations, matrices, group theory, logic, statistics, problems of mathematical foundations, imaginary numbers, vectors, etc. Original publication. 2 appendices. 2 indexes. 65 illustr. 322pp. 5⅜ x 8.   S587 Paperbound **$1.75**

MATHEMATICS IN ACTION, O. G. Sutton. Everyone with a command of high school algebra will find this book one of the finest possible introductions to the application of mathematics to physical theory. Ballistics, numerical analysis, waves and wavelike phenomena, Fourier series, group concepts, fluid flow and aerodynamics, statistical measures, and meteorology are discussed with unusual clarity. Some calculus and differential equations theory is developed by the author for the reader's help in the more difficult sections. 88 figures. Index. viii + 236pp. 5⅜ x 8.
                                                                          T440 Clothbound **$3.50**

THE FOURTH DIMENSION SIMPLY EXPLAINED, edited by H. P. Manning. 22 essays, originally Scientific American contest entries, that use a minimum of mathematics to explain aspects of 4-dimensional geometry: analogues to 3-dimensional space, 4-dimensional absurdities and curiosities (such as removing the contents of an egg without puncturing its shell), possible measurements and forms, etc. Introduction by the editor. Only book of its sort on a truly elementary level, excellent introduction to advanced works. 82 figures. 251pp. 5⅜ x 8.
                                                                          T711 Paperbound **$1.35**

BOOKS EXPLAINING SCIENCE AND MATHEMATICS

Engineering, technology, applied science etc.

TEACH YOURSELF ELECTRICITY, C. W. Wilman. Electrical resistance, inductance, capacitance, magnets, chemical effects of current, alternating currents, generators and motors, transformers, rectifiers, much more. 230 questions, answers, worked examples. List of units. 115 illus. 194pp. 6⅞ x 4¼.
Clothbound **$2.00**

ELEMENTARY METALLURGY AND METALLOGRAPHY, A. M. Shrager. Basic theory and descriptions of most of the fundamental manufacturing processes involved in metallurgy. Partial contents: the structure of metals; slip, plastic deformation, and recrystalization; iron ore and production of pig iron; chemistry involved in the metallurgy of iron and steel; basic processes such as the Bessemer treatment, open-hearth process, the electric arc furnace —with advantages and disadvantages of each; annealing, hardening, and tempering steel; copper, aluminum, magnesium, and their alloys. For freshman engineers, advanced students in technical high schools, etc. Index. Bibliography. 177 diagrams. 17 tables. 284 questions and problems. 27-page glossary. ix + 389pp. 5⅜ x 8.
S138 Paperbound **$2.25**

BASIC ELECTRICITY, Prepared by the Bureau of Naval Personnel. Originally a training course text for U.S. Navy personnel, this book provides thorough coverage of the basic theory of electricity and its applications. Best book of its kind for either broad or more limited studies of electrical fundamentals . . . for classroom use or home study. Part 1 provides a more limited coverage of theory: fundamental concepts, batteries, the simple circuit, D.C. series and parallel circuits, conductors and wiring techniques, A.C. electricity, inductance and capacitance, etc. Part 2 applies theory to the structure of electrical machines—generators, motors, transformers, magnetic amplifiers. Also deals with more complicated instruments, synchros, servo-mechanisms. The concluding chapters cover electrical drawings and blueprints, wiring diagrams, technical manuals, and safety education. The book contains numerous questions for the student, with answers. Index and six appendices. 345 illustrations. x + 448pp. 6½ x 9¼.
S973 Paperbound **$3.00**

BASIC ELECTRONICS, prepared by the U.S. Navy Training Publications Center. A thorough and comprehensive manual on the fundamentals of electronics. Written clearly, it is equally useful for self-study or course work for those with a knowledge of the principles of basic electricity. Partial contents: Operating Principles of the Electron Tube; Introduction to Transistors; Power Supplies for Electronic Equipment; Tuned Circuits; Electron-Tube Amplifiers; Audio Power Amplifiers; Oscillators; Transmitters; Transmission Lines; Antennas and Propagation; Introduction to Computers; and related topics. Appendix. Index. Hundreds of illustrations and diagrams. vi + 471pp. 6½ x 9¼.
S1076 Paperbound **$2.75**

BASIC THEORY AND APPLICATION OF TRANSISTORS, Prepared by the U.S. Department of the Army. An introductory manual prepared for an army training program. One of the finest available surveys of theory and application of transistor design and operation. Minimal knowledge of physics and theory of electron tubes required. Suitable for textbook use, course supplement, or home study. Chapters: Introduction; fundamental theory of transistors; transistor amplifier fundamentals; parameters, equivalent circuits, and characteristic curves; bias stabilization; transistor analysis and comparison using characteristic curves and charts; audio amplifiers; tuned amplifiers; wide-band amplifiers; oscillators; pulse and switching circuits; modulation, mixing, and demodulation; and additional semiconductor devices. Unabridged, corrected edition. 240 schematic drawings, photographs, wiring diagrams, etc. 2 Appendices. Glossary. Index. 263pp. 6½ x 9¼.
S380 Paperbound **$1.25**

TEACH YOURSELF HEAT ENGINES, E. De Ville. Measurement of heat, development of steam and internal combustion engines, efficiency of an engine, compression-ignition engines, production of steam, the ideal engine, much more. 318 exercises, answers, worked examples. Tables. 76 illus. 220pp. 6⅞ x 4¼.
Clothbound **$2.00**

BOOKS EXPLAINING SCIENCE AND MATHEMATICS

Miscellaneous

ON THE SENSATIONS OF TONE, Hermann Helmholtz. This is an unmatched coordination of such fields as acoustical physics, physiology, experiment, history of music. It covers the entire gamut of musical tone. Partial contents: relation of musical science to acoustics, physical vs. physiological acoustics, composition of vibration, resonance, analysis of tones by sympathetic resonance, beats, chords, tonality, consonant chords, discords, progression of parts, etc. 33 appendixes discuss various aspects of sound, physics, acoustics, music, etc. Translated by A. J. Ellis. New introduction by Prof. Henry Margenau of Yale. 68 figures. 43 musical passages analyzed. Over 100 tables. Index. xix + 576pp. 6⅛ x 9¼.
S114 Paperbound **$3.00**

THE NATURE OF LIGHT AND COLOUR IN THE OPEN AIR, M. Minnaert. Why is falling snow sometimes black? What causes mirages, the fata morgana, multiple suns and moons in the sky? How are shadows formed? Prof. Minnaert of the University of Utrecht answers these and similar questions in optics, light, colour, for non-specialists. Particularly valuable to nature, science students, painters, photographers. Translated by H. M. Kremer-Priest, K. Jay. 202 illustrations, including 42 photos. xvi + 362pp. 5⅜ x 8. **T196 Paperbound $2.00**

THE PHYSICS OF MUSIC, Alexander Wood. Introduction for musicians to the physical aspect of sound. No scientific training necessary to understand concepts, etc. Wealth of material on origin and development of instruments, physical principles involved in the production of their sounds, pitch, intensity and loudness, mechanism of the ear, dissonance and consonance, sound reproduction and recordings, concert halls, etc. Extensively revised by Dr. J. M. Bowsher. Indices. Bibliography. 16 plates. 114 illustrations. 270pp. 5⅛ x 8⅛. **T322 Paperbound $2.25**

GREAT IDEAS AND THEORIES OF MODERN COSMOLOGY, Jagjit Singh. The theories of Jeans, Eddington, Milne, Kant, Bondi, Gold, Newton, Einstein, Gamow, Hoyle, Dirac, Kuiper, Hubble, Weizsäcker and many others on such cosmological questions as the origin of the universe, space and time, planet formation, "continuous creation," the birth, life, and death of the stars, the origin of the galaxies, etc. By the author of the popular "Great Ideas of Modern Mathematics." A gifted popularizer of science, he makes the most difficult abstractions crystal-clear even to the most non-mathematical reader. Index. xii + 276 pp. 5⅜ x 8½. **T925 Paperbound $1.85**

PIONEERS OF SCIENCE, O. Lodge. Eminent scientist-expositor's authoritative, yet elementary survey of great scientific theories. Concentrating on individuals—Copernicus, Brahe, Kepler, Galileo, Descartes, Newton, Laplace, Herschel, Lord Kelvin, and other scientists—the author presents their discoveries in historical order adding biographical material on each man and full, specific explanations of their achievements. The clear and complete treatment of the post-Newtonian astronomers is a feature seldom found in other books on the subject. Index. 120 illustrations. xv + 404pp. 5⅜ x 8. **T716 Paperbound $1.65**

BIOGRAPHY OF SCIENTISTS

ISAAC NEWTON: A BIOGRAPHY, Louis Trenchard More. The definitive biography of Newton, his life and work. Presents Newton as a living man, with a critical, objective analysis of his character as well as a careful survey of his manifold accomplishments, scientific, theological, etc. The author, himself a professor of physics, has made full use of all of Newton's published works and all material in the Portsmouth Collection of Newton's personal and unpublished papers. The text includes numerous letters by Newton and his acquaintances, and many other of his papers—some translated from Latin to English by the author. A universally-esteemed work. Unabridged republication. 1 full-page plate. Index. xiii + 675pp. 5⅜ x 8½. **T579 Paperbound $2.50**

PIERRE CURIE, Marie Curie. Mme. Curie, Nobel Prize winner, creates a memorable portrait of her equally famous husband and his lifelong scientific researches. She brings to life the determined personality of a great scientist at work. Her own autobiographical notes, included in this volume, reconstruct her own work on radiation which resulted in the isolation of radium. "A delightful book. It marks one of the few instances in which the proverbially humdrum life of the student of physical science, together with the austere ideals, has been made intelligible," New York Times. Unabridged reprint. Translated by Charlotte and Vernon Kellogg. Introduction by Mrs. Wm. Brown Meloney. 8 halftones. viii + 120pp. 5⅜ x 8½. **T199 Paperbound $1.00**

THE BOOK OF MY LIFE (DE VITA PROPRIA LIBER), Jerome Cardan. The remarkable autobiography of an important Renaissance mathematician, physician, and scientist, who at the same time was a paranoid, morbid, superstitious man, consumed with ambition and self-love (and self-pity). These chronicles of his fortunes and misfortunes make absorbing reading, giving us an extremely insightful view of a man's reactions and sensations—the first psychological autobiography. Through his eyes we can also see the superstitions and beliefs of an age, Renaissance medical practices, and the problems that concerned a trained mind in the 16th century. Unabridged republication of original English edition, translated by Jean Stoner. Introduction. Notes. Bibliography. xviii + 331pp. 5⅜ x 8½. **T345 Paperbound $1.60**

THE AUTOBIOGRAPHY OF CHARLES DARWIN, AND SELECTED LETTERS, edited by **Francis Darwin.** Darwin's own record of his early life; the historic voyage aboard the "Beagle"; the furor surrounding evolution, and his replies; reminiscences of his son. Letters to Henslow, Lyell, Hooker, Huxley, Wallace, Kingsley, etc., and thoughts on religion and vivisection. We see how he revolutionized geology with his concept of ocean subsidence; how his great books on variation of plants and animals, primitive man, the expression of emotion among primates, plant fertilization, carnivorous plants, protective coloration, etc., came into being. Appendix. Index. 365pp. 5⅜ x 8. **T479 Paperbound $1.65**

MATHEMATICS, ELEMENTARY TO INTERMEDIATE

HOW TO CALCULATE QUICKLY, Henry Sticker. This handy volume offers a tried and true method for helping you in the basic mathematics of daily life—addition, subtraction, multiplication, division, fractions, etc. It is designed to awaken your "number sense" or the ability to see relationships between numbers as whole quantities. It is not a collection of tricks working only on special numbers, but a serious course of over 9,000 problems and their solutions, teaching special techniques not taught in schools: left-to-right multiplication, new fast ways of division, etc. 5 or 10 minutes daily use will double or triple your calculation speed. Excellent for the scientific worker who is at home in higher math, but is not satisfied with his speed and accuracy in lower mathematics. 256pp. 5 x 7¼.　T295 Paperbound **$1.00**

TEACH YOURSELF books. For adult self-study, for refresher and supplementary study.

The most effective series of home study mathematics books on the market! With absolutely no outside help, they will teach you as much as any similar college or high-school course, or will helpfully supplement any such course. Each step leads directly to the next, each question is anticipated. Numerous lucid examples and carefully-wrought practice problems illustrate meanings. Not skimpy outlines, not surveys, not usual classroom texts, these 204- to 380-page books are packed with the finest instruction you'll find anywhere for adult self-study.

TEACH YOURSELF ALGEBRA, P. Abbott. Formulas, coordinates, factors, graphs of quadratic functions, quadratic equations, logarithms, ratio, irrational numbers, arithmetical, geometrical series, much more. 1241 problems, solutions. Tables. 52 illus. 307pp. 6⅞ x 4¼.
Clothbound **$2.00**

TEACH YOURSELF GEOMETRY, P. Abbott. Solids, lines, points, surfaces, angle measurement, triangles, theorem of Pythagoras, polygons, loci, the circle, tangents, symmetry, solid geometry, prisms, pyramids, solids of revolution, etc. 343 problems, solutions. 268 illus. 334pp. 6⅞ x 4¼.
Clothbound **$2.00**

TEACH YOURSELF TRIGONOMETRY, P. Abbott. Geometrical foundations, indices, logarithms, trigonometrical ratios, relations between sides, angles of triangle, circular measure, trig. ratios of angles of any magnitude, much more. Requires elementary algebra, geometry. 465 problems, solutions. Tables. 102 illus. 204pp. 6⅞ x 4¼.
Clothbound **$2.00**

TEACH YOURSELF THE CALCULUS, P. Abbott. Variations in functions, differentiation, solids of revolution, series, elementary differential equations, areas by integral calculus, much more. Requires algebra, trigonometry. 970 problems, solutions. Tables. 89 illus. 380pp. 6⅞ x 4¼.
Clothbound **$2.00**

TEACH YOURSELF THE SLIDE RULE, B. Snodgrass. Fractions, decimals, A-D scales, log-log scales, trigonometrical scales, indices, logarithms. Commercial, precision, electrical, dualistic, Brighton rules. 80 problems, solutions. 10 illus. 207pp. 6⅞ x 4¼. Clothbound **$2.00**

ARITHMETICAL EXCURSIONS: AN ENRICHMENT OF ELEMENTARY MATHEMATICS, H. Bowers and J. Bowers. For students who want unusual methods of arithmetic never taught in school; for adults who want to increase their number sense. Little known facts about the most simple numbers, arithmetical entertainments and puzzles, figurate numbers, number chains, mysteries and folklore of numbers, the "Hin-dog-abic" number system, etc. First publication. Index. 529 numbered problems and diversions, all with answers. Bibliography. xiv + 320pp. 5⅜ x 8.　T770 Paperbound **$1.65**

HOW DO YOU USE A SLIDE RULE? by A. A. Merrill. Not a manual for mathematicians and engineers, but a lucid step-by-step explanation that presents the fundamental rules clearly enough to be understood by anyone who could benefit by the use of a slide rule in his work or business. This work concentrates on the 2 most important operations: multiplication and division. 10 easy lessons, each with a clear drawing, will save you countless hours in your banking, business, statistical, and other work. First publication. Index. 2 Appendixes. 10 illustrations. 78 problems, all with answers. vi + 36pp. 6⅛ x 9¼.　T62 Paperbound **60¢**

THE THEORY AND OPERATION OF THE SLIDE RULE, J. P. Ellis. Not a skimpy "instruction manual", but an exhaustive treatment that will save you hours throughout your career. Supplies full understanding of every scale on the Log Log Duplex Decitrig type of slide rule. Shows the most time-saving methods, and provides practice useful in the widest variety of actual engineering situations. Each operation introduced in terms of underlying logarithmic theory. Summary of prerequisite math. First publication. Index. 198 figures. Over 450 problems with answers. Bibliography. 12 Appendices. ix + 289pp. 5⅜ x 8.
S727 Paperbound **$1.50**

COLLEGE ALGEBRA, H. B. Fine. Standard college text that gives a systematic and deductive structure to algebra; comprehensive, connected, with emphasis on theory. Discusses the commutative, associative, and distributive laws of number in unusual detail, and goes on with undetermined coefficients, quadratic equations, progressions, logarithms, permutations, probability, power series, and much more. Still most valuable elementary-intermediate text on the science and structure of algebra. Index. 1560 problems, all with answers. x + 631pp. 5⅜ x 8.
T211 Paperbound **$2.25**

COORDINATE GEOMETRY, L. P. Eisenhart. Thorough, unified introduction. Unusual for advancing in dimension within each topic (treats together circle, sphere; polar coordinates, 3-dimensional coordinate systems; conic sections, quadric surfaces), affording exceptional insight into subject. Extensive use made of determinants, though no previous knowledge of them is assumed. Algebraic equations of 1st degree, 2 and 3 unknowns, carried further than usual in algebra courses. Over 500 exercises. Introduction. Appendix. Index. Bibliography. 43 illustrations. 310pp. 5⅜ x 8.
S600 Paperbound **$1.65**

A TREATISE ON PLANE AND ADVANCED TRIGONOMETRY, E. W. Hobson. Extraordinarily wide coverage, going beyond usual college level trig, one of the few works covering advanced trig in full detail. By a great expositor with unerring anticipation and lucid clarification of potentially difficult points. Includes circular functions; expansion of functions of multiple angle; trig tables; relations between sides and angles of triangle; complex numbers; etc. Many problems solved completely. "The best work on the subject." Nature. Formerly entitled "A Treatise on Plane Trigonometry." 689 examples. 6 figures. xvi + 383pp. 5⅜ x 8.
S353 Paperbound **$1.95**

FAMOUS PROBLEMS OF ELEMENTARY GEOMETRY, Felix Klein. Expanded version of the 1894 Easter lectures at Göttingen. 3 problems of classical geometry, in an excellent mathematical treatment by a famous mathematician: squaring the circle, trisecting angle, doubling cube. Considered with full modern implications: transcendental numbers, pi, etc. Notes by R. Archibald. 16 figures. xi + 92pp. 5⅜ x 8.
T298 Paperbound **$1.00**

MONOGRAPHS ON TOPICS OF MODERN MATHEMATICS, edited by J. W. A. Young. Advanced mathematics for persons who haven't gone beyond or have forgotten high school algebra. 9 monographs on foundation of geometry, modern pure geometry, non-Euclidean geometry, fundamental propositions of algebra, algebraic equations, functions, calculus, theory of numbers, etc. Each monograph gives proofs of important results, and descriptions of leading methods, to provide wide coverage. New introduction by Prof. M. Kline, N. Y. University. 100 diagrams. xvi + 416pp. 6⅛ x 9¼.
S289 Paperbound **$2.00**

HIGHER MATHEMATICS FOR STUDENTS OF CHEMISTRY AND PHYSICS, J. W. Mellor. Not abstract, but practical, building its problems out of familiar laboratory material, this covers differential calculus, coordinate, analytical geometry, functions, integral calculus, infinite series, numerical equations, differential equations, Fourier's theorem, probability, theory of errors, calculus of variations, determinants. "If the reader is not familiar with this book, it will repay him to examine it," CHEM. & ENGINEERING NEWS. 800 problems. 189 figures. Bibliography. xxi + 641pp. 5⅜ x 8.
S193 Paperbound **$2.25**

TRIGONOMETRY REFRESHER FOR TECHNICAL MEN, A. Albert Klaf. 913 detailed questions and answers cover the most important aspects of plane and spherical trigonometry. They will help you to brush up or to clear up difficulties in special areas. The first portion of this book covers plane trigonometry, including angles, quadrants, trigonometrical functions, graphical representation, interpolation, equations, logarithms, solution of triangle, use of the slide rule and similar topics. 188 pages then discuss application of plane trigonometry to special problems in navigation, surveying, elasticity, architecture, and various fields of engineering. Small angles, periodic functions, vectors, polar coordinates, de Moivre's theorem are fully examined. The third section of the book then discusses spherical trigonometry and the solution of spherical triangles, with their applications to terrestrial and astronomical problems. Methods of saving time with numerical calculations, simplification of principal functions of angle, much practical information make this a most useful book. 913 questions answered. 1738 problems, answers to odd numbers. 494 figures. 24 pages of useful formulae, functions. Index. x + 629pp. 5⅜ x 8.
T371 Paperbound **$2.00**

TEXTBOOK OF ALGEBRA, G. Chrystal. One of the great mathematical textbooks, still about the best source for complete treatments of the topics of elementary algebra; a chief reference work for teachers and students of algebra in advanced high school and university courses, or for the mathematician working on problems of elementary algebra or looking for a background to more advanced topics. Ranges from basic laws and processes to extensive examination of such topics as limits, infinite series, general properties of integral numbers, and probability theory. Emphasis is on algebraic form, the foundation of analytical geometry and the key to modern developments in algebra. Prior course in algebra is desirable, but not absolutely necessary. Includes theory of quotients, distribution of products, arithmetical theory of surds, theory of interest, permutations and combinations, general expansion theorems, recurring fractions, and much, much more. Two volume set. Index in each volume. Over 1500 exercises, approximately half with answers. Total of xlviii + 1187pp. 5⅜ x 8.
S750 Vol I Paperbound **$2.35**
S751 Vol II Paperbound **$2.35**
The set **$4.70**

MATHEMATICS—INTERMEDIATE TO ADVANCED

General

INTRODUCTION TO APPLIED MATHEMATICS, Francis D. Murnaghan. A practical and thoroughly sound introduction to a number of advanced branches of higher mathematics. Among the selected topics covered in detail are: vector and matrix analysis, partial and differential equations, integral equations, calculus of variations, Laplace transform theory, the vector triple product, linear vector functions, quadratic and bilinear forms, Fourier series, spherical harmonics, Bessel functions, the Heaviside expansion formula, and many others. Extremely useful book for graduate students in physics, engineering, chemistry, and mathematics. Index. 111 study exercises with answers. 41 illustrations. ix + 389pp. 5⅜ x 8½.
S1042 Paperbound $2.00

OPERATIONAL METHODS IN APPLIED MATHEMATICS, H. S. Carslaw and J. C. Jaeger. Explanation of the application of the Laplace Transformation to differential equations, a simple and effective substitute for more difficult and obscure operational methods. Of great practical value to engineers and to all workers in applied mathematics. Chapters on: Ordinary Linear Differential Equations with Constant Coefficients;; Electric Circuit Theory; Dynamical Applications; The Inversion Theorem for the Laplace Transformation; Conduction of Heat; Vibrations of Continuous Mechanical Systems; Hydrodynamics; Impulsive Functions; Chains of Differential Equations; and other related matters. 3 appendices. 153 problems, many with answers. 22 figures. xvi + 359pp. 5⅜ x 8½.
S1011 Paperbound $2.25

APPLIED MATHEMATICS FOR RADIO AND COMMUNICATIONS ENGINEERS, C. E. Smith. No extraneous material here!—only the theories, equations, and operations essential and immediately useful for radio work. Can be used as refresher, as handbook of applications and tables, or as full home-study course. Ranges from simplest arithmetic through calculus, series, and wave forms, hyperbolic trigonometry, simultaneous equations in mesh circuits, etc. Supplies applications right along with each math topic discussed. 22 useful tables of functions, formulas, logs, etc. Index. 166 exercises, 140 examples, all with answers. 95 diagrams. Bibliography. x + 336pp. 5⅜ x 8.
S141 Paperbound $1.75

Algebra, group theory, determinants, sets, matrix theory

ALGEBRAS AND THEIR ARITHMETICS, L. E. Dickson. Provides the foundation and background necessary to any advanced undergraduate or graduate student studying abstract algebra. Begins with elementary introduction to linear transformations, matrices, field of complex numbers; proceeds to order, basal units, modulus, quaternions, etc.; develops calculus of linears sets, describes various examples of algebras including invariant, difference, nilpotent, semi-simple. "Makes the reader marvel at his genius for clear and profound analysis," Amer. Mathematical Monthly. Index. xii + 241pp. 5⅜ x 8.
S616 Paperbound $1.50

THE THEORY OF EQUATIONS WITH AN INTRODUCTION TO THE THEORY OF BINARY ALGEBRAIC FORMS, W. S. Burnside and A. W. Panton. Extremely thorough and concrete discussion of the theory of equations, with extensive detailed treatment of many topics curtailed in later texts. Covers theory of algebraic equations, properties of polynomials, symmetric functions, derived functions, Horner's process, complex numbers and the complex variable, determinants and methods of elimination, invariant theory (nearly 100 pages), transformations, introduction to Galois theory, Abelian equations, and much more. Invaluable supplementary work for modern students and teachers. 759 examples and exercises. Index in each volume. Two volume set. Total of xxiv + 604pp. 5⅜ x 8.
S714 Vol I Paperbound $1.85
S715 Vol II Paperbound $1.85
The set $3.70

COMPUTATIONAL METHODS OF LINEAR ALGEBRA, V. N. Faddeeva, translated by **C. D. Benster.** First English translation of a unique and valuable work, the only work in English presenting a systematic exposition of the most important methods of linear algebra—classical and contemporary. Shows in detail how to derive numerical solutions of problems in mathematical physics which are frequently connected with those of linear algebra. Theory as well as individual practice. Part I surveys the mathematical background that is indispensable to what follows. Parts II and III, the conclusion, set forth the most important methods of solution, for both exact and iterative groups. One of the most outstanding and valuable features of this work is the 23 tables, double and triple checked for accuracy. These tables will not be found elsewhere. Author's preface. Translator's note. New bibliography and index. x + 252pp. 5⅜ x 8.
S424 Paperbound $1.95

ALGEBRAIC EQUATIONS, E. Dehn. Careful and complete presentation of Galois' theory of algebraic equations; theories of Lagrange and Galois developed in logical rather than historical form, with a more thorough exposition than in most modern books. Many concrete applications and fully-worked-out examples. Discusses basic theory (very clear exposition of the symmetric group); isomorphic, transitive, and Abelian groups; applications of Lagrange's and Galois' theories; and much more. Newly revised by the author. Index. List of Theorems. xi + 208pp. 5⅜ x 8.
S697 Paperbound $1.45

Catalogue of Dover Books

ALGEBRAIC THEORIES, L. E. Dickson. Best thorough introduction to classical topics in higher algebra develops theories centering around matrices, invariants, groups. Higher algebra, Galois theory, finite linear groups, Klein's icosahedron, algebraic invariants, linear transformations, elementary divisors, invariant factors; quadratic, bi-linear, Hermitian forms, singly and in pairs. Proofs rigorous, detailed; topics developed lucidly, in close connection with their most frequent mathematical applications. Formerly "Modern Algebraic Theories." 155 problems. Bibliography. 2 indexes. 285pp. 5⅜ x 8.
S547 Paperbound **$1.50**

LECTURES ON THE ICOSAHEDRON AND THE SOLUTION OF EQUATIONS OF THE FIFTH DEGREE, Felix Klein. The solution of quintics in terms of rotation of a regular icosahedron around its axes of symmetry. A classic & indispensable source for those interested in higher algebra, geometry, crystallography. Considerable explanatory material included. 230 footnotes, mostly bibliographic. 2nd edition, xvi + 289pp. 5⅜ x 8.
S314 Paperbound **$2.25**

LINEAR GROUPS, WITH AN EXPOSITION OF THE GALOIS FIELD THEORY, L. E. Dickson. The classic exposition of the theory of groups, well within the range of the graduate student. Part I contains the most extensive and thorough presentation of the theory of Galois Fields available, with a wealth of examples and theorems. Part II is a full discussion of linear groups of finite order. Much material in this work is based on Dickson's own contributions. Also includes expositions of Jordan, Lie, Abel, Betti-Mathieu, Hermite, etc. "A milestone in the development of modern algebra," W. Magnus, in his historical introduction to this edition. Index. xv + 312pp. 5⅜ x 8.
S482 Paperbound **$1.95**

INTRODUCTION TO THE THEORY OF GROUPS OF FINITE ORDER, R. Carmichael. Examines fundamental theorems and their application. Beginning with sets, systems, permutations, etc., it progresses in easy stages through important types of groups: Abelian, prime power, permutation, etc. Except 1 chapter where matrices are desirable, no higher math needed. 783 exercises, problems. Index. xvi + 447pp. 5⅜ x 8.
S300 Paperbound **$2.25**

THEORY OF GROUPS OF FINITE ORDER, W. Burnside. First published some 40 years ago, this is still one of the clearest introductory texts. Partial contents: permutations, groups independent of representation, composition series of a group, isomorphism of a group with itself, Abelian groups, prime power groups, permutation groups, invariants of groups of linear substitution, graphical representation, etc. 45pp. of notes. Indexes. xxiv + 512pp. 5⅜ x 8.
S38 Paperbound **$2.75**

CONTINUOUS GROUPS OF TRANSFORMATIONS, L. P. Eisenhart. Intensive study of the theory and geometrical applications of continuous groups of transformations; a standard work on the subject, called forth by the revolution in physics in the 1920's. Covers tensor analysis, Riemannian geometry, canonical parameters, transitivity, imprimitivity, differential invariants, the algebra of constants of structure, differential geometry, contact transformations, etc. "Likely to remain one of the standard works on the subject for many years . . . principal theorems are proved clearly and concisely, and the arrangement of the whole is coherent," MATHEMATICAL GAZETTE. Index. 72-item bibliography. 185 exercises. ix + 301pp. 5⅜ x 8.
S781 Paperbound **$2.00**

THE THEORY OF GROUPS AND QUANTUM MECHANICS, H. Weyl. Discussions of Schroedinger's wave equation, de Broglie's waves of a particle, Jordan-Hoelder theorem, Lie's continuous groups of transformations, Pauli exclusion principle, quantization of Maxwell-Dirac field equations, etc. Unitary geometry, quantum theory, groups, application of groups to quantum mechanics, symmetry permutation group, algebra of symmetric transformation, etc. 2nd revised edition. Bibliography. Index. xxii + 422pp. 5⅜ x 8.
S269 Paperbound **$2.35**

APPLIED GROUP-THEORETIC AND MATRIX METHODS, Bryan Higman. The first systematic treatment of group and matrix theory for the physical scientist. Contains a comprehensive, easily-followed exposition of the basic ideas of group theory (realized through matrices) and its applications in the various areas of physics and chemistry: tensor analysis, relativity, quantum theory, molecular structure and spectra, and Eddington's quantum relativity. Includes rigorous proofs available only in works of a far more advanced character. 34 figures, numerous tables. Bibliography. Index. xiii + 454pp. 5⅜ x 8⅜.
S1147 Paperbound **$2.50**

THE THEORY OF GROUP REPRESENTATIONS, Francis D. Murnaghan. A comprehensive introduction to the theory of group representations. Particular attention is devoted to those groups—mainly the symmetric and rotation groups—which have proved to be of fundamental significance for quantum mechanics (esp. nuclear physics). Also a valuable contribution to the literature on matrices, since the usual representations of groups are groups of matrices. Covers the theory of group integration (as developed by Schur and Weyl), the theory of 2-valued or spin representations, the representations of the symmetric group, the crystallographic groups, the Lorentz group, reducibility (Schur's lemma, Burnside's Theorem, etc.), the alternating group, linear groups, the orthogonal group, etc. Index. List of references. xi + 369pp. 5⅜ x 8½.
S1112 Paperbound **$2.35**

THEORY OF SETS, E. Kamke. Clearest, amplest introduction in English, well suited for independent study. Subdivision of main theory, such as theory of sets of points, are discussed, but emphasis is on general theory. Partial contents: rudiments of set theory, arbitrary sets and their cardinal numbers, ordered sets and their order types, well-ordered sets and their cardinal numbers. Bibliography. Key to symbols. Index. vii + 144pp. 5⅜ x 8.
S141 Paperbound **$1.35**

THEORY AND APPLICATIONS OF FINITE GROUPS, G. A. Miller, H. F. Blichfeldt, L. E. Dickson.
Unusually accurate and authoritative work, each section prepared by a leading specialist:
Miller on substitution and abstract groups, Blichfeldt on finite groups of linear homogeneous
transformations, Dickson on applications of finite groups. Unlike more modern works, this gives
the concrete basis from which abstract group theory arose. Includes Abelian groups, prime-
power groups, isomorphisms, matrix forms of linear transformations, Sylow groups, Galois'
theory of algebraic equations, duplication of a cube, trisection of an angle, etc. 2 Indexes.
267 problems. xvii + 390pp. 5⅜ x 8. S216 Paperbound **$2.00**

THE THEORY OF DETERMINANTS, MATRICES, AND INVARIANTS, H. W. Turnbull. Important
study includes all salient features and major theories. 7 chapters on determinants and
matrices cover fundamental properties, Laplace identities, multiplication, linear equations,
rank and differentiation, etc. Sections on invariants gives general properties, symbolic and
direct methods of reduction, binary and polar forms, general linear transformation, first
fundamental theorem, multilinear forms. Following chapters study development and proof
of Hilbert's Basis Theorem, Gordan-Hilbert Finiteness Theorem, Clebsch's Theorem, and
include discussions of apolarity, canonical forms, geometrical interpretations of algebraic
forms, complete system of the general quadric, etc. New preface and appendix. Bibliography.
xviii + 374pp. 5⅜ x 8. S699 Paperbound **$2.25**

AN INTRODUCTION TO THE THEORY OF CANONICAL MATRICES, H. W. Turnbull and A. C. Aitken.
All principal aspects of the theory of canonical matrices, from definitions and fundamental
properties of matrices to the practical applications of their reduction to canonical form.
Beginning with matrix multiplications, reciprocals, and partitioned matrices, the authors go
on to elementary transformations and bilinear and quadratic forms. Also covers such topics
as a rational canonical form for the collineatory group, congruent and conjunctive transformation for quadratic and hermitian forms, unitary and orthogonal transformations, canonical
reduction of pencils of matrices, etc. Index. Appendix. Historical notes at chapter ends.
Bibliographies. 275 problems. xiv + 200pp. 5⅜ x 8. S177 Paperbound **$1.55**

A TREATISE ON THE THEORY OF DETERMINANTS, T. Muir. Unequalled as an exhaustive compilation of nearly all the known facts about determinants up to the early 1930's. Covers notation
and general properties, row and column transformation, symmetry, compound determinants,
adjugates, rectangular arrays and matrices, linear dependence, gradients, Jacobians, Hessians,
Wronskians, and much more. Invaluable for libraries of industrial and research organizations
as well as for student, teacher, and mathematician; very useful in the field of computing
machines. Revised and enlarged by W. H. Metzler. Index. 485 problems and scores of numerical examples. iv + 766pp. 5⅜ x 8. S670 Paperbound **$3.00**

THEORY OF DETERMINANTS IN THE HISTORICAL ORDER OF DEVELOPMENT, Sir Thomas Muir.
Unabridged reprinting of this complete study of 1,859 papers on determinant theory written
between 1693 and 1900. Most important and original sections reproduced, valuable com-
mentary on each. No other work is necessary for determinant research: all types are covered—
each subdivision of the theory treated separately; all papers dealing with each type are
covered; you are told exactly what each paper is about and how important its contribution is.
Each result, theory, extension, or modification is assigned its own identifying numeral so that
the full history may be more easily followed. Includes papers on determinants in general,
determinants and linear equations, symmetric determinants, alternants, recurrents, determinants having invariant factors, and all other major types. "A model of what such histories
ought to be," NATURE. "Mathematicians must ever be grateful to Sir Thomas for his monu-
mental work," AMERICAN MATH MONTHLY. Four volumes bound as two. Indices. Bibliographies. Total of lxxxiv + 1977pp. 5⅜ x 8. S672-3 The set, Clothbound **$12.50**

Calculus and function theory, Fourier theory, infinite series, calculus of variations, real and complex functions

FIVE VOLUME "THEORY OF FUNCTIONS' SET BY KONRAD KNOPP

This five-volume set, prepared by Konrad Knopp, provides a complete and readily followed
account of theory of functions. Proofs are given concisely, yet without sacrifice of complete-
ness or rigor. These volumes are used as texts by such universities as M.I.T., University of
Chicago, N. Y. City College, and many others. "Excellent introduction . . . remarkably
readable, concise, clear, rigorous," JOURNAL OF THE AMERICAN STATISTICAL ASSOCIATION.

ELEMENTS OF THE THEORY OF FUNCTIONS, Konrad Knopp. This book provides the student
with background for further volumes in this set, or texts on a similar level. Partial contents:
foundations, system of complex numbers and the Gaussian plane of numbers, Riemann
sphere of numbers, mapping by linear functions, normal forms, the logarithm, the cyclometric
functions and binomial series. "Not only for the young student, but also for the student
who knows all about what is in it," MATHEMATICAL JOURNAL. Bibliography. Index. 140pp.
5⅜ x 8. S154 Paperbound **$1.35**

THEORY OF FUNCTIONS, PART I, Konrad Knopp. With volume II, this book provides coverage
of basic concepts and theorems. Partial contents: numbers and points, functions of a complex variable, integral of a continuous function, Cauchy's integral theorem, Cauchy's integral
formulae, series with variable terms, expansion of analytic functions in power series, analytic
continuation and complete definition of analytic functions, entire transcendental functions,
Laurent expansion, types of singularities. Bibliography. Index. vii + 146pp. 5⅜ x 8.
S156 Paperbound **$1.35**

THEORY OF FUNCTIONS, PART II, Konrad Knopp. Application and further development of general theory, special topics. Single valued functions, entire, Weierstrass, Meromorphic functions. Riemann surfaces. Algebraic functions. Analytical configuration, Riemann surface. Bibliography. Index. x + 150pp. 5⅜ x 8.
S157 Paperbound **$1.35**

PROBLEM BOOK IN THE THEORY OF FUNCTIONS, VOLUME 1, Konrad Knopp. Problems in elementary theory, for use with Knopp's THEORY OF FUNCTIONS, or any other text, arranged according to increasing difficulty. Fundamental concepts, sequences of numbers and infinite series, complex variable, integral theorems, development in series, conformal mapping. 182 problems. Answers. viii + 126pp. 5⅜ x 8.
S158 Paperbound **$1.35**

PROBLEM BOOK IN THE THEORY OF FUNCTIONS, VOLUME 2, Konrad Knopp. Advanced theory of functions, to be used either with Knopp's THEORY OF FUNCTIONS, or any other comparable text. Singularities, entire & meromorphic functions, periodic, analytic, continuation, multiple-valued functions, Riemann surfaces, conformal mapping. Includes a section of additional elementary problems. "The difficult task of selecting from the immense material of the modern theory of functions the problems just within the reach of the beginner is here masterfully accomplished," AM. MATH. SOC. Answers. 138pp. 5⅜ x 8.   S159 Paperbound **$1.35**

A COURSE IN MATHEMATICAL ANALYSIS, Edouard Goursat. Trans. by E. R. Hedrick, O. Dunkel. Classic study of fundamental material thoroughly treated. Exceptionally lucid exposition of wide range of subject matter for student with 1 year of calculus. Vol. 1: Derivatives and Differentials, Definite Integrals, Expansion in Series, Applications to Geometry. Problems. Index. 52 illus. 556pp. Vol. 2, Part I: Functions of a Complex Variable, Conformal Representations, Doubly Periodic Functions, Natural Boundaries, etc. Problems. Index. 38 illus. 269pp. Vol. 2, Part 2: Differential Equations, Cauchy-Lipschitz Method, Non-linear Differential Equations, Simultaneous Equations, etc. Problems. Index. 308pp. 5⅜ x 8.

Vol. 1 S554 Paperbound **$2.50**
Vol. 2 part 1 S555 Paperbound **$1.85**
Vol. 2 part 2 S556 Paperbound **$1.85**
3 vol. set **$6.20**

MODERN THEORIES OF INTEGRATION, H. Kestelman. Connected and concrete coverage, with fully-worked-out proofs for every step. Ranges from elementary definitions through theory of aggregates, sets of points, Riemann and Lebesgue· integration, and much more. This new revised and enlarged edition contains a new chapter on Riemann-Stieltjes integration, as well as a supplementary section of 186 exercises. Ideal for the mathematician, student, teacher, or self-studier. Index of Definitions and Symbols. General Index. Bibliography. x + 310pp. 5⅝ x 8⅜.
S572 Paperbound **$2.25**

THEORY OF MAXIMA AND MINIMA, H. Hancock. Fullest treatment ever written; only work in English with extended discussion of maxima and minima for functions of 1, 2, or n variables, problems with subsidiary constraints, and relevant quadratic forms. Detailed proof of each important theorem. Covers the Scheeffer and von Dantscher theories, homogeneous quadratic forms, reversion of series, fallacious establishment of maxima and minima, etc. Unsurpassed treatise for advanced students of calculus, mathematicians, economists, statisticians. Index. 24 diagrams. 39 problems, many examples. 193pp. 5⅜ x 8.   S665 Paperbound **$1.50**

AN ELEMENTARY TREATISE ON ELLIPTIC FUNCTIONS, A. Cayley. Still the fullest and clearest text on the theories of Jacobi and Legendre for the advanced student (and an excellent supplement for the beginner). A masterpiece of exposition by the great 19th century British mathematician (creator of the theory of matrices and abstract geometry), it covers the addition-theory, Landen's theorem, the 3 kinds of elliptic integrals, transformations, the q-functions, reduction of a differential expression, and much more. Index. xii + 386pp. 5⅜ x 8.
S728 Paperbound **$2.00**

THE APPLICATIONS OF ELLIPTIC FUNCTIONS, A. G. Greenhill. Modern books forego detail for sake of brevity—this book offers complete exposition necessary for proper understanding, use of elliptic integrals. Formulas developed from definite physical, geometric problems; examples representative enough to offer basic information in widely useable form. Elliptic integrals, addition theorem, algebraical form of addition theorem, elliptic integrals of 2nd, 3rd kind, double periodicity, resolution into factors, series, transformation, etc. Introduction. Index. 25 illus. xi + 357pp. 5⅜ x 8.
S603 Paperbound **$1.75**

THE THEORY OF FUNCTIONS OF REAL VARIABLES, James Pierpont. A 2-volume authoritative exposition, by one of the foremost mathematicians of his time. Each theorem stated with all conditions, then followed by proof. No need to go through complicated reasoning to discover conditions added without specific mention. Includes a particularly complete, rigorous presentation of theory of measure; and Pierpont's own work on a theory of Lebesgue integrals, and treatment of area of a curved surface. Partial contents, Vol. 1: rational numbers, exponentials, logarithms, point aggregates, maxima, minima, proper integrals, improper integrals, multiple proper integrals, continuity, discontinuity, indeterminate forms. Vol. 2: point sets, proper integrals, series, power series, aggregates, ordinal numbers, discontinuous functions, sub-, infra-uniform convergence, much more. Index. 95 illustrations. 1229pp. 5⅜ x 8.
S558-9, 2 volume set, paperbound **$5.20**

FUNCTIONS OF A COMPLEX VARIABLE, James Pierpont. Long one of best in the field. A thorough treatment of fundamental elements, concepts, theorems. A complete study, rigorous, detailed, with carefully selected problems worked out to illustrate each topic. Partial contents: arithmetical operations, real term series, positive term series, exponential functions, integration, analytic functions, asymptotic expansions, functions of Weierstrass, Legendre, etc. Index. List of symbols. 122 illus. 597pp. 5⅜ x 8.   S560 Paperbound **$2.45**

MODERN OPERATIONAL CALCULUS: WITH APPLICATIONS IN TECHNICAL MATHEMATICS, N. W. McLachlan. An introduction to modern operational calculus based upon the Laplace transform, applying it to the solution of ordinary and partial differential equations. For physicists, engineers, and applied mathematicians. Partial contents: Laplace transform, theorems or rules of the operational calculus, solution of ordinary and partial linear differential equations with constant coefficients, evaluation of integrals and establishment of mathematical relationships, derivation of Laplace transforms of various functions, etc. Six appendices deal with Heaviside's unit function, etc. Revised edition. Index. Bibliography. xiv + 218pp. 5⅜ x 8½.   S192 Paperbound **$1.75**

ADVANCED CALCULUS, E. B. Wilson. An unabridged reprinting of the work which continues to be recognized as one of the most comprehensive and useful texts in the field. It contains an immense amount of well-presented, fundamental material, including chapters on vector functions, ordinary differential equations, special functions, calculus of variations, etc., which are excellent introductions to these areas. For students with only one year of calculus, more than 1300 exercises cover both pure math and applications to engineering and physical problems. For engineers, physicists, etc., this work, with its 54 page introductory review, is the ideal reference and refresher. Index. ix + 566pp. 5⅜ x 8.   S504 Paperbound **$2.45**

ASYMPTOTIC EXPANSIONS, A. Erdélyi. The only modern work available in English, this is an unabridged reproduction of a monograph prepared for the Office of Naval Research. It discusses various procedures for asymptotic evaluation of integrals containing a large parameter and solutions of ordinary linear differential equations. Bibliography of 71 items. vi + 108pp. 5⅜ x 8.   S318 Paperbound **$1.35**

INTRODUCTION TO ELLIPTIC FUNCTIONS: with applications, F. Bowman. Concise, practical introduction to elliptic integrals and functions. Beginning with the familiar trigonometric functions, it requires nothing more from the reader than a knowledge of basic principles of differentiation and integration. Discussion confined to the Jacobian functions. Enlarged bibliography. Index. 173 problems and examples. 56 figures, 4 tables. 115pp. 5⅜ x 8.   S922 Paperbound **$1.25**

ON RIEMANN'S THEORY OF ALGEBRAIC FUNCTIONS AND THEIR INTEGRALS: A SUPPLEMENT TO THE USUAL TREATISES, Felix Klein. Klein demonstrates how the mathematical ideas in Riemann's work on Abelian integrals can be arrived at by thinking in terms of the flow of electric current on surfaces. Intuitive explanations, not detailed proofs given in an extremely clear exposition, concentrating on the kinds of functions which can be defined on Riemann surfaces. Also useful as an introduction to the origins of topological problems. Complete and unabridged. Approved translation by Frances Hardcastle. New introduction. 43 figures. Glossary. xii + 76pp. 5⅜ x 8½.   S1072 Paperbound **$1.25**

COLLECTED WORKS OF BERNHARD RIEMANN. This important source book is the first to contain the complete text of both 1892 Werke and the 1902 supplement, unabridged. It contains 31 monographs, 3 complete lecture courses, 15 miscellaneous papers, which have been of enormous importance in relativity, topology, theory of complex variables, and other areas of mathematics. Edited by R. Dedekind, H. Weber, M. Noether, W. Wirtinger. German text. English introduction by Hans Lewy. 690pp. 5⅜ x 8.   S226 Paperbound **$3.75**

THE TAYLOR SERIES, AN INTRODUCTION TO THE THEORY OF FUNCTIONS OF A COMPLEX VARIABLE, P. Dienes. This book investigates the entire realm of analytic functions. Only ordinary calculus is needed, except in the last two chapters. Starting with an introduction to real variables and complex algebra, the properties of infinite series, elementary functions, complex differentiation and integration are carefully derived. Also biuniform mapping, a thorough two part discussion of representation and singularities of analytic functions, overconvergence and gap theorems, divergent series, Taylor series on its circle of convergence, divergence and singularities, etc. Unabridged, corrected reissue of first edition. Preface and index. 186 examples, many fully worked out. 67 figures. xii + 555pp. 5⅜ x 8.   S391 Paperbound **$2.75**

INTRODUCTION TO BESSEL FUNCTIONS, Frank Bowman. A rigorous self-contained exposition providing all necessary material during the development, which requires only some knowledge of calculus and acquaintance with differential equations. A balanced presentation including applications and practical use. Discusses Bessel Functions of Zero Order, of Any Real Order; Modified Bessel Functions of Zero Order; Definite Integrals; Asymptotic Expansions; Bessel's Solution to Kepler's Problem; Circular Membranes; much more. "Clear and straightforward . . . useful not only to students of physics and engineering, but to mathematical students in general," Nature. 226 problems. Short tables of Bessel functions. 27 figures. Index. x + 135pp. 5⅜ x 8.   S462 Paperbound **$1.35**

Probability theory and information theory

AN ELEMENTARY INTRODUCTION TO THE THEORY OF PROBABILITY, B. V. Gnedenko and A. Ya. Khinchin. Translated by Leo F. Boron. A clear, compact introduction designed to equip the reader with a fundamental grasp of the theory of probability. It is thorough and authoritative within its purposely restricted range, yet the layman with a background in elementary mathematics will be able to follow it without difficulty. Covers such topics as the processes involved in the calculation of probabilities, conditional probabilities and the multiplication rule, Bayes's formula, Bernoulli's scheme and theorem, random variables and distribution laws, and dispersion and mean deviations. New translation of fifth (revised) Russian edition (1960)—the only translation checked and corrected by Gnedenko. New preface for Dover edition by B. V. Gnedenko. Index. Bibliography. Appendix: Table of values of function $\phi(a)$.
xii + 130pp. 5⅜ x 8½.
T155 Paperbound **$1.50**

AN INTRODUCTION TO MATHEMATICAL PROBABILITY, Julian Lowell Coolidge. A thorough introduction which presents the mathematical foundation of the theory of probability. A substantial body of material, yet can be understood with a knowledge of only elementary calculus. Contains: The Scope and Meaning of Mathematical Probability; Elementary Principles of Probability; Bernoulli's Theorem; Mean Value and Dispersion; Geometrical Probability; Probability of Causes; Errors of Observation; Errors in Many Variables; Indirect Observations; The Statistical Theory of Gases; and The Principles of Life Insurance. Six pages of logarithm tables. 4 diagrams. Subject and author indices. xii + 214pp. 5⅜ x 8½.
S258 Paperbound **$1.35**

A GUIDE TO OPERATIONS RESEARCH, W. E. Duckworth. A brief nontechnical exposition of techniques and theories of operational research. A good introduction for the layman; also can provide the initiate with new understandings. No mathematical training needed, yet not an oversimplification. Covers game theory, mathematical analysis, information theory, linear programming, cybernetics, decision theory, etc. Also includes a discussion of the actual organization of an operational research program and an account of the uses of such programs in the oil, chemical, paper, and metallurgical industries, etc. Bibliographies at chapter ends. Appendices. 36 figures. 145pp. 5¼ x 8½.
T1129 Clothbound **$3.50**

MATHEMATICAL FOUNDATIONS OF INFORMATION THEORY, A. I. Khinchin. For the first time mathematicians, statisticians, physicists, cyberneticists, and communications engineers are offered a complete and exact introduction to this relatively new field. Entropy as a measure of a finite scheme, applications to coding theory, study of sources, channels and codes, detailed proofs of both Shannon theorems for any ergodic source and any stationary channel with finite memory, and much more are covered. Bibliography. vii + 120pp. 5⅜ x 8.
S434 Paperbound **$1.35**

SELECTED PAPERS ON NOISE AND STOCHASTIC PROCESS, edited by Prof. Nelson Wax, U. of Illinois. 6 basic papers for newcomers in the field, for those whose work involves noise characteristics. Chandrasekhar, Uhlenbeck & Ornstein, Uhlenbeck & Ming, Rice, Doob. Included is Kac's Chauvenet-Prize winning Random Walk. Extensive bibliography lists 200 articles, up through 1953. 21 figures. 337pp. 6⅛ x 9¼.
S262 Paperbound **$2.50**

THEORY OF PROBABILITY, William Burnside. Synthesis, expansion of individual papers presents numerous problems in classical probability, offering many original views succinctly, effectively. Game theory, cards, selections from groups; geometrical probability in such areas as suppositions as to probability of position of point on a line, points on surface of sphere, etc. Includes methods of approximation, theory of errors, direct calculation of probabilities, etc. Index. 136pp. 5⅜ x 8.
S567 Paperbound **$1.00**

Statistics

ELEMENTARY STATISTICS, WITH APPLICATIONS IN MEDICINE AND THE BIOLOGICAL SCIENCES, F. E. Croxton. A sound introduction to statistics for anyone in the physical sciences, assuming no prior acquaintance and requiring only a modest knowledge of math. All basic formulas carefully explained and illustrated; all necessary reference tables included. From basic terms and concepts, the study proceeds to frequency distribution, linear, non-linear, and multiple correlation, skewness, kurtosis, etc. A large section deals with reliability and significance of statistical methods. Containing concrete examples from medicine and biology, this book will prove unusually helpful to workers in those fields who increasingly must evaluate, check, and interpret statistics. Formerly titled "Elementary Statistics with Applications in Medicine." 101 charts. 57 tables. 14 appendices. Index. iv + 376pp. 5⅜ x 8.
S506 Paperbound **$2.00**

ANALYSIS & DESIGN OF EXPERIMENTS, H. B. Mann. Offers a method for grasping the analysis of variance and variance design within a short time. Partial contents: Chi-square distribution and analysis of variance distribution, matrices, quadratic forms, likelihood ration tests and tests of linear hypotheses, power of analysis, Galois fields, non-orthogonal data, interblock estimates, etc. 15pp. of useful tables. x + 195pp. 5 x 7⅜.
S180 Paperbound **$1.45**

METHODS OF STATISTICS, L. H. C. Tippett. A classic in its field, this unusually complete systematic introduction to statistical methods begins at beginner's level and progresses to advanced levels for experimenters and poll-takers in all fields of statistical research. Supplies fundamental knowledge of virtually all elementary methods in use today by sociologists, psychologists, biologists, engineers, mathematicians, etc. Explains logical and mathematical basis of each method described, with examples for each section. Covers frequency distributions and measures, inference from random samples, errors in large samples, simple analysis of variance, multiple and partial regression and correlation, etc. 4th revised (1952) edition. 16 charts. 5 significance tables. 152-item bibliography. 96 tables. 22 figures. 395pp. 6 x 9.
S228 Clothbound **$7.50**

STATISTICS MANUAL, E. L. Crow, F. A. Davis, M. W. Maxfield. Comprehensive collection of classical, modern statistics methods, prepared under auspices of U. S. Naval Ordnance Test Station, China Lake, Calif. Many examples from ordnance will be valuable to workers in all fields. Emphasis is on use, with information on fiducial limits, sign tests, Chi-square runs, sensitivity, quality control, much more. "Well written . . . excellent reference work," Operations Research. Corrected edition of NAVORD Report 3360 NOTS 948. Introduction. Appendix of 32 tables, charts. Index. Bibliography. 95 illustrations. 306pp. 5⅜ x 8.
S599 Paperbound **$1.75**

Symbolic logic

AN INTRODUCTION TO SYMBOLIC LOGIC, Susanne K. Langer. Probably the clearest book ever written on symbolic logic for the philosopher, general scientist and layman. It will be particularly appreciated by those who have been rebuffed by other introductory works because of insufficient mathematical training. No special knowledge of mathematics is required. Starting with the simplest symbols and conventions, you are led to a remarkable grasp of the Boole-Schroeder and Russell-Whitehead systems clearly and quickly. PARTIAL CONTENTS: Study of forms, Essentials of logical structure, Generalization, Classes, The deductive system of classes, The algebra of logic, Abstraction of interpretation, Calculus of propositions, Assumptions of PRINCIPIA MATHEMATICA, Logistics, Logic of the syllogism, Proofs of theorems. "One of the clearest and simplest introductions to a subject which is very much alive. The style is easy, symbolism is introduced gradually, and the intelligent non-mathematician should have no difficulty in following the argument," MATHEMATICS GAZETTE. Revised, expanded second edition. Truth-value tables. 368pp. 5⅜ x 8.
S164 Paperbound **$1.85**

A SURVEY OF SYMBOLIC LOGIC: THE CLASSIC ALGEBRA OF LOGIC, C. I. Lewis. Classic survey of the field, comprehensive and thorough. Indicates content of major systems, alternative methods of procedure, and relation of these to the Boole-Schroeder algebra and to one another. Contains historical summary, as well as full proofs and applications of the classic, or Boole-Schroeder, algebra of logic. Discusses diagrams for the logical relations of classes, the two-valued algebra, propositional functions of two or more variables, etc. Chapters 5 and 6 of the original edition, which contained material not directly pertinent, have been omitted in this edition at the author's request. Appendix. Bibliography. Index. viii + 352pp. 5⅜ x 8⅜.
S643 Paperbound **$2.00**

INTRODUCTION TO SYMBOLIC LOGIC AND ITS APPLICATIONS, R. Carnap. One of the clearest, most comprehensive, and rigorous introductions to modern symbolic logic by perhaps its greatest living master. Symbolic languages are analyzed and one constructed. Applications to math (symbolic representation of axiom systems for set theory, natural numbers, real numbers, topology, Dedekind and Cantor explanations of continuity), physics (the general analysis of concepts of determination, causality, space-time-topology, based on Einstein), biology (symbolic representation of an axiom system for basic concepts). "A masterpiece," Zentralblatt für Mathematik und ihre Grenzgebiete. Over 300 exercises. 5 figures. Bibliography. Index. xvi + 241pp. 5⅜ x 8.
S453 Paperbound **$1.85**
Clothbound **$4.00**

SYMBOLIC LOGIC, C. I. Lewis, C. H. Langford. Probably the most cited book in symbolic logic, this is one of the fullest treatments of paradoxes. A wide coverage of the entire field of symbolic logic, plus considerable material that has not appeared elsewhere. Basic to the entire volume is the distinction between the logic of extensions and of intensions. Considerable emphasis is placed on converse substitution, while the matrix system presents the supposition of a variety of non-Aristotelian logics. It has especially valuable sections on strict limitations, existence of terms, 2-valued algebra and its extension to propositional functions, truth value systems, the matrix method, implication and deductibility, general theory of propositions, propositions of ordinary discourse, and similar topics. "Authoritative, most valuable," TIMES, London. Bibliography. 506pp. 5⅜ x 8.
S170 Paperbound **$2.35**

THE ELEMENTS OF MATHEMATICAL LOGIC, Paul Rosenbloom. First publication in any language. This book is intended for readers who are mature mathematically, but have no previous training in symbolic logic. It does not limit itself to a single system, but covers the field as a whole. It is a development of lectures given at Lund University, Sweden, in 1948. Partial contents: Logic of classes, fundamental theorems, Boolean algebra, logic of propositions, logic of propositional functions, expressive languages, combinatory logics, development of mathematics within an object language, paradoxes, theorems of Post and Goedel, Church's theorem, and similar topics. iv + 214pp. 5⅜ x 8.
S227 Paperbound **$1.45**

MATHEMATICS, HISTORIES AND CLASSICS

HISTORY OF MATHEMATICS, D. E. Smith. Most comprehensive non-technical history of math in English. Discusses lives and works of over a thousand major and minor figures, with footnotes supplying technical information outside the book's scheme, and indicating disputed matters. Vol I: A chronological examination, from primitive concepts through Egypt, Babylonia, Greece, the Orient, Rome, the Middle Ages, the Renaissance, and up to 1900. Vol 2: The development of ideas in specific fields and problems, up through elementary calculus. Two volumes, total of 510 illustrations, 1355pp. 5⅜ x 8. Set boxed in attractive container.
T429, 430 Paperbound, the set **$5.00**

A SHORT ACCOUNT OF THE HISTORY OF MATHEMATICS, W. W. R. Ball. Most readable non-technical history of mathematics treats lives, discoveries of every important figure from Egyptian, Phoenician mathematicians to late 19th century. Discusses schools of Ionia, Pythagoras, Athens, Cyzicus, Alexandria, Byzantium, systems of numeration; primitive arithmetic; Middle Ages, Renaissance, including Arabs, Bacon, Regiomontanus, Tartaglia, Cardan, Stevinus, Galileo, Kepler; modern mathematics of Descartes, Pascal, Wallis, Huygens, Newton, Leibnitz, d'Alembert, Euler, Lambert, Laplace, Legendre, Gauss, Hermite, Weierstrass, scores more. Index. 25 figures. 546pp. 5⅜ x 8.
S630 Paperbound **$2.25**

A HISTORY OF GEOMETRICAL METHODS, J. L. Coolidge. Full, authoritative history of the techniques which men have employed in dealing with geometric questions . . . from ancient times to the modern development of projective geometry. Critical analyses of the original works. Contents: Synthetic Geometry—the early beginnings, Greek mathematics, non-Euclidean geometries, projective and descriptive geometry; Algebraic Geometry—extension of the system of linear coordinates, other systems of point coordinates, enumerative and birational geometry, etc.; and Differential Geometry—intrinsic geometry and moving axes, Gauss and the classical theory of surfaces, and projective and absolute differential geometry. The work of scores of geometers analyzed: Pythagoras, Archimedes, Newton, Descartes, Leibniz, Lobachevski, Riemann, Hilbert, Bernoulli, Schubert, Grassman, Klein, Cauchy, and many, many others. Extensive (24-page) bibliography. Index. 13 figures. xviii + 451pp. 5⅜ x 8½.
S1006 Paperbound **$2.25**

THE MATHEMATICS OF GREAT AMATEURS, Julian Lowell Coolidge. Enlightening, often surprising, accounts of what can result from a non-professional preoccupation with mathematics. Chapters on Plato, Omar Khayyam and his work with cubic equations, Piero della Francesca, Albrecht Dürer, as the true discoverer of descriptive geometry, Leonardo da Vinci and his varied mathematical interests, John Napier, Baron of Merchiston, inventor of logarithms, Pascal, Diderot, l'Hospital, and seven others known primarily for contributions in other fields. Bibliography. 56 figures. viii + 211pp. 5⅜ x 8½.
S1009 Paperbound **$1.50**

ART AND GEOMETRY, Wm. M. Ivins, Jr. A controversial study which propounds the view that the ideas of Greek philosophy and culture served not to stimulate, but to stifle the development of Western thought. Through an examination of Greek art and geometrical inquiries and Renaissance experiments, this book offers a concise history of the evolution of mathematical perspective and projective geometry. Discusses the work of Alberti, Dürer, Pelerin, Nicholas of Cusa, Kepler, Desargues, etc. in a wholly readable text of interest to the art historian, philosopher, mathematician, historian of science, and others. x + 113pp. 5⅜ x 8⅜.
T941 Paperbound **$1.00**

A SOURCE BOOK IN MATHEMATICS, D. E. Smith. Great discoveries in math, from Renaissance to end of 19th century, in English translation. Read announcements by Dedekind, Gauss, Delamain, Pascal, Fermat, Newton, Abel, Lobachevsky, Bolyai, Riemann, De Moivre, Legendre, Laplace, others of discoveries about imaginary numbers, number congruence, slide rule, equations, symbolism, cubic algebraic equations, non-Euclidean forms of geometry, calculus, function theory, quaternions, etc. Succinct selections from 125 different treatises, articles, most unavailable elsewhere in English. Each article preceded by biographical, historical introduction. Vol. I: Fields of Number, Algebra. Index. 32 illus. 338pp. 5⅜ x 8. Vol. II: Fields of Geometry, Probability, Calculus, Functions, Quaternions. 83 illus. 432pp. 5⅜ x 8.
Vol. 1: S552 Paperbound **$2.00**
Vol. 2: S553 Paperbound **$2.00**
2 vol. set, **$4.00**

A COLLECTION OF MODERN MATHEMATICAL CLASSICS, edited by R. Bellman. 13 classic papers, complete in their original languages, by Hermite, Hardy and Littlewood, Tchebychef, Fejér, Fredholm, Fuchs, Hurwitz, Weyl, van der Pol, Birkhoff, Kellogg, von Neumann, and Hilbert. Each of these papers, collected here for the first time, triggered a burst of mathematical activity, providing useful new generalizations or stimulating fresh investigations. Topics discussed include classical analysis, periodic and almost periodic functions, analysis and number theory, integral equations, theory of approximation, non-linear differential equations, and functional analysis. Brief introductions and bibliographies to each paper. xii + 292pp. 6 x 9.
S730 Paperbound **$2.00**

THE WORKS OF ARCHIMEDES, edited by T. L. Heath. All the known works of the great Greek mathematician are contained in this one volume, including the recently discovered Method of Archimedes. Contains: On Sphere & Cylinder, Measurement of a Circle, Spirals, Conoids, Spheroids, etc. This is the definitive edition of the greatest mathematical intellect of the ancient world. 186-page study by Heath discusses Archimedes and the history of Greek mathematics. Bibliography. 563pp. 5⅜ x 8.
S9 Paperbound **$2.45**

THE THIRTEEN BOOKS OF EUCLID'S ELEMENTS, edited by **Sir Thomas Heath.** Definitive edition of one of the very greatest classics of Western world. Complete English translation of Heiberg text, together with spurious Book XIV. Detailed 150-page introduction discussing aspects of Greek and Medieval mathematics. Euclid, texts, commentators, etc. Paralleling the text is an elaborate critical apparatus analyzing each definition, proposition, postulate, covering textual matters, mathematical analysis, commentators of all times, refutations, supports, extrapolations, etc. This is the full Euclid. Unabridged reproduction of Cambridge U. 2nd edition. 3 volumes. Total of 995 figures, 1426pp. 5⅜ x 8.
$88,89,90, 3 volume set, paperbound **$6.75**

A CONCISE HISTORY OF MATHEMATICS, D. Struik. Lucid study of development of mathematical ideas, techniques from Ancient Near East, Greece, Islamic science, Middle Ages, Renaissance, modern times. Important mathematicians are described in detail. Treatment is not anecdotal, but analytical development of ideas. "Rich in content, thoughtful in interpretation," U.S. QUARTERLY BOOKLIST. Non-technical; no mathematical training needed. Index. 60 illustrations, including Egyptian papyri, Greek mss., portraits of 31 eminent mathematicians. Bibliography. 2nd edition. xix + 299pp. 5⅜ x 8.
T255 Paperbound **$1.75**

A HISTORY OF THE CALCULUS, AND ITS CONCEPTUAL DEVELOPMENT, Carl B. Boyer. Provides laymen and mathematicians a detailed history of the development of the calculus, from early beginning in antiquity to final elaboration as mathematical abstractions. Gives a sense of mathematics not as a technique, but as a habit of mind, in the progression of ideas of Zeno, Plato, Pythagoras, Eudoxus, Arabic and Scholastic mathematicians, Newton, Leibnitz, Taylor, Descartes, Euler, Lagrange, Cantor, Weierstrass, and others. This first comprehensive critical history of the calculus was originally titled "The Concepts of the Calculus." Foreword by R. Courant. Preface. 22 figures. 25-page bibliography. Index. v + 364pp. 5⅜ x 8.
S509 Paperbound **$2.00**

A MANUAL OF GREEK MATHEMATICS, Sir Thomas L. Heath. A non-technical survey of Greek mathematics addressed to high school and college students and the layman who desires a sense of historical perspective in mathematics. Thorough exposition of early numerical notation and practical calculation, Pythagorean arithmetic and geometry, Thales and the earliest Greek geometrical measurements and theorems, the mathematical theories of Plato, Euclid's "Elements" and his other works (extensive discussion), Aristarchus, Archimedes, Eratosthenes and the measurement of the earth, trigonometry (Hipparchus, Menelaus, Ptolemy), Pappus and Heron of Alexandria, and detailed coverage of minor figures normally omitted from histories of this type. Presented in a refreshingly interesting and readable style. Appendix. 2 Indexes. xvi + 552pp. 5⅜ x 8.
S279 Paperbound **$2.25**

THE GEOMETRY OF RENÉ DESCARTES. With this book Descartes founded analytical geometry. Excellent Smith-Latham translation, plus original French text with Descartes' own diagrams. Contains Problems the Construction of Which Requires Only Straight Lines and Circles; On the Nature of Curved Lines; On the Construction of Solid or Supersolid Problems. Notes. Diagrams. 258pp. 5⅜ x 8.
S68 Paperbound **$1.60**

A PHILOSOPHICAL ESSAY ON PROBABILITIES, Marquis de Laplace. This famous essay explains without recourse to mathematics the principle of probability, and the application of probability to games of chance, natural philosophy, astronomy, many other fields. Translated from the 6th French edition by F. W. Truscott, F. L. Emory, with new introduction for this edition by E. T. Bell. 204pp. 5⅜ x 8.
S166 Paperbound **$1.35**

Prices subject to change without notice.

Dover publishes books on art, music, philosophy, literature, languages, history, social sciences, psychology, handcrafts, orientalia, puzzles and entertainments, chess, pets and gardens, books explaining science, intermediate and higher mathematics, mathematical physics, engineering, biological sciences, earth sciences, classics of science, etc. Write to:

Dept. catrr.
Dover Publications, Inc.
180 Varick Street, N.Y. 14, N.Y.